English
Novel
Explication

Supplement VI

Compiled by
Christian J. W. Kloesel

ARCHON BOOKS
North Haven, Connecticut   1997

© 1997 The Shoe String Press, Inc.
All rights reserved.
First published 1997 as an Archon Book,
an imprint of The Shoe String Press, Inc.,
North Haven, Connecticut 06473.

Library of Congress Cataloging-in-Publication Data
(Revised for volume 6)

English novel explication. Supplement.
Supplements: English novel explication/
compiled by Helen H. Palmer & Anne Jane Dyson.
Supplement I / compiled by Peter L. Abernethy,
Christian J. W. Kloesel, Jeffrey R. Smitten;
supplement II / compiled by Christian J. W. Kloesel,
Jeffrey R. Smitten; supplements III–VI / compiled
by Christian J. W. Kloesel.
Includes bibliographical references and indexes.
1. English fiction—Explication—Bibliography
I. Abernethy, Peter L.   II. Kloesel, Christian J. W.
III. Smitten, Jeffrey R.   IV. Title: English novel explication

Z2014.F5P26 Suppl. [PR821]   016.823′009   84-137107
ISBN 0-208-01464-0 (v. 1)
ISBN 0-208-02418-2 (v. 6: alk. paper)

For Alicia

CONTENTS

PREFACE

This sixth supplement extends the *English Novel Explication* series from the second half of 1993 through the beginning months of 1997. Accordingly, it has been my primary responsibility to gather materials published in those nearly four years, although I have added a few earlier items not included in the fifth supplement, as well as everything published in 1997 that had arrived in nearby libraries. But readers should be reminded that it has not been possible to include all items published during that time, especially those appearing toward the very end of the period. Because *English Novel Explication* is a continuing series, it must have a fixed date of publication, and that date cannot be affected by printing and library binding schedules or by the inevitable delays in acquisitions, cataloguing, interlibrary loans, and the return of charged or overdue books. Consequently, readers not finding an item they expect to be here must consult the next supplement.

The scope of the present supplement is the same as that of the five previous ones. The very broad definition of the term "novel" is again based on Ernest A. Baker's *History of the English Novel,* and that is why such works as Malory's *Le Morte Darthur,* Bunyan's *The Pilgrim's Progress,* Swift's *Gulliver's Travels,* Johnson's *Rasselas,* and Orwell's *Down and Out in Paris and London* are included. An "English" novelist is a writer born in England, Scotland, Wales, Ireland, or the British Commonwealth (present and past) who has lived in Great Britain during some significant portion of her/his creative years. This definition excludes writers like Brian Moore and Henry James, and it includes others like Buchi Emecheta, Doris Lessing, Malcolm Lowry, Timothy Mo, V. S. Naipaul, Salman Rushdie, and Olive Schreiner. By "explication" is meant the interpretation of the significance and meaning of a novel. Consequently, discussions of theme, imagery, symbolism, diction, and structure are included here (even those of the poststructuralist, deconstructionist, and semiotic kind), whereas those wholly or exclusively devoted to sources and influence, critical reception, biography, or bibliography are ordinarily excluded.

The format of the present supplement is similar to that of the five earlier ones. I have abbreviated book titles to conserve space; full titles, together with complete bibliographical information, may be found in the *List of Books Indexed* at the end of the volume. In addition, I have used the generally accepted abbreviations of the journals of the American and Australian Modern Language Associations (*PMLA* and *AUMLA*), and have abbreviated several frequently repeated words in journal and serial titles. These words include, without periods, Academy (Acad), American (Am), Association (Assoc), British (Brit), Bulletin (Bull), Century (Cent), Chronicle (Chron), College (Coll), Comparative (Compar), Conference (Conf), Contemporary (Contemp), Critical (Crit), Department (Dept), English (Engl), History (Hist), Humanities (Hum), Institute (Inst), International (Intl), Journal (J), Language (Lang), Library (Lib), Linguistics (Ling), Literary (Liter), Literature (Lit), Magazine (Mag), Miscellany (Misc), Modern (Mod), Newsletter (Newsl), Philological (Philol), Philosophy (Philos), Proceedings (Proc), Psychology (Psych), Publications (Publs), Quarterly (Q), Religion (Rel), Research (Res), Review (R), Society (Soc), Studies (Stud), Supplement (Suppl), Transactions (Trans), University (Univ), and Yearbook (Yrbk). A few abbreviations, like *ANQ, ELH, GRAAT, PTL, S,* or *SPAN,* are themselves journal titles. (The abbreviation "nyp" appears once, under David Caute's *The Time of the Toad*; although completed several years ago, the novel remains "not yet published.") In another matter—the same article treating two or more of a single author's novels—I have continued the practice of the preceding supplement, with full citations in all instances; for though the practice of abbreviating subsequent citations may be useful for such rarely cited or moderately productive novelists as Pat Barker, Mary Rose Callaghan, Mary Gordon, Christopher Isherwood, Jennifer Johnston, and Cecil Day Lewis, it unnecessarily complicates the reader's task in such productive and much-discussed authors as Jane Austen, Charles Dickens, George Eliot, D. H. Lawrence, Doris Lessing, and Virginia Woolf.

Readers should remember that, as in the five previous supplements, page numbers in a citation correspond, in most instances, to the passage of explication for a given novel and not necessarily to the entire article or book. When an entire book is devoted to explication of the novel under which it appears, it is sometimes listed without page numbers. (Not included here are World Wide Web resources.)

As always, I am grateful to the library staffs at Indiana University–Purdue University at Indianapolis and Indiana University at Bloomington—and, especially, to English novelists and the critics who explicate them.

Indianapolis, Indiana   C.J.W.K.
June 1997

EDWIN ABBOTT

Flatland, 1884

Eco, Umberto. *Six Walks in the Fictional Woods,* 79–81.
Smith, Jonathan. *Fact and Feeling,* 201–8.

PETER ACKROYD

Chatterton, 1987

Janik, Del Ivan. "No End of History: Evidence from the Contemporary English Novel." *Twentieth Cent Lit* 41 (1995), 173–74.
Jukic, Tatjana. "Variants of *Victoriana* in the Postmodern English Novel." *Studia Romanica et Anglica Zagrabiensia* 40 (1995), 72–74.
Maack, Annegret. "Der Roman als 'Echokammer': Peter Ackroyds Erzählstrategien," in Herbert Foltinek et al., eds., *Tales and "their telling difference,"* 321–23.
Peck, John. "The Novels of Peter Ackroyd." *Engl Stud* (Amsterdam) 75 (1994), 445–47.
Wesseling, Elisabeth. *Writing History as a Prophet,* 135–38.

English Music, 1992

Janik, Del Ivan. "No End of History: Evidence from the Contemporary English Novel." *Twentieth Cent Lit* 41 (1995), 175–77.

First Light, 1989

Fokkema, Aleid. "Abandoning the Postmodern? The Case of Peter Ackroyd," in Theo D'haen and Hans Bertens, eds., *British Postmodern Fiction,* 174–77.
Janik, Del Ivan. "No End of History: Evidence from the Contemporary English Novel." *Twentieth Cent Lit* 41 (1995), 174–75.
Peck, John. "The Novels of Peter Ackroyd." *Engl Stud* (Amsterdam) 75 (1994), 447–50.

Hawksmoor, 1985

Cavaliero, Glen. *The Supernatural and English Fiction,* 224–27.
Connor, Steven. *The English Novel in History,* 143–46.
De Lange, Adriaan M. "The Complex Architectonics of Postmodern Fiction: *Hawksmoor*—A Case Study," in Theo D'haen and Hans Bertens, eds., *British Postmodern Fiction,* 145–62.
Fokkema, Aleid. "Abandoning the Postmodern? The Case of Peter Ackroyd," in Theo D'haen and Hans Bertens, eds., *British Postmodern Fiction,* 169–74.
Janik, Del Ivan. "No End of History: Evidence from the Contemporary English Novel." *Twentieth Cent Lit* 41 (1995), 172–73.
Maack, Annegret. "Der Roman als 'Echokammer': Peter Ackroyds Erzählstrategien," in Herbert Foltinek et al., eds., *Tales and "their telling difference,"* 324–28.

1

Onega, Susana. "British Historiographic Metafiction in the 1980s," in Theo D'haen and Hans Bertens, eds., *British Postmodern Fiction*, 55–57.

Onega Jaén, Susana. "Pattern and Magic in *Hawksmoor.*" *Atlantis* 12:2 (1991), 31–43.

Peck, John. "The Novels of Peter Ackroyd." *Engl Stud* (Amsterdam) 75 (1994), 442–45.

Todd, Richard. *Consuming Fictions*, 171–73.

The Last Testament of Oscar Wilde, 1983

Maack, Annegret. "Der Roman als 'Echokammer': Peter Ackroyds Erzählstrategien," in Herbert Foltinek et al., eds., *Tales and "their telling difference,"* 328–29.

RICHARD ADAMS

Watership Down, 1972

Anderson, Kathleen. "Shaping Self through Spontaneous Narration in Richard Adams' *Watership Down.*" *J of the Fantastic in the Arts* 6:1 (1993), 25–33.

Baldwin, Marc D. "The Birth of Self and Society: The Language of the Unconscious in Richard Adams's *Watership Down.*" *Intl Fiction R* 21 (1994), 39–43.

Bridgman, Joan. "The Significance of Myth in *Watership Down.*" *J of the Fantastic in the Arts* 6:1 (1993), 7–24.

Meyer, Charles A. "The Efrafan Hunt for Immortality in Richard Adams' *Watership Down.*" *J of the Fantastic in the Arts* 6:1 (1993), 71–88.

Miltner, Robert. "*Watership Down:* A Genre Study." *J of the Fantastic in the Arts* 6:1 (1993), 63–70.

Pennington, John. "From Peter Rabbit to *Watership Down:* There and Back Again to the Arcadian Ideal." *J of the Fantastic in the Arts* 3:2 (1991), 66–80.

Pennington, John. "Shamanistic Mythmaking: From Civilization to Wilderness in *Watership Down.*" *J of the Fantastic in the Arts* 6:1 (1993), 34–50.

Peters, John G. "Saturnalia and Sanctuary: The Role of the Tale in *Watership Down.*" *J of the Fantastic in the Arts* 6:1 (1993), 51–62.

Rose, Jacqueline. *The Case of Peter Pan*, 129–31.

JAMES ADDERLEY

Stephen Remarx, 1893

Hapgood, Lynne. " 'The Reconceiving of Christianity': Secularisation, Realism and the Religious Novel: 1888–1900." *Lit and Theology* 10 (1996), 344–49.

GRACE AGUILAR

The Vale of Cedars; or, The Martyr, 1850
Galchinsky, Michael. *The Origin of the Modern Jewish Woman Writer,* 164–67.
Ragussis, Michael. *Figures of Conversion,* 141–53.

WILLIAM HARRISON AINSWORTH

Jack Sheppard, 1839
Clarke, Micael M. *Thackeray and Women,* 41–43.
Joyce, Simon. "Resisting Arrest/Arresting Resistance: Crime Fiction, Cultural Studies, and the 'Turn to History.' " *Criticism* 37 (1995), 313–17, 322–31.

RICHARD ALDINGTON

The Colonel's Daughter, 1931
Gates, Norman T. "The Stereotype as Satire in the Fiction of Richard Aldington," in John Morris, ed., *Exploring Stereotyped Images,* 83–86.
Death of a Hero, 1929
Cecil, Hugh. *The Flower of Battle,* 34–37.
Gates, Norman T. "The Stereotype as Satire in the Fiction of Richard Aldington," in John Morris, ed., *Exploring Stereotyped Images,* 78–83.

BRIAN ALDISS

Dracula Unbound, 1991
Auerbach, Nina. *Our Vampires, Ourselves,* 175–77.
Frankenstein Unbound, 1973
Connor, Steven. *The English Novel in History,* 169–77.

ROSE LAURE ALLATINI

Despised and Rejected, 1918
Griffin, Gabriele. *Heavenly Love?,* 27–29.

GRANT ALLEN

The Woman Who Did, 1895
Luftig, Victor. *Seeing Together,* 97–104.
Reynolds, Kimberley, and Nicola Humble. *Victorian Heroines,* 40–44.

MARGERY ALLINGHAM

The Crime at Black Dudley, 1929

> Woods, Paula M. "The First Campion Novel," in Mary Jean DeMarr, ed., *In the Beginning*, 19–30.

Mystery Mile, 1930

> Woods, Paula M. "The First Campion Novel," in Mary Jean DeMarr, ed., *In the Beginning*, 24–28.

ERIC AMBLER

The Care of Time, 1981

> Wolfe, Peter. *Alarms and Epitaphs*, 207–15.
> Lewis, Peter. *Eric Ambler*, 198–208.

Cause for Alarm, 1938

> Ambrosetti, Ronald J. *Eric Ambler,* 44–47.
> Lewis, Peter. *Eric Ambler*, 52–61.
> Wolfe, Peter. *Alarms and Epitaphs*, 55–63.

The Dark Frontier, 1936

> Ambrosetti, Ronald J. *Eric Ambler,* 28–35.
> Lewis, Peter. *Eric Ambler*, 23–33.
> Wolfe, Peter. *Alarms and Epitaphs*, 32–39.

Dirty Story, 1967

> Ambrosetti, Ronald J. *Eric Ambler,* 112–15.
> Lewis, Peter. *Eric Ambler*, 135–41.
> Wolfe, Peter. *Alarms and Epitaphs*, 164–69.

Doctor Frigo, 1974

> Lewis, Peter. *Eric Ambler*, 172–85.
> Wolfe, Peter. *Alarms and Epitaphs*, 185–97.

Epitaph for a Spy, 1938

> Ambrosetti, Ronald J. *Eric Ambler,* 40–44.
> Lewis, Peter. *Eric Ambler,* 42–52.
> Wolfe, Peter. *Alarms and Epitaphs*, 47–53.

The Intercom Conspiracy, 1969

> Ambrosetti, Ronald J. *Eric Ambler,* 131–36.
> Lewis, Peter. *Eric Ambler,* 151–61.
> Wolfe, Peter. *Alarms and Epitaphs*, 169–75.

Journey into Fear, 1940

> Ambrosetti, Ronald J. *Eric Ambler,* 60–72.
> Lewis, Peter. *Eric Ambler,* 73–85.
> Wolfe, Peter. *Alarms and Epitaphs*, 74–82.

Judgment on Deltchev, 1951

> Ambrosetti, Ronald J. *Eric Ambler,* 74–83.
> Lewis, Peter. *Eric Ambler,* 86–100.
> Wolfe, Peter. *Alarms and Epitaphs*, 84–91.

A Kind of Anger, 1964
>   Ambrosetti, Ronald J. *Eric Ambler,* 124–31.
>   Lewis, Peter. *Eric Ambler*, 142–51.
>   Wolfe, Peter. *Alarms and Epitaphs*, 158–64.

The Levanter, 1972
>   Ambrosetti, Ronald J. *Eric Ambler,* 116–22.
>   Lewis, Peter. *Eric Ambler*, 162–72.
>   Wolfe, Peter. *Alarms and Epitaphs*, 177–85.

The Light of Day, 1962
>   Ambrosetti, Ronald J. *Eric Ambler,* 104–12.
>   Lewis, Peter. *Eric Ambler*, 125–33.
>   Wolfe, Peter. *Alarms and Epitaphs*, 151–58.

The Mask of Dimitrios, 1939
>   Ambrosetti, Ronald J. *Eric Ambler,* 49–60.
>   Lewis, Peter. *Eric Ambler*, 62–73.
>   Wolfe, Peter. *Alarms and Epitaphs*, 63–74.

The Night-Comers, 1956
>   Ambrosetti, Ronald J. *Eric Ambler,* 97–101.
>   Lewis, Peter. *Eric Ambler*, 108–14.
>   Wolfe, Peter. *Alarms and Epitaphs*, 99–106.

Passage of Arms, 1959
>   Ambrosetti, Ronald J. *Eric Ambler,* 101–4.
>   Lewis, Peter. *Eric Ambler*, 114–24.
>   Wolfe, Peter. *Alarms and Epitaphs*, 106–16.

The Schirmer Inheritance, 1953
>   Ambrosetti, Ronald J. *Eric Ambler,* 83–94.
>   Lewis, Peter. *Eric Ambler*, 100–107.
>   Wolfe, Peter. *Alarms and Epitaphs*, 91–99.

Send No More Roses, 1977
>   Lewis, Peter. *Eric Ambler*, 186–98.
>   Wolfe, Peter. *Alarms and Epitaphs*, 197–207.

Uncommon Danger, 1937
>   Ambrosetti, Ronald J. *Eric Ambler,* 35–40.
>   Lewis, Peter. *Eric Ambler*, 33–42.
>   Wolfe, Peter. *Alarms and Epitaphs*, 40–47.

KINGSLEY AMIS

The Alteration, 1976
>   Aldiss, Brian W. *The Detached Retina,* 107–11.
>   Salwak, Dale. *Kingsley Amis*, 197–207.

The Anti-Death League, 1966
>   Salwak, Dale. *Kingsley Amis*, 143–55.

Difficulties With Girls, 1988

  Salwak, Dale. *Kingsley Amis,* 251–60.

Ending Up, 1974

  Salwak, Dale. *Kingsley Amis,* 186–96.

The Folks That Live on the Hill, 1990

  Salwak, Dale. *Kingsley Amis,* 260–66.

Girl, 20, 1971

  Salwak, Dale. *Kingsley Amis,* 174–80.

The Green Man, 1969

  Jacobs, Eric. *Kingsley Amis,* 307–12.
  Salwak, Dale. *Kingsley Amis,* 165–74.

I Like It Here, 1958

  Costa, Richard Hauer. *An Appointment with Somerset Maugham,* 116–19.
  Jacobs, Eric. *Kingsley Amis,* 199–215.
  Salwak, Dale. *Kingsley Amis,* 101–7.

I Want It Now, 1969

  Jacobs, Eric. *Kingsley Amis,* 298–300.
  Salwak, Dale. *Kingsley Amis,* 155–61.

Jake's Thing, 1978

  Antor, Heinz. *Der englische Universitätsroman,* 697–700.
  Rabinovitz, Rubin. "The Reaction against Modernism: Amis, Snow, Wilson," in John Richetti et al., eds., *The Columbia History,* 900–901.
  Salwak, Dale. *Kingsley Amis,* 207–12.

Lucky Jim, 1954

  Antor, Heinz. *Der englische Universitätsroman,* 611–15.
  Costa, Richard Hauer. *An Appointment with Somerset Maugham,* 106–8.
  English, James F. *Comic Transactions,* 128–52.
  Jacobs, Eric. *Kingsley Amis,* 142–62.
  Krishnan, R. S. "Closure in Kingsley Amis's *Lucky Jim.*" *Stud in Contemp Satire* 18 (1991–92), 18–25.
  Lamarque, Peter, and Stein Haugom Olsen. *Truth, Fiction, and Literature,* 405–6.
  Salwak, Dale. *Kingsley Amis,* 60–75.
  Taylor, D. J. *After the War,* 48–50, 67–81.

The Old Devils, 1986

  Salwak, Dale. *Kingsley Amis,* 241–51.

One Fat Englishman, 1963

  Jacobs, Eric. *Kingsley Amis,* 227–29.
  Salwak, Dale. *Kingsley Amis,* 132–43.

The Riverside Villas Murder, 1973

  Salwak, Dale. *Kingsley Amis,* 180–86.

The Russian Girl, 1994

Allen, Brooke. "The Professor and the Poetess." *New Criterion* 12:9 (1994), 69–71.

Russian Hide-and-Seek, 1980

Aldiss, Brian W. *The Detached Retina,* 111–15.
Salwak, Dale. *Kingsley Amis,* 212–24.
Spiering, M. *Englishness,* 156–63, 175–77.

Stanley and the Women, 1984

Jacobs, Eric. *Kingsley Amis,* 317–21.
Rabinovitz, Rubin. "The Reaction against Modernism: Amis, Snow, Wilson," in John Richetti et al., eds., *The Columbia History,* 900–901.
Salwak, Dale. *Kingsley Amis,* 226–41.

Take A Girl Like You, 1960

Rabinovitz, Rubin. "The Reaction against Modernism: Amis, Snow, Wilson," in John Richetti et al., eds., *The Columbia History,* 900–901.
Salwak, Dale. *Kingsley Amis,* 109–28.

That Uncertain Feeling, 1955

Jacobs, Eric. *Kingsley Amis,* 177–79.
Salwak, Dale. *Kingsley Amis,* 83–101.

MARTIN AMIS

Dead Babies, 1975

Diedrick, James. *Understanding Martin Amis,* 32–40.

The Information, 1995

Diedrick, James. *Understanding Martin Amis,* 174–89.
Nash, John. "Fiction May be a Legal Paternity: Martin Amis's *The Information.*" *English* 45 (1996), 213–23.
Todd, Richard. *Consuming Fictions,* 189–90.

London Fields, 1989

Bernard, Catherine. "Dismembering/Remembering Mimesis: Martin Amis, Graham Swift," in Theo D'haen and Hans Bertens, eds., *British Postmodern Fiction,* 124–44.
Diedrick, James. *Understanding Martin Amis,* 147–61.
Finney, Brian. "Narrative and Narrated Homicides in Martin Amis's *Other People* and *London Fields.*" *Critique* (Washington, DC) 37 (1995), 8–15.
Mills, Sara. "Working with Sexism: What Can Feminist Text Analysis Do?," in Peter Verdonk and Jean Jacques Weber, eds., *Twentieth-Century Fiction,* 207–18.
Moyle, David. "Beyond the Black Hole: Emergence of Science Fiction Themes in the Recent Work of Martin Amis." *Extrapolation* 36 (1995), 309–11.

Smith, Penny. "Hell innit: The Millennium in Alasdair Gray's *Lanark*, Martin Amis's *London Fields*, and Shena Mackay's *Dunedin*," in Laurel Brake, ed., *The Endings of Epochs*, 120–23.

Todd, Richard. *Consuming Fictions*, 193–96.

Money: A Suicide Note, 1984

Bernard, Catherine. "Dismembering/Remembering Mimesis: Martin Amis, Graham Swift," in Theo D'haen and Hans Bertens, eds., *British Postmodern Fiction*, 124–44.

Brantlinger, Patrick. *Fictions of State*, 258–60.

Diedrick, James. *Understanding Martin Amis*, 70–101.

Elias, Amy J. "Meta-*mimesis*? The Problem of British Postmodern Realism," in Theo D'haen and Hans Bertens, eds., *British Postmodern Fiction*, 20–23.

Todd, Richard. *Consuming Fictions*, 190–93.

Wood, Michael. "The Contemporary Novel," in John Richetti et al., eds., *The Columbia History*, 979–80.

Other People: A Mystery Story, 1981

Diedrick, James. *Understanding Martin Amis*, 53–68.

Finney, Brian. "Narrative and Narrated Homicides in Martin Amis's *Other People* and *London Fields*." *Critique* (Washington, DC) 37 (1995), 3–8.

The Rachel Papers, 1973

Diedrick, James. *Understanding Martin Amis*, 20–31.

Success, 1978

Diedrick, James. *Understanding Martin Amis*, 40–49.

Taylor, D. J. *After the War*, 191–93.

Time's Arrow, 1991

Bernard, Catherine. "Dismembering/Remembering Mimesis: Martin Amis, Graham Swift," in Theo D'haen and Hans Bertens, eds., *British Postmodern Fiction*, 133–44.

Diedrick, James. *Understanding Martin Amis*, 161–71.

Easterbrook, Neil. " 'I Know That It Is To Do with Trash and Shit, and That It Is Wrong in Time': Narrative Reversal in Martin Amis' *Time's Arrow*." *Conf of Coll Teachers of Engl Stud* 55 (1995), 52–61.

Granofsky, Ronald. *The Trauma Novel*, 57–64.

Moyle, David. "Beyond the Black Hole: Emergence of Science Fiction Themes in the Recent Work of Martin Amis." *Extrapolation* 36 (1995), 311–15.

THOMAS AMORY

The Life of John Buncle, Esq., 1756–1766

Antor, Heinz. *Der englische Universitätsroman*, 37–39, 50–51.

JAY ASHTON

The Door From Nowhere, 1992

Filmer-Davies, Kath. *Fantasy Fiction and Welsh Myth,* 56–61.

PENELOPE AUBIN

The Noble Slaves, 1722

Snader, Joe. "The Oriental Captivity Narrative and Early English Fiction." *Eighteenth-Cent Fiction* 9 (1997), 289–97.

JANE AUSTEN

Emma, 1816

Brodie, Laura Fairchild. "Jane Austen and the Common Reader: 'Opinions of *Mansfield Park,*' 'Opinions of *Emma,*' and the Janeite Phenomenon." *Texas Stud in Lit and Lang* 37 (1995), 57–65.

Derry, Stephen. *"Emma,* the Earthly Paradise, and *The History of Nourjahad." Notes and Queries* 43 (1996), 417–18.

Derry, Stephen. "Harriet Smith's Reading." *Persuasions* 14 (1992), 70–72.

Devereux, Cecily. " 'Much, much beyond impropriety': Ludic Subversions and the Limitations of Decorum in *Emma." Mod Lang Stud* 25:4 (1995), 37–54.

Fergus, Jan. "Jane Austen: Tensions Between Security and Marginality," in Beth Fowkes Tobin, ed., *History, Gender, and Eighteenth-Century Literature,* 265–66.

Fergus, Jan. "Male Whiners in Austen's Novels." *Persuasions* 18 (1996), 102–8.

Fletcher, Loraine. "Emma: The Shadow Novelist." *Crit Survey* 4:1 (1992), 36–44.

Ginsburg, Michael Peled. *Economies of Change,* 118–37.

Gliserman, Martin. *Psychoanalysis, Language, and the Body of the Text,* 52–55.

Gordon, Jan B. *Gossip and Subversion,* 85–87.

Gorman, Anita G. *The Body in Illness and Health,* 36, 69–81, 114–16, 152–56, 178–83.

Hall, Lynda A. "Jane Austen's Attractive Rogues: Willoughby, Wickham, and Frank Churchill." *Persuasions* 18 (1996), 186–90.

Havely, Cicely Palser. *"Emma:* Portrait of the Artist as a Young Woman." *English* 42 (1993), 221–36.

Heyns, Michiel. *Expulsion and the Nineteenth-Century Novel,* 53–59.

Hollahan, Eugene. *Crisis-Consciousness,* 61–64.

Hopkins, Lisa. "Jane Austen and Money." *Wordsworth Circle* 25 (1994), 77–78.

Jager, Colin. "Renouncing the Impossible, Wishing for Nothing in *Emma*." *Persuasions* 17 (1995), 40–45.

Kestner, Joseph A. "Jane Austen: Revolutionizing Masculinities." *Persuasions* 16 (1994), 147–59.

Kittredge, Katharine. "That Excellent Miss Bates." *Persuasions* 17 (1995), 26–30.

Kohn, Denise. "Reading *Emma* as a Lesson on 'Ladyhood': A Study in the Domestic *Bildungsroman*." *Essays in Lit* (Macomb, IL) 22 (1995), 45–55.

Lane, Maggie. *Jane Austen and Food*, 153–68.

MacCarthy, B. G. *The Female Pen*, 493–97.

McMaster, Juliet. "The Children in *Emma*." *Persuasions* 14 (1992), 62–67.

McMaster, Juliet. "Emma Watson: Jane Austen's Uncompleted Heroine," in Robert M. Polhemus and Roger B. Henkle, eds., *Critical Reconstructions*, 212–16, 220–27.

McMaster, Juliet. *Jane Austen the Novelist*, 90–105, 164–67, 189–90.

Mezei, Kathy. "Who Is Speaking Here? Free Indirect Discourse, Gender, and Authority in *Emma, Howards End,* and *Mrs. Dalloway*," in Mezei, ed., *Ambiguous Discourse*, 72–78.

Myer, Valerie Grosvenor. *Ten Great English Novelists*, 73–77.

Pinch, Adela. *Strange Fits of Passion*, 142–44.

Potter, Tiffany F. " 'A Low But Very Feeling Tone': The Lesbian Continuum and Power Relations in Jane Austen's *Emma*." *Engl Stud in Canada* 20 (1994), 187–201.

Restuccia, Frances L. "A Black Morning: Kristevan Melancholia in Jane Austen's *Emma*." *Am Imago* 51 (1994), 447–68.

Ricks, Christopher. *Essays in Appreciation*, 96–99.

Rogers, Pat. " 'Caro sposo': Mrs. Elton, Burneys, Thrales, and Noels." *R of Engl Stud* 45 (1994), 70–75.

Roulston, Christine. "Discourse, Gender, and Gossip: Some Reflections on Bakhtin and *Emma*," in Kathy Mezei, ed., *Ambiguous Discourse*, 40–61.

Ruderman, Anne. "Moral Education in Jane Austen's *Emma*," in Joseph M. Knippenberg and Peter Augustine Lawler, eds., *Poets, Princes, and Private Citizens*, 271–85.

Sales, Roger. *Jane Austen and Representations*, 135–69.

Straus, Nina Pelikan. "Emma, Anna, Tess: Skepticism, Betrayal, and Displacement." *Philos and Lit* 18 (1994), 72–88.

Sutherland, John. *Is Heathcliff a Murderer?*, 14–19.

Tanaka, Toshiro. "Double Negation in Jane Austen." *Poetica* (Tokyo) 41 (1994), 137–48.

Thompson, James. "Jane Austen," in John Richetti et al., eds., *The Columbia History*, 283–85.

Tobin, Mary-Elisabeth Fowkes. "Aiding Impoverished Gentlewomen: Power and Class in *Emma*," in Arthur F. Marotti et al., eds., *Reading with a Difference*, 45–58.

Tucker, George Holbert. *Jane Austen the Woman*, 120–28.

Tumbleson, Ray. " 'It is like a woman's writing': The Alternative Epistolary Novel in *Emma.*" *Persuasions* 14 (1992), 141–43.

Waldron, Mary. "Men of Sense and Silly Wives: The Confusions of Mr. Knightley." *Stud in the Novel* 28 (1996), 141–56.

Wallace, Tara Ghoshal. *Jane Austen and Narrative Authority*, 77–97.

White, Laura Mooneyham. "Jane Austen and the Marriage Plot: Questions of Persistence," in Devoney Looser, ed., *Jane Austen*, 73–77.

York, R. A. *Strangers and Secrets*, 24–39.

Lady Susan, 1871

Alliston, April. *Virtue's Faults*, 109–11.

Ballaster, Ros. *Seductive Forms*, 208–10.

Gordon, Jan B. *Gossip and Subversion*, 70–73.

Gorman, Anita G. *The Body in Illness and Health*, 101–3, 135–36.

Wallace, Tara Ghoshal. *Jane Austen and Narrative Authority*, 1–16.

Love and Friendship, 1922

Bilger, Audrey. "Goblin Laughter: Violent Comedy and the Condition of Women in Frances Burney and Jane Austen." *Women's Stud* 24 (1995), 330–31.

Gorman, Anita G. *The Body in Illness and Health*, 31–32, 43.

MacCarthy, B. G. *The Female Pen*, 473–76.

McMaster, Juliet. *Jane Austen the Novelist*, 18–35.

Mansfield Park, 1814

Alliston, April. *Virtue's Faults*, 237–40.

Anderson, Misty G. " 'The Different Sorts of Friendship': Desire in *Mansfield Park,*" in Devoney Looser, ed., *Jane Austen*, 167–82.

Auerbach, Emily. "Jane Austen, Fanny Price and the Courage to Write." *Persuasions* 17 (1995), 152–56.

Baldridge, Cates. *The Dialogics of Dissent*, 40–62.

Bander, Elaine. "The Other Play in *Mansfield Park:* Shakespeare's *Henry VIII.*" *Persuasions* 17 (1995), 111–18.

Berglund, Birgitta. *Woman's Whole Existence*, 136–58.

Brodey, Inger Sigrun Bredkjaer. "Papas and Ha-has: Rebellion, Authority, and Landscaping in *Mansfield Park.*" *Persuasions* 17 (1995), 90–96.

Brodie, Laura Fairchild. "Jane Austen and the Common Reader: 'Opinions of *Mansfield Park,*' 'Opinions of *Emma,*' and the Janeite Phenomenon." *Texas Stud in Lit and Lang* 37 (1995), 57–65.

Brown, Penny. *The Captured World*, 29–30.

Byatt, A. S., and Ignês Sodré. *Imagining Characters*, 1–42.

Cleere, Eileen. "Reinvesting Nieces: *Mansfield Park* and the Economics of Endogomy." *Novel* 28 (1995), 113–29.

Dunn, Allen. "The Ethics of *Mansfield Park:* MacIntyre, Said, and Social Context." *Soundings* 78 (1995), 483–500.

Erwin, Jacqueline M. "Lady Bertram, Mrs. Norris and Mrs. Price: Place and Moral Identity in *Mansfield Park.*" *Persuasions* 17 (1995), 144–51.

Evans, Mary. "Henry Crawford and the 'Sphere of Love' in *Mansfield Park,*" in Nigel Wood, ed., *"Mansfield Park,"* 31–52.

Ferguson, Moira. *Colonialism and Gender Relations,* 65–89.

Gardiner, Ellen. "Privacy, Privilege, and 'Poaching' in *Mansfield Park,*" in Devoney Looser, ed., *Jane Austen,* 151–63.

Gay, Penny. "Theatricality and the Theatricals in *Mansfield Park.*" *Persuasions* 17 (1995), 121–28.

Gillooly, Eileen. "Rehabilitating Mary Crawford: *Mansfield Park* and the Relief of 'Throwing Ridicule,' " in Susan Ostrov Weisser and Jennifer Fleischner, eds., *Feminist Nightmares,* 328–38.

Ginsburg, Michael Peled. *Economies of Change,* 99–117.

Gordon, Jan B. *Gossip and Subversion,* 90–95.

Gorman, Anita G. *The Body in Illness and Health,* 34–35, 63–69, 111–14, 149–52, 175–78.

Goubert, Pierre. "L'ironie de Jane Austen." *Etudes Anglaises* 48 (1995), 44–49.

Greenfield, Susan C. "Fanny's Misreading and the Misreading of Fanny: Women, Literature, and Interiority in *Mansfield Park.*" *Texas Stud in Lit and Lang* 36 (1994), 306–22.

Hammond, Brean S. "The Political Unconscious in *Mansfield Park,*" in Nigel Wood, ed., *"Mansfield Park,"* 58–87.

Harris, Jocelyn. "Jane Austen and the Burden of the (Male) Past: The Case Reexamined," in Devoney Looser, ed., *Jane Austen,* 90–91.

Heyns, Michiel. *Expulsion and the Nineteenth-Century Novel,* 6–18, 51–89.

Hoberg, Thomas. "Fanny in Fairyland: *Mansfield Park* and the Cinderella Legend." *Persuasions* 17 (1995), 137–43.

Hopkins, Lisa. "Jane Austen and Money." *Wordsworth Circle* 25 (1994), 77–78.

Hudson, Glenda A. "Consolidated Communities: Masculine and Feminine Values in Jane Austen's Fiction," in Devoney Looser, ed., *Jane Austen,* 107–12.

Johnson, Claudia L. "Gender, Theory and Jane Austen Culture," in Nigel Wood, ed., *"Mansfield Park,"* 104–17.

Johnson, Claudia L. "What Became of Jane Austen? *Mansfield Park.*" *Persuasions* 17 (1995), 59–69.

Kelsall, Malcolm. *The Great Good Place,* 107–14.

Kestner, Joseph A. "Jane Austen: Revolutionizing Masculinities." *Persuasions* 16 (1994), 147–59.

Kirkham, Margaret. "Edmund Bertram: A Politically Correct Hero?" *Persuasions* 17 (1995), 71–76.

Knox-Shaw, Peter. "Fanny Price Refuses to Kowtow." *R of Engl Stud* 47 (1996), 212–17.

Kuwahara, Kuldip Kaur. "Jane Austen's *Mansfield Park,* Property, and the British Empire." *Persuasions* 17 (1995), 106–10.

Lamont, Claire. " 'Let other pens dwell on guilt and misery': Adultery in Jane Austen," in Nicholas White and Naomi Segal, eds., *Scarlet Letters*, 70–79.

Lew, Joseph. " 'That Abominable Traffic': *Mansfield Park* and the Dynamics of Slavery," in Beth Fowkes Tobin, ed., *History, Gender, and Eighteenth-Century Literature*, 271–94.

MacCarthy, B. G. *The Female Pen*, 489–93.

McMaster, Juliet. "Emma Watson: Jane Austen's Uncompleted Heroine," in Robert M. Polhemus and Roger B. Henkle, eds., *Critical Reconstructions*, 212–18.

McMaster, Juliet. *Jane Austen the Novelist*, 138–42, 160–63, 186–89.

McMaster, Juliet. "The Talkers and Listeners of *Mansfield Park*." *Persuasions* 17 (1995), 77–88.

Marshall, Mary Gaither. "Will Mrs. Norris Return to Harass Another Day? Continuations and Adaptations of *Mansfield Park*." *Persuasions* 17 (1995), 157–66.

Palmer, Frank. *Literature and Moral Understanding*, 116–19, 138–43.

Pedley, Colin. " 'Terrific and Unprincipled Compositions': The Reception of *Lovers' Vows* and *Mansfield Park*." *Philol Q* 74 (1995), 297–314.

Perera, Suvendrini. *Reaches of Empire*, 42–45.

Preus, Nicholas. "Power Houses and Polite Fiction." *Persuasions* 17 (1995), 167–74.

Rasmussen, Barbara. "Discovering 'A New Way of Reading': Shoshana Felman, Psychoanalysis and *Mansfield Park*," in Nigel Wood, ed., *"Mansfield Park,"* 124–53.

Reid-Walsh, Jacqueline. " 'Entering the World' of *Regency Society:* The Ballroom Scenes in *Northanger Abbey*, 'The Watsons' and *Mansfield Park*." *Persuasions* 16 (1994), 115–24.

Reid-Walsh, Jacqueline. " 'Pray, is she out, or is she not?—I am puzzled': Decoding Fanny's Position at Mansfield Park." *Persuasions* 17 (1995), 130–35.

Richardson, Alan. *Literature, Education, and Romanticism*, 194–202.

Rowen, Norma. "Reinscribing Cinderella: Jane Austen and the Fairy Tale," in Joe Sanders, ed., *Functions of the Fantastic*, 32–34.

Sales, Roger. *Jane Austen and Representations*, 87–131.

Smith, Peter. "*Mansfield Park* and the World Stage." *Cambridge Q* 23 (1994), 203–29.

Spacks, Patricia Meyer. *Desire and Truth*, 218–24.

Sparshott, Francis. "The View from Gadshill." *Philos and Lit* 20 (1996), 401–4.

Steffes, Michael. "Slavery and *Mansfield Park:* The Historical and Biographical Context." *Engl Lang Notes* 34:2 (1996), 23–36.

Sutherland, John. *Is Heathcliff a Murderer?*, 1–9.

Tanaka, Toshiro. "Double Negation in Jane Austen." *Poetica* (Tokyo) 41 (1994), 137–48.

Terry, Judith. "Sir Thomas Bertram's 'Business in Antigua.' " *Persuasions* 17 (1995), 97–104.

Thompson, James. "Jane Austen," in John Richetti et al., eds., *The Columbia History*, 290–93.

Tobin, Beth Fowkes. *"Mansfield Park,* Hannah More, and the Evangelical Redefinition of Virtue." *Stud on Voltaire and the Eighteenth Cent* 304 (1992), 787.

Tucker, George Holbert. *Jane Austen the Woman*, 80–82, 140–44, 165–67, 209–12.

Usui, Masami. "Fanny's Awakening to Herself in Quest for Privacy in Jane Austen's *Mansfield Park." Stud in Culture and the Hum* 2 (1993), 1–28.

Waldron, Mary. "The Frailties of Fanny: *Mansfield Park* and the Evangelical Movement." *Eighteenth-Cent Fiction* 6 (1994), 259–81.

Wallace, Tara Ghoshal. *Jane Austen and Narrative Authority*, 59–75.

Wilson, George M. "Edward Said on Contrapuntal Reading." *Philos and Lit* 18 (1994), 267–73.

Winnifrith, Tom. *Fallen Women,* 20–23, 26–29.

Worthington, Pepper. "Jane Austen's Image of Female Character and Personality in *Mansfield Park." Mount Olive R* 6 (1992), 61–76.

Northanger Abbey, 1818

Alliston, April. "Gender and the Rhetoric of Evidence in Early-Modern Historical Narratives." *Compar Lit Stud* 33 (1996), 233–35.

Alliston, April. *Virtue's Faults*, 226–35.

Baldridge, Cates. *The Dialogics of Dissent*, 46–48.

Barfoot, C. C. "The Gist of the Gothic in English Fiction; or, Gothic and the Invasion of Boundaries," in Valeria Tinkler-Villani and Peter Davidson, eds., *Exhibited by Candlelight*, 162–63.

Barreca, Regina. *Untamed and Unabashed,* 45–52.

Brown, Penny. *The Captured World,* 28–29.

Burton, Antoinette. " 'Invention Is What Delights Me': Jane Austen's Remaking of 'English' History," in Devoney Looser, ed., *Jane Austen*, 35–36.

Cohen, Paula Marantz. "Jane Austen's Rejection of Rousseau: A Novelistic and Feminist Initiation." *Papers on Lang and Lit* 30 (1994), 220–26, 231–33.

Derry, Stephen. "Feud, the Gothic, and Coat Symbolism in *Northanger Abbey." Persuasions* 18 (1996), 49–53.

Edgecombe, Rodney Stenning. "Legitimate Hyperbole in *Northanger Abbey." Univ of Dayton R* 22:1 (1993), 147–48.

Gordon, Jan B. *Gossip and Subversion*, 81–84.

Gorman, Anita G. *The Body in Illness and Health*, 45–50, 103–10, 136–39, 171–72.

Heyns, Michiel. *Expulsion and the Nineteenth-Century Novel,* 54–60.

Hoeveler, Diane. "Vindicating *Northanger Abbey:* Mary Wollstonecraft, Jane Austen, and Gothic Feminism," in Devoney Looser, ed., *Jane Austen*, 117–34.

Howard, Jacqueline. *Reading Gothic Fiction*, 160–82.

Jerinic, Maria. "In Defense of the Gothic: Rereading *Northanger Abbey*," in Devoney Looser, ed., *Jane Austen*, 137–48.

Kelsall, Malcolm. *The Great Good Place*, 103–7.

Lamont, Claire. "Jane Austen's Gothic Architecture," in Valeria Tinkler-Villani and Peter Davidson, eds., *Exhibited by Candlelight*, 107–15.

Looser, Devoney. "(Re)Making History and Philosophy: Austen's *Northanger Abbey*." *European Romantic R* 4:1 (1993), 34–56.

Lynch, Deidre. "At Home with Jane Austen," in Deidre Lynch and William B. Warner, eds., *Cultural Institutions of the Novel*, 176–80.

MacCarthy, B. G. *The Female Pen*, 487–89.

McMaster, Juliet. *Jane Austen the Novelist*, 43–45, 177–79.

Malina, Debra. "Rereading the Patriarchal Text: *The Female Quixote, Northanger Abbey*, and the Trace of the Absent Mother." *Eighteenth-Cent Fiction* 8 (1996), 271–92.

Middleton, Linda C. "Anxious Spectators and Voluntary Spies: The Novel Hauntings of *Northanger Abbey*." *Genre* 27 (1994), 105–18.

Minma, Shinobu. "General Tilney and Tyranny: *Northanger Abbey*." *Eighteenth-Cent Fiction* 8 (1996), 503–18.

Neill, Edward. "The Secret of *Northanger Abbey*." *Essays in Criticism* 47:1 (1997), 13–29.

Nollen, Elizabeth Mahn. "Female Detective Figures in British Fiction: Coping with Madness and Imprisonment." *Clues* 15:2 (1994), 42–45.

Oh, Jung-hwa. "Catherine Morland and Henry Tilney: Two Readers in *Northanger Abbey*." *J of Engl Lang and Lit* 40 (1994), 657–74.

Ray, Joan Klingel. "Austen's *Northanger Abbey*." *Explicator* 54 (1996), 142–44.

Reid-Walsh, Jacqueline. " 'Entering the World' of *Regency Society:* The Ballroom Scenes in *Northanger Abbey,* 'The Watsons' and *Mansfield Park*." *Persuasions* 16 (1994), 115–24.

Richter, David H. *The Progress of Romance*, 100–102.

Siskin, Clifford. "Jane Austen and the Engendering of Disciplinarity," in Devoney Looser, ed., *Jane Austen*, 60–64.

Stewart, Garrett. *Dear Reader*, 92–96.

Thompson, James. "Jane Austen," in John Richetti et al., eds., *The Columbia History*, 277–83.

Tucker, George Holbert. *Jane Austen the Woman*, 132–35.

Wallace, Tara Ghoshal. *Jane Austen and Narrative Authority*, 17–30.

Persuasion, 1818

Bander, Elaine. "Blair's *Rhetoric* and the Art of *Persuasion*." *Persuasions* 15 (1993), 124–30.

Bilger, Audrey. "Goblin Laughter: Violent Comedy and the Condition of Women in Frances Burney and Jane Austen." *Women's Stud* 24 (1995), 331–33.

Brown, Julia Prewitt. "Private and Public in *Persuasion*." *Persuasions* 15 (1993), 131–38.

Cohen, Monica F. "Persuading the Navy Home: Austen and Married Women's Professional Property." *Novel* 29 (1996), 347–64.

Copeland, Edward. "*Persuasion:* The Jane Austen Consumer's Guide." *Persuasions* 15 (1993), 111–21.

Fergus, Jan. "Male Whiners in Austen's Novels." *Persuasions* 18 (1996), 99–102.

Fergus, Jan. " 'My sore throats, you know, are always worse than anybody's': Mary Musgrove and Jane Austen's Art of Whining." *Persuasions* 15 (1993), 139–47.

Giordano, Julia. "The Word as Battleground in Jane Austen's *Persuasion,"* in Carol J. Singley and Susan Elizabeth Sweeney, eds., *Anxious Power,* 107–21.

Gordon, Jan B. *Gossip and Subversion,* 63–68.

Gorman, Anita G. *The Body in Illness and Health,* 36–38, 81–84, 116–24, 156–61.

Grundy, Isobel. "*Persuasion:* or, The Triumph of Cheerfulness." *Persuasions* 15 (1993), 89–99.

Hale, John K. "*Persuasion,* Vol. IV, Chapter XI." *Persuasions* 16 (1994), 34–35.

Harris, Jocelyn. "Jane Austen and the Burden of the (Male) Past: The Case Reexamined," in Devoney Looser, ed., *Jane Austen,* 94–97.

Heldman, James. "The Crofts and the Art of Suggestion in *Persuasion:* A Speculation." *Persuasions* 15 (1993), 46–52.

Heydt-Stevenson, Jill. " 'Unbecoming Conjunctions': Mourning the Loss of Landscape and Love in *Persuasion." Eighteenth-Cent Fiction* 8 (1995), 51–71.

Holstein, Suzy Clarkson. "Out of the Estate and into the Rescue Boat." *Persuasions* 15 (1993), 53–56.

Hopkins, Lisa. "Jane Austen and Money." *Wordsworth Circle* 25 (1994), 78.

Kaplan, Laurie. "*Persuasion:* The Accidents of Human Life." *Persuasions* 15 (1993), 157–63.

Kaufmann, David. *The Business of Common Life,* 139–48, 159–63.

Kestner, Joseph A. "Jane Austen: Revolutionizing Masculinities." *Persuasions* 16 (1994), 147–59.

Knuth, Deborah J. " 'There is so little real friendship in the world!': 'Distant civility,' conversational 'treat[s],' and good advice in *Persuasion." Persuasions* 15 (1993), 148–56.

Koppel, Gene. "Jane Austen and Anne Tyler, Sister Novelists Under the Skin: Comparison of *Persuasion* and *Saint Maybe." Persuasions* 15 (1993), 164–69.

Lambert, Ellen Zetzel. *The Face of Love,* 83–86.

MacCarthy, B. G. *The Female Pen,* 497–99.

McLean, Barbara. "Professional Persuasion: Dr. Anne Elliot." *Persuasions* 15 (1993), 170–77.

McMaster, Juliet. "Emma Watson: Jane Austen's Uncompleted Heroine," in Robert M. Polhemus and Roger B. Henkle, eds., *Critical Reconstructions*, 212–20.

McMaster, Juliet. *Jane Austen the Novelist*, 142–46, 167–69, 190–96.

Masters, Joshua J. "The Reversal of Gender Roles in *Persuasion.*" *Persuasions* 15 (1993), 251.

Millgate, Jane. "*Persuasion* and the Presence of Scott." *Persuasions* 15 (1993), 184–94.

Morgan, Susan. "Captain Wentworth, British Imperialism and Personal Romance." *Persuasions* 18 (1996), 88–96.

Myer, Valerie Grosvenor. *Ten Great English Novelists*, 77–79.

Newark, Elizabeth. "Love Comes to Penelope Clay." *Persuasions* 15 (1993), 196–99.

O'Toole, Tess. "Reconfiguring the Family in *Persuasion.*" *Persuasions* 15 (1993), 200–206.

Perera, Suvendrini. *Reaches of Empire,* 39–46.

Pinch, Adela. "Lost in a Book: Jane Austen's *Persuasion.*" *Stud in Romanticism* 32 (1993), 97–117.

Pinch, Adela. *Strange Fits of Passion*, 138–40, 144–63.

Ray, Joan Klingel. "In Defense of Lady Russell; or, The Godmother Knew Best." *Persuasions* 15 (1993), 207–15.

Reid-Walsh, Jacqueline. " 'She Learned Romance as She Grew Older': From Conduct Book to Romance in *Persuasion.*" *Persuasions* 15 (1993), 216–23.

Ricks, Christopher. *Essays in Appreciation*, 104–6.

Rowen, Norma. "Reinscribing Cinderella: Jane Austen and the Fairy Tale," in Joe Sanders, ed., *Functions of the Fantastic*, 34–36.

Rzepka, Charles J. "Making It in a Brave New World: Marriage, Profession, and Anti-Romantic *Ekstasis* in Austen's *Persuasion.*" *Stud in the Novel* 26 (1994), 99–115.

Sales, Roger. *Jane Austen and Representations*, 171–99.

Seeber, Barbara K., and Kathleen James-Cavan . " 'Unvarying, warm admiration everywhere': The Truths about Wentworth." *Persuasions* 16 (1994), 39–47.

Showalter, Elaine. "Retrenchment." *Persuasions* 15 (1993), 101–9.

Smith, Peter. "Jane Austen's *Persuasion* and the Secret Conspiracy." *Cambridge Q* 24 (1995), 279–303.

Spacks, Patricia Meyer. "Reply to David Richter: Form and Ideology— Novels at Work." *Eighteenth Cent* 37 (1996), 220–31.

Stewart, Garrett. *Dear Reader*, 100–112.

Terry, Judith. "The Slow Process of *Persuasion.*" *Persuasions* 15 (1993), 226–33.

Thompson, James. "Jane Austen," in John Richetti et al., eds., *The Columbia History*, 288–90.

Thomsen, Inger Sigrun. "*Persuasion* and Persuadability: When Vanity is a Virtue." *Persuasions* 15 (1993), 235–42.

Tracy, Laura. "Relational Competence: Jane Austen's *Persuasion.*" *Persuasions* 18 (1996), 154–58.

Tumbleson, Ray. " 'Suspense and Indecision': Austen's Revision of *Persuasion.*" *Persuasions* 15 (1993), 261–63.

Vlasopolos, Anca. "Staking Claims for No Territory: The Sea as Woman's Space," in Margaret R. Higonnet and Joan Templeton, eds., *Reconfigured Spheres*, 77–80.

Wallace, Tara Ghoshal. *Jane Austen and Narrative Authority*, 99–116.

Warhol, Robyn. "The Look, the Body, and the Heroine of *Persuasion:* A Feminist-Narratological View of Jane Austen," in Kathy Mezei, ed., *Ambiguous Discourse*, 21–38.

White, Laura Mooneyham. "Jane Austen and the Marriage Plot: Questions of Persistence," in Devoney Looser, ed., *Jane Austen*, 78–80.

Wickes, Joanne. " 'Song of the Dying Swan'?: The Nineteenth-Century Response to *Persuasion.*" *Stud in the Novel* 28 (1996), 38–53.

Wilson, Margaret Madrigal. "The Hero and the Other Man in Jane Austen's Novels." *Persuasions* 18 (1996), 182–85.

Pride and Prejudice, 1813

Allen, Dennis W. *Sexuality in Victorian Fiction*, 37–59.

Almond, Barbara, and Richard Almond. *The Therapeutic Narrative*, 23–42.

Barreca, Regina. *Untamed and Unabashed,* 55–57.

Berglund, Birgitta. *Woman's Whole Existence,* 159–63, 179–93.

Blue, Denise. "Saint Jane." *Persuasions* 16 (1994), 32–33.

Breihan, John, and Clive Caplan. "Jane Austen and the Militia." *Persuasions* 14 (1992), 18–25.

Clifford-Amos, Terence. "Some Observations on the Language of *Pride and Prejudice.*" *Lang and Lit* (San Antonio) 20 (1995), 1–10.

Cohen, Michael. *Sisters*, 96–98, 111–15.

Cohen, Paula Marantz. "Jane Austen's Rejection of Rousseau: A Novelistic and Feminist Initiation." *Papers on Lang and Lit* 30 (1994), 226–33.

Croft, Sarah Frances, and Mary Lee Moldenhauer. "Lady Catherine: A Castle Built on Sand?" *Persuasions* 16 (1994), 21–24.

Focaccia, Angelita. "*Orgoglio e pregiudizio:* Arte della conversazione e mondanità nei salotti di Jane Austen." *Lettore di Provincia* 25:91 (1994), 81–86.

Ginsburg, Michael Peled. *Economies of Change*, 124–27.

Gordon, Jan B. *Gossip and Subversion*, 87–93.

Gorman, Anita G. *The Body in Illness and Health*, 58–61, 110–11, 145–49, 172–75.

Goubert, Pierre. "L'ironie de Jane Austen." *Etudes Anglaises* 48 (1995), 44–49.

Hall, Lynda A. "Jane Austen's Attractive Rogues: Willoughby, Wickham, and Frank Churchill." *Persuasions* 18 (1996), 186–90.

Hollahan, Eugene. *Crisis-Consciousness*, 61–64.

Hopkins, Lisa. "Jane Austen and Money." *Wordsworth Circle* 25 (1994), 77.

Horwitz, Barbara. "*Pride and Prejudice* and *Framley Parsonage:* A Structural Resemblance." *Persuasions* 15 (1993), 32–35.

Juhasz, Suzanne. *Reading from the Heart,* 28–50.

Lambert, Ellen Zetzel. *The Face of Love,* 69–71.

MacCarthy, B. G. *The Female Pen,* 483–87.

McMaster, Juliet. "Emma Watson: Jane Austen's Uncompleted Heroine," in Robert M. Polhemus and Roger B. Henkle, eds., *Critical Reconstructions,* 212–27.

McMaster, Juliet. *Jane Austen the Novelist,* 76–89, 182–86.

Myer, Valerie Grosvenor. *Ten Great English Novelists,* 66–71.

Newey, Katherine. " 'What think you of books?': Reading in *Pride and Prejudice.*" *Sydney Stud in Engl* 21 (1995–96), 81–94.

O'Farrell, Mary Ann. "Austen's Blush." *Novel* 27 (1994), 125–37.

Rowen, Norma. "Reinscribing Cinderella: Jane Austen and the Fairy Tale," in Joe Sanders, ed., *Functions of the Fantastic,* 30–32.

Schneider, Matthew. "Card-playing and the Marriage Gamble in *Pride and Prejudice.*" *Dalhousie R* 73 (1993), 5–17.

Shaffer, Julie. "Not Subordinate: Empowering Women in the Marriage Plot—The Novels of Frances Burney, Maria Edgeworth, and Jane Austen," in Arthur F. Marotti et al., eds., *Reading with a Difference,* 34–38.

Siegel, Carol. *Male Masochism,* 115–16.

Tanaka, Toshiro. "Double Negation in Jane Austen." *Poetica* (Tokyo) 41 (1994), 137–48.

Thompson, James. "Jane Austen," in John Richetti et al., eds., *The Columbia History,* 285–88.

Turner, Martha A. *Mechanism and the Novel,* 43–62.

Wallace, Tara Ghoshal. *Jane Austen and Narrative Authority,* 45–58.

Wheat, Patricia H. *The Adytum of the Heart,* 35–40, 46–56.

Wiesenfarth, Joseph. "The Evolution of *Civility* in *Pride and Prejudice.*" *Persuasions* 16 (1994), 107–13.

Winnifrith, Tom. *Fallen Women,* 20–23, 31–34.

Sanditon, 1925

Axelrad, Arthur M. "Sir Edward's 'Ingenuity': A Corrected Reading in the *Sanditon* Manuscript." *Persuasions* 17 (1995), 47–48.

Ebbatson, Roger. "*Sanditon.*" *Crit Survey* 4 (1992), 45–51.

Fergus, Jan. "Jane Austen: Tensions Between Security and Marginality," in Beth Fowkes Tobin, ed., *History, Gender, and Eighteenth-Century Literature,* 266–67.

Gorman, Anita G. *The Body in Illness and Health,* 84–92.

Kaufmann, David. *The Business of Common Life,* 164–68.

Perera, Suvendrini. *Reaches of Empire,* 43–45.

Sacco, Teran Lee. *A Transcription and Analysis,* 164–76.

Sales, Roger. *Jane Austen and Representations,* 200–221.

White, Laura Mooneyham. "Jane Austen and the Marriage Plot: Questions of Persistence," in Devoney Looser, ed., *Jane Austen,* 80–83.

Sense and Sensibility, 1811

Barreca, Regina. *Untamed and Unabashed,* 53–55.

Benedict, Barbara M. *Framing Feeling,* 196–210.

Buchanan, Laurie. " 'Islands' of Peace: Female Friendships in Victorian Literature," in Janet Doubler Ward and JoAnna Stephens Mink, eds., *Communication and Women's Friendships,* 81–86.

Cohen, Michael. *Sisters,* 115–18.

Derry, Stephen. "Jane Austen's Use of *Measure for Measure* in *Sense and Sensibility.*" *Persuasions* 15 (1993), 37–40.

Derry, Stephen. "Robert Bage's *Barham Downs* and *Sense and Sensibility.*" *Notes and Queries* 41 (1994), 325–26.

Derry, Stephen. "Sources of Chapter Two of *Sense and Sensibility.*" *Persuasions* 16 (1994), 25–27.

Gobel, Walter. "Die Heldin als Detektiv: Das Ideal des Weiblichen in Jane Austens *Sense and Sensibility.*" *Sprachkunst* 25 (1994), 403–14.

Gordon, Jan B. *Gossip and Subversion,* 74–80.

Gorman, Anita G. *The Body in Illness and Health,* 33–34, 50–58, 139–45.

Goubert, Pierre. "*Sense and Sensibility:* Réflexions sur un titre." *Bull de la Société d'Etudes Anglo-Américaines des XVIIe et XVIIIe Siècles* 36 (1993), 55–60.

Hall, Lynda A. "Jane Austen's Attractive Rogues: Willoughby, Wickham, and Frank Churchill." *Persuasions* 18 (1996), 186–90.

Harding, D. W. "The Supposed Letter Form of *Sense and Sensibility.*" *Notes and Queries* 40 (1993), 464–66.

Harris, Jocelyn. "Jane Austen and the Burden of the (Male) Past: The Case Reexamined," in Devoney Looser, ed., *Jane Austen,* 89–90.

Hopkins, Lisa. "Jane Austen and Money." *Wordsworth Circle* 25 (1994), 76–77.

Lamont, Claire. " 'Let other pens dwell on guilt and misery': Adultery in Jane Austen," in Nicholas White and Naomi Segal, eds., *Scarlet Letters,* 70–72.

MacCarthy, B. G. *The Female Pen,* 478–83.

McMaster, Juliet. *Jane Austen the Novelist,* 179–82.

Prince, Michael. *Philosophical Dialogue,* 237–50.

Ricks, Christopher. *Essays in Appreciation,* 101–3.

Saisselin, Rémy G. "The Man of Taste as Social Model, or, 'Sense and Sensibility,' " in Jacques Carré, ed., *The Crisis of Courtesy,* 119–20.

Shaffer, Julie A. "The Ideological Intervention of Ambiguities in the Marriage Plot: Who Fails Marianne in Austen's *Sense and Sensibility?*," in Karen Hohne and Helen Wussow, eds., *A Dialogue of Voices,* 128–48.

Small, Helen. *Love's Madness,* 89–103.

Smith, Phoebe A. "*Sense and Sensibility* and 'The Lady's Law': The Failure of Benevolent Paternalism." *CEA Critic* 55:3 (1993), 3–20.

Spacks, Patricia Meyer. *Desire and Truth,* 204–6, 214–18.

Todd, Janet. *Gender, Art and Death,* 148–51.

Wallace, Tara Ghoshal. *Jane Austen and Narrative Authority,* 31–44.

White, Laura Mooneyham. "Jane Austen and the Marriage Plot: Questions of Persistence," in Devoney Looser, ed., *Jane Austen,* 77–78.

The Watsons, 1871

Fergus, Jan. "Jane Austen: Tensions Between Security and Marginality," in Beth Fowkes Tobin, ed., *History, Gender, and Eighteenth-Century Literature,* 263–65.

McMaster, Juliet. "Emma Watson: Jane Austen's Uncompleted Heroine," in Robert M. Polhemus and Roger B. Henkle, eds., *Critical Reconstructions,* 212–30.

McMaster, Juliet. *Jane Austen the Novelist,* 59–75.

Reid-Walsh, Jacqueline. " 'Entering the World' of *Regency Society:* The Ballroom Scenes in *Northanger Abbey,* 'The Watsons' and *Mansfield Park." Persuasions* 16 (1994), 115–24.

ROBERT BAGE

Barham Downs, 1784

Derry, Stephen. "Robert Bage's *Barham Downs* and *Sense and Sensibility." Notes and Queries* 41 (1994), 325–26.

Hermsprong, or Man as He Is Not, 1796

Johnson, Nancy E. "Rights, Property and the Law in the English Jacobin Novel." *Mosaic* 27:4 (1994), 100–104.

Perkins, Pam. "Playfulness of the Pen: Bage and the Politics of Comedy." *J of Narrative Technique* 26 (1996), 30–44.

Spacks, Patricia Meyer. "Novels of the 1790s: Action and Impasse," in John Richetti et al., eds., *The Columbia History,* 255–57, 271–73.

Man As He Is, 1792

O'Flinn, Paul. "*Man As He Is* and Romanticism As It Ought to Be." *Crit Survey* 4 (1992), 28–35.

Mt. Henneth, 1781

Perry, Ruth. "Bluestockings in Utopia," in Beth Fowkes Tobin, ed., *History, Gender, and Eighteenth-Century Literature,* 169–76.

ENID BAGNOLD

The Squire, 1938

Cosslett, Tess. *Women Writing Childbirth,* 22–27, 145–47.

BERYL BAINBRIDGE

The Bottle Factory Outing, 1974

Wennö, Elisabeth. *Ironic Formula,* 155–62.

The Dressmaker, 1973

    Wennö, Elisabeth. *Ironic Formula,* 96–110.

Harriet Said . . ., 1972

    Smith, Patricia Juliana. " 'And I Wondered If She Might Kiss Me': Lesbian Panic as Narrative Strategy in British Women's Fiction." *Mod Fiction Stud* 41 (1995), 585–92.

    Wennö, Elisabeth. *Ironic Formula,* 139–54.

Injury Time, 1977

    Wennö, Elisabeth. *Ironic Formula,* 162–74.

Sweet William, 1975

    Wennö, Elisabeth. *Ironic Formula,* 122–34.

Young Adolf, 1978

    Wennö, Elisabeth. *Ironic Formula,* 110–21.

ELIZABETH BAINES

The Birth Machine, 1983

    Adams, Alice E. *Reproducing the Womb,* 53–62.

    Cosslett, Tess. *Women Writing Childbirth,* 30–31, 36–39, 49–51, 145–47.

ROBERT MICHAEL BALLANTYNE

The Coral Island, 1858

    Hannabuss, Stuart. "Moral Islands: A Study of Robert Michael Ballantyne, Writer for Children." *Scottish Liter J* 22:2 (1995), 31–33.

    Knowles, Murray, and Kirsten Malmkjær. *Language and Control,* 93–97.

J. G. BALLARD

Concrete Island, 1974

    Parrinder, Patrick. "Landscapes of British Science Fiction," in George Slusser and Eric S. Rabkin, eds., *Styles of Creation,* 196–97.

Crash, 1972

    Broege, Valerie. "Technology and Sexuality in Science Fiction: Creating New Erotic Interfaces," in Donald Palumbo, ed., *Erotic Universe,* 108–10.

The Crystal World, 1966

    Brigg, Peter. "J. G. Ballard: Time Out of Mind." *Extrapolation* 35 (1994), 48–52.

    Jones, Mark. "J. G. Ballard: Neurographer," in Derek Littlewood and Peter Stockwell, eds., *Impossibility Fiction,* 135–38.

The Drowned World, 1962

>   Crossley, Robert. "In the Palace of Green Porcelain: Artifacts from the Museums of Science Fiction," in George Slusser and Eric S. Rabkin, eds., *Styles of Creation,* 215–17.
>   Jones, Mark. "J. G. Ballard: Neurographer," in Derek Littlewood and Peter Stockwell, eds., *Impossibility Fiction,* 132–35.
>   Rossi, Umberto. "Images from the Disaster Area: An Apocalyptic Reading of Urban Landscapes in Ballard's *The Drowned World* and *Hello America." Science-Fiction Stud* 21 (1994), 81–94.

Empire of the Sun, 1984

>   Luckhurst, Roger. "Petition, Repetition, and 'Autobiography': J. G. Ballard's *Empire of the Sun* and *The Kindness of Women." Contemp Lit* 35 (1994), 690–706.

Hello America, 1981

>   Brigg, Peter. "J. G. Ballard: Time Out of Mind." *Extrapolation* 35 (1994), 52–55.
>   Hollinger, Veronica. "Travels in Hyperreality: Jean Baudrillard's *America* and J. G. Ballard's *Hello America,"* in Joe Sanders, ed., *Functions of the Fantastic,* 188–92.
>   Rossi, Umberto. "Images from the Disaster Area: An Apocalyptic Reading of Urban Landscapes in Ballard's *The Drowned World* and *Hello America." Science-Fiction Stud* 21 (1994), 81–94.

The Kindness of Women, 1991

>   Luckhurst, Roger. "Petition, Repetition, and 'Autobiography': J. G. Ballard's *Empire of the Sun* and *The Kindness of Women." Contemp Lit* 35 (1994), 690–706.

Vermilion Sands, 1985

>   Luckhurst, Roger. "Repetition and Unreadability: J. G. Ballard's *Vermilion Sands." Extrapolation* 36 (1995), 292–303.

JOHN BANIM

The Fetches, 1825

>   Denman, Peter. "Ghosts in Anglo-Irish Literature," in Robert Welch, ed., *Irish Writers and Religion,* 63–65.

MICHAEL BANIM

The Croppy, 1826

>   Hayley, Barbara. "Religion and Society in Nineteenth Century Irish Fiction," in Robert Welch, ed., *Irish Writers and Religion,* 34–35.

IAIN BANKS

The Bridge, 1986

>Armitt, Lucie. *Theorising the Fantastic,* 103–16.

Complicity, 1994

>Sage, Victor. "The Politics of Petrifaction: Culture, Religion, History in the Fiction of Iain Banks and John Banville," in Victor Sage and Allan Lloyd Smith, eds., *Modern Gothic,* 20–24.
>
>Todd, Richard. *Consuming Fictions,* 153–56.

Consider Phlebas, 1987

>Brown, Carolyn. "Utopias and Heterotopias: The 'Culture' of Iain M. Banks," in Derek Littlewood and Peter Stockwell, eds., *Impossibility Fiction,* 64–67.

The Player of Games, 1988

>Brown, Carolyn. "Utopias and Heterotopias: The 'Culture' of Iain M. Banks," in Derek Littlewood and Peter Stockwell, eds., *Impossibility Fiction,* 68–71.

The Wasp Factory, 1984

>Sage, Victor. "The Politics of Petrifaction: Culture, Religion, History in the Fiction of Iain Banks and John Banville," in Victor Sage and Allan Lloyd Smith, eds., *Modern Gothic,* 24–28.
>
>Todd, Richard. *Consuming Fictions,* 148–53.

JOHN BANVILLE

Birchwood, 1973

>D'haen, Theo. "Irish Regionalism, Magic Realism and Postmodernism," in Theo D'haen and Hans Bertens, eds., *British Postmodern Fiction,* 42–46.
>
>Sage, Victor. "The Politics of Petrifaction: Culture, Religion, History in the Fiction of Iain Banks and John Banville," in Victor Sage and Allan Lloyd Smith, eds., *Modern Gothic,* 32–36.

The Book of Evidence, 1989

>Imhof, Rüdiger. *"The Book of Evidence." Etudes Irlandaises* 19:1 (1994), 63–80.
>
>Imhof, Rüdiger. "In Search of the Rosy Grail: The Creative Process in the Novels of John Banville," in Jacqueline Genet and Wynne Hellegouarc'h, eds., *Irish Writers,* 131–34.

Doctor Copernicus, 1976

>Imhof, Rüdiger. "In Search of the Rosy Grail: The Creative Process in the Novels of John Banville," in Jacqueline Genet and Wynne Hellegouarc'h, eds., *Irish Writers,* 126–28.
>
>McIlroy, Brian. "Pattern in Chaos: John Banville's Scientific Art." *Colby Q* 31 (1995), 74–79.

Swann, Joseph. "Banville's Faust: *Doctor Copernicus, Kepler, The Newton Letter* and *Mefisto,*" in Donald E. Morse et al., eds., *A Small Nation's Contribution*, 148–55.

Kepler, 1981

McIlroy, Brian. "Pattern in Chaos: John Banville's Scientific Art." *Colby Q* 31 (1995), 74–79.

Swann, Joseph. "Banville's Faust: *Doctor Copernicus, Kepler, The Newton Letter* and *Mefisto,*" in Donald E. Morse et al., eds., *A Small Nation's Contribution*, 154.

Mefisto, 1986

Imhof, Rüdiger. "In Search of the Rosy Grail: The Creative Process in the Novels of John Banville," in Jacqueline Genet and Wynne Hellegouarc'h, eds., *Irish Writers*, 129–30.

McIlroy, Brian. "Pattern in Chaos: John Banville's Scientific Art." *Colby Q* 31 (1995), 74–79.

Sage, Victor. "The Politics of Petrifaction: Culture, Religion, History in the Fiction of Iain Banks and John Banville," in Victor Sage and Allan Lloyd Smith, eds., *Modern Gothic*, 28–29.

Swann, Joseph. "Banville's Faust: *Doctor Copernicus, Kepler, The Newton Letter* and *Mefisto,*" in Donald E. Morse et al., eds., *A Small Nation's Contribution*, 157–58.

The Newton Letter, 1982

Imhof, Rüdiger. "In Search of the Rosy Grail: The Creative Process in the Novels of John Banville," in Jacqueline Genet and Wynne Hellegouarc'h, eds., *Irish Writers*, 128–29.

McIlroy, Brian. "Pattern in Chaos: John Banville's Scientific Art." *Colby Q* 31 (1995), 74–79.

Sage, Victor. "The Politics of Petrifaction: Culture, Religion, History in the Fiction of Iain Banks and John Banville," in Victor Sage and Allan Lloyd Smith, eds., *Modern Gothic*, 30–32.

Swann, Joseph. "Banville's Faust: *Doctor Copernicus, Kepler, The Newton Letter* and *Mefisto,*" in Donald E. Morse et al., eds., *A Small Nation's Contribution*, 155–57.

FLORENCE BARCLAY

The Rosary, 1909

Cadogan, Mary. *And Then Their Hearts Stood Still*, 53–56, 94–95.

CLIVE BARKER

The Thief of Always, 1992

Ziegler, Robert. "Fantasy's Timeless Humor in Clive Barker's *The Thief of Always.*" *Notes on Contemp Lit* 24:5 (1994), 7–9.

JANE BARKER

Exilius, or, The Banished Roman, 1715

Gonda, Caroline. *Reading Daughters' Fictions*, 51–54.

A Patch-Work Screen for the Ladies, 1723

King, Kathryn R. "Galesia, Jane Barker, and a Coming to Authorship," in Carol J. Singley and Susan Elizabeth Sweeney, eds., *Anxious Power*, 91–101.

King, Kathryn R. "The Unaccountable Wife and Other Tales of Female Desire in Jane Barker's *A Patch-Work Screen for the Ladies.*" *Eighteenth Cent* 35 (1994), 155–68.

Straub, Kristina. "Frances Burney and the Rise of the Woman Novelist," in John Richetti et al., eds., *The Columbia History*, 203–4.

PAT BARKER

Blow Your House Down, 1984

Anderson, Sue. "Life on the Street: Pat Barker's Realist Fictions," in Gina Wisker, ed., *It's My Party,* 186–88.

The Century's Daughter, 1986

Anderson, Sue. "Life on the Street: Pat Barker's Realist Fictions," in Gina Wisker, ed., *It's My Party,* 186–87, 189–90.

Union Street, 1982

Anderson, Sue. "Life on the Street: Pat Barker's Realist Fictions," in Gina Wisker, ed., *It's My Party,* 182–86.

JULIAN BARNES

Before She Met Me, 1982

Todd, Richard. *Consuming Fictions,* 267–69.

Flaubert's Parrot, 1984

Elias, Amy J. "Meta-*mimesis*? The Problem of British Postmodern Realism," in Theo D'haen and Hans Bertens, eds., *British Postmodern Fiction,* 26–28.

Gasiorek, Andrzej. *Post-War British Fiction,* 158–62.

Janik, Del Ivan. "No End of History: Evidence from the Contemporary English Novel." *Twentieth Cent Lit* 41 (1995), 168–71.

Todd, Richard. *Consuming Fictions,* 269–71.

Wesseling, Elisabeth. *Writing History as a Prophet,* 121–22, 125–27.

Wood, Michael. "The Contemporary Novel," in John Richetti et al., eds., *The Columbia History,* 973–76.

A History of the World in 10 1/2 Chapters, 1989

Connor, Steven. *The English Novel in History,* 232–38.

Gasiorek, Andrzej. *Post-War British Fiction,* 162–65.

Lozano, María. " 'How You Cuddle in the Dark Governs How You See the History of the World': A Note on Some Obsessions in Recent British Fiction," in Susana Onega, ed., *Telling Histories*, 121–29.

Todd, Richard. *Consuming Fictions*, 273–75.

Wood, Michael. "The Contemporary Novel," in John Richetti et al., eds., *The Columbia History*, 975–76.

Metroland, 1980

Todd, Richard. *Consuming Fictions*, 265–67.

Talking It Over, 1991

Todd, Richard. *Consuming Fictions*, 275–79.

EATON STANNARD BARRETT

The Heroine; or Adventures of a Fair Romance Reader, 1813

Gonda, Caroline. *Reading Daughters' Fictions*, 158–61.

Howard, Jacqueline. *Reading Gothic Fiction*, 145–60.

Jackson, Jessamyn. "Why Novels Make Bad Mothers." *Novel* 27 (1994), 161–72.

JAMES MATTHEW BARRIE

The Little White Bird, 1902

Rose, Jacqueline. *The Case of Peter Pan*, 20–34.

Wullschläger, Jackie. *Inventing Wonderland*, 123–25.

Peter and Wendy, 1911

Rose, Jacqueline. *The Case of Peter Pan*, 66–78, 83–86, 125–30.

Peter Pan in Kensington Gardens, 1906

Hunt, Peter. *An Introduction to Children's Literature*, 89–90.

Jack, R. D. S. "*Peter Pan* as Darwinian Creation Myth." *Lit and Theology* 8 (1994), 157–72.

Wullschläger, Jackie. *Inventing Wonderland*, 126–33.

STAN BARSTOW

A Kind of Loving, 1960

Sillars, Stuart. *Visualisation in Popular Fiction*, 154–57.

H. E. BATES

The Poacher, 1935

Baldwin, Dean. "H. E. Bates: *The Poacher*," in Patrick J. Quinn, ed., *Recharting the Thirties*, 126–31.

NINA BAWDEN

Carrie's War, 1973

Knowles, Murray, and Kirsten Malmkjær. *Language and Control,* 115–25.

AUBREY BEARDSLEY

Venus and Tannhäuser, 1907

Kooistra, Lorraine Janzen. *The Artist as Critic,* 226–35.

SAMUEL BEAZLEY

The Oxonians, 1830

Antor, Heinz. *Der englische Universitätsroman,* 220–22.

SAMUEL BECKETT

Company, 1980

Abbott, H. Porter. *Beckett Writing Beckett,* 9–19.

Brater, Enoch. *The Drama in the Text,* 106–22.

Davies, Paul. *The Ideal Real,* 182–95.

Finney, Brian. "Samuel Beckett's Postmodern Fictions," in John Richetti et al., eds., *The Columbia History,* 862–63.

García Landa, José Angel. " 'Till nohow on': The Later Metafiction of Samuel Beckett," in Theo D'haen and Hans Bertens, eds., *British Postmodern Fiction,* 66–69.

Henry, Anne. "*Compagnie* de Beckett: Etude d'une Réduction," in Marius Buning et al., eds., *Samuel Beckett 1970–1989,* 26–34.

Hill, Leslie. "Late Texts: Writing the Work of Mourning," in Marius Buning et al., eds., *Samuel Beckett 1970–1989,* 19–21.

Houppermans, Sjef. "Compagnie & Cie & Cie," in Marius Buning et al., eds., *Samuel Beckett 1970–1989,* 41–47.

Knowlson, James. *Damned to Fame,* 561–80.

Locatelli, Carla. *Unwording the World,* 157–84.

McCrudden, Ian C. *The Phenomenon of the Voice,* 11–29.

Madou, Jean-Pol. "La Voix et la Lumière," in Marius Buning et al., eds., *Samuel Beckett 1970–1989,* 50–57.

Merger, Andrea. *Becketts Rhetorik,* 91–177.

Miskinis, Steven. "Enduring Recurrence: Samuel Beckett's Nihilistic Poetics." *ELH* 63 (1996), 1047–64.

Murphy, P. J. "On First Looking into Beckett's *The Voice,*" in John Pilling and Mary Bryden, eds., *The Ideal Core of the Onion,* 63–78.

Olney, James. "Memory and the Narrative Imperative: St. Augustine and Samuel Beckett." *New Liter Hist* 24 (1993), 861–79.

Piette, Adam. "Ill Seen Ill Said: Allusion and Cultural Memory." *Swiss Papers in Engl Lang and Lit* 6 (1992), 179–81.

Ricks, Christopher. *Beckett's Dying Words*, 135–36, 207–8.

Schmitz, Peter. "Tracing Samuel Beckett," in Marius Buning et al., eds., *Samuel Beckett 1970–1989*, 37–39.

Sharkey, Rodney. "Irish? Au Contraire!: The Search for Identity in the Fictions of Samuel Beckett." *J of Beckett Stud* 3:2 (1994), 14–16.

Welch, Robert. *Changing States*, 176–79.

How It Is, 1964

Abbott, H. Porter. *Beckett Writing Beckett*, 95–108.

Abbott, H. Porter. "Beginning Again: The Post-Narrative Art of *Texts for Nothing* and *How It Is,*" in John Pilling, ed., *The Cambridge Companion to Beckett,* 110–20.

Balzano, Wanda. "Re-Mythologizing Beckett: The Metaphors of Metafiction in *How It Is,*" in Lois Oppenheim and Marius Buning, eds., *Beckett On and On,* 102–9.

Davies, Paul. *The Ideal Real*, 93–131, 234–45.

Finney, Brian. "Samuel Beckett's Postmodern Fictions," in John Richetti et al., eds., *The Columbia History*, 855–59.

Hansford, James. " 'Imagination Dead Imagine': The Imagination and Its Context," in S. E. Gontarski, ed., *The Beckett Studies Reader*, 146–50.

Knowlson, James. *Damned to Fame*, 400–424.

Ricks, Christopher. *Beckett's Dying Words*, 79–80, 109–10, 115–16, 137–39, 144–45.

Welch, Robert. *Changing States*, 183–86.

Ill Seen Ill Said, 1982

Baker, Phil. "Ghost Stories: Beckett and the Literature of Introjection." *J of Beckett Stud* 5:1–2 (1996), 53–59.

Brater, Enoch. *The Drama in the Text,* 122–35.

Davies, Paul. *The Ideal Real*, 196–210.

Dunn, Allen. "Pathos in Postmodernity: Beckett, Sade, and the Performance of Suffering." *Southern Hum R* 30 (1996), 341–49.

Finney, Brian. "Samuel Beckett's Postmodern Fictions," in John Richetti et al., eds., *The Columbia History*, 864–65.

Hill, Leslie. "Late Texts: Writing the Work of Mourning," in Marius Buning et al., eds., *Samuel Beckett 1970–1989*, 21–24.

Knowlson, James. *Damned to Fame*, 588–90.

Locatelli, Carla. *Unwording the World*, 188–218.

Madou, Jean-Pol. "La Voix et la Lumière," in Marius Buning et al., eds., *Samuel Beckett 1970–1989*, 51–57.

Merger, Andrea. *Becketts Rhetorik*, 178–244.

Piette, Adam. "Ill Seen Ill Said: Allusion and Cultural Memory." *Swiss Papers in Engl Lang and Lit* 6 (1992), 181–94.

Ricks, Christopher. *Beckett's Dying Words*, 94–95, 125–26, 139–40, 147–48, 151–52.

Ruyter-Tognotti, Danièle de. "Mise en Image, Mise en Texte dans *Mal*

Vu Mal Dit," in Marius Buning et al., eds., *Samuel Beckett 1970–1989*, 58–67.

The Lost Ones, 1971

Booker, M. Keith. *Literature and Domination*, 142–60.

Brater, Enoch. *The Drama in the Text*, 98–105.

Buning, Marius. "Allegory's Double Bookkeeping: The Case of Samuel Beckett," in Marius Buning et al., eds., *Samuel Beckett 1970–1989*, 73–74.

Davies, Paul. *The Ideal Real*, 145–61.

Finney, Brian. "Samuel Beckett's Postmodern Fictions," in John Richetti et al., eds., *The Columbia History*, 858–61.

Gontarski, S. E. "Refiguring, Revising, and Reprinting *The Lost Ones."* *J of Beckett Stud* 4:2 (1995), 99–101.

Miller, Tyrus. "Dismantling Authenticity: Beckett, Adorno, and the 'Post-War.' " *Textual Practice* 8 (1994), 49–55.

Malone Dies, 1956

Acheson, James. *Samuel Beckett's Artistic Theory*, 116–32.

Davies, Paul. *The Ideal Real*, 66–68, 78–81, 85–89.

Davies, Paul. "Three Novels and Four *Nouvelles:* Giving Up the Ghost Be Born At Last," in John Pilling, ed., *The Cambridge Companion to Beckett*, 47–63.

Finney, Brian. "Samuel Beckett's Postmodern Fictions," in John Richetti et al., eds., *The Columbia History*, 850–52.

Knowlson, James. *Damned to Fame*, 336–39.

Ricks, Christopher. *Beckett's Dying Words*, 1–3, 111–16, 118–20, 129–30, 142–44, 201–2.

Schwalm, Helga. *Dekonstruktion im Roman*, 221–29.

Vandervlist, Harry. " 'A Voice from Elsewhere': Impossible Survivals and the Annihilating Power of Language in Beckett's Fiction," in Lois Oppenheim and Marius Buning, eds., *Beckett On and On*, 178–85.

Welch, Robert. *Changing States*, 171–76.

Mercier and Camier, 1970

Acheson, James. *Samuel Beckett's Artistic Theory*, 89–95.

Davies, Paul. *The Ideal Real*, 50–56.

Ricks, Christopher. *Beckett's Dying Words*, 69–73, 76–78.

Molloy, 1955

Baker, Phil. "Beckett's Bilingualism and a Possible Source for the Name of Moran in *Molloy." J of Beckett Stud* 3:2 (1994), 81–82.

Baker, Phil. "The Stamp of the Father in *Molloy." J of Beckett Stud* 5:1–2 (1996), 143–54.

Acheson, James. *Samuel Beckett's Artistic Theory*, 99–115.

Brater, Enoch. *The Drama in the Text*, 3–8.

Butler, Lance St. John. " 'A Mythology with which I Am Perfectly Familiar': Samuel Beckett and the Absence of God," in Robert Welch, ed., *Irish Writers and Religion*, 173–75, 177–79.

Davies, Paul. *The Ideal Real*, 76–89.

Davies, Paul. "Three Novels and Four *Nouvelles:* Giving Up the Ghost Be Born At Last," in John Pilling, ed., *The Cambridge Companion to Beckett*, 47–63.

Finney, Brian. "Samuel Beckett's Postmodern Fictions," in John Richetti et al., eds., *The Columbia History*, 850–51.

Gray, Margaret E. "Beckett Backwards and Forwards: The Rhetoric of Retraction in *Molloy.*" *French Forum* 19:2 (1994), 161–74.

Harrison, Robert Pogue. *Forests,* 151–52.

Knowlson, James. *Damned to Fame*, 336–42.

Matton, Frank. "Beckett's Trilogy and the Limits of Autobiography," in Lois Oppenheim and Marius Buning, eds., *Beckett On and On*, 69–80.

Moorjani, Angela. "Mourning, Schopenhauer, and Beckett's Art of Shadows," in Lois Oppenheim and Marius Buning, eds., *Beckett On and On*, 86–88.

O'Hara, J. D. "Jung and the 'Molloy' Narrative," in S. E. Gontarski, ed., *The Beckett Studies Reader*, 129–45.

Ricks, Christopher. *Beckett's Dying Words*, 74–75, 91–92, 116–17, 123–24, 182–83, 195–96.

Schwalm, Helga. *Dekonstruktion im Roman*, 211–20.

Sharkey, Rodney. "Irish? Au Contraire!: The Search for Identity in the Fictions of Samuel Beckett." *J of Beckett Stud* 3:2 (1994), 5–10.

Smyth, John Vignaux. "A Glance at SunSet: Numerical Fundaments in Frege, Wittgenstein, Shakespeare, Beckett." *South Atlantic Q* 94 (1995), 640–44.

Vandervlist, Harry. " 'A Voice from Elsewhere': Impossible Survivals and the Annihilating Power of Language in Beckett's Fiction," in Lois Oppenheim and Marius Buning, eds., *Beckett On and On*, 178–85.

Welch, Robert. *Changing States,* 170–71.

Zelter, Joachim. *Sinnhafte Fiktion und Wahrheit*, 229–31.

Murphy, 1938

Acheson, James. *"Murphy's* Metaphysics," in S. E. Gontarski, ed., *The Beckett Studies Reader*, 78–91.

Acheson, James. *Samuel Beckett's Artistic Theory*, 41–58.

Bernstein, Stephen. "The Gothicism of Beckett's *Murphy.*" *Notes on Mod Irish Lit* 6 (1994), 25–30.

Davies, Paul. *The Ideal Real*, 33–38, 41–43, 45–47.

Finney, Brian. "Samuel Beckett's Postmodern Fictions," in John Richetti et al., eds., *The Columbia History*, 845–47.

Knowlson, James. *Damned to Fame*, 189–215.

Matton, Frank. "Beckett's Trilogy and the Limits of Autobiography," in Lois Oppenheim and Marius Buning, eds., *Beckett On and On*, 69–80.

Menaghan, John M. "A Wilderness of Mirrors: Modernist Mimesis in Joyce's *Portrait* and Beckett's *Murphy.*" *Colby Q* 30 (1994), 258–63.

Murphy, P. J. "Beckett and the Philosophers," in John Pilling, ed., *The Cambridge Companion to Beckett*, 224–29.

Pilling, John. "Beckett's English Fiction," in Pilling, ed., *The Cambridge Companion to Beckett*, 30–36.

Pilling, John. "From a (W)horoscope to *Murphy,*" in John Pilling and Mary Bryden, eds., *The Ideal Core of the Onion*, 1–20.

Ricks, Christopher. *Beckett's Dying Words*, 6–8, 37–38, 52–53, 57–60, 62–63, 98–101, 108–9, 111–12, 169–70, 202–3.

Schwalm, Helga. *Dekonstruktion im Roman*, 186–97.

Welch, Robert. *Changing States*, 164–66.

The Unnamable, 1958

Acheson, James. *Samuel Beckett's Artistic Theory*, 132–40.

Beck, Andrea. "Selbstreferentialität und Schweigen in S. Becketts *Endgame* und *The Unnamable.*" *Anglia* 112 (1994), 95–99.

Begam, Richard. "Splitting the *Différance:* Beckett, Derrida and the Unnamable." *Mod Fiction Stud* 38 (1992), 873–88.

Brockmeier, Peter. "Der namenlose Ich-Erzähler: Beckett, *L'innomable*, und Tante Léonie in Proust, *Du côté de chez Swann,*" in Eberhard Lämmert and Barbara Naumann, eds., *Wer sind wir?*, 108–13.

Davies, Paul. *The Ideal Real*, 81–92, 99–101, 117–19.

Davies, Paul. "Three Novels and Four *Nouvelles:* Giving Up the Ghost Be Born At Last," in John Pilling, ed., *The Cambridge Companion to Beckett*, 47–63.

Finney, Brian. "Samuel Beckett's Postmodern Fictions," in John Richetti et al., eds., *The Columbia History*, 852–55.

Heumakers, Arnold. "L'Enfer Abstrait de Samuel Beckett," in Marius Buning et al., eds., *Samuel Beckett 1970–1989*, 79–83.

Jeffers, Jennifer. "Beyond Irony: *The Unnamable*'s Appropriation of its Criticism in a Humorous Reading of the Text." *J of Narrative Technique* 25 (1995), 47–64.

Knowlson, James. *Damned to Fame*, 353–55.

Levy, Eric. "*The Unnamable:* The Metaphysics of Beckettian Introspection." *J of Beckett Stud* 5:1–2 (1996), 81–97.

Matton, Frank. "Beckett's Trilogy and the Limits of Autobiography," in Lois Oppenheim and Marius Buning, eds., *Beckett On and On*, 69–80.

Moorjani, Angela. "Mourning, Schopenhauer, and Beckett's Art of Shadows," in Lois Oppenheim and Marius Buning, eds., *Beckett On and On*, 86–88.

Olney, James. "Memory and the Narrative Imperative: St. Augustine and Samuel Beckett." *New Liter Hist* 24 (1993), 857–79.

Pol, Popovic. "Beckett et l'espace de l'écriture." *LittéRéalité* 2:1 (1990), 14–25.

Schwalm, Helga. *Dekonstruktion im Roman*, 229–39.

Sharkey, Rodney. "Irish? Au Contraire!: The Search for Identity in the Fictions of Samuel Beckett." *J of Beckett Stud* 3:2 (1994), 10–11.

Vandervlist, Harry. " 'A Voice from Elsewhere': Impossible Survivals and the Annihilating Power of Language in Beckett's Fiction," in Lois Oppenheim and Marius Buning, eds., *Beckett On and On*, 178–85.

Welch, Robert. *Changing States*, 179–83.

Watt, 1953

Acheson, James. *Samuel Beckett's Artistic Theory,* 59–79.

Booker, M. Keith. *Literature and Domination,* 20–42.

Butler, Lance St. John. " 'A Mythology with which I Am Perfectly Familiar': Samuel Beckett and the Absence of God," in Robert Welch, ed., *Irish Writers and Religion,* 171–73.

Cousineau, Thomas J. *"Watt:* Language as Interdiction and Consolation," in S. E. Gontarski, ed., *The Beckett Studies Reader,* 64–75.

Davies, Paul. *The Ideal Real,* 28–35, 37–56.

Finney, Brian. "Samuel Beckett's Postmodern Fictions," in John Richetti et al., eds., *The Columbia History,* 847–49.

Howard, Alane. "The Roots of Beckett's Aesthetic: Mathematical Allusions in *Watt." Papers on Lang and Lit* 30 (1994), 346–51.

Kevorkian, Martin. "Misreading *Watt:* The Scottish Psychoanalysis of Samuel Beckett." *ELH* 61 (1994), 427–40.

Knowlson, James. *Damned to Fame,* 355–58.

Lees, Heath. *"Watt:* Music, Tuning, and Tonality," in S. E. Gontarski, ed., *The Beckett Studies Reader,* 167–84.

McCormack, W. J. *From Burke to Beckett,* 391–95.

Murphy, P. J. "Beckett and the Philosophers," in John Pilling, ed., *The Cambridge Companion to Beckett,* 229–33.

Pilling, John. "Beckett's English Fiction," in Pilling, ed., *The Cambridge Companion to Beckett,* 36–39.

Pilling, John. "A Short Statement with Long Shadows: *Watt's* Arsene and His Kind(s)," in Lois Oppenheim and Marius Buning, eds., *Beckett On and On,* 61–64.

Ricks, Christopher. *Beckett's Dying Words,* 40–41, 74–76, 100–101, 196–97, 205–6.

Schwalm, Helga. *Dekonstruktion im Roman,* 197–209.

Welch, Robert. *Changing States,* 166–70.

Wolff, Ellen. "Watt . . . Knott . . Anglo-Ireland: Samuel Beckett's *Watt." J of Beckett Stud* 5:1–2 (1996), 107–31.

WILLIAM BECKFORD

Arabella Bloomville, 1796

Lenz, Bernd. "Popularisierung und Wandlung der Empfindsamkeit im englischen Roman des 18. Jahrhunderts," in Klaus P. Hansen, ed., *Empfindsamkeiten,* 70–72.

Schlaeger, Jürgen. "Die Unwirklichkeit des Wirklichen: Zur Wandlungsdynamik des englischen Romans im 18. Jahrhundert." *Poetica* (Munich) 25 (1993), 332–37.

Azemia, 1797

Lenz, Bernd. "Popularisierung und Wandlung der Empfindsamkeit im englischen Roman des 18. Jahrhunderts," in Klaus P. Hansen, ed., *Empfindsamkeiten,* 70–72.

Spacks, Patricia Meyer. "Novels of the 1790s: Action and Impasse," in
John Richetti et al., eds., *The Columbia History*, 257–58.

Vathek, 1786

Alamoudi, Carmen. "Un Sourire déchiré: l'ironie dans le *Vathek* de
Beckford." *Eighteenth-Cent Fiction* 8 (1996), 401–14.

Botting, Fred. *Gothic*, 59–61.

Haggerty, George E. "The Gothic Novel, 1764–1824," in John Richetti
et al., eds., *The Columbia History*, 232–34.

Jack, Malcolm. *William Beckford*, 19–21, 79–82.

Knox-Shaw, P. H. "The West Indian *Vathek.*" *Essays in Criticism* 43
(1993), 284–304.

Knox-Shaw, Peter. "*Vathek* and 'The Seven Fountains' by Sir William
Jones." *Notes and Queries* 42 (1995), 75–76.

Magnier, Mireille. "*Vathek:* Hommage à Voltaire ou avatar de Faust?"
Mythes, Croyances et Religions dans le Monde Anglo-Saxon 4 (1986),
98–108.

Roberts, Adam, and Eric Robertson. "The Giaour's Sabre: A Reading of
Beckford's *Vathek.*" *Stud in Romanticism* 35 (1996), 199–211.

MAX BEERBOHM

The Happy Hypocrite, 1896

Lane, Christopher. "Framing Fears, Reading Designs: The Homosexual
Art of Painting in James, Wilde, and Beerbohm." *ELH* 61 (1994),
943–50.

APHRA BEHN

The Fair Jilt, 1688

Bowers, Toni O'Shaughnessy. "Sex, Lies, and Invisibility: Amatory Fiction from the Restoration to Mid-Century," in John Richetti et al.,
eds., *The Columbia History*, 56–57.

Fitzmaurice, James. "The Narrator in Aphra Behn's *The Fair Jilt.*" *Zeitschrift für Anglistik und Amerikanistik* 42 (1994), 131–37.

MacCarthy, B. G. *The Female Pen*, 139–43.

Nováková, Soňa. "The Narrator in Aphra Behn's Fiction." *Litteraria
Pragensia* 4:7 (1994), 23–24.

The History of the Nun; or, The Fair Vow-Breaker, 1689

Bowers, Toni O'Shaughnessy. "Sex, Lies, and Invisibility: Amatory Fiction from the Restoration to Mid-Century," in John Richetti et al.,
eds., *The Columbia History*, 65–67.

MacCarthy, B. G. *The Female Pen*, 143–48.

Nováková, Soňa. "The Narrator in Aphra Behn's Fiction." *Litteraria
Pragensia* 4:7 (1994), 22–23.

Love Letters Between a Nobleman and His Sister, 1683–1687

Ballaster, Ros. *Seductive Forms,* 106–13.

Ballaster, Ros. "Seizing the Means of Seduction: Fiction and Feminine Identity in Aphra Behn and Delarivier Manley," in Isobel Grundy and Susan Wiseman, eds., *Women, Witing, History,* 97–102.

Fludernik, Monika. "Narrative Strategies in Early English Fiction: From Renaissance Prose to Aphra Behn," in Wolfgang Görtschacher and Holger Klein, eds., *Narrative Strategies,* 18–22.

Howlett, Kathy. "The Entangled History of Legal and Fictional Discourse *in The Trial of Ford Lord Grey of Werk* and Aphra Behn's *Love Letters Between a Nobleman and His Sister." CEA Critic* 58:1 (1995), 25–33.

Nováková, Soňa. "The Narrator in Aphra Behn's Fiction." *Litteraria Pragensia* 4:7 (1994), 24–25.

Richards, Cynthia. " 'The Pleasures of Complicity': Sympathetic Identification and the Female Reader in Early Eighteenth-Century Women's Amatory Fiction." *Eighteenth Cent* 36 (1995), 223–26.

Todd, Janet. *Gender, Art and Death,* 40–43.

Todd, Janet. *The Sign of Angellica,* 78–83.

Warner, William B. "Formulating Fiction: Romancing the General Reader in Early Modern Britain," in Deidre Lynch and William B. Warner, eds., *Cultural Institutions of the Novel,* 286–89.

Oroonoko, 1688

Alliston, April. "Gender and the Rhetoric of Evidence in Early-Modern Historical Narratives." *Compar Lit Stud* 33 (1996), 243–52.

Andrade, Susan Z. "White Skin, Black Masks: Colonialism and the Sexual Politics of *Oroonoko." Cultural Critique* 27 (1994), 189–214.

Athey, Stephanie, and Daniel Cooper Alarcon. "*Oroonoko*'s Gendered Economies of Honor/Horror: Reframing Colonial Discourse Studies in the Americas." *Am Lit* 65 (1993), 415–43.

Azim, Firdous. *The Colonial Rise of the Novel,* 34–60.

Ballaster, Ros. *Seductive Forms,* 95–98, 201–3.

Boesky, Amy. *Founding Fictions,* 162–77.

David, Deirdre. *Rule Britannia,* 47–49.

Dhuicq, Bernard. "*Oroonoko:* La Rencontre de trois mondes." *Bull de la Société d'Etudes Anglo-Américaines des XVIIe et XVIIIe Siècles* 38 (1994), 33–43.

Doyle, Laura. "The Folk, the Nobles, and the Novel: The Racial Subtext of Sentimentality." *Narrative* 3 (1995), 170–74.

Frohock, Richard. "Violence and Awe: The Foundations of Government in Aphra Behn's New World Settings." *Eighteenth-Cent Fiction* 8 (1996), 437–52.

Hoegberg, David E. "Caesar's Toils: Allusion and Rebellion in *Oroonoko." Eighteenth-Cent Fiction* 7 (1995), 239–58.

Kaul, Suvir. "Reading Literary Symptoms: Colonial Pathologies and the

Oroonoko Fictions of Behn, Southerne, and Hawkesworth." *Eighteenth Cent Life* 18:3 (1994), 81–88.

MacCarthy, B. G. *The Female Pen,* 151–65.

Nováková, Soňa. "The Narrator in Aphra Behn's Fiction." *Litteraria Pragensia* 4:7 (1994), 25–26.

Overton, Bill. "Countering *Crusoe:* Two Colonial Narratives." *Crit Survey* 4 (1992), 302–10.

Paxman, David. "Oral and Literate Discourse in Aphra Behn's *Oroonoko.*" *Restoration* 18 (1994), 88–102.

Rosenthal, Laura J. "Owning *Oroonoko:* Behn, Southerne, and the Contingencies of Property." *Renaissance Drama* 23 (1992), 25–38.

Todd, Janet. *Gender, Art and Death,* 43–49, 51–61.

Vermillion, Mary. "Buried Heroism: Critiques of Female Authorship in Southerne's Adaptation of Behn's *Oroonoko.*" *Restoration* 16 (1992), 28–35.

ARNOLD BENNETT

Anna of the Five Towns, 1902

De Stasio, Clotilde. "Arnold Bennett and Late-Victorian *Woman.*" *Victorian Periodicals R* 28 (1995), 46–49.

Lamarque, Peter, and Stein Haugom Olsen. *Truth, Fiction, and Literature,* 452–54.

Marroni, Francesco. "The Paradigm of Negativity in *Anna of the Five Towns.*" *Cahiers Victoriens et Edouardiens* 41 (1995), 99–118.

Helen with the High Hand, 1911

De Stasio, Clotilde. "Arnold Bennett and Late-Victorian *Woman.*" *Victorian Periodicals R* 28 (1995), 47–49.

Hilda Lessways, 1911

Miller, Jane Eldridge. *Rebel Women,* 110–13.

Leonora, 1903

Miller, Jane Eldridge. *Rebel Women,* 67–69.

A Man from the North, 1898

Trotter, David. "The Avoidance of Naturalism: Gissing, Moore, Grand, Bennett, and Others," in John Richetti et al., eds., *The Columbia History,* 623–24.

The Old Wives' Tale, 1908

Squillace, Robert. "Bennett, Wells, and the Persistence of Realism," in John Richetti et al., eds., *The Columbia History,* 675–76.

Squillace, Robert. "Self-Isolation and Self-Advertisement in *The Old Wives' Tale,*" in Carola M. Kaplan and Anne B. Simpson, eds., *Seeing Double,* 79–95.

Trotter, David. "The Avoidance of Naturalism: Gissing, Moore, Grand,

Bennett, and Others," in John Richetti et al., eds., *The Columbia History*, 625–27.

Trotter, David. *The English Novel in History*, 138–41.

Riceyman Steps, 1923

Rothfield, Lawrence. *Vital Signs*, 152–57.

Squillace, Robert. "Bennett, Wells, and the Persistence of Realism," in John Richetti et al., eds., *The Columbia History*, 677–83.

These Twain, 1915

Trotter, David. "The Avoidance of Naturalism: Gissing, Moore, Grand, Bennett, and Others," in John Richetti et al., eds., *The Columbia History*, 626–27.

Trotter, David. *The English Novel in History*, 137–38.

Whom God Hath Joined, 1906

Harris, Janice Hubbard. *Edwardian Stories of Divorce*, 120–25.

Miller, Jane Eldridge. *Rebel Women*, 65–67.

ROBERT HUGH BENSON

Lord of the World, 1907

Jenkins, Philip. "Naming the Beast: Contemporary Apocalyptic Novels." *Chesterton R* 22 (1996), 489–93.

Menges, Thomas. " 'Trauet nicht jedem, sondern prüft die Geister': Apokalyptik und Wissenschaftsglaube in Robert Hugh Bensons Roman *Der Herr der Welt.*" *Inklings* 11 (1993), 97–110.

JOHN BERGER

G., 1972

Wesseling, Elisabeth. *Writing History as a Prophet*, 131–33.

Pig Earth, 1979

Blaustone, Jeff. "Ethnography as Art: Polymorphous Point of View in John Berger's *Pig Earth.*" *Arkansas Q* 2 (1993), 299–307.

SIMON BERINGTON

The Memoirs of Signior Gaudentio di Lucca, 1737

Rees, Christine. *Utopian Imagination and Eighteenth-Century Fiction*, 105–9.

WALTER BESANT

All Sorts and Conditions of Man, 1882

Neetens, Wim. "Problems of a 'Democratic Text': Walter Besant's Impossible Story in *All Sorts and Conditions of Men* (1882)," in Barbara

Leah Harman and Susan Meyer, eds., *The New Nineteenth Century*, 135–56.

Dorothy Forster, 1884

Orel, Harold. *The Historical Novel*, 50–59.

CLEMENTINA BLACK

An Agitator, 1896

Hapgood, Lynne. "The Novel and Political Agency: Socialism and the Work of Margaret Harkness, Constance Howell and Clementina Black: 1888–1896." *Lit and Hist* 5:2 (1996), 47–50.

TERENCE BLACKER

Fixx, 1989

Taylor, D. J. *After the War*, 271–76.

RICHARD D. BLACKMORE

Clara Vaughan, 1864

Parker, Christopher. "Gender Roles and Sexuality in R. D. Blackmore's Other Novels," in Parker, ed., *Gender Roles and Sexuality*, 85–87, 92.

Cradock Nowell: A Tale of the New Forest, 1865–1866

Parker, Christopher. "Gender Roles and Sexuality in R. D. Blackmore's Other Novels," in Parker, ed., *Gender Roles and Sexuality*, 90–93.

Erema, 1877

Parker, Christopher. "Gender Roles and Sexuality in R. D. Blackmore's Other Novels," in Parker, ed., *Gender Roles and Sexuality*, 88–89.

Lorna Doone, 1869

Horsman, Alan. *The Victorian Novel*, 196–97.

Parker, Christopher. "Gender Roles and Sexuality in R. D. Blackmore's Other Novels," in Parker, ed., *Gender Roles and Sexuality*, 83–85.

The Maid of Sker, 1872

Parker, Christopher. "Gender Roles and Sexuality in R. D. Blackmore's Other Novels," in Parker, ed., *Gender Roles and Sexuality*, 95–98.

Springhaven, 1881

Orel, Harold. *The Historical Novel*, 60–69.

HORACE WILLIAM BLEACKLEY

Une Culotte; or, A New Woman, 1894

Antor, Heinz. *Der englische Universitätsroman*, 459–62.

DERMOT BOLGER

The Journey Home, 1991

Fierobe, Claude. "Irlande et Europe 1990: *The Journey Home* de Dermot Bolger." *Etudes Irlandaises* 19:2 (1994), 41–49.

Night Shift, 1985

Kearney, Colbert. "Dermot Bolger and the Dual Carriageway." *Etudes Irlandaises* 19:2 (1994), 25–30.

The Woman's Daughter, 1987

Kearney, Colbert. "Dermot Bolger and the Dual Carriageway." *Etudes Irlandaises* 19:2 (1994), 30–39.

NANCY BOND

A String in the Harp, 1974

Filmer-Davies, Kath. *Fantasy Fiction and Welsh Myth,* 99–110.

CAROLINE BOWDER

Birth Rites, 1983

Cosslett, Tess. *Women Writing Childbirth,* 51–53, 59–62, 89–94.

ELIZABETH BOWEN

The Death of the Heart, 1938

Barreca, Regina. *Untamed and Unabashed,* 111–13.
Bennett, Andrew, and Nicholas Royle. *Elizabeth Bowen,* 63–81.
Joannou, Maroula. *'Ladies, Please Don't Smash These Windows,'* 127–58.
Jordan, Heather Bryant. *How Will the Heart Endure,* 26–27.

Eva Trout, 1969

Bennett, Andrew, and Nicholas Royle. *Elizabeth Bowen,* 140–57.
Hoogland, Renée C. *Elizabeth Bowen,* 206–90.
Jordan, Heather Bryant. *How Will the Heart Endure,* 184–89.

Friends and Relations, 1931

Bennett, Andrew, and Nicholas Royle. *Elizabeth Bowen,* 28–34.
Hoogland, Renée C. "Elizabeth Bowen: Unconscious Undertows— Queer Perspectives on *Friends and Relations,*" in Patrick J. Quinn, ed., *Recharting the Thirties,* 85–97.
Hoogland, Renée C. *Lesbian Configurations,* 81–105.

The Heat of the Day, 1949

Bennett, Andrew, and Nicholas Royle. *Elizabeth Bowen,* 82–103.
Hoogland, Renée C. *Elizabeth Bowen,* 107–205.

Jordan, Heather Bryant. *How Will the Heart Endure*, 153–68.

Leray, Josette. "The Big House and the Second World War in Elizabeth Bowen's *The Heat of the Day*." *Etudes Irlandaises* 19:1 (1994), 33–40.

Plain, Gill. *Women's Fiction of the Second World War*, 166–87.

Schneider, Karen. *Loving Arms*, 89–100.

The Hotel, 1927

Bennett, Andrew, and Nicholas Royle. *Elizabeth Bowen*, 1–14.

Jordan, Heather Bryant. *How Will the Heart Endure*, 23–26, 39–42.

The House in Paris, 1935

Bennett, Andrew, and Nicholas Royle. *Elizabeth Bowen*, 42–62.

Coates, John. "Emotional Need and Cultural Codes in *The House in Paris*." *Renascence* 47 (1994), 11–28.

Jordan, Heather Bryant. *How Will the Heart Endure*, 73–78.

The Last September, 1929

Backus, Margot Gayle. "Exploring the Ethical Implications of Narrative in a Sophomore-level Course on Same-sex Love: *Mrs. Dalloway* and *The Last September*," in Eileen Barrett and Patricia Cramer, eds., *Re: Reading*, 102–5.

Bennett, Andrew, and Nicholas Royle. *Elizabeth Bowen*, 14–22.

Hoogland, Renée C. *Elizabeth Bowen*, 24–106.

Innes, C. L. *Woman and Nation in Irish Literature*, 165–77.

Jordan, Heather Bryant. *How Will the Heart Endure*, 47–59.

Williams, Julia McElhattan. " 'Fiction with the Texture of History': Elizabeth Bowen's *The Last September*." *Mod Fiction Stud* 41 (1995), 219–38.

The Little Girls, 1964

Bennett, Andrew, and Nicholas Royle. *Elizabeth Bowen*, 121–39.

Jordan, Heather Bryant. *How Will the Heart Endure*, 182–84.

To the North, 1932

Barreca, Regina. *Untamed and Unabashed*, 125–31.

Bennett, Andrew, and Nicholas Royle. *Elizabeth Bowen*, 23–29, 31–33, 35–41.

Jordan, Heather Bryant. *How Will the Heart Endure*, 67–73.

A World of Love, 1955

Bennett, Andrew, and Nicholas Royle. *Elizabeth Bowen*, 104–20.

Jordan, Heather Bryant. *How Will the Heart Endure*, 175–78.

McCormack, W. J. *From Burke to Beckett*, 406–7.

CLARE BOYLAN

Black Baby, 1989

Giovannangeli, Jean-Louis. "Joyce and Boylan's *Black Baby:* 'Swiftly and Silently,' " in Theresa O'Connor, ed., *The Comic Tradition*, 171–82.

Holy Pictures, 1983

   Weekes, Anne Owens. "Ordinary Women: Themes in Contemporary
   Fiction by Irish Women." *Colby Q* 31 (1995), 92–93.

T. CORAGHESSAN BOYLE

Water Music, 1980

   Bauer, Matthias. *Im Fuchsbau der Geschichten,* 203–5.
   Witte, Arnd. "Fremd- und Eigenerfahrung in Westafrika: Am Beispiel
   von Gertraud Heises *Reise in die schwarze Haut* und T. Coraghessan
   Boyles *Water Music,"* in Anne Fuchs and Theo Harden, eds., *Reisen
   im Diskurs,* 382–88.

MALCOLM BRADBURY

Cuts, 1987

   Antor, Heinz. *Der englische Universitätsroman,* 683–86.

Eating People Is Wrong, 1959

   Antor, Heinz. *Der englische Universitätsroman,* 658–62.
   Taylor, D. J. *After the War,* 136–42.

The History Man, 1975

   Antor, Heinz. *Der englische Universitätsroman,* 662–63, 672–77.
   Lamarque, Peter, and Stein Haugom Olsen. *Truth, Fiction, and Litera-
   ture,* 418–23.
   Palmer, Frank. *Literature and Moral Understanding,* 147–48.

Stepping Westward, 1965

   Taylor, D. J. *After the War,* 142–49.

MARY ELIZABETH BRADDON

Aurora Floyd, 1863

   Reynolds, Kimberley, and Nicola Humble. *Victorian Heroines,* 111–17.

Barbara, 1880

   Helfield, Randa. "Poisonous Plots: Women Sensation Novelists and Murderesses of the Victorian Period." *Victorian R* 21 (1995), 178–80.

The Doctor's Wife, 1864

   Horsman, Alan. *The Victorian Novel,* 219–20.

Lady Audley's Secret, 1862

   Bernstein, Susan David. *Confessional Subjects,* 73–103.
   Bernstein, Susan David. "Dirty Reading: Sensation Fiction, Women, and
   Primitivism." *Criticism* 36 (1994), 215–25.
   Brewer, Pamela Didlake. "Pre-Raphaelitism in *Lady Audley's Secret."
   Publs of the Arkansas Philol Assoc* 19:1 (1993), 1–10.

Gilbert, Pamela K. "Madness and Civilization: Generic Opposition in Mary Elizabeth Braddon's *Lady Audley's Secret.*" *Essays in Lit* (Macomb, IL) 23 (1996), 218–31.

Hart, Lynda. "The Victorian Villainess and the Patriarchal Unconscious." *Lit and Psych* 40:3 (1994), 4–22.

Helfield, Randa. "Poisonous Plots: Women Sensation Novelists and Murderesses of the Victorian Period." *Victorian R* 21 (1995), 180–82.

Horsman, Alan. *The Victorian Novel*, 217–18.

Marks, Patricia. " 'The Boy on the Wooden Horse': Robert Audley and the Failure of Reason." *Clues* 15:2 (1994), 1–12.

Matus, Jill L. *Unstable Bodies*, 186–205.

Nemesvari, Richard. "Robert Audley's Secret: Male Homosocial Desire in *Lady Audley's Secret.*" *Stud in the Novel* 27 (1995), 515–27.

Reynolds, Kimberley, and Nicola Humble. *Victorian Heroines*, 107–10.

Thomas, Ronald R. "Wilkie Collins and the Sensation Novel," in John Richetti et al., eds., *The Columbia History*, 494–95, 501–2.

Tilley, Elizabeth. "Gender and Role-playing in *Lady Audley's Secret,*" in Valeria Tinkler-Villani and Peter Davidson, eds., *Exhibited by Candlelight*, 197–204.

The Trail of the Serpent, 1861

Helfield, Randa. "Poisonous Plots: Women Sensation Novelists and Murderesses of the Victorian Period." *Victorian R* 21 (1995), 177–78.

EDWARD BRADLEY

The Adventures of Mr. Verdant Green, an Oxford Undergraduate, 1853

Antor, Heinz. *Der englische Universitätsroman*, 154–56, 168–71.

JOHN BRAINE

Room at the Top, 1957

Wagner, Hans-Peter. "Learning to Read the Female Body: On the Function of Manet's *Olympia* in John Braine's *Room at the Top.*" *Zeitschrift für Anglistik und Amerikanistik* 42 (1994), 38–50.

WALTER BRIERLY

Means-Test Man, 1935

Fox, Pamela. *Class Fictions*, 107–8, 135–43.

VERA BRITTAIN

Account Rendered, 1945

Cadogan, Mary. *And Then Their Hearts Stood Still*, 104–6.

GEORGE BRITTAINE

Irish Priests and English Landlords, 1830

Hayley, Barbara. "Religion and Society in Nineteenth Century Irish Fiction," in Robert Welch, ed., *Irish Writers and Religion*, 33–34.

ANNE BRONTË

Agnes Grey, 1847

Baldridge, Cates. *The Dialogics of Dissent*, 64–79.

Bell, A. Craig. *The Novels of Anne Brontë*, 1–30.

Berry, Elizabeth Hollis. *Anne Brontë's Radical Vision*, 39–70, 108–10.

Frawley, Maria H. *Anne Brontë*, 82–116.

Horsman, Alan. *The Victorian Novel*, 163–64.

Matus, Jill L. *Unstable Bodies*, 90–113.

Meyer, Susan. "Words on 'Great Vulgar Sheets': Writing and Social Resistance in Anne Brontë's *Agnes Grey* (1847)," in Barbara Leah Harman and Susan Meyer, eds., *The New Nineteenth Century*, 3–15.

The Tenant of Wildfell Hall, 1848

Banerjee, Jacqueline. "The Impossible Goal: The Struggle for Manhood in Victorian Fiction." *Victorian Newsl* 89 (1996), 2–3.

Bell, A. Craig. *The Novels of Anne Brontë*, 31–133.

Berry, Elizabeth Hollis. *Anne Brontë's Radical Vision*, 71–110.

Berry, Laura C. "Acts of Custody and Incarceration in *Wuthering Heights* and *The Tenant of Wildfell Hall.*" *Novel* 30 (1996), 32–53.

Frawley, Maria H. *Anne Brontë*, 9–14, 117–39.

Horsman, Alan. *The Victorian Novel*, 178–79.

Lerner, Laurence. "Stereotypes of Woman in Victorian England," in John Morris, ed., *Exploring Stereotyped Images*, 41–44.

Poole, Russell. "Cultural Reformation and Cultural Reproduction in Anne Brontë's *The Tenant of Wildfell Hall.*" *Stud in Engl Lit, 1500–1900* 33 (1993), 859–71.

Signorotti, Elizabeth. " 'A Frame Perfect and Glorious': Narrative Structure in Anne Brontë's *The Tenant of Wildfell Hall.*" *Victorian Newsl* 87 (1995), 20–24.

Stuart, Barbara. "Lawless Mothers," in Barbara Thaden, ed., *New Essays on the Maternal Voice*, 55–64.

Sutherland, John. *Is Heathcliff a Murderer?*, 73–77.

Thormählen, Marianne. "The Villain of *Wildfell Hall:* Aspects and Prospects of Arthur Huntingdon." *Mod Lang R* 88 (1993), 831–41.

Waddington-Feather, John. "Religion, Love and Marriage in *The Tenant of Wildfell Hall.*" *Brontë Newsl* 11 (1995), 2.

Würzbach, Natascha. "The Mother Image as Cultural Concept and Literary Theme in the Nineteenth- and Twentieth-Century English Novel: A Feminist Reading within the Context of New Historicism and the

History of Mentalities," in Rüdiger Ahrens and Laurenz Volkmann, eds., *Why Literature Matters*, 375.

CHARLOTTE BRONTË

Jane Eyre, 1847

Allen, Dennis W. "*Jane Eyre* and the Politics of Style," in Diane Long Hoeveler and Beth Lau, eds., *Approaches,* 110–15.

Almond, Barbara, and Richard Almond. *The Therapeutic Narrative,* 43–61.

Armitt, Lucie. *Theorising the Fantastic,* 133–35.

Azim, Firdous. *The Colonial Rise of the Novel,* 99–101, 105–7, 175–97.

Bailin, Miriam. *The Sickroom in Victorian Fiction,* 69–73.

Barreca, Regina. *Untamed and Unabashed,* 61–68.

Beattie, Valerie. "The Mystery at Thornfield: Representations of Madness in *Jane Eyre.*" *Stud in the Novel* 28 (1996), 493–503.

Beaty, Jerome. "*Jane Eyre* Cubed: The Three Dimensions of the Text." *Narrative* 4 (1996), 74–89.

Beaty, Jerome. *Misreading "Jane Eyre,"* 11–222.

Bewell, Alan. "*Jane Eyre* and Victorian Medical Geography." *ELH* 63 (1996), 773–804.

Brown, Penny. *The Captured World,* 139–49.

Bump, Jerome. "*Jane Eyre* and Family Systems Therapy," in Diane Long Hoeveler and Beth Lau, eds., *Approaches,* 130–38.

Burgan, Mary. "Fire and Light in *Jane Eyre,*" in Diane Long Hoeveler and Beth Lau, eds., *Approaches,* 82–86.

Cadogan, Mary. *And Then Their Hearts Stood Still,* 11–13, 92–93.

Carter, Angela. "Charlotte Brontë: *Jane Eyre.*" *Revista de Occidente* 139 (1992), 25–40.

Cavaliero, Glen. *The Supernatural and English Fiction,* 94–95.

Clarke, Micael M. *Thackeray and Women,* 83–86.

Conover, Robin St. John. "Jane Eyre's Triptych and Milton's *Paradise Lost.*" *Victorian R* 22 (1996), 171–85.

Dalgarno, Emily. "Ideology into Fiction: Virginia Woolf's 'A Sketch of the Past.' " *Novel* 27 (1994), 188–92.

David, Deirdre. *Rule Britannia,* 77–97, 107–17.

Demoor, Marysa. "Male Monsters or Monstrous Males in Victorian Women's Fiction," in Valeria Tinkler-Villani and Peter Davidson, eds., *Exhibited by Candlelight,* 174–77.

Dickerson, Vanessa D. *Victorian Ghosts in the Noontide,* 50–66.

Diedrick, James. "*Jane Eyre* and *A Vindication of the Rights of Woman,*" in Diane Long Hoeveler and Beth Lau, eds., *Approaches,* 22–27.

Duncker, Patricia. *Sisters and Strangers,* 24–27.

Ermarth, Elizabeth Deeds. *The English Novel in History,* 8–13.

Farkas, Carol-Ann. " 'Beyond What Language Can Express': Transcending the Limits of the Self in *Jane Eyre.*" *Victorian R* 20 (1994), 49–67.

Fraiman, Susan. "Jane Eyre's Fall from Grace," in Beth Newman, ed., *Charlotte Brontë: "Jane Eyre,"* 614–31.

Franklin, J. Jeffrey. "The Merging of Spiritualities: Jane Eyre as Missionary of Love." *Nineteenth-Cent Lit* 49 (1995), 456–82.

Gallagher, Susan VanZanten. *"Jane Eyre* and Christianity," in Diane Long Hoeveler and Beth Lau, eds., *Approaches,* 62–68.

Gilbert, Sandra M. "Plain Jane's Progress," in Beth Newman, ed., *Charlotte Brontë: "Jane Eyre,"* 475–501.

Gliserman, Martin. *Psychoanalysis, Language, and the Body of the Text,* 84–111.

Gordon, Lyndall. *Charlotte Brontë,* 152–65, 335–37.

Goscilo, Margaret. *"Jane Eyre* and Pictorial Representation," in Diane Long Hoeveler and Beth Lau, eds., *Approaches,* 97–102.

Haroian-Guerin, Gil. *The Fatal Hero,* 9–48.

Heller, Tamar. *"Jane Eyre,* Bertha, and the Female Gothic," in Diane Long Hoeveler and Beth Lau, eds., *Approaches,* 49–55.

Hennelly, Mark M., Jr. "Contrast and Liminality: Structure and Antistructure in *Jane Eyre,*" in Diane Long Hoeveler and Beth Lau, eds., *Approaches,* 87–96.

Hennelly, Mark M., Jr. " 'In a State Between': A Reading of Liminality in *Jane Eyre.*" *Victorian Lit and Culture* 22 (1994), 103–22.

Hoeveler, Diane Long. *"Jane Eyre* through the Body: Food, Sex, Discipline," in Diane Long Hoeveler and Beth Lau, eds., *Approaches,* 116–23.

Horsman, Alan. *The Victorian Novel,* 172–78.

Ifkovic, David. "Conflict Resolution by the Brontës: *Jane Eyre*—A Case in Point." *Brontë Newsl* 10 (1994), 4–5.

Imlay, Elizabeth. "Freemasonry, the Brontës, and the Hidden Text of *Jane Eyre,*" in Marie Mulvey Roberts and Hugh Ormsby-Lennon, eds., *Secret Texts,* 210–25.

Jadwin, Lisa. " 'Caricatured, not faithfully rendered': *Bleak House* as a Revision of *Jane Eyre.*" *Mod Lang Stud* 26: 2–3 (1996), 111–31.

Jenkins, Keith A. *"Jane Eyre:* Charlotte Brontë's New Bible," in Diane Long Hoeveler and Beth Lau, eds., *Approaches,* 69–75.

Johnson, Patricia E. "Charlotte Brontë and Desire (to Write): Pleasure, Power, and Prohibition," in Carol J. Singley and Susan Elizabeth Sweeney, eds., *Anxious Power,* 175–78.

Johnston, Ruth D. "Dis-membrance of Things Past: Re-Vision of Wordsworthian Retrospection in *Jane Eyre* and *Villette.*" *Victorian Lit and Culture* 22 (1994), 78–84.

Jordan, John O. *"Jane Eyre* and Narrative Voice," in Diane Long Hoeveler and Beth Lau, eds., *Approaches,* 76–81.

Jordan, John O. "Partings Welded Together: Self-Fashioning in *Great Expectations* and *Jane Eyre.*" *Dickens Q* 13 (1996), 19–32.

Juhasz, Suzanne. *Reading from the Heart,* 115–55.

Kamel, Rose. " 'Before I Was Set Free': The Creole Wife in *Jane Eyre* and *Wide Saragasso Sea.*" *J of Narrative Technique* 25 (1995), 1–18.

Kaplan, Carla. "Girl Talk: *Jane Eyre* and the Romance of Women's Narration." *Novel* 30 (1996), 5–27.

Kaye, Richard A. "A Good Woman on Five Thousand Pounds: *Jane Eyre, Vanity Fair,* and Literary Rivalry." *Stud in Engl Lit, 1500–1900* 35 (1995), 723–35.

Kendrick, Robert. "Edward Rochester and the Margins of Masculinity in *Jane Eyre* and *Wide Saragasso Sea.*" *Papers on Lang and Lit* 30 (1994), 235–55.

Knoepflmacher, U. C. "Afterword: Endings as Beginnings," in Alison Booth, ed., *Famous Last Words,* 354–57, 362–66.

Kucich, John. "*Jane Eyre* and Imperialism," in Diane Long Hoeveler and Beth Lau, eds., *Approaches,* 104–9.

Lambert, Ellen Zetzel. *The Face of Love,* 98–103, 110–16.

Lee, Hsiao-Hung. *"Possibilities of Hidden Things,"* 13–57.

Lee, So-hee. "Women's Writing in *Jane Eyre:* Focussed on the First-Person Narrative." *J of Engl Lang and Lit* 41 (1995), 45–60.

Lerner, Laurence. *Angels and Absences,* 134–38.

Levy, Anita. "*Jane Eyre,* the Woman Writer, and the History of Experience." *Mod Lang Q* 56 (1995), 77–95.

McKnight, Natalie J. *Suffering Mothers,* 63–71, 76–83.

Marcus, Sharon. "The Profession of the Author: Abstraction, Advertising, and *Jane Eyre.*" *PMLA* 110 (1995), 206–17.

Meyer, Susan. *Imperialism at Home,* 60–95.

Michie, Elsie. "White Chimpanzees and Oriental Despots: Racial Stereotyping and Edward Rochester," in Beth Newman, ed., *Charlotte Brontë: "Jane Eyre,"* 584–97.

Michie, Elsie B. *Outside the Pale,* 11–16, 46–78, 152–55, 161–63.

Miller, Jane Eldridge. *Rebel Women,* 118–20.

Mitchell, Judith. *The Stone and the Scorpion,* 44–58.

Myer, Valerie Grosvenor. *Ten Great English Novelists,* 120–23.

Newman, Judie. *The Ballistic Bard,* 13–17.

Nichols, Nina daVinci. *Ariadne's Lives,* 26–38.

Nixon, Nicola. "*Wide Saragasso Sea* and Jean Rhys's Interrogation of the 'nature wholly alien' in *Jane Eyre.*" *Essays in Lit* (Macomb, IL) 21 (1994), 267–82.

Nollen, Elizabeth Mahn. "Female Detective Figures in British Fiction: Coping with Madness and Imprisonment." *Clues* 15:2 (1994), 42–45.

Novy, Marianne. *Engaging with Shakespeare,* 38–43.

Nudd, Donna Marie. "Rediscovering Jane Eyre through Its Adaptations," in Diane Long Hoeveler and Beth Lau, eds., *Approaches,* 139–45.

Paris, Bernard J. "*Jane Eyre* as a Novel of Vindication," in Diane Long Hoeveler and Beth Lau, eds., *Approaches,* 124–29.

Patten, Robert L. "Taking a Walk; or, Setting Forth from Gateshead," in Diane Long Hoeveler and Beth Lau, eds., *Approaches,* 148–53.

Pearson, Nels C. "Voice of My Voice: Mutual Submission and Transcendental Potentiality in *Jane Eyre.*" *Victorian Newsl* 90 (1996), 28–32.

Perera, Suvendrini. *Reaches of Empire*, 84–94.

Perkin, J. Russell. "Locking George Sand in the Attic: Female Passion and Domestic Realism in the Victorian Novel." *Univ of Toronto Q* 63 (1993–94), 421–25.

Peters, John G. "Inside and Outside: *Jane Eyre* and Marginalization Through Labeling." *Stud in the Novel* 28 (1996), 57–73.

Poovey, Mary. "Jane Eyre and the Governess in Nineteenth-Century Britain," in Diane Long Hoeveler and Beth Lau, eds., *Approaches*, 43–48.

Qualls, Barry V. " 'Speak what we think': The Brontës and Women Writers," in John Richetti et al., eds., *The Columbia History*, 352–59.

Ralph, Phyllis C. " 'Beauty and the Beast': Growing Up with Jane Eyre," in Diane Long Hoeveler and Beth Lau, eds., *Approaches*, 56–61.

Rapaport, Herman. *Between the Sign and the Gaze*, 109–22.

Rennert, Laura J. "Narrative in *Jane Eyre:* The Dialectic of Image and Exposition." *Victorians Inst J* 21 (1993), 155–87.

Reynolds, Kimberley, and Nicola Humble. *Victorian Heroines*, 122–24.

Richter, David H. *The Progress of Romance*, 106–8.

Rosenwasser, David. "A Kristevan Reading of the Marriage Plot in *Jane Eyre*," in Diane Long Hoeveler and Beth Lau, eds., *Approaches*, 154–61.

Sadoff, Dianne F. "The Father, Castration, and Female Fantasy in *Jane Eyre*," in Beth Newman, ed., *Charlotte Brontë: "Jane Eyre*," 518–34.

Sanders, Valerie. *Eve's Renegades*, 47–53, 55–59.

Schwartz, Nina. "No Place Like Home: The Logic of the Supplement in *Jane Eyre*," in Beth Newman, ed., *Charlotte Brontë: "Jane Eyre*," 549–64.

Shumway, Suzanne Rosenthal. "The Chronotype of the Asylum: *Jane Eyre*, Feminism, and Bakhtinian Theory," in Karen Hohne and Helen Wussow, eds., *A Dialogue of Voices*, 158–68.

Shuttleworth, Sally. *Charlotte Brontë and Victorian Psychology*, 148–82.

Small, Helen. *Love's Madness*, 154–78.

Smith, Patricia Juliana. " 'And I Wondered If She Might Kiss Me': Lesbian Panic as Narrative Strategy in British Women's Fiction." *Mod Fiction Stud* 41 (1995), 574–75.

Stewart, Garrett. *Dear Reader*, 242–49, 267–74.

Sutherland, John. *Is Heathcliff a Murderer?*, 59–65.

Thaden, Barbara. "Elizabeth Gaskell and the Dead Mother Plot," in Thaden, ed., *New Essays on the Maternal Voice*, 36–38.

Tkacz, Catherine Brown. "The Bible in *Jane Eyre*." *Christianity and Lit* 44 (1994), 3–19.

Tong, Q. S., and Jane Roberts. "Diachronyed Synchrony: A Comparative Study of the Opening Paragraphs of *Jane Eyre* and *Wide Saragasso Sea*." *Anglistik* 6:2 (1995), 64–74.

Tournebize, Cassilde. "Complexité et ambivalence de l'espace 'gothique' dans *Jane Eyre*." *Caliban* 33 (1996), 83–91.

48 BRONTË

Warhol, Robyn R. "Double Gender, Double Genre in *Jane Eyre* and *Villette.*" *Stud in Engl Lit, 1500–1900* 36 (1996), 857–71.
Watson, Daphne. *Their Own Worst Enemies*, 17–21.
Weisser, Susan Ostrov. *A "Craving Fancy,"* 53–72.
Wheat, Patricia H. *The Adytum of the Heart*, 46–59, 79–81.
Wheeler, Michael. *English Fiction of the Victorian Period*, 62–70.
Winnifrith, Tom. *Fallen Women*, 32–36.
Witt, Amanda B. " 'I Read It in Your Eye': Spiritual Vision in *Jane Eyre.*" *Victorian Newsl* 85 (1994), 29–34.
Wyatt, Jean. *Reconstructing Desire*, 23–40, 46–48.
York, R. A. *Strangers and Secrets*, 57–74.
Zare, Bonnie. "*Jane Eyre*'s Excruciating Ending." *Coll Lang Assoc J* 37 (1993), 204–20.
Zonana, Joyce. "The Sultan and the Slave: Feminist Orientalism and the Structure of *Jane Eyre.*" *Signs* 18 (1993), 592–615.

The Professor, 1857

Azim, Firdous. *The Colonial Rise of the Novel*, 147–71.
Federico, Annette R. "The Other Case: Gender and Narration in Charlotte Brontë's *The Professor.*" *Papers on Lang and Lit* 30 (1994), 323–44.
Gordon, Lyndall. *Charlotte Brontë*, 102–5, 126–31.
Haxell, Nichola Anne. "Woman As Lacemaker: The Development of a Literary Stereotype in Texts by Charlotte Brontë, Nerval, Lainé, and Chawaf." *Mod Lang R* 89 (1994), 546–50.
Horsman, Alan. *The Victorian Novel*, 161–63.
McIntyre, Elizabeth. "Charlotte Brontë's New Corinne: Re-reading *The Professor.*" *Victorian Newsl* 85 (1994), 34–39.
Malone, Catherine. " 'We have learnt to love her more than her books': The Critical Reception of Brontë's *Professor.*" *R of Engl Stud* 47 (1996), 175–87.
Millard, Kenneth. "My Father's Will: Self-determination and Mental Breakdown in *Basil, The Professor,* and *The Ordeal of Richard Feverel.*" *English* 44 (1995), 62–78.
Mitchell, Judith. *The Stone and the Scorpion*, 31–44.
Morphet, Fiona. "Playing with *The Professor.*" *Coll Lang Assoc J* 37 (1994), 348–57.
Shuttleworth, Sally. *Charlotte Brontë and Victorian Psychology*, 123–47.
Winnifrith, Tom. *Fallen Women*, 32–37.

Shirley, 1849

Argyle, Gisela. "Gender and Generic Mixing in Charlotte Brontë's *Shirley.*" *Stud in Engl Lit, 1500–1900* 35 (1995), 741–55.
Azim, Firdous. *The Colonial Rise of the Novel*, 197–213.
Bailin, Miriam. *The Sickroom in Victorian Fiction*, 53–77.
Dolin, Tim. "Fictional Territory and a Woman's Place: Regional and Sexual Difference in *Shirley.*" *ELH* 62 (1995), 197–212.

Gordon, Lyndall. *Charlotte Brontë*, 179–84, 187–200.

Greene, Sally. "Apocalypse When? *Shirley*'s Vision and the Politics of Reading." *Stud in the Novel* 26 (1994), 350–69.

Harsh, Constance D. *Subversive Heroines,* 115–45.

Horsman, Alan. *The Victorian Novel*, 179–83.

Ingham, Patricia. *The Language of Gender and Class*, 31–54.

Jenkins, Ruth Y. *Reclaiming Myths of Power,* 74–91.

Johnson, Patricia E. "Charlotte Brontë and Desire (to Write): Pleasure, Power, and Prohibition," in Carol J. Singley and Susan Elizabeth Sweeney, eds., *Anxious Power*, 178–80.

Johnston, Ruth D. "Narrative Diversion in *Shirley,* or the Perversion of Fetishism." *Victorian Lit and Culture* 23 (1995), 89–110.

Kahane, Claire. *Passions of the Voice*, 53–57.

Lawson, Kate. "Imagining Eve: Charlotte Brontë, Kate Millett, Hélène Cixous." *Women's Stud* 24 (1995), 411–24.

McKnight, Natalie J. *Suffering Mothers*, 70–83.

Mitchell, Judith. *The Stone and the Scorpion*, 58–69.

Myer, Valerie Grosvenor. *Ten Great English Novelists*, 122–24.

Novy, Marianne. *Engaging with Shakespeare,* 32–38.

O'Brien, Susie. "Lying Back and Thinking of England: Sex and Nationalism in Charlotte Brontë's *Shirley.*" *Frontenac R* 10–11 (1993–94), 54–79.

Orel, Harold. *The Historical Novel*, 29–31.

Qualls, Barry V. " 'Speak what we think': The Brontës and Women Writers," in John Richetti et al., eds., *The Columbia History*, 357–60.

Shuttleworth, Sally. *Charlotte Brontë and Victorian Psychology*, 183–218.

Thaden, Barbara. "Elizabeth Gaskell and the Dead Mother Plot," in Thaden, ed., *New Essays on the Maternal Voice,* 41–43.

Vanskike, Elliott. "Consistent Inconsistencies: The Transvestite Actress Madame Vestris and Charlotte Brontë's *Shirley.*" *Nineteenth-Cent Lit* 50 (1996), 464–88.

Vrettos, Athena. *Somatic Fictions*, 39–44.

Wheat, Patricia H. *The Adytum of the Heart*, 22–25, 65–73.

Winnifrith, Tom. *Fallen Women,* 42–45.

Villette, 1853

Azim, Firdous. *The Colonial Rise of the Novel*, 101–4.

Bailin, Miriam. *The Sickroom in Victorian Fiction,* 61–64, 71–73.

Barfoot, C. C. "The Gist of the Gothic in English Fiction; or, Gothic and the Invasion of Boundaries," in Valeria Tinkler-Villani and Peter Davidson, eds., *Exhibited by Candlelight*, 163–64.

Barreca, Regina. *Untamed and Unabashed,* 68–79.

Bernstein, Susan David. *Confessional Subjects*, 41–72.

Breen, Margaret Soenser. "Who Are You, Lucy Snowe?: Disoriented *Bildung* in *Villette.*" *Dickens Stud Annual* 24 (1996), 241–55.

Byatt, A. S., and Ignês Sodré. *Imagining Characters*, 43–77.

Ciolkowski, Laura E. "Charlotte Brontë's *Villette:* Forgeries of Sex and Self." *Stud in the Novel* 26 (1994), 218–31.

Dames, Nicholas. "The Clinical Novel: Phrenology and *Villette.*" *Novel* 29 (1996), 367–88.

Fasick, Laura. *Vessels of Meaning*, 103–14.

Fimland, Marit. "On the Margins of the Acceptable: Charlotte Brontë's *Villette.*" *Lit and Theology* 10 (1996), 148–57.

Gordon, Lyndall. *Charlotte Brontë*, 247–74, 282–86.

Horsman, Alan. *The Victorian Novel*, 183–88.

Johnston, Ruth D. "Dis-membrance of Things Past: Re-Vision of Wordsworthian Retrospection in *Jane Eyre* and *Villette.*" *Victorian Lit and Culture* 22 (1994), 84–97.

Kahane, Claire. *Passions of the Voice*, 57–63.

Johnson, Patricia E. "Charlotte Brontë and Desire (to Write): Pleasure, Power, and Prohibition," in Carol J. Singley and Susan Elizabeth Sweeney, eds., *Anxious Power*, 181–84.

Klaver, Claudia. "Homely Aesthetics: *Villette*'s Canny Narrator." *Genre* 26 (1993), 409–28.

Knezevic, Borislav. "The Impossible Things: Quest for Knowledge in Charlotte Brontë's *Villette.*" *Lit and Psych* 42:1–2 (1996), 65–95.

Knoepflmacher, U. C. "Afterword: Endings as Beginnings," in Alison Booth, ed., *Famous Last Words*, 363–66.

Lambert, Ellen Zetzel. *The Face of Love*, 116–18, 120–22, 131–33.

Lawrence, Karen R. *Penelope Voyages*, 25–27.

Lee, Hsiao-Hung. *"Possibilities of Hidden Things,"* 59–100.

McGlamery, Gayla. " 'This Unlicked Wolf-Club': Anti-Catholicism in Charlotte Brontë's *Villette.*" *Cahiers Victoriens et Edouardiens* 37 (1993), 55–68.

McKnight, Natalie J. *Suffering Mothers*, 78–83.

Matus, Jill L. *Unstable Bodies,* 131–48.

Mitchell, Judith. *The Stone and the Scorpion*, 69–81.

Myer, Valerie Grosvenor. *Ten Great English Novelists*, 124–25.

Qualls, Barry V. " 'Speak what we think': The Brontës and Women Writers," in John Richetti et al., eds., *The Columbia History*, 360–64.

Schiefelbein, Michael. "A Catholic Baptism for *Villette*'s Lucy Snowe." *Christianity and Lit* 45 (1996), 319–28.

Shaw, Margaret L. "Narrative Surveillance and Social Control in *Villette.*" *Stud in Engl Lit, 1500–1900* 34 (1994), 813–32.

Shuttleworth, Sally. *Charlotte Brontë and Victorian Psychology*, 219–42.

Stewart, Garrett. *Dear Reader*, 249–66.

Stewart, Garrett. "A Valediction For Bidding Mourning: Death and Narratee in Brontë's *Villette,*" in Sarah Webster Goodwin and Elisabeth Bronfen, eds., *Death and Representation*, 51–75.

Surridge, Lisa. "Representing the 'Latent Vashti': Theatricality in Charlotte Brontë's *Villette.*" *Victorian Newsl* 87 (1995), 4–13.

Sutherland, John. *Is Heathcliff a Murderer?,* 99–109.

Voskuil, Lynn M. "Acting Naturally: Brontë, Lewes, and the Problem of Gender Performance." *ELH* 62 (1995), 424–38.

Vrettos, Athena. *Somatic Fictions*, 59–69, 75–80.

Warhol, Robyn R. "Double Gender, Double Genre in *Jane Eyre* and *Villette*." *Stud in Engl Lit, 1500–1900* 36 (1996), 857–71.

Weinstone, Ann. "The Queerness of Lucy Snowe." *Nineteenth-Cent Contexts* 18 (1995), 367–79.

Weisser, Susan Ostrov. *A "Craving Fancy,"* 73–91.

Wheat, Patricia H. *The Adytum of the Heart*, 25–29, 85–90.

Wheeler, Michael. *English Fiction of the Victorian Period*, 63–65.

Wiesenthal, C. S. "Anti-bodies of Disease and Defense: Spirit-Body Relations in Nineteenth-Century Culture and Fiction." *Victorian Lit and Culture* 22 (1994), 195–200.

Wills, Jack C. "*Villette* and *The Marble Faun*." *Stud in the Novel* 25 (1993), 272–85.

EMILY BRONTË

Wuthering Heights, 1847

Banerjee, Jacqueline. "Girls' Education and the Crisis of the Heroine in Victorian Fiction." *Engl Stud* (Amsterdam) 75 (1994), 34–36.

Barfoot, C. C. "The Gist of the Gothic in English Fiction; or, Gothic and the Invasion of Boundaries," in Valeria Tinkler-Villani and Peter Davidson, eds., *Exhibited by Candlelight*, 164–66.

Berg, Maggie. *"Wuthering Heights": The Writing in the Margin*, 23–117.

Berry, Laura C. "Acts of Custody and Incarceration in *Wuthering Heights* and *The Tenant of Wildfell Hall*." *Novel* 30 (1996), 32–53.

Botting, Fred. *Gothic*, 128–31.

Brown, Penny. *The Captured World*, 149–61.

Cadogan, Mary. *And Then Their Hearts Stood Still*, 13–15.

Cavaliero, Glen. *The Supernatural and English Fiction*, 2–7.

Chazal, Roger. "Imagologie et narratologie: Actualité d'un lieu anglophone classique—*Wuthering Heights*," in Gisèle Mathieu-Castellani, ed., *La Pensée de l'image*, 173–81.

Collick, John. "Dismembering Devils: The Demonology of *Arashi ga oka* (1988) *and Wuthering Heights* (1939)," in Peter Reynolds, ed., *Novel Images*, 34–47.

Craig, Sheryl. "Brontë's *Wuthering Heights*." *Explicator* 52 (1994), 157–59.

Demoor, Marysa. "Male Monsters or Monstrous Males in Victorian Women's Fiction," in Valeria Tinkler-Villani and Peter Davidson, eds., *Exhibited by Candlelight*, 180–81.

Dickerson, Vanessa D. *Victorian Ghosts in the Noontide*, 71–79.

Ermarth, Elizabeth Deeds. *The English Novel in History*, 13–15.

Flintoff, Everard. "Branwell at the Heights: An Investigation into the

Possible Influence of Branwell Brontë upon *Wuthering Heights.*" *Durham Univ J* 86 (1994), 241–49.

Fragola, Anthony. "Buñuel's Re-vision of *Wuthering Heights:* The Triumph of *L'Amour Fou* over Hollywood Romanticism." *Lit/Film Q* 22 (1994), 50–55.

Frith, Gillian. "Decoding *Wuthering Heights,*" in Thomas John Winnifrith, ed., *Critical Essays on Emily Brontë*, 243–61.

Ghnassia, Jill Dix. *Metaphysical Rebellion*, 3–5, 44, 47, 131–33, 205–7, 212–14.

Gordon, Jan B. *Gossip and Subversion*, 97–154.

Grove, Robin. "The Poor Man's Daughter's Tale: Narrative and System in *Wuthering Heights.*" *Crit R* 36 (1996), 32–40.

Helsinger, Elizabeth K. *Rural Scenes and National Representation*, 175–77, 204–16.

Heywood, Christopher. " 'The Helks Lady' and Other Legends Surrounding *Wuthering Heights.*" *Lore and Lang* 11:2 (1992–93), 127–42.

Heywood, Christopher. "A Yorkshire Background for *Wuthering Heights.*" *Mod Lang R* 88 (1993), 817–30.

Hill, James L. "Joseph's Currants: The Hermeneutic Challenge of *Wuthering Heights.*" *Victorian Lit and Culture* 22 (1994), 267–83.

Hollahan, Eugene. *Crisis-Consciousness*, 65–67.

Horsman, Alan. *The Victorian Novel*, 164–72.

Juhasz, Suzanne. *Reading from the Heart*, 71–114.

Kauhl, Gudrun. "Myths of Enclosure and Myths of the Open in *The Monk* and *Wuthering Heights,*" in Valeria Tinkler-Villani and Peter Davidson, eds., *Exhibited by Candlelight*, 187–96.

Kearns, Katherine. *Nineteenth-Century Literary Realism,* 144–77.

Kelly Patrick. "The Sublimity of Catherine and Heathcliff." *Victorian Newsl* 86 (1994), 24–30.

Kullmann, Thomas. "Nature and Psychology in *Melmoth the Wanderer* and *Wuthering Heights,*" in Valeria Tinkler-Villani and Peter Davidson, eds., *Exhibited by Candlelight*, 102–6.

Lanone, Catherine. "*Wuthering Heights* ou le labyrinthe de l'obsession." *Caliban* 33 (1996), 73–82.

LaValva, Rosamaria. "Sortilegi della menzogna: *Wuthering Heights* e Elsa Morante." *Italian Q* 32:123–124 (1995), 49–59.

Levy, Eric P. "The Psychology of Loneliness in *Wuthering Heights.*" *Stud in the Novel* 28 (1996), 158–74.

Lovell-Smith, Rosemary. "Childhood and Adoption in Scott and the Writing of *Wuthering Heights.*" *Scottish Liter J* 21:1 (1994), 24–31.

McGuire, Kathryn B. "Second Chances: Doubling in *Wuthering Heights.*" *Conf of Coll Teachers of Engl Stud* 58 (1993), 56–62.

McMaster, Juliet. "The Courtship and Honeymoon of Mr. and Mrs. Linton Heathcliff: Emily Brontë's Sexual Imagery." *Victorian R* 18:1 (1992), 28–45.

Macovski, Michael. *Dialogue and Literature,* 134–50.

Meaney, Gerardine. *(Un)Like Subjects*, 39–43.

Medoro, Dana. " 'This Thing of Darkness I/Acknowledge Mine': Heathcliff as Fetish in *Wuthering Heights.*" *Engl Stud in Canada* 22 (1996), 267–80.

Mengel, Ewald. "Der Konflikt zwischen Natur und Zivilisation in Emily Brontës *Wuthering Heights,*" in Konrad Groß et al., eds., *Das Natur/ Kultur-Paradigma,* 62–78.

Meyer, Susan. *Imperialism at Home,* 96–125.

Michie, Elsie B. *Outside the Pale,* 13–16, 46–78.

Myer, Valerie Grosvenor. *Ten Great English Novelists,* 129–31.

Neilson, Heather. " 'The face at the window': Gothic Thematics in *Frankenstein, Wuthering Heights,* and *The Turn of the Screw.*" *Sydney Stud in Engl* 19 (1993–94), 80–83.

Nussbaum, Martha. "*Wuthering Heights:* The Romantic Ascent." *Philos and Lit* 20 (1996), 362–81.

Perkin, J. Russell. "Inhabiting *Wuthering Heights:* Jane Urquhart's Re-writing of Emily Brontë." *Victorian R* 21 (1995), 115–27.

Qualls, Barry V. " 'Speak what we think': The Brontës and Women Writers," in John Richetti et al., eds., *The Columbia History,* 373–80.

Siegel, Carol. *Male Masochism,* 147–49.

Sneidern, Maja-Lisa von. "*Wuthering Heights* and the Liverpool Slave Trade." *ELH* 62 (1995), 171–88.

Stewart, Garrett. *Dear Reader,* 237–42.

Stoneman, Patsy. "Catherine Earnshaw's Journey to her Home among the Dead: Fresh Thoughts on *Wuthering Heights* and 'Epipsychidion.' " *R of Engl Stud* 47 (1996), 521–33.

Stoneman, Patsy. "Feminist Criticism of *Wuthering Heights.*" *Crit Survey* 4 (1992), 147–53.

Strobos, Semon. "Heathcliff and Nelly Dean as Dialogical Elements in *Wuthering Heights.*" *Nassau R* 6:4 (1992), 146–52.

Sutherland, John. *Is Heathcliff a Murderer?,* 53–58.

Thompson, Nicola. "The Unveiling of Ellis Bell: Gender and the Reception of *Wuthering Heights.*" *Women's Stud* 24 (1995), 341–62.

Vine, Steven. "The Wuther of the Other in *Wuthering Heights.*" *Nineteenth-Cent Lit* 49 (1994), 339–59.

Weisser, Susan Ostrov. *A "Craving Fancy,"* 92–113.

Wheat, Patricia H. *The Adytum of the Heart,* 74–84.

Wheeler, Michael. *English Fiction of the Victorian Period,* 70–75.

Wiesenthal, C. S. "Anti-bodies of Disease and Defense: Spirit-Body Relations in Nineteenth-Century Culture and Fiction." *Victorian Lit and Culture* 22 (1994), 195–200.

York, R. A. *Strangers and Secrets,* 40–56.

EMMA BROOKE

A Superfluous Woman, 1894

Nelson, Carolyn Christensen. *British Women Fiction Writers,* 55–57.

Transition, 1895

Nelson, Carolyn Christensen. *British Women Fiction Writers,* 57–58.

FRANCES BROOKE

The History of Emily Montague, 1769

> Benedict, Barbara M. *Framing Feeling,* 106–16.
> Ellison, Julie. "There and Back: Transatlantic Novels and Anglo-American Careers," in Carla H. Hay and Syndy M. Conger, eds., *The Past as Prologue,* 311–15.
> MacCarthy, B. G. *The Female Pen,* 316–18.
> Teague, Frances. "Frances Brooke's Imagined Epistles." *Stud on Voltaire and the Eighteenth Cent* 304 (1992), 711–12.

Lady Julia Mandeville, 1763

> Benedict, Barbara M. *Framing Feeling,* 99–106.
> Todd, Janet. *The Sign of Angellica,* 177–83.

HENRY BROOKE

The Fool of Quality, 1764–1770

> Benedict, Barbara M. *Framing Feeling,* 117–26.
> Nelson, T. G. A. *Children, Parents, and the Rise of the Novel,* 185–88.
> Spacks, Patricia Meyer. *Desire and Truth,* 125–29.

CHRISTINE BROOKE-ROSE

Amalgamemnon, 1984

> Birch, Sarah. *Christine Brooke-Rose and Contemporary Fiction,* 102–11, 117–20, 219–21.
> Connor, Steven. *The English Novel in History,* 39–41.
> Friedman, Ellen G. " 'Utterly Other Discourse': The Anticanon of Experimental Women Writers from Dorothy Richardson to Christine Brooke-Rose," in Ellen G. Friedman and Richard Martin, eds., *Utterly Other Discourse,* 226–27.
> Maack, Annegret. "Narrative Techniques in *Thru* and *Amalgamemnon,*" in Ellen G. Friedman and Richard Martin, eds., *Utterly Other Discourse,* 137–39.
> McHale, Brian. " 'I draw the line as a rule between one solar system and another': The Postmodernism(s) of Christine Brooke-Rose," in Ellen G. Friedman and Richard Martin, eds., *Utterly Other Discourse,* 201–4.
> Martin, Richard. " 'Just Words on a Page': The Novels of Christine Brooke-Rose," in Ellen G. Friedman and Richard Martin, eds., *Utterly Other Discourse,* 47–48.
> Martin, Richard. " 'Stepping Stones into the Dark': Redundancy and Generation in *Amalgamemnon,*" in Ellen G. Friedman and Richard Martin, eds., *Utterly Other Discourse,* 143–51.

Between, 1968

> Birch, Sarah. *Christine Brooke-Rose and Contemporary Fiction,* 69–74, 82–89.
> Lawrence, Karen R. " 'Floating on a Pinpoint': Travel and Place in Brooke-Rose's *Between,*" in Ellen G. Friedman and Richard Martin, eds., *Utterly Other Discourse,* 76–93.
> Lawrence, Karen R. *Penelope Voyages,* 208–31.
> Little, Judy. "S(t)imulating Origins: Self-Subversion in the Early Brooke-Rose Texts," in Ellen G. Friedman and Richard Martin, eds., *Utterly Other Discourse,* 70–74.
> McHale, Brian. " 'I draw the line as a rule between one solar system and another': The Postmodernism(s) of Christine Brooke-Rose," in Ellen G. Friedman and Richard Martin, eds., *Utterly Other Discourse,* 197–99.
> Martin, Richard. " 'Just Words on a Page': The Novels of Christine Brooke-Rose," in Ellen G. Friedman and Richard Martin, eds., *Utterly Other Discourse,* 44–45.
> Suleiman, Susan Rubin. "Living Between: The Lo//n/v//eliness of the 'Alonestanding Woman,' " in Ellen G. Friedman and Richard Martin, eds., *Utterly Other Discourse,* 97–103.

The Dear Deceit, 1960

> Birch, Sarah. *Christine Brooke-Rose and Contemporary Fiction,* 35–40.
> Martin, Richard. " 'Just Words on a Page': The Novels of Christine Brooke-Rose," in Ellen G. Friedman and Richard Martin, eds., *Utterly Other Discourse,* 41.

The Intercom Quartet, 1984–1991

> Birch, Sarah. *Christine Brooke-Rose and Contemporary Fiction,* 113–44.

The Languages of Love, 1957

> Birch, Sarah. *Christine Brooke-Rose and Contemporary Fiction,* 24–30.
> Martin, Richard. " 'Just Words on a Page': The Novels of Christine Brooke-Rose," in Ellen G. Friedman and Richard Martin, eds., *Utterly Other Discourse,* 38–40.

The Middlemen: A Satire, 1961

> Birch, Sarah. *Christine Brooke-Rose and Contemporary Fiction,* 40–44.
> Martin, Richard. " 'Just Words on a Page': The Novels of Christine Brooke-Rose," in Ellen G. Friedman and Richard Martin, eds., *Utterly Other Discourse,* 41–42.

Out, 1964

> Birch, Sarah. *Christine Brooke-Rose and Contemporary Fiction,* 54–63.
> Little, Judy. "S(t)imulating Origins: Self-Subversion in the Early Brooke-Rose Texts," in Ellen G. Friedman and Richard Martin, eds., *Utterly Other Discourse,* 67–70.
> McHale, Brian. " 'I draw the line as a rule between one solar system and

another': The Postmodernism(s) of Christine Brooke-Rose," in Ellen
G. Friedman and Richard Martin, eds., *Utterly Other Discourse*,
193–94.

Martin, Richard. " 'Just Words on a Page': The Novels of Christine
Brooke-Rose," in Ellen G. Friedman and Richard Martin, eds., *Utterly
Other Discourse*, 42–43.

Such, 1966

Birch, Sarah. *Christine Brooke-Rose and Contemporary Fiction*, 63–69.

Little, Judy. "S(t)imulating Origins: Self-Subversion in the Early
Brooke-Rose Texts," in Ellen G. Friedman and Richard Martin, eds.,
Utterly Other Discourse, 70.

McHale, Brian. " 'I draw the line as a rule between one solar system and
another': The Postmodernism(s) of Christine Brooke-Rose," in Ellen
G. Friedman and Richard Martin, eds., *Utterly Other Discourse*,
194–97.

Martin, Richard. " 'Just Words on a Page': The Novels of Christine
Brooke-Rose," in Ellen G. Friedman and Richard Martin, eds., *Utterly
Other Discourse*, 43–44.

The Sycamore Tree, 1958

Birch, Sarah. *Christine Brooke-Rose and Contemporary Fiction*, 30–35.

Martin, Richard. " 'Just Words on a Page': The Novels of Christine
Brooke-Rose," in Ellen G. Friedman and Richard Martin, eds., *Utterly
Other Discourse*, 39–41.

Textermination, 1991

Birch, Sarah. *Christine Brooke-Rose and Contemporary Fiction*,
135–43.

Maack, Annegret. "Narrative Techniques in *Thru* and *Amalgamemnon,"*
in Ellen G. Friedman and Richard Martin, eds., *Utterly Other Discourse*, 140–41.

McHale, Brian. " 'I draw the line as a rule between one solar system and
another': The Postmodernism(s) of Christine Brooke-Rose," in Ellen
G. Friedman and Richard Martin, eds., *Utterly Other Discourse*,
205–9.

Thru, 1975

Berressem, Hanjo. "*Thru* the Looking Glass: A Journey into the Universe of Discourse," in Ellen G. Friedman and Richard Martin, eds.,
Utterly Other Discourse, 104–15.

Birch, Sarah. *Christine Brooke-Rose and Contemporary Fiction*, 89–
102, 217–19.

Garbero, Maria del Sapio. "The Fictionality of Fiction: Christine
Brooke-Rose's *Sense of Absence*," in Theo D'haen and Hans Bertens,
eds., *British Postmodern Fiction*, 93–96.

Grant, Damian. "The Emperor's New Clothes: Narrative Anxiety in
Thru," in Ellen G. Friedman and Richard Martin, eds., *Utterly Other
Discourse*, 117–28.

Maack, Annegret. "Narrative Techniques in *Thru* and *Amalgamemnon*," in Ellen G. Friedman and Richard Martin, eds., *Utterly Other Discourse*, 133–36.

McHale, Brian. " 'I draw the line as a rule between one solar system and another': The Postmodernism(s) of Christine Brooke-Rose," in Ellen G. Friedman and Richard Martin, eds., *Utterly Other Discourse*, 199–200.

Martin, Richard. " 'Just Words on a Page': The Novels of Christine Brooke-Rose," in Ellen G. Friedman and Richard Martin, eds., *Utterly Other Discourse*, 45–47.

Verbivore, 1990

Birch, Sarah. *Christine Brooke-Rose and Contemporary Fiction*, 126–34, 221–23.

Garbero, Maria del Sapio. "The Fictionality of Fiction: Christine Brooke-Rose's *Sense of Absence*," in Theo D'haen and Hans Bertens, eds., *British Postmodern Fiction*, 96–99.

Konkle, Lincoln. " 'Histrionic' vs. 'Hysterical': Deconstructing Gender as Genre in *Xorandor* and *Verbivore*," in Ellen G. Friedman and Richard Martin, eds., *Utterly Other Discourse*, 176–90.

Maack, Annegret. "Narrative Techniques in *Thru* and *Amalgamemnon*," in Ellen G. Friedman and Richard Martin, eds., *Utterly Other Discourse*, 140.

McHale, Brian. " 'I draw the line as a rule between one solar system and another': The Postmodernism(s) of Christine Brooke-Rose," in Ellen G. Friedman and Richard Martin, eds., *Utterly Other Discourse*, 202–4.

Xorandor, 1986

Birch, Sarah. *Christine Brooke-Rose and Contemporary Fiction*, 120–26, 221–23.

Garbero, Maria del Sapio. "The Fictionality of Fiction: Christine Brooke-Rose's *Sense of Absence*," in Theo D'haen and Hans Bertens, eds., *British Postmodern Fiction*, 90–93.

Hawkins, Susan E. "Memory and Discourse: Fictionalizing the Present in *Xorandor*," in Ellen G. Friedman and Richard Martin, eds., *Utterly Other Discourse*, 170–75.

Konkle, Lincoln. " 'Histrionic' vs. 'Hysterical': Deconstructing Gender as Genre in *Xorandor* and *Verbivore*," in Ellen G. Friedman and Richard Martin, eds., *Utterly Other Discourse*, 176–90.

Maack, Annegret. "Narrative Techniques in *Thru* and *Amalgamemnon*," in Ellen G. Friedman and Richard Martin, eds., *Utterly Other Discourse*, 139–40.

McHale, Brian. " 'I draw the line as a rule between one solar system and another': The Postmodernism(s) of Christine Brooke-Rose," in Ellen G. Friedman and Richard Martin, eds., *Utterly Other Discourse*, 202–4.

Martin, Richard. " 'Just Words on a Page': The Novels of Christine

Brooke-Rose," in Ellen G. Friedman and Richard Martin, eds., *Utterly Other Discourse*, 48–50.

ANITA BROOKNER

Family and Friends, 1985

Bowen, Deborah. "Preserving Appearances: Photography and the Post-modern Realism of Anita Brookner." *Mosaic* 28:2 (1995), 137–46.

Skinner, John. *The Fictions of Anita Brookner*, 83–97.

A Friend from England, 1987

Skinner, John. *The Fictions of Anita Brookner*, 113–28.

Smith, Patricia Juliana. " 'And I Wondered If She Might Kiss Me': Lesbian Panic as Narrative Strategy in British Women's Fiction." *Mod Fiction Stud* 41 (1995), 579–85.

Hotel du Lac, 1984

Giltrow, Janet. "Ironies of Politeness in Anita Brookner's *Hotel du Lac*," in Kathy Mezei, ed., *Ambiguous Discourse*, 215–35.

McGuirk, Carol. "Drabble to Carter: Fiction by Women, 1962–1992," in John Richetti et al., eds., *The Columbia History*, 959–60.

Skinner, John. *The Fictions of Anita Brookner*, 66–83.

Watson, Daphne. *Their Own Worst Enemies*, 40–44.

Latecomers, 1988

Skinner, John. *The Fictions of Anita Brookner*, 128–43.

Lewis Percy, 1989

Skinner, John. *The Fictions of Anita Brookner*, 143–58.

Look at Me, 1983

Bowen, Deborah. "Preserving Appearances: Photography and the Post-modern Realism of Anita Brookner." *Mosaic* 28:2 (1995), 128–37.

Skinner, John. *The Fictions of Anita Brookner*, 51–65.

A Misalliance, 1986

Skinner, John. *The Fictions of Anita Brookner*, 97–112.

Providence, 1982

Skinner, John. *The Fictions of Anita Brookner*, 36–50.

A Start in Life, 1981

Skinner, John. *The Fictions of Anita Brookner*, 22–35.

BRIGID BROPHY

The Finishing Touch, 1963

Blackmer, Corinne E. "*The Finishing Touch* and the Tradition of Homoerotic Girls' School Fictions." *R of Contemp Fiction* 15:3 (1995), 32–38.

Flesh, 1962

    Hopkins, Chris. "The Neglect of Brigid Brophy." *R of Contemp Fiction* 15:3 (1995), 13–15.

Hackenfeller's Ape, 1953

    Axelrod, Mark. "Mozart, Moonshots, and Monkey Business in Brigid Brophy's *Hackenfeller's Ape." R of Contemp Fiction* 15:3 (1995), 18–22.

In Transit, 1969

    Hopkins, Chris. "The Neglect of Brigid Brophy." *R of Contemp Fiction* 15:3 (1995), 16–17.

    Horvath, Brooke. "Brigid Brophy's It's-All-Right-I'm-Only-Dying Comedy of Modern Manners: Notes on *In Transit." R of Contemp Fiction* 15:3 (1995), 46–53.

    Lawrence, Karen R. *Penelope Voyages,* 231–36.

    Lee, Patricia. "Communication Breakdown and the 'Twin Genius' of Brophy's *In Transit." R of Contemp Fiction* 15:3 (1995), 62–67.

    Maack, Annegret. "Concordia Discors: Brigid Brophy's *In Transit." R of Contemp Fiction* 15:3 (1995), 40–45.

The King of a Rainy Country, 1956

    Smith, Patricia Juliana. "Desperately Seeking Susan[na]: Closeted Quests and Mozartean Gender Bending in Brigid Brophy's *The King of a Rainy Country." R of Contemp Fiction* 15:3 (1995), 23–30.

Palace without Chairs, 1978

    Hopkins, Chris. "The Neglect of Brigid Brophy." *R of Contemp Fiction* 15:3 (1995), 15–16.

RHODA BROUGHTON

Cometh Up as a Flower, 1867

    Demoor, Marysa. "Women Authors and their Selves: Autobiography in the Work of Charlotte Yonge, Rhoda Broughton, Mary Cholmondeley and Lucy Clifford." *Cahiers Victoriens et Edouardiens* 39 (1994), 55–58.

Not Wisely But Too Well, 1867

    Cadogan, Mary. *And Then Their Hearts Stood Still,* 45–49.

GEORGE DOUGLAS BROWN

The House with the Green Shutters, 1901

    Campbell, Ian, and Brian Vogel. "*The House with the Green Shutters* and the Seeing Eye." *Stud in Scottish Lit* 27 (1992), 89–104.

    Egan, Joseph J. "The Indebtedness of George Douglas Brown to *The Mayor of Casterbridge." Stud in Scottish Lit* 27 (1992), 203–17.

    Pick, J. B. *The Great Shadow House,* 50–52, 59–65.

Royle, Nicholas. "The Ghost of Hamlet in *The House with the Green Shutters.*" *Stud in Scottish Lit* 27 (1992), 105–12.

GEORGE MACKAY BROWN

Greenvoe, 1972
  Schoene, Berthold. *The Making of Orcadia,* 134–37, 170–85.
Magnus, 1973
  D'Arcy, Julian Meldon. *Scottish Skalds and Sagamen,* 262–70.
  Schoene, Berthold. *The Making of Orcadia,* 216–39.
Time in a Red Coat, 1984
  Schoene, Berthold. *The Making of Orcadia,* 240–51.
Vinland, 1992
  D'Arcy, Julian Meldon. *Scottish Skalds and Sagamen,* 271–79.

IVOR BROWN

Years of Plenty, 1915
  Antor, Heinz. *Der englische Universitätsroman,* 554–56, 568–70.

MARY BRUNTON

Discipline, 1814
  Gonda, Caroline. *Reading Daughters' Fictions,* 191–94.
Self-Control, 1811
  Gonda, Caroline. *Reading Daughters' Fictions,* 195–97.

WINIFRED BRYHER

Two Selves, 1923
  Collecott, Diana. "Bryher's *Two Selves* as Lesbian Romance," in Lynne Pearce and Jackie Stacey, eds., *Romance Revisited,* 128–40.

JOHN BUCHAN

The Blanket of the Dark, 1931
  Lownie, Andrew. *John Buchan,* 179–81.
The Courts of the Morning, 1929
  Lownie, Andrew. *John Buchan,* 162–64.
The Dancing Floor, 1926
  Lownie, Andrew. *John Buchan,* 166–68.

Greenmantle, 1916

    Lownie, Andrew. *John Buchan,* 139–42.

Huntingtower, 1922

    Lownie, Andrew. *John Buchan,* 169–71.

The Island of Sheep, 1936

    D'Arcy, Julian Meldon. *Scottish Skalds and Sagamen,* 122–30.

John Macnab, 1925

    Lownie, Andrew. *John Buchan,* 165–66.

Mr. Standfast, 1918

    Lownie, Andrew. *John Buchan,* 141–43.

Prester John, 1910

    Lownie, Andrew. *John Buchan,* 111–14.
    Smith, Craig. "Every Man Must Kill the Thing He Loves: Empire, Homoerotics, and Nationalism in John Buchan's *Prester John.*" *Novel* 28 (1995), 173–97.

A Prince of the Captivity, 1933

    Lownie, Andrew. *John Buchan,* 174–76.

Sick Heart River, 1941

    Pick, J. B. *The Great Shadow House,* 67–72.

The Thirty-Nine Steps, 1915

    Lownie, Andrew. *John Buchan,* 119–22.

The Three Hostages, 1924

    Greenslade, William. *Degeneration, Culture, and the Novel,* 247–49.
    Hagemann, Susanne. "Marginality: A Bifocal Approach to John Buchan's *The Three Hostages.*" *Zeitschrift für Anglistik und Amerikanistik* 44 (1996), 240–47.
    Lownie, Andrew. *John Buchan,* 161–62.
    Pick, J. B. *The Great Shadow House,* 69–70.

Witch Wood, 1927

    Lownie, Andrew. *John Buchan,* 177–79.
    Pick, J. B. *The Great Shadow House,* 66–68.

EDWARD BULWER-LYTTON

The Coming Race, 1871

    Dentith, Simon. "Imagination and Inversion in Nineteenth-Century Utopian Writing," in David Seed, ed., *Anticipations,* 141–43.
    Derry, Stephen. "The Time Traveller's Utopian Books and his Reading of the Future." *Foundation* 65 (1995), 18–22.
    Snyder, Charles W. *Liberty and Morality,* 207–9.

Ernest Maltravers, 1837

    Horsman, Alan. *The Victorian Novel,* 62–63.

Eugene Aram, 1832
> Horsman, Alan. *The Victorian Novel,* 61–62.

The Last of the Barons, 1843
> Horsman, Alan. *The Victorian Novel,* 63–64.

Leila; or, The Siege of Granada, 1892
> Ragussis, Michael. *Figures of Conversion,* 137–41.

Lucretia; or, The Children of the Night, 1846
> Small, Helen. *Love's Madness,* 142–53.

Night and Morning, 1841
> Roberts, Adam. "Dickens's Jarndyce and Lytton's Gawtrey." *Notes and Queries* 43 (1996), 45–46.

Paul Clifford, 1830
> Horsman, Alan. *The Victorian Novel,* 60–61.

Pelham, 1828
> Horsman, Alan. *The Victorian Novel,* 59–60.
> Stewart, Garrett. *Dear Reader,* 140–43.

Rienzi, 1835
> Horsman, Alan. *The Victorian Novel,* 63–64.

A Strange Story, 1862
> Cavaliero, Glen. *The Supernatural and English Fiction,* 66–68.

Zanoni, 1842
> Cavaliero, Glen. *The Supernatural and English Fiction,* 64–66.

JOHN BUNYAN

The Pilgrim's Progress, 1678
> Danielson, Dennis. "Catechism, *The Pilgrim's Progress,* and the Pilgrim's Progress." *JEGP* 94 (1995), 42–58.
> Garnier, Marie-Dominique. " 'Like burrs': les capitules du *Pilgrim's Progress."* *Recherches Anglaises et Nord-Américaines* 26 (1993), 13–26.
> Greenfield, Sayre N. "Bunyan, Non-Conformism, and the Limits of Allegory." *Stud on Voltaire and the Eighteenth Cent* 303 (1992), 439–41.
> Himy, Armand. "Errance et élection dans *The Pilgrim's Progress."* *Bull de la Société d'Etudes Anglo-Américaines des XVIIe et XVIIIe Siècles* 35 (1992), 57–68.
> Josipovici, Gabriel. *The World and the Book,* 132–33.
> Luxon, Thomas H. *Literal Figures,* 159–207.
> Madsen, Deborah L. *Rereading Allegory,* 104–7.
> Mailloux, Steven. "Persuasions Good and Bad: Bunyan, Iser, and Fish on Rhetoric and Hermeneutics in Literature." *Stud in the Liter Imagination* 28:2 (1995), 43–59.

Newey, Vincent. *Centring the Self,* 71–86.

Pfatteicher, Philip H. "Plashing Pears in Augustine and Bunyan." *Lit and Theology* 9 (1995), 26–28.

Pickering, Samuel F., Jr. *Moral Instruction and Fiction for Children,* 150–53.

Sus, Jacques. "Le Verbe et le regard: *The Pilgrim's Progress* et la dramatique chrétienne." *Bull de la Société d'Etudes Anglo-Américaines des XVIIe et XVIIIe Siècles* 35 (1992), 69–89.

KATHARINE BURDEKIN

Swastika Night, 1937

Joannou, Maroula. *'Ladies, Please Don't Smash These Windows,'* 159–63, 179–83.

McKay, George. "Katharine Burdekin: An Alien Presence in Her Own Time," in Patrick J. Quinn, ed., *Recharting the Thirties,* 188–98.

McKay, George. "Metapropaganda: Self-Reading Dystopian Fiction—Burdekin's *Swastika Night* and Orwell's *Nineteen Eightry-Four.*" *Science-Fiction Stud* 21 (1994), 302–12.

Schneider, Karen. *Loving Arms,* 40–56.

ANTHONY BURGESS

A Clockwork Orange, 1962

García Mainar, Luis Miguel. "*La naranja mecánica* o el código sin contexto." *Atlantis* 14:1–2 (1992), 63–80.

Mariani, Guido. "*A Clockwork Orange* di Anthony Burgess: problemi di traduzione." *Lingua e Stile* 29 (1994), 457–76.

Earthly Powers, 1980

Schluter, Kurt. "Onomastic Identity versus the Convention of Single Naming in Anthony Burgess' *Earthly Powers.*" *Anglia* 112 (1994), 411–20.

The End of the World News, 1982

Connor, Steven. *The English Novel in History,* 213–18.

1985, 1978

Spiering, M. *Englishness,* 151–55.

A Vision of Battlements, 1965

Colakis, Marianthe. "*Sum Ineptus Aeneas:* Anthony Burgess's *A Vision of Battlements.*" *Classical and Mod Lit* 14 (1994), 141–47.

The Wanting Seed, 1962

Kone, Boubacar. "Sex, Good, Evil in *The Wanting Seed.*" *Bridges* 6 (1995), 115–28.

FRANCES HODGSON BURNETT

Little Lord Fauntleroy, 1889

Brown, Penny. *The Captured World,* 56–57.

Bruzelius, Margaret. "Influence versus Speech: Representing the Maternal in Frances Hodgson-Burnett," in Barbara Thaden, ed., *New Essays on the Maternal Voice,* 24–28.

Sara Crewe, 1888

Lerner, Laurence. *Angels and Absences,* 89–90.

The Secret Garden, 1911

Almond, Barbara, and Richard Almond. *The Therapeutic Narrative,* 107–23.

Bixler, Phyllis. "*The Secret Garden* 'Misread': The Broadway Musical as Creative Interpretation." *Children's Lit* 22 (1994), 101–21.

Bruzelius, Margaret. "Influence versus Speech: Representing the Maternal in Frances Hodgson-Burnett," in Barbara Thaden, ed., *New Essays on the Maternal Voice,* 19–24.

Darcy, Jane. "The Representation of Nature in *The Wind in the Willows* and *The Secret Garden.*" *Lion and the Unicorn* 19 (1995), 213–21.

Knowles, Murray, and Kirsten Malmkjær. *Language and Control,* 58–60, 76–80.

Phillips, Jerry. "The Mem Sahib, the Worthy, the Rajah and His Minions: Some Reflections on the Class Politics of *The Secret Garden.*" *Lion and the Unicorn* 17 (1993), 169–88.

FANNY BURNEY

Camilla, 1796

Burgess, Miranda J. "Courting Ruin: The Economic Romances of Frances Burney." *Novel* 28 (1995), 135–40.

Fasick, Laura. *Vessels of Meaning,* 50–70.

Gonda, Caroline. *Reading Daughters' Fictions,* 132–39.

Gruner, Elisabeth Rose. "The Bullfinch and the Brother: Marriage and Family in Frances Burney's *Camilla.*" *JEGP* 93 (1994), 18–34.

Haggerty, George E. "A Friend, a Fop, and a Feminist: The Failure of Community in Burney." *Eighteenth Cent* 36 (1995), 253–58.

Lambert, Ellen Zetzel. *The Face of Love,* 58–67.

MacCarthy, B. G. *The Female Pen,* 362–67.

Spacks, Patricia Meyer. " 'Ev'ry Woman is at Heart a Rake,' " in Carla H. Hay and Syndy M. Conger, eds., *The Past as Prologue,* 56–60.

Straub, Kristina. "Frances Burney and the Rise of the Woman Novelist," in John Richetti et al., eds., *The Columbia History,* 208–10.

Todd, Janet. *The Sign of Angellica,* 275–87.

Cecilia, 1782

Haggerty, George E. "A Friend, a Fop, and a Feminist: The Failure of Community in Burney." *Eighteenth Cent* 36 (1995), 251–53.

MacCarthy, B. G. *The Female Pen,* 357–61.

Pitcher, E. W. "Frances Burney's *Cecilia* and the 'Q in the Corner.' " *Notes and Queries* 42 (1995), 71–72.

Spacks, Patricia Meyer. "Oscillations of Sensibility." *New Liter Hist* 25 (1994), 513–16.

Straub, Kristina. "Frances Burney and the Rise of the Woman Novelist," in John Richetti et al., eds., *The Columbia History,* 212–16.

Evelina, 1778

Bilger, Audrey. "Goblin Laughter: Violent Comedy and the Condition of Women in Frances Burney and Jane Austen." *Women's Stud* 24 (1995), 335–36.

Donoghue, Frank. *The Fame Machine,* 169–74.

Dykstal, Timothy. "*Evelina* and the Culture Industry." *Criticism* 37 (1995), 559–77.

Fasick, Laura. *Vessels of Meaning,* 50–70.

Forbes, Joan. "Anti-Romantic Discourse as Resistance: Women's Fiction 1775–1820," in Lynne Pearce and Jackie Stacey, eds., *Romance Revisited,* 294–304.

Galperin, William. "The Radical Work of Frances Burney's London." *Eighteenth-Cent Life* 20:3 (1996), 37–47.

Gonda, Caroline. *Reading Daughters' Fictions,* 111–31.

Hart, John. "Frances Burney's *Evelina:* Mirvan and Mezzotint." *Eighteenth-Cent Fiction* 7 (1994), 51–70.

Kowaleski-Wallace, Beth. "A Night at the Opera: The Body, Class, and Art in *Evelina* and Frances Burney's *Early Diaries,*" in Beth Fowkes Tobin, ed., *History, Gender, and Eighteenth-Century Literature,* 141–44, 148–55.

Lenz, Bernd. "Popularisierung und Wandlung der Empfindsamkeit im englischen Roman des 18. Jahrhunderts," in Klaus P. Hansen, ed., *Empfindsamkeiten,* 67–69.

Löffler, Arno. " 'The world . . . what it appears to a girl of seventeen': Fanny Burneys *Evelina* als satirischer Roman." *Anglia* 112 (1994), 50–74.

MacCarthy, B. G. *The Female Pen,* 342–57.

Rosenberg, Beth Carole. " '. . . in the wake of the matrons': Virginia Woolf's Rewriting of Fanny Burney," in Beth Rigel Daugherty and Eileen Barrett, eds., *Virginia Woolf,* 118–22.

Severance, Mary. "An Unerring Rule: The Reformation of the Father in Frances Burney's *Evelina.*" *Eighteenth Cent* 36 (1995), 119–35.

Shaffer, Julie. "Not Subordinate: Empowering Women in the Marriage Plot—The Novels of Frances Burney, Maria Edgeworth, and Jane Austen," in Arthur F. Marotti et al., eds., *Reading with a Difference,* 28–31.

Spacks, Patricia Meyer. *Desire and Truth,* 140–45.

Straub, Kristina. "Frances Burney and the Rise of the Woman Novelist," in John Richetti et al., eds., *The Columbia History,* 196–97, 208–9.

Thaden, Barbara. "Elizabeth Gaskell and the Dead Mother Plot," in Thaden, ed., *New Essays on the Maternal Voice*, 35–36.

The Wanderer, 1814

Austin, Andrea. "Between Women: Frances Burney's *The Wanderer*." *Engl Stud in Canada* 22 (1996), 253–64.

Bilger, Audrey. "Goblin Laughter: Violent Comedy and the Condition of Women in Frances Burney and Jane Austen." *Women's Stud* 24 (1995), 336–38.

Burgess, Miranda J. "Courting Ruin: The Economic Romances of Frances Burney." *Novel* 28 (1995), 144–48.

Doody, Margaret Anne. "Heliodorus Rewritten: Samuel Richardson's *Clarissa* and Frances Burney's *Wanderer*," in James Tatum, ed., *The Search for the Ancient Novel*, 117–30.

Haggerty, George E. "A Friend, a Fop, and a Feminist: The Failure of Community in Burney." *Eighteenth Cent* 36 (1995), 258–64.

Lawrence, Karen R. *Penelope Voyages*, 50–72.

Lynch, Deidre. "Domesticating Fictions and Nationalizing Women: Edmund Burke, Property, and the Reproduction of Englishness," in Alan Richardson and Sonia Hofkosch, eds., *Romanticism, Race, and Imperial Culture*, 57–62.

Perkins, Pam. "Private Men and Public Women: Social Criticism in Fanny Burney's *The Wanderer*." *Essays in Lit* (Macomb, IL) 23 (1996), 69–81.

Straub, Kristina. "Frances Burney and the Rise of the Woman Novelist," in John Richetti et al., eds., *The Columbia History*, 206–11.

DOROTHY BUSSY

Olivia, 1949

Tarr, Carrie. "Ambivalent Desires in Jacqueline Audry's *Olivia*." *Nottingham French Stud* 32:1 (1993), 32–42.

SAMUEL BUTLER

Erewhon, 1872

Dentith, Simon. "Imagination and Inversion in Nineteenth-Century Utopian Writing," in David Seed, ed., *Anticipations*, 139–41.

Nellist, Brian. "Imagining the Future: Predictive Fiction in the Nineteenth Century," in David Seed, ed., *Anticipations*, 122–25.

The Way of All Flesh, 1903

Devoize, Jeanne. "Le problème du dédoublement dans *The Way of All Flesh* de Samuel Butler." *Caliban* 31 (1994), 107–13.

Federico, Annette R. "Samuel Butler's *The Way of All Flesh*: Rewriting the Family." *Engl Lit in Transition, 1880–1920* 38 (1995), 466–80.

Fleming, Bruce E. "Mr. Overton's Solution: On Systems in Thought." *New Orleans R* 19:3–4 (1992), 146–52.

Salemi, Joseph S. "The Canvas of His Life: Epitaphs in Samuel Butler's *The Way of All Flesh.*" *Victorians Inst J* 22 (1994), 165–76.

SARAH BUTLER

Irish Tales, 1716

Ross, Ian Campbell. " 'One of the Principal Nations in Europe': The Representation of Ireland in Sarah Butler's *Irish Tales.*" *Eighteenth-Cent Fiction* 7 (1994), 2–16.

ISAAC BUTT

The Gap of Barnesmore, 1848

Spence, Joseph. "Allegories for a Protestant Nation: Irish Tory Historical Fiction, 1820–1850." *Rel and Lit* 28:2–3 (1996), 73–76.

HARRY JOHN WILMOT BUXTON

The Mysteries of Isis; or, The College Life of Paul Romaine, 1866
Antor, Heinz. *Der englische Universitätsroman,* 387–90.

A. S. BYATT

The Game, 1967

Kelly, Kathleen Cloyne. *A. S. Byatt,* 24–35.

Possession, 1990

Belsey, Catherine. "Postmodern Love: Questioning the Metaphysics of Desire." *New Liter Hist* 25 (1994), 693–96.

Bronfen, Elisabeth. "Romancing Difference, Courting Coherence: A. S. Byatt's *Possession* as Postmodern Moral Fiction," in Rüdiger Ahrens and Laurenz Volkmann, eds., *Why Literature Matters,* 117–34.

Bronfen, Elisabeth. "Wissenschaftler suchen ihre Autoren: A. S. Byatts Romanze *Possession,*" in Eberhard Lämmert and Barbara Naumann, eds., *Wer sind wir?,* 205–20.

Buxton, Jackie. " 'What's Love Got to Do With It?': Postmodernism and *Possession.*" *Engl Stud in Canada* 22 (1996), 199–217.

Connor, Steven. *The English Novel in History,* 147–51.

Giobbi, Giuliana. "Know the Past: Know Thyself—Literary Pursuits and Quest for Identity in A. S. Byatt's *Possession* and in F. Duranti's *Effetti Personali.*" *J of European Stud* 24:1 (1994), 41–54.

Holmes, Frederick M. "The Historical Imagination and the Victorian Past: A. S. Byatt's *Possession.*" *Engl Stud in Canada* 20 (1994), 319–33.

Janik, Del Ivan. "No End of History: Evidence from the Contemporary English Novel." *Twentieth Cent Lit* 41 (1995), 163–66.

Jukic, Tatjana. "Variants of *Victoriana* in the Postmodern English Novel." *Studia Romanica et Anglica Zagrabiensia* 40 (1995), 74–76.

Kelly, Kathleen Cloyne. *A. S. Byatt*, 78–98.

Maack, Annegret. "Die *romance* als postmoderne Romanform?" *Literatur in Wissenschaft und Unterricht* 26 (1993), 276–79.

McGuirk, Carol. "Drabble to Carter: Fiction by Women, 1962–1992," in John Richetti et al., eds., *The Columbia History*, 941–43, 945–47.

Marsh, Kelly A. "The Neo-Sensation Novel: A Contemporary Genre in the Victorian Tradition." *Philol Q* 74 (1995), 99–121.

Sanchez, Victoria. "A. S. Byatt's *Possession:* A Fairytale Romance." *Southern Folklore* 52:1 (1995), 33–52.

Shinn, Thelma J. " 'What's in a Word?': Possessing A. S. Byatt's Meronymic Novel." *Papers on Lang and Lit* 31 (1995), 164–82.

Todd, Richard. *Consuming Fictions*, 25–54.

Shadow of a Sun, 1964

Kelly, Kathleen Cloyne. *A. S. Byatt*, 14–24.

Still Life, 1985

Cosslett, Tess. *Women Writing Childbirth*, 24–26, 59–62, 138–40, 145–47.

Kelly, Kathleen Cloyne. *A. S. Byatt*, 65–76.

Taylor, D. J. *After the War*, 38–41, 90–94.

The Virgin in the Garden, 1978

Kelly, Kathleen Cloyne. *A. S. Byatt*, 63–65, 67–76.

McGuirk, Carol. "Drabble to Carter: Fiction by Women, 1962–1992," in John Richetti et al., eds., *The Columbia History*, 950–51.

Taylor, D. J. *After the War*, 91–103.

KATHLEEN MANNINGTON CAFFYN

A Yellow Aster, 1894

Nelson, Carolyn Christensen. *British Women Fiction Writers*, 45–48.

HALL CAINE

The Woman of Knockaloe, 1923

Cadogan, Mary. *And Then Their Hearts Stood Still*, 161–63.

MONA CAIRD

The Daughters of Danaus, 1894

Kranidis, Rita S. *Subversive Discourse*, 79–81, 91–92.

Nelson, Carolyn Christensen. *British Women Fiction Writers*, 31–33.

Pykett, Lyn. "The Cause of Women and the Course of Fiction: The Case of Mona Caird," in Christopher Parker, ed., *Gender Roles and Sexuality,* 135–37.

Pathway of the Gods, 1898

Pykett, Lyn. "The Cause of Women and the Course of Fiction: The Case of Mona Caird," in Christopher Parker, ed., *Gender Roles and Sexuality,* 137–40.

The Wing of Azrael, 1889

Pykett, Lyn. "The Cause of Women and the Course of Fiction: The Case of Mona Caird," in Christopher Parker, ed., *Gender Roles and Sexuality,* 132–35.

MARY ROSE CALLAGHAN

The Awkward Girl, 1990

Wessel-Felter, Maryanne. "Commedia: The Fiction of Mary Rose Callaghan." *Eire-Ireland* 29:2 (1994), 139–45.

Confessions of a Prodigal Daughter, 1985

Wessel-Felter, Maryanne. "Commedia: The Fiction of Mary Rose Callaghan." *Eire-Ireland* 29:2 (1994), 139–43.

Mothers, 1982

Wessel-Felter, Maryanne. "Commedia: The Fiction of Mary Rose Callaghan." *Eire-Ireland* 29:2 (1994), 139–41.

LEWIS CARROLL

Alice's Adventures in Wonderland, 1865

Armitt, Lucie. *Theorising the Fantastic*, 150–64.

Armstrong, Nancy. "The Occidental Alice." *Differences* 2:2 (1990), 3–40.

Bakewell, Michael. *Lewis Carroll*, 139–51.

Beckmann, Ulrich. "Carroll's Play with Possibilities: Aspects of Coherence in *Alice's Adventures in Wonderland,"* in Rachel Fordyce and Carla Marello, eds., *Semiotics and Linguistics*, 102–13.

Bivona, Daniel. *Desire and Contradiction,* 51–74.

Bókay, Antal. "Alice in Analysis: Interpretation of the Personal Meaning of Texts," in Rachel Fordyce and Carla Marello, eds., *Semiotics and Linguistics*, 79–91.

Boldrini, Paola, Manuela Nocentini, and Piero Ricci. " 'Was It a Cat I Saw?': The Vanishing Sign," in Rachel Fordyce and Carla Marello, eds., *Semiotics and Linguistics*, 43–52.

Brandt, Per Aage. "Curiouser and Curiouser: A Brief Analysis of *Alice's Adventures in Wonderland,"* in Rachel Fordyce and Carla Marello, eds., *Semiotics and Linguistics*, 26–33.

Burstein, Sandor. "Alice's Accordion, A Quest." *Jabberwocky* 22:2 (1993), 33–36.

Christopher, Joe R. "Alice's Adventures in Narnia; or, Through the Wardrobe, and What Alice Found There." *Jabberwocky* 22:3 (1993), 3–13.

Christopher, Joe R. "Superman's Adventure in Wonderland." *Jabberwocky* 22:4 (1993), 13–19.

Del Ninno, Maurizio. "Naked, Raw Alice," in Rachel Fordyce and Carla Marello, eds., *Semiotics and Linguistics*, 34–42.

Goodacre, Selwyn. "The De La Rue *Alice* Card Game." *Jabberwocky* 22:3 (1993), 28–33.

Harrison, Peter D. " 'Off With Their Heads': *Alice in Wonderland* and the Last Emperor of China." *Jabberwocky* 22:2 (1993), 23–24.

Holthuis, Susanne. "Alice in Wonderland: Aspects of Intertextuality," in Rachel Fordyce and Carla Marello, eds., *Semiotics and Linguistics*, 127–38.

Hunt, Peter. *An Introduction to Children's Literature*, 78–82.

Knowles, Murray, and Kirsten Malmkjær. *Language and Control*, 225–37.

Lakoff, Robin Tolmach. "Lewis Carroll: Subversive Pragmaticist." *Pragmatics* 3 (1993), 367–85.

Lecercle, Jean-Jacques. "À propos d'*Alice's Adventures in Wonderland*: le conte pour enfants à l'ère de sa reproductibilité technique." *Etudes Anglaises* 47 (1994), 407–16.

Lecercle, Jean-Jacques. *Philosophy of Nonsense*, 82–85, 88–100, 118–24.

Marello, Carla. "Alice's Omissions," in Rachel Fordyce and Carla Marello, eds., *Semiotics and Linguistics*, 176–92.

Montegrandi, Guido. "The Willing Fields: The Role of Modality in the Birth of a Character," in Rachel Fordyce and Carla Marello, eds., *Semiotics and Linguistics*, 115–25.

Nières, Isabelle. "Tenniel: The Logic behind his Interpretation of the Alice Books," in Rachel Fordyce and Carla Marello, eds., *Semiotics and Linguistics*, 194–208.

Nöth, Winfried. "Alice's Adventures in Semiosis," in Rachel Fordyce and Carla Marello, eds., *Semiotics and Linguistics*, 11–24.

Palumbo, Donald. "Sexuality and the Allure of the Fantastic in Literature," in Palumbo, ed., *Erotic Universe*, 13–17.

Partridge, Brian. "The Jury and the Number 42." *Jabberwocky* 22:2 (1993), 41–42.

Pennington, John. "Reader Response and Fantasy Literature: The Uses and Abuses of Interpretation in *Queen Victoria's Alice in Wonderland,*" in Joe Sanders, ed., *Functions of the Fantastic*, 55–64.

Petrilli, Susan, and Augusto Ponzio. "Exchange in Alice's World," in Rachel Fordyce and Carla Marello, eds., *Semiotics and Linguistics*, 74–78.

Rackin, Donald. *"Alice's Adventures in Wonderland,"* 35–152.

Rackin, Donald. "Mind over Matter: Sexuality and Where the 'body happens to be' in the *Alice* Books," in Lori Hope Lefkovitz, ed., *Textual Bodies*, 161–62, 169–74.

Roncada, Zena. "Alice's Body: Arrhythmias and Dystonias," in Rachel Fordyce and Carla Marello, eds., *Semiotics and Linguistics*, 53–61.

Rosenthal, M. L. "Alice, Huck, Pinocchio, and the Blue Fairy: Bodies Real and Imagined." *Southern R* (Baton Rouge) 29 (1993), 486–90.

Salsa, Patrice. " 'Did you say pig, or fig?': Alice's Travels—An Approach through the Concepts and Tools of Conversational Analysis," in Rachel Fordyce and Carla Marello, eds., *Semiotics and Linguistics*, 157–74.

Sasveld, Karen J. "Logic in *Alice's Adventures in Wonderland.*" *Jabberwocky* 22:1 (1992/93), 3–11.

Sherer, Susan. "Secrecy and Autonomy in Lewis Carroll." *Philos and Lit* 20 (1996), 1–18.

Spence, George. "Further Thoughts on Forty-Two." *Jabberwocky* 22:2 (1993), 43.

Tassinari, Maria Giovanna. "Texts and Metatexts in Alice," in Rachel Fordyce and Carla Marello, eds., *Semiotics and Linguistics*, 140–55.

Thomas, Donald. *Lewis Carroll*, 142–67, 356–69.

Turci, Mario. "What Is Alice, What Is This Thing, Who Are You?: The Reasons of the Body in Alice," in Rachel Fordyce and Carla Marello, eds., *Semiotics and Linguistics*, 63–72.

Vitacolonna, Luciano. "Aspects of Coherence in Alice," in Rachel Fordyce and Carla Marello, eds., *Semiotics and Linguistics*, 93–100.

Ward, Ian. *Law and Literature,* 101–4.

Wright, Julia M. " 'Which is to be Master': Classifying the Language of Alice's 'Antipathies.' " *Engl Stud in Canada* 20 (1994), 301–15.

Wullschläger, Jackie. *Inventing Wonderland*, 41–55.

Sylvie and Bruno, 1889

Bakewell, Michael. *Lewis Carroll*, 299–302.

Through the Looking-Glass, 1871

Armitt, Lucie. *Theorising the Fantastic*, 150–64.

Bakewell, Michael. *Lewis Carroll*, 190–94.

Bókay, Antal. "Alice in Analysis: Interpretation of the Personal Meaning of Texts," in Rachel Fordyce and Carla Marello, eds., *Semiotics and Linguistics*, 79–91.

Davies, Ivor Ll. "The Six Little Brooks in *Through the Looking-Glass.*" *Jabberwocky* 22:1 (1992/93), 13.

Del Ninno, Maurizio. "Naked, Raw Alice," in Rachel Fordyce and Carla Marello, eds., *Semiotics and Linguistics*, 34–42.

Hunt, Peter. *An Introduction to Children's Literature*, 78–82.

Lakoff, Robin Tolmach. "Lewis Carroll: Subversive Pragmaticist." *Pragmatics* 3 (1993), 367–85.

Lange, Bernd-Peter. "Der Meisterdiskurs: Symbolische Herrschaft in

Lewis Carrolls *Through the Looking-Glass."* *Arbeiten aus Anglistik und Amerikanistik* 18:1 (1993), 91–125.

Lecercle, Jean-Jacques. *Philosophy of Nonsense*, 7–20, 135–61.

Marello, Carla. "Alice's Omissions," in Rachel Fordyce and Carla Marello, eds., *Semiotics and Linguistics*, 176–92.

Nières, Isabelle. "Tenniel: The Logic behind his Interpretation of the Alice Books," in Rachel Fordyce and Carla Marello, eds., *Semiotics and Linguistics*, 194–208.

Nöth, Winfried. "Alice's Adventures in Semiosis," in Rachel Fordyce and Carla Marello, eds., *Semiotics and Linguistics*, 11–24.

Palumbo, Donald. "Sexuality and the Allure of the Fantastic in Literature," in Palumbo, ed., *Erotic Universe*, 13–17.

Polhemus, Robert M. "Lewis Carroll and the Child in Victorian Fiction," in John Richetti et al., eds., *The Columbia History*, 579–81, 595–97, 600–602.

Rackin, Donald. *"Alice's Adventures in Wonderland,"* 68–152.

Rackin, Donald. "Mind over Matter: Sexuality and Where the 'body happens to be' in the *Alice* Books," in Lori Hope Lefkovitz, ed., *Textual Bodies*, 161–63, 165–67.

Salsa, Patrice. " 'Did you say pig, or fig?': Alice's Travels—An Approach through the Concepts and Tools of Conversational Analysis," in Rachel Fordyce and Carla Marello, eds., *Semiotics and Linguistics*, 157–74.

Sasveld, Karen J. "Logic in *Through the Looking-Glass." Jabberwocky* 22:2 (1993), 25–32.

Sherer, Susan. "Secrecy and Autonomy in Lewis Carroll." *Philos and Lit* 20 (1996), 1–18.

Speranza, J. L. "Dealing with Humpty Dumpty's Conversational Impenetrability: Carroll, Grice and Meaning." *Jabberwocky* 22:4 (1993), 20–25.

Tassinari, Maria Giovanna. "Texts and Metatexts in Alice," in Rachel Fordyce and Carla Marello, eds., *Semiotics and Linguistics*, 140–55.

Thomas, Donald. *Lewis Carroll*, 163–68.

Turci, Mario. "What Is Alice, What Is This Thing, Who Are You?: The Reasons of the Body in Alice," in Rachel Fordyce and Carla Marello, eds., *Semiotics and Linguistics*, 63–72.

Vitacolonna, Luciano. "Aspects of Coherence in Alice," in Rachel Fordyce and Carla Marello, eds., *Semiotics and Linguistics*, 93–100.

Wullschläger, Jackie. *Inventing Wonderland*, 44–52.

ANGELA CARTER

Heroes and Villains, 1969

Gass, Joanne. "Written on the Body: The Materiality of Myth in Angela Carter's *Heroes and Villains." Arkansas R* 4:1 (1995), 12–30.

Hallab, Mary Y. "Carter and Blake: The Dangers of Innocence," in Joe Sanders, ed., *Functions of the Fantastic*, 179–83.

Landon, Brooks. "Eve at the End of the World: Sexuality and the Reversal of Expectations in Novels by Joanna Russ, Angela Carter, and Thomas Berger," in Donald Palumbo, ed., *Erotic Universe*, 67–70.

Meaney, Gerardine. *(Un)Like Subjects*, 91–95, 98–110, 118–20.

Parrinder, Patrick. "Landscapes of British Science Fiction," in George Slusser and Eric S. Rabkin, eds., *Styles of Creation*, 198–201.

Sage, Lorna. *Angela Carter*, 17–20.

The Infernal Desire Machines of Doctor Hoffmann, 1972

Bonca, Cornel. "In Despair of the Old Adams: Angela Carter's *The Infernal Desire Machines of Dr. Hoffmann.*" *R of Contemp Fiction* 14:3 (1994), 56–61.

Christensen, Peter. "The Hoffmann Connection: Demystification in Angela Carter's *The Infernal Desire Machines of Dr. Hoffmann.*" *R of Contemp Fiction* 14:3 (1994), 63–69.

Galván, Fernando. "Travel Writing in British Metafiction: A Proposal for Analysis," in Theo D'haen and Hans Bertens, eds., *British Postmodern Fiction*, 84–87.

Gasiorek, Andrzej. *Post-War British Fiction*, 128–31.

Granofsky, Ronald. *The Trauma Novel*, 26–33.

Habermeier, Steffi. "Autoerotismus und Pikareske in Angela Carters *The Infernal Desire Machines of Doctor Hoffmann,*" in Annette Keck and Dietmar Schmidt, eds., *Auto(r)erotik*, 102–18.

Hallab, Mary Y. "Carter and Blake: The Dangers of Innocence," in Joe Sanders, ed., *Functions of the Fantastic*, 180–83.

McGuirk, Carol. "Drabble to Carter: Fiction by Women, 1962–1992," in John Richetti et al., eds., *The Columbia History*, 950–52.

Neumeier, Beate. "Postmodern Gothic: Desire and Reality in Angela Carter's Writing," in Victor Sage and Allan Lloyd Smith, eds., *Modern Gothic*, 142–45.

Sage, Lorna. *Angela Carter*, 33–35.

Sceats, Sarah. "Eating the Evidence: Women, Power, and Food," in Sarah Sceats and Gail Cunningham, eds., *Image and Power*, 122–23.

Love, 1987

Britzolakis, Christina. "Angela Carter's Fetishism." *Textual Practice* 9 (1995), 461–66.

Hallab, Mary Y. "Carter and Blake: The Dangers of Innocence," in Joe Sanders, ed., *Functions of the Fantastic*, 178–83.

Sage, Lorna. *Angela Carter*, 20–23.

Sage, Lorna. *Women in the House of Fiction*, 171–73.

Smith, Patricia Juliana. "All You Need Is *Love:* Angela Carter's Novel of Sixties Sex and Sensibility." *R of Contemp Fiction* 14:3 (1994), 24–29.

The Magic Toyshop, 1967

Sage, Lorna. *Angela Carter*, 15–16.

Sage, Lorna. *Women in the House of Fiction*, 169–70.

Sceats, Sarah. "Eating the Evidence: Women, Power, and Food," in Sarah Sceats and Gail Cunningham, eds., *Image and Power*, 121–22.

Schmid, Susanne. "Angela Carter: 'Mythomania and Demythologising,' " in Neil Thomas and Françoise Le Saux, eds., *Myth and Its Legacy*, 145–50.

Nights at the Circus, 1984

Bell, Michael. *Literature, Modernism and Myth*, 211–22.

Blodgett, Harriet. "Fresh Iconography: Subversive Fantasy by Angela Carter." *R of Contemp Fiction* 14:3 (1994), 52–54.

Boehm, Beth A. "Feminist Metafiction and Androcentric Reading Strategies: Angela Carter's Reconstructed Reader in *Nights at the Circus.*" *Critique* (Washington, DC) 37 (1995), 35–48.

Britzolakis, Christina. "Angela Carter's Fetishism." *Textual Practice* 9 (1995), 470–72.

Fernihough, Anne. " 'Is she fact or is she fiction?': Angela Carter and the Enigma of Woman." *Textual Practice* 11:1 (1997), 89–105.

Gasiorek, Andrzej. *Post-War British Fiction,* 133–35.

Gass, Joanne M. "Panopticism in *Nights at the Circus.*" *R of Contemp Fiction* 14:3 (1994), 71–76.

Littlewood, Derek. "Uneasy Readings/Unspeakable Dialogics," in Derek Littlewood and Peter Stockwell, eds., *Impossibility Fiction*, 198–99, 202–5.

Mergenthal, Silvia. " 'Seeing Is Believing': The Rhetoric of Looking in Angela Carter's *Nights at the Circus* and Fay Weldon's *Life and Loves of a She-Devil.*" *GRAAT* 11 (1993), 105–17.

Michael, Magali Cornier. "Angela Carter's *Nights at the Circus:* An Enraged Feminism via Subversive Postmodern Strategies." *Contemp Lit* 35 (1994), 492–519.

Michael, Magali Cornier. *Feminism and the Postmodern Impulse*, 171–208.

Neumeier, Beate. "Postmodern Gothic: Desire and Reality in Angela Carter's Writing," in Victor Sage and Allan Lloyd Smith, eds., *Modern Gothic*, 146–49.

Sage, Lorna. *Angela Carter*, 47–51.

Sage, Lorna. *Women in the House of Fiction,* 176–77.

Schmid, Susanne. "Angela Carter: 'Mythomania and Demythologising,' " in Neil Thomas and Françoise Le Saux, eds., *Myth and Its Legacy*, 145–50.

Siegel, Carol. *Male Masochism,* 152–55.

Todd, Richard. *Consuming Fictions*, 182–86.

Wisker, Gina. "Weaving Our Own Web: Demythologising/Remythologising and Magic in the Work of Contemporary Women Writers," in Wisker, ed., *It's My Party,* 110–13.

Wood, Michael. "The Contemporary Novel," in John Richetti et al., eds., *The Columbia History*, 981–83.

The Passion of New Eve, 1977

Armitt, Lucie. *Theorising the Fantastic,* 164–79.

Blodgett, Harriet. "Fresh Iconography: Subversive Fantasy by Angela Carter." *R of Contemp Fiction* 14:3 (1994), 49–52.

Bono, Paola. "The Passion for Sexual Difference: On (Re)Reading Angela Carter's *The Passion of New Eve.*" *Tessera* 11 (1991), 31–46.

Britzolakis, Christina. "Angela Carter's Fetishism." *Textual Practice* 9 (1995), 467–69.

Connor, Steven. *The English Novel in History,* 33–35.

Gasiorek, Andrzej. *Post-War British Fiction,* 128–31.

Johnson, Heather. "Textualizing the Double-Gendered Body: Forms of the Grotesque in *The Passion of New Eve.*" *R of Contemp Fiction* 14:3 (1994), 43–48.

Ledwon, Lenora. "The Passion of the Phallus and Angela Carter's *The Passion of New Eve.*" *J of the Fantastic in the Arts* 5:4 (1993), 26–41.

Lee, Alison. "Angela Carter's New Eve(lyn): De/En-Gendering Narrative," in Kathy Mezei, ed., *Ambiguous Discourse,* 238–49.

Neumeier, Beate. "Postmodern Gothic: Desire and Reality in Angela Carter's Writing," in Victor Sage and Allan Lloyd Smith, eds., *Modern Gothic,* 149–50.

Sage, Lorna. *Angela Carter,* 35–38.

Sage, Lorna. *Women in the House of Fiction,* 173–76.

Schmid, Susanne. "Angela Carter: 'Mythomania and Demythologising,' " in Neil Thomas and Françoise Le Saux, eds., *Myth and Its Legacy,* 149–52.

Siegel, Carol. *Male Masochism,* 158–59.

Vallorani, Nicoletta. "The Body of the City: Angela Carter's *The Passion of the New Eve.*" *Science-Fiction Stud* 21 (1994), 365–77.

Several Perceptions, 1968

Sage, Lorna. *Angela Carter,* 16–17.

Shadow Dance, 1966

Sage, Lorna. *Angela Carter,* 9–15.

Wise Children, 1991

Boehm, Beth A. "*Wise Children:* Angela Carter's Swan Song." *R of Contemp Fiction* 14:3 (1994), 84–89.

Britzolakis, Christina. "Angela Carter's Fetishism." *Textual Practice* 9 (1995), 472.

Connor, Steven. *The English Novel in History,* 36–38.

Deleyto, Celestino. " 'We Are No Angels': Woman versus History in Angela Carter's *Wise Children,*" in Susana Onega, ed., *Telling Histories,* 163–80.

Gasiorek, Andrzej. *Post-War British Fiction,* 134–37.

Hardin, Michael. "The Other Other: Self-Definition Outside Patriarchal Institutions in Angela Carter's *Wise Children.*" *R of Contemp Fiction* 14:3 (1994), 77–82.

Meaney, Gerardine. *(Un)Like Subjects*, 127–32, 135–40.
Mohr, Hans-Ulrich. "Drei Konstrukte weiblicher Verhaltensräume: Charlotte Smith, Olive Schreiner, Angela Carter." *Arbeiten aus Anglistik und Amerikanistik* 20 (1995), 317–33.
Novy, Marianne. *Engaging with Shakespeare,* 166–68.
Sage, Lorna. *Angela Carter*, 54–59.
Todd, Richard. *Consuming Fictions*, 186–88.
Wood, Michael. "The Contemporary Novel," in John Richetti et al., eds., *The Columbia History*, 963–64.

BARBARA CARTLAND

The Proud Princess, 1976
Hughes, Helen. *The Historical Romance*, 21–24.

JOYCE CARY

An American Visitor, 1933
Belliappa, K. C. "The Outsider's Perceptions of Africa: A Consideration of Joyce Cary and Joseph Conrad," in P. K. Rajan et al., eds., *Commonwealth Literature*, 169–70.
Castle Corner, 1938
Welch, Robert. *Changing States*, 124–29.
Except the Lord, 1953
Roberts, Alan. "Rhythm in Prose and the Serial Correlation of Sentence Lengths: A Joyce Cary Case Study." *Liter & Linguistic Computing* 11 (1996), 35–39.
Herself Surprised, 1941
Welch, Robert. *Changing States*, 132–35.
The Horse's Mouth, 1944
Levitt, Annette Shandler. *The Intertextuality of Joyce Cary's "The Horse's Mouth,"* 1–136.
Welch, Robert. *Changing States*, 132–35.
A House of Children, 1941
Welch, Robert. *Changing States*, 129–32.
Mister Johnson, 1939
Belliappa, K. C. "The Outsider's Perceptions of Africa: A Consideration of Joyce Cary and Joseph Conrad," in P. K. Rajan et al., eds., *Commonwealth Literature*, 170–73.
Harris, Michael. *Outsiders and Insiders*, 79–94.
Not Honour More, 1955
Roberts, Alan. "Rhythm in Prose and the Serial Correlation of Sentence Lengths: A Joyce Cary Case Study." *Liter & Linguistic Computing* 11 (1996), 35–39.

Prisoner of Grace, 1952

> Roberts, Alan. "Rhythm in Prose and the Serial Correlation of Sentence Lengths: A Joyce Cary Case Study." *Liter & Linguistic Computing* 11 (1996), 35–39.
>
> Welch, Robert. *Changing States,* 135–37.

To Be a Pilgrim, 1942

> Kraemer, Alfred R. "Two Female Bookends to a Long Life: Lucy and Ann in Joyce Cary's *To Be a Pilgrim." Engl Lang Notes* 33:4 (1996), 71–76.
>
> Welch, Robert. *Changing States,* 132–35.

DAVID CAUTE

At Fever Pitch, 1959

> Tredell, Nicolas. *Caute's Confrontations,* 8–11.

Comrade Jacob, 1961

> Tredell, Nicolas. *Caute's Confrontations,* 11–15.

The Decline of the West, 1966

> Tredell, Nicolas. *Caute's Confrontations,* 15–22.

Dr. Orwell and Mr. Blair, 1994

> Tredell, Nicolas. *Caute's Confrontations,* 87–103.

The K-Factor, 1983

> Tredell, Nicolas. *Caute's Confrontations,* 49–52.

News from Nowhere, 1989

> Tredell, Nicolas. *Caute's Confrontations,* 52–64.

The Occupation, 1971

> Tredell, Nicolas. *Caute's Confrontations,* 26–42.

The Time of the Toad, nyp

> Tredell, Nicolas. *Caute's Confrontations,* 103–15.

Veronica or The Two Nations, 1989

> Tredell, Nicolas. *Caute's Confrontations,* 65–78.

The Women's Hour, 1991

> Antor, Heinz. *Der englische Universitätsroman,* 708–11.
>
> Tredell, Nicolas. *Caute's Confrontations,* 78–86.

MARGARET CAVENDISH

The Description of a New Blazing-World, 1666

> Boesky, Amy. *Founding Fictions,* 132–40.
>
> Jacobs, Naomi. "The Frozen Landscape in Women's Utopian and Science Fiction," in Jane L. Donawerth and Carol A. Kolmerten, eds., *Utopian and Science Fiction,* 191–92.

Khanna, Lee Cullen. "The Subject of Utopia: Margaret Cavendish and Her *Blazing-World*," in Jane L. Donawerth and Carol A. Kolmerten, eds., *Utopian and Science Fiction*, 15–34.
MacCarthy, B. G. *The Female Pen*, 107–12.

Sociable Letters, 1664

MacCarthy, B. G. *The Female Pen*, 244–48.

SID CHAPLIN

The Day of the Sardine, 1961

Taylor, D. J. *After the War*, 111–18.

MARIA CHARLESWORTH

Ministering Children: A Tale Dedicated to Childhood, 1854

Brown, Penny. *The Captured World*, 50–54.

HENRIETTA CHATTERTON

Compensation: A Story of Real Life Thirty Years Ago, 1856

Tush, Susan Rowland. *George Eliot and . . . Popular Women's Fiction*, 126–47.

BRUCE CHATWIN

On the Black Hill, 1983

Kane, Richard. "A Contemporary Anomaly: Bruce Chatwin's Pastoral Novel, *On the Black Hill.*" *Arkansas R* 3:2 (1994), 168–92.

GEORGE CHESNEY

The Dilemma, 1876

Paxton, Nancy L. "Mobilizing Chivalry: Rape in Flora Annie Steel's *On the Face of the Waters* (1896) and Other British Novels about the Indian Uprising of 1857," in Barbara Leah Harman and Susan Meyer, eds., *The New Nineteenth Century*, 256–59.

G. K. CHESTERTON

The Ball and the Cross, 1910

Coates, John. "*The Ball and the Cross* and the Edwardian Novel of Ideas." *Chesterton R* 18 (1992), 49–79.
Gardner, Martin. "Levels of Allegory in *The Ball and the Cross.*" *Chesterton R* 18 (1992), 37–47.

Pearce, Joseph. *Wisdom and Innocence*, 151–53.
Slevin, Gerard. "Chesterton's Scottish Characters." *Chesterton R* 18 (1992), 84–86.

The Club of Queer Trades, 1905
Scheick, William J. *The Ethos of Romance*, 102–9.

The Man Who Was Thursday, 1908
Carlin, Russell. "The Hero Who Was Thursday: A Modern Myth." *Mythlore* 19:3 (1993), 27–30.
Isley, William L., Jr. "Knowledge and Mystery in Chesterton's *The Man Who Was Thursday*." *Christianity and Lit* 42 (1993), 279–93.

Manalive, 1912
Pearce, Joseph. *Wisdom and Innocence*, 173–76.

The Napoleon of Notting Hill, 1904
Bergonzi, Bernard. "*The Napoleon of Notting Hill:* An Introduction." *Chesterton R* 19 (1993), 515–31.
Pearce, Joseph. *Wisdom and Innocence*, 87–90.

The Return of Don Quixote, 1927
Morris, Kevin L. "Chesterton Sees Red: The Metaphysics of a Colour." *Chesterton R* 21 (1995), 505–16.

WILLIAM RUFUS CHETWOOD

The Voyages and Adventures of Captain Robert Boyle, 1726
Snader, Joe. "The Oriental Captivity Narrative and Early English Fiction." *Eighteenth-Cent Fiction* 9 (1997), 281–88.

JAMES SAXON CHILDERS

Laurel and Straw, 1927
Antor, Heinz. *Der englische Universitätsroman*, 516–18, 566–68.

MARY CHOLMONDELEY

Red Pottage, 1899
Demoor, Marysa. "Women Authors and their Selves: Autobiography in the Work of Charlotte Yonge, Rhoda Broughton, Mary Cholmondeley and Lucy Clifford." *Cahiers Victoriens et Edouardiens* 39 (1994), 58–60.
Kranidis, Rita S. *Subversive Discourse*, 81–84.
Nelson, Carolyn Christensen. *British Women Fiction Writers*, 32–36.
Scheick, William J. *The Ethos of Romance*, 151–53.

AGATHA CHRISTIE

The Murder at the Vicarage, 1930

> Knepper, Marty S. "Reading Agatha Christie's Miss Marple Series: The Thirteen Problems," in Mary Jean DeMarr, ed., *In the Beginning,* 33–55.

The Murder of Roger Ackroyd, 1926

> Eco, Umberto. *Six Walks in the Fictional Woods,* 27–29.
> Gibelli, Dario. "Le Paradoxe du narrateur dans *Roger Ackroyd.*" *Poetique* 23:92 (1992), 387–97.

Murder on the Orient Express, 1934

> Thomas, G. W. "Murder in Mesopotamia: Agatha Christie in the Middle East." *Armchair Detective* 27 (1994), 276–83.
> Vagstad, Kristi. "Yankees on the Orient Express." *Armchair Detective* 28 (1995), 82–90.

Sleeping Murder, 1976

> Thompson, Jon. *Fiction, Crime, and Empire,* 124–26, 131–33.

JANE HUME CLAPPERTON

Margaret Dunmore; or, A Socialist Home, 1888
> Lewes, Darby. *Dream Revisionaries,* 95–97.

ALLEN CLARKE

The Knobstick: A Story of Love and Labour, 1893
> Fox, Pamela. *Class Fictions,* 178–80.
Lancashire Lasses and Lads, 1896
> Fox, Pamela. *Class Fictions,* 123–27.

ARTHUR C. CLARKE

Childhood's End, 1953
> Connolly, John. "A Progressive End: Arthur C. Clarke and Teilhard de Chardin." *Foundation* 61 (1994), 66–75.

LINDSAY CLARKE

The Chymical Wedding, 1990
> Harper, Anthony J. "*Mysterium Conjunctionis:* On the Attraction of 'Chymical Weddings.'" *German Life and Letters* 47 (1994), 449–55.
> Meakin, David. *Hermetic Fictions,* 144–50.

Rowland, Susan. "The Body's Sacred: Romance and Sacrifice in Religious and Jungian Narratives." *Lit and Theology* 10 (1996), 163–70.

JOHN CLELAND

Fanny Hill, 1748

Anderson, Antje Schaum. "Gendered Pleasure, Gendered Plot: Defloration as Climax in *Clarissa* and *Memoirs of a Woman of Pleasure.*" *J of Narrative Technique* 25 (1995), 108–21.

Badir, Magdy Gabriel. "L'Ascension de la courtisane au dix-huitième siècle dans *Les Egarements* et *Fanny Hill.*" *Stud on Voltaire and the Eighteenth Cent* 305 (1992), 1435–38.

Gautier, Gary. "Fanny Hill's Mapping of Sexuality, Female Identity, and Maternity." *Stud in Engl Lit, 1500–1900* 35 (1995), 473–88.

Gautier, Gary. "Fanny's Fantasies: Class, Gender, and the Unreliable Narrator in Cleland's *Memoirs of a Woman of Pleasure.*" *Style* 28 (1994), 133–43.

Gliserman, Martin. *Psychoanalysis, Language, and the Body of the Text,* 33–36.

Kopelson, Kevin. "Seeing Sodomy: *Fanny Hill's* Blinding Vision," in Claude J. Summers, ed., *Homosexuality,* 173–82.

Mengay, Donald H. "The Sodomitical Muse: *Fanny Hill* and the Rhetoric of Crossdressing," in Claude J. Summers, ed., *Homosexuality,* 185–96.

Nussbaum, Felicity A. "One Part of Womankind: Prostitution and Sexual Geography in *Memoirs of a Woman of Pleasure.*" *Differences* 7:2 (1995), 17–40.

Spacks, Patricia Meyer. *Desire and Truth,* 95–98.

LUCY CLIFFORD

Mrs Keith's Crime, 1885

Demoor, Marysa. "Women Authors and their Selves: Autobiography in the Work of Charlotte Yonge, Rhoda Broughton, Mary Cholmondeley and Lucy Clifford." *Cahiers Victoriens et Edouardiens* 39 (1994), 60–62.

DESMOND COKE

Sandford of Merton: A Story of Oxford Life, 1903

Antor, Heinz. *Der englische Universitätsroman,* 450–53.

WILKIE COLLINS

Antonina, 1850

Orel, Harold. *The Historical Novel,* 20–22.

Armadale, 1866

>   Caracciolo, Peter L. "Wilkie Collins and 'The God Almighty of Novelists': The Example of Scott in *No Name* and *Armadale,*" in Nelson Smith and R. C. Terry, eds., *Wilkie Collins to the Forefront,* 171–74.
>
>   Gates, Barbara T. "Wilkie Collins' Suicides: 'Truth As It Is in Nature,' " in Nelson Smith and R. C. Terry, eds., *Wilkie Collins to the Forefront,* 246–47.
>
>   Hall, Donald E. *Fixing Patriarchy,* 164–69.
>
>   Horsman, Alan. *The Victorian Novel,* 211–12.
>
>   Thomas, Ronald R. "Wilkie Collins and the Sensation Novel," in John Richetti et al., eds., *The Columbia History,* 497–98.

Basil, 1852

>   Kent, Christopher. "Probability, Reality and Sensation in the Novels of Wilkie Collins," in Nelson Smith and R. C. Terry, eds., *Wilkie Collins to the Forefront,* 58–60.
>
>   Millard, Kenneth. "My Father's Will: Self-determination and Mental Breakdown in *Basil, The Professor,* and *The Ordeal of Richard Feverel.*" *English* 44 (1995), 62–78.

The Dead Secret, 1857

>   Thomas, Ronald R. "Wilkie Collins and the Sensation Novel," in John Richetti et al., eds., *The Columbia History,* 489–91.
>
>   Vrettos, Athena. *Somatic Fictions,* 44–47.

The Fallen Leaves, 1879

>   Gates, Barbara T. "Wilkie Collins' Suicides: 'Truth As It Is in Nature,' " in Nelson Smith and R. C. Terry, eds., *Wilkie Collins to the Forefront,* 247–49.

The Haunted Hotel, 1879

>   Wolfreys, Julian. *Being English,* 110–19.

Heart and Science, 1883

>   Gates, Barbara T. "Wilkie Collins' Suicides: 'Truth As It Is in Nature,' " in Nelson Smith and R. C. Terry, eds., *Wilkie Collins to the Forefront,* 252–53.
>
>   Wiesenthal, C. S. "From Charcot to Plato: The History of Hysteria in *Heart and Science,*" in Nelson Smith and R. C. Terry, eds., *Wilkie Collins to the Forefront,* 257–65.

The Law and the Lady, 1875

>   Gates, Barbara T. "Wilkie Collins' Suicides: 'Truth As It Is in Nature,' " in Nelson Smith and R. C. Terry, eds., *Wilkie Collins to the Forefront,* 249–51.
>
>   O'Fallon, Kathleen. "Breaking the Laws about Ladies: Wilkie Collins' Questioning of Gender Roles," in Nelson Smith and R. C. Terry, eds., *Wilkie Collins to the Forefront,* 231–39.
>
>   Wolfreys, Julian. *Being English,* 105–7.

Man and Wife, 1870

Hall, Donald E. *Fixing Patriarchy,* 169–73.

Surridge, Lisa. "Unspeakable Histories: Hester Dethridge and the Narration of Domestic Violence in *Man and Wife." Victorian R* 22 (1996), 102–22.

Wolfreys, Julian. *Being English,* 119–26.

The Moonstone, 1868

Burgan, William M. "Masonic Symbolism in *The Moonstone* and *The Mystery of Edwin Drood,"* in Nelson Smith and R. C. Terry, eds., *Wilkie Collins to the Forefront,* 101–26.

Calanchi, Alessandra. "Visite guidate: La complicità dello scenario domestico in *The Moonstone." Paragone* 43:32–34 (1992), 28–46.

David, Deirdre. *Rule Britannia,* 17–20, 49–51, 142–47.

Duncan, Ian. *"The Moonstone,* the Victorian Novel, and Imperialist Panic." *Mod Lang Q* 55 (1994), 297–319.

Escuret, Annie. *"The Moonstone:* 'J'enquête donc je lis'—Lecture, Epistémologique." *Q/W/E/R/T/Y* 5 (1995), 129–40.

Hollington, Michael. " 'To the Droodstone': Or, From *The Moonstone* to *Edwin Drood* via *No Thoroughfare." Q/W/E/R/T/Y* 5 (1995), 141–49.

Horsman, Alan. *The Victorian Novel,* 212–14.

Kresge, Delphine. "Voix et voies: *The Moonstone* et *The Big Sleep." Q/W/E/R/T/Y* 5 (1995), 151–58.

Kucich, John. *The Power of Lies,* 97–104.

Martin, Françoise. "Le Corps dans tous ses éclats: Maux et mots du corps dans *The Moonstone." Q/W/E/R/T/Y* 5 (1995), 159–68.

Milligan, Barry. *Pleasures and Pains,* 69–82.

Naugrette, Jean-Pierre. *"The Moonstone:* signes indiens." *Etudes Anglaises* 48 (1995), 407–17.

Reed, John R. "The Stories of *The Moonstone,"* in Nelson Smith and R. C. Terry, eds., *Wilkie Collins to the Forefront,* 91–99.

Thomas, Ronald R. "Wilkie Collins and the Sensation Novel," in John Richetti et al., eds., *The Columbia History,* 500–502.

Thornton, Sara. "Dealing with *Disjecta Membra:* Strategies of Homogenization and Interment in *The Moonstone." Q/W/E/R/T/Y* 5 (1995), 169–76.

Zander, Andela. " 'Spot the Source': Wilkie Collins' *The Moonstone* und John Fowles' *The French Lieutenant's Woman." Zeitschrift für Anglistik und Amerikanistik* 41 (1993), 341–47.

The New Magdalen, 1873

Cohen, Michael. *Sisters,* 138–40.

Leavy, Barbara Fass. "Wilkie Collins' *The New Magdalen* and the Folklore of the Kind and the Unkind Girls," in Nelson Smith and R. C. Terry, eds., *Wilkie Collins to the Forefront,* 209–22.

No Name, 1862

Caracciolo, Peter L. "Wilkie Collins and 'The God Almighty of Novelists': The Example of Scott in *No Name* and *Armadale,"* in Nelson Smith and R. C. Terry, eds., *Wilkie Collins to the Forefront,* 174–77.

Chattman, Lauren. "Actresses at Home and on the Stage: Spectacular Domesticity and the Victorian Theatrical Novel." *Novel* 28 (1994), 80–86.

Cohen, Michael. *Sisters*, 138–40, 142–44.

David, Deirdre. "Rewriting the Male Plot in Wilkie Collins's *No Name* (1862): Captain Wragge Orders an Omelette and Mrs. Wragge Goes into Custody," in Barbara Leah Harman and Susan Meyer, eds., *The New Nineteenth Century*, 33–43.

Gates, Barbara T. "Wilkie Collins' Suicides: 'Truth As It Is in Nature,' " in Nelson Smith and R. C. Terry, eds., *Wilkie Collins to the Forefront*, 244–46.

Kucich, John. *The Power of Lies*, 83–85.

Reynolds, Kimberley, and Nicola Humble. *Victorian Heroines*, 116–20.

Thomas, Ronald R. "Wilkie Collins and the Sensation Novel," in John Richetti et al., eds., *The Columbia History*, 492–93.

Poor Miss Finch, 1872

Callander, Margaret M. "Variations on Blindness: Wilkie Collins' *Poor Miss Finch* and André Gide's *Symphonie Pastorale.*" *New Comparison* 17 (1994), 23–34.

The Woman in White, 1860

Andres, Sophia. "Pre-Raphaelite Paintings and Jungian Images in Wilkie Collins's *The Woman in White.*" *Victorian Newsl* 88 (1995), 26–30.

Ascari, Maurizio. "Più di una penna, più di un testimone: Tecniche narrative in *The Woman in White.*" *Paragone* 43:32–34 (1992), 9–27.

Bernstein, Stephen. "Reading Blackwater Park: Gothicism, Narrative, and Ideology in *The Woman in White.*" *Stud in the Novel* 25 (1993), 291–302.

Botting, Fred. *Gothic*, 131–34.

Bury, Laurent. "Shutting In, Shutting Out, Shutting Up: variations sur l'enfermement dans *The Woman in White* de Wilkie Collins." *Cahiers Victoriens et Edouardiens* 43 (1996), 31–46.

Cohen, Michael. *Sisters*, 140–42.

Hall, Donald E. *Fixing Patriarchy*, 156–65.

Horsman, Alan. *The Victorian Novel*, 208–10.

Kucich, John. *The Power of Lies*, 84–98, 106–17.

Ledwon, Lenora. "Veiled Women, the Law of Coverture, and Wilkie Collins's *The Woman in White.*" *Victorian Lit and Culture* 22 (1994), 1–20.

May, Leila Silvana. "Sensational Sisters: Wilkie Collins's *The Woman in White.*" *Pacific Coast Philology* 30:1 (1995), 82–102.

Milbank, Alison. "From the Sublime to the Uncanny: Victorian Gothic and Sensation Fiction," in Allan Lloyd Smith and Victor Sage, eds., *Gothick Origins and Innovations*, 171–74.

Müller, Wolfgang G. "The Homology of Syntax and Narrative Form in English and American Fiction," in Herbert Foltinek et al., eds., *Tales and "their telling difference,"* 90–92.

Reynolds, Kimberley, and Nicola Humble. *Victorian Heroines*, 52–56.

Schmitt, Cannon. "Alien Nation: Gender, Genre, and English Nationality in Wilkie Collins's *The Woman in White.*" *Genre* 26 (1993), 283–307.

Small, Helen. *Love's Madness*, 193–207.

Sutherland, John. *Is Heathcliff a Murderer?*, 117–22.

Sutherland, John. *Victorian Fiction*, 28–54.

Sutherland, John. "Wilkie Collins and the Origins of the Sensation Novel," in Nelson Smith and R. C. Terry, eds., *Wilkie Collins to the Forefront*, 75–81, 86–89.

Taylor, Michael. " 'In the name of her sacred weakness': Romance, Destiny, and Woman's Revenge in Wilkie Collins's *The Woman in White.*" *Univ of Toronto Q* 64 (1995), 289–301.

Thomas, Peter. "Escaping the Plot: The Quest for Selfhood in *The Woman in White,*" in Nelson Smith and R. C. Terry, eds., *Wilkie Collins to the Forefront*, 183–204.

Thomas, Ronald R. "Wilkie Collins and the Sensation Novel," in John Richetti et al., eds., *The Columbia History*, 485–89, 499–502.

York, R. A. *Strangers and Secrets*, 104–18.

GERTRUDE COLMORE

Suffragette Sally, 1911
Miller, Jane Eldridge. *Rebel Women*, 144–54.

IVY COMPTON-BURNETT

Manservant and Maidservant, 1947
Seeber, Hans Ulrich. "Macht und Erotik in Ivy Compton-Burnetts Dialogroman *Manservant and Maidservant,*" in Konrad Groß et al., eds., *Das Natur/Kultur-Paradigma*, 190–207.

The Mighty and Their Fall, 1961
Gasiorek, Andrzej. *Post-War British Fiction*, 27–31.

WILLIAM CONGREVE

Incognita, 1692
Bonheim, Helmut. "Defining the Novel: Congreve's *Incognita,*" in Herbert Foltinek et al., eds., *Tales and "their telling difference,"* 165–82.

Ogée, Frédéric. " 'For show and form': feinte et fiction dans l'*Incognita* de Congreve." *Recherches Anglaises et Nord-Américaines* 26 (1993), 31–50.

CYRIL VERNON CONNOLLY

The Rock Pool, 1936
Hopkins, Chris. "Cyril Vernon Connolly: Inside *The Rock Pool,*" in Patrick J. Quinn, ed., *Recharting the Thirties*, 159–70.

JOSEPH CONRAD

Almayer's Folly, 1895

Batchelor, John. *The Life of Joseph Conrad*, 46–50, 53–55.

Fredriksson, Gunnar. "In Joseph Conrad's Waters," in Jakob Lothe, ed., *Conrad in Scandinavia*, 43–48.

GoGwilt, Christopher. *The Invention of the West*, 81–85.

Griffith, John W. *Joseph Conrad and the Anthropological Dilemma*, 141–44.

Harpham, Geoffrey Galt. *One of Us*, 121–23.

Krenn, Heliéna M. "The 'Beautiful' World of Women: Women as Reflections of Colonial Issues in Conrad's Malay Novels," in Keith Carabine et al., eds., *Contexts for Conrad*, 106–15.

Lesage, Claudine. "Marguerite Poradocoska écrivain et *Le Mariage du Fils Grandsire.*" *L'Epoque Conradienne* 21 (1995), 57–62.

Maisonnat, Claude. "Castration symbolique et problématique de l'identité dans *Almayer's Folly.*" *L'Epoque Conradienne* 20 (1994), 57–74.

Maisonnat, Claude. "Discursive Deception and the Quest for Meaning in *Almayer's Folly,*" in Keith Carabine et al., eds., *Conrad's Literary Career*, 3–20.

Pendleton, Robert. *Graham Greene's Conradian Masterplot*, 14–17.

Schwarz, Daniel R. "Joseph Conrad," in John Richetti et al., eds., *The Columbia History*, 688–89.

Stott, Rebecca. *The Fabrication*, 148–50.

Walton, Priscilla L. " 'This vague feeling of their difference': Race, Gender, and the Originary Impetus in Conrad's *Almayer's Folly.*" *Ariel* 26:2 (1995), 95–108.

Wexler, Joyce Piell. *Who Paid for Modernism*, 26–27.

White, Andrea. "Conrad and Imperialism," in J. H. Stape, ed., *The Cambridge Companion*, 187–90.

Williams, Mary Frances. "*Almayer's Folly* and the Golden Fleece: Conrad's Malaysian *Argonautica.*" *Classical and Mod Lit* 15 (1995), 145–62.

Wilson, Robert. *Joseph Conrad*, 15–16.

The Arrow of Gold, 1919

Batchelor, John. *The Life of Joseph Conrad*, 256–62.

Hampson, Robert. "The Late Novels," in J. H. Stape, ed., *The Cambridge Companion*, 146–50.

Pendleton, Robert. *Graham Greene's Conradian Masterplot*, 21–23.

Wilson, Robert. *Joseph Conrad*, 119–24.

Chance, 1913

Armstrong, Paul B. "Misogyny and the Ethics of Reading: The Problem of Conrad's *Chance,*" in Keith Carabine et al., eds., *Contexts for Conrad*, 151–70.

Batchelor, John. *The Life of Joseph Conrad*, 200–218.

Hampson, Robert. "The Late Novels," in J. H. Stape, ed., *The Cambridge Companion*, 142–44.

Luftig, Victor. *Seeing Together*, 143–47.

McLauchlan, Juliet. "Conrad: The 'Few Simple Ideas,' " in Keith Carabine et al., eds., *Conrad's Literary Career*, 240–44.

Monk, Leland. *Standard Deviations*, 75–80, 83–109.

Pendleton, Robert. *Graham Greene's Conradian Masterplot*, 20–21.

Schwarz, Daniel R. "Joseph Conrad," in John Richetti et al., eds., *The Columbia History*, 708–10.

Wexler, Joyce Piell. *Who Paid for Modernism*, 44–47.

Wilson, Robert. *Joseph Conrad*, 132–35.

Lord Jim, 1900

Ambrosini, Richard. "Conrad's 'Paper Boats,' " in Keith Carabine et al., eds., *Conrad's Literary Career*, 47–56.

Batchelor, John. *The Life of Joseph Conrad*, 95–113.

Born, Daniel. *The Birth of Liberal Guilt*, 105–19.

Browne, Andrew K. M. "An Original for 'Gentleman' Brown." *Conradiana* 26 (1994), 76–79.

Clarke, Michael Tavel. "Reclaiming Literary Territory: Paule Marshall's Response to Joseph Conrad." *Conradiana* 28 (1996), 138–50.

Conroy, Mark. "Colonial Self-Fashioning in Conrad: Writing and Remembrance in *Lord Jim.*" *L'Epoque Conradienne* 19 (1993), 25–36.

Gass, Joanne. " 'The Significant Fact of an Unforgotten Grave': Encrypting the Feminine in *Lord Jim.*" *Conradiana* 27 (1995), 250–57.

Gillon, Adam. *Joseph Conrad*, 129–35.

GoGwilt, Christopher. *The Invention of the West*, 87–105.

GoGwilt, Christopher. "Lord Jim and the Invention of the West." *Conradiana* 27 (1995), 45–61.

Griffith, John W. *Joseph Conrad and the Anthropological Dilemma*, 48–50, 82–85, 172–74, 183–87.

Hagen, Erik Bjerck. "*Lord Jim* and the Perils of Interpretation," in Jakob Lothe, ed., *Conrad in Scandinavia*, 195–209.

Hampson, Robert G. "Conrad and the Formation of Legends," in Keith Carabine et al., eds., *Conrad's Literary Career*, 167–70, 182–83.

Harpham, Geoffrey Galt. *One of Us*, 173–76.

Heyns, Michiel. *Expulsion and the Nineteenth-Century Novel*, 39–42, 187–226.

Hollahan, Eugene. *Crisis-Consciousness*, 161–62.

Jackson, Tony E. *The Subject of Modernism*, 67–98.

Jackson, Tony E. "Turning into Modernism: *Lord Jim* and the Alteration of the Narrative Subject." *Lit and Psych* 39:4 (1993), 65–84.

Koh, Boo Eung. "Contradictions in Colonial History in *Lord Jim.*" *Conradiana* 28 (1996), 163–78.

Kurtz, R. "Lloyd Fernando's *Scorpion Orchid* and Lord Jim's Dilemma: Another Descendant, In Other Words." *Conradiana* 28 (1996), 115–24.

Lange, Robert J. G. "The Eyes Have It: Homoeroticism in *Lord Jim.*" *West Virginia Univ Philol Papers* 38 (1992), 59–68.

Lothe, Jakob. "Conradian Narrative," in J. H. Stape, ed., *The Cambridge Companion*, 169–72.

Lothe, Jakob. "Narrators and Characters in *Lord Jim,*" in Keith Carabine et al., eds., *Conrad's Literary Career*, 113–25.

Mongia, Padmini. "Empire, Narrative and the Feminine in *Lord Jim* and *Heart of Darkness,*" in Keith Carabine et al., eds., *Contexts for Conrad*, 135–40, 143–47.

Moses, Michael Valdez. *The Novel and the Globalization of Culture*, 67–104.

Nishihara, Laverne. " 'The Fetters of that Strange Freedom': Boundary as Regulating Technique in *Lord Jim.*" *Conradiana* 28 (1996), 54–64.

Pecora, Vincent P. "The Sorcerer's Apprentices: Romance, Anthropology, and Literary Theory." *Mod Lang Q* 55 (1994), 359–64, 377–82.

Pendleton, Robert. *Graham Greene's Conradian Masterplot*, 33–37.

Peters, John G. "Skin's Collections: Order and Chaos in *Lord Jim.*" *Conradiana* 28 (1996), 48–52.

Pettersson, Torsten. "*Lord Jim:* The Prison-House of Consciousness," in Jakob Lothe, ed., *Conrad in Scandinavia*, 169–91.

Phillips, Gene D. *Conrad and Cinema*, 97–112.

Ray, Martin. *Joseph Conrad*, 32–47.

Schwarz, Daniel R. "Joseph Conrad," in John Richetti et al., eds., *The Columbia History*, 698–702.

Stape, J. H. " 'Gaining Conviction': Conradian Borrowing and the *Patna* Episode in *Lord Jim.*" *Conradiana* 25 (1993), 222–34.

Stape, J. H. "*Lord Jim,*" in J. H. Stape, ed., *The Cambridge Companion*, 63–78.

Thomas, Mark Ellis. "Doubling and Difference in Conrad: 'The Secret Sharer,' *Lord Jim,* and *The Shadow Line.*" *Conradiana* 27 (1995), 226–29.

Trotter, David. *The English Novel in History*, 253–54.

Wexler, Joyce Piell. *Who Paid for Modernism*, 36–39.

Wheatley, Alison E. "The Function of Epithets in Conrad." *Conradiana* 29 (1997), 16–20.

White, Andrea. "Conrad and Imperialism," in J. H. Stape, ed., *The Cambridge Companion*, 192–93.

Williams, Mary Frances. "Cicero's *De Officiis* and Conrad's *Lord Jim:* A Philosophical Paradigm for the Novel." *Classical and Mod Lit* 16 (1996), 131–47.

Wilson, Robert. *Joseph Conrad*, 42–48.

The Nigger of the "Narcissus," 1897

Bailin, Miriam. *The Sickroom in Victorian Fiction*, 139–40.

Batchelor, John. *The Life of Joseph Conrad*, 61–69.

Bendelli, Giuliana. "Le configurazioni discorsive in *The Nigger of the*

'Narcissus' di Joseph Conrad." *Confronto Letterario* 6:12 (1989), 267–86.

Greenslade, William. *Degeneration, Culture, and the Novel,* 108–10.

Griffith, John W. *Joseph Conrad and the Anthropological Dilemma,* 37–39.

Harpham, Geoffrey Galt. *One of Us,* 84–87.

Hawthorn, Jeremy. "Narrative and Ideology: Race and Class in *The Nigger of the 'Narcissus,'* " in Jakob Lothe, ed., *Conrad in Scandinavia,* 53–88.

Kane, Michael. "Insiders/Outsiders: Conrad's *The Nigger of the 'Narcissus'* and Bram Stoker's *Dracula.*" *Mod Lang R* 92 (1997), 1–7.

de Lange, Adriaan M. "Conrad and Impressionism: Problems and (Possible) Solutions," in Keith Carabine et al., eds., *Conrad's Literary Career,* 29–36.

Lothe, Jakob. "Conradian Narrative," in J. H. Stape, ed., *The Cambridge Companion,* 162–64.

McLauchlan, Juliet. "Conrad: The 'Few Simple Ideas,' " in Keith Carabine et al., eds., *Conrad's Literary Career,* 236–39.

Melfi, Mary Ann. "Changing Perspective: Conrad's Treatment of Doubt in *The Nigger of the 'Narcissus.'"* *J of Evolutionary Psych* 15 (1994), 204–11.

Schwarz, Daniel R. "Joseph Conrad," in John Richetti et al., eds., *The Columbia History,* 689–91.

Wexler, Joyce Piell. *Who Paid for Modernism,* 30–33.

Wilson, Robert. *Joseph Conrad,* 31–32.

Wilson, Robert Rawdon. "The Space of the Untold: Conrad's Allusiveness." *Victorian R* 16:1 (1990), 25–30 and 16:2 (1990), 24–36.

Nostromo, 1904

Batchelor, John. *The Life of Joseph Conrad,* 126–46.

Bivona, Daniel. *Desire and Contradiction,* 124–27.

Bonney, William. "Conrad's Nostromo: Money and Mystification on the Frontier," in Keith Carabine et al., eds., *Contexts for Conrad,* 207–38.

Brantlinger, Patrick. *Fictions of State,* 213–17.

Brigham, Cathy. "Costaguana's Other Coup: The Failed Insurrection of Private Lyric Speech against Official Doublespeak in *Nostromo.*" *Conradiana* 26 (1994), 157–67.

Caracciola, Peter L. "The Use of the Expatrial Allusion in Conrad's Fiction," in Keith Carabine et al., eds., *Contexts for Conrad,* 198–202.

Delany, Paul. "*Nostromo:* Economism and its Discontents," in Carola M. Kaplan and Anne B. Simpson, eds., *Seeing Double,* 215–31.

Erdinast-Vulcan, Daphna. "*Nostromo* and the Failure of Myth," in Elaine Jordan, ed., *Joseph Conrad,* 128–43.

Gallix, François. "*Nostromo:* Pour une défense du titre, I." *L'Epoque Conradienne* 20 (1994), 47–56.

Gillon, Adam. *Joseph Conrad,* 46–57.

GoGwilt, Christopher. *The Invention of the West,* 190–219.

Goodman, Daniel. "Overseeing the Metropolis: Edward Said as Border Intellectual." *L'Epoque Conradienne* 20 (1994), 123–40.

Hampson, Robert G. "Conrad and the Formation of Legends," in Keith Carabine et al., eds., *Conrad's Literary Career*, 170–78.

Hay, Eloise Knapp. *"Nostromo,"* in J. H. Stape, ed., *The Cambridge Companion*, 81–96.

Hollahan, Eugene. *Crisis-Consciousness*, 162–63.

Issa, Mahmoud. "Involvement and Detachment in *Nostromo*," in Jakob Lothe, ed., *Conrad in Scandinavia*, 211–23.

Jameson, Fredric. "Romance and Reification: Plot Construction and Ideological Closure in *Nostromo*," in Elaine Jordan, ed., *Joseph Conrad*, 116–26.

Lesage, Claudine. "Et si Mitchell disait vrai?" *L'Epoque Conradienne* 20 (1994), 43–46.

Lothe, Jakob. "Conradian Narrative," in J. H. Stape, ed., *The Cambridge Companion*, 172–74.

Luftig, Victor. *Seeing Together*, 136–38.

Moses, Michael Valdez. *The Novel and the Globalization of Culture*, 69–71.

Moyer, Guy L. " 'Inner Secrets' in Conrad's *Nostromo." Conradiana* 27 (1995), 235–43.

Paccaud-Huguet, Josiane. "Betrayal and Corruptible Values in *Nostromo." L'Epoque Conradienne* 20 (1994), 17–31.

Pendleton, Robert. *Graham Greene's Conradian Masterplot*, 37–42.

Phillips, Gene D. *Conrad and Cinema*, 145–49.

Ray, Martin. *Joseph Conrad*, 48–68.

Reilly, Jim. "A Play of Signs: *Nostromo*," in Elaine Jordan, ed., *Joseph Conrad*, 146–56.

Said, Edward W. "The Novel as Beginning Intention: *Nostromo*," in Elaine Jordan, ed., *Joseph Conrad*, 103–14.

Schwarz, Daniel R. "Joseph Conrad," in John Richetti et al., eds., *The Columbia History*, 702–6.

Szczypien, Jean M. "Twirling Moustaches and Equestrian Statuary: Polish Semiotics in Conrad's *Nostromo." Mosaic* 28:3 (1995), 31–55.

Trotter, David. *The English Novel in History*, 257–59.

Vinciguerra, Marie-Jean. " 'Cervoni–Nostromo–Garibaldi': Un Regard corse et garibaldien sur *Nostromo." L'Epoque Conradienne* 21 (1995), 33–43.

Watts, Cedric. "Four Rather Obscure Allusions in *Nostromo." Conradiana* 28 (1996), 77–80.

Watts, Cedric. "*Nostromo* and the Unitary Theory of Conradian Narrative Verve." *L'Epoque Conradienne* 20 (1994), 33–41.

Wheatley, Alison E. "The Function of Epithets in Conrad." *Conradiana* 29 (1997), 20–24.

White, Andrea. "Conrad and Imperialism," in J. H. Stape, ed., *The Cambridge Companion*, 194–96.

Whitebrook, Maureen. *Real Toads in Imaginary Gardens,* 101–22.

Wilding, Michael. *Social Visions,* 77–94.
Wilson, Robert. *Joseph Conrad,* 64–82.

The Rescue, 1920

Batchelor, John. *The Life of Joseph Conrad,* 262–65.
GoGwilt, Christopher. *The Invention of the West,* 69–81.
Griffith, John W. *Joseph Conrad and the Anthropological Dilemma,*
50–52.
Harpham, Geoffrey Galt. *One of Us,* 97–111.
Krenn, Heliéna M. "The 'Beautiful' World of Women: Women as Re-
flections of Colonial Issues in Conrad's Malay Novels," in Keith Cara-
bine et al., eds., *Contexts for Conrad,* 115–18.
Phillips, Gene D. *Conrad and Cinema,* 22–24.
Wilson, Robert. *Joseph Conrad,* 136–37.

The Rover, 1923

Batchelor, John. *The Life of Joseph Conrad,* 265–68.
Hampson, Robert. "The Late Novels," in J. H. Stape, ed., *The Cam-
bridge Companion,* 150–53.
La Bossiere, Camille R. "Pop Conrad and Child's Play: A Context for
The Rover." L'Epoque Conradienne 20 (1994), 75–94.
Pendleton, Robert. *Graham Greene's Conradian Masterplot,* 23–25.
Phillips, Gene D. *Conrad and Cinema,* 113–16.
Schwarz, Daniel R. "Joseph Conrad," in John Richetti et al., eds., *The
Columbia History,* 712–13.
Wilson, Robert. *Joseph Conrad,* 125–26.

The Secret Agent, 1907

Armstrong, Paul B. "The Politics of Irony in Reading Conrad." *Conra-
diana* 26 (1994), 85–99.
Batchelor, John. *The Life of Joseph Conrad,* 151–64.
Bernstein, Stephen. "Modernist Spatial Nostalgia: Forster, Conrad,
Woolf," in Beth Rigel Daugherty and Eileen Barrett, eds., *Virginia
Woolf,* 40–44.
Berthoud, Jacques. *"The Secret Agent,"* in J. H. Stape, ed., *The Cam-
bridge Companion,* 100–119.
Cohen, Paula Marantz. "The Ideological Transformation of Conrad's
The Secret Agent into Hitchcock's *Sabotage." Lit/Film Q* 22 (1994),
199–208.
Crick, Brian. "Conrad's Polish Joke: *The Secret Agent* as Domestic
Art." *Cambridge Q* 25 (1996), 124–51.
DiBattista, Maria. "The Lowly Art of Murder: Modernism and the Case
of the Free Woman," in Maria DiBattista and Lucy McDiarmid, eds.,
High and Low Moderns, 186–91.
Eagleton, Terry. "Form, Ideology and *The Secret Agent,"* in Elaine Jor-
dan, ed., *Joseph Conrad,* 158–67.

English, James F. *Comic Transactions*, 34–66.

Fogel, Aaron. "The Fragmentation of Sympathy in *The Secret Agent*," in Elaine Jordan, ed., *Joseph Conrad*, 168–90.

Gillon, Adam. *Joseph Conrad*, 142–43.

GoGwilt, Christopher. *The Invention of the West*, 160–87.

Greenslade, William. *Degeneration, Culture, and the Novel*, 114–18.

Humphries, Reynold. "C'est la faute à l'autre: Le Non-dit idéologique dans *The Secret Agent*." *L'Epoque Conradienne* 21 (1995), 93–102.

Kauhl, Gudrun. "Strategies of Reappraisal: Joseph Conrad's *The Secret Agent*." *Conradiana* 26 (1994), 103–17.

Leavis, L. R. "Marriage, Murder, and Morality: *The Secret Agent* and *Tess*." *Neophilologus* 80 (1996), 161–69.

Mageean, Michael. "*The Secret Agent*'s (T)extimacies: A Traumatic Reading Beyond Rhetoric," in Carola M. Kaplan and Anne B. Simpson, eds., *Seeing Double*, 235–56.

Moffat, Wendy. "Domestic Violence: The Simple Tale within *The Secret Agent*." *Engl Lit in Transition, 1880–1920* 37 (1994), 465–83.

Monk, Leland. *Standard Deviations*, 77–79.

Moseley, William W., Jr. "The Vigilant Society: *The Secret Agent* and Victorian Panopticism." *Conradiana* 29 (1997), 59–75.

Pendleton, Robert. *Graham Greene's Conradian Masterplot*, 42–44, 65–68.

Phillips, Gene D. *Conrad and Cinema*, 51–65.

Ray, Martin. *Joseph Conrad*, 69–90.

Rignall, John. *Realist Fiction*, 137–51.

Sandison, Alan. *Robert Louis Stevenson*, 119–25.

Schwarz, Daniel R. "Joseph Conrad," in John Richetti et al., eds., *The Columbia History*, 706–7.

Shaffer, Brian W. " 'The Commerce of Shady Wares': Politics and Pornography in Conrad's *The Secret Agent*." *ELH* 62 (1995), 443–62.

Stott, Rebecca. *The Fabrication*, 152–62.

Stott, Rebecca. "The Woman in Black: Unravelling Race and Gender in *The Secret Agent*," in Elaine Jordan, ed., *Joseph Conrad*, 193–212.

Sturgess, Philip J. M. *Narrativity*, 106–9.

Thompson, Jon. *Fiction, Crime, and Empire*, 95–107.

Trotter, David. *The English Novel in History*, 254–56.

Turner, Martha A. *Mechanism and the Novel*, 119–33.

Wheatley, Alison E. "The Function of Epithets in Conrad." *Conradiana* 29 (1997), 24–27.

Wilson, Robert. *Joseph Conrad*, 82–102.

Suspense, 1925

Hampson, Robert. "The Late Novels," in J. H. Stape, ed., *The Cambridge Companion*, 153–56.

Under Western Eyes, 1911

Armstrong, Paul B. "Cultural Differences in Conrad and James: *Under Western Eyes* and *The Ambassadors." REAL: Yrbk of Res in Engl and Am Lit* 12 (1996), 146–52.

Batchelor, John. *The Life of Joseph Conrad,* 165–85.

Busza, Andrzej. "Conrad's Tale of Two Cities." *L'Epoque Conradienne* 19 (1993), 107–18.

Carabine, Keith. "Conrad, Apollo Korzeniowski, and Dostoevsky." *Conradiana* 28 (1996), 11–18.

Carabine, Keith. "Construing 'Secrets' and 'Diabolism' in *Under Western Eyes:* A Response to Frank Kermode," in Carabine et al., eds., *Conrad's Literary Career,* 187–207.

Carabine, Keith. *"Under Western Eyes,"* in J. H. Stape, ed., *The Cambridge Companion,* 122–36.

Dalipagic-Csizmazia, Catherine. "Razumov and Raskolnikov: The Path of Torments." *L'Epoque Conradienne* 19 (1993), 71–84.

Erdinast-Vulcan, Daphna. "On the Edge of the Subject: The Heterobiography of Joseph K. Conrad." *Genre* 28 (1995), 307–20.

Gillon, Adam. *Joseph Conrad,* 59–67, 135–41, 146–48.

GoGwilt, Christopher. *The Invention of the West,* 150–75.

Hawthorn, Jeremy. "Joseph Conrad's Theory of Reading," in Andrew Kennedy and Orm Øverland, eds., *Excursions in Fiction,* 102–5.

Kaplan, Carola M. "Conrad's Narrative Occupation of/by Russia in *Under Western Eyes." Conradiana* 27 (1995), 97–112.

Larson, Jil. "Promises, Lies, and Ethical Agency in *Under Western Eyes." Conradiana* 29 (1997), 41–56.

Lothe, Jakob. "Conradian Narrative," in J. H. Stape, ed., *The Cambridge Companion,* 174–75.

Luftig, Victor. *Seeing Together,* 139–43.

Paccaud-Huguet, Josiane. *"Under Western Eyes* and *Hamlet:* Where Angels Fear to Tread." *Conradiana* 26 (1994), 169–84.

Pendleton, Robert. *Graham Greene's Conradian Masterplot,* 44–51, 87–89.

Phillips, Gene D. *Conrad and Cinema,* 43–51.

Ray, Martin. *Joseph Conrad,* 91–108.

Rødstøl, Knut. "The Subversions of the 'Debauch of the Imagination': Ethics and Aesthetics in *Under Western Eyes,"* in Jakob Lothe, ed., *Conrad in Scandinavia,* 225–48.

Schwarz, Daniel R. "Joseph Conrad," in John Richetti et al., eds., *The Columbia History,* 707–8.

Sturgess, Philip J. M. *Narrativity,* 166–88.

Thomas, Brian. "The Symbolism of Textuality in Joseph Conrad's *Under Western Eyes:* Razumov as Literalist of the Imagination." *Conradiana* 28 (1996), 215–27.

Trotter, David. *The English Novel in History,* 256–57.

Wilson, Robert. *Joseph Conrad,* 129–32.

Victory, 1915

> Batchelor, John. *The Life of Joseph Conrad,* 223–27.
> Gillon, Adam. *Joseph Conrad,* 21–40.
> Gordon, Jan B. *Gossip and Subversion,* 367–71.
> Hampson, Robert. "The Late Novels," in J. H. Stape, ed., *The Cambridge Companion,* 144–46.
> Heywood, Leslie. "The Unreadable Text: Conrad and 'The Enigma of Woman' in *Victory." Conradiana* 26 (1994), 3–16.
> Hollahan, Eugene. *Crisis-Consciousness,* 163–64.
> Pendleton, Robert. *Graham Greene's Conradian Masterplot,* 51–55.
> Phillips, Gene D. *Conrad and Cinema,* 25–41.
> Roberts, Andrew Michael. "Economies of Empire and Masculinity in Conrad's *Victory." Kunapipi* 18:1 (1996), 158–67.
> Schwarz, Daniel R. "Joseph Conrad," in John Richetti et al., eds., *The Columbia History,* 708–11.
> Vanderwielen, Betty. "Gender Performance in *Victory." Conradiana* 26 (1994), 201–9.
> Watts, Cedric. "*The Ebb-Tide* and *Victory." Conradiana* 28 (1996), 133–36.
> Wilson, Robert. *Joseph Conrad,* 135–36.
> Yoshida, Tetsuo. "On Captain Davidson." *Stud in Engl Lang and Lit* (Fukuoka) 43 (1993), 49–58.

JOSEPH CONRAD AND FORD MADOX FORD

The Inheritors, 1901

> White, Andrea. "Conrad and Imperialism," in J. H. Stape, ed., *The Cambridge Companion,* 193–94.

Romance, 1903

> Pendleton, Robert. *Graham Greene's Conradian Masterplot,* 12–13.
> Phillips, Gene D. *Conrad and Cinema,* 20–22.

WILLIAM JOHN CONYBEARE

Perversion; or, The Causes and Consequences of Infidelity, 1856
> Antor, Heinz. *Der englische Universitätsroman,* 147–49.

SUSAN MARY COOPER

The Dark Is Rising, 1965

> Krips, Valerie. "Finding One's Place in the Fantastic: Susan Cooper's *The Dark Is Rising,"* in Joe Sanders, ed., *Functions of the Fantastic,* 169–73.

The Grey King, 1977

    Filmer-Davies, Kath. *Fantasy Fiction and Welsh Myth*, 110–16.

Silver on the Tree, 1979

    Filmer-Davies, Kath. *Fantasy Fiction and Welsh Myth*, 116–19.

MARIE CORELLI

Boy: A Sketch, 1900

    Brown, Penny. *The Captured World*, 110–12.

The Mighty Atom, 1896

    Brown, Penny. *The Captured World*, 112–13.

A Romance of Two Worlds, 1886

    Kranidis, Rita S. *Subversive Discourse*, 67–68.

The Sorrows of Satan, 1896

    Kershner, R. B. "Modernism's Mirror: The Sorrows of Marie Corelli," in Nikki Lee Manos and Meri-Jane Rochelson, eds., *Transforming Genres*, 75–77.

ANNIE SOPHIE CORY

Anna Lombard, 1901

    Knapp, Shoshana Milgram. "Revolutionary Androgyny in the Fiction of 'Victoria Cross,' " in Carola M. Kaplan and Anne B. Simpson, eds., *Seeing Double*, 10–11.

Six Chapters of a Man's Life, 1903

    Knapp, Shoshana Milgram. "Revolutionary Androgyny in the Fiction of 'Victoria Cross,' " in Carola M. Kaplan and Anne B. Simpson, eds., *Seeing Double*, 12–16.

PEARL RICHARDS CRAIGIE

The School for Saints, 1897

    Nelson, Carolyn Christensen. *British Women Fiction Writers*, 65–69.

CHARLOTTE DACRE

The Passions, 1811

    Small, Helen. *Love's Madness*, 80–89.

Zofloya, 1806

    Haggerty, George E. "The Gothic Novel, 1764–1824," in John Richetti et al., eds., *The Columbia History*, 234–35.

ANDREW DAVIES

A Very Peculiar Practice: The New Frontier, 1988
  Antor, Heinz. *Der englische Universitätsroman,* 681–83.

MARY DAVYS

The Reform'd Coquet, 1724
  Saje, Natasha. " 'The Assurance to Write, the Vanity of Expecting to be
  Read': Deception and Reform in Mary Davys's *The Reform'd Co-
  quet.*" *Essays in Lit* (Macomb, IL) 23 (1996), 165–75.

W. J. DAWSON

The Redemption of Edward Strahan, 1891
  Hapgood, Lynne. " 'The Reconceiving of Christianity': Secularisation,
  Realism and the Religious Novel: 1888–1900." *Lit and Theology* 10
  (1996), 340–43.

J. P. DAY

The Banner of David, 1992
  Filmer-Davies, Kath. *Fantasy Fiction and Welsh Myth,* 130–35.

WARWICK DEEPING

The Secret Sanctuary, 1923
  Greenslade, William. *Degeneration, Culture, and the Novel,* 235–37.
Sorrell and Son, 1925
  Greenslade, William. *Degeneration, Culture, and the Novel,* 238–40.

DANIEL DEFOE

Captain Singleton, 1720
  Brantlinger, Patrick. *Fictions of State,* 79–85.
  Chambers, Douglas. *The Reinvention of the World,* 61–63.
  Kroll, Richard. "Defoe and Early Narrative," in John Richetti et al., eds.,
  The Columbia History, 35–39.
  Warner, John M. *Joyce's Grandfathers,* 34–38.
  Zhang, Zaixin. *Voices of the Self,* 65–74.
Colonel Jacque, 1722
  Bauer, Matthias. *Im Fuchsbau der Geschichten,* 103–5.
  Kroll, Richard. "Defoe and Early Narrative," in John Richetti et al., eds.,
  The Columbia History, 36–38.

Nelson, T. G. A. *Children, Parents, and the Rise of the Novel*, 199–202.

Novak, Maximillian E. "Defoe and the Art of War." *Philol Q* 75 (1996), 203–11.

Warner, John M. *Joyce's Grandfathers*, 47–49.

Warner, Nicholas O. "The Drunken Wife in Defoe's *Colonel Jack:* An Early Description of Alcohol Addiction." *Dionysos* 1:1 (1989), 3–9.

A Journal of the Plague Year, 1722

Juengel, Scott J. "Writing Decomposition: Defoe and the Corpse." *J of Narrative Technique* 25 (1995), 139–50.

Kroll, Richard. "Defoe and Early Narrative," in John Richetti et al., eds., *The Columbia History*, 31–34.

MacLelland, Jackie. "The Rhetoric of Orality in Defoe's *A Journal of the Plague Year.*" *Conf of Coll Teachers of Engl Stud* 58 (1993), 36–39.

Warner, John M. *Joyce's Grandfathers*, 44–47.

The Memoirs of a Cavalier, 1720

Kroll, Richard. "Defoe and Early Narrative," in John Richetti et al., eds., *The Columbia History*, 39–40.

Novak, Maximillian E. "Defoe and the Art of War." *Philol Q* 75 (1996), 203–11.

Moll Flanders, 1722

Azim, Firdous. *The Colonial Rise of the Novel*, 70–74, 83–86.

Bauer, Matthias. *Im Fuchsbau der Geschichten*, 100–103.

Bauer, Matthias. *Der Schelmenroman*, 168–71.

Bowers, Toni. *The Politics of Motherhood*, 98–111, 121–23.

Cole, David L. "Working Class Culture in the New World: Moll Flanders in America." *Illinois Engl Bull* 83:2 (1996), 8–13.

Di Giuseppe, Rita. "The Ghost in the Machine: *Moll Flanders* and the Body Politic." *Quaderni di Lingue e Letterature* 18 (1993), 311–26.

Hummel, William E. " 'The Gift of My Father's Bounty': Patriarchal Patronization in *Moll Flanders* and *Roxana.*" *Rocky Mountain R of Lang and Lit* 48:2 (1994), 119–41.

Hunter, J. Paul. "Editing for the Classroom: Texts in Contexts." *Stud in the Novel* 27 (1995), 292–94.

Kibbie, Ann Louise. "Monstrous Generation: The Birth of Capital in Defoe's *Moll Flanders* and *Roxana.*" *PMLA* 110 (1995), 1023–28.

Kroll, Richard. "Defoe and Early Narrative," in John Richetti et al., eds., *The Columbia History*, 35–37, 40–46.

Lovitt, Carl R. "Defoe's 'Almost Invisible Hand': Narrative Logic as a Structuring Principle in *Moll Flanders.*" *Eighteenth-Cent Fiction* 6 (1993), 1–28.

Michael, Steven C. "Thinking Parables: What *Moll Flanders* Does Not Say." *ELH* 63 (1996), 367–90.

Nelson, T. G. A. *Children, Parents, and the Rise of the Novel*, 25–27, 137–42.

Rauseo, Chris. "Die gentlewoman und der chevalier: Standesgemäße Erzähler in *Moll Flanders* und *Manon Lescaut.*" *Archiv für das Studium der neueren Sprachen und Literaturen* 231 (1994), 91–101.

Shankman, Steven. "Genre, Didacticism, and the Ethics of Fiction in *Moll Flanders*," in his *In Search of the Classic,* 263–75.

Sherman, Sandra. "Commercial Paper, Commercial Fiction: 'The Compleat English Tradesman' and Defoe's Reluctant Novels." *Criticism* 37 (1995), 393–96.

Siegel, Carol. *Male Masochism,* 112–15.

Stadler, Eva Maria. "Addressing Social Boundaries: Dressing the Female Body in Early Realist Fiction," in Margaret R. Higonnet and Joan Templeton, eds., *Reconfigured Spheres,* 21–25.

Warner, John M. *Joyce's Grandfathers,* 38–44.

Zhang, Zaixin. *Voices of the Self,* 88–112.

A New Voyage Round the World, 1724

Markley, Robert. " 'So Inexhaustible a Treasure of Gold': Defoe, Capitalism, and the Romance of the South Seas." *Eighteenth Cent Life* 18:3 (1994), 148–64.

Robinson Crusoe, 1719

Baines, Paul. " 'Able Mechanick': *The Life and Adventures of Peter Wilkins* and the Eighteenth-Century Fantastic Voyage," in David Seed, ed., *Anticipations,* 5–9.

Bellver, Catherine G. "Robinson Crusoe Revisited: *El año de Gracia* and the Postmodern Ethic." *J of Interdisciplinary Liter Stud* 7:1 (1995), 105–18.

Bertrand, Didier. "Order and Chaos in Paradise: Colonial and 'Postcolonial' Constructions of Religious Identity through the Robinson Crusoe Story." *Rel and Lit* 27:3 (1995), 29–47.

Blewett, David. *The Illustration of "Robinson Crusoe,"* 11–175.

Bond, Clinton. "Representing Reality: Strategies of Realism in the Early English Novel." *Eighteenth-Cent Fiction* 6 (1994), 128–29.

Bonnici, Thomas. "*Robinson Crusoé,* de Defoe, e o Problema do 'Outro.' " *Revista de Letras* 33 (1993), 259–66.

Brown, Homer Obed. *Institutions of the English Novel,* 51–81.

Chambers, Douglas. *The Reinvention of the World,* 56–64.

Connor, Steven. *The English Novel in History,* 182–84.

David, Deirdre. *Rule Britannia,* 49–51.

Donoghue, Frank. "Inevitable Politics: Rulership and Identity in *Robinson Crusoe .*" *Stud in the Novel* 27 (1995), 1–9.

Engélibert, Jean-Paul. "Réécrire *Robinson Crusoé:* mythe littéraire et deuil de la modernité." *Revue de Littérature Comparée* 70 (1996), 52–70.

Fougère, Eric. "Genèse et exégèse du texte dans Robinson Crusoé: l'écriture réflexive de Daniel Defoe." *Stud on Voltaire and the Eighteenth Cent* 341 (1996), 225–37.

Gliserman, Martin. *Psychoanalysis, Language, and the Body of the Text,* 58–83.

Henderson, Andrea K. *Romantic Identities*, 158–60.

Hoegberg, David E. " 'Your pen, your ink': Coetzee's *Foe, Robinson Crusoe,* and the Politics of Parody." *Kunapipi* 17:3 (1995), 86–99.

Hopes, Jeffrey. "Real and Imaginary Stories: *Robinson Crusoe* and the *Serious Reflections.*" *Eighteenth-Cent Fiction* 8 (1996), 313–28.

Hutton, Margaret-Anne. "Getting Away from it All: The Island as a Space of Transformation in Defoe's *Robinson Crusoe* and Tournier's *Vendredi ou les Limbes du Pacifique,*" in Richard Maber, ed., *Nouveaux Mondes*, 121–24.

Kroll, Richard. "Defoe and Early Narrative," in John Richetti et al., eds., *The Columbia History*, 31–36, 39–46.

Lawrence, Karen R. *Penelope Voyages*, 49–56.

McFarlane, Cameron. "Reading Crusoe Reading Providence." *Engl Stud in Canada* 21 (1995), 257–65.

Malchow, H. L. *Gothic Images of Race*, 42–50.

Monk, Leland. *Standard Deviations,* 31–45.

Morrissey, Lee. "Robinson Crusoe and South Sea Trade, 1710–1720," in John Louis DiGaetani, ed., *Money*, 209–14.

Novak, Maximillian E. "Picturing the Thing Itself, or Not: Defoe, Painting, Prose Fiction, and the Arts of Describing." *Eighteenth-Cent Fiction* 9 (1996), 13–20.

Overton, Bill. "Countering *Crusoe:* Two Colonial Narratives." *Crit Survey* 4 (1992), 302–10.

Pickering, Samuel F., Jr. *Moral Instruction and Fiction for Children*, 58–80.

Rees, Christine. *Utopian Imagination and Eighteenth-Century Fiction*, 2–5, 73–102.

Rennie, Neil. *Far-Fetched Facts*, 54–57, 61–63, 73–76.

Rommel, Thomas. "Aspects of Verisimilitude: Temporal and Topographical References in *Robinson Crusoe.*" *Liter & Linguistic Computing* 10 (1995), 279–85.

Sill, Geoffrey M. "Crusoe in the Cave: Defoe and the Semiotics of Desire." *Eighteenth-Cent Fiction* 6 (1994), 215–32.

Sill, Geoffrey M. "A Source for Crusoe's Tobacco Cure." *Engl Lang Notes* 32:4 (1995), 46–48.

Soupel, Serge. "Note sur quelques échos de la mythologie et de la littérature classiques dans *Robinson Crusoe:* Hercule, Crusoe, Enée." *Bull de la Société d'Etudes Anglo-Américaines des XVIIe et XVIIIe Siècles* 35 (1992), 123–28.

Sturgess, Philip J. M. "*Robinson Crusoe:* The Character of Representation." *Recherches Anglaises et Nord-Américaines* 26 (1993), 75–86.

Suerbaum, Ulrich. " 'I Repeat and Repeat': Repetition as Structure in Defoe's *Robinson Crusoe,*" in Elmar Lehmann and Bernd Lenz, eds., *Telling Stories*, 69–83.

Svilpis, Janis. "Bourgeois Solitude in *Robinson Crusoe.*" *Engl Stud in Canada* 22 (1996), 35–42.

Vickers, Ilse. *Defoe and the New Sciences*, 99–131.

Warner, John M. *Joyce's Grandfathers*, 26–34.

Wheeler, Roxann. " 'My Savage,' 'My Man': Racial Multiplicity in *Robinson Crusoe.*" *ELH* 62 (1995), 821–53.

Wiegman, Robyn. "Economies of the Body: Gendered Sites in *Robinson Crusoe* and *Roxana,*" in Arthur F. Marotti et al., eds., *Reading with a Difference*, 217–23.

Zhang, Zaixin. *Voices of the Self,* 52–64.

Roxana, 1724

Azim, Firdous. *The Colonial Rise of the Novel*, 61–87.

Bowers, Toni. *The Politics of Motherhood*, 98–101, 111–23.

Brantlinger, Patrick. "Cashing in on the Real: Money and the Failure of Mimesis in Defoe and Trollope." *Stud in the Liter Imagination* 29:1 (1996), 11–13.

Brantlinger, Patrick. *Fictions of State*, 75–79.

Brown, Homer Obed. *Institutions of the English Novel*, 71–73.

Furbank, P. N., and W. R. Owens. "The 'Lost' Continuation of Defoe's *Roxana.*" *Eighteenth-Cent Fiction* 9 (1997), 299–305.

Hummel, William E. " 'The Gift of My Father's Bounty': Patriarchal Patronization in *Moll Flanders* and *Roxana.*" *Rocky Mountain R of Lang and Lit* 48:2 (1994), 119–41.

Kelly, Veronica. "The Paranormal Roxana," in Bill Readings and Bennet Schaber, eds., *Postmodernism Across the Ages*, 138–49.

Kibbie, Ann Louise. "Monstrous Generation: The Birth of Capital in Defoe's *Moll Flanders* and *Roxana.*" *PMLA* 110 (1995), 1028–32.

Kroll, Richard. "Defoe and Early Narrative," in John Richetti et al., eds., *The Columbia History*, 43–47.

Lawson, Jacqueline Elaine. *Domestic Misconduct,* 35–72.

Nelson, T. G. A. *Children, Parents, and the Rise of the Novel*, 142–51.

New, Peter. "Why Roxana Can Never Find Herself." *Mod Lang R* 91 (1996), 317–29.

Newman, Judie. *The Ballistic Bard*, 96–98.

Osland, Dianne. "Loose Ends in *Roxana* and *The French Lieutenant's Woman.*" *Stud in the Novel* 25 (1993), 381–93.

Snow, Malinda. "Arguments to the Self in Defoe's *Roxana.*" *Stud in Engl Lit, 1500–1900* 34 (1994), 523–34.

Todd, Janet. *The Sign of Angellica*, 261–68.

Warner, John M. *Joyce's Grandfathers*, 49–56.

Wiegman, Robyn. "Economies of the Body: Gendered Sites in *Robinson Crusoe* and *Roxana,*" in Arthur F. Marotti et al., eds., *Reading with a Difference*, 210–16.

Zhang, John Z. "Defoe's 'Man-Woman' Roxana: Gender, Reversal, and Androgyny." *Etudes Anglaises* 46 (1993), 272–86.

Zhang, Zaixin. *Voices of the Self,* 74–87, 113–48.

Zomchick, John P. *Family and the Law,* 32–57.

WALTER DE LA MARE

Henry Brocken, 1904
> Whistler, Theresa. *Imagination of the Heart,* 109–16.

Memoirs of a Midget, 1921
> Whistler, Theresa. *Imagination of the Heart,* 301–10.

The Return, 1910
> Cavaliero, Glen. *The Supernatural and English Fiction,* 125–27.

ETHEL M. DELL

The Way of an Eagle, 1912
> Cadogan, Mary. *And Then Their Hearts Stood Still,* 77–80, 141–42.

THOMAS DELONEY

Jack of Newbury, 1597
> Kegl, Rosemary. *The Rhetoric of Concealment,* 127–66.
> Mesa-Pelly, Judith Broome. "Fantasy and Social Change in Thomas Deloney's *Jack of Newbury* and *Thomas of Reading.*" *Stud in the Hum* 23:1 (1996), 84–96.
> Stemmler, Theo. "The Rise of a New Literary Genre: Thomas Deloney's Bourgeois Novel *Jack of Newbury,*" in Elmar Lehmann and Bernd Lenz, eds., *Telling Stories,* 47–55.
> Suzuki, Mihoko. "The London Apprentice Riots of the 1590s and the Fiction of Thomas Deloney." *Criticism* 38 (1996), 189–98, 206–8.
> Tribble, Evelyn B. " 'We Will Do No Harm without Swords': Royal Representation, Civic Pageantry, and the Displacement of Popular Protest in Thomas Deloney's *Jacke of Newberie,*" in Alvin Vos, ed., *Place and Displacement,* 145–57.

Thomas of Reading, 1597
> Mesa-Pelly, Judith Broome. "Fantasy and Social Change in Thomas Deloney's *Jack of Newbury* and *Thomas of Reading.*" *Stud in the Hum* 23:1 (1996), 84–96.
> Suzuki, Mihoko. "The London Apprentice Riots of the 1590s and the Fiction of Thomas Deloney." *Criticism* 38 (1996), 198–208.

CLAIRE DE PRATZ

Elisabeth Davenay, 1909
> Miller, Jane Eldridge. *Rebel Women,* 136–38.

COLIN DEXTER

Last Bus to Woodstock, 1989

> Reynolds, William. "Paradigm Established, Paradigm Surpassed: Colin Dexter's *Last Bus to Woodstock,"* in Mary Jean DeMarr, ed., *In the Beginning,* 203–22.

The Way Through the Woods, 1992

> Reynolds, William. "Paradigm Established, Paradigm Surpassed: Colin Dexter's *Last Bus to Woodstock,"* in Mary Jean DeMarr, ed., *In the Beginning,* 214–22.

CHARLES DICKENS

Barnaby Rudge, 1841

> Andrews, Malcolm. *Dickens and the Grown-up Child,* 75–77.
> Collins, Philip. *Dickens and Crime,* 44–51, 221–23, 274–76.
> Connor, Steven. "Space, Place and the Body of Riot in *Barnaby Rudge,"* in Connor, ed., *Charles Dickens,* 211–28.
> Horsman, Alan. *The Victorian Novel,* 108–12.
> Johnson, Derek. *Pastoral in . . . Dickens,* 233–35, 237–38.
> Joyce, Simon. "Resisting Arrest/Arresting Resistance: Crime Fiction, Cultural Studies, and the 'Turn to History.' " *Criticism* 37 (1995), 317–22.
> McGuire, Matthew J. *The Role of Women,* 19–21.
> Marlow, James E. *Charles Dickens,* 42–44, 83–85.
> Marshall, Tim. *Murdering to Dissect,* 38–44, 110–26.
> Netto, Jeffrey A. "Dickens with Kant and Sade." *Style* 29 (1995), 451–52.
> Reed, John R. *Dickens and Thackeray,* 122–33.
> Rosenberg, Brian. *Little Dorrit's Shadows,* 71, 107, 120–21.
> Stone, Harry. *The Night Side of Dickens,* 225–28.
> Tambling, Jeremy. *Dickens, Violence and the Modern State,* 131–34.
> Visser, Nicholas. "Roaring Beasts and Raging Floods: The Representation of Political Crowds in the Nineteenth-Century British Novel." *Mod Lang R* 89 (1994), 302–4.

Bleak House, 1853

> Allen, Dennis W. *Sexuality in Victorian Fiction,* 84–109.
> Benton, Graham. " 'And Dying Thus Around Us Every Day': Pathology, Ontology and the Discourse of the Diseased Body—A Study of Illness and Contagion in *Bleak House." Dickens Q* 11 (1994), 69–79.
> Blum, Virginia L. *Hide and Seek,* 128–30, 148–54.
> Budd, Dona. "Language Couples in *Bleak House." Nineteenth-Cent Lit* 49 (1994), 196–220.
> Clarkson, Carrol. "Alias and Alienation in *Bleak House:* Identity in Language." *Dickens Stud Annual* 23 (1994), 121–34.

Collins, Philip. *Dickens and Crime*, 203–11.

Dever, Carolyn M. "Broken Mirror, Broken Words: Autobiography, Prosopopeia, and the Dead Mother in *Bleak House*." *Stud in the Novel* 27 (1995), 515–27.

Fasik, Laura. "Dickens and the Diseased Body in *Bleak House*." *Dickens Stud Annual* 24 (1996), 135–46.

Felber, Lynette. " 'Delightfully Irregular': Esther's Nascent *écriture féminine* in *Bleak House*." *Victorian Newsl* 85 (1994), 13–19.

Fielding, Kenneth. "*Bleak House* and Dickens' Originals: 'The Romantic Side of Familiar Things.' " *Dickens Stud Annual* 24 (1996), 119–31.

Foltinek, Herbert. "Charles Dickens and the Identity of the Narrator," in Herbert Foltinek et al., eds., *Tales and "their telling difference,"* 205–20.

Foor, Sheila M. *Dickens' Rhetoric*, 4–9, 13–24, 27–43, 45–60, 63–82, 85–94, 99–106, 109–24, 127–32, 135–40.

Fulweiler, Howard W. "*Here A Captive Heart Busted,*" 63–93.

Ginsburg, Michael Peled. *Economies of Change*, 143–48.

Gordon, Jan B. "Dickens and the Political Economy of the Eye." *Dickens Stud Annual* 24 (1996), 24–31.

Gordon, Jan B. *Gossip and Subversion*, 155–236.

Gottfried, Barbara. "Household Arrangements and the Patriarchal Order in *Bleak House*." *J of Narrative Technique* 24 (1994), 1–13.

Hall, Jasmine Yong. "What Troubling About Esther?: Narrating, Policing and Resisting Arrest in *Bleak House*." *Dickens Stud Annual* 22 (1993), 171–91.

Hara, Eiichi. "*Bleak House* and the Reign of Metaphor." *Poetica* (Tokyo) 36 (1992), 55–68.

Horsman, Alan. *The Victorian Novel*, 126–32.

Houston, Gail Turley. *Consuming Fictions*, 123–33.

Jacoby, N. M. "Krook's Dyslexia." *Dickensian* 91 (1995), 102–6.

Jadwin, Lisa. " 'Caricatured, not faithfully rendered': *Bleak House* as a Revision of *Jane Eyre*." *Mod Lang Stud* 26: 2–3 (1996), 111–31.

Johnson, Derek. *Pastoral in . . . Dickens*, 153–54, 247–49.

Kucich, John. "Dickens," in John Richetti et al., eds., *The Columbia History*, 402–4.

Landon, Philip. "Great Exhibitions: Representations of the Crystal Palace in Mayhew, Dickens, and Dostoevsky." *Nineteenth-Cent Contexts* 20:1 (1997), 36–43.

Lerner, Laurence. *Angels and Absences*, 121–24.

Lucas, John. "Past and Present: *Bleak House* and *A Child's History of England*," in John Schad, ed., *Dickens Refigured*, 136–55.

McGuire, Matthew J. *The Role of Women*, 45–48.

McKnight, Natalie J. *Suffering Mothers*, 45–47.

Maglavera, Soultana. *Time Patterns in Later Dickens*, 38–64.

Marlow, James E. *Charles Dickens*, 52–56, 159–62.

Michie, Elsie B. *Outside the Pale*, 8–11, 98–105, 109–11.

Miller, D. A. "Discipline in Different Voices: Bureaucracy, Police, Family, and *Bleak House*," in Steven Connor, ed., *Charles Dickens*, 135–47.

Miller, J. Hillis. "Dickens's *Bleak House*," in Steven Connor, ed., *Charles Dickens*, 59–75.

Miller, J. Hillis. "The Topography of Jealousy in *Our Mutual Friend*," in John Schad, ed., *Dickens Refigured*, 218–20.

Mota, Miguel M. "The Construction of the Christian Community in Charles Dickens' *Bleak House*." *Renascence* 46 (1994), 187–96.

Murray, Brian. *Charles Dickens*, 137–46.

Nord, Deborah Epstein. *Walking the Victorian Streets*, 96–109, 241–44.

Norman, Ralph V. "The Importance of Being Esther." *Soundings* 75 (1992), 199–214.

O'Hara, Kieron. "Self-Deception in *Bleak House:* A Reply to David Cowles." *Dickensian* 91 (1995), 118–22.

Reed, John R. *Dickens and Thackeray*, 207–18.

Rignall, John. *Realist Fiction*, 62–79.

Roberts, Adam. "Dickens's Megalosaurus." *Notes and Queries* 40 (1993), 478–79.

Roberts, Adam. "Skimpole, Leigh Hunt and Dickens's 'Remonstrance.' " *Dickensian* 92 (1996), 177–85.

Rosenberg, Brian. *Little Dorrit's Shadows*, 74–75, 140–43.

Sadrin, Anny. *Parentage and Inheritance*, 64–73.

Schad, John. "Dickens's Cryptic Church: Drawing on *Pictures from Italy*," in Schad, ed., *Dickens Refigured*, 9–11.

Smith, Monika Rydygier. "The W/hole Remains: Consumerist Politics in *Bleak House, Great Expectations*, and *Our Mutual Friend*." *Victorian R* 19:1 (1993), 1–16.

Spiegel, Maura. "Managing Pain: Suffering and Reader Sympathy in *Bleak House*." *Dickens Q* 12 (1995), 3–9.

Stone, Harry. *The Night Side of Dickens*, 139–50.

Sutherland, John. *Is Heathcliff a Murderer?*, 90–98.

Tambling, Jeremy. *Dickens, Violence and the Modern State*, 71–97.

Thomas, Ronald R. "Making Darkness Visible: Capturing the Criminal and Observing the Law in Victorian Photography and Detective Fiction," in Carol T. Christ and John O. Jordan, eds., *Victorian Literature*, 137–46.

Thoms, Peter. " 'The Narrow Track of Blood': Detection and Storytelling in *Bleak House*." *Nineteenth-Cent Lit* 50 (1995), 147–67.

Trotter, David. "Dickens's Idle Men," in John Schad, ed., *Dickens Refigured*, 210–13.

Turner, Martha A. *Mechanism and the Novel*, 79–98.

West, Gilian. "Family Connections: The Influence of the Crewe Family on *Bleak House*." *Dickensian* 91 (1995), 5–24.

West, John B. "Krook's Death by Spontaneous Combustion and the Controversy between Dickens and Lewes: A Physiologist's View." *Dickensian* 90 (1994), 125–28.

Wheeler, Michael. *English Fiction of the Victorian Period*, 90–91.

Wilson, Brendan. " 'He thought it a very good Philosophy': Moral Taxonomy in *Bleak House." Poetica* (Tokyo) 38 (1993), 116–37.

The Chimes, 1844

Johnson, Derek. *Pastoral in . . . Dickens,* 241–44.

Reed, John R. *Dickens and Thackeray,* 155–57.

A Christmas Carol, 1843

Andrews, Malcolm. *Dickens and the Grown-up Child,* 102–11.

Callahan, Charles W., Jr. "Tiny Tim: The Child with a Crippling Fatal Illness." *Dickensian* 89 (1993), 214–17.

Collins, Philip. "The Reception and Status of the *Carol." Dickensian* 89 (1993), 170–75.

Eigner, Edwin M. "On Becoming Pantaloon." *Dickensian* 89 (1993), 177–82.

Grossman, Jonathan H. "The Absent Jew in Dickens: Narrators in *Oliver Twist, Our Mutual Friend,* and *A Christmas Carol." Dickens Stud Annual* 24 (1996), 49–53.

Jaffe, Audrey. "Spectacular Sympathy: Visuality and Ideology in Dickens's *A Christmas Carol." PMLA* 109 (1994), 254–63. (Also in Carol T. Christ and John O. Jordan, eds., *Victorian Literature,* 327–40.)

Lerner, Laurence. *Angels and Absences,* 114–16.

McCracken-Flesher, Caroline. "The Incorporation of *A Christmas Carol:* A Tale of Seasonal Screening." *Dickens Stud Annual* 24 (1996), 93–116.

Miller, J. Hillis. "The Genres of *A Christmas Carol." Dickensian* 89 (1993), 193–206.

Patterson, Arthur P. "Sponging the Stone: Transformation in *A Christmas Carol." Dickens Q* 11 (1994), 172–76.

Reed, John R. *Dickens and Thackeray,* 154–55.

Sasaki, Toru. "Ghosts in *A Christmas Carol:* A Japanese View." *Dickensian* 92 (1996), 187–94.

Shainess, Natalie. "Charles Dickens: The First (Interpersonal) Psychoanalyst; or, *A Christmas Carol:* A Literary Psychoanalysis." *Am J of Psychoanalysis* 52 (1992), 351–62.

Slater, Michael. "The Triumph of Humour: The *Carol* Revisited." *Dickensian* 89 (1993), 184–91.

Stone, Harry. *The Night Side of Dickens,* 465–70.

Tillotson, Kathleen. "A Background for *A Christmas Carol." Dickensian* 89 (1993), 165–69.

David Copperfield, 1850

Andrews, Malcolm. *Dickens and the Grown-up Child,* 135–70.

Bauer, Matthias. "Orpheus and the Shades: The Myth of the Poet in *David Copperfield." Univ of Toronto Q* 63 (1993–94), 308–24.

Bottum, Joseph. "The Gentleman's True Name: *David Copperfield* and the Philosophy of Naming." *Nineteenth-Cent Lit* 49 (1995), 435–55.

Cain, Tom. "Tolstoy's Use of *David Copperfield,*" in W. Gareth Jones, ed., *Tolstoi and Britain*, 67–78.

Collier, Peter, and Carola Hicks. "Proust and Dickens: The Windows of Memory and the Influence of Anxiety." *New Comparison* 14 (1992), 172–80.

Collins, Philip. *Dickens and Crime*, 113–15, 155–63.

Cronin, Mark. "The Rake, The Writer, and *The Stranger:* Textual Relations between *Pendennis* and *David Copperfield.*" *Dickens Stud Annual* 24 (1996), 215–37.

Darby, Margaret Flanders. "Dora and Doady." *Dickens Stud Annual* 22 (1993), 155–68.

Davies, James A. "Dickens and the Region in *David Copperfield.*" *Swansea R* 1994, 187–96.

Friedman, Stanley. "Heep and Powell: Dickensian Revenge?" *Dickensian* 90 (1994), 36–42.

Gager, Valerie L. *Shakespeare and Dickens*, 175–77, 193–200, 225–44.

Gervais, David. "Dickens's Comic Speech: Inventing the Self." *Yrbk of Engl Stud* 25 (1995), 131–33.

Hager, Kelly. "Estranging *David Copperfield:* Reading the Novel of Divorce." *ELH* 63 (1996), 989–1017.

Heyns, Michiel. *Expulsion and the Nineteenth-Century Novel*, 106–10.

Horsman, Alan. *The Victorian Novel*, 118–25.

Houston, Gail Turley. *Consuming Fictions*, 99–122.

Houston, Gail Turley. "Gender Construction and the Künstlerroman: *David Copperfield* and *Aurora Leigh.*" *Philol Q* 72 (1993), 213–34.

Johnson, Derek. *Pastoral in . . . Dickens*, 21–29.

Kucich, John. "Dickens," in John Richetti et al., eds., *The Columbia History*, 402–5.

Lee, Hsiao-Hung. *"Possibilities of Hidden Things,"* 101–34.

Leger, J. Michael. "Triangulation and Homoeroticism in *David Copperfield.*" *Victorian Lit and Culture* 23 (1995), 301–20.

Lerner, Laurence. "Stereotypes of Woman in Victorian England," in John Morris, ed., *Exploring Stereotyped Images*, 44–46.

Levenson, Michael H. "The Private Life of a Public Form: Freud, Fantasy, and the Novel," in Robert M. Polhemus and Roger B. Henkle, eds., *Critical Reconstructions*, 58–60, 64–70.

McGuire, Matthew J. *The Role of Women*, 36–39.

McSweeney, Kerry. *"David Copperfield* and the Music of Memory." *Dickens Stud Annual* 23 (1994), 93–117.

Marlow, James E. *Charles Dickens*, 49–52, 155–59.

Michie, Elsie B. *Outside the Pale*, 93–95.

Mugglestone, Lynda. "Fictions of Speech: Literature and the Literate Speaker in the Nineteenth-Century Novel." *Yrbk of Engl Stud* 25 (1995), 123–27.

Murray, Brian. *Charles Dickens*, 123–36.

Olson, Ted. "His Changing Nature: Comparing Dickens's Two 'Autobiographical' Novels." *Publs of the Mississippi Philol Assoc* 1992, 119–24.

Polhemus, Robert M. "Lewis Carroll and the Child in Victorian Fiction," in John Richetti et al., eds., *The Columbia History*, 593–94.

Reed, John R. *Dickens and Thackeray,* 187–206.

Reynolds, Kimberley, and Nicola Humble. *Victorian Heroines,* 157–62.

Rosenberg, Brian. *Little Dorrit's Shadows,* 107–8.

Sadrin, Anny. *Parentage and Inheritance,* 1–3, 10–11.

Schad, John. "Dickens's Cryptic Church: Drawing on *Pictures from Italy,"* in Schad, ed., *Dickens Refigured,* 13–15.

Shires, Linda M. "Literary Careers, Death, and the Body Politics of *David Copperfield,"* in John Schad, ed., *Dickens Refigured,* 117–33.

Sroka, Kenneth M. "Dickens' Metafiction: Readers and Writers in *Oliver Twist, David Copperfield,* and *Our Mutual Friend." Dickens Stud Annual* 22 (1993), 42–51.

Stone, Harry. *The Night Side of Dickens,* 107–24, 353–56.

Wheeler, Michael. *English Fiction of the Victorian Period,* 85–87, 93–95.

Wilt, Judith. *Abortion, Choice, and Contemporary Fiction,* 120–23.

Winkgens, Meinhard. "Natur als Palimpsest: Der eingeschriebene Subtext in Charles Dickens' *David Copperfield,"* in Konrad Groß et al., eds., *Das Natur/Kultur-Paradigma,* 35–61.

Winnifrith, Tom. *Fallen Women,* 93–96, 105–8.

Zhang, Yu. "Acculturation beyond Recognition: Lin Shu's Treatment of Women Characters in His Translation of *David Copperfield,"* in Cristina Bacchilega and Cornelia N. Moore, eds., *Constructions and Confrontations,* 170–79.

Dombey and Son, 1848

Alter, Robert. "Reading Style in Dickens." *Philos and Lit* 19 (1995), 131–33.

Andrews, Malcolm. *Dickens and the Grown-up Child,* 112–34.

Armstrong, Mary. "Pursuing Perfection: *Dombey and Son,* Female Homoerotic Desire, and the Sentimental Heroine." *Stud in the Novel* 28 (1996), 281–98.

Cohen, Michael. *Sisters,* 126–31.

David, Deirdre. *Rule Britannia,* 64–76.

Elfenbein, Andrew. "Managing the House in *Dombey and Son:* Dickens and the Uses of Analogy." *Stud in Philology* 92 (1995), 361–82.

Ermarth, Elizabeth Deeds. *The English Novel in History,* 31–33.

Gager, Valerie L. *Shakespeare and Dickens,* 201–7, 213–22.

Gomel, Elana. "The Body of Parts: Dickens and the Poetics of Synecdoche." *J of Narrative Technique* 26 (1996), 48–50.

Henkle, Roger B. "The Crisis of Representation in *Dombey and Son,"* in Robert M. Polhemus and Roger B. Henkle, eds., *Critical Reconstructions,* 90–110.

Heyns, Michiel. *Expulsion and the Nineteenth-Century Novel,* 97–101.

Horsman, Alan. *The Victorian Novel*, 116–20.

Houston, Gail Turley. *Consuming Fictions*, 90–99.

John, Juliet. "Dickens' Deviant Women: A Reassessment." *Crit R* 34 (1994), 68–78.

Johnson, Derek. *Pastoral in . . . Dickens*, 199–203.

Klaver, Claudia. "Revaluing Money: *Dombey and Son*'s Moral Critique," in Anthony Purdy, ed., *Literature and Money*, 105–32.

Kucich, John. "Dickens," in John Richetti et al., eds., *The Columbia History*, 397–98.

Lerner, Laurence. *Angels and Absences*, 82–94, 117–20, 185–87.

McBride, Mary G. "Contemporary Economic Metaphors in *Dombey and Son*." *Dickensian* 90 (1994), 19–23.

McGuire, Matthew J. *The Role of Women*, 28–32.

McKnight, Natalie J. *Suffering Mothers*, 42–44.

Marks, Patricia. "Paul Dombey and the Milk of Human Kindness." *Dickens Q* 11 (1994), 14–23.

Murray, Brian. *Charles Dickens*, 111–23.

Nord, Deborah Epstein. *Walking the Victorian Streets*, 86–99.

Nygaard, Susan. "Redecorating Dombey: The Power of a 'A Woman's Anger' versus Upholstery in *Dombey and Son*." *Crit Matrix* 8:1 (1994), 40–80.

Perera, Suvendrini. *Reaches of Empire*, 59–77.

Polhemus, Robert M. "Lewis Carroll and the Child in Victorian Fiction," in John Richetti et al., eds., *The Columbia History*, 595–96.

Reed, John R. *Dickens and Thackeray*, 169–86.

Sadrin, Anny. *Parentage and Inheritance*, 44–63.

Sage, Victor. "Gothic Laughter: Farce and Horror in Five Texts," in Allan Lloyd Smith and Victor Sage, eds., *Gothick Origins and Innovations*, 195–97.

Stone, Harry. *The Night Side of Dickens*, 198–215.

Suchoff, David. *Critical Theory and the Novel*, 41–43.

Tambling, Jeremy. "Death and Modernity in *Dombey and Son*." *Essays in Criticism* 43 (1993), 308–27.

Tambling, Jeremy. *Dickens, Violence and the Modern State*, 48–70.

Wiley, Margaret. "Mother's Milk and Dombey's Son." *Dickens Q* 13 (1996), 217–25.

Great Expectations, 1861

Andrews, Malcolm. *Dickens and the Grown-up Child*, 94–96.

Bailin, Miriam. *The Sickroom in Victorian Fiction*, 88–89.

Brooks, Peter. "Repetition, Repression and Return: The Plotting of *Great Expectations*," in Steven Connor, ed., *Charles Dickens*, 34–57.

Burgan, William M. "Orlick's Hammers and Pip's Third Degree," in Marie Mulvey Roberts and Hugh Ormsby-Lennon, eds., *Secret Texts*, 258–65.

Campbell, Elizabeth. "*Great Expectations*: Dickens and the Language of Fortune." *Dickens Stud Annual* 24 (1996), 153–63.

Cohen, William A. *Sex Scandal*, 29–33, 35–72.

Crowley, James P. "Pip's Spiritual Exercise: The Meditative Mode in Dickens' *Great Expectations.*" *Renascence* 46 (1994), 133–41.

Cunningham, John. "Christian Allusion, Comedic Structure, and the Metaphor of Baptism in *Great Expectations.*" *South Atlantic R* 59:2 (1994), 35–49.

Dessner, Lawrence Jay. "Arthur Havisham or Mr Arthur?" *Dickensian* 91 (1995), 123–25.

Dutheil, Martine Hennard. "*Great Expectations* as Reading Lesson." *Dickens Q* 13 (1996), 164–72.

Edgecombe, Rodney Stenning. "Violence, Death and Euphemism in *Great Expectations.*" *Victorians Inst J* 22 (1994), 85–98.

Galbraith, Mary. "Pip as 'Infant Tongue' and as Adult Narrator in Chapter One of *Great Expectations,*" in Elizabeth Goodenough et al., eds., *Infant Tongues*, 123–39.

Gardner, Colin. "Transition and Transformation: Shakespeare, Dickens, Serote." *Engl Stud in Africa* 37:2 (1994), 5–6.

Gordon, Jan B. "Dickens and the Political Economy of the Eye." *Dickens Stud Annual* 24 (1996), 1–10.

Hall, Donald E. *Fixing Patriarchy*, 175–95.

Hannon, Patrice. "The Aesthetics of Humour in *Great Expectations.*" *Dickensian* 92 (1996), 91–105.

Hennard, Martine. "La Leçon de lecture de *Great Expectations.*" *Etudes de Lettres* 3 (1993), 105–19.

Heyns, Michiel. *Expulsion and the Nineteenth-Century Novel*, 115–17.

Horsman, Alan. *The Victorian Novel*, 144–49.

Houston, Gail Turley. *Consuming Fictions*, 157–70.

Jordan, John O. "Partings Welded Together: Self-Fashioning in *Great Expectations* and *Jane Eyre.*" *Dickens Q* 13 (1996), 19–32.

Kucich, John. "Dickens," in John Richetti et al., eds., *The Columbia History*, 389–91.

McGuire, Matthew J. *The Role of Women*, 41–44.

McKnight, Natalie J. *Suffering Mothers*, 43–45.

Maglavera, Soultana. *Time Patterns in Later Dickens*, 138–62.

Marlow, James E. *Charles Dickens*, 98–102.

Morris, Christopher D. "The Bad Faith of Pip's Bad Faith: Deconstructing *Great Expectations*," in Steven Connor, ed., *Charles Dickens*, 76–88.

Murray, Brian. *Charles Dickens*, 168–77.

Olson, Ted. "His Changing Nature: Comparing Dickens's Two 'Autobiographical' Novels." *Publs of the Mississippi Philol Assoc* 1992, 119–24.

Reed, John R. *Dickens and Thackeray*, 270–88.

Sadrin, Anny. *Parentage and Inheritance*, 95–120.

Siegel, Carol. *Male Masochism*, 141–48.

Small, Helen. *Love's Madness*, 207–20.

Smith, Grahame. *Charles Dickens*, 159–78.

Smith, Monika Rydygier. "The W/hole Remains: Consumerist Politics in *Bleak House, Great Expectations,* and *Our Mutual Friend." Victorian R* 19:1 (1993), 1–16.

Stone, Harry. *The Night Side of Dickens,* 11–15, 125–39, 342–45, 364–71.

Tambling, Jeremy. *Dickens, Violence and the Modern State,* 17–47.

Tambling, Jeremy. "Prison-Bound: Dickens and Foucault (*Great Expectations*)," in Steven Connor, ed., *Charles Dickens,* 117–34.

Tatham, Michael. "The Curious Connection: The Role of Millwood in *Great Expectations." Dickensian* 92 (1996), 106–9.

Walsh, Susan. "Bodies of Capital: *Great Expectations* and the Climacteric Economy." *Victorian Stud* 37 (1993), 73–96.

Wheeler, Michael. *English Fiction of the Victorian Period,* 112–14.

York, R. A. *Strangers and Secrets,* 119–33.

Hard Times, 1854

Carr, Jean Ferguson. "Writing as a Woman: Dickens, *Hard Times* and and Feminine Discourses," in Steven Connor, ed., *Charles Dickens,* 159–73.

Colby, Robin B. *"Some Appointed Work To Do,"* 26–28.

Dahmane, Razak. " 'A Mere Question of Figures': Measures, Mystery, and Metaphor in *Hard Times." Dickens Stud Annual* 23 (1994), 137–58.

Duncan, Edwin. "*Adam Bede, Hard Times,* and Melodrama." *Lamar J of the Hum* 19:1 (1993), 43–55.

Fowler, Roger. "Polyphony and Problematic in *Hard Times,*" in Steven Connor, ed., *Charles Dickens,* 100–115.

Guy, Josephine M. *The Victorian Social-Problem Novel,* 13–17, 52–57, 121–37.

Harsh, Constance D. *Subversive Heroines,* 50–55, 68–72, 85–88.

Horsman, Alan. *The Victorian Novel,* 132–34.

Ingham, Patricia. *The Language of Gender and Class,* 78–101.

Kearns, Katherine. *Nineteenth-Century Literary Realism,* 179–204.

Levy, Eric P. "Dickens' Pathology of Time in *Hard Times." Philol Q* 74 (1995), 189–205.

McGuire, Matthew J. *The Role of Women,* 48–49.

Maglavera, Soultana. *Time Patterns in Later Dickens,* 65–92.

Marlow, James E. *Charles Dickens,* 55–59, 108–10, 162–64.

Michie, Elsie B. *Outside the Pale,* 122–31.

Murray, Brian. *Charles Dickens,* 146–53.

Nayak, Jatindra, and Himansu Mohapatra. "Utilitarianism at Home and Abroad: A Comparative Study of Charles Dickens's *Hard Times* and Fakir Mohan Senapati's *Chha Mana Atha Guntha." Intl Fiction R* 22 (1995), 80–88.

van Peer, Willie. "Literature, Imagination, and Human Rights." *Philos and Lit* 19 (1995), 284–89.

Pulsford, Stephen. "The Aesthetic and the Closed Shop: The Ideology of the Aesthetic in Dickens's *Hard Times.*" *Victorian R* 21 (1995), 145–58.

Reed, John R. *Dickens and Thackeray,* 219–33.

Retan, Katherine A. "Lower-Class Angels in the Middle-Class House: The Domestic Woman's 'Progress' in *Hard Times* and *Ruth.*" *Dickens Stud Annual* 23 (1994), 183–92.

Sicher, Efraim. "Acts of Enclosure: The Moral Landscape of Dickens' *Hard Times.*" *Dickens Stud Annual* 22 (1993), 195–213.

Stewart, Garrett. *Dear Reader*, 221–24.

Terry, R. C. " 'Have at the Masters!': Working-Class Stereotypes in Some Nineteenth-Century Novels," in John Morris, ed., *Exploring Stereotyped Images,* 177–83.

Thatcher, Barry. "Dickens' Bow to the Language Theory Debate." *Dickens Stud Annual* 23 (1994), 17–45.

Toker, Leona. "*Hard Times* and a Critique of Utopia: A Typological Study." *Narrative* 4 (1996), 218–31.

Wheeler, Michael. *English Fiction of the Victorian Period*, 88–90.

Zander, Horst. " 'A Jaundiced Jail' oder 'Die Familie als Zelle der Gesellschaft': Die Darstellung der Familie im früh- und mittviktorianischen Roman." *Zeitschrift für Anglistik und Amerikanistik* 43 (1995), 330–35.

The Haunted Man, 1847

Carse, Wendy K. "Domestic Transformation in Dickens' 'The Haunted Man.' " *Dickens Stud Annual* 23 (1994), 163–77.

Rosenberg, Brian. *Little Dorrit's Shadows*, 121–23.

Stone, Harry. *The Night Side of Dickens*, 463–69.

Little Dorrit, 1857

Bakhtin, Mikhail. "Heteroglossia in the Novel: *Little Dorrit*," in Steven Connor, ed., *Charles Dickens*, 91–99.

Bennett, Rachel. "Hajji and Mermaid in *Little Dorrit.*" *R of Engl Stud* 46 (1995), 174–90.

Born, Daniel. *The Birth of Liberal Guilt,* 30–51.

Cohen, Michael. *Sisters*, 131–37.

Collins, Philip. *Dickens and Crime*, 137–39.

Easson, Angus. "A Novel Scarcely Historical? Time and History in Dickens's *Little Dorrit.*" *Essays and Stud* (London) 44 (1991), 27–40.

Edgecombe, Rodney Stenning. "Reading through the Past: 'Archaeological' Conceits and Procedures in *Little Dorrit.*" *Yrbk of Engl Stud* 26 (1996), 65–72.

Eigner, Edwin M. "Dogmatism and Puppyism: The Novelist, the Reviewer, and the Serious Subject: The Case of *Little Dorrit.*" *Dickens Stud Annual* 22 (1993), 217–34.

Elam, Diane. " 'Another day done and I'm deeper in debt': *Little Dorrit* and the Debt of the Everyday," in John Schad, ed., *Dickens Refigured*, 157–74.

Gordon, Jan B. "Dickens and the Political Economy of the Eye." *Dickens Stud Annual* 24 (1996), 11–19.

Hall, Donald E. *Fixing Patriarchy*, 107–30.

Harsh, Constance D. *Subversive Heroines*, 148–58, 163–65.

Heyns, Michiel. *Expulsion and the Nineteenth-Century Novel*, 112–16.

Horsman, Alan. *The Victorian Novel*, 134–41.

Houston, Gail Turley. *Consuming Fictions*, 133–53.

Ingham, Patricia. "Nobody's Fault: The Scope of the Negative in *Little Dorrit*," in John Schad, ed., *Dickens Refigured*, 98–116.

Innes, Christopher. "Adapting Dickens to the Modern Eye: *Nicholas Nickleby* and *Little Dorrit*," in Peter Reynolds, ed., *Novel Images*, 73–78.

Johnson, Derek. *Pastoral in . . . Dickens*, 27–30, 43–45.

Kucich, John. "Dickens," in John Richetti et al., eds., *The Columbia History*, 388–90.

Lapinski, Piya Pal. "Dickens's Miss Wade and J. S. Le Fanu's Carmilla: The Female Vampire in *Little Dorrit*." *Dickens Q* 11 (1994), 81–86.

McGuire, Matthew J. *The Role of Women*, 50–54.

Maglavera, Soultana. *Time Patterns in Later Dickens*, 93–120.

Marlow, James E. *Charles Dickens*, 59–63, 167–76.

Marsh, Joss Lutz. "Inimitable Double Vision: Dickens, *Little Dorrit*, Photography, Film." *Dickens Stud Annual* 22 (1993), 239–82.

Michie, Elsie B. *Outside the Pale*, 150–52, 155–59.

Murray, Brian. *Charles Dickens*, 155–68.

Peters, Laura. "The Histories of Two Self-Tormentors: Orphans and Power in *Little Dorrit*." *Dickensian* 91 (1995), 187–96.

Philpotts, Trey. "Trevelyan, Treasury, and Circumlocution." *Dickens Stud Annual* 22 (1993), 283–99.

Rainsford, Dominic. "Flatness and Ethical Responsibility in *Little Dorrit*." *Victorian Newsl* 88 (1995), 11–17.

Reed, John R. *Dickens and Thackeray*, 234–46.

Rosenberg, Brian. *Little Dorrit's Shadows*, 31–48.

Sadrin, Anny. *Parentage and Inheritance*, 74–94.

Schad, John. "Dickens's Cryptic Church: Drawing on *Pictures from Italy*," in Schad, ed., *Dickens Refigured*, 8–11.

Sirabian, Robert. "Dickens's *Little Dorrit*." *Explicator* 54 (1996), 216–19.

Spiegel, Maura. "Unfelt Feelings: An Evolving Grammar of Hidden Motives." *Victorian Lit and Culture* 23 (1995), 256–58.

Suchoff, David. *Critical Theory and the Novel*, 44–88.

Tambling, Jeremy. *Dickens, Violence and the Modern State*, 98–128.

Wall, William G. "Mrs. Affery Flintwinch's Dreams: Reading and Remembering in *Little Dorrit*." *Dickens Q* 10 (1993), 202–6.

Wheeler, Michael. *English Fiction of the Victorian Period*, 95–98.

Martin Chuzzlewit, 1844

Andrews, Malcolm. *Dickens and the Grown-up Child*, 92–94.

Baubles, Raymond L., Jr. "Displaced Persons: The Cost of Speculation in Charles Dickens' *Martin Chuzzlewit,"* in John Louis DiGaetani, ed., *Money,* 245–51.

Collins, Philip. *Dickens and Crime,* 276–80.

Connor, Steven. "Babel Unbuilding: The Anti-archi-rhetoric of *Martin Chuzzlewit,"* in John Schad, ed., *Dickens Refigured,* 178–99.

Edgecombe, Rodney Stenning. "Topographic Disaffection in Dickens's *American Notes* and *Martin Chuzzlewit."* *JEGP* 93 (1994), 35–54.

Edgecombe, Rodney Stenning. "The Urban Idyll in *Martin Chuzzlewit."* *R of Engl Stud* 45 (1994), 370–83.

Gervais, David. "Dickens's Comic Speech: Inventing the Self." *Yrbk of Engl Stud* 25 (1995), 133–36.

Greenstein, Michael. *"Martin Chuzzlewit's* Connections." *Dickens Q* 11 (1994), 5–12.

Hall, Donald E. *Fixing Patriarchy,* 21–43.

Horsman, Alan. *The Victorian Novel,* 112–16.

Houston, Gail Turley. *Consuming Fictions,* 73–89.

Joseph, Gerhard. "Charles Dickens, International Copyright, and the Discretionary Silence of *Martin Chuzzlewit,"* in Martha Woodmansee and Peter Jaszi, eds., *The Construction of Authorship,* 259–70.

Joseph, Gerhard. "Construing the Inimitable's Silence: Pecksniff's Grammar School and International Copyright." *Dickens Stud Annual* 22 (1993), 121–33.

Joseph, Gerhard. "The Labyrinth and the Library *en abyme:* Eco, Borges, Dickens . . .," in Mary Ann Caws, ed., *City Images,* 44–58.

Kissel, Susan S. *In Common Cause,* 115–17, 119–21.

Kucich, John. "Dickens," in John Richetti et al., eds., *The Columbia History,* 400–401.

Lougy, Robert E. "Desire and the Ideology of Violence: America in Charles Dickens's *Martin Chuzzlewit."* *Criticism* 36 (1994), 569–90.

McGuire, Matthew J. *The Role of Women,* 32–34.

Marlow, James E. *Charles Dickens,* 86–90.

Metz, Nancy Aycock. "Dickens and The Quack Architectural." *Dickens Q* 11 (1994), 59–67.

Murray, Brian. *Charles Dickens,* 105–10.

Netto, Jeffrey A. "Dickens with Kant and Sade." *Style* 29 (1995), 443–45.

Reed, John R. *Dickens and Thackeray,* 134–53.

Rosenberg, Brian. *Little Dorrit's Shadows,* 71–74, 105–7.

Stone, Harry. *The Night Side of Dickens,* 228–30.

Sutherland, John. *Is Heathcliff a Murderer?,* 46–52.

Tambling, Jeremy. *Dickens, Violence and the Modern State,* 25–28.

Trotter, David. "Dickens's Idle Men," in John Schad, ed., *Dickens Refigured,* 204–6.

The Mystery of Edwin Drood, 1870

Burgan, William M. "Masonic Symbolism in *The Moonstone* and *The Mystery of Edwin Drood,"* in Nelson Smith and R. C. Terry, eds., *Wilkie Collins to the Forefront,* 126–42.

Collins, Philip. *Dickens and Crime*, 283–85, 291–309.

Connor, Steven. "Dead? Or Alive?: *Edwin Drood* and the Work of Mourning." *Dickensian* 89 (1993), 85–102.

Cox, Don Richard. " 'Can't You See A Hint?': The Mysterious 'Thirteenth Illustration' to *Edwin Drood.*" *Dickensian* 92 (1996), 5–17.

Dubberke, Ray. "Who Drew the *Drood* Cover?" *Dickensian* 91 (1995), 108–12.

Faulkner, David. "The Confidence Man: Empire and the Destruction of Muscular Christianity in *The Mystery of Edwin Drood,*" in Donald E. Hall, ed., *Muscular Christianity*, 175–89.

Hardman, Malcolm. "*The Mystery of Edwin Drood* and James Lobley's 'Little Nell.' " *Notes and Queries* 42 (1995), 193–95.

Hollington, Michael. " 'To the Droodstone': Or, From *The Moonstone* to *Edwin Drood* via *No Thoroughfare.*" *Q/W/E/R/T/Y* 5 (1995), 141–49.

Horsman, Alan. *The Victorian Novel*, 155–58.

Joseph, Gerhard. "Who Cares Who Killed Edwin Drood? Or, On the Whole, I'd Rather Be in Philadelphia." *Nineteenth-Cent Lit* 51 (1996), 161–75.

Karbacz, Elsie, and Robert Raven. "The Many Mysteries of *Edwin Drood.*" *Dickensian* 90 (1994), 5–17.

Lloyd Smith, Allan. "The Phantoms of *Drood* and *Rebecca:* The Uncanny Reencountered through Abraham and Torok's 'Cryptonymy.' " *Poetics Today* 13 (1992), 285–308.

McGuire, Matthew J. *The Role of Women*, 59–65.

Meyer, Susan. *Imperialism at Home*, 1–3.

Milligan, Barry. *Pleasures and Pains,* 96–99, 103–11.

Murray, Brian. *Charles Dickens,* 180–86.

Parker, David. "Drood Redux: Mystery and the Art of Fiction." *Dickens Stud Annual* 24 (1996), 185–95.

Perera, Suvendrini. *Reaches of Empire,* 103–22.

Robson, W. W. *Critical Enquiries*, 139–59.

Rosenberg, Brian. *Little Dorrit's Shadows*, 104–5, 126–27.

Tambling, Jeremy. *Dickens, Violence and the Modern State*, 155–85.

Wheeler, Michael. *English Fiction of the Victorian Period*, 118–20.

Nicholas Nickleby, 1839

Bowen, John. "Performing Business, Training Ghosts: Transcoding *Nickleby.*" *ELH* 63 (1996), 153–72.

Horsman, Alan. *The Victorian Novel*, 104–7.

Innes, Christopher. "Adapting Dickens to the Modern Eye: *Nicholas Nickleby* and *Little Dorrit,*" in Peter Reynolds, ed., *Novel Images*, 68–73.

Johnson, Derek. *Pastoral in . . . Dickens,* 205–7.

Manning, Sylvia. "*Nicholas Nickleby:* Parody on the Plains of Syria." *Dickens Stud Annual* 23 (1994), 73–90.

Marlow, James E. *Charles Dickens,* 80–82, 126–33.

Michie, Helena. "The Avuncular and Beyond: Family (Melo)drama in *Nicholas Nickleby,*" in John Schad, ed., *Dickens Refigured*, 80–97.

Murray, Brian. *Charles Dickens,* 89–98.

Reed, John R. *Dickens and Thackeray,* 90–105.

Rem, Tore. "Melodrama *and* Parody: A Reading that *Nicholas Nickleby* Requires?" *Engl Stud* (Amsterdam) 77 (1996), 240–54.

Robson, W. W. *Critical Enquiries,* 126–38.

Stein, Richard L. "Street Figures: Victorian Urban Iconography," in Carol T. Christ and John O. Jordan, eds., *Victorian Literature,* 236–40.

Stone, Harry. *The Night Side of Dickens,* 345–48.

Trotter, David. "Dickens's Idle Men," in John Schad, ed., *Dickens Refigured,* 202–4.

The Old Curiosity Shop, 1841

Bailin, Miriam. *The Sickroom in Victorian Fiction,* 89–97.

Birch, Dinah. "Beauty and the Victorian Body." *Essays in Criticism* 44 (1994), 105–6.

Buckley, Jerome H. "Little Nell's Curious Grandfather." *Dickens Stud Annual* 24 (1996), 81–87.

Clark, Timothy. "Dickens Through Blanchot: The Nightmare Fascination of a World Without Interiority," in John Schad, ed., *Dickens Refigured,* 31–33.

David, Deirdre. *Rule Britannia,* 58–64.

Gawel, Angela. "Subordinating the Other: Illustrations in Dickens's *Old Curiosity Shop.*" *Metaphor and Symbolic Activity* 8 (1993), 169–79.

Hennelly, Mark M., Jr. "Carnivalesque 'Unlawful Games' in *The Old Curiosity Shop.*" *Dickens Stud Annual* 22 (1993), 67–110.

Horne, Lewis. "*The Old Curiosity Shop* and the Limits of Melodrama." *Dalhousie R* 72 (1992–93), 494–505.

Horsman, Alan. *The Victorian Novel,* 107–8.

Houston, Gail Turley. *Consuming Fictions,* 61–73.

Johnson, Derek. *Pastoral in . . . Dickens,* 7–9, 155–57.

Kucich, John. "Dickens," in John Richetti et al., eds., *The Columbia History,* 396–98.

Lerner, Laurence. *Angels and Absences,* 94–97, 101–13, 174–83.

McGuire, Matthew J. *The Role of Women,* 22–27.

Marlow, James E. *Charles Dickens,* 82–85.

Murray, Brian. *Charles Dickens,* 98–105.

Polhemus, Robert M. "Comic and Erotic Faith Meet Faith in the Child: Charles Dickens's *The Old Curiosity Shop* ('The Old Cupiosity Shape')," in Robert M. Polhemus and Roger B. Henkle, eds., *Critical Reconstructions,* 71–89.

Polhemus, Robert M. "Lewis Carroll and the Child in Victorian Fiction," in John Richetti et al., eds., *The Columbia History,* 593–96.

Pope, Norris. "The Old Curiosity Shop and the New: Dickens and the Age of Machinery." *Dickens Q* 13 (1996), 3–14.

Reed, John R. *Dickens and Thackeray,* 107–21.

Rowlinson, Matthew. "Reading Capital with Little Nell." *Yale J of Criticism* 9:2 (1996), 347–76.

Schiefelbein, Michael. "Bringing to Earth the 'Good Angel of the Race.' " *Victorian Newsl* 84 (1993), 25–28.

Sillars, Stuart. *Visualisation in Popular Fiction*, 21–26.

Steig, Michael. "Abuse and the Comic-Grotesque in *The Old Curiosity Shop:* Problems of Response." *Dickens Q* 11 (1994), 103–13.

Stewart, Garrett. *Dear Reader*, 184–205, 287–89.

Stone, Harry. *The Night Side of Dickens*, 216–20.

Terry, R. C. " 'Have at the Masters!': Working-Class Stereotypes in Some Nineteenth-Century Novels," in John Morris, ed., *Exploring Stereotyped Images,* 161–62.

Wheeler, Michael. *English Fiction of the Victorian Period*, 30–32.

Zemka, Sue. "From the Punchmen to Pugin's Gothics: The Broad Road to a Sentimental Death in *The Old Curiosity Shop." Nineteenth-Cent Lit* 48 (1993), 291–309.

Oliver Twist, 1838

Baldridge, Cates. *The Dialogics of Dissent*, 79–90.

Baumgarten, Murray. "Seeing Double: Jews in the Fiction of F. Scott Fitzgerald, Charles Dickens, Anthony Trollope, and George Eliot," in Bryan Cheyette, ed., *Between 'Race' and Culture*, 45–51.

Birch, Dinah. "Beauty and the Victorian Body." *Essays in Criticism* 44 (1994), 106–7.

Blum, Virginia L. *Hide and Seek,* 130–34, 142–46, 154–56, 162–64.

Cohen, William A. *Sex Scandal*, 27–29.

Collins, Philip. *Dickens and Crime*, 41–43, 256–72.

Dellamora, Richard. "Pure Oliver; or, Representation without Agency," in John Schad, ed., *Dickens Refigured*, 55–77.

Gager, Valerie L. *Shakespeare and Dickens*, 75–77.

Grossman, Jonathan H. "The Absent Jew in Dickens: Narrators in *Oliver Twist, Our Mutual Friend,* and *A Christmas Carol." Dickens Stud Annual* 24 (1996), 38–45.

Horsman, Alan. *The Victorian Novel*, 101–4.

Houston, Gail Turley. *Consuming Fictions,* 14–37.

Johnson, Derek. *Pastoral in . . . Dickens,* 173–75, 213–18.

Kucich, John. "Dickens," in John Richetti et al., eds., *The Columbia History*, 399–401.

Long, Pamela H. "Fagin and Monipodio: The Sources of *Oliver Twist* in Cervantes's *Rinconete y Cortadillo." Dickensian* 90 (1994), 117–23.

McGuire, Matthew J. *The Role of Women*, 14–19.

Marlow, James E. *Charles Dickens,* 76–80.

Marshall, Tim. *Murdering to Dissect,* 64–68, 106–10.

Michael, Steven. "Criminal Slang in *Oliver Twist:* Dickens's Survival Code." *Style* 27 (1993), 41–59.

Mothersole, Brenda. "The 'Fallen Woman' in the Victorian Novel," in John Morris, ed., *Exploring Stereotyped Images,* 198–201.

Murray, Brian. *Charles Dickens,* 78–89.

Netto, Jeffrey A. "Dickens with Kant and Sade." *Style* 29 (1995), 445–46, 452–54.

Pache, Walter. "Bedroht und bedrohlich: Zum Formwandel der viktorianischen Idylle," in Herbert Foltinek et al., eds., *Tales and "their telling difference,"* 224–27.

Reed, John R. *Dickens and Thackeray,* 76–89.

Sadrin, Anny. *Parentage and Inheritance,* 30–43.

Sroka, Kenneth M. "Dickens' Metafiction: Readers and Writers in *Oliver Twist, David Copperfield,* and *Our Mutual Friend." Dickens Stud Annual* 22 (1993), 35–42.

Stone, Harry. *The Night Side of Dickens,* 81–83.

Sutherland, John. *Is Heathcliff a Murderer?,* 35–45.

Tambling, Jeremy. "Dangerous Crossings: Dickens, Digression, and Montage." *Yrbk of Engl Stud* 26 (1996), 47–53.

Tambling, Jeremy. *Dickens, Violence and the Modern State,* 157–67.

Weston, Nancy. "Dickens, Daniel Maclise and the Real Bill Sikes." *Dickensian* 90 (1994), 189–96.

Wilkes, David. "Dickens, Bakhtin, and the Neopastoral Shepherd in *Oliver Twist." Dickens Stud Annual* 24 (1996), 59–75.

Winnifrith, Tom. *Fallen Women,* 93–95.

Wolff, Larry. " 'The Boys are Pickpockets, and the Girl is a Prostitute': Gender and Juvenile Criminality in Early Victorian England from *Oliver Twist* to *London Labour." New Liter Hist* 27 (1996), 227–48.

Our Mutual Friend, 1865

Alter, Robert. "Reading Style in Dickens." *Philos and Lit* 19 (1995), 131–37.

Bailin, Miriam. *The Sickroom in Victorian Fiction,* 96–106.

Baumgarten, Murray. "Seeing Double: Jews in the Fiction of F. Scott Fitzgerald, Charles Dickens, Anthony Trollope, and George Eliot," in Bryan Cheyette, ed., *Between 'Race' and Culture,* 51–54.

Collins, Philip. *Dickens and Crime,* 283–89, 296–99.

Connor, Steven. *The English Novel in History,* 124–26.

Curry, Mary Jane Chilton. "Anaphoric and Cataphoric Reference in Dickens's *Our Mutual Friend* and James's *The Golden Bowl,"* in Cynthia Goldin Bernstein, ed., *The Text and Beyond,* 30–52.

DeMarcus, Cynthia. "Wolves Within and Without: Dickens's Transformation of 'Little Red Riding Hood' in *Our Mutual Friend." Dickens Q* 12 (1995), 11–17.

Edgecombe, Rodney Stenning. " 'The Ring of Cant': Formulaic Elements in *Our Mutual Friend." Dickens Stud Annual* 24 (1996), 167–83.

Edgecombe, Rodney Stenning. "Two Oblique Allusions in *Our Mutual Friend." Notes and Queries* 41 (1994), 352–53.

Edgecombe, Rodney Stenning. "The 'Veiled-prophet' in *Our Mutual Friend." Dickensian* 92 (1996), 208–9.

Fasick, Laura. *Vessels of Meaning,* 138–40.

Fulweiler, Howard W. " 'A Dismal Swamp': Darwin, Design, and Evolution in *Our Mutual Friend." Nineteenth-Cent Lit* 49 (1994), 50–74.

Ginsburg, Michael Peled. *Economies of Change*, 142–56.

Gomel, Elana. "The Body of Parts: Dickens and the Poetics of Synecdoche." *J of Narrative Technique* 26 (1996), 63–66.

Gordon, Jan B. "Dickens and the Political Economy of the Eye." *Dickens Stud Annual* 24 (1996), 19–23.

Green, Paul. "Two Venal Girls: A Study in Dickens and Zola." *Recovering Lit* 19 (1993), 21–33.

Grossman, Jonathan H. "The Absent Jew in Dickens: Narrators in *Oliver Twist, Our Mutual Friend,* and *A Christmas Carol.*" *Dickens Stud Annual* 24 (1996), 45–49.

Handy, Ellen. "Dust Piles and Damp Pavements: Excrement, Repression, and the Victorian City in Photography and Literature," in Carol T. Christ and John O. Jordan, eds., *Victorian Literature,* 118–20, 122–24.

Hecimovich, Gregg A. "The Cup and the Lip and the Riddle of *Our Mutual Friend.*" *ELH* 62 (1995), 955–72.

Hennelly, Mark M., Jr. " 'Toy Wonders' in *Our Mutual Friend.*" *Dickens Q* 12 (1995), 60–71 and 95–105.

Heyns, Michiel. *Expulsion and the Nineteenth-Century Novel,* 117–35.

Horsman, Alan. *The Victorian Novel,* 148–54.

Houston, Gail Turley. *Consuming Fictions,* 170–82.

Johnson, Derek. *Pastoral in . . . Dickens,* 263–66.

King, James Roy. "Defense Mechanisms in *Our Mutual Friend.*" *Dickens Q* 12 (1995), 45–58.

Kucich, John. "Dickens," in John Richetti et al., eds., *The Columbia History,* 395–97.

Kucich, John. "Repression and Representation: Dickens's General Economy (*Our Mutual Friend*)," in Steven Connor, ed., *Charles Dickens,* 197–209.

Lerner, Laurence. *Angels and Absences,* 107–11.

McGuire, Matthew J. *The Role of Women,* 54–59.

Maglavera, Soultana. *Time Patterns in Later Dickens,* 163–80.

Marlow, James E. *Charles Dickens,* 65–67, 179–89, 214–16.

Miller, J. Hillis. "The Topography of Jealousy in *Our Mutual Friend,*" in John Schad, ed., *Dickens Refigured,* 218–35.

Murray, Brian. *Charles Dickens,* 177–80.

O'Hea, Michael. "Hidden Harmony: Marcus Stone's Wrapper Design for *Our Mutual Friend.*" *Dickensian* 91 (1995), 198–207.

Reed, John R. *Dickens and Thackeray,* 289–303.

Royle, Nicholas. "Our Mutual Friend," in John Schad, ed., *Dickens Refigured,* 39–53.

Sadrin, Anny. *Parentage and Inheritance,* 121–47.

Sedgwick, Eve Kosofsky. "Homophobia, Misogyny and Capital: The Example of *Our Mutual Friend,*" in Steven Connor, ed., *Charles Dickens,* 178–95.

Shuman, Cathy. "Invigilating *Our Mutual Friend:* Gender and the Legitimation of Professional Authority." *Novel* 28 (1995), 154–69.

Smith, Jonathan. "Heat and Modern Thought: The Forces of Nature in *Our Mutual Friend.*" *Victorian Lit and Culture* 23 (1995), 37–67.

Smith, Monika Rydygier. "The W/hole Remains: Consumerist Politics in *Bleak House, Great Expectations,* and *Our Mutual Friend.*" *Victorian R* 19:1 (1993), 1–16.

Spiegel, Maura. "Unfelt Feelings: An Evolving Grammar of Hidden Motives." *Victorian Lit and Culture* 23 (1995), 259–67.

Sroka, Kenneth M. "Dickens' Metafiction: Readers and Writers in *Oliver Twist, David Copperfield,* and *Our Mutual Friend.*" *Dickens Stud Annual* 22 (1993), 51–61.

Stewart, Garrett. *Dear Reader,* 231–34.

Stone, Harry. *The Night Side of Dickens,* 151–61, 371–78.

Tambling, Jeremy. *Dickens, Violence and the Modern State,* 186–215.

Wheeler, Michael. *English Fiction of the Victorian Period,* 114–18.

Winnifrith, Tom. *Fallen Women,* 93–98.

The Pickwick Papers, 1837

Cronin, Mark. "Thackeray's First Fashioned Response to Dickens: *The Yellowplush Papers* Cast a Cynical Eye on the 'Admiral Boz's' *Pickwick Papers.*" *Dickens Q* 10 (1993), 191–201.

Fein, Mara H. "The Politics of Family in *The Pickwick Papers.*" *ELH* 61 (1994), 363–77.

Gager, Valerie L. *Shakespeare and Dickens,* 188–90.

Glavin, John. "Pickwick on the Wrong Side of the Door." *Dickens Stud Annual* 22 (1993), 1–16.

Horsman, Alan. *The Victorian Novel,* 98–100.

Houston, Gail Turley. *Consuming Fictions,* 14–37.

Johnson, Derek. *Pastoral in . . . Dickens,* 104–6, 122–27.

Knott, John. "In Search of Dingley Dell." *Dickensian* 91 (1995), 179–85.

McGuire, Matthew J. *The Role of Women,* 11–14.

Marlow, James E. *Charles Dickens,* 74–76, 103–5.

Murray, Brian. *Charles Dickens,* 73–78.

Myers, Richard M. "Politics of Hatred in *A Tale of Two Cities,*" in Joseph M. Knippenberg and Peter Augustine Lawler, eds., *Poets, Princes, and Private Citizens,* 63–73.

Newsom, Robert. "Pickwick in the Utilitarian Sense." *Dickens Stud Annual* 23 (1994), 49–64.

Nord, Deborah Epstein. *Walking the Victorian Streets,* 70–72.

Reed, John R. *Dickens and Thackeray,* 69–75.

Rosenberg, Brian. *Little Dorrit's Shadows,* 67–69.

Sadrin, Anny. "Fragmentation in *The Pickwick Papers.*" *Dickens Stud Annual* 22 (1993), 21–34.

Sestito, Marisa. "Divided Dickens." *Yrbk of Engl Stud* 26 (1996), 34–42.

Stone, Harry. *The Night Side of Dickens,* 77–79.

Wheeler, Michael. *English Fiction of the Victorian Period,* 25–29.

A Tale of Two Cities, 1859

Adams, James Eli. *Dandies and Desert Saints,* 55–60, 160–62.

Adams, James Eli. "The Hero as Spectacle: Carlyle and the Persistence of Dandyism," in Carol T. Christ and John O. Jordan, eds., *Victorian Literature,* 223–29.

Baldridge, Cates. *The Dialogics of Dissent,* 144–66.

Collins, Philip. *Dickens and Crime,* 133–38.

Gomel, Elana. "The Body of Parts: Dickens and the Poetics of Synecdoche." *J of Narrative Technique* 26 (1996), 59–63.

Hamilton, J. F. "Dickens's *A Tale of Two Cities." Explicator* 53 (1995), 204–7.

Hochberg, Shifra. "Madame Defarge and a Possible Carlylean Source." *Dickensian* 91 (1995), 99–101.

Horsman, Alan. *The Victorian Novel,* 141–44.

Kucich, John. "Dickens," in John Richetti et al., eds., *The Columbia History,* 401–2.

McGuire, Matthew J. *The Role of Women,* 39–41.

Maglavera, Soultana. *Time Patterns in Later Dickens,* 121–37.

Myers, Richard M. "Politics of Hatred in *A Tale of Two Cities,*" in Joseph M. Knippenberg and Peter Augustine Lawler, eds., *Poets, Princes, and Private Citizens,* 63–73.

Orel, Harold. *The Historical Novel,* 31–33.

Reed, John R. *Dickens and Thackeray,* 257–69.

Robson, Lisa. "The 'Angels' in Dickens's House: Representation of Women in *A Tale of Two Cities." Dalhousie R* 72 (1992), 311–31.

Rosenberg, Brian. *Little Dorrit's Shadows,* 123–26.

Sanders, Andrew. " 'Sixty Years Since': Victorian Historical Fiction from Dickens to Eliot," in Susana Onega, ed., *Telling Histories,* 27–30.

Schad, John. "Dickens's Cryptic Church: Drawing on *Pictures from Italy,*" in Schad, ed., *Dickens Refigured,* 7–9.

Stewart, Garrett. *Dear Reader,* 224–31.

Stone, Harry. *The Night Side of Dickens,* 162–98, 358–64, 437–40.

Tambling, Jeremy. *Dickens, Violence and the Modern State,* 129–54.

Visser, Nicholas. "Roaring Beasts and Raging Floods: The Representation of Political Crowds in the Nineteenth-Century British Novel." *Mod Lang R* 89 (1994), 304–8.

Wolf, Werner. "Die Domestizierung der Geschichte: Eine These zur Funktion des englischen historischen Romans im 19. Jahrhundert am Beispiel von Scott, Thackeray und Dickens." *Archiv für das Studium der neueren Sprachen und Literaturen* 231 (1994), 288–95.

BENJAMIN DISRAELI

Coningsby, 1844

Antor, Heinz. *Der englische Universitätsroman,* 223–25.

Bivona, Daniel. *Desire and Contradiction,* 5–12.

Brantlinger, Patrick. *Fictions of State*, 175–84.
Childers, Joseph W. *Novel Possibilities,* 38–51, 52–68.
Horsman, Alan. *The Victorian Novel*, 70–72.
Kelsall, Malcolm. *The Great Good Place,* 124–37.
Milton, Paul. "Inheritance as the Key to all Mythologies: George Eliot and Legal Practice." *Mosaic* 28:1 (1995), 55–57.
Poovey, Mary. "Disraeli, Gaskell, and the Condition of England," in John Richetti et al., eds., *The Columbia History*, 512–20.

Contarini Fleming, 1832

Antor, Heinz. *Der englische Universitätsroman*, 127–29.

Lothair, 1870

Ragussis, Michael. *Figures of Conversion*, 225–27.

Sybil, 1845

Bivona, Daniel. *Desire and Contradiction,* 12–17.
Brantlinger, Patrick. *Fictions of State*, 175–84.
Colby, Robin B. *"Some Appointed Work To Do,"* 19–22.
Guy, Josephine M. *The Victorian Social-Problem Novel,* 180–86.
Harsh, Constance D. *Subversive Heroines,* 95–99.
Horsman, Alan. *The Victorian Novel*, 72–73.
Kelsall, Malcolm. *The Great Good Place,* 124–37.
Milton, Paul. "Inheritance as the Key to all Mythologies: George Eliot and Legal Practice." *Mosaic* 28:1 (1995), 55–56.
Poovey, Mary. "Disraeli, Gaskell, and the Condition of England," in John Richetti et al., eds., *The Columbia History*, 520–21.
Ragussis, Michael. *Figures of Conversion*, 189–94.
Terry, R. C. " 'Have at the Masters!': Working-Class Stereotypes in Some Nineteenth-Century Novels," in John Morris, ed., *Exploring Stereotyped Images,* 163–64, 166–67.
Visser, Nicholas. "Roaring Beasts and Raging Floods: The Representation of Political Crowds in the Nineteenth-Century British Novel." *Mod Lang R* 89 (1994), 298–99.
Wheeler, Michael. *English Fiction of the Victorian Period*, 40–41.

Tancred, 1847

Bivona, Daniel. *Desire and Contradiction,* 17–25.
Brantlinger, Patrick. *Fictions of State*, 175–84.
Horsman, Alan. *The Victorian Novel*, 73–74.
Ragussis, Michael. *Figures of Conversion*, 194–99, 206–12, 217–20.

The Young Duke, 1831

Antor, Heinz. *Der englische Universitätsroman*, 197–99.

FLORENCE DIXIE

Gloriana; or, The Revolution of 1900, 1890

Lewes, Darby. *Dream Revisionaries*, 69–72.

ELLA HEPWORTH DIXON

The Story of a Modern Woman, 1894
  Nelson, Carolyn Christensen. *British Women Fiction Writers,* 48–51.

J. P. DONLEAVY

The Destinies of Darcy Dancer, Gentleman, 1977
  Seed, David. "Parables of Estrangement: The Fiction of J. P. Donleavy,"
    in Paul Hyland and Neil Sammells, eds., *Irish Writing,* 219–21.
The Ginger Man, 1955
  Seed, David. "Parables of Estrangement: The Fiction of J. P. Donleavy,"
    in Paul Hyland and Neil Sammells, eds., *Irish Writing,* 209–14.
Leila, 1983
  Seed, David. "Parables of Estrangement: The Fiction of J. P. Donleavy,"
    in Paul Hyland and Neil Sammells, eds., *Irish Writing,* 221–22.
The Onion Eaters, 1971
  Seed, David. "Parables of Estrangement: The Fiction of J. P. Donleavy,"
    in Paul Hyland and Neil Sammells, eds., *Irish Writing,* 214–15.

MENIE MURIEL DOWIE

Gallia, 1895
  Nelson, Carolyn Christensen. *British Women Fiction Writers,* 51–55.

ARTHUR CONAN DOYLE

The Hound of the Baskervilles, 1902
  Coren, Michael. *Conan Doyle,* 104–6.
  DiBattista, Maria. "The Lowly Art of Murder: Modernism and the Case
    of the Free Woman," in Maria DiBattista and Lucy McDiarmid, eds.,
    High and Low Moderns, 183–85.
  Greenslade, William. *Degeneration, Culture, and the Novel,* 100–101.
The Sign of the Four, 1890
  Coren, Michael. *Conan Doyle,* 57–61.
  Frank, Lawrence. "Dreaming the Medusa: Imperialism, Primitivism, and
    Sexuality in Arthur Conan Doyle's *The Sign of Four." Signs* 22
    (1996), 52–81.
  Thompson, Jon. *Fiction, Crime, and Empire,* 69–73.
A Study in Scarlet, 1887
  Atkinson, Michael. *The Secret Marriage of Sherlock Holmes,* 65–90.
  Coren, Michael. *Conan Doyle,* 49–53.
  Van Dover, J. K. *You Know My Method,* 72–79.

The White Company, 1891

Hughes, Helen. *The Historical Romance,* 25–27, 44–51, 60–74.
Orel, Harold. *The Historical Novel,* 87–101.

MARGARET DRABBLE

The Garrick Year, 1964

Stovel, Nora Foster. "Rebelling Against the Regency: Jane Austen and Margaret Drabble." *Persuasions* 16 (1994), 165–66.

The Gates of Ivory, 1992

de la Concha, Angeles. "Drabble's Gate to the End of History," in Susana Onega, ed., *Telling Histories,* 154–62.
Druxes, Helga. *Resisting Bodies,* 155–58.
Knutsen, Karen Patrick. "Leaving Dr. Leavis: A Farewell to the Great Tradition?—Margaret Drabble's *The Gates of Ivory.*" *Engl Stud* (Amsterdam) 77 (1996), 579–91.
Rubenstein, Roberta. "Fragmented Bodies/Selves/Narratives: Margaret Drabble's Postmodern Turn." *Contemp Lit* 35 (1994), 142–54.

The Ice Age, 1977

Connor, Steven. *The English Novel in History,* 59–64.
de la Concha, Angeles. "Drabble's Gate to the End of History," in Susana Onega, ed., *Telling Histories,* 152–53.
Sage, Lorna. *Women in the House of Fiction,* 95–96.
Stovel, Nora Foster. "Rebelling Against the Regency: Jane Austen and Margaret Drabble." *Persuasions* 16 (1994), 170–71.

Jerusalem the Golden, 1967

Druxes, Helga. *Resisting Bodies,* 123–25.
Sage, Lorna. *Women in the House of Fiction,* 91–92.
Stovel, Nora Foster. "Rebelling Against the Regency: Jane Austen and Margaret Drabble." *Persuasions* 16 (1994), 167.
Taylor, D. J. *After the War,* 248–51.

The Middle Ground, 1980

Allan, Tuzyline Jita. *Womanist and Feminist Aesthetics,* 45–68.
Druxes, Helga. *Resisting Bodies,* 124–29.
Rubenstein, Roberta. "Fragmented Bodies/Selves/Narratives: Margaret Drabble's Postmodern Turn." *Contemp Lit* 35 (1994), 138–39.
Sage, Lorna. *Women in the House of Fiction,* 89, 96–97.
Stovel, Nora Foster. "Rebelling Against the Regency: Jane Austen and Margaret Drabble." *Persuasions* 16 (1994), 171–72.
Wilt, Judith. *Abortion, Choice, and Contemporary Fiction,* 59–66.
Wyatt, Jean. *Reconstructing Desire,* 192–94.

The Millstone, 1965

Cosslett, Tess. *Women Writing Childbirth,* 94–103.
Saccucci, Sandra. "The Dilemmas of the Professional Woman in Margaret Drabble's *The Millstone.*" *Crit Mass* 3:2 (1993), 3–25.

Stovel, Nora Foster. "Rebelling Against the Regency: Jane Austen and Margaret Drabble." *Persuasions* 16 (1994), 166–67.

Taylor, D. J. *After the War*, 163–66.

Wilt, Judith. *Abortion, Choice, and Contemporary Fiction*, 52–59.

A Natural Curiosity, 1989

Marsh, Kelly A. "The Neo-Sensation Novel: A Contemporary Genre in the Victorian Tradition." *Philol Q* 74 (1995), 99–121.

Rubenstein, Roberta. "Fragmented Bodies/Selves/Narratives: Margaret Drabble's Postmodern Turn." *Contemp Lit* 35 (1994), 140–42.

Wood, Michael. "The Contemporary Novel," in John Richetti et al., eds., *The Columbia History*, 962–63.

The Needle's Eye, 1972

Almond, Barbara, and Richard Almond. *The Therapeutic Narrative*, 63–76.

Stovel, Nora Foster. "Rebelling Against the Regency: Jane Austen and Margaret Drabble." *Persuasions* 16 (1994), 169–70.

The Radiant Way, 1987

Connor, Steven. *The English Novel in History*, 64–69.

de la Concha, Angeles. "Drabble's Gate to the End of History," in Susana Onega, ed., *Telling Histories*, 153–62.

Druxes, Helga. *Resisting Bodies*, 130–40, 145–55.

Marsh, Kelly A. "The Neo-Sensation Novel: A Contemporary Genre in the Victorian Tradition." *Philol Q* 74 (1995), 99–121.

Stovel, Nora Foster. "Rebelling Against the Regency: Jane Austen and Margaret Drabble." *Persuasions* 16 (1994), 172–74.

Thompson, Lee Briscoe. "Atwood and Drabble: Life After Radiance," in Gillian Whitlock and Helen Tiffin, eds., *Re-Siting Queen's English*, 38–46.

Wood, Michael. "The Contemporary Novel," in John Richetti et al., eds., *The Columbia History*, 964–65.

Realms of Gold, 1975

de la Concha, Angeles. "Drabble's Gate to the End of History," in Susana Onega, ed., *Telling Histories*, 150–52.

Novy, Marianne. *Engaging with Shakespeare*, 151–53.

Stovel, Nora Foster. "Rebelling Against the Regency: Jane Austen and Margaret Drabble." *Persuasions* 16 (1994), 170.

A Summer Bird-Cage, 1963

Lambert, Ellen Zetzel. *The Face of Love*, 90–94.

Sage, Lorna. *Women in the House of Fiction*, 90–91.

Stovel, Nora Foster. "Rebelling Against the Regency: Jane Austen and Margaret Drabble." *Persuasions* 16 (1994), 164–65.

Wood, Michael. "The Contemporary Novel," in John Richetti et al., eds., *The Columbia History*, 961–62.

The Waterfall, 1969

de la Concha, Angeles. "Drabble's Gate to the End of History," in Susana Onega, ed., *Telling Histories,* 149–50.

Emmitt, Helen V. " 'Drowned in a Willing Sea': Freedom and Drowning in Eliot, Chopin, and Drabble." *Tulsa Stud in Women's Lit* 12 (1993), 324–29.

Greene, Gayle. "Ambiguous Benefits: Reading and Writing in Feminist Metafiction," in Carol J. Singley and Susan Elizabeth Sweeney, eds., *Anxious Power,* 323–25.

Kelly, Darlene. " 'Either Way, I Stand Condemned': A Woman's Place in Margaret Atwood's *The Edible Woman* and Margaret Drabble's *The Waterfall." Engl Stud in Canada* 21 (1995), 320–31.

Stovel, Nora Foster. "Rebelling Against the Regency: Jane Austen and Margaret Drabble." *Persuasions* 16 (1994), 167–69.

Wyatt, Jean. *Reconstructing Desire,* 126–48.

Zelter, Joachim. *Sinnhafte Fiktion und Wahrheit,* 215–17.

DAPHNE DU MAURIER

The Flight of the Falcon, 1965

Forster, Margaret. *Daphne du Maurier,* 336–38.

I'll Never Be Young Again, 1932

Forster, Margaret. *Daphne du Maurier,* 78–81.

Jamaica Inn, 1936

Forster, Margaret. *Daphne du Maurier,* 120–22.

The King's General, 1946

Forster, Margaret. *Daphne du Maurier,* 196–99.

The Loving Spirit, 1931

Forster, Margaret. *Daphne du Maurier,* 76–78.

My Cousin Rachel, 1951

Forster, Margaret. *Daphne du Maurier,* 252–54.

The Parasites, 1949

Forster, Margaret. *Daphne du Maurier,* 241–44.

The Progress of Julius, 1933

Forster, Margaret. *Daphne du Maurier,* 83–86.

Rebecca, 1938

Auffret-Boucé, Hélène. "*Rebecca* ou 'lepérie en la demeure.' " *Caliban* 33 (1996), 93–100.

Berglund, Birgitta. "Mrs Radcliffe and *Rebecca." Studia Neophilologica* 68 (1996), 73–80.

Cadogan, Mary. *And Then Their Hearts Stood Still,* 20–22, 108–9.

Forster, Margaret. *Daphne du Maurier,* 136–40.

Horner, Avril, and Sue Zlosnik. "A 'disembodied spirit': The Letters and Fiction of Daphne du Maurier." *Prose Stud* 19 (1996), 186–93.

Lloyd Smith, Allan. "The Phantoms of *Drood* and *Rebecca:* The Uncanny Reencountered through Abraham and Torok's 'Cryptonymy.' " *Poetics Today* 13 (1992), 285–308.

Nollen, Elizabeth Mahn. "Female Detective Figures in British Fiction: Coping with Madness and Imprisonment." *Clues* 15:2 (1994), 45–47.

Sillars, Stuart. *Visualisation in Popular Fiction*, 113–31.

Watson, Daphne. *Their Own Worst Enemies*, 17–23.

Williams, Tony. "Respecting Daphne DuMaurier's *Rebecca.*" *Notes on Contemp Lit* 26:2 (1996), 10–12.

The Scapegoat, 1957

Forster, Margaret. *Daphne du Maurier*, 285–90.

Horner, Avril, and Sue Zlosnik. "A 'disembodied spirit': The Letters and Fiction of Daphne du Maurier." *Prose Stud* 19 (1996), 196–97.

GEORGE DU MAURIER

The Martian, 1897

Golden, Catherine. "Turning Life into Literature: The Romantic Fiction of George Du Maurier." *CEA Critic* 58:1 (1995), 47–50.

Peter Ibbetson, 1891

Golden, Catherine. "Turning Life into Literature: The Romantic Fiction of George Du Maurier." *CEA Critic* 58:1 (1995), 44–46.

Trilby, 1894

Golden, Catherine. "Turning Life into Literature: The Romantic Fiction of George Du Maurier." *CEA Critic* 58:1 (1995), 46–47.

Grossman, Jonathan H. "The Mythic Svengali: Anti-Aestheticism in *Trilby.*" *Stud in the Novel* 28 (1996), 525–38.

Hait, Elizabeth A. "Parisian Street Names in George Du Maurier's *Trilby.*" *Names* 42 (1994), 19–25.

Piquet, Martine. "Dans les griffes de Svengali: caricature antisémite littéraire et graphique dans *Trilby* de George du Maurier." *Cahiers Victoriens et Edouardiens* 43 (1996), 62–63.

Stewart, Garrett. " 'Count Me In': *Dracula,* Hypnotic Participation, and the Late-Victorian Gothic of Reading." *LIT: Literature, Interpretation, Theory* 5 (1994), 5–6.

Stewart, Garrett. *Dear Reader*, 352–57.

Titus, Mary. "Cather's Creative Women and DuMaurier's Cozy Men: *The Song of the Lark* and *Trilby.*" *Mod Lang Stud* 24:2 (1994), 29–36.

Vrettos, Athena. *Somatic Fictions*, 102–5.

LAWRENCE DURRELL

The Alexandria Quartet, 1961

Alexandre-Garner, Corinne. "Villes de la mémoire, écriture de l'oubli: voyage à travers l'œuvre de Lawrence Durrell." *Etudes Anglaises* 46 (1993), 302–12.

Ashworth, Ann. "Anima and Individuation Issues in *The Alexandria Quartet.*" *J of Evolutionary Psych* 15 (1994), 244–48.

Beard, Pauline. "The Usufruct of Time in Lawrence Durrell's *Alexandria Quartet.*" *Deus Loci* 3 (1994), 75–97.

Bynum, Paige Matthey. "The Artist as Shaman: Durrell's *Alexandria Quartet,*" in Julius Rowan Raper et al., eds., *Lawrence Durrell,* 82–97.

Hollahan, Eugene. *Crisis-Consciousness,* 179–87.

Kaczvinsky, Donald P. *Lawrence Durrell's Major Novels,* 36–87.

Lemon, Lee T. "Durrell, Derrida, and the Heraldic Universe," in Julius Rowan Raper et al., eds., *Lawrence Durrell,* 62–69.

Peirce, Carol. "A Fellowship in Time: Durrell, Eliot, and the Quest of the Grail," in Julius Rowan Raper et al., eds., *Lawrence Durrell,* 73–81.

Peirce, Carol. " 'Some Worthwhile Work to Be Done': Is Nessim the Leader of the World Today?" *Deus Loci* 2 (1993), 164–66.

Pine, Richard. *Lawrence Durrell,* 169–244.

Vipond, Dianne L. "Lawrence Durrell's *Alexandria Quartet:* The Missing Link to Postmodernism." *Deus Loci* 2 (1993), 54–66.

Zelter, Joachim. *Sinnhafte Fiktion und Wahrheit,* 287–91.

The Avignon Quintet, 1974–1985

Alastrué, Ramón Plo. "Chaos and Cosmos in *The Avignon Quintet.*" *Deus Loci* 2 (1993), 116–25.

Alexandre-Garner, Corinne. "Villes de la mémoire, écriture de l'oubli: voyage à travers l'œuvre de Lawrence Durrell." *Etudes Anglaises* 46 (1993), 302–12.

Enscore, Melody L. " 'Members one another': Systemic Imagery in Durrell's *Avignon Quintet,*" in Julius Rowan Raper et al., eds., *Lawrence Durrell,* 151–60.

Ingersoll, Earl G. "*Mise-en-Abyme* in *The Avignon Quintet.*" *Deus Loci* 3 (1994), 113–19.

Kaczvinsky, Donald P. *Lawrence Durrell's Major Novels,* 105–51.

Lorenz, Paul H. "Angkor Wat, the Kundalini, and the Quinx: The Human Architecture of Divine Renewal in the *Quincunx,*" in Julius Rowan Raper et al., eds., *Lawrence Durrell,* 161–71.

Nichols, James R. "The Quest for Self: The Labyrinth in the Fiction of Lawrence Durrell." *Intl Fiction R* 22 (1995), 57–60.

Pine, Richard. *Lawrence Durrell,* 325–87.

Raper, Julius Rowan. "The Philosopher's Stone and Durrell's Psychological Vision in *The Avignon Quintet,*" in Julius Rowan Raper et al., eds., *Lawrence Durrell,* 137–50.

Vander Closter, Susan. "The Medieval Art of Lawrence Durrell's *Avignon Quintet.*" *Deus Loci* 2 (1993), 43–53.

Zelter, Joachim. *Sinnhafte Fiktion und Wahrheit*, 291–326.

Balthazar, 1958

Kaczvinsky, Donald P. *Lawrence Durrell's Major Novels*, 48–58.

Pine, Richard. *Lawrence Durrell*, 169–244.

Raper, Julius Rowan. "Lawrence Durrell's *Balthazar* (1958): Breaking the Modernist Mold." *Deus Loci* 2 (1993), 69–84.

The Black Book, 1938

Christensen, Peter G. "The Achievement and Failure: Durrell's Three Early Novels," in Julius Rowan Raper et al., eds., *Lawrence Durrell*, 30–32.

Kaczvinsky, Donald P. *Lawrence Durrell's Major Novels*, 20–35.

MacNiven, Ian S. "Ur-Durrell," in Julius Rowan Raper et al., eds., *Lawrence Durrell*, 16–20.

Pelletier, Jacques. "*Le Carnet noir* de Lawrence Durrell et le roman de la transition." *Etudes Littéraires* 27:2 (1994), 123–33.

Pine, Richard. *Lawrence Durrell*, 146–66.

Thomas, Gordon K. "The 'Romanticism" of *The Black Book:* Zoroaster in the Garden," in Julius Rowan Raper et al., eds., *Lawrence Durrell*, 55–61.

Constance, 1982

Kaczvinsky, Donald P. *Lawrence Durrell's Major Novels*, 125–35.

Pine, Richard. *Lawrence Durrell*, 325–87.

The Dark Labyrinth, 1947

Nichols, James R. "The Quest for Self: The Labyrinth in the Fiction of Lawrence Durrell." *Intl Fiction R* 22 (1995), 54–57.

Pine, Richard. *Lawrence Durrell*, 146–66.

Justine, 1957

Kaczvinsky, Donald P. *Lawrence Durrell's Major Novels*, 38–48.

Pine, Richard. *Lawrence Durrell*, 169–244.

Livia, 1978

Kaczvinsky, Donald P. *Lawrence Durrell's Major Novels*, 118–25.

Pine, Richard. *Lawrence Durrell*, 325–87.

Raper, Julius Rowan. "The Philosopher's Stone and Durrell's Psychological Vision in *The Avignon Quintet,*" in Julius Rowan Raper et al., eds., *Lawrence Durrell*, 138–42.

Monsieur; or, The Prince of Darkness, 1974

Kaczvinsky, Donald P. *Lawrence Durrell's Major Novels*, 106–18.

Moore, Stephanie. "Turning in the Trap: Can You Escape the Prince of Darkness? A Reader's Guide to *Monsieur.*" *Deus Loci* 2 (1993), 100–115.

Pine, Richard. *Lawrence Durrell*, 325–87.

Raper, Julius Rowan. "The Philosopher's Stone and Durrell's Psychological Vision in *The Avignon Quintet,"* in Julius Rowan Raper et al., eds., *Lawrence Durrell*, 140–42.

Mountolive, 1958

    Kaczvinsky, Donald P. *Lawrence Durrell's Major Novels*, 58–70.

    Pine, Richard. *Lawrence Durrell*, 169–244.

Nunquam, 1970

    Kaczvinsky, Donald P. " 'Bringing him to the lure': Postmodern Society and the Modern Artist's felix culpa in Durrell's *Tunc/Nunquam."* *South Atlantic R* 59:4 (1994), 63–74.

    Kaczvinsky, Donald P. *Lawrence Durrell's Major Novels*, 97–104.

    Pine, Richard. *Lawrence Durrell*, 247–321.

Panic Spring, 1937

    Christensen, Peter G. "The Achievement and Failure: Durrell's Three Early Novels," in Julius Rowan Raper et al., eds., *Lawrence Durrell*, 27–30.

    Kaczvinsky, Donald P. *"Panic Spring* and Durrell's 'Heraldic' Birds of Rebirth," in Julius Rowan Raper et al., eds., *Lawrence Durrell*, 33–44.

    MacNiven, Ian S. "Ur-Durrell," in Julius Rowan Raper et al., eds., *Lawrence Durrell*, 14–19.

    Pine, Richard. *Lawrence Durrell*, 146–66.

Pied Piper of Lovers, 1935

    Christensen, Peter G. "The Achievement and Failure: Durrell's Three Early Novels," in Julius Rowan Raper et al., eds., *Lawrence Durrell*, 22–26.

    MacNiven, Ian S. "Ur-Durrell," in Julius Rowan Raper et al., eds., *Lawrence Durrell*, 12–14.

    Pine, Richard. *Lawrence Durrell*, 146–66.

Quinx, or The Ripper's Tale, 1983

    Kaczvinsky, Donald P. *Lawrence Durrell's Major Novels*, 144–51.

    Pine, Richard. *Lawrence Durrell*, 325–87.

The Revolt of Aphrodite, 1970

    Kaczvinsky, Donald P. *Lawrence Durrell's Major Novels*, 88–104.

    Orr, Leonard. "Pleasures of the Immachination: Transformations of the Inanimate in Durrell and Pynchon," in Julius Rowan Raper et al., eds., *Lawrence Durrell*, 127–36.

    Pine, Richard. *Lawrence Durrell*, 247–321.

Sebastian; or, Ruling Passions, 1983

    Kaczvinsky, Donald P. *Lawrence Durrell's Major Novels*, 135–44.

    Pine, Richard. *Lawrence Durrell*, 325–87.

Tunc, 1968

    Kaczvinsky, Donald P. " 'Bringing him to the lure': Postmodern Society and the Modern Artist's felix culpa in Durrell's *Tunc/Nunquam."* *South Atlantic R* 59:4 (1994), 63–74.

Kaczvinsky, Donald P. *Lawrence Durrell's Major Novels*, 89–97.
Pine, Richard. *Lawrence Durrell*, 247–321.

White Eagles over Serbia, 1957

Pine, Richard. *Lawrence Durrell*, 87–88, 250–52.

MARIA EDGEWORTH

The Absentee, 1812

Corbett, Mary Jean. "Public Affections and Familial Politics: Burke, Edgeworth, and the 'Common Naturalization' of Great Britain." *ELH* 61 (1994), 882–86, 890–94.

Almeria, 1809

Chuilleanáin, Eiléan Ní. "The Voices of Maria Edgeworth's Comedy," in Theresa O'Connor, ed., *The Comic Tradition*, 22–24.

Belinda, 1801

Chuilleanáin, Eiléan Ní. "The Voices of Maria Edgeworth's Comedy," in Theresa O'Connor, ed., *The Comic Tradition*, 32–34.

Fitzgerald, Laurie. "Multiple Genres and Questions of Gender in Maria Edgeworth's *Belinda*." *Stud on Voltaire and the Eighteenth Cent* 304 (1992), 821–23.

Gonda, Caroline. *Reading Daughters' Fictions*, 214–20.

Jones, Darryl. "Frekes, Monsters and the Ladies: Attitudes to Female Sexuality in the 1790s." *Lit and Hist* 4:2 (1995), 15–19.

Kelly, Gary. "Class, Gender, Nation, and Empire: Money and Merit in the Writings of the Edgeworths." *Wordsworth Circle* 25 (1994), 92–93.

Kirkpatrick, Kathryn J. " 'Gentlemen Have Horrors Upon This Subject': West Indian Suitors in Maria Edgeworth's *Belinda*." *Eighteenth-Cent Fiction* 5 (1993), 331–48.

McCann, Andrew. "Conjugal Love and the Enlightenment Subject: The Colonial Context of Non-identity in Maria Edgeworth's *Belinda*." *Novel* 30 (1996), 56–75.

McFadyen, Heather. "Lady Delacour's Library: Maria Edgeworth's *Belinda* and Fashionable Reading." *Nineteenth-Cent Lit* 48 (1994), 423–39.

Mellor, Anne K. "A Novel of Their Own: Romantic Women's Fiction, 1790–1830," in John Richetti et al., eds., *The Columbia History*, 332–34.

Michals, Teresa. "Commerce and Character in Maria Edgeworth." *Nineteenth-Cent Lit* 49 (1994), 5–6, 9–20.

Perera, Suvendrini. *Reaches of Empire*, 15–34.

Richardson, Alan. *Literature, Education, and Romanticism*, 189–94.

Shaffer, Julie. "Not Subordinate: Empowering Women in the Marriage Plot—The Novels of Frances Burney, Maria Edgeworth, and Jane Austen," in Arthur F. Marotti et al., eds., *Reading with a Difference*, 31–34.

Smith, Patricia Juliana. " 'And I Wondered If She Might Kiss Me': Lesbian Panic as Narrative Strategy in British Women's Fiction." *Mod Fiction Stud* 41 (1995), 573–75.

Castle Rackrent, 1800

Corbett, Mary Jean. "Another Tale to Tell: Postcolonial Theory and the Case of *Castle Rackrent.*" *Criticism* 36 (1994), 383–98.

Deane, Seamus. *Strange Country*, 38–41, 44–47.

Ferris, Ina. *The Achievement of Literary Authority*, 105–22.

Hack, Daniel. "Inter-Nationalism: *Castle Rackrent* and Anglo-Irish Union." *Novel* 29 (1996), 145–62.

Kirkpatrick, Kathryn. "Putting Down the Rebellion: Notes and Glosses on *Castle Rackrent*, 1800." *Eire-Ireland* 30:1 (1995), 77–90.

Michals, Teresa. "Commerce and Character in Maria Edgeworth." *Nineteenth-Cent Lit* 49 (1994), 3–5.

Ó hÓgáin, Dáithí. "The Word, the Lore, and the Spirit: Folk Religion and the Supernatural in Modern Irish Literature," in Robert Welch, ed., *Irish Writers and Religion*, 43–44, 48–49.

Sturgess, Philip J. M. *Narrativity,* 289–97, 300–311.

Ennui, 1809

Ferris, Ina. "Narrating Cultural Encounter: Lady Morgan and the Irish National Tale." *Nineteenth-Cent Lit* 51 (1996), 300–301.

Myers, Mitzi. " 'Like the Pictures in a Magic Lantern': Gender, History, and Edgeworth's Rebellion Narratives." *Nineteenth-Cent Contexts* 19 (1996), 376–88.

Harrington, 1817

Brown, Penny. *The Captured World*, 26–28.

Gonda, Caroline. *Reading Daughters' Fictions*, 221–25.

Ragussis, Michael. *Figures of Conversion*, 57–88.

Helen, 1834

Gonda, Caroline. *Reading Daughters' Fictions*, 226–37.

Leonora, 1806

Kelly, Gary. "Class, Gender, Nation, and Empire: Money and Merit in the Writings of the Edgeworths." *Wordsworth Circle* 25 (1994), 92–93.

The Modern Griselda, 1805

Kelly, Gary. "Class, Gender, Nation, and Empire: Money and Merit in the Writings of the Edgeworths." *Wordsworth Circle* 25 (1994), 92–93.

Ormond, 1817

Chuilleanáin, Eiléan Ní. "The Voices of Maria Edgeworth's Comedy," in Theresa O'Connor, ed., *The Comic Tradition*, 35–39.

Gonda, Caroline. *Reading Daughters' Fictions*, 225–26.

ANNIE EDWARDS

A Girton Girl, 1885

Antor, Heinz. *Der englische Universitätsroman,* 451–53, 456–57, 462–64.

AMELIA EDWARDES

Hand and Glove, 1858

Rees, Joan. *Writings on the Nile,* 75–78.

GEORGE EGERTON

Keynotes, 1893

McCullough, Kate. "Mapping the *'Terra Incognita'* of Woman: George Egerton's *Keynotes* (1893) and New Woman Fiction," in Barbara Leah Harman and Susan Meyer, eds., *The New Nineteenth Century,* 205–22.

GEORGE ELIOT

Adam Bede, 1859

Bellringer, Alan W. *George Eliot,* 18–42.

Bodenheimer, Rosemarie. *The Real Life of Mary Ann Evans,* 130–34, 171–74.

Carroll, David. *George Eliot and the Conflict of Interpretations,* 73–105.

Crick, Brian. "George Eliot 'Tries to Run Away From Her Shadow': The Hold of the Familial on Sexual Passion." *Crit R* 35 (1995), 138–39.

Duncan, Edwin. "*Adam Bede, Hard Times,* and Melodrama." *Lamar J of the Hum* 19:1 (1993), 43–55.

Eifrig, Gail McGrew. "History and Memory in *Adam Bede.*" *Soundings* 76 (1993), 407–20.

Erickson, Joyce Quiring. "Multiculturalism and the Question of Audience: *Adam Bede* as a Test Case." *Victorian Newsl* 85 (1994), 20–25.

Granlund, Helena. *The Paradox of Self-Love,* 35–41, 51–58, 103–8, 128–30.

Gribble, Jennifer. "The Hidden Shame: Telling Hetty Sorrel's Story." *Sydney Stud in Engl* 22 (1996–97), 102–19.

Heidt, Edward R. *The Image of the Church Minister,* 40–46.

Heyns, Michiel. *Expulsion and the Nineteenth-Century Novel,* 148–53.

Homans, Margaret. "Dinah's Blush, Maggie's Arm: Class, Gender, and Sexuality in George Eliot's Early Novels." *Victorian Stud* 36 (1993), 158–68.

Horsman, Alan. *The Victorian Novel,* 298–302.

Houston, Natalie M. "George Eliot's Material History: Clothing and Realist Narrative." *Stud in the Liter Imagination* 29:1 (1996), 24–26.

Jackson, Tony E. *The Subject of Modernism,* 41–46.

Johnstone, Peggy Fitzhugh. *The Transformation of Rage*, 24–40.

Jones, W. Gareth. "George Eliot's *Adam Bede* and Tolstoy's Conception of *Anna Karenina,*" in Jones, ed., *Tolstoi and Britain*, 79–92.

Lambert, Ellen Zetzel. *The Face of Love,* 143–45.

Logan, Deborah A. "Am I My Sister's Keeper? Sexual Deviance and the Social Community." *Victorian Newsl* 90 (1996), 18–27.

Luftig, Victor. *Seeing Together*, 63–68.

McKnight, Natalie J. *Suffering Mothers*, 115–24.

McLaughlin, Mark Warren. "*Adam Bede:* History, Narrative, Culture." *Victorians Inst J* 22 (1994), 55–73.

Martin, Carol A. *George Eliot's Serial Fiction*, 95–105.

Matus, Jill. " 'The Unnaturalness of her Crime': Mid-Victorian Representations of Maternal Deviance," in Barbara Thaden, ed., *New Essays on the Maternal Voice,* 80–88.

Matus, Jill L. *Unstable Bodies,* 167–79.

Mitchell, Judith. *The Stone and the Scorpion*, 92–104.

Mothersole, Brenda. "The 'Fallen Woman' in the Victorian Novel," in John Morris, ed., *Exploring Stereotyped Images,* 201–5.

Mugglestone, Lynda. " 'Grammatical fair ones': Women, Men, and Attitudes to Language in the Novels of George Eliot." *R of Engl Stud* 46 (1995), 13–16.

Novy, Marianne. *Engaging with Shakespeare,* 59–61.

Panek, Jennifer. "Constructions of Masculinity in *Adam Bede* and *Wives and Daughters." Victorian R* 22 (1996), 127–48.

Pyle, Forest. *The Ideology of Imagination*, 155–60.

Pyle, Forest. "A Novel Sympathy: The Imagination of Community in George Eliot." *Novel* 27 (1993), 7–23.

Ruth, Katrina. "The Imaginary Vision in *Adam Bede:* Hetty's Mirrors and the *objet a." George Eliot R* 27 (1996), 49–55.

Spittles, Brian. *George Eliot*, 52–54, 97–100, 176–78.

Sutherland, John. *Is Heathcliff a Murderer?,* 110–16.

Terry, R. C. " 'Have at the Masters!': Working-Class Stereotypes in Some Nineteenth-Century Novels," in John Morris, ed., *Exploring Stereotyped Images,* 156–58.

Tush, Susan Rowland. *George Eliot and . . . Popular Women's Fiction,* 15–58.

Weisser, Susan Ostrov. *A "Craving Fancy,"* 126–29.

Winnifrith, Tom. *Fallen Women,* 52–56, 67–69.

Wolfreys, Julian. *Being English,* 132–36.

Daniel Deronda, 1876

Bailin, Miriam. *The Sickroom in Victorian Fiction,* 132–34.

Barfoot, C. C. "The Gist of the Gothic in English Fiction; or, Gothic and the Invasion of Boundaries," in Valeria Tinkler-Villani and Peter Davidson, eds., *Exhibited by Candlelight,* 169–72.

Baumgarten, Murray. "Seeing Double: Jews in the Fiction of F. Scott Fitzgerald, Charles Dickens, Anthony Trollope, and George Eliot," in Bryan Cheyette, ed., *Between 'Race' and Culture*, 54–56.

Beer, Gillian. "George Eliot and the Novel of Ideas," in John Richetti et al., eds., *The Columbia History*, 430–31, 449–50.

Bellringer, Alan W. *George Eliot*, 90–100.

Bernstein, Susan David. *Confessional Subjects*, 105–41.

Bodenheimer, Rosemarie. *The Real Life of Mary Ann Evans,* 173–75, 181–88, 257–66.

Bonaparte, Felicia. "*Daniel Deronda:* Theology in a Secular Age." *Rel and Lit* 25:3 (1993), 17–41.

Born, Daniel. *The Birth of Liberal Guilt,* 54–70.

Brantlinger, Patrick. *Fictions of State*, 178–82.

Byatt, A. S., and Ignês Sodré. *Imagining Characters*, 78–117.

Carroll, David. *George Eliot and the Conflict of Interpretations*, 273–312.

Demoor, Marysa. "Male Monsters or Monstrous Males in Victorian Women's Fiction," in Valeria Tinkler-Villani and Peter Davidson, eds., *Exhibited by Candlelight*, 178–80.

Dowling, Andrew. " 'The Other Side of Silence': Matrimonial Conflict and the Divorce Court in George Eliot's Fiction." *Nineteenth-Cent Lit* 50 (1995), 331–36.

Dupeyron-Lafay, Françoise. "Savoir ancien, savoir nouveau dans *Daniel Deronda.*" *Cahiers Victoriens et Edouardiens* 43 (1996), 197–209.

During, Lisabeth. "The Concept of Dread: Sympathy and Ethics in *Daniel Deronda.*" *Crit R* 33 (1993), 88–109.

Ermarth, Elizabeth Deeds. "George Eliot and the World as Language," in John Rignall, ed., *George Eliot and Europe*, 40–43.

Granlund, Helena. *The Paradox of Self-Love*, 45–51, 58–66, 113–24, 134–42.

Haroian-Guerin, Gil. *The Fatal Hero*, 163–90.

Helsinger, Elizabeth K. *Rural Scenes and National Representation*, 230–32.

Heyns, Michiel. *Expulsion and the Nineteenth-Century Novel,* 34–39, 153–82.

Hirsch, Pam. "Women and Jews in *Daniel Deronda.*" *George Eliot R* 25 (1994), 45–49.

Hochberg, Shifra. "*Daniel Deronda* and Wordsworth's 'The White Doe of Rylstone.' " *Engl Lang Notes* 31:3 (1994), 43–49.

Hollahan, Eugene. *Crisis-Consciousness*, 84–95.

Horsman, Alan. *The Victorian Novel*, 323–30.

Jackson, Tony E. *The Subject of Modernism,* 47–66.

Johnstone, Peggy Fitzhugh. *The Transformation of Rage*, 159–80.

Knapp, Shoshana Milgram. " 'Too intensely French for my taste': Victor Hugo as Read by George Eliot and George Henry Lewes," in John Rignall, ed., *George Eliot and Europe*, 204–9.

Kuczynski, Ingrid. "Der Blick auf das Andere: Das Konstrukt des Judentums in George Eliots Roman *Daniel Deronda,* " in Inge Stephan et al., eds., *Jüdische Kultur und Weiblichkeit,* 73–82.

Lambert, Ellen Zetzel. *The Face of Love,* 145–49.

Law-Viljoen, Bronwyn. "Midrash, Myth, and Prophecy: George Eliot's Reinterpretation of Biblical Stories." *Lit and Theology* 11:1 (1997), 83–90.

Luftig, Victor. *Seeing Together,* 59–61, 76–90.

McKnight, Natalie J. *Suffering Mothers,* 130–38.

McMullen, Bonnie. " 'The Interest of Spanish Sights': From Ronda to *Daniel Deronda,*" in John Rignall, ed., *George Eliot and Europe,* 123–37.

Marshall, Gail. "Actresses, Statues and Speculation in *Daniel Deronda.*" *Essays in Criticism* 44 (1994), 117–37.

Martin, Carol A. *George Eliot's Serial Fiction,* 211–37, 238–59.

Meyer, Susan. *Imperialism at Home,* 157–201.

Miller, Derek. "*Daniel Deronda* and Allegories of Empire," in John Rignall, ed., *George Eliot and Europe,* 113–22.

Miller, Derek. "A Note on Hermione in *Daniel Deronda.*" *George Eliot R* 24 (1993), 46.

Mitchell, Judith. *The Stone and the Scorpion,* 134–53.

Myer, Valerie Grosvenor. *Ten Great English Novelists,* 141–44.

Novy, Marianne. *Engaging with Shakespeare,* 117–37.

Nurbhai, Saleel. "Metafiction and Metaphor: *Daniel Deronda* as Golem." *George Eliot R* 25 (1994), 39–43.

Ragussis, Michael. *Figures of Conversion,* 60–62, 234–40, 260–98.

Rignall, John. "George Eliot, Balzac and Proust," in Rignall, ed., *George Eliot and Europe,* 215–24.

Rignall, John. *Realist Fiction,* 103–13.

Robertson, Linda K. "From Reality to Fiction: Benefits and Hazards in Continental Education," in John Rignall, ed., *George Eliot and Europe,* 160–64.

Rowe, Margaret Moan. *Doris Lessing,* 52–56.

Shaw, Harry E. "Loose Narrators: Display, Engagement, and the Search for a Place in History in Realist Fiction." *Narrative* 3 (1995), 109–13.

Sousa Correa, Delia de. "George Eliot and the Germanic 'Musical Magus,' " in John Rignall, ed., *George Eliot and Europe,* 98–112.

Spittles, Brian. *George Eliot,* 83–87, 139–41, 167–70, 185–87.

Stewart, Garrett. *Dear Reader,* 301–28.

Stone, Carole. "George Eliot's *Daniel Deronda:* 'The Case History of Gwendolen H.' " *Nineteenth Cent Stud* 7 (1993), 57–66.

Swann, Charles. "A George Eliot Debt to George Meredith: From *Rhoda Fleming* to *Daniel Deronda.*" *Notes and Queries* 43 (1996), 46–47.

Swann, Charles. "Miss Harleth, Miss Mackenzie: Mirror Images?" *Notes and Queries* 43 (1996), 47–48.

Sypher, Eileen. "Resisting Gwendolen's 'Subjection': *Daniel Deronda*'s Proto-Feminism." *Stud in the Novel* 28 (1996), 506–21.

Vitaglione, Daniel. *George Eliot and George Sand,* 1–5.

Vrettos, Athena. *Somatic Fictions*, 58–64, 69–80.

Weisser, Susan Ostrov. *A "Craving Fancy,"* 141–49.

Weliver, Phyllis. "Music as a Sign in *Daniel Deronda.*" *George Eliot R* 27 (1996), 43–47.

Wheeler, Michael. *English Fiction of the Victorian Period*, 152–54.

Winnifrith, Tom. *Fallen Women*, 64–69, 156–58.

Wolfreys, Julian. *Being English*, 129–50.

Wolfreys, Julian. "The Ideology of Englishness: The Paradoxes of Tory-Liberal Culture and National Identity in *Daniel Deronda.*" *George Eliot–George Henry Lewes Stud* 26–27 (1994), 15–33.

Würzbach, Natascha. "The Mother Image as Cultural Concept and Literary Theme in the Nineteenth- and Twentieth-Century English Novel: A Feminist Reading within the Context of New Historicism and the History of Mentalities," in Rüdiger Ahrens and Laurenz Volkmann, eds., *Why Literature Matters*, 377–78.

Zimmerman, Bonnie. "George Eliot's Sacred Chest of Language," in Alison Booth, ed., *Famous Last Words*, 154–73.

Felix Holt, 1866

Beer, Gillian. "George Eliot and the Novel of Ideas," in John Richetti et al., eds., *The Columbia History*, 430–31, 450–51.

Bellringer, Alan W. *George Eliot*, 101–4.

Bode, Rita. "Power and Submission in *Felix Holt, the Radical.*" *Stud in Engl Lit, 1500–1900* 35 (1995), 769–86.

Carroll, David. *George Eliot and the Conflict of Interpretations*, 201–33.

Cohen, Monica F. "Professing Renunciation: Domesticity in *The Cloister and the Hearth* and *Felix Holt.*" *Victorian Lit and Culture* 23 (1995), 280–96.

Colby, Robin B. *"Some Appointed Work To Do,"* 28–31.

Ermarth, Elizabeth Deeds. *The English Novel in History*, 91–93.

Gray, Beryl. "The Power of Provincial Culture: *Felix Holt.*" *George Eliot–George Henry Lewes Stud* 24–25:2 (1993), 17–35.

Guy, Josephine M. *The Victorian Social-Problem Novel*, 186–203.

Harsh, Constance D. *Subversive Heroines*, 148–57, 160–65.

Hochberg, Shifra. "Nomenclature and the Historical Matrix of *Felix Holt.*" *Engl Lang Notes* 31:2 (1993), 46–53.

Hollahan, Eugene. *Crisis-Consciousness*, 67–79.

Horsman, Alan. *The Victorian Novel*, 309–16.

Ingham, Patricia. *The Language of Gender and Class*, 113–36.

Johnstone, Peggy Fitzhugh. *The Transformation of Rage*, 111–31.

Lesjak, Carolyn. "A Modern Odyssey: Realism, the Masses, and Nationalism in George Eliot's *Felix Holt.*" *Novel* 30 (1996), 78–95.

Milton, Paul. "Inheritance as the Key to all Mythologies: George Eliot and Legal Practice." *Mosaic* 28:1 (1995), 54–57.

Mugglestone, Lynda. " 'Grammatical fair ones': Women, Men, and Attitudes to Language in the Novels of George Eliot." *R of Engl Stud* 46 (1995), 17–20.

Novy, Marianne. *Engaging with Shakespeare,* 69–93.

Spittles, Brian. *George Eliot,* 115–17, 150–55, 180–82.

Visser, Nicholas. "Roaring Beasts and Raging Floods: The Representation of Political Crowds in the Nineteenth-Century British Novel." *Mod Lang R* 89 (1994), 308–10.

Vitaglione, Daniel. *George Eliot and George Sand,* 80–83, 99–101.

Winnifrith, Tom. *Fallen Women,* 60–62, 67–69.

Würzbach, Natascha. "The Mother Image as Cultural Concept and Literary Theme in the Nineteenth- and Twentieth-Century English Novel: A Feminist Reading within the Context of New Historicism and the History of Mentalities," in Rüdiger Ahrens and Laurenz Volkmann, eds., *Why Literature Matters,* 379–80.

Middlemarch, 1872

Andres, Sophia. "The Unhistoric in History: George Eliot's Challenge to Victorian Historiography." *Clio* 26:1 (1996), 79–95.

apRoberts, Ruth. "The Clergy in *Middlemarch:* A Note." *George Eliot–George Henry Lewes Stud* 26–27 (1994), 33–35.

Barrat, Alain. "*Middlemarch:* A Darkening Vision of Provincial Life." *Cahiers Victoriens et Edouardiens* 38 (1993), 105–14.

Barreca, Regina. *Untamed and Unabashed,* 97–108.

Beer, Gillian. "George Eliot and the Novel of Ideas," in John Richetti et al., eds., *The Columbia History,* 430–32, 437–43, 447–49, 451–55.

Bellringer, Alan W. *George Eliot,* 104–21.

Blumberg, Edwina Jannie. "Tolstoy and the English Novel: A Note on *Middlemarch* and *Anna Karenina,*" in W. Gareth Jones, ed., *Tolstoi and Britain,* 93–104.

Bodenheimer, Rosemarie. *The Real Life of Mary Ann Evans,* 53–55, 151–57, 174–76, 220–24.

Carroll, David. *George Eliot and the Conflict of Interpretations,* 234–72.

Clifford, David. "The Dead Hand in *Middlemarch.*" *George Eliot R* 27 (1996), 64–65.

Cohen, Michael. *Sisters,* 98–101, 162–71.

Crick, Brian. "George Eliot 'Tries to Run Away From Her Shadow': The Hold of the Familial on Sexual Passion." *Crit R* 35 (1995), 153–65.

Demoor, Marysa. "Male Monsters or Monstrous Males in Victorian Women's Fiction," in Valeria Tinkler-Villani and Peter Davidson, eds., *Exhibited by Candlelight,* 181–82.

Dowling, Andrew. " 'The Other Side of Silence': Matrimonial Conflict and the Divorce Court in George Eliot's Fiction." *Nineteenth-Cent Lit* 50 (1995), 329–31.

Ermarth, Elizabeth Deeds. *The English Novel in History,* 160–64.

Ermarth, Elizabeth Deeds. "George Eliot and the World as Language," in John Rignall, ed., *George Eliot and Europe,* 34–38.

Ferris, David. *Theory and the Evasion of History,* 183–230.

Franklin, J. Jeffrey. "The Victorian Discourse of Gambling: Speculations on *Middlemarch* and *The Duke's Children.*" *ELH* 61 (1994), 899–918.

Furst, Lilian R. "Struggling for Medical Reform in Middlemarch." *Nineteenth-Cent Lit* 48 (1993), 341–61.

Gervais, David. "Televising *Middlemarch*." *English* 43 (1994), 59–64.

Gordon, Jan B. *Gossip and Subversion*, 237–94.

Gowdy, Anne Razey. "The Illusory Angel: The Perfect Victorian Wife." *Univ of Mississippi Stud in Engl* 11–12 (1993–95), 11–23.

Granlund, Helena. *The Paradox of Self-Love*, 66–74, 84–88, 108–13, 142–45.

Green, Janet M. "Eliot's *Middlemarch*." *Explicator* 53 (1995), 89–92.

Green, Laura. " 'At once narrow and promiscuous': Emily Davies, George Eliot, and *Middlemarch*." *Nineteenth Cent Stud* 9 (1995), 1–27.

Guth, Deborah. "Strategies of Surprise in *Middlemarch*." *Cahiers Victoriens et Edouardiens* 38 (1993), 115–25.

Hardy, Barbara. "The Miserable Marriages in *Middlemarch, Anna Karenina,* and *Effi Briest,*" in John Rignall, ed., *George Eliot and Europe*, 64–83.

Hardy, Barbara. "Rome in *Middlemarch*: A Need for Foreignness." *George Eliot–George Henry Lewes Stud* 24–25:2 (1993), 1–16.

Harris, Margaret. "Whose *Middlemarch*? The 1994 British Broadcasting Corporation Television Production." *Sydney Stud in Engl* 21 (1995–96), 95–102.

Harter, Deborah A. *Bodies in Pieces*, 114–22.

Hollahan, Eugene. *Crisis-Consciousness*, 79–84.

Horsman, Alan. *The Victorian Novel*, 315–23.

Houston, Natalie M. "George Eliot's Material History: Clothing and Realist Narrative." *Stud in the Liter Imagination* 29:1 (1996), 26–29.

Jenkins, Ruth Y. *Reclaiming Myths of Power*, 117–21, 126–40, 142–44.

Johnson, Patricia E. "The Gendered Politics of the Gaze: Henry James and George Eliot." *Mosaic* 30:1 (1997), 39–40, 46–53.

Johnstone, Peggy Fitzhugh. *The Transformation of Rage*, 132–58.

Jumeau, Alain. "*Middlemarch: a Study of Provincial Life*—réflexions et spéculations sur un titre de George Eliot." *Cahiers Victoriens et Edouardiens* 38 (1993), 129–44.

Knapp, Shoshana Milgram. " 'Too intensely French for my taste': Victor Hugo as Read by George Eliot and George Henry Lewes," in John Rignall, ed., *George Eliot and Europe*, 199–203.

Lamarque, Peter, and Stein Haugom Olsen. *Truth, Fiction, and Literature*, 140–42, 334–36.

Lambert, Ellen Zetzel. *The Face of Love*, 129–36.

Langland, Elizabeth. "Inventing Reality: The Ideological Commitments of George Eliot's *Middlemarch*." *Narrative* 2 (1994), 87–106.

Lerner, Laurence. "Stereotypes of Woman in Victorian England," in John Morris, ed., *Exploring Stereotyped Images*, 50–52.

McKnight, Natalie J. *Suffering Mothers*, 124–30.

McMaster, Juliet. "Will Ladislaw and Other Italians with White Mice." *Victorian R* 16:2 (1990), 1–6.

Majumdar, Santanu. "Memory and Identity in Wordsworth and in George Eliot's *Middlemarch*." *Crit R* 36 (1996), 41–61.

Martin, Bruce K. "Fred Vincy and the Unravelling of *Middlemarch*." *Papers on Lang and Lit* 30 (1994), 3–23.

Martin, Carol A. *George Eliot's Serial Fiction*, 182–209, 241–54.

Matus, Jill L. "Saint Teresa, Hysteria, and *Middlemarch*." *J of the Hist of Sexuality* 1 (1990), 215–40.

Matus, Jill L. *Unstable Bodies*, 213–44.

Maxwell, Catherine. "The Brooking of Desire: Dorothea and Deferment in *Middlemarch*." *Yrbk of Engl Stud* 26 (1996), 116–26.

Meaney, Gerardine. *(Un)Like Subjects*, 124–27.

Michie, Elsie B. *Outside the Pale*, 155–66, 168–71.

Mills, Chester St. H. "Eliot's Spanish Connection: Casaubon, the Avatar of Quixote." *George Eliot–George Henry Lewes Stud* 26–27 (1994), 1–6.

Milton, Paul. "Inheritance as the Key to all Mythologies: George Eliot and Legal Practice." *Mosaic* 28:1 (1995), 57–67.

Mitchell, Judith. *The Stone and the Scorpion*, 121–34.

Monk, Leland. *Standard Deviations*, 51–73.

Moscovici, Claudia. "Allusive Mischaracterization in *Middlemarch*." *Nineteenth-Cent Lit* 49 (1995), 513–31.

Mugglestone, Lynda. " 'Grammatical fair ones': Women, Men, and Attitudes to Language in the Novels of George Eliot." *R of Engl Stud* 46 (1995), 11–25.

Newey, Vincent. *Centring the Self*, 211–13.

Novy, Marianne. *Engaging with Shakespeare*, 94–116.

Perkin, J. Russell. "Locking George Sand in the Attic: Female Passion and Domestic Realism in the Victorian Novel." *Univ of Toronto Q* 63 (1993–94), 421–25.

Pyle, Forest. *The Ideology of Imagination*, 160–65.

Ricks, Christopher. *Essays in Appreciation*, 210–12, 225–28, 230–33, 280–83.

Rignall, John. *Realist Fiction*, 99–104.

Rischin, Abigail S. "Beside the Reclining Statue: Ekphrasis, Narrative, and Desire in *Middlemarch*." *PMLA* 111 (1996), 1121–30.

Robertson, Linda K. "From Reality to Fiction: Benefits and Hazards in Continental Education," in John Rignall, ed., *George Eliot and Europe*, 161–64.

Rothfield, Lawrence. *Vital Signs*, 84–119.

Seeber, Hans Ulrich. "Cultural Synthesis in George Eliot's *Middlemarch*," in John Rignall, ed., *George Eliot and Europe*, 17–32.

Shuttleworth, Sally. "Sexuality and Knowledge in *Middlemarch*." *Nineteenth-Cent Contexts* 19 (1996), 425–36.

Spittles, Brian. *George Eliot*, 6–10, 47–52, 79–81, 110–16, 121–27, 141–46, 181–85.

Stewart, Garrett. *Dear Reader*, 323–25.

Sutherland, John. *Is Heathcliff a Murderer?*, 146–55.

Tush, Susan Rowland. *George Eliot and . . . Popular Women's Fiction*, 111–66.

Vitaglione, Daniel. *George Eliot and George Sand*, 25–27, 128–35.

Vrettos, Athena. *Somatic Fictions*, 105–10.

Wheeler, Michael. *English Fiction of the Victorian Period*, 146–53.

Winnifrith, Tom. *Fallen Women*, 62–64, 145–47.

Wormald, Mark. "Microscopy and Semiotic in *Middlemarch*." *Nineteenth-Cent Lit* 50 (1996), 501–24.

Yoon, Hae-ryung. "George Eliot's *Middlemarch* as 'The Novel of Vocation.' " *J of Engl Lang and Lit* 41 (1995), 983–1004.

York, R. A. *Strangers and Secrets*, 134–49.

Zimmerman, Bonnie. "George Eliot's Sacred Chest of Language," in Alison Booth, ed., *Famous Last Words*, 157–60.

The Mill on the Floss, 1860

Banerjee, Jacqueline. "Girls' Education and the Crisis of the Heroine in Victorian Fiction." *Engl Stud* (Amsterdam) 75 (1994), 36–38.

Barreca, Regina. *Untamed and Unabashed,* 89–97.

Barreca, Regina. "Writing as Voodoo: Sorcery, Hysteria, and Art," in Sarah Webster Goodwin and Elisabeth Bronfen, eds., *Death and Representation*, 184–85.

Beer, Gillian. "George Eliot and the Novel of Ideas," in John Richetti et al., eds., *The Columbia History*, 433–37.

Bellringer, Alan W. *George Eliot*, 43–62.

Bodenheimer, Rosemarie. *The Real Life of Mary Ann Evans,* 101–11, 146–48.

Brown, Penny. *The Captured World,* 161–70.

Carroll, David. *George Eliot and the Conflict of Interpretations*, 106–39.

Cohen, William A. *Sex Scandal*, 130–58.

Crick, Brian. "George Eliot 'Tries to Run Away From Her Shadow': The Hold of the Familial on Sexual Passion." *Crit R* 35 (1995), 139–52.

Dickerson, Vanessa D. "Feminine Transactions: Money and Nineteenth-Century British Women Writers," in John Louis DiGaetani, ed., *Money*, 233–36.

Emmitt, Helen V. " 'Drowned in a Willing Sea': Freedom and Drowning in Eliot, Chopin, and Drabble." *Tulsa Stud in Women's Lit* 12 (1993), 317–20.

Esty, Joshua D. "Nationhood, Adulthood, and the Ruptures of *Bildung*: Arresting Development in *The Mill on the Floss*." *Narrative* 4 (1996), 142–56.

Frith, Gill. "Playing with Shawls: George Eliot's Use of *Corinne* in *The Mill on the Floss*," in John Rignall, ed., *George Eliot and Europe*, 225–39.

Fuchs, Eva. "Eliot's *The Mill on the Floss*." *Explicator* 52 (1994), 79–80.

Granlund, Helena. *The Paradox of Self-Love*, 77–84.

Gray, Beryl. " 'Animated Nature': *The Mill on the Floss*," in John Rignall, ed., *George Eliot and Europe*, 138–55.

Helsinger, Elizabeth K. *Rural Scenes and National Representation*, 225–30, 232–34.

Homans, Margaret. "Dinah's Blush, Maggie's Arm: Class, Gender, and Sexuality in George Eliot's Early Novels." *Victorian Stud* 36 (1993), 168–77.

Horsman, Alan. *The Victorian Novel*, 302–5.

Hottle, Karen E. "Thou Shalt Not Read: Maggie's Arrested Development in *The Mill on the Floss.*" *George Eliot R* 26 (1995), 35–40.

Houston, Natalie M. "George Eliot's Material History: Clothing and Realist Narrative." *Stud in the Liter Imagination* 29:1 (1996), 29–31.

Johnstone, Peggy Fitzhugh. *The Transformation of Rage*, 41–67.

Lambert, Ellen Zetzel. *The Face of Love,* 138–41.

Luftig, Victor. *Seeing Together*, 67–73.

Martin, Carol A. *George Eliot's Serial Fiction*, 106–20.

Meyer, Susan. *Imperialism at Home*, 126–56.

Mitchell, Judith. *The Stone and the Scorpion*, 104–21.

Nichols, Nina daVinci. *Ariadne's Lives,* 79–94.

Polhemus, Robert M. "Lewis Carroll and the Child in Victorian Fiction," in John Richetti et al., eds., *The Columbia History*, 596–97.

Pyle, Forest. *The Ideology of Imagination*, 150–55, 160–64.

Pyle, Forest. "A Novel Sympathy: The Imagination of Community in George Eliot." *Novel* 27 (1993), 7–23.

Reynolds, Kimberley, and Nicola Humble. *Victorian Heroines,* 89–93.

Rignall, John. "Metaphor, Truth and the Mobile Imagination in *The Mill on the Floss.*" *George Eliot R* 24 (1993), 36–40.

Robertson, Linda K. "Horses and Hounds: The Importance of Animals in *The Mill on the Floss.*" *George Eliot R* 26 (1995), 61–63.

Smith, Jonathan. *Fact and Feeling,* 130–51.

Spittles, Brian. *George Eliot*, 88–90, 94–99, 173–75.

Szirotny, June Skye. "Maggie Tulliver's Sad Sacrifice: Confusing But Not Confused." *Stud in the Novel* 28 (1996), 178–94.

Tush, Susan Rowland. *George Eliot and . . . Popular Women's Fiction*, 63–106.

Weisser, Susan Ostrov. *A "Craving Fancy,"* 129–41.

Winnifrith, Tom. *Fallen Women,* 57–59.

Wyatt, Jean. *Reconstructing Desire,* 134–36.

Yoon, Hye-joon. "Dorlcote Mill: A Note on Social History in George Eliot's *The Mill on the Floss.*" *J of Engl Lang and Lit* 40 (1994), 689–99.

Romola, 1863

Bailin, Miriam. *The Sickroom in Victorian Fiction,* 123–31.

Beer, Gillian. "George Eliot and the Novel of Ideas," in John Richetti et al., eds., *The Columbia History*, 444–47.

Bellringer, Alan W. *George Eliot*, 80–90.

Booth, Alison. "The Silence of Great Men: Statuesque Femininity and the Ending of *Romola,*" in Booth, ed., *Famous Last Words*, 110–28.

Bullen, J. B. *The Myth of the Renaissance*, 208–38.

Carroll, David. *George Eliot and the Conflict of Interpretations*, 167–200.

Fontana, Ernest. "George Eliot's *Romola* and Emerson's 'The American Scholar.' " *Engl Lang Notes* 32:4 (1995), 70–75.

Fraser, Hilary. "Titian's *Il Bravo* and George Eliot's Tito: A Painted Record." *Nineteenth-Cent Lit* 50 (1995), 210–17.

Gordon, Lesley. "Greek Scholarship and Renaissance Florence in George Eliot's *Romola*," in John Rignall, ed., *George Eliot and Europe*, 179–89.

Gordon, Lesley. "Tito, Dionysus and Apollo: An Examination of Tito Melema in *Romola*." *George Eliot R* 25 (1994), 34–37.

Granlund, Helena. *The Paradox of Self-Love*, 32–45, 88–103, 130–34.

Han, Ae-kyung. "A Study of *Romola*: Focussing on Romola's Life." *J of Engl Lang and Lit* 41 (1995), 377–401.

Horsman, Alan. *The Victorian Novel*, 307–9.

Johnstone, Peggy Fitzhugh. *The Transformation of Rage*, 86–110.

Malley, Shawn. " 'The Listening Look': Visual and Verbal Metaphor in Frederic Leighton's Illustrations to George Eliot's *Romola*." *Nineteenth-Cent Contexts* 19 (1996), 259–78.

Martin, Carol A. *George Eliot's Serial Fiction*, 123–52.

Michie, Elsie B. *Outside the Pale*, 147–49.

Orel, Harold. *The Historical Novel*, 22–25.

Ragussis, Michael. *Figures of Conversion*, 281–83.

Ricks, Christopher. *Essays in Appreciation*, 227–29.

Sanders, Andrew. " 'Sixty Years Since': Victorian Historical Fiction from Dickens to Eliot," in Susana Onega, ed., *Telling Histories*, 25–27.

Schiefelbein, Michael. "Crucifixes and Madonnas: George Eliot's Fascination with Catholicism in *Romola*." *Victorian Newsl* 88 (1995), 31–34.

Spittles, Brian. *George Eliot*, 126–29.

Sweeney, Kevin W., and Elizabeth Winston. "Redirecting Melodrama: Gish, Henry King, and *Romola*." *Lit/Film Q* 23 (1995), 137–43.

Vitaglione, Daniel. *George Eliot and George Sand*, 43–57.

Winnifrith, Tom. "Renaissance and Risorgimento in *Romola*," in John Rignall, ed., *George Eliot and Europe*, 166–78.

Scenes of Clerical Life, 1858

Bailin, Miriam. *The Sickroom in Victorian Fiction*, 111–22.

Barrat, Alain. "Nostalgia and Reform in *Scenes of Clerical Life*." *Cahiers Victoriens et Edouardiens* 41 (1995), 47–57.

Bellringer, Alan W. *George Eliot*, 63–71.

Bodenheimer, Rosemarie. *The Real Life of Mary Ann Evans*, 49–51, 169–71, 180–82.

Carroll, David. *George Eliot and the Conflict of Interpretations*, 38–72.

Dickerson, Vanessa D. *Victorian Ghosts in the Noontide*, 95–102.

Heidt, Edward R. *The Image of the Church Minister,* 46–50.

Horsman, Alan. *The Victorian Novel,* 297–98.

Johnstone, Peggy Fitzhugh. *The Transformation of Rage,* 19–21.

Luftig, Victor. *Seeing Together,* 69–76.

Martin, Carol A. *George Eliot's Serial Fiction,* 32–93.

Ricks, Christopher. *Essays in Appreciation,* 221–23.

Shaw, Harry E. "Loose Narrators: Display, Engagement, and the Search for a Place in History in Realist Fiction." *Narrative* 3 (1995), 104–8.

Vitaglione, Daniel. *George Eliot and George Sand,* 128–32.

Weisser, Susan Ostrov. *A "Craving Fancy,"* 118–26.

Winnifrith, T. J. " 'Subtle Shadowy Suggestions': Fact and Fiction in *Scenes of Clerical Life." George Eliot–George Henry Lewes Stud* 24–25:2 (1993), 65–75.

Silas Marner, 1861

Almond, Barbara, and Richard Almond. *The Therapeutic Narrative,* 93–106.

Bailin, Miriam. *The Sickroom in Victorian Fiction,* 129–30.

Beer, Gillian. "George Eliot and the Novel of Ideas," in John Richetti et al., eds., *The Columbia History,* 447–48.

Bellringer, Alan W. *George Eliot,* 73–79.

Bodenheimer, Rosemarie. *The Real Life of Mary Ann Evans,* 204–8.

Brown, Penny. *The Captured World,* 57–60.

Carroll, David. *George Eliot and the Conflict of Interpretations,* 140–66.

Fujisawa, Matoshi. "Yasushi Inone's *Aru onna no shi* and George Eliot's *Silas Marner:* Some Notes on Influence." *Compar Lit Stud* 33 (1996), 69–73.

Horsman, Alan. *The Victorian Novel,* 306–7.

Johnstone, Peggy Fitzhugh. *The Transformation of Rage,* 68–85.

Mugglestone, Lynda. " 'Grammatical fair ones': Women, Men, and Attitudes to Language in the Novels of George Eliot." *R of Engl Stud* 46 (1995), 16–18.

Nunokawa, Jeff. "The Miser's Two Bodies: *Silas Marner* and the Sexual Possibilities of the Commodity." *Victorian Stud* 36 (1993), 273–90.

Spittles, Brian. *George Eliot,* 57–59, 85–87, 175–77, 185–87.

Swinden, Patrick. *"Silas Marner,"* 23–115.

Wheeler, Michael. *English Fiction of the Victorian Period,* 140–46.

Wolfreys, Julian. *Being English,* 132–36.

ALICE THOMAS ELLIS

The Birds of the Air, 1980

Conradi, Peter. "Alice Thomas Ellis: Kinder, Kirche und Küche," in Sarah Sceats and Gail Cunningham, eds., *Image and Power,* 155–56.

The Other Side of the Fire, 1983

Conradi, Peter. "Alice Thomas Ellis: Kinder, Kirche und Küche," in Sarah Sceats and Gail Cunningham, eds., *Image and Power,* 156–57.

The Sin Eater, 1977

Conradi, Peter. "Alice Thomas Ellis: Kinder, Kirche und Küche," in Sarah Sceats and Gail Cunningham, eds., *Image and Power*, 154–55.

The 27th Kingdom, 1982

Conradi, Peter. "Alice Thomas Ellis: Kinder, Kirche und Küche," in Sarah Sceats and Gail Cunningham, eds., *Image and Power*, 157–58.

Unexplained Laughter, 1985

Conradi, Peter. "Alice Thomas Ellis: Kinder, Kirche und Küche," in Sarah Sceats and Gail Cunningham, eds., *Image and Power*, 150–52, 158.

SARAH STICKNEY ELLIS

The Mother's Mistake, 1856

Davenport, Randi L. "*The Mother's Mistake:* Sarah Stickney Ellis and Dreams of Empire." *Victorian Lit and Culture* 22 (1994), 173–84.

BUCHI EMECHETA

The Joys of Motherhood, 1979

Andrade, Susan Z. "The Joys of Daughterhood: Gender, Nationalism, and the Making of Literary Tradition(s)," in Deidre Lynch and William B. Warner, eds., *Cultural Institutions of the Novel*, 264–72.
Cosslett, Tess. *Women Writing Childbirth*, 40–42.

The Rape of Shavi, 1983

Cosslett, Tess. *Women Writing Childbirth*, 40–42.
Hunter, Eva. " 'What Exactly Is Civilisation?': 'Africa,' 'The West' and Gender in Buchi Emecheta's *The Rape of Shavi*." *Engl Stud in Africa* 37:1 (1994), 47–59.
Newman, Judie. *The Ballistic Bard*, 105–15.

BARBARA ERSKINE

Child of the Phoenix, 1992

Filmer-Davies, Kath. *Fantasy Fiction and Welsh Myth*, 140–42.

Lady of Hay, 1987

Filmer-Davies, Kath. *Fantasy Fiction and Welsh Myth*, 135–40.

LEONORA EYLES

Margaret Protests, 1919

Joannou, Maroula. *'Ladies, Please Don't Smash These Windows,'* 67–74.

ZOE FAIRBAIRNS

Stand We At Last, 1983
Duncker, Patricia. *Sisters and Strangers,* 124–26.

JOHN MEADE FALKNER

The Nebuly Coat, 1903
Derry, Stephen. "John Meade Falkner's Use of *Desperate Remedies* and *A Laodicean* in *The Nebuly Coat.*" *Thomas Hardy J* 9:1 (1993), 102–3.

JEFFREY FARNOL

The Broad Highway, 1910
Hughes, Helen. *The Historical Romance,* 84–86.

FREDERICK WILLIAM FARRAR

Julian Home: A Tale of College Life, 1859
Antor, Heinz. *Der englische Universitätsroman,* 403–6.

J. G. FARRELL

A Girl in the Head, 1967
Cichon, Anna. *The Realm of Personality and History,* 18–32.
Cichon, Anna Izabela. "Politics, Ideology and Reality in J. G. Farrell's Early Novels." *Anglica Wratislaviensia* 25 (1993), 35–38.
The Lung, 1965
Cichon, Anna. *The Realm of Personality and History,* 18–32.
Cichon, Anna Izabela. "Politics, Ideology and Reality in J. G. Farrell's Early Novels." *Anglica Wratislaviensia* 25 (1993), 35.
A Man from Elsewhere, 1963
Cichon, Anna. *The Realm of Personality and History,* 18–32.
Cichon, Anna Izabela. "Politics, Ideology and Reality in J. G. Farrell's Early Novels." *Anglica Wratislaviensia* 25 (1993), 23–34.
The Siege of Krishnapur, 1973
Cichon, Anna. *The Realm of Personality and History,* 33–84.
McLeod, John. "Exhibiting Empire in J. G. Farrell's *The Siege of Krishnapur.*" *J of Commonwealth Lit* 29:2 (1994), 117–31.
The Singapore Grip, 1978
Cichon, Anna. *The Realm of Personality and History,* 33–84.

Troubles, 1970

Cichon, Anna. *The Realm of Personality and History*, 33–84.

SUSAN FERRIER

Marriage, 1818

Craik, Wendy. " 'Man, Vain Man' in Susan Ferrier, Margaret Oliphant and Elizabeth Gaskell." *Gaskell Soc J* 9 (1995), 55–65.

MacCarthy, B. G. *The Female Pen,* 458–60.

Mellor, Anne K. "A Novel of Their Own: Romantic Women's Fiction, 1790–1830," in John Richetti et al., eds., *The Columbia History,* 334–36.

Richardson, Alan. *Literature, Education, and Romanticism,* 198–202.

HENRY FIELDING

Amelia, 1752

Benedict, Barbara M. *Framing Feeling,* 30–46.

Campbell, Jill. "Fielding and the Novel at Mid-Century," in John Richetti et al., eds., *The Columbia History*, 123–25.

Campbell, Jill. *Natural Masques*, 203–41.

Conway, Alison. "Fielding's *Amelia* and the Aesthetics of Virtue." *Eighteenth-Cent Fiction* 8 (1995), 35–50.

Haggerty, George E. "Amelia's Nose; or, Sensibility and Its Symptoms." *Eighteenth Cent* 36 (1995), 151–54.

Haggerty, George E. "Fielding's Novel of Atonement: Confessional Form in *Amelia.*" *Eighteenth-Cent Fiction* 8 (1996), 383–400.

Johnson, Christopher. " 'British Championism': Early Pugilism and the Works of Fielding." *R of Engl Stud* 47 (1996), 348–51.

Kraft, Elizabeth. "The Two Amelias: Henry Fielding and Elizabeth Justice." *ELH* 62 (1995), 313–25.

Lawson, Jacqueline Elaine. *Domestic Misconduct,* 111–44.

Mace, Nancy A. *Henry Fielding's Novels*, 73–80, 95–101.

Nelson, T. G. A. *Children, Parents, and the Rise of the Novel*, 177–81.

Schellenberg, Betty A. *The Conversational Circle*, 69–87.

Spacks, Patricia Meyer. "Reply to David Richter: Form and Ideology— Novels at Work." *Eighteenth Cent* 37 (1996), 220–31.

Staves, Susan. "Fielding and the Comedy of Attempted Rape," in Beth Fowkes Tobin, ed., *History, Gender, and Eighteenth-Century Literature*, 98–100.

Uglow, Jenny. *Henry Fielding*, 75–84.

Zomchick, John P. *Family and the Law,* 130–53.

Jonathan Wild, 1743

Bauer, Matthias. *Der Schelmenroman*, 172–74.

Campbell, Jill. "Fielding and the Novel at Mid-Century," in John Richetti et al., eds., *The Columbia History*, 114–18.

Gautier, Gary. "Marriage and Family in Fielding's Fiction." *Stud in the Novel* 27 (1995), 118–19.

Goldgar, Bertrand A. "The *Champion* and the Chapter on Hats in *Jonathan Wild.*" *Philol Q* 72 (1993), 443–48.

Mace, Nancy A. *Henry Fielding's Novels*, 68–70, 86–89.

Medrano, Isabel. "Apuntes para una lectura bakhtiniana de *Jonathan Wild,*" in José Romera Castillo et al., eds., *Bajtín y la literatura*, 325–30.

Nelson, T. G. A. *Children, Parents, and the Rise of the Novel*, 166–70.

Pettit, Alexander. "What the Drama Does in Fielding's *Jonathan Wild.*" *Eighteenth-Cent Fiction* 6 (1994), 153–68.

Uglow, Jenny. *Henry Fielding*, 43–49.

Joseph Andrews, 1742

Battersby, James. "The Importance of Putting Joseph's Fanny on the Road." *Hypotheses* 6 (1993), 2–4.

Bauer, Matthias. *Im Fuchsbau der Geschichten*, 111–16.

Campbell, Jill. "Fielding and the Novel at Mid-Century," in John Richetti et al., eds., *The Columbia History*, 105–7, 119–21.

Campbell, Jill. *Natural Masques*, 61–130.

Cantrell, Pamela. "Writing the Picture: Fielding, Smollett, and Hogarthian Pictorialism." *Stud in Eighteenth-Cent Culture* 24 (1995), 70–72.

Frank, Judith. "The Comic Novel and the Poor: Fielding's Preface to *Joseph Andrews.*" *Eighteenth-Cent Stud* 27 (1993–94), 217–34.

Frank, Judith. "Literacy, Desire, and the Novel: From *Shamela* to *Joseph Andrews.*" *Yale J of Criticism* 6 (1993), 157–74.

Gautier, Gary. "Marriage and Family in Fielding's Fiction." *Stud in the Novel* 27 (1995), 111–16.

Guilhamet, Leon. "The Function of Mixed Genres in Fielding's Fiction: The Case of *Joseph Andrews.*" *Stud on Voltaire and the Eighteenth Cent* 305 (1992), 1356–59.

Johnson, Christopher. " 'British Championism': Early Pugilism and the Works of Fielding." *R of Engl Stud* 47 (1996), 339–42.

Mace, Nancy A. *Henry Fielding's Novels*, 65–73, 89–92, 100–103.

McLoughlin, Tim. "Fielding's *Essay on Conversation:* A Courtesy Guide to *Joseph Andrews*?," in Jacques Carré, ed., *The Crisis of Courtesy*, 93–102.

Mortimer, Anthony. " 'The Manner of Cervantes': Some Notes on *Joseph Andrews* and *Don Quixote.*" *Colloquium Helveticum* 16 (1992), 69–83.

Myer, Valerie Grosvenor. *Ten Great English Novelists*, 31–34.

Nelson, T. G. A. *Children, Parents, and the Rise of the Novel*, 119–21, 162–66.

Ogée, Frédéric. "Against 'metaphysical rubbish': The Real Beginning of *Joseph Andrews.*" *Stud on Voltaire and the Eighteenth Cent* 305 (1992), 1362–65.

Rees, Christine. *Utopian Imagination and Eighteenth-Century Fiction*, 181–84.

Soupel, Serge. "Lady Booby au pouvoir de l'amour dans *Joseph Andrews.*" *Bull de la Société d'Etudes Anglo-Américaines des XVIIe et XVIIIe Siècles* 41 (1995), 103–12.

Spacks, Patricia Meyer. *Desire and Truth,* 59–62.

Staves, Susan. "Fielding and the Comedy of Attempted Rape," in Beth Fowkes Tobin, ed., *History, Gender, and Eighteenth-Century Literature*, 90–95.

Stewart, Garrett. *Dear Reader*, 39–42, 63–68, 97–100.

Suhamy, Henri. "La Religion de Fielding dans *Joseph Andrews.*" *Mythes, Croyances et Religions dans le Monde Anglo-Saxon* 5 (1987), 187–96.

Toise, David W. " 'A More Culpable Passion': *Pamela, Joseph Andrews,* and the History of Desire." *Clio* 25 (1996), 409–19.

Turner, James Grantham. "Richardson and His Circle," in John Richetti et al., eds., *The Columbia History*, 84–86.

Uglow, Jenny. *Henry Fielding*, 34–42.

Shamela, 1741

Frank, Judith. "Literacy, Desire, and the Novel: From *Shamela* to *Joseph Andrews.*" *Yale J of Criticism* 6 (1993), 157–74.

Gooding, Richard. *"Pamela, Shamela,* and the Politics of the *Pamela* Vogue." *Eighteenth-Cent Fiction* 7 (1995), 125–30.

Keymer, Tom. *Richardson's "Clarissa,"* 24–27, 29–31.

Turner, James Grantham. "Richardson and His Circle," in John Richetti et al., eds., *The Columbia History*, 84–86.

Uglow, Jenny. *Henry Fielding*, 28–33.

Wilputte, Earla A. "Ambiguous Language and Ambiguous Gender: The 'Bisexual' Text of *Shamela.*" *Mod Lang R* 89 (1994), 561–71.

Tom Jones, 1749

Antor, Heinz. *Der englische Universitätsroman*, 75–77.

Bauer, Matthias. *Im Fuchsbau der Geschichten*, 111–16.

Bauer, Matthias. *Der Schelmenroman*, 175–77.

Braverman, Richard. "Rebellion Redux: Figuring Whig History in *Tom Jones.*" *Clio* 24 (1995), 251–68.

Brown, Homer Obed. *Institutions of the English Novel*, 82–115.

Butler, Gerald J. "Making Fielding's Novels Speak for Law and Order." *Eighteenth Cent* 37 (1996), 232–41.

Campbell, Jill. "Fielding and the Novel at Mid-Century," in John Richetti et al., eds., *The Columbia History*, 105–7, 121–23.

Campbell, Jill. *Natural Masques*, 160–91.

Gautier, Gary. "Marriage and Family in Fielding's Fiction." *Stud in the Novel* 27 (1995), 116–18.

Harding, James M. " 'He's a Gallus un'': Excess, Restriction, and Narrative Reprieve at the Gallows in *Tom Jones.*" *Eighteenth Cent Life* 18:2 (1994), 15–32.

Hipchen, Emily A. "Fielding's *Tom Jones.*" *Explicator* 53 (1994), 16–18.

Johnson, Christopher. " 'British Championism': Early Pugilism and the Works of Fielding." *R of Engl Stud* 47 (1996), 342–48.

Mace, Nancy A. *Henry Fielding's Novels*, 66–76, 79–85, 92–95, 100–104.

Müller, Wolfgang G. "The Homology of Syntax and Narrative Form in English and American Fiction," in Herbert Foltinek et al., eds., *Tales and "their telling difference,"* 84–86.

Myer, Valerie Grosvenor. *Ten Great English Novelists*, 34–38.

Nelson, T. G. A. *Children, Parents, and the Rise of the Novel*, 171–77, 218–20.

Peternel, Joan. "Readers, Characters, and Identity: *Tom Jones* and *Ulysses.*" *McNeese R* 33 (1990–94), 48–57.

Peternel, Joan. *"Tom Jones:* An Alchemical Opus." *J of Unconventional Hist* 5:2 (1994), 37–42.

Rees, Christine. *Utopian Imagination and Eighteenth-Century Fiction*, 185–90.

Richetti, John. "Reply to David Richter: Ideology and Literary Form in Fielding's *Tom Jones.*" *Eighteenth Cent* 37 (1996), 205–16.

Rizzo, Betty. "The Gendering of Divinity in *Tom Jones.*" *Stud in Eighteenth-Cent Culture* 24 (1995), 259–75.

Sayres, William G. "A Loophole in the Law: The Case of Black George and the Purse in *Tom Jones.*" *JEGP* 94 (1995), 207–19.

Spacks, Patricia Meyer. *Desire and Truth,* 34–54, 76–83.

Staves, Susan. "Fielding and the Comedy of Attempted Rape," in Beth Fowkes Tobin, ed., *History, Gender, and Eighteenth-Century Literature*, 103–7.

Stevenson, John Allen. "Black George and the Black Act." *Eighteenth-Cent Fiction* 8 (1996), 355–82.

Stevenson, John Allen. "Tom Jones and the Stuarts." *ELH* 61 (1994), 571–89.

Stevenson, John Allen. *"Tom Jones,* Jacobitism, and the Rise of Gothic," in Allan Lloyd Smith and Victor Sage, eds., *Gothick Origins and Innovations*, 16–22.

Stocker, Susan. "The Commercialization of *Tom Jones.*" *Recovering Lit* 19 (1993), 49–52.

Stratmann, Gerd. "Undermining Public Opinion: The Function of Narrative in Fielding's *Tom Jones,"* in Elmar Lehmann and Bernd Lenz, eds., *Telling Stories*, 84–96.

Tumbleson, Raymond D. "The Novel's Progress: Faction, Fiction, and Fielding." *Stud in the Novel* 27 (1995), 12–23.

Uglow, Jenny. *Henry Fielding*, 54–70.

Walker, William. "The Determination of Locke, Hume, and Fielding." *Eighteenth-Cent Life* 20:2 (1996), 81–90.

Yoshida, Naoki. "The Power Within: *Tom Jones* and the Egyptian Majesty." *Shiron* 32 (1993), 17–30.

SARAH FIELDING

The Countess of Dellwyn, 1759

    Bree, Linda. *Sarah Fielding,* 125–34.

The Cry, 1754

    Bree, Linda. *Sarah Fielding,* 91–107..

    Woodward, Carolyn. " 'My Heart So Wrapt': Lesbian Disruptions in Eighteenth-Century British Fiction." *Signs* 18 (1993), 855–57.

David Simple, 1744–1753

    Barchas, Janine. "Sarah Fielding's Dashing Style and Eighteenth-Century Print Culture." *ELH* 63 (1996), 633–52.

    Bree, Linda. *Sarah Fielding,* 29–45, 80–90.

    Cooke, Stewart J. " 'Good Heads and Good Hearts': Sarah Fielding's Moral Romance." *Engl Stud in Canada* 21 (1995), 268–80.

    MacCarthy, B. G. *The Female Pen,* 232–37.

    Nickel, Terri. " 'Ingenious Torment': Incest, Family, and the Structure of Community in the Work of Sarah Fielding." *Eighteenth Cent* 36 (1995), 236–46.

    Schellenberg, Betty A. *The Conversational Circle,* 22–35, 117–30.

    Todd, Janet. *The Sign of Angellica,* 165–75.

    Woodward, Carolyn. " 'My Heart So Wrapt': Lesbian Disruptions in Eighteenth-Century British Fiction." *Signs* 18 (1993), 855–57.

The Governess; or, Little Female Academy, 1749

    Bree, Linda. *Sarah Fielding,* 58–72.

    Nickel, Terri. " 'Ingenious Torment': Incest, Family, and the Structure of Community in the Work of Sarah Fielding." *Eighteenth Cent* 36 (1995), 236–46.

    Richardson, Alan. *Literature, Education, and Romanticism,* 135–37.

    Wilner, Arlene Fish. "Education and Ideology in Sarah Fielding's *The Governess.*" *Stud in Eighteenth-Cent Culture* 24 (1995), 308–20.

The History of Ophelia, 1760

    Bree, Linda. *Sarah Fielding,* 134–45.

EVA FIGES

The Tree of Knowledge, 1990

    Rozett, Martha Tuck. "Constructing a World: How Postmodern Historical Fiction Reimagines the Past." *Clio* 25 (1996), 157–59.

DARRELL FIGGIS

The Return of the Hero, 1923

    Lanters, Jose. "Darrell Figgis, The Return of the Hero, and the Making of the Irish Nation." *Colby Q* 31 (1995), 204–12.

PATRICIA FINNEY

Firedrake's Eye, 1992

Rozett, Martha Tuck. "Constructing a World: How Postmodern Historical Fiction Reimagines the Past." *Clio* 25 (1996), 153–57.

FORD MADOX FORD

The Fifth Queen Trilogy, 1962

Galef, David. "Forster, Ford, and the New Novel of Manners," in John Richetti et al., eds., *The Columbia History*, 833–34.

The Good Soldier, 1915

Bailin, Miriam. *The Sickroom in Victorian Fiction,* 140–42.

Foata, Anne. " 'Beati Immaculati': À propos de l'épigraphe de *The Good Soldier* de Ford Madox Ford." *Etudes Anglaises* 48 (1995), 148–59.

Galef, David. "Forster, Ford, and the New Novel of Manners," in John Richetti et al., eds., *The Columbia History*, 834–37.

Kahane, Claire. *Passions of the Voice,* 138–47.

Levenson, Michael. *Modernism and the Fate of Individuality,* 102–20.

May, Brian. "Ford Madox Ford and the Politics of Impressionism." *Essays in Lit* (Macomb, IL) 21 (1994), 82–94.

Rignall, John. *Realist Fiction,* 127–36.

Robertson, Robert M.. "The Wrong 'Saddest Story': Reading the Appearance of Postmodernity in Ford's *Good Soldier,*" in Bill Readings and Bennet Schaber, eds., *Postmodernism Across the Ages*, 171–85.

Mr. Fleight, 1913

Trotter, David. *The English Novel in History,* 165–66.

Parade's End, 1950

Calderaro, Michela A. *A Silent New World: Ford Madox Ford's "Parade's End."*

Galef, David. "Forster, Ford, and the New Novel of Manners," in John Richetti et al., eds., *The Columbia History*, 837–38.

E. M. FORSTER

Howards End, 1910

Beauman, Nicola. *E. M. Forster,* 216–25.

Beer, John. *Romantic Influences,* 202–6.

Bernstein, Stephen. "Modernist Spatial Nostalgia: Forster, Conrad, Woolf," in Beth Rigel Daugherty and Eileen Barrett, eds., *Virginia Woolf,* 40–44.

Born, Daniel. *The Birth of Liberal Guilt,* 120–35.

Buck, R. A. "Forster's *Howards End.*" *Explicator* 53 (1995), 221–24.

Buck, R. A., and Timothy R. Austin. "Dialogue and Power in E. M.

Forster's *Howards End,"* in Peter Verdonk and Jean Jacques Weber, eds., *Twentieth-Century Fiction*, 63–76.

Childs, Peter. " 'One may as well begin with Helen's letters . . .': Corresponding but not Connecting in the Writings of E. M. Forster." *Prose Stud* 19 (1996), 203–8.

Doyle, T. Douglas. "Forster's *Howards End." Explicator* 52 (1994), 226–28.

Firchow, Peter E. "Not an Aspect of the Novel: E. M. Forster on Point of View in Fiction," in Herbert Foltinek et al., eds., *Tales and "their telling difference,"* 277–78.

Foata, Anne. "The Knocking at the Door: A Fantasy on Fate, Forster and Beethoven's Fifth." *Cahiers Victoriens et Edouardiens* 44 (1996), 135–44.

Galef, David. "Forster, Ford, and the New Novel of Manners," in John Richetti et al., eds., *The Columbia History*, 825–30.

Galef, David. *The Supporting Cast,* 65–112.

Greenslade, William. *Degeneration, Culture, and the Novel,* 202–5, 214–20.

Hollahan, Eugene. *Crisis-Consciousness*, 141–47.

Kershner, R. Brandon. "Teaching *Howards End* through *Ulysses* through Bakhtin," in Robert Newman, ed., *Pedagogy, Praxis, "Ulysses,"* 153–64.

Kohl, Stephan. "Rural England in Moderne und Zwischenkriegszeit: Zur Nachgeschichte eines literarischen Konstrukts." *Poetica* (Munich) 27 (1995), 378–80.

Lago, Mary. *E. M. Forster,* 40–47.

Levenson, Michael. *Modernism and the Fate of Individuality,* 78–101.

Lucas, John. "The Sunlight on the Garden," in Carola M. Kaplan and Anne B. Simpson, eds., *Seeing Double*, 65–70.

May, Brian. *The Modernist as Pragmatist,* 53–71, 76–95, 101–9.

Messenger, Nigel. *How to Study,* 109–38.

Mezei, Kathy. "Who Is Speaking Here? Free Indirect Discourse, Gender, and Authority in *Emma, Howards End,* and *Mrs. Dalloway,"* in Mezei, ed., *Ambiguous Discourse*, 76–83.

Miller, Jane Eldridge. *Rebel Women,* 49–54.

Niederhoff, Burkhard. "E. M. Forster and the Suppression of Plot by Leitmotif: A Reading of *Aspects of the Novel* and *Howards End." Anglia* 112 (1994), 341–63.

Stern, Michael Lynn. " 'It has been itself a dream': The Oneiric Plot of *Howards End." Lit and Psych* 41:1–2 (1995), 19–35.

Stewart, Garrett. "Film's Victorian Retrofit." *Victorian Stud* 38 (1995), 174–78.

Stone, Wilfred H. "Forster, the Environmentalist," in Carola M. Kaplan and Anne B. Simpson, eds., *Seeing Double*, 172–83.

The Longest Journey, 1907

Beauman, Nicola. *E. M. Forster*, 178–90.

Galef, David. "Forster, Ford, and the New Novel of Manners," in John Richetti et al., eds., *The Columbia History*, 822–23, 825–26.

Lago, Mary. *E. M. Forster*, 32–40.

May, Brian. "Modernism and Other Modes in Forster's *The Longest Journey.*" *Twentieth Cent Lit* 42 (1996), 234–53.

May, Brian. *The Modernist as Pragmatist*, 39–49.

Messenger, Nigel. *How to Study*, 80–108.

Zelter, Joachim. *Sinnhafte Fiktion und Wahrheit*, 191–97.

Maurice, 1971

Beauman, Nicola. *E. M. Forster*, 226–37.

Dukes, Thomas. "From Fairy Tale to Film: The Coming Out and Completion of Forster's *Maurice.*" *West Virginia Univ Philol Papers* 38 (1992), 91–98.

Galef, David. "Forster, Ford, and the New Novel of Manners," in John Richetti et al., eds., *The Columbia History*, 832–33.

Hammond, Paul. *Love between Men*, 196–203.

Lago, Mary. *E. M. Forster*, 135–39.

Messenger, Nigel. *How to Study*, 8–23.

Miller, Jane Eldridge. *Rebel Women*, 52–54.

Zelter, Joachim. *Sinnhafte Fiktion und Wahrheit*, 191–97.

A Passage to India, 1924

Beauman, Nicola. *E. M. Forster*, 319–32.

Beer, John. *Romantic Influences*, 206–9, 212–14.

Begum, Khani. "E. M. Forster's and David Lean's (Re)Presentations and (Re)Productions of Empire." *West Virginia Univ Philol Papers* 40 (1994), 20–29.

Brantlinger, Patrick. " 'The Bloomsbury Fraction' Versus War and Empire," in Carola M. Kaplan and Anne B. Simpson, eds., *Seeing Double*, 155–57.

Cavaliero, Glen. *The Supernatural and English Fiction*, 14–16.

Das, Prasanta. " 'The Common Iora' in *A Passage to India.*" *Notes and Queries* 43 (1996), 54–55.

Dolin, Kieran. "Freedom, Uncertainty, and Diversity: *A Passage to India* as a Critique of Imperialist Law." *Texas Stud in Lit and Lang* 36 (1994), 328–49.

Favre, Albert. "Christianisme et Hindouisme: Murailles, barrières et échos chez E. M. Forster (*A Passage to India*)." *Mythes, Croyances et Religions dans le Monde Anglo-Saxon* 5 (1987), 91–110.

Galef, David. "Forster, Ford, and the New Novel of Manners," in John Richetti et al., eds., *The Columbia History*, 829–32.

Gorra, Michael. "Rudyard Kipling to Salman Rushdie: Imperialism to Postcolonialism," in John Richetti et al., eds., *The Columbia History*, 640–43.

Harrex, Syd. "The Game & the Goal: Kipling, Forster & the Indian English Novel," in Annie Greet et al., eds., *Raj Nostalgia*, 80–86.

Herz, Judith Scherer. "Forster's Ghosts: *A Passage to India* and the Emptying of Narrative," in Daniel Fischlin, ed., *Negation, Critical Theory, and Postmodern Textuality*, 191–200.

Herz, Judith Scherer. *"A Passage to India": Nation and Narration*, 45–134.

Hollahan, Eugene. *Crisis-Consciousness*, 147–51.

Horatschek, Annegreth. " 'The beautiful naked god': Der ästhetische Körper in E. M. Forsters *A Passage to India,"* in Konrad Groß et al., eds., *Das Natur/Kultur-Paradigma*, 113–33.

Kumar, Manjushree S. "An Inscrutability: Forster's Vision of India," in R. K. Dhawan and L. S. R. Krishna Sastry, eds., *Commonwealth Writing*, 107–11.

Lago, Mary. *E. M. Forster*, 65–91.

Lichtenstein, Leonie. "Reading Stereotypes: Changing the Lighting in *A Passage to India,"* in John Morris, ed., *Exploring Stereotyped Images*, 99–146.

May, Brian. *The Modernist as Pragmatist*, 101–13, 115–48, 150–53.

Messenger, Nigel. *How to Study*, 139–72.

Monk, Leland. "Apropos of Nothing: Chance and Narrative in Forster's *A Passage to India." Stud in the Novel* 26 (1994), 392–402.

Pether, Penelope. "Their Fathers' House: Forster, Woolf, and the Aesthetics of Patriotism." *Lit and Aesthetics* 2 (1992), 35–42.

Pintchman, Tracy. "Snakes in the Cave: Religion and the Echo in E. M. Forster's *A Passage to India." Soundings* 75:1 (1992), 61–78.

Poll, Eve Dawkins. "The Colonization of the Ingenue in E. M. Forster's *A Passage to India." SPAN* 38 (1994), 46–64.

Werth, Paul. " 'World enough, and time': Deictic Space and the Interpretation of Prose," in Peter Verdonk and Jean Jacques Weber, eds., *Twentieth-Century Fiction*, 190–202.

Winn, Harbour. "Parallel Inward Journeys: *A Passage to India* and *St. Mawr." Engl Lang Notes* 31:2 (1993), 62–66.

A Room with a View, 1908

Beauman, Nicola. *E. M. Forster*, 204–15.

Galef, David. "Forster, Ford, and the New Novel of Manners," in John Richetti et al., eds., *The Columbia History*, 823–26.

Goscilo, Margaret. "Forster's Italian Comedies: Que[e]rying Heterosexuality Abroad," in Carola M. Kaplan and Anne B. Simpson, eds., *Seeing Double*, 203–11.

Heath, Jeffrey. "Kissing and Telling: Turning Round in *A Room with a View." Twentieth Cent Lit* 40 (1994), 393–429.

Kohl, Stephan. "Rural England in Moderne und Zwischenkriegszeit: Zur Nachgeschichte eines literarischen Konstrukts." *Poetica* (Munich) 27 (1995), 380–81.

Lago, Mary. *E. M. Forster*, 24–27.

Messenger, Nigel. *How to Study*, 53–79.

Miller, Jane Eldridge. *Rebel Women*, 47–49.

Where Angels Fear to Tread, 1905

Beauman, Nicola. *E. M. Forster*, 160–70.

Galef, David. "Forster, Ford, and the New Novel of Manners," in John Richetti et al., eds., *The Columbia History*, 820–21.

Goscilo, Margaret. "Forster's Italian Comedies: Que[e]rying Heterosexuality Abroad," in Carola M. Kaplan and Anne B. Simpson, eds., *Seeing Double*, 193–203.

Lago, Mary. *E. M. Forster*, 27–32.

Messenger, Nigel. *How to Study*, 24–52.

MARGARET FORSTER

Mother, Can You Hear Me?, 1979

Würzbach, Natascha. "The Mother Image as Cultural Concept and Literary Theme in the Nineteenth- and Twentieth-Century English Novel: A Feminist Reading within the Context of New Historicism and the History of Mentalities," in Rüdiger Ahrens and Laurenz Volkmann, eds., *Why Literature Matters*, 388–89.

JOHN FOWLES

The Collector, 1963

Brink, Andrew. *Obsession and Culture*, 148–50.

Eriksson, Bo H. T. *The "Structuring Forces" of Detection*, 125–50.

Foster, Thomas C. *Understanding John Fowles*, 20–37.

Onega, Susana. "Self, World, and Art in the Fiction of John Fowles." *Twentieth Cent Lit* 42 (1996), 39–40.

Taylor, D. J. *After the War*, 158–62.

Daniel Martin, 1977

Arlett, Robert. *Epic Voices*, 144–68.

Brandt, Peter. "Somewhere Else in the Forest." *Twentieth Cent Lit* 42 (1996), 145–62.

Brink, Andrew. *Obsession and Culture*, 156–60.

Eriksson, Bo H. T. *The "Structuring Forces" of Detection*, 170–81.

Foster, Thomas C. *Understanding John Fowles*, 119–38.

Onega, Susana. "Self, World, and Art in the Fiction of John Fowles." *Twentieth Cent Lit* 42 (1996), 42–45.

Späth, Eberhard. "*Daniel Martin:* 'The word as game. The word as tool'—John Fowles's Poetological Experiment," in Rüdiger Ahrens and Laurenz Volkmann, eds., *Why Literature Matters*, 311–23.

Wilson, Raymond J. III. "Overcoming Reification in *Daniel Martin:* John Fowles's Response to Georg Lukács." *J of Narrative Technique* 25 (1995), 301–14.

The French Lieutenant's Woman, 1969

Behrens, Volker. *Das Spiel mit der Illusion in "The French Lieutenant's Woman."*

Bowen, Deborah. "John Fowles's Uncrucified Jesus." *Christianity and Lit* 45 (1996), 373–84.

Bowen, Deborah. "The Riddler Riddled: Reading the Epigraphs in John

Fowles's *French Lieutenant's Woman.*" *J of Narrative Technique* 25 (1995), 67–88.

Foster, Thomas C. *Understanding John Fowles,* 67–89.

Gasiorek, Andrzej. *Post-War British Fiction,* 112–16.

Jukic, Tatjana. "Variants of *Victoriana* in the Postmodern English Novel." *Studia Romanica et Anglica Zagrabiensia* 40 (1995), 70–72.

Martin, Joseph. "Postmodernist Play in Karel Reisz's *The French Lieutenant's Woman.*" *Lit/Film Q* 22 (1994), 151–58.

Osland, Dianne. "Loose Ends in *Roxana* and *The French Lieutenant's Woman.*" *Stud in the Novel* 25 (1993), 381–93.

Shields, Ellen F. "Hysteria, Sexual Assault, and the Military: The Trial of Emile de La Roncière and *The French Lieutenant's Woman.*" *Mosaic* 28:3 (1995), 83–107.

Steed, Tonia. "Exploring the Cave: The Search for a Feminist Mimesis in *The French Lieutenant's Woman.*" *Text and Presentation* 8 (1992), 71–76.

Stewart, Garrett. "Film's Victorian Retrofit." *Victorian Stud* 38 (1995), 158–60.

Sturgess, Philip J. M. *Narrativity,* 252–56.

Tarbox, Katherine. "*The French Lieutenant's Woman* and the Evolution of Narrative." *Twentieth Cent Lit* 42 (1996), 88–113.

Warburton, Eileen. "Ashes, Ashes, We All Fall Down: *Ourika, Cinderella,* and *The French Lieutenant's Woman.*" *Twentieth Cent Lit* 42 (1996), 165–84.

Zander, Andela. " 'Spot the Source': Wilkie Collins' *The Moonstone* und John Fowles' *The French Lieutenant's Woman.*" *Zeitschrift für Anglistik und Amerikanistik* 41 (1993), 341–47.

A Maggot, 1985

Connor, Steven. *The English Novel in History,* 146–47.

Eriksson, Bo H. T. *The "Structuring Forces" of Detection,* 196–229.

Foster, Thomas C. *Understanding John Fowles,* 140–67.

Onega, Susana. "British Historiographic Metafiction in the 1980s," in Theo D'haen and Hans Bertens, eds., *British Postmodern Fiction,* 53–55.

Onega, Susana. "Self, World, and Art in the Fiction of John Fowles." *Twentieth Cent Lit* 42 (1996), 46–51.

The Magus, 1966

Almond, Barbara, and Richard Almond. *The Therapeutic Narrative,* 131–48.

Aubrey, James R. "Eleusinian Mysteries in the Trial Scene of John Fowles's *The Magus.*" *J of Evolutionary Psych* 15 (1994), 129–33.

Aubrey, James R. "Jungian 'Synchronicity' and John Fowles' *The Magus.*" *Notes on Contemp Lit* 24:2 (1994), 11–12.

Brink, Andrew. *Obsession and Culture,* 151–56.

Cavaliero, Glen. *The Supernatural and English Fiction,* 187–89.

Eriksson, Bo H. T. *The "Structuring Forces" of Detection,* 181–86, 193–95.

Foster, Thomas C. *Understanding John Fowles,* 38–65.

Fowles, John. "Behind *The Magus." Twentieth Cent Lit* 42 (1996), 58–68.

Kefalea, Circe. " 'Was diese Griechen zu telefonieren haben!': Literarische Griechenlandbilder zwischen Erfahrung und Klischee." *Neohelicon* 21:2 (1994), 325–43.

Lorenz, Paul H. "Heraclitus Against the Barbarians: John Fowles's *The Magus." Twentieth Cent Lit* 42 (1996), 69–85.

Onega, Susana. "Self, World, and Art in the Fiction of John Fowles." *Twentieth Cent Lit* 42 (1996), 40–42.

Mantissa, 1982

Brink, Andrew. *Obsession and Culture,* 160–61.

Foster, Thomas C. *Understanding John Fowles,* 111–17.

Onega, Susana. "Self, World, and Art in the Fiction of John Fowles." *Twentieth Cent Lit* 42 (1996), 45–46.

Schaff, Barbara. "*Mantissa:* Männerphantasien um Macht und Musen—Zu einem Roman von John Fowles," in Annette Keck and Dietmar Schmidt, eds., *Auto(r)erotik,* 102–18.

GILBERT FRANKAU

Peter Jackson, 1920

Cecil, Hugh. *The Flower of Battle,* 202–11.

JOHN GALSWORTHY

The Country House, 1907

Miller, Jane Eldridge. *Rebel Women,* 61–63.

The Forsyte Saga, 1922

Harvey, Geoffrey. "Reading *The Forsyte Saga." Yrbk of Engl Stud* 26 (1996), 127–34.

The Man of Property, 1906

Miller, Jane Eldridge. *Rebel Women,* 59–61.

JOHN GALT

Bogle Corbet, 1831

Harper, Marjory. "Adventure or Exile? The Scottish Emigrant in Fiction." *Scottish Liter J* 23:1 (1996), 24–25.

Trumpener, Katie. "The Abbotsford Guide to India: Romantic Fictions of Empire and the Narratives of Canadian Literature," in Deidre Lynch and William B. Warner, eds., *Cultural Institutions of the Novel*, 209–16.

The Last of the Lairds, 1826

Harper, Marjory. " Adventure or Exile? The Scottish Emigrant in Fiction." *Scottish Liter J* 23:1 (1996), 23–24.

The Provost, 1822

Visser, Nicholas. "Roaring Beasts and Raging Floods: The Representation of Political Crowds in the Nineteenth-Century British Novel." *Mod Lang R* 89 (1994), 289–92, 296–97.

Ringan Gilhaize, 1823

Ferris, Ina. *The Achievement of Literary Authority*, 176–85.

ALAN GARNER

The Owl Service, 1967

Beach, Sarah. "Breaking the Pattern: Alan Garner's *The Owl Service* and the *Mabinogion.*" *Mythlore* 20:1 (1994), 10–14.
Cavaliero, Glen. *The Supernatural and English Fiction*, 219–20.
Filmer-Davies, Kath. *Fantasy Fiction and Welsh Myth*, 23–26.

DAVID GARNETT

Lady into Fox, 1922

Presley, John Woodrow. "Fox, Vampire, Witch: Two Novels of Fantasy by Graves and Garnett." *Focus on Robert Graves and His Contemporaries* 2:2 (1994), 26–30.

GEORGE GASCOIGNE

The Adventures of Master F. J., 1573

Austen, Gillian. "Gascoigne's *Master FJ* and its Revision, or, 'You ain't heard nothin' yet!,'" in Wolfgang Görtschacher and Holger Klein, eds., *Narrative Strategies*, 67–83.
Billingsley, Dale B. "The Pastime of Master F. J." *Renaissance and Reformation* 17:3 (1993), 5–18.
Eriksen, Roy. "The Mimesis of Change: Gascoigne's *Aduentures of Master F. J.* (1573)," in Eriksen, ed., *Contexts of Pre-Novel Narrative*, 185–228.
Müller, Wolfgang G. "The Modernity of the Second Version of George Gascoigne's *Master FJ,*" in Wolfgang Görtschacher and Holger Klein, eds., *Narrative Strategies*, 87–100.
Relihan, Constance C. *Fashioning Authority*, 21–24.

ELIZABETH GASKELL

Cousin Phillis, 1865

Bonaparte, Felicia. *The Gypsy-Bachelor of Manchester*, 229–31.

Curtis, Jeni. " 'Manning the World': The Role of the Male Narrator in Elizabeth Gaskell's *Cousin Phillis.*" *Victorian R* 21 (1995), 129–41.

Flint, Kate. *Elizabeth Gaskell*, 53–55.

Horsman, Alan. *The Victorian Novel*, 290–91.

James, Harumi. "Secrecy in Elizabeth Gaskell's *Cousin Phillis.*" *Gaskell Soc J* 8 (1994), 28–41.

Rogers, Philip. "The Education of Cousin Phillis." *Nineteenth-Cent Lit* 50 (1995), 27–50.

Vrettos, Athena. *Somatic Fictions*, 35–39.

Wolfreys, Julian. *Being English,* 88–102.

Wright, Terence. *Elizabeth Gaskell*, 147–62.

Cranford, 1853

Allen, Dennis W. *Sexuality in Victorian Fiction*, 60–83.

Bonaparte, Felicia. *The Gypsy-Bachelor of Manchester*, 153–61.

Cohen, Michael. *Sisters*, 155–57.

Colby, Robin B. *"Some Appointed Work To Do,"* 65–72.

Craik, Wendy. " 'Man, Vain Man' in Susan Ferrier, Margaret Oliphant and Elizabeth Gaskell." *Gaskell Soc J* 9 (1995), 55–65.

Dolin, Tim. "*Cranford* and the Victorian Collection." *Victorian Stud* 36 (1993), 179–203.

Fasick, Laura. *Vessels of Meaning*, 92–103.

Flint, Kate. *Elizabeth Gaskell*, 31–35.

Gavin, Adrienne E. "Language Among the Amazons: Conjuring and Creativity in *Cranford.*" *Dickens Stud Annual* 23 (1994), 205–23.

Horsman, Alan. *The Victorian Novel*, 274–76.

Kucich, John. *The Power of Lies,* 138–40, 145–57.

Miller, Andrew H. "Subjectivity Ltd: The Discourse of Liability in the Joint Stock Companies Act of 1856 and Gaskell's *Cranford.*" *ELH* 61 (1994), 139–54.

Mulvihill, James. "Economies of Living in Mrs. Gaskell's *Cranford.*" *Nineteenth-Cent Lit* 50 (1995), 337–56.

Rosenthal, Rae. "Gaskell's Feminist Utopia: The Cranfordians and the Reign of Goodwill," in Jane L. Donawerth and Carol A. Kolmerten, eds., *Utopian and Science Fiction*, 73–92.

Wright, Terence. *Elizabeth Gaskell*, 129–45.

Mary Barton, 1848

Baldridge, Cates. *The Dialogics of Dissent*, 119–29.

Bonaparte, Felicia. *The Gypsy-Bachelor of Manchester*, 133–52.

Brown, Penny. *The Captured World*, 76–78.

Childers, Joseph W. *Novel Possibilities,* 158–78.

Colby, Robin B. *"Some Appointed Work To Do,"* 33–45.

Edgecombe, R. S. "Two Female Saviours in Nineteenth-Century Fiction:

Jeanie Deans and Mary Barton." *Engl Stud* (Amsterdam) 77 (1996), 51–58.

Flint, Kate. *Elizabeth Gaskell*, 11–19.

Guy, Josephine M. *The Victorian Social-Problem Novel*, 48–50, 137–61.

Harsh, Constance D. *Subversive Heroines*, 66–68, 77–79, 99–101.

Horsman, Alan. *The Victorian Novel*, 270–74.

Kissel, Susan S. *In Common Cause*, 123–26.

Kucich, John. *The Power of Lies*, 125–33.

Marshall, Tim. *Murdering to Dissect*, 331–39.

Matus, Jill L. *Unstable Bodies*, 56–83.

Michie, Elsie B. *Outside the Pale*, 115–18, 127–31.

Nord, Deborah Epstein. *Walking the Victorian Streets*, 142–60.

Perera, Suvendrini. *Reaches of Empire*, 52–56.

Poovey, Mary. "Disraeli, Gaskell, and the Condition of England," in John Richetti et al., eds., *The Columbia History*, 521–30.

Preston, Peter. "Manchester and Milton-Northern: Elizabeth Gaskell and the Industrial Town," in Peter Preston and Paul Simpson-Housley, eds., *Writing the City*, 38–43.

Sutherland, John. *Is Heathcliff a Murderer?*, 78–83.

Terry, R. C. " 'Have at the Masters!': Working-Class Stereotypes in Some Nineteenth-Century Novels," in John Morris, ed., *Exploring Stereotyped Images*, 170–72.

Thaden, Barbara. "Elizabeth Gaskell and the Dead Mother Plot," in Thaden, ed., *New Essays on the Maternal Voice*, 39–40.

Wheeler, Michael. *English Fiction of the Victorian Period*, 39–41.

Wright, Terence. *Elizabeth Gaskell*, 21–41.

My Lady Ludlow, 1859

Horsman, Alan. *The Victorian Novel*, 284–85.

Wright, Terence. *Elizabeth Gaskell*, 119–27.

North and South, 1855

Baldridge, Cates. *The Dialogics of Dissent*, 119–21, 130–43.

Bonaparte, Felicia. *The Gypsy-Bachelor of Manchester*, 167–93.

Brown, Susan. " 'Money is Virtue': Sexual and Economic Exchange in Mid-Victorian Literary Discourse," in Anthony Purdy, ed., *Literature and Money*, 82–85.

Colby, Robin B. *"Some Appointed Work To Do,"* 47–61.

Elliott, Dorice Williams. "The Female Visitor and the Marriage of Classes in Gaskell's *North and South." Nineteenth-Cent Lit* 49 (1994), 21–49.

Fasick, Laura. *Vessels of Meaning*, 118–23, 135–37.

Flint, Kate. *Elizabeth Gaskell*, 36–44.

Guy, Josephine M. *The Victorian Social-Problem Novel*, 161–73.

Harsh, Constance D. *Subversive Heroines*, 21–46, 69–71, 81–85.

Horsman, Alan. *The Victorian Novel*, 280–84.

Ingham, Patricia. *The Language of Gender and Class*, 55–77.

Johnson, Patricia E. "Elizabeth Gaskell's *North and South:* A National *Bildungsroman." Victorian Newsl* 85 (1994), 1–9.

Kissel, Susan S. *In Common Cause*, 121–27.

Kucich, John. *The Power of Lies,* 124–26.

Michie, Elsie B. *Outside the Pale*, 131–40.

Nord, Deborah Epstein. *Walking the Victorian Streets,* 166–75.

Perera, Suvendrini. *Reaches of Empire,* 46–51.

Preston, Peter. "Manchester and Milton-Northern: Elizabeth Gaskell and the Industrial Town," in Peter Preston and Paul Simpson-Housley, eds., *Writing the City,* 44–56.

Terry, R. C. " 'Have at the Masters!': Working-Class Stereotypes in Some Nineteenth-Century Novels," in John Morris, ed., *Exploring Stereotyped Images,* 162–63, 173–75.

Visser, Nicholas. "Roaring Beasts and Raging Floods: The Representation of Political Crowds in the Nineteenth-Century British Novel." *Mod Lang R* 89 (1994), 299–300.

Wainwright, Valerie. "Discovering Autonomy and Authenticity in *North and South:* Elizabeth Gaskell, John Stuart Mill, and the Liberal Ethic." *Clio* 23 (1994), 149–65.

Wheeler, Michael. *English Fiction of the Victorian Period*, 77–80.

Wright, Terence. *Elizabeth Gaskell*, 97–117.

York, R. A. *Strangers and Secrets*, 75–88.

Ruth, 1853

Bonaparte, Felicia. *The Gypsy-Bachelor of Manchester*, 77–95.

Buchanan, Laurie. " 'Islands' of Peace: Female Friendships in Victorian Literature," in Janet Doubler Ward and JoAnna Stephens Mink, eds., *Communication and Women's Friendships*, 86–95.

Demoor, Marysa. "Male Monsters or Monstrous Males in Victorian Women's Fiction," in Valeria Tinkler-Villani and Peter Davidson, eds., *Exhibited by Candlelight*, 177–78.

Flint, Kate. *Elizabeth Gaskell*, 20–28.

Horsman, Alan. *The Victorian Novel*, 276–80.

Jenkins, Ruth Y. *Reclaiming Myths of Power,* 94–115.

Matus, Jill L. *Unstable Bodies,* 113–31.

Michie, Elsie B. *Outside the Pale*, 82–84, 105–10, 123–27.

Mothersole, Brenda. "The 'Fallen Woman' in the Victorian Novel," in John Morris, ed., *Exploring Stereotyped Images,* 195–98.

Nord, Deborah Epstein. *Walking the Victorian Streets,* 159–66.

Retan, Katherine A. "Lower-Class Angels in the Middle-Class House: The Domestic Woman's 'Progress' in *Hard Times* and *Ruth." Dickens Stud Annual* 23 (1994), 193–201.

Thaden, Barbara. "Elizabeth Gaskell and the Dead Mother Plot," in Thaden, ed., *New Essays on the Maternal Voice,* 40–41, 43–47.

Wright, Terence. *Elizabeth Gaskell*, 73–95.

Würzbach, Natascha. "The Mother Image as Cultural Concept and Literary Theme in the Nineteenth- and Twentieth-Century English Novel:

A Feminist Reading within the Context of New Historicism and the
History of Mentalities," in Rüdiger Ahrens and Laurenz Volkmann,
eds., *Why Literature Matters*, 375–76.

Sylvia's Lovers, 1863

Bonaparte, Felicia. *The Gypsy-Bachelor of Manchester*, 194–208.

Flint, Kate. *Elizabeth Gaskell*, 45–52.

Horsman, Alan. *The Victorian Novel*, 286–90.

Krueger, Christine L. " 'Speaking like a woman': How to Have the Last
Word on *Sylvia's Lovers,*" in Alison Booth, ed., *Famous Last Words*,
135–50.

Kucich, John. *The Power of Lies,* 126–34.

Shaw, Marion. "Elizabeth Gaskell, Tennyson and the Fatal Return: *Sylvia's Lovers* and *Enoch Arden."* *Gaskell Soc J* 9 (1995), 43–54.

Wright, Terence. *Elizabeth Gaskell*, 163–83.

Wives and Daughters, 1866

Bonaparte, Felicia. *The Gypsy-Bachelor of Manchester*, 55–76.

Cohen, Michael. *Sisters*, 98–101, 157–61.

Colby, Robin B. *"Some Appointed Work To Do,"* 89–103.

Flint, Kate. *Elizabeth Gaskell*, 53–59.

Harsh, Constance D. *Subversive Heroines,* 158–65.

Horsman, Alan. *The Victorian Novel*, 291–94.

Kucich, John. *The Power of Lies,* 129–32.

Lambert, Ellen Zetzel. *The Face of Love,* 86–88.

Panek, Jennifer. "Constructions of Masculinity in *Adam Bede* and *Wives
and Daughters."* *Victorian R* 22 (1996), 127–48.

Price, Leah. "The *Life of Charlotte Brontë* and the Death of Miss Eyre."
Stud in Engl Lit, 1500–1900 35 (1995), 757–67.

Waters, Mary. "Elizabeth Gaskell, Mary Wollstonecraft and the Conduct
Books: Mrs. Gibson as the Product of a Conventional Education in
Wives and Daughters." *Gaskell Soc J* 9 (1995), 13–20.

Wheeler, Michael. *English Fiction of the Victorian Period*, 80–82.

Wright, Terence. *Elizabeth Gaskell*, 43–71.

MAGGIE GEE

The Burning Book, 1983

Connor, Steven. *The English Novel in History*, 238–45.

WILLIAM ALEXANDER GERHARDIE

My Wife's the Least of It, 1939

Loewenstein, Andrea Freud. "The Protection of Masculinity: Jews as
Projective Pawns in the Texts of William Gerhardi and George Orwell," in Bryan Cheyette, ed., *Between 'Race' and Culture*, 152–55.

PHILLIP GIBBS

Blood Relations, 1935
Cadogan, Mary. *And Then Their Hearts Stood Still,* 167–69.

GEORGE GISSING

Born in Exile, 1892
Selig, Robert. "Gissing's *Born in Exile* and Théodule-Armand Ribot's L'hérédité psychologique." *Gissing J* 32:4 (1996), 1–9.
Selig, Robert L. *George Gissing,* 53–60.
The Crown of Life, 1899
Selig, Robert L. *George Gissing,* 87–89.
Demos, 1886
Selig, Robert L. *George Gissing,* 28–30.
Denzil Quarrier, 1892
Selig, Robert L. *George Gissing,* 75–77.
The Emancipated, 1890
Dupeyron, Françoise. "*The Emancipated*: A Comedy in Italy." *Gissing J* 30:1 (1994), 12–24.
Fasick, Laura. *Vessels of Meaning,* 155–57.
Kranidis, Rita S. *Subversive Discourse,* 118–19.
Selig, Robert L. *George Gissing,* 41–45.
Sjöholm, Christina. *"The Vice of Wedlock,"* 36–51.
Eve's Ransom, 1895
Selig, Robert L. *George Gissing,* 77–80.
In the Year of Jubilee, 1894
Harsh, Constance D. "Gissing's *In the Year of Jubilee* and the Epistemology of Resistance." *Stud in Engl Lit, 1500–1900* 34 (1994), 853–73.
Selig, Robert L. *George Gissing,* 66–69.
Sjöholm, Christina. *"In the Year of Jubilee* and American Grundyism." *Gissing J* 33:1 (1997), 1–9.
Sjöholm, Christina. *"The Vice of Wedlock,"* 85–106.
Isabel Clarendon, 1886
Selig, Robert L. *George Gissing,* 36–39.
A Life's Morning, 1888
Selig, Robert L. *George Gissing,* 39–41.
The Nether World, 1889
Born, Daniel. *The Birth of Liberal Guilt,* 78–85.
Harman, Barbara Leah. "Joy behind the Screen: The Problem of 'Presentability' in George Gissing's *The Nether World* (1889)," in Barbara

Leah Harman and Susan Meyer, eds., *The New Nineteenth Century*, 181–93.

Selig, Robert L. *George Gissing,* 33–35.

Trotter, David. "The Avoidance of Naturalism: Gissing, Moore, Grand, Bennett, and Others," in John Richetti et al., eds., *The Columbia History*, 611–13.

Wheeler, Michael. *English Fiction of the Victorian Period*, 187–89.

New Grub Street, 1891

Hollahan, Eugene. *Crisis-Consciousness*, 110–14.

Kranidis, Rita S. *Subversive Discourse*, 119–21.

Selig, Robert L. *George Gissing,* 46–53.

Sjöholm, Christina. *"The Vice of Wedlock,"* 52–63.

Stetz, Margaret Diane. "*New Grub Street* and the Woman Writer of the 1890s," in Nikki Lee Manos and Meri-Jane Rochelson, eds., *Transforming Genres*, 21–34.

Stewart, Garrett. *Dear Reader*, 330–39.

Wheeler, Michael. *English Fiction of the Victorian Period*, 190–92.

The Odd Women, 1893

Comitini, Patricia. "A Feminist Fantasy: Conflicting Ideologies in *The Odd Women.*" *Stud in the Novel* 27 (1995), 529–42.

Cronin, Michael. "The Unclassed in *The Odd Women.*" *Gissing J* 31:2 (1995), 1–14.

Ermarth, Elizabeth Deeds. *The English Novel in History*, 206–8.

Nord, Deborah Epstein. *Walking the Victorian Streets*, 200–202.

Selig, Robert L. *George Gissing,* 61–66.

Sjöholm, Christina. *"The Vice of Wedlock,"* 64–84.

Takeda, Mihoko. "Between Emancipation and Restraint—Reading the Body in *The Odd Women.*" *Gissing J* 32:2 (1996), 10–13.

Zare, Bonnie. "*The Odd Women*'s Creation of a Desire for Romantic Fulfillment." *Gissing J* 30:4 (1994), 1–16.

Our Friend the Charlatan, 1901

Selig, Robert L. *George Gissing,* 89–91.

The Paying Guest, 1895

Coustillas, Pierre. "*The Paying Guest* and the Praise it Won in 1896." *Gissing J* 32:4 (1996), 20–23.

Selig, Robert L. *George Gissing,* 82–84.

The Private Papers of Henry Ryecroft, 1903

Born, Daniel. *The Birth of Liberal Guilt*, 91–96.

Selig, Robert L. *George Gissing,* 112–14.

Sleeping Fires, 1895

Selig, Robert L. *George Gissing,* 80–82.

Thyrza, 1887

Harsh, Constance. "George Gissing's *Thyrza:* Romantic Love and Ideological Co-Conspiracy." *Gissing J* 30:1 (1994), 1–11.

Lott, Sydney. "Thyrza's Eastbourne." *Gissing J* 33:1 (1997), 28–32.
Selig, Robert L. *George Gissing*, 31–33.

The Town Traveller, 1898
Selig, Robert L. *George Gissing*, 85–87.

The Unclassed, 1884
Ingham, Patricia. *The Language of Gender and Class*, 137–59.
Selig, Robert L. *George Gissing*, 25–28.
Trotter, David. "The Avoidance of Naturalism: Gissing, Moore, Grand, Bennett, and Others," in John Richetti et al., eds., *The Columbia History*, 611–12.

Veranilda, 1904
Selig, Robert L. *George Gissing*, 93–94.
Yahata, Masahiko. "A Forgotten Assessment of *Veranilda."* *Gissing J* 32:2 (1996), 19–23.

The Whirlpool, 1897
Greenslade, William. *Degeneration, Culture, and the Novel,* 134–50.
Neale, Gwyn. *All the Days Were Glorious*, 25–52.
Selig, Robert L. *George Gissing*, 70–73.
Sjöholm, Christina. *"The Vice of Wedlock,"* 107–31 .

Will Warburton, 1905
Selig, Robert L. *George Gissing*, 91–93.

Workers in the Dawn, 1880
Born, Daniel. *The Birth of Liberal Guilt,* 75–77.
Selig, Robert L. *George Gissing*, 21–25.
Trotter, David. "The Avoidance of Naturalism: Gissing, Moore, Grand, Bennett, and Others," in John Richetti et al., eds., *The Columbia History*, 611–12.

ELINOR GLYN

Three Weeks, 1907
Cadogan, Mary. *And Then Their Hearts Stood Still*, 73–77.

RUMER GODDEN

The Battle of the Villa Fiorita, 1963
Rosenthal, Lynne M. *Rumer Godden Revisited*, 77–83.

Black Narcissus, 1939
Bagchi, Alaknanda. "Of Nuns and Palaces: Rumer Godden's *Black Narcissus." Christianity and Lit* 45 (1995), 53–64.

Breakfast with the Nikolides, 1942
Rosenthal, Lynne M. *Rumer Godden Revisited*, 19–23.

A Candle for St. Jude, 1948
>   Rosenthal, Lynne M. *Rumer Godden Revisited,* 33–35.

China Court, 1961
>   Rosenthal, Lynne M. *Rumer Godden Revisited,* 73–77.

An Episode of Sparrows, 1955
>   Rosenthal, Lynne M. *Rumer Godden Revisited,* 47–54.

A Fugue in Time, 1945
>   Rosenthal, Lynne M. *Rumer Godden Revisited,* 23–27.

The Greengage Summer, 1958
>   Rosenthal, Lynne M. *Rumer Godden Revisited,* 54–58.

Kingfishers Catch Fire, 1953
>   Rosenthal, Lynne M. *Rumer Godden Revisited,* 40–47.

The River, 1946
>   Rosenthal, Lynne M. *Rumer Godden Revisited,* 27–30.

FRANCIS GODWIN

The Man in the Moon, 1638
>   Guthke, Karl S. *The Last Frontier,* 153–58.

WILLIAM GODWIN

Caleb Williams, 1794
>   Balfour, Ian. "Promises, Promises: Social and Other Contracts in the English Jacobins (Godwin/Inchbald)," in David L. Clark and Donald C. Goellnicht, eds., *New Romanticisms,* 234–39.
>   Bender, John. "Impersonal Violence: The Penetrating Gaze and the Field of Narration in *Caleb Williams,*" in Robert M. Polhemus and Roger B. Henkle, eds., *Critical Reconstructions,* 111–26.
>   Botting, Fred. *Gothic,* 94–98.
>   Corber, Robert J. "Representing the 'Unspeakable': William Godwin and the Politics of Homophobia." *J of the Hist of Sexuality* 1:1 (1990), 85–101.
>   Daffron, Eric. " 'Magnetical Sympathy': Strategies of Power and Resistance in Godwin's *Caleb Williams.*" *Criticism* 37 (1995), 213–29.
>   Graham, Kenneth W. "Narrative Method in *Caleb Williams:* Contrasting Perceptions of Evil." *Stud on Voltaire and the Eighteenth Cent* 305 (1992), 1389–90.
>   Handwerk, Gary. "Of Caleb's Guilt and Godwin's Truth: Ideology and Ethics in *Caleb Williams.*" *ELH* 60 (1993), 939–56.
>   Helfield, Randa. "Constructive Treason and Godwin's Treasonous Constructions." *Mosaic* 28:2 (1995), 49–61.
>   Hill-Miller, Katherine C. *"My Hideous Progeny,"* 68–75.

Johnson, Nancy E. "Rights, Property and the Law in the English Jacobin Novel." *Mosaic* 27:4 (1994), 113–18.

Juengel, Scott J. "Godwin, Lavater, and the Pleasures of Surface." *Stud in Romanticism* 35 (1996), 79–97.

Kilgour, Maggie. *The Rise of the Gothic Novel*, 53–75.

Leaver, Kristen. "Pursuing Conversations: *Caleb Williams* and the Romantic Construction of the Reader." *Stud in Romanticism* 33 (1994), 589–610.

Logan, Peter Melville. "Narrating Hysteria: *Caleb Williams* and the Cultural History of Nerves." *Novel* 29 (1996), 206–20.

McCormack, W. J. *From Burke to Beckett*, 99–106.

Mücke, Dorothea von. " 'To Love a Murderer'—Fantasy, Sexuality and the Political Novel: The Case of *Caleb Williams*," in Deidre Lynch and William B. Warner, eds., *Cultural Institutions of the Novel*, 306–33.

Rizzo, Betty. "The Gothic *Caleb Williams*." *Stud on Voltaire and the Eighteenth Cent* 305 (1992), 1387–89.

Spacks, Patricia Meyer. "Novels of the 1790s: Action and Impasse," in John Richetti et al., eds., *The Columbia History*, 268–72.

Sullivan, Garrett A., Jr. " 'A Story To Be Hastily Gobbled Up': *Caleb Williams* and Print Culture." *Stud in Romanticism* 32 (1993), 323–37.

Verhoeven, W. M. "Opening the Text: The Locked-Trunk Motif in Late Eighteenth-Century British and American Gothic Fiction," in Valeria Tinkler-Villani and Peter Davidson, eds., *Exhibited by Candlelight*, 208–13.

Zomchick, John P. *Family and the Law*, 177–92.

Deloraine, 1833

Hill-Miller, Katherine C. *"My Hideous Progeny,"* 166–73.

Fleetwood, 1805

Robertson, Fiona. *Legitimate Histories*, 113–15.

St. Leon, 1799

Hill-Miller, Katherine C. *"My Hideous Progeny,"* 170–73.

Kilgour, Maggie. *The Rise of the Gothic Novel*, 96–109.

Lévy, Ellen. "The Philosophical Gothic of *St Leon*." *Caliban* 33 (1996), 51–62.

Maertz, Gregory. "Family Resemblances: Intertextual Dialogue Between Father and Daughter Novelists in Godwin's *St. Leon* and Shelley's *Frankenstein*." *Univ of Mississippi Stud in Engl* 11–12 (1993–95), 303–17.

Maertz, Gregory. "Generic Fusion and Appropriation in Godwin's *St. Leon*." *European Romantic R* 5 (1995), 214–29.

WILLIAM GOLDING

Close Quarters, 1987

Dicken-Fuller, Nicola C. *William Golding's Use of Symbolism*, 55–59.

McCarron, Kevin. *The Coincidence of Opposites*, 101–19.

Darkness Visible, 1979

    Cavaliero, Glen. *The Supernatural and English Fiction,* 192–94.
    Dicken-Fuller, Nicola C. *William Golding's Use of Symbolism,* 43–46.
    Lamarque, Peter, and Stein Haugom Olsen. *Truth, Fiction, and Literature,* 430–34.
    McCarron, Kevin. *The Coincidence of Opposites,* 15–70.
    McCarron, Kevin. "*Darkness Visible* and *The Dunciad.*" *Crit Survey* 7:1 (1995), 44–50.
    Miyahara, Kazunari. "One Redeemer for Each Sinner: Individual Salvations in *Darkness Visible.*" *Stud in Engl Lang and Lit* (Fukuoka) 45 (1995), 65–82.

Fire Down Below, 1989

    Dicken-Fuller, Nicola C. *William Golding's Use of Symbolism,* 60–69.
    McCarron, Kevin. *The Coincidence of Opposites,* 123–39.

Free Fall, 1959

    Dicken-Fuller, Nicola C. *William Golding's Use of Symbolism,* 29–33.
    Granofsky, Ronald. *The Trauma Novel,* 81–84.

The Inheritors, 1955

    Black, Elizabeth. "Metaphor, Simile and Cognition in Golding's *The Inheritors.*" *Lang and Lit* 2 (1993), 37–48.
    Dicken-Fuller, Nicola C. *William Golding's Use of Symbolism,* 18–21.
    Josipovici, Gabriel. *The World and the Book,* 238–43.
    Timmons, Daniel. "Sub-Creation in William Golding's *The Inheritors.*" *Engl Stud in Canada* 22 (1996), 399–411.

Lord of the Flies, 1954

    Dicken-Fuller, Nicola C. *William Golding's Use of Symbolism,* 13–17.
    Hawlin, Stefan. "The Savages in the Forest: Decolonising William Golding." *Crit Survey* 7:2 (1995), 125–35.
    Hollahan, Eugene. *Crisis-Consciousness,* 177–78.
    Josipovici, Gabriel. *The World and the Book,* 236–38.
    Sugimura, Yasunori. "Self-Destructive Community and the Improbability of War in *Lord of the Flies.*" *Stud in Engl Lit* (Tokyo) 70 (English Number 1994), 47–64.
    Ward, Ian. *Law and Literature,* 110–12.

The Paper Men, 1984

    Dicken-Fuller, Nicola C. *William Golding's Use of Symbolism,* 51–54.
    McCarron, Kevin. *The Coincidence of Opposites,* 145–93.

Pincher Martin, 1956

    Dicken-Fuller, Nicola C. *William Golding's Use of Symbolism,* 22–24.
    Granofsky, Ronald. *The Trauma Novel,* 78–81.
    Josipovici, Gabriel. *The World and the Book,* 243–46, 252–54.
    Surette, Leon. "A Matter of Belief: Pincher Martin's Afterlife." *Twentieth Cent Lit* 40 (1994), 205–23.
    Tanzman, Lea. "Poe's 'A Tale of the Ragged Mountains' as a Source for

Golding's Post Mortem Consciousness Technique in *Pincher Martin.*" *Notes on Contemp Lit* 25:4 (1995), 6–7.

The Pyramid, 1967

Dicken-Fuller, Nicola C. *William Golding's Use of Symbolism*, 38–42.

Taniguchi, Hideko Jojima. " 'A Fulfilled Woman, a Wife and Mother'?: Female Characters in William Golding's *The Pyramid." Stud in Engl Lang and Lit* (Fukuoka) 45 (1995), 51–63.

Rites of Passage, 1980

Connor, Steven. *The English Novel in History*, 150–62.

Dicken-Fuller, Nicola C. *William Golding's Use of Symbolism*, 47–50.

McCarron, Kevin. *The Coincidence of Opposites*, 75–97.

Nadal, Marita. "William Golding's *Rites of Passage:* A World in Transition," in Susana Onega, ed., *Telling Histories*, 85–102.

Savage, Meredyth. "Golding and Van Gennep, *Rites of Passage:* Between the Sacred and the Profane, I." *Confronto Letterario* 9:17 (1992), 15–58.

The Spire, 1964

Dicken-Fuller, Nicola C. *William Golding's Use of Symbolism*, 34–37.

Hooker, Jeremy. *Writers in a Landscape*, 142–47.

Josipovici, Gabriel. *The World and the Book*, 247–51.

OLIVER GOLDSMITH

The Vicar of Wakefield, 1766

Baldridge, Cates. *The Dialogics of Dissent*, 21–39.

Benedict, Barbara M. *Framing Feeling*, 50–60.

Donoghue, Frank. *The Fame Machine*, 99–109.

Dykstal, Timothy. "The Story of O: Politics and Pleasure in *The Vicar of Wakefield." ELH* 62 (1995), 329–43.

Flint, Christopher. " 'The Family Piece': Oliver Goldsmith and the Politics of the Everyday in Eighteenth-Century Domestic Portraiture." *Eighteenth-Cent Stud* 29 (1995–96), 128–32, 137–40.

Murray, David Aaron. "From Patrimony to Paternity in *The Vicar of Wakefield." Eighteenth-Cent Fiction* 9 (1997), 327–36.

Zomchick, John P. *Family and the Law*, 154–76.

MARY GORDON

The Company of Women, 1980

Labrie, Ross. "Women and the Catholic Church in the Fiction of Mary Gordon." *Engl Stud in Canada* 22 (1996), 172–74.

Final Payments, 1978

Johnston, Eileen Fess. "The Biblical Matrix of Mary Gordon's *Final Payments." Christianity and Lit* 44 (1995), 145–64.

Labrie, Ross. "Women and the Catholic Church in the Fiction of Mary Gordon." *Engl Stud in Canada* 22 (1996), 170–72.

Good Boys and Dead Girls, 1991

Labrie, Ross. "Women and the Catholic Church in the Fiction of Mary Gordon." *Engl Stud in Canada* 22 (1996), 168–70.

Men and Angels, 1985

Labrie, Ross. "Women and the Catholic Church in the Fiction of Mary Gordon." *Engl Stud in Canada* 22 (1996), 174–77.

The Other Side, 1989

Labrie, Ross. "Women and the Catholic Church in the Fiction of Mary Gordon." *Engl Stud in Canada* 22 (1996), 177–79.

CATHERINE GORE

Cecil, a Peer, 1845

Hughes, Winifred. "Elegies for the Regency: Catherine Gore's Dandy Novels." *Nineteenth-Cent Lit* 50 (1995), 189–209.

Cecil; or, The Adventures of a Coxcomb, 1841

Hughes, Winifred. "Elegies for the Regency: Catherine Gore's Dandy Novels." *Nineteenth-Cent Lit* 50 (1995), 189–209.

KENNETH GRAHAME

The Wind in the Willows, 1908

Darcy, Jane. "The Representation of Nature in *The Wind in the Willows* and *The Secret Garden." Lion and the Unicorn* 19 (1995), 213–21.

Gaarden, Bonnie. "The Inner Family of *The Wind in the Willows." Children's Lit* 22 (1994), 43–54.

Hunt, Peter. *An Introduction to Children's Literature,* 95–99.

Hunt, Peter. *"The Wind in the Willows,"* 25–124.

Marshall, Cynthia. "Bodies and Pleasures in *The Wind in the Willows." Children's Lit* 22 (1994), 58–67.

Wullschläger, Jackie. *Inventing Wonderland,* 161–70.

SARAH GRAND

The Beth Book, 1897

Brown, Penny. *The Captured World,* 170–77.

Doughty, Terri. "Sarah Grand's *The Beth Book:* The New Woman and the Ideology of the Romance Ending," in Carol J. Singley and Susan Elizabeth Sweeney, eds., *Anxious Power,* 185–93.

Kranidis, Rita S. *Subversive Discourse,* 93–94.

Kucich, John. *The Power of Lies,* 261–65, 270–78.

Mangum, Teresa. "Style Wars of the 1890s: The New Woman and the

Decadent," in Nikki Lee Manos and Meri-Jane Rochelson, eds., *Transforming Genres*, 47–49, 52–64.

Nelson, Carolyn Christensen. *British Women Fiction Writers*, 8–20, 37–39.

Reynolds, Kimberley, and Nicola Humble. *Victorian Heroines*, 93–95.

The Heavenly Twins, 1893

Brown, Penny. *The Captured World,* 177–80.

Greenslade, William. *Degeneration, Culture, and the Novel,* 165–67.

Kranidis, Rita S. *Subversive Discourse*, 77–79.

Kucich, John. "Curious Dualities: *The Heavenly Twins* (1893) and Sarah Grand's Belated Modernist Aesthetics," in Barbara Leah Harman and Susan Meyer, eds., *The New Nineteenth Century*, 195–203.

Kucich, John. *The Power of Lies,* 239–41, 248–58, 261–67, 269–72.

Montgomery, Fiona. " 'Women who Dids, and all that kind of thing. . . .' Male Perceptions of 'Wholesome' Literature," in Christopher Parker, ed., *Gender Roles and Sexuality,* 178–83.

Nelson, Carolyn Christensen. *British Women Fiction Writers*, 8–20, 35–37.

Trotter, David. *The English Novel in History*, 117–18.

Ideala: A Study from Life, 1888

Kranidis, Rita S. *Subversive Discourse*, 94–95.

Nelson, Carolyn Christensen. *British Women Fiction Writers*, 8–20.

JAMES GRANT

First Love and Last Love: A Tale of the Indian Mutiny, 1868

Paxton, Nancy L. "Mobilizing Chivalry: Rape in Flora Annie Steel's *On the Face of the Waters* (1896) and Other British Novels about the Indian Uprising of 1857," in Barbara Leah Harman and Susan Meyer, eds., *The New Nineteenth Century*, 253–56.

ROBERT GRAVES

Claudius the God, 1934

Burton, Philip. "The Values of a Classical Education: Satirical Elements in Robert Graves's *Claudius* Novels." *R of Engl Stud* 46 (1995), 191–218.

Homer's Daughter, 1955

Swan, George Steven. " 'Who Was Homer's Daughter': Robert Graves and T. E. Lawrence." *Focus on Robert Graves and His Contemporaries* 2:2 (1994), 17–23.

I, Claudius, 1934

Burton, Philip. "The Values of a Classical Education: Satirical Elements in Robert Graves's *Claudius* Novels." *R of Engl Stud* 46 (1995), 191–218.

Watch the North Wind Rise, 1949

Presley, John Woodrow. "Fox, Vampire, Witch: Two Novels of Fantasy by Graves and Garnett." *Focus on Robert Graves and His Contemporaries* 2:2 (1994), 26–30.

ALASDAIR GRAY

The Fall of Kevin Walker, 1985

Bernstein, Stephen. "Scottish Enough: The London Novels of Alasdair Gray." *R of Contemp Fiction* 15:2 (1995), 170–74.

Lanark, 1981

Donaldson, George, and Alison Lee. "Is Eating People Really Wrong? Dining with Alasdair Gray." *R of Contemp Fiction* 15:2 (1995), 158–61.

Harrison, William M. "The Power of Work in the Novels of Alasdair Gray." *R of Contemp Fiction* 15:2 (1995), 162–68.

Smith, Penny. "Hell innit: The Millennium in Alasdair Gray's *Lanark,* Martin Amis's *London Fields,* and Shena Mackay's *Dunedin,*" in Laurel Brake, ed., *The Endings of Epochs,* 116–19.

Todd, Richard. *Consuming Fictions,* 141–45.

McGrotty and Ludmilla, 1990

Bernstein, Stephen. "Scottish Enough: The London Novels of Alasdair Gray." *R of Contemp Fiction* 15:2 (1995), 170–74.

Harrison, William M. "The Power of Work in the Novels of Alasdair Gray." *R of Contemp Fiction* 15:2 (1995), 162–68.

1982 Janine, 1984

Donaldson, George, and Alison Lee. "Is Eating People Really Wrong? Dining with Alasdair Gray." *R of Contemp Fiction* 15:2 (1995), 155–58.

Harrison, William M. "The Power of Work in the Novels of Alasdair Gray." *R of Contemp Fiction* 15:2 (1995), 162–68.

Poor Things, 1992

Diamond-Nigh, Lynne. "Gray's Anatomy: When Words and Images Collide." *R of Contemp Fiction* 15:2 (1995), 178–83.

Hawley, John C. "Bell, Book, and Candle: Poor Things and the Exorcism of Victorian Sentiment." *R of Contemp Fiction* 15:2 (1995), 175–77.

Todd, Richard. *Consuming Fictions,* 145–47.

Something Leather, 1991

Donaldson, George, and Alison Lee. "Is Eating People Really Wrong? Dining with Alasdair Gray." *R of Contemp Fiction* 15:2 (1995), 155–58.

HENRY GREEN

Caught, 1943

    Gasiorek, Andrzej. *Post-War British Fiction,* 35–39.

    Sharrock, Roger. *New Insights on English Authors,* 146–47.

Doting, 1952

    Gasiorek, Andrzej. *Post-War British Fiction,* 39–42.

Living, 1929

    Hitchcock, Peter. "Passing: Henry Green and Working-Class Identity." *Mod Fiction Stud* 40 (1994), 9–25.

Nothing, 1950

    Gasiorek, Andrzej. *Post-War British Fiction,* 39–42.

GRAHAM GREENE

Brighton Rock, 1938

    Gordon, Haim. *Fighting Evil,* 11–15, 59–62, 88–90.

    Macdonald, Andrew and Gina. "Graham Greene's Female Hard-Boiled Detective: Ida in *Brighton Rock.*" *Clues* 15:2 (1994), 99–115.

    Mudford, Peter. *Graham Greene,* 21–24, 26–28.

    Pendleton, Robert. *Graham Greene's Conradian Masterplot,* 91–95.

    Pierloot, Roland A. *Psychoanalytic Patterns,* 74–81.

    Shelden, Michael. *Graham Greene,* 195–204.

    Wilkes, G. A. "The Narrator of *Brighton Rock.*" *Sydney Stud in Engl* 20 (1994–95), 91–103.

A Burnt-Out Case, 1961

    Gordon, Haim. *Fighting Evil,* 45–51, 93–96, 122–25.

    Mudford, Peter. *Graham Greene,* 52–53.

    Pendleton, Robert. *Graham Greene's Conradian Masterplot,* 109–16.

    Pierloot, Roland A. *Psychoanalytic Patterns,* 151–57.

    Shelden, Michael. *Graham Greene,* 362–65.

The Captain and the Enemy, 1988

    Pendleton, Robert. *Graham Greene's Conradian Masterplot,* 156–57.

The Comedians, 1966

    Gordon, Haim. *Fighting Evil,* 62–64, 69–71, 99–104, 121–25.

    Mudford, Peter. *Graham Greene,* 44–46, 50–51.

    Pendleton, Robert. *Graham Greene's Conradian Masterplot,* 128–32.

    Pierloot, Roland A. *Psychoanalytic Patterns,* 167–74.

    Shelden, Michael. *Graham Greene,* 367–73.

The Confidential Agent, 1939

    Gordon, Haim. *Fighting Evil,* 64–68, 72–74, 113–15.

    Pendleton, Robert. *Graham Greene's Conradian Masterplot,* 77–79.

    Shelden, Michael. *Graham Greene,* 124–26, 235–38.

Doctor Fisher of Geneva, 1980

   Gordon, Haim. *Fighting Evil,* 111–15.
   Pendleton, Robert. *Graham Greene's Conradian Masterplot,* 142–44.
   Pierloot, Roland A. *Psychoanalytic Patterns,* 81–83.

The End of the Affair, 1951

   Cavaliero, Glen. *The Supernatural and English Fiction,* 106–7.
   Mudford, Peter. *Graham Greene,* 24–27.
   Pendleton, Robert. *Graham Greene's Conradian Masterplot,* 96–97.
   Pierloot, Roland A. *Psychoanalytic Patterns,* 123–28, 227–29.
   Sharrock, Roger. *New Insights on English Authors,* 134–42.
   Shelden, Michael. *Graham Greene,* 313–18.

England Made Me, 1935

   Gordon, Haim. *Fighting Evil,* 29–31, 90–94, 122–24.
   Hopkins, Chris. "Greene's *England Made Me:* Krogh, Kreuger and En-
      glish Marxist Criticism in the Nineteen Thirties." *Engl Lang Notes*
      33:1 (1995), 61–63.
   Pendleton, Robert. *Graham Greene's Conradian Masterplot,* 71–73.
   Pierloot, Roland A. *Psychoanalytic Patterns,* 138–45.
   Shelden, Michael. *Graham Greene,* 169–72.

A Gun for Sale, 1936

   Mockler, Anthony. *Graham Greene,* 117–26.
   Pendleton, Robert. *Graham Greene's Conradian Masterplot,* 132–37.
   Shelden, Michael. *Graham Greene,* 180–86.

The Heart of the Matter, 1948

   Gordon, Haim. *Fighting Evil,* 20–21, 85–87.
   Malamet, Elliott. "Penning the Police/Policing the Pen: The Case of Gra-
      ham Greene's *The Heart of the Matter." Twentieth Cent Lit* 39 (1993),
      283–303.
   Mudford, Peter. *Graham Greene,* 7–9, 32–36.
   Pendleton, Robert. *Graham Greene's Conradian Masterplot,* 105–9.
   Pierloot, Roland A. *Psychoanalytic Patterns,* 100–112.
   Sharrock, Roger. *New Insights on English Authors,* 134–42.
   Shelden, Michael. *Graham Greene,* 291–98.

The Honorary Consul, 1973

   Higgins, Michael W. "Greene's Priest: A Sort of Rebel." *Essays in Gra-
      ham Greene* 3 (1992), 15–23.
   Mudford, Peter. *Graham Greene,* 46–49.
   Pendleton, Robert. *Graham Greene's Conradian Masterplot,* 132–35.
   Pierloot, Roland A. *Psychoanalytic Patterns,* 186–92.

The Human Factor, 1978

   Gordon, Haim. *Fighting Evil,* 38–41.
   Mudford, Peter. *Graham Greene,* 39–42.
   Pendleton, Robert. *Graham Greene's Conradian Masterplot,* 135–38.
   Shelden, Michael. *Graham Greene,* 399–403.

It's a Battlefield, 1934

> Diemert, Brian. "The Pursuit of Justice: Graham Greene's Refiguring of the Detective Story in *It's a Battlefield." Papers on Lang and Lit* 30 (1994), 285–306.
> McCartney, George. "Satire between the Wars: Evelyn Waugh and Others," in John Richetti et al., eds., *The Columbia History,* 874–75.
> Mockler, Anthony. *Graham Greene,* 79–83.
> Pendleton, Robert. *Graham Greene's Conradian Masterplot,* 65–68.
> Shelden, Michael. *Graham Greene,* 148–52.

The Man Within, 1929

> Mockler, Anthony. *Graham Greene,* 53–55.
> Pendleton, Robert. *Graham Greene's Conradian Masterplot,* 57–59.
> Pierloot, Roland A. *Psychoanalytic Patterns,* 178–82.
> Shelden, Michael. *Graham Greene,* 96–101.

The Ministry of Fear, 1943

> Pendleton, Robert. *Graham Greene's Conradian Masterplot,* 79–82.
> Pierloot, Roland A. *Psychoanalytic Patterns,* 85–99.
> Shelden, Michael. *Graham Greene,* 280–85.

Monsignor Quixote, 1982

> Christensen, Peter G. "The Art of Self-Preservation: Monsignor Quixote's Resistance to Don Quixote." *Essays in Graham Greene* 3 (1992), 25–41.
> Duran, Leopoldo. *Graham Greene,* 212–30.
> Gordon, Haim. *Fighting Evil,* 47–51, 93–95, 105–8.
> Heidt, Edward R. *The Image of the Church Minister,* 89–100.
> Higgins, Michael W. "Greene's Priest: A Sort of Rebel." *Essays in Graham Greene* 3 (1992), 12–23.
> Mudford, Peter. *Graham Greene,* 56–58.
> Pendleton, Robert. *Graham Greene's Conradian Masterplot,* 150–55.
> Pierloot, Roland A. *Psychoanalytic Patterns,* 157–60.
> Sharrock, Roger. *New Insights on English Authors,* 134–42.

The Name of Action, 1930

> Mockler, Anthony. *Graham Greene,* 57–59.
> Pendleton, Robert. *Graham Greene's Conradian Masterplot,* 59–62.
> Shelden, Michael. *Graham Greene,* 118–23.

Our Man in Havana, 1958

> McCartney, George. "Satire between the Wars: Evelyn Waugh and Others," in John Richetti et al., eds., *The Columbia History,* 875–76.
> Pendleton, Robert. *Graham Greene's Conradian Masterplot,* 144–46.
> Pierloot, Roland A. *Psychoanalytic Patterns,* 163–67.
> Shelden, Michael. *Graham Greene,* 356–60.

The Power and the Glory, 1940

> Gordon, Haim. *Fighting Evil,* 46–50.
> Heidt, Edward R. *The Image of the Church Minister,* 81–89.

Higgins, Michael W. "Greene's Priest: A Sort of Rebel." *Essays in Graham Greene* 3 (1992), 13–23.

Malamet, Elliott. "The Uses of Delay in *The Power and the Glory.*" *Renascence* 46 (1994), 211–22.

Mudford, Peter. *Graham Greene*, 27–32.

Pendleton, Robert. *Graham Greene's Conradian Masterplot*, 97–101.

Pierloot, Roland A. *Psychoanalytic Patterns*, 210–26.

Sharrock, Roger. *New Insights on English Authors*, 135–36.

Shelden, Michael. *Graham Greene*, 220–29.

The Quiet American, 1955

Gordon, Haim. *Fighting Evil*, 17–19, 30–36, 58–60, 75–78, 88–90, 93–96, 104–6.

Mudford, Peter. *Graham Greene*, 42–45.

Pendleton, Robert. *Graham Greene's Conradian Masterplot*, 119–28.

Pierloot, Roland A. *Psychoanalytic Patterns*, 199–203.

Shelden, Michael. *Graham Greene*, 333–38.

Rumour at Nightfall, 1941

Pendleton, Robert. *Graham Greene's Conradian Masterplot*, 62–64.

Shelden, Michael. *Graham Greene*, 131–33.

Stamboul Train, 1932

Pendleton, Robert. *Graham Greene's Conradian Masterplot*, 68–71.

Shelden, Michael. *Graham Greene*, 137–43.

The Tenth Man, 1985

Pendleton, Robert. *Graham Greene's Conradian Masterplot*, 87–89.

Stemmler, Theo. "Literary Amnesia: Graham Greene's Novel and Somerset Maugham's Play *The Tenth Man.*" *Essays in Graham Greene* 3 (1992), 55–57.

The Third Man, 1950

Blayac, Alain. "Vienne et Berlin dans la littérature anglaise de l'Entre-Deux-Guerres." *Cahiers d'Etudes Germaniques* 24 (1993), 97–99.

Man, Glenn K. S. "*The Third Man:* Pulp Fiction and Art Film." *Lit/Film Q* 21 (1993), 171–77.

Pendleton, Robert. *Graham Greene's Conradian Masterplot*, 82–87.

Shelden, Michael. *Graham Greene*, 265–79.

Travels with My Aunt, 1969

Gordon, Haim. *Fighting Evil*, 90–94.

Pendleton, Robert. *Graham Greene's Conradian Masterplot*, 146–50.

Shelden, Michael. *Graham Greene*, 383–87.

ROBERT GREENE

Ciceronis Amor: Tullies Love, 1589

Barbour, Reid. *Deciphering Elizabethan Fiction*, 37–40.

Mamillia, 1580

Barbour, Reid. *Deciphering Elizabethan Fiction,* 27–29.

Menaphon, 1589

Barbour, Reid. *Deciphering Elizabethan Fiction,* 40–42.

McCluskey, Peter M. " 'Humors to Delight': *Menaphon* as Burlesque." *Publs of the Arkansas Philol Assoc* 21:1 (1995), 69–74.

Wilson, Katharine. " 'The Ironicall Recreation of the Reader': Robert Greene's *Menaphon,* Pastoral and Parody," in Wolfgang Görtschacher and Holger Klein, eds., *Narrative Strategies,* 207–23.

Pandosto, 1588

Margolies, David. "Fortune and Agency in Greene's *Pandosto,*" in Wolfgang Görtschacher and Holger Klein, eds., *Narrative Strategies,* 195–206.

Newcomb, Lori Humphrey. " 'Social Things': The Production of Popular Culture in the Reception of Robert Greene's *Pandosto.*" *ELH* 61 (1994), 753–73.

WALTER GREENWOOD

Love on the Dole, 1933

Fox, Pamela. *Class Fictions,* 79–83, 132–34, 184–88.

Hopkins, Chris. "Dialect and Dialectic: Region and Nations in Walter Greenwood's *Love on the Dole.*" *Lit of Region and Nation* 3:4 (1993), 1–8.

GERALD GRIFFIN

The Collegians, 1828

Deane, Seamus. *Strange Country,* 56–63.

Hayley, Barbara. "Religion and Society in Nineteenth Century Irish Fiction," in Robert Welch, ed., *Irish Writers and Religion,* 41–42.

ELIZABETH GRIFFITH

The Delicate Distress, 1769

MacCarthy, B. G. *The Female Pen,* 318–20.

The History of Lady Barton, 1771

MacCarthy, B. G. *The Female Pen,* 320–22.

JOSEPH GUINAN

The Soggarth Aroon, 1907

Murphy, James H. *Catholic Fiction and Social Reality in Ireland,* 116–19.

NEIL GUNN

Bloodhunt, 1952
> Pick, J. B. *The Great Shadow House,* 126–32.

Highland River, 1937
> Curtis, Jan. "The Celtic Tradition of the Winged Poet and the Mythical Salmon of Wisdom in Neil Gunn's *Highland River." Scottish Liter J* 22:2 (1995), 60–72.
> D'Arcy, Julian Meldon. *Scottish Skalds and Sagamen,* 78–81.

The Key of the Chest, 1945
> Pick, J. B. *The Great Shadow House,* 124–25.

The Other Landscape, 1954
> Pick, J. B. *The Great Shadow House,* 132–46.

The Silver Darlings, 1941
> D'Arcy, Julian Meldon. *Scottish Skalds and Sagamen,* 82–85.
> Inness, Sherrie A. " 'They must worship industry or starve': Scottish Resistance to British Imperialism in Gunn's *The Silver Darlings." Stud in Scottish Lit* 28 (1993), 133–49.

Sun Circle, 1933
> D'Arcy, Julian Meldon. *Scottish Skalds and Sagamen,* 68–78.

SUSANNAH GUNNING

Coombe Wood, 1783
> Todd, Janet. *The Sign of Angellica,* 179–85.

The Memoirs of Mary, 1793
> MacCarthy, B. G. *The Female Pen,* 307–9.

RONALD GURNER

Pass Guard at Ypres, 1930
> Cecil, Hugh. *The Flower of Battle,* 213–17.

HENRY RIDER HAGGARD

Allan Quartermain, 1887
> Bassnett, Susan. "Lost in the Past: A Tale of Heroes and Englishness." *Kunapipi* 18:1 (1996), 51–53, 59–60.
> Ching-Liang Low, Gail. *White Skins/Black Masks,* 37–49.
> Demoor, Marysa. "Ritual Celebrations as Rites of Passage in Rider Haggard's Dark Romances." *Cahiers Victoriens et Edouardiens* 39 (1994), 209–12.

Ayesha, 1905

Stott, Rebecca. *The Fabrication*, 99–101.

Eric Brighteyes, 1898

Orel, Harold. *The Historical Novel*, 133–50.

King Solomon's Mines, 1885

Ching-Liang Low, Gail. *White Skins/Black Masks*, 47–50, 59–63, 76–83, 96–98.

Cole, David L. "Maps and the Discovery Motif in *Treasure Island, King Solomon's Mines,* and *The Treasure of the Sierra Maddre.*" *Illinois Engl Bull* 83:2 (1996), 4–7.

David, Deirdre. *Rule Britannia*, 188–92.

Demoor, Marysa. "Ritual Celebrations as Rites of Passage in Rider Haggard's Dark Romances." *Cahiers Victoriens et Edouardiens* 39 (1994), 205–7.

Dixon, Robert. *Writing the Colonial Adventure*, 62–81.

Harris, Michael. *Outsiders and Insiders*, 47–61.

Pocock, Tom. *Rider Haggard and the Lost Empire*, 62–66.

Scheick, William J. *The Ethos of Romance*, 44–56.

Stott, Rebecca. *The Fabrication*, 92–95, 112–14.

Vrettos, Athena. *Somatic Fictions*, 158–60.

Mr. Meeson's Will, 1888

Stewart, Garrett. *Dear Reader*, 157–63.

She, 1887

Bivona, Daniel. *Desire and Contradiction*, 79–84.

Ching-Liang Low, Gail. *White Skins/Black Masks*, 63–65.

David, Deirdre. *Rule Britannia*, 192–99.

Demoor, Marysa. "Ritual Celebrations as Rites of Passage in Rider Haggard's Dark Romances." *Cahiers Victoriens et Edouardiens* 39 (1994), 207–9.

Dixon, Robert. *Writing the Colonial Adventure*, 83–85.

Gold, Barri J. "Embracing the Corpse: Discursive Recycling in H. Rider Haggard's *She.*" *Engl Lit in Transition, 1880–1920* 38 (1995), 302–25.

Pocock, Tom. *Rider Haggard and the Lost Empire*, 66–71.

Stott, Rebecca. *The Fabrication*, 95–121.

Vrettos, Athena. *Somatic Fictions*, 155–75.

Westerweel, Bart. " 'An Immense Snake Uncoiled': H. Rider Haggard's Heart of Darkness and Imperial Gothic," in Valeria Tinkler-Villani and Peter Davidson, eds., *Exhibited by Candlelight*, 257–70.

MARGUERITE RADCLYFFE HALL

The Unlit Lamp, 1924

Joannou, Maroula. *'Ladies, Please Don't Smash These Windows,'* 80–95.

Würzbach, Natascha. "The Mother Image as Cultural Concept and Literary Theme in the Nineteenth- and Twentieth-Century English Novel: A Feminist Reading within the Context of New Historicism and the History of Mentalities," in Rüdiger Ahrens and Laurenz Volkmann, eds., *Why Literature Matters*, 382–83.

The Well of Loneliness, 1928

Backus, Margot Gayle. "Sexual Orientation in the (Post)Imperial Nation: Celticism and Inversion Theory in Radclyffe Hall's *The Well of Loneliness.*" *Tulsa Stud in Women's Lit* 15 (1996), 253–63.

Cadogan, Mary. *And Then Their Hearts Stood Still,* 240–45.

Duncker, Patricia. *Sisters and Strangers,* 167–69.

Griffin, Gabriele. *Heavenly Love?,* 20–24.

Joannou, Maroula. *'Ladies, Please Don't Smash These Windows,'* 102–26.

Parkes, Adam. "Lesbianism, History, and Censorship: *The Well of Loneliness* and the Suppressed Randiness of Virginia Woolf's *Orlando.*" *Twentieth Cent Lit* 40 (1994), 434–46.

Parkes, Adam. *Modernism and the Theater of Censorship,* 144–62.

Rauch, Christina. "Vom Umgang mit Krankheit und Natur in Radclyffe Halls *The Well of Loneliness:* Zur Rezeptionsgeschichte." *Forum Homosexualität und Literatur* 23 (1995), 71–81.

Skinner, Shelly. "The House in Order: Lesbian Identity and *The Well of Loneliness.*" *Women's Stud* 23 (1994), 19–33.

Strobel, Christina. "Vom Umgang mit Krankheit und Natur in Radclyffe Halls *The Well of Loneliness.*" *Forum Homosexualität und Literatur* 23 (1995), 83–97.

CICELY HAMILTON

William—An Englishman, 1919

Goldman, Dorothy. *Women Writers and the Great War,* 57–60.

MARY HAMILTON

Munster Village, 1778

Johns, Alessa. "Mary Hamilton, Daniel Defoe, and a Case of Plagiarism in Eighteenth-Century England." *Engl Lang Notes* 31:4 (1994), 25–30.

Perry, Ruth. "Bluestockings in Utopia," in Beth Fowkes Tobin, ed., *History, Gender, and Eighteenth-Century Literature*, 163–66.

PATRICK HAMILTON

The Plains of Cement, 1934

McKenna, Brian. "The British Communist Novel of the 1930s and 1940s: A 'Party of Equals'? (And Does That Matter?)." *R of Engl Stud* 47 (1996), 372–75.

JAMES HANLEY

The Furys, 1935

Williams, Patrick. " 'No Struggle But the Home': James Hanley's *The Furys,"* in Patrick J. Quinn, ed., *Recharting the Thirties,* 135–44.

THOMAS HARDY

Desperate Remedies, 1871

Dalziel, Pamela. "Exploiting the *Poor Man:* The Genesis of Hardy's *Desperate Remedies." JEGP* 94 (1995), 220–32.

Ebbatson, Roger. *Hardy,* 13–39.

Fisher, Joe. *The Hidden Hardy,* 20–37.

Gibson, James. *Thomas Hardy,* 40–46.

Jedrzejewski, Jan. *Thomas Hardy and the Church,* 70–73, 130–32.

Levine, George. "Shaping Hardy's Art: Vision, Class, and Sex," in John Richetti et al., eds., *The Columbia History,* 544–51.

Millgate, Michael. *Thomas Hardy,* 29–35.

Morgan, Rosemarie. "Bodily Transactions: Toni Morrison and Thomas Hardy in Literary Discourse," in Charles P. C. Pettit, ed., *Celebrating Thomas Hardy,* 148–51.

Neale, Catherine. *"Desperate Remedies:* The Merits and Demerits of Popular Fiction." *Crit Survey* 5 (1993), 117–22.

Sasaki, Toru. "Viewer and Victim in *Desperate Remedies:* Links between Hardy's Life and His Fiction." *Thomas Hardy J* 10:1 (1994), 77–85.

Seymour-Smith, Martin. *Hardy,* 121–37.

Stave, Shirley A. *The Decline of the Goddess,* 8–10.

Far from the Madding Crowd, 1874

Blythe, Ronald. "Thomas Hardy and John Clare: A Soil Observed, a Soil Ploughed," in Charles P. C. Pettit, ed., *Celebrating Thomas Hardy,* 59–61.

Davis, Rocio G. " 'Cedit Amor Rebus': Love and Circumstance in Hardy's *Far from the Madding Crowd." Thomas Hardy Yrbk* 22 (1996), 5–11.

Doheny, [Prof.]. " 'The race for money and good things': *Far from the Madding Crowd." Thomas Hardy Yrbk* 21 (1995), 8–26.

Elbarbary, Samir. "The Male Bias of Language and Gender Hierarchy: Hardy's Bathsheba Everdene and his Vision of Feminine Reality Reconsidered." *Cahiers Victoriens et Edouardiens* 41 (1995), 59–76.

Fisher, Joe. *The Hidden Hardy,* 38–62.

Gatrell, Simon. *"Far from the Madding Crowd* Revisited." *Thomas Hardy J* 10:2 (1994), 38–50.

Gibson, James. *Thomas Hardy,* 62–67.

Hands, Timothy. *Thomas Hardy,* 124–28, 138–40.

Jedrzejewski, Jan. *Thomas Hardy and the Church,* 81–86, 136–40.

Kucich, John. *The Power of Lies,* 228–30.

Kurzon, Dennis. "The Anatomy of Two Promises: The Cases of 'The Rash Bride' and Bathsheba Everdene." *Thomas Hardy Yrbk* 22 (1996), 13–20.

Langbaum, Robert. *Thomas Hardy in Our Time,* 10–12, 78–94.

Millgate, Michael. *Thomas Hardy,* 79–94.

Mitchell, Judith. *The Stone and the Scorpion,* 162–74.

Morgan, Rosemarie. *Cancelled Words,* 13–151.

Rothermel, Peter. "The Far and the Near: On Reading Thomas Hardy Today," in Charles P. C. Pettit, ed., *Celebrating Thomas Hardy,* 166–69, 171–73.

Seymour-Smith, Martin. *Hardy,* 178–82, 184–204.

Sprechman, Ellen Lew. *Seeing Women as Men,* 12–14, 25–39.

Stave, Shirley A. *The Decline of the Goddess,* 23–45.

Winnifrith, Tom. *Fallen Women,* 116–18.

The Hand of Ethelberta, 1876

Blishen, Edward. "Hardy, *The Hand of Ethelberta,* and Some Persisting English Discomforts," in Charles P. C. Pettit, ed., *Celebrating Thomas Hardy,* 182–94.

Davies, Sarah. "*The Hand of Ethelberta:* De-Mythologising 'Woman.' " *Crit Survey* 5 (1993), 123–30.

Fisher, Joe. *The Hidden Hardy,* 63–81.

Gibson, James. *Thomas Hardy,* 68–72.

Jedrzejewski, Jan. *Thomas Hardy and the Church,* 86–90.

Levine, George. "Shaping Hardy's Art: Vision, Class, and Sex," in John Richetti et al., eds., *The Columbia History,* 538–39.

Millgate, Michael. *Thomas Hardy,* 105–16.

Roberts, Patrick. "*Ethelberta:* Portrait of the Artist as a Young Woman—Love and Ambition." *Thomas Hardy J* 10:1 (1994), 87–94.

Seymour-Smith, Martin. *Hardy,* 210–19.

Stave, Shirley A. *The Decline of the Goddess,* 13–16.

Jude the Obscure, 1895

Antor, Heinz. *Der englische Universitätsroman,* 412–14.

Bauer, Margaret D. "Failed Quests for Ideal Love: *Jude the Obscure* as a Paradigm for *The Wild Palms.*" *Univ of Mississippi Stud in Engl* 11–12 (1993–95), 282–89.

Casagrande, Peter J. " 'Something More to be Said': Hardy's Creative Process and the Case of *Tess* and *Jude,*" in Charles P. C. Pettit, ed., *New Perspectives,* 23–37.

Davis, William A., Jr. "Happy Days in *Jude the Obscure:* Hardy and the Crawford-Dilke Divorce Case." *Thomas Hardy J* 13:1 (1997), 64–73.

Dutta, Shanta. "Sue's 'Obscure' Sisters." *Thomas Hardy J* 12:2 (1996), 60–70.

Elbarbary, Samir. "The Context and Analogies of Hardy's Sue's Sexless Fixation and Procreative Deconstructionist Argument." *Thomas Hardy Yrbk* 22 (1996), 54–60.

Fisher, Joe. *The Hidden Hardy*, 174–92.

Fulweiler, Howard W. *"Here A Captive Heart Busted,"* 121–48.

Gatrell, Simon. *Thomas Hardy and the Proper Study of Mankind*, 140–71.

Gibson, James. *Thomas Hardy*, 129–34.

Gordon, Jan B. *Gossip and Subversion*, 307–12, 316–26.

Green, Laura. " 'Strange [in]difference of sex': Thomas Hardy, the Victorian Man of Letters, and the Temptations of Androgyny." *Victorian Stud* 38 (1995), 534–47.

Greenslade, William. *Degeneration, Culture, and the Novel*, 170–75, 177–81.

Hands, Timothy. *Thomas Hardy*, 75–79, 126–30.

Hands, Timothy. "Jude in Oxford." *Thomas Hardy J* 11:3 (1995), 61–65.

Harding, James M. "The Signification of Arabella's Missile: Feminine Sexuality, Masculine Anxiety and Revision in *Jude the Obscure*." *J of Narrative Technique* 26 (1996), 85–105.

Ingham, Patricia. *The Language of Gender and Class*, 160–82.

Jedrzejewski, Jan. *Thomas Hardy and the Church*, 105–11, 155–61.

Kranidis, Rita S. *Subversive Discourse*, 123–25.

Kucich, John. *The Power of Lies*, 229–34.

Lainsbury, G. P " 'Outside the gates of everything': The Problem of Tragic Sensibility in *Jude the Obscure*." *Thomas Hardy Yrbk* 23 (1996), 5–16.

Langbaum, Robert. *Thomas Hardy in Our Time*, 16–24.

Levine, George. "Shaping Hardy's Art: Vision, Class, and Sex," in John Richetti et al., eds., *The Columbia History*, 554–58.

Luftig, Victor. *Seeing Together*, 108–19.

Mallett, Phillip. *"Jude the Obscure:* A Farewell to Wessex." *Thomas Hardy J* 11:3 (1995), 48–58.

Miller, Jane Eldridge. *Rebel Women*, 33–36.

Millgate, Michael. *Thomas Hardy*, 317–35.

Mills, Howard. " 'The World of Substance': Lawrence, Hardy, Cézanne, and Shelley." *English* 43 (1994), 210–12.

Mitchell, Judith. *The Stone and the Scorpion*, 198–207.

Morrison, Ronald D. *"Jude the Obscure* and *The Well-Beloved:* Sibling Novels." *Thomas Hardy Yrbk* 22 (1996), 34–50.

Myer, Valerie Grosvenor. *Ten Great English Novelists*, 153–54.

Nemesvari, Richard. "Appropriating the Word: *Jude the Obscure* as Subversive Apocrypha." *Victorian R* 19:2 (1993), 48–65.

Newey, Vincent. *Centring the Self,* 214–38.

Otis, Laura. *Organic Memory*, 176–80.

Prentiss, Norman D. "The Tortured Form of *Jude the Obscure*." *Colby Q* 31 (1995), 179–93.

Pyle, Forest. "Demands of History: Narrative Crisis in *Jude the Obscure*." *New Liter Hist* 26 (1995), 359–75.

Reynolds, Kimberley, and Nicola Humble. *Victorian Heroines*, 43–46.

Seymour-Smith, Martin. *Hardy*, 505–36, 541–48.

Sprechman, Ellen Lew. *Seeing Women as Men*, 20–23, 101–20.

Stave, Shirley A. *The Decline of the Goddess*, 123–56.

Stewart, Garrett. *Dear Reader*, 294–300.

Sumner, Rosemary. "Discoveries of Dissonance: Hardy's Late Fiction." *Thomas Hardy J* 11:3 (1995), 79–88.

Sutherland, John. *Is Heathcliff a Murderer?*, 221–23.

Taylor, Dennis. "The Chronology of *Jude the Obscure*." *Thomas Hardy J* 12:3 (1996), 65–68.

Thorpe, Michael. "Sue the Obscure: Hardy's Female Readers." *Thomas Hardy J* 11:3 (1995), 66–75.

Trotter, David. *The English Novel in History*, 36–38.

Watts, Cedric. "Hardy's Sue Bridehead and the 'New Woman.' " *Crit Survey* 5 (1993), 152–56.

Wheeler, Michael. *English Fiction of the Victorian Period*, 210–13.

Wilson, Martin. " 'Lovely Conundrum' and Locus for Conflict: The Figure of Sue Bridehead in Hardy's *Jude the Obscure*." *Thomas Hardy J* 11:3 (1995), 90–99.

A Laodicean, 1881

Fisher, Joe. *The Hidden Hardy*, 99–114.

Gatrell, Simon. *Thomas Hardy and the Proper Study of Mankind*, 53–55.

Gibson, James. *Thomas Hardy*, 82–87.

Jedrzejewski, Jan. *Thomas Hardy and the Church*, 94–100, 194–96.

Levine, George. "Shaping Hardy's Art: Vision, Class, and Sex," in John Richetti et al., eds., *The Columbia History*, 539–40.

Millgate, Michael. *Thomas Hardy*, 165–73.

Morgan, Rosemarie. "Bodily Transactions: Toni Morrison and Thomas Hardy in Literary Discourse," in Charles P. C. Pettit, ed., *Celebrating Thomas Hardy*, 154–57.

Seymour-Smith, Martin. *Hardy*, 265–73.

Stave, Shirley A. *The Decline of the Goddess,* 17–19.

The Mayor of Casterbridge, 1886

Easingwood, Peter. "*The Mayor of Casterbridge* and the Irony of Literary Production." *Thomas Hardy J* 9:3 (1993), 64–74.

Ebbatson, Roger. *Thomas Hardy*, 55–117.

Egan, Joseph J. "The Indebtedness of George Douglas Brown to *The Mayor of Casterbridge*." *Stud in Scottish Lit* 27 (1992), 203–17.

Fisher, Joe. *The Hidden Hardy*, 115–35.

Gatrell, Simon. *Thomas Hardy and the Proper Study of Mankind*, 68–96.

Gibson, James. *Thomas Hardy*, 95–99.

Greenslade, William. *Degeneration, Culture, and the Novel,* 54–64.

Hands, Timothy. *Thomas Hardy*, 73–75, 162–65.

Hennelly, Mark M., Jr. "The Unknown 'Character' of *The Mayor of Casterbridge,* Part I." *J of Evolutionary Psych* 16:1–2 (1995), 92–101.

Hooker, Jeremy. *Writers in a Landscape*, 118–38.

Jedrzejewski, Jan. *Thomas Hardy and the Church*, 144–47.

Jones, Tod E. "Michael Henchard: Hardy's Male Homosexual." *Victorian Newsl* 86 (1994), 9–13.

Langbaum, Robert. *Thomas Hardy in Our Time,* 127–41.

Millgate, Michael. *Thomas Hardy,* 221–34, 238–43.

Moses, Michael Valdez. *The Novel and the Globalization of Culture,* 29–67.

Prentiss, Norman D. "Compilation and Design in *The Mayor of Casterbridge.*" *Thomas Hardy J* 11:1 (1995), 60–72.

Raine, Craig. "Conscious Artistry in *The Mayor of Casterbridge,*" in Charles P. C. Pettit, ed., *New Perspectives,* 156–69.

Rothermel, Peter. "The Far and the Near: On Reading Thomas Hardy Today," in Charles P. C. Pettit, ed., *Celebrating Thomas Hardy,* 167–74.

Seymour-Smith, Martin. *Hardy,* 321–29, 331–42.

Sprechman, Ellen Lew. *Seeing Women as Men,* 16–18, 59–76.

Wheeler, Michael. *English Fiction of the Victorian Period,* 204–7.

A Pair of Blue Eyes, 1873

Gibson, James. *Thomas Hardy,* 55–60.

Green, Laura. " 'Strange [in]difference of sex': Thomas Hardy, the Victorian Man of Letters, and the Temptations of Androgyny." *Victorian Stud* 38 (1995), 527–34.

Jedrzejewski, Jan. *Thomas Hardy and the Church,* 76–80.

Levine, George. "Shaping Hardy's Art: Vision, Class, and Sex," in John Richetti et al., eds., *The Columbia History,* 538–41.

Millgate, Michael. *Thomas Hardy,* 66–76.

Pinion, F. B. "Questions Arising from Hardy's Visits to Cornwall," in Charles P. C. Pettit, ed., *New Perspectives,* 198–208.

Seymour-Smith, Martin. *Hardy,* 152–71.

Stave, Shirley A. *The Decline of the Goddess,* 11–13.

The Return of the Native, 1878

Dalziel, Pamela. "Anxieties of Representation: The Serial Illustrations to Hardy's *The Return of the Native.*" *Nineteenth-Cent Lit* 51 (1996), 84–110.

Ermarth, Elizabeth Deeds. *The English Novel in History,* 48–50.

Fisher, Joe. *The Hidden Hardy,* 82–98.

Gallet, René. "*The Return of the Native:* logique tragique et logique sacrificielle." *Cahiers Victoriens et Edouardiens* 41 (1995), 81–94.

Gatrell, Simon. *Thomas Hardy and the Proper Study of Mankind,* 35–37, 42–49, 69–71.

Gibson, James. *Thomas Hardy,* 76–79.

Gribble, Jennifer. "The Quiet Women of Egdon Heath." *Essays in Criticism* 46 (1996), 234–55.

Heusser, Martin. "*Déjà vu* with a Difference: Repetition and the Tragic in Thomas Hardy's Novels," in Andreas Fischer, ed., *Repetition,* 171–86.

Hooker, Jeremy. *Writers in a Landscape,* 96–101.

Jedrzejewski, Jan. *Thomas Hardy and the Church*, 90–93.

Langbaum, Robert. *Thomas Hardy in Our Time*, 64–67, 95–111.

Larson, Dixie Lee. "Eustacia Vye's Drowning: Defiance versus Convention." *Thomas Hardy J* 9:3 (1993), 55–62.

Magee, John. "Hardy's *The Return of the Native*." *Explicator* 53 (1995), 216–17.

Millgate, Michael. *Thomas Hardy*, 130–44.

Mitchell, Judith. *The Stone and the Scorpion*, 174–87.

Seymour-Smith, Martin. *Hardy*, 225–40.

Smith, J. B. " 'Bees Up Flues' and 'Chips in Porridge': Two Proverbial Sayings in Thomas Hardy's *The Return of the Native*." *Thomas Hardy J* 12:1 (1996), 52–55. (Also in *Proverbium* 12 [1995], 315–22.)

Sprechman, Ellen Lew. *Seeing Women as Men*, 14–15, 41–57.

Stave, Shirley A. *The Decline of the Goddess*, 49–68.

Swann, Charles. "Clym Ancient and Modern: Oedipus, Bunyan and *The Return of the Native*." *Victorian Newsl* 90 (1996), 15–18.

Thomas, Brian. *"The Return of the Native,"* 27–131.

Wheeler, Michael. *English Fiction of the Victorian Period*, 202–4.

Winnifrith, Tom. *Fallen Women*, 120–22.

Tess of the d'Urbervilles, 1891

Allan, Janice M. "The Art of Nature: A Study of Hardy's *Tess of the D'Urbervilles*." *Thomas Hardy Yrbk* 22 (1996), 28–33.

Allen, Dennis W. *Sexuality in Victorian Fiction*, 43–46.

Bernstein, Susan David. *Confessional Subjects*, 143–63.

Bonnell, William. "Broken Communion in *Tess of the D'Urbervilles*." *Engl Lang Notes* 31:4 (1994), 63–69.

Bushloper, Lida. "Hardy's *Tess of the D'Urbervilles*." *Explicator* 52 (1994), 222–24.

Caminero-Santangelo, Byron. "A Moral Dilemma: Ethics in *Tess of the D'Urbervilles*." *Engl Stud* (Amsterdam) 75 (1994), 46–61.

Casagrande, Peter J. " 'Something More to be Said': Hardy's Creative Process and the Case of *Tess* and *Jude*," in Charles P. C. Pettit, ed., *New Perspectives*, 23–37.

Craik, Roger. "Hardy's *Tess of the D'Urbervilles*." *Explicator* 53 (1994), 41–43.

Ermarth, Elizabeth Deeds. *The English Novel in History*, 222–26.

Fisher, Joe. *The Hidden Hardy*, 153–73.

Gallet, René. "L'insistance et la distraction: Hopkins et Hardy, essai pour situer le poète." *Etudes Anglaises* 48 (1995), 423–28.

Gatrell, Simon. *Thomas Hardy and the Proper Study of Mankind*, 97–139, 155–58.

Gibson, James. *Thomas Hardy*, 110–19.

Greenslade, William. *Degeneration, Culture, and the Novel*, 153–63.

Grossman, Julie. "Hardy's *Tess* and 'The Photograph': Images to Die for." *Criticism* 35 (1993), 609–26.

Hands, Timothy. *Thomas Hardy*, 79–84, 127–32.

Heidt, Edward R. *The Image of the Church Minister*, 58–64.

Jedrzejewski, Jan. *Thomas Hardy and the Church*, 101–5, 151–55, 203–5.

Jones, Bernard. "Hardy, Chesterton, the 'Epitaphs' and *Tess of the D'Urbervilles.*" *Thomas Hardy J* 12:2 (1996), 72–80.

Kucich, John. *The Power of Lies*, 206–9, 211–13, 219–22, 230–32.

Langbaum, Robert. *Thomas Hardy in Our Time*, 12–15, 20–24.

Leavis, L. R. "Marriage, Murder, and Morality: *The Secret Agent* and *Tess.*" *Neophilologus* 80 (1996), 161–69.

Levine, George. "Shaping Hardy's Art: Vision, Class, and Sex," in John Richetti et al., eds., *The Columbia History*, 552–54.

Manzer, Patricia K. " 'In Some Old Book, Somebody Just Like Me': Eliot's Tessa and Hardy's Tess." *Engl Lang Notes* 33:3 (1996), 33–37.

Millgate, Michael. *Thomas Hardy*, 263–80.

Mistichelli, William J. " 'This Pageantry of Fear': The Sublime in Thomas Hardy." *Cahiers Victoriens et Edouardiens* 44 (1996), 97–104.

Mitchell, Judith. *The Stone and the Scorpion*, 187–98.

Monk, Leland. *Standard Deviations*, 158–60.

Mothersole, Brenda. "The 'Fallen Woman' in the Victorian Novel," in John Morris, ed., *Exploring Stereotyped Images*, 205–8.

Myer, Valerie Grosvenor. *Ten Great English Novelists*, 151–53.

Nichols, Nina daVinci. *Ariadne's Lives*, 97–113.

Otis, Laura. *Organic Memory*, 162–72.

Otis, Laura. "Organic Memory: History, Bodies and Texts in *Tess of the d'Urbervilles.*" *Nineteenth Cent Stud* 8 (1994), 1–20.

Pache, Walter. "Bedroht und bedrohlich: Zum Formwandel der viktorianischen Idylle," in Herbert Foltinek et al., eds., *Tales and "their telling difference,"* 227–31.

Pettit, Charles P. C. "Hardy's Vision of the Individual in *Tess of the d'Urbervilles,*" in Pettit, ed., *New Perspectives*, 172–89.

Rothermel, Peter. "The Far and the Near: On Reading Thomas Hardy Today," in Charles P. C. Pettit, ed., *Celebrating Thomas Hardy*, 159–71.

Seymour-Smith, Martin. *Hardy*, 406–13, 423–51.

Shumaker, Jeanette. "Breaking with the Conventions: Victorian Confession Novels and *Tess of the D'Urbervilles.*" *Engl Lit in Transition, 1880–1920* 37 (1994), 445–59.

Siegel, Carol. *Male Masochism*, 35–47.

Sprechman, Ellen Lew. *Seeing Women as Men*, 18–19, 77–100.

Stave, Shirley A. *The Decline of the Goddess*, 101–20.

Stott, Rebecca. *The Fabrication*, 163–99.

Straus, Nina Pelikan. "Emma, Anna, Tess: Skepticism, Betrayal, and Displacement." *Philos and Lit* 18 (1994), 72–88.

Sutherland, John. *Is Heathcliff a Murderer?*, 202–12.

Sutton, Max Keith. "Hardy's Fiddler and the Bull: A Debt to Baring-Gould?" *Engl Lang Notes* 32:2 (1994), 45–52.

Trezise, Simon. "Places in Time: Discovering the Chronotype in *Tess of the D'Urbervilles.*" *Crit Survey* 5 (1993), 136–42.

Trotter, David. *The English Novel in History*, 199–200.

Wahl, P. "Tess: Moral Heroism and the Earth Goddess." *Thomas Hardy Yrbk* 22 (1996), 22–26.

Wheeler, Michael. *English Fiction of the Victorian Period*, 210–12.

Widdowson, Peter. " 'Moments of Vision': Postmodernising *Tess of the d'Urbervilles;* or, *Tess of the d'Urbervilles* Faithfully Presented," in Charles P. C. Pettit, ed., *New Perspectives,* 80–98.

Widdowson, Peter. "*Tess of the d'Urbervilles* Faithfully Presented," in Widdowson, ed., *"Tess of the d'Urbervilles,"* 1–20.

Winnifrith, Tom. *Fallen Women,* 127–30.

The Trumpet-Major, 1880

Ebbatson, Roger. *Hardy*, 43–59.

Gatrell, Simon. *Thomas Hardy and the Proper Study of Mankind*, 50–53.

Gibson, James. *Thomas Hardy*, 78–81.

Levine, George. "Shaping Hardy's Art: Vision, Class, and Sex," in John Richetti et al., eds., *The Columbia History*, 540–41.

Millgate, Michael. *Thomas Hardy*, 147–56, 159–65.

Mistichelli, William J. "The Trumpet Major's Signal: Kinship and Sexual Rivalry in the Novels of Thomas Hardy." *CEA Critic* 56:3 (1994), 43–59.

Seymour-Smith, Martin. *Hardy*, 250–57.

Spurr, Barry. " 'Splendid Words': Hardy's *Trumpet-Major* and 'Church Verse.' " *Thomas Hardy J* 13:1 (1997), 77–82.

Subils, Pierre Claude. "Le Miroir perdu: *The Lady of Shalott* de Tennyson et *The Trumpet-Major* de Thomas Hardy aux fils du texte." *Cahiers Victoriens et Edouardiens* 42 (1995), 55–63.

Two on a Tower, 1882

Evers, Alma. " 'Two Devotions, Two Thoughts, Two Hopes, and Two Blessings': Dualism as Theme and Patterning in *Two on a Tower.*" *Thomas Hardy Yrbk* 21 (1995), 52–58.

Gatrell, Simon. *Thomas Hardy and the Proper Study of Mankind*, 55–67.

Gibson, James. *Thomas Hardy*, 87–92.

Jedrzejewski, Jan. *Thomas Hardy and the Church*, 25–26, 143–44, 196–99.

Levine, George. "Shaping Hardy's Art: Vision, Class, and Sex," in John Richetti et al., eds., *The Columbia History*, 539–41.

Millgate, Michael. *Thomas Hardy*, 183–93.

Seymour-Smith, Martin. *Hardy*, 280–95.

Sylvia, Richard D. "Hardy's Feminism: Apollonian Myth and *Two on a Tower.*" *Thomas Hardy J* 12:2 (1996), 48–57.

Winnifrith, Tom. *Fallen Women,* 123–26.

Under the Greenwood Tree, 1872

Blishen, Edward. "Hardy, *The Hand of Ethelberta*, and Some Persisting English Discomforts," in Charles P. C. Pettit, ed., *Celebrating Thomas Hardy*, 179–81.

Gatrell, Simon. *Thomas Hardy and the Proper Study of Mankind*, 10–23, 25–28.

Gibson, James. *Thomas Hardy*, 52–55.

Jedrzejewski, Jan. *Thomas Hardy and the Church*, 73–75, 132–36, 187–90.

Langbaum, Robert. *Thomas Hardy in Our Time*, 70–78.

Millgate, Michael. *Thomas Hardy*, 42–61.

Seymour-Smith, Martin. *Hardy*, 137–44.

Takemori, Tetsushi. "Who Can 'Onriddle' Her?: Thomas Hardy's *Under the Greenwood Tree* and the Problematic of the Look." *Shiron* 34 (1995), 45–60.

The Well-Beloved, 1892

Beer, Gillian. "Hardy and Decadence," in Charles P. C. Pettit, ed., *Celebrating Thomas Hardy*, 99–101.

Bennett, Brandon B. "Hardy's Noble Melancholics." *Novel* 27 (1993), 30–32.

Gibson, James. *Thomas Hardy*, 122–25.

Jedrzejewski, Jan. *Thomas Hardy and the Church*, 111–13.

Kucich, John. *The Power of Lies,* 211–20, 223–27.

Langbaum, Robert. *Thomas Hardy in Our Time*, 141–55.

Levine, George. "Shaping Hardy's Art: Vision, Class, and Sex," in John Richetti et al., eds., *The Columbia History*, 538–39.

Millgate, Michael. *Thomas Hardy*, 293–307.

Morrison, Ronald D. *"Jude the Obscure* and *The Well-Beloved:* Sibling Novels." *Thomas Hardy Yrbk* 22 (1996), 34–50.

Noland, Richard W. "The Migrating Anima in Thomas Hardy's *The Well-Beloved." J of Evolutionary Psych* 15:1–2 (1994), 104–11.

Otis, Laura. *Organic Memory*, 173–76.

O'Toole, Tess. "Genealogy and Narrative Jamming in Hardy's *The Well-Beloved." Narrative* 1 (1993), 207–21.

Pilgrim, Anne C. "Hardy's Retroactive Self-Censorship: The Case of *The Well-Beloved,"* in Judith Kennedy, ed., *Victorian Authors and their Works,* 125–37.

Schur, Owen. "Desire in *The Well-Beloved." CEA Critic* 57:2 (1995), 77–84.

Seymour-Smith, Martin. *Hardy*, 594–600.

Sumner, Rosemary. "Discoveries of Dissonance: Hardy's Late Fiction." *Thomas Hardy J* 11:3 (1995), 79–88.

The Woodlanders, 1887

Bennett, Brandon B. "Hardy's Noble Melancholics." *Novel* 27 (1993), 26–30, 32–39.

Dutta, Shanta. "The 'Lovingkindness' of Hardy's Revising Hand." *Thomas Hardy J* 12:3 (1996), 79–80.

Fisher, Joe. *The Hidden Hardy*, 136–52.

Gibson, James. *Thomas Hardy*, 100–106.

Hands, Timothy. *Thomas Hardy*, 67–69, 76–84, 125–31.

Kucich, John. *The Power of Lies,* 228–30.
Langbaum, Robert. *Thomas Hardy in Our Time,* 111–26.
Millgate, Michael. *Thomas Hardy,* 249–60.
Morgan, Rosemarie. "Bodily Transactions: Toni Morrison and Thomas
    Hardy in Literary Discourse," in Charles P. C. Pettit, ed., *Celebrating
    Thomas Hardy,* 151–54.
Ozguren, Azize. "*The Woodlanders:* A Metaphor of Character," in Nor-
    man Page and Peter Preston, eds., *The Literature of Place,* 64–74.
Reisner, Thomas A. "The Narrative Time-Scheme of *The Woodlanders.*"
    Notes and Queries 43 (1996), 434–35.
Seymour-Smith, Martin. *Hardy,* 352–73.
Stave, Shirley A. *The Decline of the Goddess,* 71–99.
Wheeler, Michael. *English Fiction of the Victorian Period,* 207–10.

MARGARET HARKNESS

A City Girl, 1887

Nord, Deborah Epstein. *Walking the Victorian Streets,* 193–95.
Visser, Nicholas. "Roaring Beasts and Raging Floods: The Representa-
    tion of Political Crowds in the Nineteenth-Century British Novel."
    Mod Lang R 89 (1994), 315–17.

Out of Work, 1888

Hapgood, Lynne. "The Novel and Political Agency: Socialism and the
    Work of Margaret Harkness, Constance Howell and Clementina Black:
    1888–1896." *Lit and Hist* 5:2 (1996), 46–47.

MARY KINGSLEY HARRISON

The History of Sir Richard Calmady, 1901

Srebrnik, Patricia. "The Re-Subjection of 'Lucas Malet': Charles Kings-
    ley's Daughter and the Response to Muscular Christianity," in Donald
    E. Hall, ed., *Muscular Christianity,* 200–206.

The Wages of Sin, 1891

Srebrnik, Patricia. "The Re-Subjection of 'Lucas Malet': Charles Kings-
    ley's Daughter and the Response to Muscular Christianity," in Donald
    E. Hall, ed., *Muscular Christianity,* 197–99.

L. P. HARTLEY

The Betrayal, 1966
    Wright, Adrian. *Foreign Country,* 223–29.
The Boat, 1949
    Wright, Adrian. *Foreign Country,* 155–59.

The Brickfield, 1964

    Wright, Adrian. *Foreign Country,* 218–21, 225–28.

Eustace and Hilda, 1947

    Wright, Adrian. *Foreign Country,* 146–49.

Facial Justice, 1960

    Wright, Adrian. *Foreign Country,* 205–8.

The Go-Between, 1953

    Blum, Virginia L. *Hide and Seek,* 95–120.

    Kobus, Isabel. "Repetitionsstrategien als Oralisierungsmerkmal in der Literaturverfilmung *The Go-Between,*" in Hildegard L. C. Tristram, ed., *(Re)Oralisierung,* 425–40.

    Wright, Adrian. *Foreign Country,* 160–73.

The Harness Room, 1971

    Wright, Adrian. *Foreign Country,* 249–52, 261–63.

The Hireling, 1957

    Wright, Adrian. *Foreign Country,* 185–90.

My Fellow Devils, 1951

    Wright, Adrian. *Foreign Country,* 161–66.

A Perfect Woman, 1955

    Wright, Adrian. *Foreign Country,* 183–85.

Poor Clare, 1968

    Wright, Adrian. *Foreign Country,* 242–45.

The Shrimp and the Anemone, 1944

    Wright, Adrian. *Foreign Country,* 124–29.

Simonetta Perkins, 1925

    Wright, Adrian. *Foreign Country,* 84–87.

JOHN MACDOUGALL HAY

Gillespie, 1914

    Pick, J. B. *The Great Shadow House,* 59–65.

MARY HAYS

The Memoirs of Emma Courtney, 1796

    Rajan, Tilottama. "Autonarration and Genotext in Mary Hays' *Memoirs of Emma Courtney.*" *Stud in Romanticism* 32 (1993), 149–76.

    Spacks, Patricia Meyer. "Novels of the 1790s: Action and Impasse," in John Richetti et al., eds., *The Columbia History,* 259–60.

    Todd, Janet. *The Sign of Angellica,* 241–48.

    Ty, Eleanor. *Unsex'd Revolutionaries,* 46–59.

The Victim of Prejudice, 1799
Ty, Eleanor. *Unsex'd Revolutionaries,* 60–72.

SIAN HAYTON

Cells of Knowledge, 1989
Whyte, Christopher. "Postmodernism, Gender and Belief in Recent Scottish Fiction." *Scottish Liter J* 23:1 (1996), 51–55.

ELIZA HAYWOOD

The Adventures of Eovaai, 1736
MacCarthy, B. G. *The Female Pen,* 271–73.
Wilputte, Earla A. "The Textual Architecture of Eliza Haywood's *Adventures of Eovaai.*" *Essays in Lit* (Macomb, IL) 22 (1995), 31–42.

Betsy Thoughtless, 1751
Ellis, Lorna Beth. "Engendering the *Bildungsroman:* The *Bildung* of Betsy Thoughtless." *Genre* 28 (1995), 279–98.
MacCarthy, B. G. *The Female Pen,* 221–24.
Nestor, Deborah J. "Virtue Rarely Rewarded: Ideological Subversion and Narrative Form in Haywood's Later Fiction." *Stud in Engl Lit, 1500–1900* 34 (1994), 580–89.
Todd, Janet. *The Sign of Angellica,* 146–51.

The British Recluse, 1722
Bowers, Toni O'Shaughnessy. "Sex, Lies, and Invisibility: Amatory Fiction from the Restoration to Mid-Century," in John Richetti et al., eds., *The Columbia History,* 60–61.
MacCarthy, B. G. *The Female Pen,* 212–15.
Richards, Cynthia. " 'The Pleasures of Complicity': Sympathetic Identification and the Female Reader in Early Eighteenth-Century Women's Amatory Fiction." *Eighteenth Cent* 36 (1995), 226–31.

Fantomina, 1724
Ballaster, Ros. *Seductive Forms,* 187–92.

The Fatal Secret, 1724
Gonda, Caroline. *Reading Daughters' Fictions,* 54–55.

The Force of Nature, 1725
Bowers, Toni. *The Politics of Motherhood,* 135–41.

The Fortunate Foundlings, 1744
Gonda, Caroline. *Reading Daughters' Fictions,* 55–59.

The History of Jemmy and Jenny Jessamy, 1753
MacCarthy, B. G. *The Female Pen,* 224–26.
Nestor, Deborah J. "Virtue Rarely Rewarded: Ideological Subversion

and Narrative Form in Haywood's Later Fiction." *Stud in Engl Lit, 1500–1900* 34 (1994), 589–94.

The Injur'd Husband, 1723

MacCarthy, B. G. *The Female Pen,* 216–19.

Love in Excess, 1719–1720

Ballaster, Ros. *Seductive Forms,* 175–77.

Bowers, Toni O'Shaughnessy. "Sex, Lies, and Invisibility: Amatory Fiction from the Restoration to Mid-Century," in John Richetti et al., eds., *The Columbia History,* 54–55, 60–61, 68–69.

Warner, William B. "Formulating Fiction: Romancing the General Reader in Early Modern Britain," in Deidre Lynch and William B. Warner, eds., *Cultural Institutions of the Novel,* 290–300.

Love-Letters on All Occasions, 1730

MacCarthy, B. G. *The Female Pen,* 258–60.

The Masqueraders, 1724

Ballaster, Ros. *Seductive Forms,* 181–87.

The Rash Resolve, 1724

Bowers, Toni. *The Politics of Motherhood,* 125–35.

G. A. HENTY

In Times of Peril, 1881

Nünning, Vera. "Viktorianische Populärliteratur als imperialistische Propaganda: G. A. Hentys historischer Roman *In Time of Peril." Literatur in Wissenschaft und Unterricht* 28 (1995), 189–201.

Rujub the Juggler, 1893

Paxton, Nancy L. "Mobilizing Chivalry: Rape in Flora Annie Steel's *On the Face of the Waters* (1896) and Other British Novels about the Indian Uprising of 1857," in Barbara Leah Harman and Susan Meyer, eds., *The New Nineteenth Century,* 264–65.

HAROLD HESLOP

The Gate of a Strange Field, 1933

Fox, Pamela. *Class Fictions,* 83–85, 188–90.

Last Cage Down, 1935

Fox, Pamela. *Class Fictions,* 190–91.

JOSEPH HEWLETT

College Life: or, The Proctor's Notebook, 1843

Antor, Heinz. *Der englische Universitätsroman,* 102–5, 151–53, 187–88, 213–15.

Peter Priggins, the College Scout, 1841
  Antor, Heinz. *Der englische Universitätsroman,* 117–19, 135–37, 175–76, 202–5.

GEORGETTE HEYER

Regency Buck, 1935
  Hughes, Helen. *The Historical Romance,* 115–24.

WILLIAM EDWARD HEYGATE

Godfrey Davenant at College, 1849
  Antor, Heinz. *Der englische Universitätsroman,* 233–35, 239–44.

ROBERT HICHENS

The Garden of Allah, 1904
  Cadogan, Mary. *And Then Their Hearts Stood Still,* 117–22.

AIDAN HIGGINS

Balcony of Europe, 1972
  Wall, Eamonn. "Aidan Higgins's *Balcony of Europe:* Stephen Dedalus Hits the Road." *Colby Q* 31 (1995), 81–87.
Langrishe, Go Down, 1966
  Imhof, Rüdiger. "The Prose Works of Aidan Higgins: Fiction, Fictionalised Autobiography, Travelogue." *Anglia* 114 (1996), 64–75.

SUSAN HILL

The Woman in Black, 1983
  Cavaliero, Glen. *The Supernatural and English Fiction,* 223–24.

ALEC HILTON

Shrink, 1973
  Bach, Susanne. "*Shrink* oder: Die Umkehrung der geschlechtsdeterminierten Rezeptionssteuerung im Trivialroman." *Arbeiten aus Anglistik und Amerikanistik* 20:1 (1995), 147–70.

WILLIAM HOPE HODGSON

The Boats of the "Glen Carrig," 1907
  Hurley, Kelly. *The Gothic Body,* 147–48, 157–59.

DESMOND HOGAN

A Curious Street, 1984

D'haen, Theo. "Irish Regionalism, Magic Realism and Postmodernism," in Theo D'haen and Hans Bertens, eds., *British Postmodern Fiction*, 42–46.

JAMES HOGG

The Brownie of Bodsbeck, 1818

Ferris, Ina. *The Achievement of Literary Authority*, 185–94.

The Private Memoirs and Confessions of a Justified Sinner, 1824

Botting, Fred. *Gothic*, 110–12.

Cavaliero, Glen. *The Supernatural and English Fiction*, 159–62.

Elphinstone, Margaret. "Contemporary Feminist Fantasy in the Scottish Literary Tradition," in Robert A. Latham and Robert A. Collins, eds., *Modes of the Fantastic*, 85–87.

Glance, Jonathan C. "Ambiguity and the Dreams in James Hogg's *The Private Memoirs and Confessions of a Justified Sinner.*" *Stud in Scottish Lit* 28 (1993), 165–77.

Haggerty, George E. "The Gothic Novel, 1764–1824," in John Richetti et al., eds., *The Columbia History*, 243–44.

Monnickendam, Andrew. "The Paradigm of Borders in *The Private Memoirs and Confessions of a Justified Sinner.*" *Stud in Hogg and His World* 5 (1994), 55–69.

Pick, J. B. *The Great Shadow House*, 18–24.

Pope, Rebecca A. "Hogg, Wordsworth, and Gothic Autobiography." *Stud in Scottish Lit* 27 (1992), 218–40.

Richter, David H. *The Progress of Romance*, 93–95.

Robertson, Fiona. *Legitimate Histories*, 246–48.

Schoenfield, Mark L. "Butchering James Hogg: Romantic Identity in the Magazine Market," in Mary A. Favret and Nicola J. Watson, eds., *At the Limits of Romanticism*, 209–13, 215–20.

Smith, Iain Crichton. "A Work of Genius: James Hogg's *Justified Sinner.*" *Stud in Scottish Lit* 28 (1993), 1–11.

Steig, Michael. "Unearthing Buried Affects and Associations in Reading: The Case of the Justified Sinner," in Daniel Rancour-Laferriere, ed., *Self-Analysis in Literary Study*, 193–205.

The Three Perils of Man, 1822

Fielding, Penny. *Writing and Orality*, 8–98.

The Three Perils of Woman, 1823

Groves, David. "Urban Corruption and the Pastoral Ideal in James Hogg's *Three Perils of Woman.*" *Stud in Scottish Lit* 27 (1992), 80–88.

THOMAS HOLCROFT

The Adventures of Hugh Trevor, 1797

Antor, Heinz. *Der englische Universitätsroman,* 86–88.

Bour, Isabel. "Raison, esprit, psyché dans les romans révolutionnaires de Thomas Holcroft." *Bull de la Société d'Etudes Anglo-Américaines des XVIIe et XVIIIe Siècles* 36 (1993), 71–82.

Anna St. Ives, 1792

Bour, Isabel. "Raison, esprit, psyché dans les romans révolutionnaires de Thomas Holcroft." *Bull de la Société d'Etudes Anglo-Américaines des XVIIe et XVIIIe Siècles* 36 (1993), 71–82.

Spacks, Patricia Meyer. "Novels of the 1790s: Action and Impasse," in John Richetti et al., eds., *The Columbia History,* 249–54.

ETHEL CARNIE HOLDSWORTH

Helen of Four Gates, 1917

Fox, Pamela. *Class Fictions,* 158–63.

Fox, Pamela. "The 'Revolt of the Gentle': Romance and the Politics of Resistance in Working-Class Women's Writing." *Novel* 27 (1994), 148–51.

Miss Nobody, 1913

Fox, Pamela. *Class Fictions,* 154–58.

Fox, Pamela. "The 'Revolt of the Gentle': Romance and the Politics of Resistance in Working-Class Women's Writing." *Novel* 27 (1994), 145–48.

This Slavery, 1925

Fox, Pamela. *Class Fictions,* 163–70.

Fox, Pamela. "The 'Revolt of the Gentle': Romance and the Politics of Resistance in Working-Class Women's Writing." *Novel* 27 (1994), 151–56.

CONSTANCE HOLME

The Old Road from Spain, 1915

Cavaliero, Glen. *The Supernatural and English Fiction,* 143–44.

VICTORIA HOLT

Mistress of Mellyn, 1960

Cadogan, Mary. *And Then Their Hearts Stood Still,* 22–24.

WINIFRED HOLTBY

Anderby World, 1923

  Brown, Sally. "Love and Marriage in the Works of Winifred Holtby," in Gina Wisker, ed., *It's My Party,* 165–67.

The Land of the Green Ginger, 1927

  Brown, Sally. "Love and Marriage in the Works of Winifred Holtby," in Gina Wisker, ed., *It's My Party,* 155–58, 167–68.

South Riding, 1936

  Brown, Sally. "Love and Marriage in the Works of Winifred Holtby," in Gina Wisker, ed., *It's My Party,* 156–58, 162–65.

ANTHONY HOPE

Mrs. Maxon Protests, 1911

  Harris, Janice Hubbard. *Edwardian Stories of Divorce,* 132–35.

The Prisoner of Zenda, 1894

  Cadogan, Mary. *And Then Their Hearts Stood Still,* 205–8.

Rupert of Hentzau, 1898

  Cadogan, Mary. *And Then Their Hearts Stood Still,* 208–10.

Simon Dale, 1898

  Orel, Harold. *The Historical Novel,* 115–32.

CONSTANCE HOWELL

A More Excellent Way, 1888

  Hapgood, Lynne. "The Novel and Political Agency: Socialism and the Work of Margaret Harkness, Constance Howell and Clementina Black: 1888–1896." *Lit and Hist* 5:2 (1996), 44–46.

RICHARD HUGHES

A High Wind in Jamaica, 1929

  Morgan, Paul. *The Art of Richard Hughes,* 19–51.

The Human Predicament, 1961–1973

  Morgan, Paul. *The Art of Richard Hughes,* 89–136.

In Hazard: A Sea Story, 1938

  Morgan, Paul. *The Art of Richard Hughes,* 52–88.

THOMAS HUGHES

Tom Brown's School Days, 1857

Allen, Dennis W. "Young England: Muscular Christianity and the Politics of the Body in *Tom Brown's Schooldays,"* in Donald E. Hall, ed., *Muscular Christianity,* 114–30.

Antor, Heinz. *Der englische Universitätsroman,* 357–58, 398–99.

Dingley, Robert. "Shades of the Prison House: Discipline and Surveillance in *Tom Brown's Schooldays." Victorian R* 22 (1996), 1–10.

Hall, Donald E. *Fixing Patriarchy,* 131–48.

Horsman, Alan. *The Victorian Novel,* 199–200.

Puccio, Paul M. "At the Heart of *Tom Brown's Schooldays:* Thomas Arnold and Christian Friendship." *Mod Lang Stud* 25:4 (1995), 57–72.

E. M. HULL

The Sheik, 1919

Cadogan, Mary. *And Then Their Hearts Stood Still,* 126–30.

Trotter, David. *The English Novel in History,* 185–87, 190–93.

ALDOUS HUXLEY

After Many a Summer Dies the Swan, 1939

Baker, Robert S. "The Nightmare of the Frankfurt School: The Marquis de Sade and the Problem of Modernity in Aldous Huxley's Dystopian Narrative," in Bernfried Nugel, ed., *Now More Than Ever,* 250–60.

Rosenthal, Michael. "Isherwood, Huxley, and the Thirties," in John Richetti et al., eds., *The Columbia History,* 749–50, 753–54.

Ape and Essence, 1949

Marovitz, Sanford E. "*Ape and Essence:* Fright or Fantasy?," in Bernfried Nugel, ed., *Now More Than Ever,* 159–73.

Brave New World, 1932

Adams, Alice E. *Reproducing the Womb,* 96–103.

Attarian, John. "*Brave New World* and the Flight from God." *Mod Age* 38 (1996), 332–42.

Booker, M. Keith. *The Dystopian Impulse in Modern Literature,* 47–66.

Bradshaw, David. "The Best of Companions: J. W. N. Sullivan, Aldous Huxley, and the New Physics." *R of Engl Stud* 47 (1996), 205–6, 352–68.

Broege, Valerie. "Technology and Sexuality in Science Fiction: Creating New Erotic Interfaces," in Donald Palumbo, ed., *Erotic Universe,* 113–15.

Deery, June. *Aldous Huxley,* 32–38, 52–53.

Fietz, Lothar. "The Fragmentariness of the Self: Continuity and Discontinuity in the Works of Aldous Huxley," in Bernfried Nugel, ed., *Now More Than Ever*, 352–55.

Maule, Victoria. "On the Subversion of Character in the Literature of Identity Anxiety," in Derek Littlewood and Peter Stockwell, eds., *Impossibility Fiction*, 109–12.

Meckier, Jerome. "Aldous Huxley, from Poet to Mystic: The Poetry of Ideas, the Idea of Poetry," in Bernfried Nugel, ed., *Now More Than Ever*, 130–32.

Rindisbacher, Hans J. "Sweet Scents and Stench: Traces of Post/Modernism in Aldous Huxley's *Brave New World,*" in Bernfried Nugel, ed., *Now More Than Ever*, 209–23.

Rosenthal, Michael. "Isherwood, Huxley, and the Thirties," in John Richetti et al., eds., *The Columbia History*, 750–52.

Zelter, Joachim. *Sinnhafte Fiktion und Wahrheit*, 204–9.

Crome Yellow, 1921

Deery, June. *Aldous Huxley*, 27–30.

Meckier, Jerome. "Aldous Huxley, from Poet to Mystic: The Poetry of Ideas, the Idea of Poetry," in Bernfried Nugel, ed., *Now More Than Ever*, 125–28.

Rosenthal, Michael. "Isherwood, Huxley, and the Thirties," in John Richetti et al., eds., *The Columbia History*, 749–51.

Eyeless in Gaza, 1936

Deery, June. *Aldous Huxley*, 28–33, 123–26.

Gill, Kulwant Singh. "Crisis of Double Consciousness in the Huxley Canon," in Bernfried Nugel, ed., *Now More Than Ever*, 287–90.

Rosenthal, Michael. "Isherwood, Huxley, and the Thirties," in John Richetti et al., eds., *The Columbia History*, 750–53.

Vitoux, Pierre. "Aldous Huxley on D. H. Lawrence's Philosophy of Life," in Bernfried Nugel, ed., *Now More Than Ever*, 310–13.

The Genius and the Goddess, 1955

Deery, June. *Aldous Huxley*, 35–37.

Zelter, Joachim. *Sinnhafte Fiktion und Wahrheit*, 209–13.

Island, 1962

Cupers, Jean-Louis. "Huxley's Variations on a Musical Theme:From the Mendelssohnian Chord in 'Farcical History of Richard Greenow' to the (Syn)Aesthetic Experience of Music in *Island,*" in Bernfried Nugel, ed., *Now More Than Ever*, 83–105.

Deery, June. *Aldous Huxley*, 33–36, 111–18, 121–26.

Gill, Kulwant Singh. "Crisis of Double Consciousness in the Huxley Canon," in Bernfried Nugel, ed., *Now More Than Ever*, 289–93.

May, Keith M. "Huxley's Marriage of Heaven and Hell," in Bernfried Nugel, ed., *Now More Than Ever*, 335–45.

Nance, Guin A. "Dragons and Dragomen: Huxley's Heroines," in Bernfried Nugel, ed., *Now More Than Ever*, 153–56.

Nugel, Bernfried. "Aldous Huxley's Revisions in the Final Typescript of *Island*," in Nugel, ed., *Now More Than Ever*, 225–42.

Rohmann, Gerd. "*Island:* Huxley's Ecological Utopia," in Bernfried Nugel, ed., *Now More Than Ever*, 175–84.

Thody, Philip. "Huxley and Religion: From Agnosticism to Mystical Disbelief," in Bernfried Nugel, ed., *Now More Than Ever*, 277–80.

Point Counter Point, 1928

Baker, Robert S. "The Nightmare of the Frankfurt School: The Marquis de Sade and the Problem of Modernity in Aldous Huxley's Dystopian Narrative," in Bernfried Nugel, ed., *Now More Than Ever*, 253–54.

Deery, June. *Aldous Huxley*, 27–32, 35–42.

Fietz, Lothar. "The Fragmentariness of the Self: Continuity and Discontinuity in the Works of Aldous Huxley," in Bernfried Nugel, ed., *Now More Than Ever*, 350–53.

Lerner, Laurence. *Angels and Absences*, 162–70.

Meckier, Jerome. "Aldous Huxley, from Poet to Mystic: The Poetry of Ideas, the Idea of Poetry," in Bernfried Nugel, ed., *Now More Than Ever*, 128–30.

Nance, Guin A. "Dragons and Dragomen: Huxley's Heroines," in Bernfried Nugel, ed., *Now More Than Ever*, 149–54.

Rosenthal, Michael. "Isherwood, Huxley, and the Thirties," in John Richetti et al., eds., *The Columbia History*, 748–52.

Thody, Philip. "Huxley and Religion: From Agnosticism to Mystical Disbelief," in Bernfried Nugel, ed., *Now More Than Ever*, 274–76.

Vitoux, Pierre. "Aldous Huxley on D. H. Lawrence's Philosophy of Life," in Bernfried Nugel, ed., *Now More Than Ever*, 304–7.

Those Barren Leaves, 1925

Meckier, Jerome. "Aldous Huxley, from Poet to Mystic: The Poetry of Ideas, the Idea of Poetry," in Bernfried Nugel, ed., *Now More Than Ever*, 123–27.

Nance, Guin A. "Dragons and Dragomen: Huxley's Heroines," in Bernfried Nugel, ed., *Now More Than Ever*, 148–50.

Rosenthal, Michael. "Isherwood, Huxley, and the Thirties," in John Richetti et al., eds., *The Columbia History*, 749–52.

Time Must Have a Stop, 1944

Deery, June. *Aldous Huxley*, 28–30, 117–20, 123–26.

Meckier, Jerome. "Aldous Huxley, from Poet to Mystic: The Poetry of Ideas, the Idea of Poetry," in Bernfried Nugel, ed., *Now More Than Ever*, 135–37.

Singh, Kirpal. "Aldous Huxley through Asian Eyes: A Re-consideration of *Time Must Have a Stop*," in Bernfried Nugel, ed., *Now More Than Ever*, 263–68.

ELSPETH HUXLEY

A Thing to Love, 1954

Harris, Michael. *Outsiders and Insiders*, 111–25.

ELIZABETH INCHBALD

Nature and Art, 1796

MacCarthy, B. G. *The Female Pen,* 438–41.
Ty, Eleanor. *Unsex'd Revolutionaries,* 101–14.

A Simple Story, 1791

Balfour, Ian. "Promises, Promises: Social and Other Contracts in the English Jacobins (Godwin/Inchbald)," in David L. Clark and Donald C. Goellnicht, eds., *New Romanticisms,* 239–44.

Boardman, Michael. "Inchbald's *A Simple Story:* An Anti-Ideological Reading." *Eighteenth Cent* 37 (1996), 271–83.

Ford, Susan Allen. " 'A name more dear': Daughters, Fathers, and Desire in *A Simple Story, The False Friend,* and *Mathilda,* " in Carol Shiner Wilson and Joel Haefner, eds., *Re-Visioning Romanticism,* 52–56, 62–67.

Gonda, Caroline. *Reading Daughters' Fictions,* 181–91, 199–203.

Haggerty, George E. "Female Abjection in Inchbald's *A Simple Story.*" *Stud in Engl Lit, 1500–1900* 36 (1996), 655–70.

MacCarthy, B. G. *The Female Pen,* 435–38.

Spacks, Patricia Meyer. *Desire and Truth,* 197–202.

Spacks, Patricia Meyer. "Novels of the 1790s: Action and Impasse," in John Richetti et al., eds., *The Columbia History,* 260–64.

Spacks, Patricia Meyer. "Oscillations of Sensibility." *New Liter Hist* 25 (1994), 516–20.

Ty, Eleanor. *Unsex'd Revolutionaries,* 85–100.

CHRISTOPHER ISHERWOOD

All the Conspirators, 1928

Ferres, Kay. *Christopher Isherwood,* 26–33.
Fryer, Jonathan. *Eye of the Camera,* 62–67.
Rosenthal, Michael. "Isherwood, Huxley, and the Thirties," in John Richetti et al., eds., *The Columbia History,* 755–57.

Down There on a Visit, 1962

Ferres, Kay. *Christopher Isherwood,* 87–101.
Fryer, Jonathan. *Eye of the Camera,* 196–98.

Goodbye to Berlin, 1939

Blayac, Alain. "Vienne et Berlin dans la littérature anglaise de l'Entre-Deux-Guerres." *Cahiers d'Etudes Germaniques* 24 (1993), 97–99.
Ferres, Kay. *Christopher Isherwood,* 53–63.
Rosenthal, Michael. "Isherwood, Huxley, and the Thirties," in John Richetti et al., eds., *The Columbia History,* 761–63.

Lions and Shadows, 1938

Rosenthal, Michael. "Isherwood, Huxley, and the Thirties," in John Richetti et al., eds., *The Columbia History,* 756–58.

A Meeting by the River, 1967

> Ferres, Kay. *Christopher Isherwood,* 114–24.
> Fryer, Jonathan. *Eye of the Camera,* 206–8.

The Memorial, 1932

> Ferres, Kay. *Christopher Isherwood,* 34–42.
> Rosenthal, Michael. "Isherwood, Huxley, and the Thirties," in John Richetti et al., eds., *The Columbia History,* 757–59.

Mr. Norris Changes Trains, 1935

> Ferres, Kay. *Christopher Isherwood,* 46–53.
> Fryer, Jonathan. *Eye of the Camera,* 99–101.
> Rosenthal, Michael. "Isherwood, Huxley, and the Thirties," in John Richetti et al., eds., *The Columbia History,* 759–61.

Prater Violet, 1946

> Ferres, Kay. *Christopher Isherwood,* 68–76.

A Single Man, 1964

> Ferres, Kay. *Christopher Isherwood,* 106–14.
> Fryer, Jonathan. *Eye of the Camera,* 190–203.

The World in the Evening, 1954

> Ferres, Kay. *Christopher Isherwood,* 76–85.
> Fryer, Jonathan. *Eye of the Camera,* 183–85.

KAZUO ISHIGURO

An Artist of the Floating World, 1986

> Purton, Valerie. "The Reader in a Floating World," in Norman Page and Peter Preston, eds., *The Literature of Place,* 174–79.

A Pale View of Hills, 1982

> Mergenthal, Silvia. "Acculturation and Family Structure: Mo's *Sour Sweet,* Kureishi's *The Buddha of Suburbia,* Ishiguro's *A Pale View of Hills,*" in Eckhard Breitinger, ed., *Defining New Idioms,* 124–27.
> Purton, Valerie. "The Reader in a Floating World," in Norman Page and Peter Preston, eds., *The Literature of Place,* 171–74.
> Wong, Cynthia F. "The Shame of Memory: Blanchot's Self-Dispossession in Ishiguro's *A Pale View of Hills.*" *Clio* 24 (1995), 127–45.
> Wood, Michael. "The Contemporary Novel," in John Richetti et al., eds., *The Columbia History,* 972–73.

The Remains of the Day, 1989

> Connor, Steven. *The English Novel in History,* 104–12.
> Griffiths, M. "Great English Houses/New Homes in England?: Memory and Identity in Kazuo Ishiguro's *The Remains of the Day* and V. S. Naipaul's *The Enigma of Arrival.*" *SPAN* 36 (1993), 488–503.
> Janik, Del Ivan. "No End of History: Evidence from the Contemporary English Novel." *Twentieth Cent Lit* 41 (1995), 166–68.

O'Brien, Susie. "Serving a New World Order: Postcolonial Politics in Kazuo Ishiguro's *The Remains of the Day.*" *Mod Fiction Stud* 42 (1996), 787–804.

Rothfork, John. "Zen Comedy in Postcolonial Literature: Kazuo Ishiguro's *The Remains of the Day.*" *Mosaic* 29:1 (1996), 79–100.

Wall, Kathleen. *"The Remains of the Day* and Its Challenges to Theories of Unreliable Narration." *J of Narrative Technique* 24 (1994), 18–39.

HOWARD JACOBSON

Coming From Behind, 1983

Antor, Heinz. *Der englische Universitätsroman,* 615–18, 679–81.

P. D. JAMES

The Black Tower, 1975

Leonard, John. "Conservative Fiction(s): P. D. James' *The Black Tower.*" *AUMLA* 83 (1995), 31–39.

Cover Her Face, 1962

Kotker, Joan G. "P. D. James's Adam Dalgliesh Series," in Mary Jean DeMarr, ed., *In the Beginning,* 139–53.

Devices and Desires, 1989

Kotker, Joan G. "P. D. James's Adam Dalgliesh Series," in Mary Jean DeMarr, ed., *In the Beginning,* 139–53.

Wood, Michael. "The Contemporary Novel," in John Richetti et al., eds., *The Columbia History,* 971–72.

Innocent Blood, 1980

Campbell, SueEllen. "The Detective Heroine and the Death of Her Hero: Dorothy Sayers to P. D. James," in Glenwood Irons, ed., *Feminism in Women's Detective Fiction,* 12–15, 20–24.

The Skull Beneath the Skin, 1982

Campbell, SueEllen. "The Detective Heroine and the Death of Her Hero: Dorothy Sayers to P. D. James," in Glenwood Irons, ed., *Feminism in Women's Detective Fiction,* 25–26.

Nixon, Nicola. "Gray Areas: P. D. James's Unsuiting of Cordelia," in Glenwood Irons, ed., *Feminism in Women's Detective Fiction,* 29–44.

A Taste for Death, 1986

Majeske, Penelope K. "P. D. James' Dark Interiors." *Clues* 15:2 (1994), 119–30.

An Unsuitable Job for a Woman, 1973

Campbell, SueEllen. "The Detective Heroine and the Death of Her Hero: Dorothy Sayers to P. D. James," in Glenwood Irons, ed., *Feminism in Women's Detective Fiction,* 12–15, 17–20.

Clark, S. L. "*Gaudy Night's* Legacy: P. D. James' *An Unsuitable Job for a Woman.*" *Sayers R* 4 (Sept. 1980), 1–12.

Nixon, Nicola. "Gray Areas: P. D. James's Unsuiting of Cordelia," in Glenwood Irons, ed., *Feminism in Women's Detective Fiction*, 29–44.

RICHARD JEFFERIES

After London, or Wild England, 1885

Hooker, Jeremy. *Writers in a Landscape*, 38–55.

Nellist, Brian. "Imagining the Future: Predictive Fiction in the Nineteenth Century," in David Seed, ed., *Anticipations*, 125–29.

GERALDINE JEWSBURY

The Half-Sisters, 1848

Chattman, Lauren. "Actresses at Home and on the Stage: Spectacular Domesticity and the Victorian Theatrical Novel." *Novel* 28 (1994), 75–80.

Rosen, Judith. "At Home upon a Stage: Domesticity and Genius in Geraldine Jewsbury's *The Half Sisters* (1848)," in Barbara Leah Harman and Susan Meyer, eds., *The New Nineteenth Century*, 17–30.

Zoe, 1845

Perkin, J. Russell. "Locking George Sand in the Attic: Female Passion and Domestic Realism in the Victorian Novel." *Univ of Toronto Q* 63 (1993–94), 416–20.

WILLIAM EARLE JOHNS

Desert Night, 1938

Cadogan, Mary. *And Then Their Hearts Stood Still*, 133–35.

SAMUEL JOHNSON

Rasselas, 1759

Folkenflik, Robert. "*Rasselas* and the Closed Field." *Huntington Lib Q* 57 (1994), 337–50.

Foy, Roslyn Reso. "Johnson's *Rasselas:* Women in the 'Stream of Life.'" *Engl Lang Notes* 32:1 (1994), 39–51.

García Landa, José Angel. "'The Enthusiastick Fit': The Function and Fate of the Poet in Johnson's *Rasselas.*" *Cuadernos de Investigación Filológica* 17:1–2 (1991), 103–26.

Hinnant, Charles H. *'Steel for the Mind,'* 142–51.

MacCarthy, B. G. *The Female Pen*, 277–79.

New, Melvyn. "*Rasselas* in an Eighteenth-Century Novels Course," in

David R. Anderson and Gwin J. Kolb, eds., *Approaches to Teaching*, 121–27.

Power, Stephen S. "Through the Lens of *Orientalism:* Samuel Johnson's *Rasselas." West Virginia Univ Philol Papers* 40 (1994), 6–10.

Prince, Michael. *Philosophical Dialogue*, 229–37.

Rees, Christine. *Utopian Imagination and Eighteenth-Century Fiction*, 241–65.

Rosenberg, Beth Carole. *Virginia Woolf and Samuel Johnson*, 43–47.

Smith, Duane H. "Repetitive Patterns in Samuel Johnson's *Rasselas." Stud in Engl Lit, 1500–1900* 36 (1996), 623–37.

Spacks, Patricia Meyer. " 'Ev'ry Woman is at Heart a Rake,' " in Carla H. Hay and Syndy M. Conger, eds., *The Past as Prologue*, 53–55.

Tomarken, Edward. *A History of the Commentary*, 62–91.

Wiltshire, John. *Samuel Johnson in the Medical World*, 165–94.

JENNIFER JOHNSTON

The Captains and the Kings, 1972

Berge, Marit. "The Big House in Jennifer Johnston's Novels," in Andrew Kennedy and Orm Øverland, eds., *Excursions in Fiction*, 15–16.

Fool's Sanctuary, 1987

Berge, Marit. "The Big House in Jennifer Johnston's Novels," in Andrew Kennedy and Orm Øverland, eds., *Excursions in Fiction*, 22–24.

The Gates, 1973

Berge, Marit. "The Big House in Jennifer Johnston's Novels," in Andrew Kennedy and Orm Øverland, eds., *Excursions in Fiction*, 18–20.

How Many Miles to Babylon?, 1974

Berge, Marit. "The Big House in Jennifer Johnston's Novels," in Andrew Kennedy and Orm Øverland, eds., *Excursions in Fiction*, 16–18.

The Invisible Worm, 1991

Berge, Marit. "The Big House in Jennifer Johnston's Novels," in Andrew Kennedy and Orm Øverland, eds., *Excursions in Fiction*, 24–26.

The Old Jest, 1979

Berge, Marit. "The Big House in Jennifer Johnston's Novels," in Andrew Kennedy and Orm Øverland, eds., *Excursions in Fiction*, 20–22.

The Railway Station Man, 1984

Berge, Marit. "The Big House in Jennifer Johnston's Novels," in Andrew Kennedy and Orm Øverland, eds., *Excursions in Fiction*, 26–30.

Shadows on Our Skin, 1977

Weekes, Anne Owens. "Ordinary Women: Themes in Contemporary Fiction by Irish Women." *Colby Q* 31 (1995), 88–89.

GWYNETH A. JONES

Escape Plans, 1986

Wolmark, Jenny. "The Postmodern Romances of Feminist Science Fiction," in Lynne Pearce and Jackie Stacey, eds., *Romance Revisited*, 165–67.

LEWIS JONES

Cwmardy, 1937

Fox, Pamela. *Class Fictions*, 191–93.

We Live, 1939

Fox, Pamela. *Class Fictions*, 191–93.

JAMES JOYCE

Finnegans Wake, 1939

Anspaugh, Kelly. "How Butt Shot the Chamber Pot: *Finnegans Wake* II.3." *James Joyce Q* 32 (1994), 71–79.

Anspaugh, Kelly. "Powers of Ordure: James Joyce and the Excremental Vision(s)." *Mosaic* 27:1 (1994), 91–96.

Anspaugh, Kelly. " 'When Lovely Wooman Stoops to Conk Him': Virginia Woolf in *Finnegans Wake*." *Joyce Stud Annual 1996*, 176–91.

Attridge, Derek. "Countlessness of Livestories: Narrativity in *Finnegans Wake*," in Morris Beja and David Norris, eds., *Joyce in the Hibernian Metropolis*, 290–95.

Barger, Jorn. "A Preliminary Stratigraphy of *Scribbledehobble*," in Andrew Treip, ed., *Finnegans Wake*, 127–34.

Beckman, Richard. "Perils of Marriage in *Finnegans Wake*." *James Joyce Q* 33 (1995), 83–97.

Benstock, Bernard. "Quinet in the *Wake:* The Proof or The Pudding?," in John Harty, III, ed., *James Joyce's "Finnegans Wake,"* 57–68.

Black, Martha Fodaski. *Shaw and Joyce*, 19–23, 50–53, 261–405, 407–10.

Blumenbach, Ulrich. "Irish Views on British Wars: Joyce's Museyroom Memorial—Metaphors of Memory and Recollection." *Zeitschrift für Anglistik und Amerikanistik* 44 (1996), 44–49.

Bolt, Sydney. *A Preface to James Joyce*, 155–86.

Booker, M. Keith. *Joyce, Bakhtin, and the Literary Tradition*, 8–10, 91–103, 141–44.

Borodin, David. " 'Group drinkards maaks grope thinkards or how reads rotary' *FW* 312.31): *Finnegans Wake* and the Group Reading Experience," in John Harty, III, ed., *James Joyce's "Finnegans Wake,"* 151–62.

Brivic, Sheldon. "The Femasculine Obsubject: A Lacanian Reading of

FW 606–607," in John Harty, III, ed., *James Joyce's "Finnegans Wake,"* 45–53.

Brivic, Sheldon. *Joyce's Waking Women,* 3–135.

Brivic, Sheldon. *The Veil of Signs,* 151–81.

Burns, Christy. "An Erotics of the Word: Female 'Assaucyetiams' in *Finnegans Wake.*" *James Joyce Q* 31:3 (1994), 315–32.

Burrell, Harry. "Chemistry and Physics in *Finnegans Wake.*" *Joyce Stud Annual 1996,* 192–218.

Burrell, Harry. *Narrative Design in "Finnegans Wake,"* 1–220.

Cahalan, James M. " 'Dear Reader' and 'Drear Writer': Joyce's Direct Addresses to His Readers in *Finnegans Wake.*" *Twentieth Cent Lit* 41 (1995), 306–15.

Campbell, Joseph. *Mythic Worlds, Modern Words,* 189–248.

Carnell, Simon. "*Finnegans Wake:* 'the most formidable anti-fascist book produced between the two wars'?," in Andrew Treip, ed., *Finnegans Wake,* 139–63.

Cheng, Vincent J. "*Finnegans Wake:* All the World's a Stage," in John Harty, III, ed., *James Joyce's "Finnegans Wake,"* 69–82.

Cheng, Vincent J. *Joyce, Race, and Empire,* 251–96.

Conrad, Kathryn, and Darryl Wadsworth. "Joyce and the Irish Body Politic: Sexuality and Colonization in *Finnegans Wake.*" *James Joyce Q* 31:3 (1994), 301–12.

Culleton, Claire A. *Names and Naming in Joyce,* 49–55, 68–71.

Day, Robert Adams. "Joyce's AquaCities," in Morris Beja and David Norris, eds., *Joyce in the Hibernian Metropolis,* 17–19.

Deane, Vincent. "Bywaters and the Original Crime," in Andrew Treip, ed., *Finnegans Wake,* 165–79.

Dettmar, Kevin J. H. *The Illicit Joyce,* 9–11, 168–70, 209–17.

Devlin, Kimberly J. "The Female Word," in John Harty, III, ed., *James Joyce's "Finnegans Wake,"* 141–47.

Diament, Henri. "Gallic Joys of Joyce: On Translating Some Names in *Finnegans Wake* into French." *Names* 44 (1996), 83–98.

Duszenko, Andrzej. "The Joyce of Science: Quantum Physics in *Finnegans Wake.*" *Irish Univ R* 24 (1994), 272–82.

Duszenko, Andrzej. "The Relativity Theory in *Finnegans Wake.*" *James Joyce Q* 32 (1994), 61–70.

Eckley, Grace. *The Steadfast "Finnegans Wake,"* 1–299.

Erzgräber, Willi. "The Narrative Presentation of Orality in James Joyce's *Finnegans Wake.*" *Oral Tradition* 7:1 (1992), 150–70.

Fairhall, James. *James Joyce and the Question of History,* 57–60, 214–47.

Ferris, Kathleen. *James Joyce and the Burden of Disease,* 120–47.

Froula, Christine. *Modernism's Body,* 199–249.

Gordon, John. "The Convertshems of the Tchoose: Judaism and Jewishness in *Finnegans Wake,*" in John Harty, III, ed., *James Joyce's "Finnegans Wake,"* 85–96.

Gordon, John. "Joyce Egg and Claddagh Ring: Joycean Artifacts in

Ulysses and *Finnegans Wake.*" *Notes on Mod Irish Lit* 5 (1993), 43–51.

Gordon, John. "Joycean Heroes, Joycean Counterparts." *Essays in Lit* (Macomb, IL) 21 (1994), 251–64.

Gottfried, Roy. *Joyce's Iritis*, 9–12, 17–20, 57–60, 134–36.

Gregory, Shelly. "Rewaking the Mother Tongue in *Finnegans Wake:* A Kristevan Interpretation." *Engl Lang Notes* 34:1 (1996), 63–75.

Harty, John, III. "*FW* 26.25–36: 'Belly the First.' " *Notes on Mod Irish Lit* 6 (1994), 12–15.

Harty, John, III. "Is Beckett's 'Come in' in *Finnegans Wake?*" *Notes on Mod Irish Lit* 5 (1993), 52–56.

Hayman, David. "Dreaming Up the *Wake,*" in John Harty, III, ed., *James Joyce's "Finnegans Wake,"* 13–21.

Hayman, David. "Substantial Time: The Temporalities of Mamalujo," in Andrew Treip, ed., *Finnegans Wake*, 95–105.

Heller, Vivian. *Joyce, Decadence, and Emancipation*, 158–63.

Herman, David. "The Mutt and Jute Dialogue in Joyce's *Finnegans Wake:* Some Gricean Perspectives." *Style* 28 (1994), 219–36.

Hofheinz, Thomas C. *Joyce and the Invention of Irish History*, 1–187.

Hogan, Patrick Colm. *Joyce, Milton,* 51–53, 132–34, 154–203.

Hollahan, Eugene. *Crisis-Consciousness*, 169–73.

Kenner, Hugh. "SHEM THE TEXTMAN," in John Harty, III, ed., *James Joyce's "Finnegans Wake,"* 33–41.

Klein, Scott W. *The Fictions of James Joyce and Wyndham Lewis,* 153–97.

Kopcewicz, Andrzej. "*Finnegans Wake* and *The Dead Father:* An Intertextual Transaction." *REAL: Yrbk of Res in Engl and Am Lit* 9 (1993), 149–86.

Kostelanetz, Richard. *An ABC of Contemporary Reading*, 133–38.

Lernout, Geert. "Time and the *Wakean* Person," in Andrew Treip, ed., *Finnegans Wake*, 119–25.

Lewiecki-Wilson, Cynthia. *Writing Against the Family*, 205–41.

Loxterman, Alan S. "Every Man His Own God: From *Ulysses* to *Finnegans Wake,*" in John Harty, III, ed., *James Joyce's "Finnegans Wake,"* 115–25.

McBride, Margaret. "*Finnegans Wake:* The Issue of Issy's Schizophrenia." *Joyce Stud Annual 1996*, 145–73.

MacCabe, Colin. "An Introduction to *Finnegans Wake,*" in John Harty, III, ed., *James Joyce's "Finnegans Wake,"* 23–31.

McCarthy, Patrick A. "The World as Book, the Book as Machine: Art and Life in Joyce and Lowry," in Patrick A. McCarthy and Paul Tiessen, eds., *Joyce/Lowry*, 153–56.

McCormack, W. J. *From Burke to Beckett*, 278–86.

McDowell, Lesley. "Daughter's Time: Issy's Problematics of Time in *Finnegans Wake,*" in Andrew Treip, ed., *Finnegans Wake*, 81–93.

McGee, Patrick. *Telling the Other*, 78–83, 85–93.

Mailhos, Jacques. " 'Begin to forget it': The Preprovided emory of *Finnegans Wake,"* in Andrew Treip, ed., *Finnegans Wake*, 41–67.

Meakin, David. *Hermetic Fictions*, 132–36.

Meaney, Gerardine. *(Un)Like Subjects*, 136–39.

Milesi, Laurent. *"Finnegans Wake:* The Obliquity of Trans-lations," in Morris Beja and David Norris, eds., *Joyce in the Hibernian Metropolis*, 279–85.

Milesi, Laurent. "Killing Lewis with Einstein: 'Secting Time' in *Finnegans Wake,"* in Andrew Treip, ed., *Finnegans Wake*, 9–20.

Moliterno, Gino. "The Candlebearer at the *Wake:* Bruno's *Candelaio* in Joyce's Book of the Dark." *Compar Lit Stud* 30 (1993), 269–90.

Montesi, Albert. "Joyce's "Blue Guitar": Wallace Stevens and *Finnegans Wake,"* in John Harty, III, ed., *James Joyce's "Finnegans Wake,"* 99–108.

Nolan, Emer. *James Joyce and Nationalism*, 139–62, 179–81.

O'Connor, Theresa. "History, Gender, and the Postcolonial Condition: Julia O'Faolain's Comic Rewriting of *Finnegans Wake,"* in O'Connor, ed., *The Comic Tradition*, 124–47.

Piette, Adam. *"Finnegans Wake* and Familial Memory." *Swiss Papers in Engl Lang and Lit* 9 (1996), 249–54.

Polhemus, Robert M. "Dantellising Peaches and Miching Daddy, the Gushy Old Goof: The Browning Case and *Finnegans Wake." Joyce Stud Annual 1994*, 75–103.

Rabaté, Jean-Michel. "On Joycean and Wildean Sodomy." *James Joyce Q* 31:3 (1994), 163–65.

Radford, Fred. "Anticipating *Finnegans Wake: The United Irishman* and *La Belle Iseult." James Joyce Q* 33 (1996), 237–43.

Rapaport, Herman. *Between the Sign and the Gaze*, 219–23.

Rice, Thomas Jackson. "The Complexity of *Finnegans Wake." Joyce Stud Annual 1995*, 79–98.

Rice, Thomas Jackson. *Joyce, Chaos, and Complexity*, 112–40.

Robinson, David W. "Joyce's Nonce-Symbolic Calculus: A *Finnegans Wake* Trajectory," in John Harty, III, ed., *James Joyce's "Finnegans Wake,"* 131–38.

Rogers, Margaret. "Thoughts on Making Music From the Hundred-Letter Words in *Finnegans Wake,"* in John Harty, III, ed., *James Joyce's "Finnegans Wake,"* 189–96.

Rose, Danis. *The Textual Diaries of James Joyce*, 41–136.

Sailer, Susan Shaw. *On the Void to Be*, 11–203.

Sawyer-Lauçanno, Christopher. *The World's Words*, 12–40.

Schork, R. J. "By Jingo: Genetic Criticism of *Finnegans Wake." Joyce Stud Annual 1994*, 104–27.

Seidel, Michael. "James Joyce," in John Richetti et al., eds., *The Columbia History*, 767–68, 770–72, 774–78, 784–88.

Senn, Fritz. *Inductive Scrutinies*, 48–51, 220–23, 226–37.

Senn, Fritz.. " 'The Same Renew': *Finnegans Wake* as a Chamber of Echoes," in Andreas Fischer, ed., *Repetition*, 195–206.

Slote, Sam. "Needles in the Camel's Eye: Concerning a Time of the 'Collideorscape,' " in Andrew Treip, ed., *Finnegans Wake*, 69–80.

Stocker, Barry. "The Return of the Law in *Finnegans Wake.*" *Oxford Liter R* 14:1–2 (1992), 45–69.

Theall, Donald. "Joyce's Techno-Poetics of Artifice: Machines, Media, Memory, and Modes of Communication in *Ulysses* and *Finnegans Wake,*" in R. B. Kershner, ed., *Joyce and Popular Culture*, 139–51.

Treip, Andrew. " 'As per periodicity': Vico, Freud and the Serial Awakening of Book III Chapter 4," in Treip, ed., *Finnegans Wake*, 21–40.

Treip, Andrew. "Histories of Sexuality: Vico and Roman Marriage Law in *Finnegans Wake.*" *Revue des Lettres Modernes* 1173–82 (1994), 179–99.

Treip, Andrew. "Lost Histereve: Vichian Soundings and Reverberations in the Genesis of *Finnegans Wake* II.4." *James Joyce Q* 32 (1995), 641–53.

Tymoczko, Maria. *The Irish "Ulysses,"* 277–85, 299–301.

Valente, Joseph. *James Joyce and the Problem of Justice*, 122–31, 245–47, 252–56.

Vespa, Jack. "Another Book at the *Wake:* Indian Mysticism and the *Bhagavad-Gita* in I.4 of *Finnegans Wake.*" *James Joyce Q* 31 (1994), 81–86.

Weir, David. *James Joyce and the Art of Mediation*, 185–206.

Wexler, Joyce Piell. *Who Paid for Modernism*, 67–70.

Whittier-Ferguson, John. *Framing Pieces*, 56–72.

Williams, Keith. "Joyce's 'Chinese alphabet': *Ulysses* and the Proletarians," in Paul Hyland and Neil Sammells, eds., *Irish Writing*, 173–75.

Yee, Cordell D. K. *The Word according to James Joyce*, 68–86.

A Portrait of the Artist as a Young Man, 1917

Anspaugh, Kelly. "Powers of Ordure: James Joyce and the Excremental Vision(s)." *Mosaic* 27:1 (1994), 87–89.

Astier, Colette. "Mythe et roman du poète dans *A Portrait of the Artist as a Young Man.*" *Littératures* 33 (1995), 125–38.

Ayotte, Jean. "Le fin mot de la durée: Aspects du temps dans *Portrait de l'artiste en jeune homme* de James Joyce." *Cahiers Victoriens et Edouardiens* 37 (1993), 107–16.

Bartlett, Sally A. "Spectral Thought and Psychological Mimesis in *A Portrait of the Artist as a Young Man.*" *Notes on Mod Irish Lit* 5 (1993), 57–66.

Black, Martha Fodaski. *Shaw and Joyce*, 54–57, 69–88.

Bolt, Sydney. *A Preface to James Joyce*, 59–95.

Booker, M. Keith. *Joyce, Bakhtin, and the Literary Tradition*, 38–41, 74–76, 126–29, 196–98.

Bowen, Zack. *Bloom's Old Sweet Song*, 77–79, 85–90, 100–106.

Brenner, Rachel Feldhay. "The Grammar of the Portrait: The Construct of the Artist in David Grossman, *The Book of Internal Grammar,* and James Joyce, *A Portrait of the Artist as a Young Man.*" *Compar Lit Stud* 31 (1994), 270–90.

Brivic, Sheldon. "Stephen Haunted by His Gender: The Uncanny *Portrait,*" in Morris Beja and David Norris, eds., *Joyce in the Hibernian Metropolis*, 205–12.

Brivic, Sheldon. *The Veil of Signs*, 37–58.

Buehrer, David. "Clothes Make the Man-Child: Masks, Costumes, and Fashion-Fragments in Joyce's *A Portrait.*" *J of Evolutionary Psych* 15:1–2 (1994), 2–8.

Campbell, Joseph. *Mythic Worlds, Modern Words*, 23–50.

Carlson, Sandy. James Joyce's Irish Nationalism, A Response to His Time: *A Portrait of the Artist as a Young Man.*" *Arkansas Q* 2:4 (1993), 282–98.

Chardin, Philippe. "La Femme, l'artiste, le prêtre et la poésie dans *Portrait de l'artiste en jeune homme* de Joyce ou comment un adieu peut en cacher un autre." *Littératures* 33 (1995), 113–23.

Davison, Neil R. *James Joyce . . . and the Construction of Jewish Identity*, 1–3.

Davison, Neil R. "Joyce's Homosocial Reckoning: Italo Svevo, Aesthetics, and *A Portrait of the Artist as a Young Man.*" *Mod Lang Stud* 24:3 (1994), 69–87.

Day, Robert Adams. "Joyce's AquaCities," in Morris Beja and David Norris, eds., *Joyce in the Hibernian Metropolis*, 10–11.

Deane, Seamus. *Strange Country*, 94–96.

Dettmar, Kevin J. H. *The Illicit Joyce*, 107–12, 117–24, 130–35, 211–13.

Dettmar, Kevin J. H. "Joyce/'Irishness'/Modernism," in John S. Rickard, ed., *Irishness and (Post)Modernism*, 103–25.

Dettmar, Kevin J. H. "*Ulysses* and the Preemptive Power of Plot," in Robert Newman, ed., *Pedagogy, Praxis, "Ulysses,"* 26–29.

Diment, Galya. *The Autobiographical Novel,* 114–16.

Duffy, Enda. *The Subaltern "Ulysses,"* 11–14.

Echeruo, Michael J. C. "Joyce's 'Epical Equidistance.' " *Engl Stud in Africa* 39:1 (1996), 1–11.

Fairhall, James. *James Joyce and the Question of History*, 44–47, 112–60.

Ferris, Kathleen. *James Joyce and the Burden of Disease,* 19–22, 33–35.

Feshbach, Sidney. "The Magic Lantern of Tradition on *A Portrait of the Artist as a Young Man.*" *Joyce Stud Annual 1996*, 3–66.

Fleischmann, Ruth. "Knowledge of the World as the Forbidden Fruit: Canon Sheehan and Joyce on the Sacrificium Intellectus," in Donald E. Morse et al., eds., *A Small Nation's Contribution*, 131–35.

Froula, Christine. *Modernism's Body*, 33–83.

Galef, David. *The Supporting Cast,* 140–42.

Grayson, Janet. "The Consecration of Stephen Dedalus." *Engl Lang Notes* 34:1 (1996), 55–62.

Heidt, Edward R. *The Image of the Church Minister,* 65–80.

Heller, Vivian. *Joyce, Decadence, and Emancipation*, 47–77.

Hickman, Alan Forrest. "Growing Up Irish: An Update on Stephen Dedalus." *Publs of the Arkansas Philol Assoc* 22:1 (1996), 9–18.

Hogan, Patrick Colm. *Joyce, Milton,* 50–52, 60–63, 97–109.

Hollahan, Eugene. *Crisis-Consciousness,* 165–69.

Hubier, Sebastien. " 'La Chambre noire de l'imagination' ou le 'roman familial' du poète." *Littératures* 33 (1995), 93–112.

Hughes, Eamonn. "Joyce and Catholicism," in Robert Welch, ed., *Irish Writers and Religion,* 129–35.

Innes, C. L. *Woman and Nation in Irish Literature,* 63–68.

Kestner, Joseph A. "Youth by the Sea: The Ephebe in *A Portrait of the Artist as a Young Man* and *Ulysses.*" *James Joyce Q* 31:3 (1994), 233–55.

Kim, Suzanne. "*A Portrait of the Artist as a Young Man* and *Ultramarine:* Two Exercises in Identification," in Patrick A. McCarthy and Paul Tiessen, eds., *Joyce/Lowry,* 109–24.

Lambert, Ellen Zetzel. *The Face of Love,* 49–50.

Leonard, Garry. "The City, Modernism, and Aesthetic Theory in *A Portrait of the Artist as a Young Man.*" *Novel* 29 (1995), 79–99.

Lewiecki-Wilson, Cynthia. *Writing Against the Family,* 121–37.

Lozes, Jean. "James Joyce dans la tradition 'gothique'?" *Caliban* 33 (1996), 127–36.

MacCabe, Colin. "An Introduction to *Finnegans Wake,*" in John Harty, III, ed., *James Joyce's "Finnegans Wake,"* 23–25.

McCormack, W. J. *From Burke to Beckett,* 268–75.

Mahaffey, Vicki. "Père-version and Im-mère-sion: Idealized Corruption in *A Portrait of the Artist as a Young Man* and *The Picture of Dorian Gray.*" *James Joyce Q* 31:3 (1994), 189–96.

Martin, Augustine. *Bearing Witness,* 56–61.

Meakin, David. *Hermetic Fictions,* 122–28.

Melnick, Daniel C. *Fullness of Dissonance,* 108–13.

Menaghan, John M. "A Wilderness of Mirrors: Modernist Mimesis in Joyce's *Portrait* and Beckett's *Murphy.*" *Colby Q* 30 (1994), 252–58.

Morrisson, Mark. "Stephen Dedalus and the Ghost of the Mother." *Mod Fiction Stud* 39 (1993), 345–62.

Muller, Jill. "John Henry Newman and the Education of Stephen Dedalus." *James Joyce Q* 33 (1996), 593–602.

Murphy, James H. *Catholic Fiction and Social Reality in Ireland,* 139–40, 145–47.

Nalbantian, Suzanne. *Aesthetic Autobiography,* 118–22.

Nolan, Emer. *James Joyce and Nationalism,* 37–46, 171–72.

Norris, David. "The 'unhappy mania' and Mr. Bloom's Cigar: Homosexuality in the Works of James Joyce." *James Joyce Q* 31:3 (1994), 365–69.

O'Neill, William. "Myth and Identity in Joyce's Fiction: Disentangling the Image." *Twentieth Cent Lit* 40 (1994), 383–91.

Osteen, Mark. "The Treasure-House of Language: Managing Symbolic Economies in Joyce's *Portrait.*" *Stud in the Novel* 27 (1995), 154–65.

Rabaté, Jean-Michel. "Joyce, the Edwardian," in Carola M. Kaplan and Anne B. Simpson, eds., *Seeing Double,* 104–7.

Rice, Thomas Jackson. *Joyce, Chaos, and Complexity*, 52–81.

Richter, David H. *The Progress of Romance*, 34–36.

Scott, Bonnie Kime. "James Joyce: A Subversive Geography of Gender," in Paul Hyland and Neil Sammells, eds., *Irish Writing*, 164–71.

Seed, David. *James Joyce's "A Portrait of the Artist as a Young Man,"* 45–174.

Seed, David. "The Voices of the Church: A Dialogical Aproach to the Retreat Section of Joyce's *A Portrait of the Artist."* *Lit and Theology* 9 (1995), 153–63.

Seidel, Michael. "James Joyce," in John Richetti et al., eds., *The Columbia History*, 767–68, 771–74.

Senn, Fritz.. " 'The Same Renew': *Finnegans Wake* as a Chamber of Echoes," in Andreas Fischer, ed., *Repetition*, 192–95.

Smith, Evans Lansing. *Ricorso and Revelation*, 64–66, 94–96.

Spoo, Robert. *James Joyce and the Language of History*, 38–65.

Teal, Laurie. "Batlike Souls and Penile Temptresses: Gender Inversions in *A Portrait of the Artist as a Young Man."* *Novel* 29 (1995), 63–78.

Thornton, Weldon. *The Antimodernism of Joyce's "Portrait,"* 85–158.

Thornton, Weldon. "Authorial Omniscience and Cultural Psyche: The Antimodernism of Joyce's *Ulysses,"* in John S. Rickard, ed., *Irishness and (Post)Modernism*, 84–92.

Tratner, Michael. *Modernism and Mass Politics,* 116–32.

Trotter, David. *The English Novel in History*, 95–98, 290–94.

Tymoczko, Maria. *The Irish "Ulysses,"* 107–9, 187–89.

Valente, Joseph. *James Joyce and the Problem of Justice*, 42–47, 183–85.

Valente, Joseph. "Thrilled by His Touch: Homosexual Panic and the Will to Artistry in *A Portrait of the Artist as a Young Man."* *James Joyce Q* 31:3 (1994), 167–87.

Watson, G. J. *Irish Identity and the Literary Revival*, 179–98, 200–203.

Weir, David. *Decadence and the Making of Modernism,* 122–33.

Weir, David. "Epiphanoumenon." *James Joyce Q* 31 (1994), 55–64.

Weir, David. *James Joyce and the Art of Mediation*, 21–31, 54–60, 111–14, 119–33.

Weir, David. "A Womb of His Own: Joyce's Sexual Aesthetics." *James Joyce Q* 31:3 (1994), 212–18.

Wexler, Joyce Piell. *Who Paid for Modernism*, 58–61.

Yee, Cordell D. K. *The Word according to James Joyce*, 35–44.

Stephen Hero, 1944

Black, Martha Fodaski. *Shaw and Joyce*, 54–70.

Bolt, Sydney. *A Preface to James Joyce*, 59–63.

Dettmar, Kevin J. H. *The Illicit Joyce*, 85–87.

Diment, Galya. *The Autobiographical Novel,* 113–16.

Fairhall, James. *James Joyce and the Question of History*, 117–20, 146–53.

Froula, Christine. *Modernism's Body*, 34–37, 60–66, 192–94.

Hogan, Patrick Colm. *Joyce, Milton,* 73–75.
Lewiecki-Wilson, Cynthia. *Writing Against the Family,* 120–22.
Muller, Jill. "John Henry Newman and the Education of Stephen Dedalus." *James Joyce Q* 33 (1996), 596–602.
Nalbantian, Suzanne. *Aesthetic Autobiography,* 115–18.
Nolan, Emer. *James Joyce and Nationalism,* 36–45.
O'Neill, William. "Myth and Identity in Joyce's Fiction:Disentangling the Image." *Twentieth Cent Lit* 40 (1994), 379–83.
Tratner, Michael. *Modernism and Mass Politics,* 119–21.
Watson, G. J. *Irish Identity and the Literary Revival,* 156–60, 164–66.
Weir, David. *Decadence and the Making of Modernism,* 124–26.
Weir, David. *James Joyce and the Art of Mediation,* 20–22.
Welch, Robert. *Changing States,* 102–7.

Ulysses, 1922

Ackerley, Chris. " 'Living in the Same Place': Joyce's *Ulysses* in T. S. Eliot's *After Strange Gods.*" *AUMLA* 84 (1995), 111–14.
Ackerley, Chris. " 'Well, of course, if we knew all the things': Coincidence and Design in *Ulysses* and *Under the Volcano,*" in Patrick A. McCarthy and Paul Tiessen, eds., *Joyce/Lowry,* 41–58.
Anspaugh, Kelly. " 'Jean qui rit' and 'Jean qui pleure': James Joyce, Wyndham Lewis and the High Modern Grotesque," in Michael J. Meyer, ed., *Literature and the Grotesque,* 130–39.
Anspaugh, Kelly. "Powers of Ordure: James Joyce and the Excremental Vision(s)." *Mosaic* 27:1 (1994), 89–91.
Anspaugh, Kelly. "Ulysses Upon Ajax? Joyce, Harrington, and the Question of 'Cloacal' Imperialism." *South Atlantic R* 60:2 (1995), 11–26.
Armstrong, Paul B. "James Joyce and the Politics of Reading: Power, Belief, and Justice in *Ulysses.*" *REAL: Yrbk of Res in Engl and Am Lit* 11 (1995), 325–43.
Attridge, Derek. "The Postmodernity of Joyce: Chance, Coincidence, and the Reader." *Joyce Stud Annual 1995,* 11–18.
Aubert, Jacques. "On Friendship in Joyce." *Joyce Stud Annual 1995,* 5–9.
Barta, Peter I. *Bely, Joyce, and Döblin,* 47–75.
Bazargan, Susan. "Mapping Gibraltar: Colonialism, Time, and Narrative in 'Penelope,' " in Richard Pearce, ed., *Molly Blooms,* 119–33.
Begnal, Michael H. "Molly Bloom and Lady Hester Stanhope," in R. B. Kershner, ed., *Joyce and Popular Culture,* 64–73.
Beja, Morris. "Some Points of Departure for Teaching *Ulysses,*" in Kathleen McCormick and Erwin R. Steinberg, eds., *Approaches,* 129–38.
Bell, Michael. *Literature, Modernism and Myth,* 67–93.
Benstock, Bernard. "Middle-Class Values in *Ulysses*—and the Value of the Middle Class." *James Joyce Q* 31 (1994), 439–52.
Bishop, Edward L. "Re: Covering *Ulysses.*" *Joyce Stud Annual 1994,* 22–54.

Black, Martha Fodaski. *Shaw and Joyce*, 17–19, 50–52, 194–259, 331–34, 341–43.

Blamires, Harry. *The New Bloomsday Book*, 3–249.

Blumenbach, Ulrich. "Joyce's Handiwork on Myth." *Zeitschrift für Anglistik und Amerikanistik* 41 (1993), 331–39.

Bock, Martin. "Syphilisation and Its Discontents: Somatic Indications of Psychological Ills in Joyce and Lowry," in Patrick A. McCarthy and Paul Tiessen, eds., *Joyce/Lowry*, 135–36, 137–39.

Bolt, Sydney. *A Preface to James Joyce*, 97–154.

Booker, M. Keith. "Decolonizing Literature: *Ulysses* and the Postcolonial Novel in English," in Robert Newman, ed., *Pedagogy, Praxis, "Ulysses,"* 135–49.

Booker, M. Keith. *Joyce, Bakhtin, and the Literary Tradition*, 7–9, 18–20, 93–97, 153–55, 185–87, 201–4.

Bowen, Zack. *Bloom's Old Sweet Song*, 10–24, 25–75, 77–84, 87–90, 92–106, 107–14, 115–23, 124–34.

Bowen, Zack. "Wilde About Joyce," in R. B. Kershner, ed., *Joyce and Popular Culture*, 105–15.

Brammer, Marsanne. "Joyce's 'hallucinian via': Mysteries, Gender, and the Staging of 'Circe.' " *Joyce Stud Annual 1996*, 86–122.

Breuer, Horst. "Who Narrates Joyce's 'Eumaeus'?," in Konrad Groß et al., eds., *Das Natur/Kultur-Paradigma*, 134–49.

Briggs, Austin. "The Full Stop at the End of 'Ithaca': Thirteen Ways—and Then Some—of Looking at a Black Dot." *Joyce Stud Annual 1996*, 125–41.

Briggs, Austin. "Helping Students Read *Ulysses*," in Kathleen McCormick and Erwin R. Steinberg, eds., *Approaches*, 149–54.

Brivic, Sheldon. "Consciousness as Conflict: A Psychoanalytic Approach to *Ulysses*," in Kathleen McCormick and Erwin R. Steinberg, eds., *Approaches*, 59–66.

Brivic, Sheldon. "Dialogic Monologue, or Divided Discourse in *Ulysses* and *Othello*," in Robert Newman, ed., *Pedagogy, Praxis, "Ulysses,"* 253–65.

Brivic, Sheldon. *The Veil of Signs*, 79–147.

Brockman, William S. "American Librarians and Early Censorship of *Ulysses:* 'Aiding the Cause of Free Expression'?" *Joyce Stud Annual 1994*, 56–74.

Burkdall, Thomas L. "Cinema Fakes: Film and Joycean Fantasy," in Morris Beja and David Norris, eds., *Joyce in the Hibernian Metropolis*, 260–68.

Campbell, Joseph. *Mythic Worlds, Modern Words*, 51–188.

Castle, Gregory. "Ousted Possibilities: Critical Histories in James Joyce's *Ulysses*." *Twentieth Cent Lit* 39 (1993), 306–24.

Chace, William M. "Joycean Realism," in Robert M. Polhemus and Roger B. Henkle, eds., *Critical Reconstructions*, 150–67.

Cheng, Vincent J. *Joyce, Race, and Empire*, 151–248.

Cheng, Vincent J. "The Joycean Unconscious, or Getting Respect in the

Real World," in R. B. Kershner, ed., *Joyce and Popular Culture*, 187–92.

Childress, Lynn. "The Missing 'Cicones' Episode of *Ulysses*." *James Joyce Q* 33 (1995), 69–81.

Collins, Floyd. "The Polytropic Potential of Language in the 'Hades' Chapter of Joyce's *Ulysses*." *Arkansas Q* 2:4 (1993), 268–80.

Conely, James. "Sounding the Sirens Again: An Evaluation of Musical Structure in the Sirens Chapter of James Joyce's *Ulysses*." *Ars Lyrica* 7 (1993), 107–15.

Cornwell, Neil. "More on Joyce and Russia: Or *Ulysses* on the Moscow Rover." *Joyce Stud Annual 1994*, 175–86.

Couturier, Maurice. "Censorship and the Authorial Figure in *Ulysses* and *Lolita*." *Cycnos* 12:2 (1995), 29–42.

Cross, Richard K. "*Ulysses* and *Under the Volcano*: The Difficulty of Loving," in Patrick A. McCarthy and Paul Tiessen, eds., *Joyce/Lowry*, 63–79.

Culleton, Claire A. *Names and Naming in Joyce*, 8–42, 55–68, 75–91, 95–108, 113–25.

Davison, Neil R. *James Joyce . . . and the Construction of Jewish Identity*, 185–239.

Day, Robert Adams. "Joyce's AquaCities," in Morris Beja and David Norris, eds., *Joyce in the Hibernian Metropolis*, 11–17.

Deane, Vincent. "Greek Gifts: *Ulysses* into Fox in VI.B.10." *Joyce Stud Annual 1994*, 163–75.

Dettmar, Kevin J. H. *The Illicit Joyce*, 8–11, 106–208.

Dettmar, Kevin J. H. "Joyce/'Irishness'/Modernism," in John S. Rickard, ed., *Irishness and (Post)Modernism*, 103–25.

Dettmar, Kevin J. H. "Selling *Ulysses*." *James Joyce Q* 30:4/31:1 (1993), 795–807.

Dettmar, Kevin J. H. "*Ulysses* and the Preemptive Power of Plot," in Robert Newman, ed., *Pedagogy, Praxis, "Ulysses,"* 21–43.

Devlin, Kimberly J. "Bloom and the Police: Regulatory Vision and Visions in *Ulysses*." *Novel* 29 (1995), 45–62.

Devlin, Kimberly J. "Pretending in 'Penelope': Masquerade, Mimicry, and Molly Bloom," in Richard Pearce, ed., *Molly Blooms*, 80–100.

Diment, Galya. *The Autobiographical Novel*, 3–10, 109–42.

Duffy, Enda. *The Subaltern "Ulysses,"* 1–191.

Ellmann, Maud. " 'Aeolus': Reading Backward," in Morris Beja and David Norris, eds., *Joyce in the Hibernian Metropolis*, 198–201.

Erzgräber, Willi. "Varianten des inneren Monologs in James Joyces *Ulysses*," in Herbert Foltinek et al., eds., *Tales and "their telling difference,"* 279–94.

Fairhall, James. *James Joyce and the Question of History*, 32–38, 43–48, 52–56, 161–213, 223–25, 238–41, 243–46, 252–55.

Ferrer, Daniel. "Between *Inventio* and *Memoria*: Locations of 'Aeolus,' " in Morris Beja and David Norris, eds., *Joyce in the Hibernian Metropolis*, 190–96.

Ferris, Kathleen. *James Joyce and the Burden of Disease,* 39–65.

Finneran, Richard J. " 'That Word Known to All Men' in *Ulysses:* A Reconsideration." *James Joyce Q* 33 (1996), 569–79.

Froula, Christine. *Modernism's Body,* 87–196.

Füger, Wilhelm. "Stimmbrüche: Varianten und Spielräume narrativer Fokalisation," in Herbert Foltinek et al., eds., *Tales and "their telling difference,"* 54–57.

Gaipa, Mark. "Culture, Anarchy, and the Politics of Modernist Style in Joyce's 'Oxen of the Sun.' " *Mod Fiction Stud* 41 (1995), 195–212.

Galef, David. *The Supporting Cast,* 140–42, 148–50.

Garvey, Johanna X. K. "City Limits: Reading Gender and Urban Space in *Ulysses." Twentieth Cent Lit* 41 (1995), 108–19.

Garvey, Johanna X. K. " 'If We Were All Suddenly Somebody Else': *Orlando* as the New *Ulysses." Women's Stud* 23 (1994), 1–13.

Gillespie, Michael Patrick. " 'In the buginning is the woid': Opening Lines and the Protocols of Reading," in Robert Newman, ed., *Pedagogy, Praxis, "Ulysses,"* 9–20.

Giovannangeli, Jean-Louis. "La Rupture des Pactes dans *Ulysses." Cahiers Victoriens et Edouardiens* 44 (1996), 167–82.

Gordon, John. "Approaching Reality in 'Circe.' " *Joyce Stud Annual 1994,* 3–21.

Gordon, John. "Joyce Egg and Claddagh Ring: Joycean Artifacts in *Ulysses* and *Finnegans Wake." Notes on Mod Irish Lit* 5 (1993), 43–51.

Gordon, John. " 'Ithaca' as the Letter 'C.' " *James Joyce Q* 32 (1994), 45–55.

Gordon, John. "Joycean Heroes, Joycean Counterparts." *Essays in Lit* (Macomb, IL) 21 (1994), 252–64.

Gordon, John. "Some Joyce Skies." *James Joyce Q* 33 (1996), 411–25.

Gottfried, Roy. *Joyce's Iritis,* 8–166.

Gottfried, Roy. "Reading the Text of *Ulysses,* 'Reading' Other 'Texts': Representation and the Limits of Visual and Verbal Narratives," in Robert Newman, ed., *Pedagogy, Praxis, "Ulysses,"* 181–93.

Grace, Sherrill. "Midsummer Madness and the Day of the Dead: Joyce, Lowry, and Expressionism," in Patrick A. McCarthy and Paul Tiessen, eds., *Joyce/Lowry,* 9–18.

Haroian-Guerin, Gil. *The Fatal Hero,* 93–120.

Harper, Margaret Mills. "Bread and Wine, Coke and Peanuts: Teaching Sacrificial Feasts," in Robert Newman, ed., *Pedagogy, Praxis, "Ulysses,"* 63–74.

Harper, Margaret Mills. " 'Taken in Drapery': Dressing the Narrative in the *Odyssey* and 'Penelope,' " in Richard Pearce, ed., *Molly Blooms,* 237–56.

Hayman, David. "Dreaming Up the *Wake,"* in John Harty, III, ed., *James Joyce's "Finnegans Wake,"* 17–19.

Heininger, Joseph. "Molly Bloom's Ad Language and Goods Behavior:

Advertising as Social Communication in *Ulysses*," in Richard Pearce, ed., *Molly Blooms*, 237–56.

Heininger, Joseph. "Understanding *Ulysses* through Irish and British Popular Culture," in Kathleen McCormick and Erwin R. Steinberg, eds., *Approaches*, 78–86.

Heller, Vivian. *Joyce, Decadence, and Emancipation*, 78–156, 165–76.

Herman, David. " 'Sirens' after Schönberg." *James Joyce Q* 31 (1994), 473–87.

Herr, Cheryl. " 'Penelope' as Period Piece," in Richard Pearce, ed., *Molly Blooms*, 63–78.

Herr, Cheryl, and Chris Connell. "Political Contexts for *Ulysses*," in Kathleen McCormick and Erwin R. Steinberg, eds., *Approaches*, 31–41.

Herrick, Casey. "Joyce's *Ulysses*." *Explicator* 53 (1994), 45–47.

Hill, Marylu. " 'Amor Matris':Mother and Self in the Telemachiad Episode of *Ulysses*." *Twentieth Cent Lit* 39 (1993), 329–41.

Hogan, Patrick Colm. *Joyce, Milton*, 48–51, 53–57, 93–153, 164–67.

Hughes, Eamonn. "Joyce and Catholicism," in Robert Welch, ed., *Irish Writers and Religion*, 120–25.

Innes, C. L. *Woman and Nation in Irish Literature*, 71–74.

Jackson, Tony E. *The Subject of Modernism*, 170–88.

Jones, Ellen Carol. "Commodious Recirculation: Commodity and Dream in Joyce's *Ulysses*." *James Joyce Q* 30:4/31:1 (1993), 739–55.

Kenner, Hugh. "Joyce and Modernism," in Kathleen McCormick and Erwin R. Steinberg, eds., *Approaches*, 21–30.

Kenner, Hugh. "SHEM THE TEXTMAN," in John Harty, III, ed., *James Joyce's "Finnegans Wake*," 38–41.

Kershner, R. Brandon. "Teaching *Howards End* through *Ulysses* through Bakhtin," in Robert Newman, ed., *Pedagogy, Praxis, "Ulysses*," 153–64.

Kestner, Joseph A. "Youth by the Sea: The Ephebe in *A Portrait of the Artist as a Young Man* and *Ulysses*." *James Joyce Q* 31:3 (1994), 233–55.

Kimball, Jean. "An Ambiguous Faithlessness: Molly Bloom and the Widow of Ephesus." *James Joyce Q* 31 (1994), 455–70.

Kirchhofer, Anton. "The Text in the Closet: Concealment and Disclosure in James Joyce's *Ulysses*." *Zeitschrift für Anglistik und Amerikanistik* 44 (1996), 27–43.

Klein, Scott W. *The Fictions of James Joyce and Wyndham Lewis*, 66–152.

Klein, Scott W. "Searching for Lost Keys: Epic and Linguistic Dislocations in *Ulysses*," in Kathleen McCormick and Erwin R. Steinberg, eds., *Approaches*, 105–12.

Knowles, Sebastian D. G. "That Form Endearing: A Performance of Siren Songs; or, 'I was only vamping, man,' " in Morris Beja and David Norris, eds., *Joyce in the Hibernian Metropolis*, 213–32.

Lamos, Colleen. "Signatures of the Invisible: Homosexual Secrecy and Knowledge in *Ulysses.*" *James Joyce Q* 31:3 (1994), 337–53.

Leerssen, Joep. *Remembrance and Imagination*, 228–31.

Lentin, Louis. "I Don't Understand. I Fail To Say. I Dearsee You Too," in Morris Beja and David Norris, eds., *Joyce in the Hibernian Metropolis*, 61–68.

Leonard, Garry. "Molly Bloom's 'Lifestyle': The Performative as Normative," in Richard Pearce, ed., *Molly Blooms*, 196–230.

Leonard, Garry M. "Advertising and Religion in James Joyce's Fiction: The New (Improved) Testament," in R. B. Kershner, ed., *Joyce and Popular Culture*, 125–38.

Levine, Jennifer. "A Brief Allegory of Readings: 1972–1992," in Morris Beja and David Norris, eds., *Joyce in the Hibernian Metropolis*, 181–88.

Levine, Jennifer. "James Joyce, Tattoo Artist: Tracing the Outlines of Homosocial Desire." *James Joyce Q* 31:3 (1994), 277–96.

Levine, Jennifer. " 'Nausicaa': For [Wo]men Only?," in Morris Beja and David Norris, eds., *Joyce in the Hibernian Metropolis*, 128–34.

Lewiecki-Wilson, Cynthia. *Writing Against the Family*, 139–76.

Lloyd, David. *Anomalous States*, 100–110.

Loss, Archie K. "*Ulysses,* Cubism, and MTV," in Robert Newman, ed., *Pedagogy, Praxis, "Ulysses,"* 195–205.

Lowe-Evans, Mary. "Approaching *Ulysses* through the New Historicism," in Kathleen McCormick and Erwin R. Steinberg, eds., *Approaches*, 67–75.

Loxterman, Alan S. "Every Man His Own God: From *Ulysses* to *Finnegans Wake,*" in John Harty, III, ed., *James Joyce's "Finnegans Wake,"* 115–25.

McCarthy, Patrick A. "The World as Book, the Book as Machine: Art and Life in Joyce and Lowry," in Patrick A. McCarthy and Paul Tiessen, eds., *Joyce/Lowry*, 145–56.

McCormack, W. J. *From Burke to Beckett*, 269–76.

McCormick, Kathleen. "Reading *Ulysses* within the History of Its Production and Reception," in Kathleen McCormick and Erwin R. Steinberg, eds., *Approaches*, 87–96.

McCormick, Kathleen. "Reproducing Molly Bloom: A Revisionist History of the Reception of 'Penelope,' 1922–1970," in Richard Pearce, ed., *Molly Blooms*, 17–35.

McCormick, Kathleen. *"Ulysses," 'Wandering Rocks,' and the Reader*, 59–168.

McDonald, Michael Bruce. " 'Circe' and the Uncanny, or Joyce From Freud to Marx." *James Joyce Q* 33 (1995), 49–65.

McGee, Patrick. *Telling the Other*, 3–9.

McGee, Patrick. "When Is a Man Not a Man? or, The Male Feminist Approaches 'Nausicaa,' " in Morris Beja and David Norris, eds., *Joyce in the Hibernian Metropolis*, 122–27.

McMahon, Timothy G. "Cultural Nativism and Irish-Ireland: *The Leader* as a Source for Joyce's *Ulysses*." *Joyce Stud Annual 1996*, 67–85.

McWilliams, Jim. "Joyce's *Ulysses*." *Explicator* 53 (1995), 106–7.

Mahaffey, Vicki. "The Importance of Playing Earnest: The Stakes of Reading *Ulysses*," in Kathleen McCormick and Erwin R. Steinberg, eds., *Approaches*, 139–48.

Martin, Augustine. *Bearing Witness*, 67–77.

Meakin, David. *Hermetic Fictions*, 128–37.

Melnick, Daniel C. *Fullness of Dissonance*, 112–25.

Mercier, Vivian. *Modern Irish Literature*, 242–311.

Mitchell, J. Lawrence. "Joyce and Boxing: Famous Fighters in *Ulysses*." *James Joyce Q* 31 (1994), 21–28.

Monk, Leland. *Standard Deviations*, 110–44.

Montresor, Jaye Berman. "Joyce's Jewish Stew: The Alimentary Lists in *Ulysses*." *Colby Q* 31 (1995), 194–202.

Moretti, Franco. *Modern Epic*, 123–229.

Moretti, Franco. *Signs Taken For Wonders*, 182–208.

Morrisson, Mark. "Stephen Dedalus and the Ghost of the Mother." *Mod Fiction Stud* 39 (1993), 345–62.

Morse, Donald E. "Starting from the Earth, Starting from the Stars: The Fantastic in Samuel Beckett's Plays and James Joyce's *Ulysses*," in Donald E. Morse et al., eds., *A Small Nation's Contribution*, 10–18.

Murphy, James J. "A Collective Exploration of *Ulysses*," in Kathleen McCormick and Erwin R. Steinberg, eds., *Approaches*, 155–60.

Nalbantian, Suzanne. *Aesthetic Autobiography*, 123–33.

Newman, Robert. "Discovering Body Tropes through *Ulysses*," in Newman, ed., *Pedagogy, Praxis, "Ulysses*," 207–19.

Nolan, Emer. *James Joyce and Nationalism*, 55–119, 124–28, 131–38, 163–69, 173–79.

Norris, David. "The 'unhappy mania' and Mr. Bloom's Cigar: Homosexuality in the Works of James Joyce." *James Joyce Q* 31:3 (1994), 369–71.

Norris, Margot. "Theater of the Mind: 'Circe' and Avant-Garde Form," in Robert Newman, ed., *Pedagogy, Praxis, "Ulysses*," 79–93.

Ochoa, Peter. "Joyce's 'Nausicaa': The Paradox of Advertising Narcissism." *James Joyce Q* 30:4/31:1 (1993), 783–91.

Osteen, Mark. "Cribs in the Countinghouse: Plagiarism, Proliferation, and Labor in 'Oxen of the Sun,' " in Morris Beja and David Norris, eds., *Joyce in the Hibernian Metropolis*, 237–47.

Osteen, Mark. *The Economy of "Ulysses*," 1–444.

Osteen, Mark. "The Money Question at the Back of Everything: Clichés, Counterfeits and Forgeries in Joyce's 'Eumaeus.' " *Mod Fiction Stud* 38 (1992), 821–39.

Osteen, Mark. "Seeking Renewal: Bloom, Advertising, and the Domestic Economy." *James Joyce Q* 30:4/31:1 (1993), 717–35.

Palumbo, Donald. "Sexuality and the Allure of the Fantastic in Literature," in Palumbo, ed., *Erotic Universe*, 10–13.

Parkes, Adam. *Modernism and the Theater of Censorship,* 65–106.

Pearce, Richard. "How Does Molly Bloom Look Through the Male Gaze?," in Pearce, ed., *Molly Blooms,* 40–57.

Pearce, Richard. " 'Nausicaa': Monologue as Monologic," in Morris Beja and David Norris, eds., *Joyce in the Hibernian Metropolis,* 106–13.

Pearce, Richard. "Teaching for the (W)Holes," in Kathleen McCormick and Erwin R. Steinberg, eds., *Approaches,* 97–104.

Peternel, Joan. "Readers, Characters, and Identity: *Tom Jones* and *Ulysses." McNeese R* 33 (1990–94), 48–57.

Rabaté, Jean-Michel. "Joyce, the Edwardian," in Carola M. Kaplan and Anne B. Simpson, eds., *Seeing Double,* 101–6.

Rabaté, Jean-Michel. "On Joycean and Wildean Sodomy." *James Joyce Q* 31:3 (1994), 159–65.

Rader, Ralph W. "Mulligan and Molly: The Beginning and the End," in Morris Beja and David Norris, eds., *Joyce in the Hibernian Metropolis,* 270–76.

Rado, Lisa. " 'Hypsos' or 'Spadia'? Rethinking Androgyny in *Ulysses* with Help from Sacher-Masoch." *Twentieth Cent Lit* 42 (1996), 193–205.

Rainsford, Dominic. "Pity in Joyce: The Significance of the Blind Stripling." *Engl Lang Notes* 34:1 (1996), 47–54.

Reichert, Klaus. "Ich-Fluchten: Leopold Bloom und Zeno Cosini—James Joyce, *Ulysses,* und Italo Svevo, *Zeno Cosini,"* in Eberhard Lämmert and Barbara Naumann, eds., *Wer sind wir?,* 25–36.

Reizbaum, Marilyn. "A Nightmare of History: Ireland's Jews and Joyce's *Ulysses,"* in Bryan Cheyette, ed., *Between 'Race' and Culture,* 102–13.

Rice, Thomas Jackson. *Joyce, Chaos, and Complexity,* 82–111.

Rice, Thomas Jackson. "The (Tom) Swiftean Comedy of 'Scylla and Charybdis,' " in R. B. Kershner, ed., *Joyce and Popular Culture,* 116–24.

Rice, Thomas Jackson. "Ulysses, Chaos, and Complexity." *James Joyce Q* 31 (1994), 41–50.

Rickard, John S. "The Irish Undergrounds of Joyce and Heaney," in Morris Beja and David Norris, eds., *Joyce in the Hibernian Metropolis,* 250–58.

Rocco, John. "Drinking *Ulysses:* Joyce, Bass Ale, and the Typography of Cubism." *James Joyce Q* 33 (1996), 399–406.

Sailer, Susan Shaw. "Women in Rooms, Women in History," in Robert Newman, ed., *Pedagogy, Praxis, "Ulysses,"* 97–118.

Sandquist, Brigitte L. "The Tree Wedding in 'Cyclops' and the Ramifications of Catalogic." *James Joyce Q* 33 (1996), 195–207.

Scott, Bonnie Kime. "Feminist Approaches to Teaching *Ulysses,"* in Kathleen McCormick and Erwin R. Steinberg, eds., *Approaches,* 49–58.

Scott, Bonnie Kime. "James Joyce: A Subversive Geography of Gender," in Paul Hyland and Neil Sammells, eds., *Irish Writing*, 169–71.

Scott, Shirley Clay. "Man, Mind, and Monster: Polyphemus from Homer through Joyce." *Classical and Mod Lit* 16 (1996), 62–75.

Segall, Jeffrey. "Culture, Politics, and Ideology in the Reception of *Ulysses*," in Kathleen McCormick and Erwin R. Steinberg, eds., *Approaches*, 42–48.

Seidel, Michael. "James Joyce," in John Richetti et al., eds., *The Columbia History*, 765–79, 781–85.

Senn, Fritz. *Inductive Scrutinies,* 7–48, 51–56, 59–72, 75–95, 97–109, 111–30, 133–53, 156–214, 216–20.

Senn, Fritz.. " 'The Same Renew': *Finnegans Wake* as a Chamber of Echoes," in Andreas Fischer, ed., *Repetition*, 192–95.

Shaffer, Brian W. "Nationalism at the Bar: Anti-Semitism in *Ulysses* and *Under the Volcano*," in Patrick A. McCarthy and Paul Tiessen, eds., *Joyce/Lowry*, 84–93.

Shaffer, Brian W. "Negotiating Self and Culture: Narcissism, Competing Discourses, and Ideological Becoming in 'Penelope,' " in Richard Pearce, ed., *Molly Blooms*, 139–50.

Shaffer, Brian W. "Teaching Freud through 'Nausicaa,' " in Robert Newman, ed., *Pedagogy, Praxis, "Ulysses,"* 121–29.

Sherry, Vincent. "Distant Music: 'Wandering Rocks' and the Art of Gratuity." *James Joyce Q* 31 (1994), 31–39.

Sherry, Vincent. *James Joyce: "Ulysses,"* 1–113.

Shloss, Carol. "Molly's Resistance to the Union: Marriage and Colonialism in Dublin, 1904," in Richard Pearce, ed., *Molly Blooms*, 105–17.

Shloss, Carol. "Teaching Joyce Teaching Kristeva: Estrangement in the Modern World," in Robert Newman, ed., *Pedagogy, Praxis, "Ulysses,"* 47–60.

Sicker, Philip. "Leopold's Travels: Swiftian Optics in Joyce's 'Cyclops.' " *Joyce Stud Annual 1995*, 59–78.

Siegel, Carol. *Male Masochism*, 48–76.

Slack, John. "Regular Hotbed: *Ulysses,* Gambling, and the Ascot Gold Cup Race." *Aethlon* 11:2 (1994), 1–11.

Smith, Evans Lansing. *Ricorso and Revelation*, 130–34.

Somer, John. "The Self-Reflexive Arranger in the Initial Style of Joyce's *Ulysses*." *James Joyce Q* 31 (1994), 65–76.

Soud, Stephen E. "Blood-Red Wombs and Monstrous Births: Aristotle's Masterpiece and *Ulysses*." *James Joyce Q* 32 (1995), 195–203.

Spoo, Robert. *James Joyce and the Language of History*, 66–162.

Stanier, Michael. " 'The Void Awaits Surely All Them That Weave the Wind': 'Penelope' and 'Sirens' in *Ulysses*." *Twentieth Cent Lit* 41 (1995), 319–29.

Stanzel, F. K. "All Europe Contributed to the Making of Bloom: New Light on Leopold Bloom's Ancestors." *James Joyce Q* 32 (1995), 619–26.

Steinberg, Erwin R. "Point of View, the Narrator(s), and the Stream of

Consciousness," in Kathleen McCormick and Erwin R. Steinberg, eds., *Approaches*, 113–21.

Steiner, Wendy. *Pictures of Romance*, 122–31.

Steppe, Wolfhard. "The Merry Greeks: (With a Farewell *epideti*)." *James Joyce Q* 32 (1995), 597–612.

Stevenson, Randall. *A Reader's Guide*, 40–42.

Strobos, Semon. "Freudian *Symbolizierung* and *Traumarbeit* in *Ulysses'* Construction and Streams of Consciousness." *Lang and Lit* (San Antonio) 20 (1995), 35–51.

Strub, Christian. "Odysseus hört Argonautenmusik oder: Warum die Sirenen nicht singen—Zur Handlungsstruktur im 'Sirens'-Kapitel des *Ulysses.*" *Zeitschrift für Anglistik und Amerikanistik* 41 (1993), 318–29.

Sturgess, Philip J. M. *Narrativity*, 189–234.

Theall, Donald. "Joyce's Techno-Poetics of Artifice: Machines, Media, Memory, and Modes of Communication in *Ulysses* and *Finnegans Wake*," in R. B. Kershner, ed., *Joyce and Popular Culture*, 139–51.

Theoharis, Theoharis Constantine. "Making Much of Nothing." *James Joyce Q* 33 (1996), 583–91.

Thornton, Weldon. "Authorial Omniscience and Cultural Psyche: The Antimodernism of Joyce's *Ulysses*," in John S. Rickard, ed., *Irishness and (Post)Modernism*, 92–99.

Thornton, Weldon. "Discovering *Ulysses:* The 'Immersive' Experience," in Kathleen McCormick and Erwin R. Steinberg, eds., *Approaches*, 122–28.

Tratner, Michael. *Modernism and Mass Politics*, 33–53, 64–68, 183–216.

Tratner, Michael. "Sex and Credit: Consumer Capitalism in *Ulysses.*" *James Joyce Q* 30:4/31:1 (1993), 695–715.

Trotter, David. *The English Novel in History*, 95–107, 217–20, 294–303.

Tymoczko, Maria. *The Irish "Ulysses,"* 21–350.

Ulmer, Gregory L. "The Heurectics of Odyssey: Ulysses in Florida," in Robert Newman, ed., *Pedagogy, Praxis, "Ulysses,"* 253–65.

Ungar, Andras P. "Ulysses in *Ulysses:* What the Nolan Said," in Donald E. Morse et al., eds., *A Small Nation's Contribution*, 138–47.

Valente, Joseph. *James Joyce and the Problem of Justice*, 46–48, 93–95, 187–241.

Vanderham, Paul. "Ezra Pound's Censorship of *Ulysses.*" *James Joyce Q* 32 (1995), 583–94.

Vanderham, Paul. "Lifting the Ban on Ulysses: The Well-Intentioned Lies of the Woolsey Decision." *Mosaic* 27:4 (1994), 179–96.

Vice, Sue. "The Construction of Femininity in *Ulysses* and *Under the Volcano:* A Bakhtinian Analysis of the Late Draft Versions," in Patrick A. McCarthy and Paul Tiessen, eds., *Joyce/Lowry*, 96–106.

Voelker, Joseph C. "Clown Meets Cops: Comedy and Paranoia in *Under the Volcano* and *Ulysses*," in Patrick A. McCarthy and Paul Tiessen, eds., *Joyce/Lowry*, 21–39.

Walkiewicz, E. P. "*Ulysses,* Order, Myth: Classification and Modern Literature," in Robert Newman, ed., *Pedagogy, Praxis, "Ulysses,"* 241–50.

Warner, John M. *Joyce's Grandfathers,* 120–55.

Watson, G. J. *Irish Identity and the Literary Revival,* 197–244.

Watt, Stephen. "Brief Exposures: Commodification, Exchange Value, and the Figure of Woman in 'Eumaeus.' " *James Joyce Q* 30:4/31:1 (1993), 757–79.

Watt, Stephen. " 'Nothing for a Woman in That': James Lovebirch and Masochistic Fantasy in *Ulysses,*" in R. B. Kershner, ed., *Joyce and Popular Culture,* 74–88.

Webb, Caroline. "Listing to the Right: Authority and Inheritance in *Orlando* and *Ulysses.*" *Twentieth Cent Lit* 40 (1994), 190–202.

Weinstein, Philip. "For Gerty Had Her Dreams that No-one Knew Of," in Morris Beja and David Norris, eds., *Joyce in the Hibernian Metropolis,* 115–20.

Weir, David. "Epiphanoumenon." *James Joyce Q* 31 (1994), 60–64.

Weir, David. *James Joyce and the Art of Mediation,* 13–181.

Weir, David. "A Womb of His Own: Joyce's Sexual Aesthetics." *James Joyce Q* 31:3 (1994), 207–12, 218–29.

Welch, Robert. *Changing States,* 107–18.

Werner, Craig. " 'Cyclops,' 'Sirens,' and the Myths of Multicultural Modernism," in Robert Newman, ed., *Pedagogy, Praxis, "Ulysses,"* 225–39.

Wexler, Joyce Piell. *Who Paid for Modernism,* 14–18, 61–69, 130–32.

Whittaker, Stephen, and Francis X. Jordan. "The Three Whistles and the Aesthetic of Mediation: Modern Physics and Platonic Metaphysics in Joyce's *Ulysses.*" *James Joyce Q* 33 (1995), 27–45.

Wicke, Jennifer. " 'Who's She When She's at Home?': Molly Bloom and the Work of Consumption," in Richard Pearce, ed., *Molly Blooms,* 174–93.

Williams, Keith. "Joyce's 'Chinese alphabet': *Ulysses* and the Proletarians," in Paul Hyland and Neil Sammells, eds., *Irish Writing,* 173–86.

Wollaeger, Mark A. "Stephen/Joyce, Joyce/Haacke: Modernism and the Social Function of Art." *ELH* 62 (1995), 691–703.

Yee, Cordell D. K. *The Word according to James Joyce,* 45–67, 102–5, 127–32.

Ziarek, Ewa. "The Female Body, Technology, and Memory in 'Penelope,' " in Richard Pearce, ed., *Molly Blooms,* 264–81.

ANNA KAVAN

The House of Sleep, 1947

Garrity, Jane. "Nocturnal Transgressions in *The House of Sleep:* Anna Kavan's Maternal Registers." *Mod Fiction Stud* 40 (1994), 253–73.

M. M. KAYE

Shadow of the Moon, 1957

Hand, Felicity. "In the Shadow of the Mutiny: Reflections on Two Post Independence Novels on the 1857 Uprising," in Susana Onega, ed., *Telling Histories,* 67–70.

ROBERT KEABLE

Simon Called Peter, 1921

Cecil, Hugh. *The Flower of Battle,* 154–57.

MOLLY KEANE

Good Behaviour, 1981

Lynch, Rachael Jane. "The Crumbling Fortress: Molly Keane's Comedies of Anglo-Irish Manners," in Theresa O'Connor, ed., *The Comic Tradition,* 77–85.

Sceats, Sarah. "Eating the Evidence: Women, Power, and Food," in Sarah Sceats and Gail Cunningham, eds., *Image and Power,* 120–21.

Weekes, Anne Owens. "Ordinary Women: Themes in Contemporary Fiction by Irish Women." *Colby Q* 31 (1995), 92–93.

Loving and Giving, 1988

Lynch, Rachael Jane. "The Crumbling Fortress: Molly Keane's Comedies of Anglo-Irish Manners," in Theresa O'Connor, ed., *The Comic Tradition,* 92–96.

Loving without Tears, 1951

Lynch, Rachael Jane. "The Crumbling Fortress: Molly Keane's Comedies of Anglo-Irish Manners," in Theresa O'Connor, ed., *The Comic Tradition,* 75–77.

Time After Time, 1983

Lynch, Rachael Jane. "The Crumbling Fortress: Molly Keane's Comedies of Anglo-Irish Manners," in Theresa O'Connor, ed., *The Comic Tradition,* 85–92.

GEORGE KEATE

Sketches from Nature; Taken, and Coloured, in a Journey to Margate, 1779

Williams, Anne Patricia. "Description and Tableau in the Eighteenth-Century British Sentimental Novel." *Eighteenth-Cent Fiction* 8 (1996), 482–84.

A. L. KENNEDY

Looking for the Possible Dance, 1993
> Todd, Richard. *Consuming Fictions,* 156–61.

CHARLES J. KICKHAM

Knocknagow, 1873
> Murphy, James H. *Catholic Fiction and Social Reality in Ireland,* 80–87.

CHARLES KINGSLEY

Alton Locke, 1850
> Adams, James Eli. *Dandies and Desert Saints,* 143–47.
> Adams, James Eli. "Pater's Muscular Aestheticism," in Donald E. Hall, ed., *Muscular Christianity,* 223–25.
> Antor, Heinz. *Der englische Universitätsroman,* 156–57.
> Childers, Joseph W. *Novel Possibilities,* 132–57.
> Colby, Robin B. *"Some Appointed Work To Do,"* 22–26.
> Guy, Josephine M. *The Victorian Social-Problem Novel,* 173–80.
> Hall, Donald E. *Fixing Patriarchy,* 63–83.
> Harsh, Constance D. *Subversive Heroines,* 91–94, 105–7.
> Horsman, Alan. *The Victorian Novel,* 258–61.
> Terry, R. C. " 'Have at the Masters!': Working-Class Stereotypes in Some Nineteenth-Century Novels," in John Morris, ed., *Exploring Stereotyped Images,* 167–68.
> Visser, Nicholas. "Roaring Beasts and Raging Floods: The Representation of Political Crowds in the Nineteenth-Century British Novel." *Mod Lang R* 89 (1994), 299.
> Wee, C. J. W.-L. "Christian Manliness and National Identity: The Problematic Construction of a Racially 'Pure' Nation," in Donald E. Hall, ed., *Muscular Christianity,* 71–76.

Hypatia, 1853
> Horsman, Alan. *The Victorian Novel,* 193–94.
> Lackey, Lionel. "Kingsley's *Hypatia:* Foes Ever New." *Victorian Newsl* 87 (1995), 1–4.
> Litvack, Leon B. "Callista, Martyrdom, and the Early Christian Novel in the Victorian Age." *Nineteenth-Cent Contexts* 17 (1993), 164–65.

Two Years Ago, 1857
> Adams, James Eli. *Dandies and Desert Saints,* 136–41.
> Fasick, Laura. "Charles Kingsley's Scientific Treatment of Gender," in Donald E. Hall, ed., *Muscular Christianity,* 96–100, 103–5.

The Water-Babies, 1863
> Horsman, Alan. *The Victorian Novel,* 262–64.
> Hunt, Peter. *An Introduction to Children's Literature,* 77–78.

Rapple, Brendon. "The Motif of Water in Charles Kingsley's *The Water-Babies.*" *Univ of Mississippi Stud in Engl* 11–12 (1993–95), 259–69.

Stevenson, Deborah. "Sentiment and Significance: The Impossibility of Recovery in the Children's Literature Canon or, The Drowning of *The Water-Babies.*" *Lion and the Unicorn* 21 (1997), 112–28.

Wood, Naomi. "A (Sea) Green Victorian: Charles Kingsley and *The Water-Babies.*" *Lion and the Unicorn* 19 (1995), 233–49.

Westward Ho!, 1855

Adams, James Eli. *Dandies and Desert Saints,* 123–25, 129–32, 134–36.

Horsman, Alan. *The Victorian Novel,* 194–95.

Wee, C. J. W.-L. "Christian Manliness and National Identity: The Problematic Construction of a Racially 'Pure' Nation," in Donald E. Hall, ed., *Muscular Christianity,* 76–86.

Yeast, 1848

Hall, Donald E. *Fixing Patriarchy,* 63–83.

Horsman, Alan. *The Victorian Novel,* 256–58.

HENRY KINGSLEY

Geoffry Hamlyn, 1859

Horsman, Alan. *The Victorian Novel,* 265–67.

The Hillyars and the Burtons, 1865

Lee, Christopher. "Representing Failure: Gender and Madness in Henry Kingsley's *The Hillyars and the Burtons.*" *AUMLA* 82 (1994), 35–47.

Ravenshoe, 1861–1862

Horsman, Alan. *The Victorian Novel,* 264–69.

RUDYARD KIPLING

Kim, 1901

Adam, Ian. "Oral/Literate/Transcendent: The Politics of Language Modes in *Kim.*" *Yrbk of Engl Stud* 27 (1997), 66–78.

Bivona, Daniel. *Desire and Contradiction,* 41–51.

Ching-Liang Low, Gail. *White Skins/Black Masks,* 200–215.

Clark, Stephen R. L. "Alien Dreams: Kipling," in David Seed, ed., *Anticipations,* 172–74.

Dixon, Robert. *Writing the Colonial Adventure,* 173–75.

Gorra, Michael. "Rudyard Kipling to Salman Rushdie: Imperialism to Postcolonialism," in John Richetti et al., eds., *The Columbia History,* 637–40.

Gournay, Jean-François. " 'The Great Game': de l'histoire à la parabole dans *Kim.*" *Etudes Anglaises* 47 (1994), 418–26.

Harrex, Syd. "The Game & the Goal: Kipling, Forster & the Indian English Novel," in Annie Greet et al., eds., *Raj Nostalgia,* 78–80.

Harris, Michael. *Outsiders and Insiders*, 17–30.

Hervoche, Brigitte. "L'Inde de Kipling dans *Kim.*" *Cahiers Victoriens et Edouardiens* 39 (1994), 227–38.

Koh, Boo Eung. "The Illusion of Permanence in Rudyard Kipling's *Kim.*" *J of Engl Lang and Lit* 40 (1994), 721–41.

McCutchan, Corinne. "Who Is Kim?," in Nikki Lee Manos and Meri-Jane Rochelson, eds., *Transforming Genres*, 131–51.

Phillips, Jerry, and Ian Wojcik-Andrews. "Telling Tales to Children: The Pedagogy of Empire in MGM's *Kim* and Disney's *Aladdin.*" *Lion and the Unicorn* 20 (1996), 69–79.

Randall, Don. "Ethnography and the Hybrid Boy in Rudyard Kipling's *Kim.*" *Ariel* 27:3 (1996), 79–101.

Rich, Paul. "Kim and the Magic House: Freemasonry and Kipling," in Marie Mulvey Roberts and Hugh Ormsby-Lennon, eds., *Secret Texts*, 322–35.

Sparshott, Francis. "The View from Gadshill." *Philos and Lit* 20 (1996), 404–7.

Sutherland, John. *Is Heathcliff a Murderer?*, 239–43.

Thompson, Jon. *Fiction, Crime, and Empire*, 83–94.

Tulloch, Graham. "Voices of the Raj: Linguistic Diversity in *Kim,*" in Annie Greet et al., eds., *Raj Nostalgia*, 35–46.

Wegner, Phillip E. " 'Life as He Would Have It': The Invention of India in Kipling's *Kim.*" *Cultural Critique* 26 (1993–94), 129–59.

The Light That Failed, 1890

Ching-Liang Low, Gail. *White Skins/Black Masks*, 169–71.

Lane, Christopher. "Passion's 'Cumulative Poison': Colonial Desire and Friendship in Kipling's Early Fiction." *Kunapipi* 18:1 (1996), 174–80.

Rodstein, Susan de Sola. "Kipling's Decadent Empire: *The Light That Failed* and the *Fin-de-Siècle,*" in Peter Liebregts and Wim Tigges, eds., *Beauty and the Beast*, 233–47.

ELLIS CORNELIA KNIGHT

Dinarbas, 1790

MacCarthy, B. G. *The Female Pen*, 277–79.

RONALD A. KNOX

Let Dons Delight, 1939

Antor, Heinz. *Der englische Universitätsroman*, 521–24.

JUNE KNOX-MAWER

Sandstorm, 1991

Cadogan, Mary. *And Then Their Hearts Stood Still*, 137–40.

ARTHUR KOESTLER

Darkness at Noon, 1940

George, Alexander. "Inconsistency in *Darkness at Noon:* Slip or Tip?" *North Am R* 279:3 (1994), 24–25.
Sturgess, Philip J. M. *Narrativity,* 260–86.

HANIF KUREISHI

The Buddha of Suburbia, 1988

Hashmi, Alamgir. "Hanif Kureishi and the Tradition of the Novel." *Crit Survey* 5:1 (1993), 25–33.
Mergenthal, Silvia. "Acculturation and Family Structure: Mo's *Sour Sweet,* Kureishi's *The Buddha of Suburbia,* Ishiguro's *A Pale View of Hills,*" in Eckhard Breitinger, ed., *Defining New Idioms,* 122–24.

LADY CAROLINE LAMB

Glenarvon, 1816

Small, Helen. *Love's Madness,* 117–20.
Watson, Nicola J. "Trans-figuring Byronic Identity," in Mary A. Favret and Nicola J. Watson, eds., *At the Limits of Romanticism,* 190–92.

MARY ANN LAMB

Mrs. Leicester's School, 1807

Marsden, Jean I. "Letters on a Tombstone: Mothers and Literacy in Mary Lamb's *Mrs. Leicester's School." Children's Lit* 23 (1995), 31–44.

GEORGE LAMMING

The Emigrants, 1954

Nair, Supriya. *Caliban's Curse,* 57–61, 63–66, 71–73.
Vijayasree, C. "George Lamming and the Caribbean Experience of Expatriation," in R. K. Dhawan and L. S. R. Krishna Sastry, eds., *Commonwealth Writing,* 102–3.

In the Castle of My Skin, 1953

Donnelly, Mary E. "*In the Castle of My Skin* and Oedipal Structures of Colonialism." *Ariel* 26:4 (1995), 7–18.
Harris, Michael. *Outsiders and Insiders,* 158–75.
Nair, Supriya. *Caliban's Curse,* 6–9, 61–64, 79–91, 93–103, 138–41.
Vijayasree, C. "George Lamming and the Caribbean Experience of Expatriation," in R. K. Dhawan and L. S. R. Krishna Sastry, eds., *Commonwealth Writing,* 102.

Natives of My Person, 1972

 Hulme, Peter. "The Profit of Language: George Lamming and the Post-colonial Novel," in Jonathan White, ed., *Recasting the World,* 125–26.
 Nair, Supriya. *Caliban's Curse,* 29–39, 41–46, 48–55.

Of Age and Innocence, 1958

 Chukwu, A. "West Indian Manifesto: A Reading of George Lamming's *Of Age and Innocence.*" *Ilorin J of Lang and Lit* 2(1989), 25–40.
 Nair, Supriya. *Caliban's Curse,* 17–20, 105–8, 125–37.
 Vijayasree, C. "George Lamming and the Caribbean Experience of Expatriation," in R. K. Dhawan and L. S. R. Krishna Sastry, eds., *Commonwealth Writing,* 103–4.

Season of Adventure, 1958

 Nair, Supriya. *Caliban's Curse,* 107–11, 115–26.

Water with Berries, 1971

 Hulme, Peter. "The Profit of Language: George Lamming and the Post-colonial Novel," in Jonathan White, ed., *Recasting the World,* 126–35.
 Nair, Supriya. *Caliban's Curse,* 15–17, 65–75, 125–30.
 Vijayasree, C. "George Lamming and the Caribbean Experience of Expatriation," in R. K. Dhawan and L. S. R. Krishna Sastry, eds., *Commonwealth Writing,* 104–6.

D. H. LAWRENCE

Aaron's Rod, 1922

 Fjågesund, Peter. *The Apocalyptic World,* 121–23.
 Goodheart, Eugene. "Censorship and Self-Censorship in the Fiction of D. H. Lawrence," in George Bornstein, ed., *Representing Modernist Texts,* 229–30.
 Jones, Carolyn M. "Male Friendship and the Construction of Identity in D. H. Lawrence's Novels." *Lit and Theology* 9 (1995), 72–76.
 Pecora, Vincent P. "D. H. Lawrence," in John Richetti et al., eds., *The Columbia History,* 717–18, 735–36.
 Scherr, Barry J. " 'Love Battle' in *Aaron's Rod.*" *Recovering Lit* 20 (1994), 23–45.
 Turner, John. "Comedy and Hysteria in *Aaron's Rod,*" in Paul Eggert and John Worthen, eds., *Lawrence and Comedy,* 70–87.
 Worthen, John. *D. H. Lawrence,* 67–74.

John Thomas and Lady Jane, 1972

 Ellis, David. "D. H. Lawrence and the Female Body." *Essays in Criticism* 46 (1996), 137–38.
 Fjågesund, Peter. *The Apocalyptic World,* 161–64.
 Worthen, John. *D. H. Lawrence,* 105–10.

Kangaroo, 1923

Baxter, Gisèle Marie. " 'After such knowledge, what forgiveness?': Exile, Marriage and the Resistance to Commitment in D. H. Lawrence's *Kangaroo.*" *J of Narrative Technique* 24 (1994), 127–38.

Eggert, Paul. "Comedy and Provisionality: Lawrence's Address to His Audience and Material in His Australian Novels," in Paul Eggert and John Worthen, eds., *Lawrence and Comedy*, 138–44.

Feinstein, Elaine. *Lawrence and the Women*, 176–79.

Fjågesund, Peter. *The Apocalyptic World*, 123–29.

LaChapelle, Dolores. *D. H. Lawrence*, 141–43.

Pecora, Vincent P. "D. H. Lawrence," in John Richetti et al., eds., *The Columbia History*, 720–21, 724–25.

Wexler, Joyce Piell. *Who Paid for Modernism*, 110–11.

Worthen, John. *D. H. Lawrence*, 78–84.

Worthen, John. "Drama and Mimicry in Lawrence," in Paul Eggert and John Worthen, eds., *Lawrence and Comedy*, 37–39.

Lady Chatterley's Lover, 1928

Blanchard, Lydia. "Lawrence, Foucault and the Language of Sexuality (*Lady Chatterley's Lover*)," in Peter Widdowson, ed., *D. H. Lawrence*, 119–33.

Buckley, William K. *"Lady Chatterley's Lover,"* 27–107.

Cadogan, Mary. *And Then Their Hearts Stood Still*, 100-101.

DuPlessis, Rachel Blau. "Seismic Orgasm: Sexual Intercourse and Narrative Meaning in Mina Loy," in Kathy Mezei, ed., *Ambiguous Discourse*, 205–8.

Edwards, Duane. "The Problem of Narcissism in Lawrence's Late Fiction." *D. H. Lawrence R* 25:1–3 (1993/1994), 71–73.

Ellis, David. "D. H. Lawrence and the Female Body." *Essays in Criticism* 46 (1996), 146–50.

Fasick, Laura. *Vessels of Meaning*, 157–66.

Feinstein, Elaine. *Lawrence and the Women*, 221–26.

Fjågesund, Peter. *The Apocalyptic World*, 146–61.

Fulweiler, Howard W. *"Here A Captive Heart Busted,"* 150–56.

Gordon, Jan B. *Gossip and Subversion*, 374–79.

Hollahan, Eugene. *Crisis-Consciousness*, 133–40.

Hyde, George. "Deconstructing the Phallic: Lawrence, Shklovsky and Rozanov." *New Comparison* 19 (1995), 79–88.

LaChapelle, Dolores. *D. H. Lawrence*, 169–71.

Martin, Graham. "D. H. Lawrence and Class," in Peter Widdowson, ed., *D. H. Lawrence*, 44–47.

Mester, Terri A. *Movement and Modernism*, 120–22.

Millett, Kate. "D. H. Lawrence (*Lady Chatterley's Lover, The Plumed Serpent,* 'The Woman Who Rode Away')," in Peter Widdowson, ed., *D. H. Lawrence*, 69–77.

Montgomery, Robert E. *The Visionary D. H. Lawrence*, 212–14.

Newman, Judie. *The Ballistic Bard*, 100–102.

Parkes, Adam. *Modernism and the Theater of Censorship,* 107–43.

Pecora, Vincent P. "D. H. Lawrence," in John Richetti et al., eds., *The Columbia History,* 719–22, 736–39.

Squires, Michael. "Editing the Cambridge *Lady Chatterley:* Collaboration and Compromise," in Charles L. Ross and Dennis Jackson, eds., *Editing D. H. Lawrence,* 117–34.

Taylor, Neil. "A Woman's Love: D. H. Lawrence on Film," in Peter Reynolds, ed., *Novel Images,* 106–20.

Wexler, Joyce Piell. *Who Paid for Modernism,* 115–21.

Worthen, John. *D. H. Lawrence,* 100–105, 110–21.

The Lost Girl, 1920

Pecora, Vincent P. "D. H. Lawrence," in John Richetti et al., eds., *The Columbia History,* 735–36.

Simpson, Hilary. "Lawrence, Feminism and the War ('Tickets, Please,' *The Lost Girl*)," in Peter Widdowson, ed., *D. H. Lawrence,* 96–101.

Wexler, Joyce Piell. *Who Paid for Modernism,* 101–4.

Worthen, John. *D. H. Lawrence,* 57–62.

Mr. Noon, 1984

Blanchard, Lydia. "D. H. Lawrence and his 'Gentle Reader': The Furious Comedy of *Mr Noon,*" in Paul Eggert and John Worthen, eds., *Lawrence and Comedy,* 89–105.

Ellis, David. "D. H. Lawrence and the Female Body." *Essays in Criticism* 46 (1996), 136–37.

Vichy, Thérèse. "Autobiography, Poetry and Fiction in *Look! We Have Come Through!* and *Mr Noon.*" *Cahiers Victoriens et Edouardiens* 39 (1994), 101–12.

Wexler, Joyce Piell. *Who Paid for Modernism,* 105–9.

Worthen, John. *D. H. Lawrence,* 62–67.

The Plumed Serpent, 1926

Bell, Michael. *Literature, Modernism and Myth,* 156–58.

Brantlinger, Patrick. *Fictions of State,* 201–5.

Carpenter, Rebecca. " 'Bottom-Dog Insolence' and 'The Harem Mentality': Race and Gender in *The Plumed Serpent.*" *D. H. Lawrence R* 25:1–3 (1993/1994), 119–27.

Clark, L. D. "Editing *The Plumed Serpent* for Cambridge: Or, Crossing the Communication Gap," in Charles L. Ross and Dennis Jackson, eds., *Editing D. H. Lawrence,* 99–115.

Edwards, Duane. "The Problem of Narcissism in Lawrence's Late Fiction." *D. H. Lawrence R* 25:1–3 (1993/1994), 69–73.

Fjågesund, Peter. *The Apocalyptic World,* 129–44.

Gates, Larry. "The Reconciliation of Opposites in *The Plumed Serpent.*" *J of Evolutionary Psych* 15 (1994), 274–82.

Hyde, Virginia, and L. D. Clark. "The Sense of an Ending in *The Plumed Serpent.*" *D. H. Lawrence R* 25:1–3 (1993/1994), 140–44.

Ian, Marcia. *Remembering the Phallic Mother,* 107–19.

Jones, Carolyn M. "Male Friendship and the Construction of Identity in D. H. Lawrence's Novels." *Lit and Theology* 9 (1995), 76–82.

LaChapelle, Dolores. *D. H. Lawrence*, 146–61.

Mester, Terri A. *Movement and Modernism*, 116–20.

Millett, Kate. "D. H. Lawrence (*Lady Chatterley's Lover, The Plumed Serpent,* 'The Woman Who Rode Away')," in Peter Widdowson, ed., *D. H. Lawrence*, 77–80.

Montgomery, Robert E. *The Visionary D. H. Lawrence*, 194–97, 199–207.

Pecora, Vincent P. "D. H. Lawrence," in John Richetti et al., eds., *The Columbia History*, 717–19, 734–36.

Roberts, Neil. "The Novelist as Travel Writer: *The Plumed Serpent." D. H. Lawrence R* 25:1–3 (1993/1994), 130–39.

VanHoosier-Carey, Kimberly. "Struggling With the Master: The Position of Kate and the Reader in Lawrence's 'Quetzalcoatl' and *The Plumed Serpent." D. H. Lawrence R* 25:1–3 (1993/1994), 104–16.

Wexler, Joyce Piell. *Who Paid for Modernism*, 111–16.

Worthen, John. *D. H. Lawrence*, 90–99.

Young, William. "D. H. Lawrence's Pastoral Allegory: *The Plumed Serpent." Arkansas R* 3:1 (1994), 63–79.

The Rainbow, 1915

Black, Michael. "Visiting the Bottom of the Monstrous World: Allusion as Metaphor in Lawrence." *Cambridge Q* 24 (1995), 140–41.

Blanchard, Lydia. "D. H. Lawrence and his 'Gentle Reader': The Furious Comedy of *Mr Noon,"* in Paul Eggert and John Worthen, eds., *Lawrence and Comedy*, 89–91.

Davies, Alistair. "Contexts of Reading: The Reception of D. H. Lawrence's *The Rainbow* and *Women in Love,"* in Peter Widdowson, ed., *D. H. Lawrence*, 171–80.

Feinstein, Elaine. *Lawrence and the Women*, 126–31.

Goodheart, Eugene. "Censorship and Self-Censorship in the Fiction of D. H. Lawrence," in George Bornstein, ed., *Representing Modernist Texts,* 232–35.

Holderness, Graham. "Transition (*The Rainbow*)," in Peter Widdowson, ed., *D. H. Lawrence*, 49–60.

Lewiecki-Wilson, Cynthia. *Writing Against the Family*, 95–102.

Mester, Terri A. *Movement and Modernism*, 104–11.

Pecora, Vincent P. "D. H. Lawrence," in John Richetti et al., eds., *The Columbia History*, 722–24, 726–29.

Pinkney, Tony. "Northernness and Modernism (*The Rainbow, Women in Love),"* in Peter Widdowson, ed., *D. H. Lawrence*, 182–91.

Ross, Charles L. "Editing as Interpretation: Self-Censorship and Collaboration in the Cambridge Edition of *The Rainbow* and *Women in Love,"* in Charles L. Ross and Dennis Jackson, eds., *Editing D. H. Lawrence*, 79–87.

Sklenicka, Carol, and Mark Spilka. "A Womb of His Own: Lawrence's

Passional/Parental View of Childhood," in Elizabeth Goodenough et al., eds., *Infant Tongues*, 171–77.

Smith, Evans Lansing. *Ricorso and Revelation*, 96–100.

Squires, Michael. "D. H. Lawrence's Narrators, Sources of Knowledge, and the Problem of Coherence." *Criticism* 37 (1995), 479–82.

Taylor, Neil. "A Woman's Love: D. H. Lawrence on Film," in Peter Reynolds, ed., *Novel Images*, 106–20.

Wexler, Joyce Piell. *Who Paid for Modernism*, 91–93, 96–98, 101–3.

Worthen, John. *D. H. Lawrence*, 43–49.

Worthen, John. "Drama and Mimicry in Lawrence," in Paul Eggert and John Worthen, eds., *Lawrence and Comedy*, 39–41.

Sons and Lovers, 1913

Adams, Judith E. "Economic Factors in the Oedipal Complex of D. H. Lawrence's *Sons and Lovers.*" *Conf of Coll Teachers of Engl Stud* 55 (1995), 18–25.

Baron, Helen. "Some Theoretical Issues Raised by Editing *Sons and Lovers,*" in Charles L. Ross and Dennis Jackson, eds., *Editing D. H. Lawrence*, 59–76.

Bergquist, Carolyn. "Lawrence's *Sons and Lovers.*" *Explicator* 53 (1995), 167–70.

Black, Michael. "A Kind of Bristling in the Darkness: Memory and Metaphor in Lawrence." *Crit R* 32 (1992), 29–43.

Doherty, Gerald. "The Dialectic of Space in D. H. Lawrence's *Sons and Lovers.*" *Mod Fiction Stud* 39 (1993), 327–41.

Eagleton, Terry. "Psychoanalysis (*Sons and Lovers*)," in Peter Widdowson, ed., *D. H. Lawrence*, 62–66.

Gavin, Adrienne E. "Miriam's Mirror: Reflections on the Labelling of Miriam Leivers." *D. H. Lawrence R* 24 (1992), 27–41.

Jackson, S. H.. "A World 'intertwining among itself': D. H. Lawrence's *Sons and Lovers.*" *Publs of the Arkansas Philol Assoc* 21:2 (1995), 21–27.

Lewiecki-Wilson, Cynthia. *Writing Against the Family*, 68–95.

Luftig, Victor. *Seeing Together*, 148–55.

Mester, Terri A. *Movement and Modernism*, 100–102.

Montgomery, Robert E. *The Visionary D. H. Lawrence*, 63–64, 70–72.

Pecora, Vincent P. "D. H. Lawrence," in John Richetti et al., eds., *The Columbia History*, 727–29.

Siegel, Carol. *Male Masochism,* 88–91.

Sklenicka, Carol, and Mark Spilka. "A Womb of His Own: Lawrence's Passional/Parental View of Childhood," in Elizabeth Goodenough et al., eds., *Infant Tongues*, 169–71.

Squires, Michael. "D. H. Lawrence's Narrators, Sources of Knowledge, and the Problem of Coherence." *Criticism* 37 (1995), 472–79.

Thompson, David M. "Calling in the Realists: The Revision and Reputation of Lawrence's *Sons and Lovers.*" *Novel* 27 (1994), 233–54.

Trotter, David. *The English Novel in History*, 76–78, 211–13.

Wexler, Joyce Piell. *Who Paid for Modernism*, 81–89.

Worthen, John. *D. H. Lawrence*, 21–31.

Worthen, John. "Orts and Slarts: Two Biographical Pieces on D. H. Lawrence." *R of Engl Stud* 46 (1995), 32–40.

The Trespasser, 1912

Bjorken, Cecilia. *Into the Isle of Self*, 11–236.

Miller, Jane Eldridge. *Rebel Women,* 105–7.

Squires, Michael. "D. H. Lawrence's Narrators, Sources of Knowledge, and the Problem of Coherence." *Criticism* 37 (1995), 472–79.

Worthen, John. *D. H. Lawrence*, 13–18.

The White Peacock, 1911

Black, Michael. "Visiting the Bottom of the Monstrous World: Allusion as Metaphor in Lawrence." *Cambridge Q* 24 (1995), 136–40.

Goodheart, Eugene. "Censorship and Self-Censorship in the Fiction of D. H. Lawrence," in George Bornstein, ed., *Representing Modernist Texts,* 225–27.

Gu, Ming Dong. "Lawrence's Childhood Traumas and the Problematic Form of *The White Peacock.*" *D. H. Lawrence R* 24 (1992), 127–43.

Hammond, Paul. *Love between Men*, 189–92.

Mester, Terri A. *Movement and Modernism*, 96–100.

Montgomery, Robert E. *The Visionary D. H. Lawrence*, 52–60.

Pecora, Vincent P. "D. H. Lawrence," in John Richetti et al., eds., *The Columbia History*, 729–31.

Squires, Michael. "D. H. Lawrence's Narrators, Sources of Knowledge, and the Problem of Coherence." *Criticism* 37 (1995), 471–72.

Worthen, John. *D. H. Lawrence*, 7–13.

Women in Love, 1920

Bell, Michael. *Literature, Modernism and Myth*, 94–97, 112–16, 150–53.

Black, Michael. "Visiting the Bottom of the Monstrous World: Allusion as Metaphor in Lawrence." *Cambridge Q* 24 (1995), 141–44.

Blanchard, Lydia. "D. H. Lawrence and his 'Gentle Reader': The Furious Comedy of *Mr Noon,*" in Paul Eggert and John Worthen, eds., *Lawrence and Comedy,* 89–91.

Carpenter, Lucas. "The Name 'Minette' in *Women in Love.*" *Engl Lang Notes* 32:1 (1994), 70–73.

Daly, Macdonald. "D. H. Lawrence and Labour in the Great War." *Mod Lang R* 89 (1994), 25–32.

Davies, Alistair. "Contexts of Reading: The Reception of D. H. Lawrence's *The Rainbow* and *Women in Love,*" in Peter Widdowson, ed., *D. H. Lawrence*, 171–80.

Doherty, Gerald. "*Ars Erotica* or *Scientia Sexualis*?: Narrative Vicissitudes in D. H. Lawrence's *Women in Love.*" *J of Narrative Technique* 26 (1996), 137–52.

Doherty, Gerald. "Death and the Rhetoric of Representation in D. H. Lawrence's *Women in Love.*" *Mosaic* 27:1 (1994), 55–71.

Eggert, Paul. "Comedy and Provisionality: Lawrence's Address to His Audience and Material in His Australian Novels," in Paul Eggert and John Worthen, eds., *Lawrence and Comedy*, 135–37.

Erzgräber, Willi. "Formen des Bewußtseins im technologischen Zeitalter: Zu D. H. Lawrences Roman *Women in Love*," in Konrad Groß et al., eds., *Das Natur/Kultur-Paradigma*, 94–112.

Feinstein, Elaine. *Lawrence and the Women*, 151–58.

Fjågesund, Peter. *The Apocalyptic World*, 31–42.

Fulweiler, Howard W. *"Here A Captive Heart Busted,"* 152–54.

Goodheart, Eugene. "Censorship and Self-Censorship in the Fiction of D. H. Lawrence," in George Bornstein, ed., *Representing Modernist Texts*, 235–37.

Hammond, Paul. *Love between Men*, 192–95.

Ingersoll, Earl. "Staging the Gaze in D. H. Lawrence's *Women in Love*." *Stud in the Novel* 26 (1994), 268–79.

Jones, Carolyn M. "Male Friendship and the Construction of Identity in D. H. Lawrence's Novels." *Lit and Theology* 9 (1995), 66–72.

Kaplan, Carola M. "Totem, Taboo, and *Blutbrüderschaft* in D. H. Lawrence's *Women in Love*," in Carola M. Kaplan and Anne B. Simpson, eds., *Seeing Double*, 113–27.

Kim, Sung Ryol. "The Vampire Lust in D. H. Lawrence." *Stud in the Novel* 25 (1993), 438–47.

Levenson, Michael. *Modernism and the Fate of Individuality*, 145–65.

Lewiecki-Wilson, Cynthia. *Writing Against the Family*, 102–8.

Martin, Graham. "D. H. Lawrence and Class," in Peter Widdowson, ed., *D. H. Lawrence*, 39–43.

Mester, Terri A. *Movement and Modernism*, 111–16.

Miller, Donna R. "D. H. Lawrence Revisited: By Way of Bakhtin." *Lingua e Stile* 29 (1994), 307–20.

Mills, Howard. "Mischief or Merriment, Amazement and Amusement—and Malice: *Women in Love*," in Paul Eggert and John Worthen, eds., *Lawrence and Comedy*, 45–66.

Montgomery, Robert E. *The Visionary D. H. Lawrence*, 111–31, 152–67.

O'Hara, Daniel. "The Power of Nothing in *Women in Love*," in Peter Widdowson, ed., *D. H. Lawrence*, 146–58.

Pecora, Vincent P. "D. H. Lawrence," in John Richetti et al., eds., *The Columbia History*, 718–20, 722–24, 726–29, 731–35.

Perkins, Wendy. "Reading Lawrence's Frames: Chapter Division in *Women in Love*." *D. H. Lawrence R* 24 (1992), 229–45.

Pinkney, Tony. "Northernness and Modernism (*The Rainbow, Women in Love*)," in Peter Widdowson, ed., *D. H. Lawrence*, 191–94.

Ross, Charles L. "Editing as Interpretation: Self-Censorship and Collaboration in the Cambridge Edition of *The Rainbow* and *Women in Love*," in Charles L. Ross and Dennis Jackson, eds., *Editing D. H. Lawrence*, 87–96.

Salgâdo, Gâmini. "Taking a Nail for a Walk: On Reading *Women in Love,*" in Peter Widdowson, ed., *D. H. Lawrence,* 137–44.

Siegel, Carol. *Male Masochism,* 91–95.

Sklenicka, Carol, and Mark Spilka. "A Womb of His Own: Lawrence's Passional/Parental View of Childhood," in Elizabeth Goodenough et al., eds., *Infant Tongues,* 165–67.

Smith, Evans Lansing. *Ricorso and Revelation,* 69–75, 101–6.

Squires, Michael. "D. H. Lawrence's Narrators, Sources of Knowledge, and the Problem of Coherence." *Criticism* 37 (1995), 482–88.

Stevenson, Randall. *A Reader's Guide,* 34–36.

Stewart, Jack F. "The Myth of the Fall in *Women in Love.*" *Philol Q* 74 (1995), 443–60.

Taylor, Neil. "A Woman's Love: D. H. Lawrence on Film," in Peter Reynolds, ed., *Novel Images,* 106–20.

Trotter, David. "The Avoidance of Naturalism: Gissing, Moore, Grand, Bennett, and Others," in John Richetti et al., eds., *The Columbia History,* 621–23.

Trotter, David. *The English Novel in History,* 124–27, 189–93.

Turner, Martha A. *Mechanism and the Novel,* 135–52.

Wexler, Joyce Piell. *Who Paid for Modernism,* 94–97, 101–3.

Worthen, John. *D. H. Lawrence,* 50–56.

JOHN LE CARRÉ

The Spy Who Came in from the Cold, 1963

Thompson, Jon. *Fiction, Crime, and Empire,* 152–60.

HARRIET LEE

Kruitzner, 1801

Shaffer, Julie. "Non-Canonical Women's Novels of the Romantic Era: Romantic Ideologies and the Problematics of Gender and Genre." *Stud in the Novel* 28 (1996), 474–80.

SOPHIA LEE

The Recess, 1785

Alliston, April. *Virtue's Faults,* 148–87.

Botting, Fred. *Gothic,* 56–59.

Haggerty, George E. "The Gothic Novel, 1764–1824," in John Richetti et al., eds., *The Columbia History,* 226–27.

Isaac, Megan Lynn. "Sophia Lee and the Gothic of Female Community." *Stud in the Novel* 28 (1996), 200–216.

Lewis, Jayne Elizabeth. " 'Ev'ry Lost Relation': Historical Fictions and

Sentimental Incidents in Sophia Lee's *The Recess." Eighteenth-Cent Fiction* 7 (1995), 165–84.

MacCarthy, B. G. *The Female Pen,* 381–84.

JOSEPH SHERIDAN LEFANU

Carmilla, 1872

Andriano, Joseph. *Our Ladies of Darkness,* 98–105.

Auerbach, Nina. *Our Vampires, Ourselves,* 38–59, 94–96.

Botting, Fred. *Gothic,* 144–45.

Heller, Tamar. "The Vampire in the House: Hysteria, Female Sexuality, and Female Knowledge in Le Fanu's 'Carmilla' (1872)," in Barbara Leah Harman and Susan Meyer, eds., *The New Nineteenth Century,* 77–91.

Lapinski, Piya Pal. "Dickens's Miss Wade and J. S. Le Fanu's Carmilla: The Female Vampire in *Little Dorrit." Dickens Q* 11 (1994), 81–86.

Signorotti, Elizabeth. "Repossessing the Body: Transgressive Desire in 'Carmilla' and *Dracula." Criticism* 38 (1996), 607–19.

The Cock and Anchor, 1845

Spence, Joseph. "Allegories for a Protestant Nation: Irish Tory Historical Fiction, 1820–1850." *Rel and Lit* 28:2–3 (1996), 70–73.

Guy Deverell, 1865

Achilles, Jochen. "Fantasy as Psychological Necessity: Sheridan Le Fanu's Fiction," in Allan Lloyd Smith and Victor Sage, eds., *Gothick Origins and Innovations,* 156–58.

The House by the Churchyard, 1863

Achilles, Jochen. "Fantasy as Psychological Necessity: Sheridan Le Fanu's Fiction," in Allan Lloyd Smith and Victor Sage, eds., *Gothick Origins and Innovations,* 154–56.

Uncle Silas, 1864

McCormack, W. J. *From Burke to Beckett,* 182–85, 190–92.

Milbank, Alison. "From the Sublime to the Uncanny: Victorian Gothic and Sensation Fiction," in Allan Lloyd Smith and Victor Sage, eds., *Gothick Origins and Innovations,* 174–77.

Sage, Victor. "Gothic Laughter: Farce and Horror in Five Texts," in Allan Lloyd Smith and Victor Sage, eds., *Gothick Origins and Innovations,* 193–95.

Wylder's Hand, 1864

Horsman, Alan. *The Victorian Novel,* 226–28.

ROSAMOND LEHMANN

Dusty Answer, 1927

> Griffin, Gabriele. *Heavenly Love?*, 29–31.

The Weather in the Streets, 1936

> Joannou, Maroula. *'Ladies, Please Don't Smash These Windows,'* 127–58.
>
> Simons, Judy. "Rosamond Lehmann: *The Weather in the Streets,*" in Patrick J. Quinn, ed., *Recharting the Thirties*, 174–84.

CHARLOTTE LENNOX

Euphemia, 1790

> Berg, Temma F. "Getting the Mother's Story Right: Charlotte Lennox and the New World." *Papers on Lang and Lit* 32 (1996), 371–95.
>
> Ellison, Julie. "There and Back: Transatlantic Novels and Anglo-American Careers," in Carla H. Hay and Syndy M. Conger, eds., *The Past as Prologue*, 315–21.

The Female Quixote, 1752

> Barreca, Regina. *Untamed and Unabashed*, 34–44.
>
> Bartolomeo, Joseph F. "Female Quixotism v. 'Feminine' Tragedy: Lennox's Comic Revision of *Clarissa,*" in Albert J. Rivero, ed., *New Essays*, 163–73.
>
> Gardiner, Ellen. "Writing Men Reading in Charlotte Lennox's *The Female Quixote.*" *Stud in the Novel* 28 (1996), 1–9.
>
> MacCarthy, B. G. *The Female Pen,* 295–301.
>
> Malina, Debra. "Rereading the Patriarchal Text: *The Female Quixote, Northanger Abbey,* and the Trace of the Absent Mother." *Eighteenth-Cent Fiction* 8 (1996), 271–92.
>
> Motooka, Wendy. "Coming to a Bad End: Sentimentalism, Hermeneutics, and *The Female Quixote.*" *Eighteenth-Cent Fiction* 8 (1996), 251–70.
>
> Spacks, Patricia Meyer. *Desire and Truth,* 12–33.
>
> Todd, Janet. *The Sign of Angellica,* 152–60.
>
> Woodward, Carolyn. " 'My Heart So Wrapt': Lesbian Disruptions in Eighteenth-Century British Fiction." *Signs* 18 (1993), 857–60.

Henrietta, 1758

> MacCarthy, B. G. *The Female Pen,* 301–4.

The Life of Harriot Stuart, 1751

> Berg, Temma F. "Getting the Mother's Story Right: Charlotte Lennox and the New World." *Papers on Lang and Lit* 32 (1996), 369–95.

JOSEPHINE CAMPBELL LESLIE

The Ghost and Mrs. Muir, 1945

Stetz, Margaret D. "*The Ghost and Mrs. Muir:* Laughing With the Captain in the House." *Stud in the Novel* 28 (1996), 93–111.

DORIS LESSING

Briefing for a Descent into Hell, 1971

Armitt, Lucie. *Theorising the Fantastic,* 89–103.

Carter, Nancy Corson. "Shamanism in a Threatened World: Doris Lessing's *Briefing for a Descent into Hell.*" *J of the Fantastic in the Arts* 2:3 (1990), 5–13.

Cederstrom, Lorelei. *Fine-Tuning the Feminine Psyche,* 135–49.

Franko, Carol. "Authority, Truthtelling, and Parody: Doris Lessing and 'the Book.' " *Papers on Lang and Lit* 31 (1995), 275–83.

Galván, Fernando. "Travel Writing in British Metafiction: A Proposal for Analysis," in Theo D'haen and Hans Bertens, eds., *British Postmodern Fiction,* 84–87.

Hynes, Joseph. "Doris Lessing's *Briefing* as Structural Life and Death." *Renascence* 46 (1994), 225–43.

Rowe, Margaret Moan. *Doris Lessing,* 62–67.

Rowland, Susan. "Esoteric Lessing: C. G. Jung, Rudolf Steiner and the Colonial Author." *Doris Lessing Newsl* 17:2 (1995), 5, 13–15.

Rubenstein, Roberta. "Fixing the Past: Yearning and Nostalgia in Woolf and Lessing," in Ruth Saxton and Jean Tobin, eds., *Woolf and Lessing,* 22–24.

Smith, Evans Lansing. "Doris Lessing's Descent into Hades." *Doris Lessing Newsl* 17:2 (1995), 4, 11–13.

Canopus in Argos, 1979–1983

Cederstrom, Lorelei. *Fine-Tuning the Feminine Psyche,* 191–207.

Hanley, Lynne. "Sleeping with the Enemy: Doris Lessing in the Century of Destruction," in John Richetti et al., eds., *The Columbia History,* 932–35.

Meaney, Gerardine. *(Un)Like Subjects,* 69–72.

Rowe, Margaret Moan. *Doris Lessing,* 77–90.

Sage, Lorna. *Women in the House of Fiction,* 21–23.

Turner, Martha A. *Mechanism and the Novel,* 155–70.

Children of Violence, 1952–1969

Cederstrom, Lorelei. *Fine-Tuning the Feminine Psyche,* 31–116.

Greene, Gayle. *Doris Lessing,* 35–56.

Nichols, Nina daVinci. *Ariadne's Lives,* 130–45.

Sceats, Sarah. "Eating the Evidence: Women, Power, and Food," in Sarah Sceats and Gail Cunningham, eds., *Image and Power,* 118–20.

Schneider, Karen. *Loving Arms,* 137–53, 161–73.

Tyler, Lisa. "Self-Hatred and the Demonic in Doris Lessing's Fiction." *Doris Lessing Newsl* 16:2 (1994), 4–5, 13.

The Diaries of Jane Somers, 1984

Greene, Gayle. *Doris Lessing*, 189–204.

Rowe, Margaret Moan. *Doris Lessing*, 93–97.

Saxton, Ruth. "The Female Body Veiled: From Crocus to Clitoris," in Ruth Saxton and Jean Tobin, eds., *Woolf and Lessing*, 117–18.

The Fifth Child, 1988

Hanley, Lynne. "Sleeping with the Enemy: Doris Lessing in the Century of Destruction," in John Richetti et al., eds., *The Columbia History*, 925–26.

Held, Helmuth. "Fokalisierung und Ironie in Doris Lessings Roman *The Fifth Child:* Ein Beitrag zur Rehabilitierung des unschuldigen Protagonisten." *Literatur in Wissenschaft und Unterricht* 28 (1995), 277–84.

Marinovich, Sarolta. "The Discourse of the Other: Female Gothic in Contemporary Women's Writing." *Neohelicon* 21:1 (1994), 201–5.

Perrakis, Phyllis Sternberg. "The Female Gothic and the (M)other in Atwood and Lessing." *Doris Lessing Newsl* 17:1 (1995), 11–14.

Rowe, Margaret Moan. *Doris Lessing*, 103–9.

Rowen, Norma. "Frankenstein Revisited: Doris Lessing's *The Fifth Child.*" *J of the Fantastic in the Arts* 2:3 (1990), 41–49.

The Four-Gated City, 1969

Cederstrom, Lorelei. *Fine-Tuning the Feminine Psyche*, 95–116.

Greene, Gayle. *Doris Lessing*, 73–91.

Hanley, Lynne. "Sleeping with the Enemy: Doris Lessing in the Century of Destruction," in John Richetti et al., eds., *The Columbia History*, 922–23.

Rowe, Margaret Moan. *Doris Lessing*, 47–58.

Saxton, Ruth. "The Female Body Veiled: From Crocus to Clitoris," in Ruth Saxton and Jean Tobin, eds., *Woolf and Lessing*, 115–16.

Schneider, Karen. *Loving Arms*, 161–68, 171–73.

Sizemore, Christine W. "The 'Outsider-Within': Virginia Woolf and Doris Lessing as Urban Novelists in *Mrs. Dalloway* and *The Four-Gated City,*" in Ruth Saxton and Jean Tobin, eds., *Woolf and Lessing*, 66–71.

The Golden Notebook, 1962

Arlett, Robert. *Epic Voices*, 23–66.

Boehm, Beth A. "Reeducating Readers: Creating New Expectations for *The Golden Notebook.*" *Narrative* 5:1 (1997), 88–97.

Bridgeporte, Virginia Eliot. "The Image of a Woman Moving from Chaos to Order in Doris Lessing's *The Golden Notebook.*" *Mount Olive R* 6 (1992), 9–24.

Brightwell, Gerri. "Flags and Filters: The Influence of Color in *The Golden Notebook.*" *Doris Lessing Newsl* 16:1 (1994), 3, 7, 14–15.

Cederstrom, Lorelei. *Fine-Tuning the Feminine Psyche*, 117–34.

Davis, Rick. "*The Golden Notebook* as Auto-Vivisection." *Doris Lessing Newsl* 16:1 (1994), 1, 10–12.

English, James F. *Comic Transactions*, 160–205.

Fahim, Shadia S. *Doris Lessing*, 51–84.

Franko, Carol. "Authority, Truthtelling, and Parody: Doris Lessing and 'the Book.' " *Papers on Lang and Lit* 31 (1995), 264–74.

Gasiorek, Andrzej. *Post-War British Fiction*, 84–92.

Greene, Gayle. *Doris Lessing*, 93–121.

Hanley, Lynne. "Sleeping with the Enemy: Doris Lessing in the Century of Destruction," in John Richetti et al., eds., *The Columbia History*, 923–27.

Meaney, Gerardine. *(Un)Like Subjects*, 67–69.

Mepham, John. "The Intellectual as Heroine: Reading and Gender," in Sarah Sceats and Gail Cunningham, eds., *Image and Power*, 17–27.

Michael, Magali Cornier. *Feminism and the Postmodern Impulse*, 79–108.

Michael, Magali Cornier. "Woolf's *Between the Acts* and Lessing's *The Golden Notebook:* From Modern to Postmodern Subjectivity," in Ruth Saxton and Jean Tobin, eds., *Woolf and Lessing*, 46–54.

Roberts, Nora Ruth. "Three Generations of Radical Women's Man-Talk," in Janet Doubler Ward and JoAnna Stephens Mink, eds., *Communication and Women's Friendships*, 138–43.

Rowe, Margaret Moan. *Doris Lessing*, 36–45.

Sage, Lorna. *Women in the House of Fiction*, 13–17.

Schneider, Karen. *Loving Arms*, 153–61.

Sprague, Claire. "Multipersonal and Dialogic Modes in *Mrs. Dalloway* and *The Golden Notebook*," in Ruth Saxton and Jean Tobin, eds., *Woolf and Lessing*, 8–13.

Tobin, Jean. "On Creativity: Woolf's *The Waves* and Lessing's *The Golden Notebook*," in Ruth Saxton and Jean Tobin, eds., *Woolf and Lessing*, 160–79.

Tyler, Lisa. "Self-Hatred and the Demonic in Doris Lessing's Fiction." *Doris Lessing Newsl* 16:2 (1994), 4–5, 13.

Wyatt, Jean. *Reconstructing Desire*, 149–63.

Zelter, Joachim. *Sinnhafte Fiktion und Wahrheit*, 214–17.

The Good Terrorist, 1985

Boschman, Robert. "Excrement and 'Kitsch' in Doris Lessing's *The Good Terrorist*." *Ariel* 25:3 (1994), 7–26.

Füger, Wilhelm. "Stimmbrüche: Varianten und Spielräume narrativer Fokalisation," in Herbert Foltinek et al., eds., *Tales and "their telling difference*," 53–54.

Greene, Gayle. *Doris Lessing*, 205–19.

Rowe, Margaret Moan. *Doris Lessing*, 97–103.

The Grass Is Singing, 1950

Cederstrom, Lorelei. *Fine-Tuning the Feminine Psyche*, 17–29.

Fahim, Shadia S. *Doris Lessing*, 19–50.

Fishburn, Katherine. "The Manichean Allegories of Doris Lessing's *The Grass Is Singing." Res in African Literatures* 25:4 (1994), 1–15.

Hanley, Lynne. "Sleeping with the Enemy: Doris Lessing in the Century of Destruction," in John Richetti et al., eds., *The Columbia History*, 928–29.

Mergenthal, Silvia. "Miranda and Caliban: White Mistresses and Black Servants in Blixen's *Out of Africa,* Lessing's *The Grass Is Singing,* and Gordimer's *July's People." Zeitschrift für Anglistik und Amerikanistik* 44 (1996), 235–37.

Roberts, Sheila. "Sites of Paranoia and Taboo: Lessing's *The Grass Is Singing* and Gordimer's *July's People." Res in African Literatures* 24:3 (1993), 73–85.

Rowe, Margaret Moan. *Doris Lessing,* 14–20.

Landlocked, 1965

Cederstrom, Lorelei. *Fine-Tuning the Feminine Psyche,* 75–94.

Greene, Gayle. *Doris Lessing,* 57–71.

Meaney, Gerardine. *(Un)Like Subjects,* 34–51.

Nichols, Nina daVinci. *Ariadne's Lives,* 138–45.

The Making of the Representative for Planet 8, 1982

Cederstrom, Lorelei. *Fine-Tuning the Feminine Psyche,* 201–3.

Rowe, Margaret Moan. *Doris Lessing,* 86–89.

The Marriages between Zones Three, Four, and Five, 1980

Cederstrom, Lorelei. *Fine-Tuning the Feminine Psyche,* 196–98.

Greene, Gayle. *Doris Lessing,* 177–88.

Meaney, Gerardine. *(Un)Like Subjects,* 87–89.

Rowe, Margaret Moan. *Doris Lessing,* 83–86.

Tiger, Virginia. " 'The words had been right and necessary': Doris Lessing's Transformations of Utopian and Dystopian Modalities in *The Marriages between Zones Three, Four, and Five." Style* 27 (1993), 63–76.

Weinhouse-Richmond, Linda. "The Politics of Motherhood." *Doris Lessing Newsl* 18:1 (1996), 3, 10–13.

Martha Quest, 1952

Cederstrom, Lorelei. *Fine-Tuning the Feminine Psyche,* 35–47.

Greene, Gayle. *Doris Lessing,* 40–43.

Nichols, Nina daVinci. *Ariadne's Lives,* 132–35.

Rowe, Margaret Moan. *Doris Lessing,* 20–24, 30–32.

Schneider, Karen. *Loving Arms,* 137–43.

The Memoirs of a Survivor, 1974

Cederstrom, Lorelei. *Fine-Tuning the Feminine Psyche,* 169–90.

Connor, Steven. *The English Novel in History,* 228–32.

Fahim, Shadia S. *Doris Lessing,* 85–135.

Granofsky, Ronald. *The Trauma Novel,* 33–43.

Greene, Gayle. *Doris Lessing,* 141–57.

Hanley, Lynne. "Sleeping with the Enemy: Doris Lessing in the Century of Destruction," in John Richetti et al., eds., *The Columbia History*, 927–28.

Rowe, Margaret Moan. *Doris Lessing*, 70–76.

Rubenstein, Roberta. "Fixing the Past: Yearning and Nostalgia in Woolf and Lessing," in Ruth Saxton and Jean Tobin, eds., *Woolf and Lessing*, 30–32.

Sage, Lorna. *Women in the House of Fiction*, 17–20.

A Proper Marriage, 1954

Adams, Alice E. *Reproducing the Womb*, 35–37.

Cederstrom, Lorelei. *Fine-Tuning the Feminine Psyche*, 49–62.

Cosslett, Tess. *Women Writing Childbirth*, 27–29, 31–33.

Greene, Gayle. *Doris Lessing*, 43–50.

Nichols, Nina daVinci. *Ariadne's Lives,* 135–38.

Rowe, Margaret Moan. *Doris Lessing*, 31–35.

Saxton, Ruth. "The Female Body Veiled: From Crocus to Clitoris," in Ruth Saxton and Jean Tobin, eds., *Woolf and Lessing*, 111–14, 119–21.

Schneider, Karen. *Loving Arms*, 143–46.

A Ripple from the Storm, 1958

Cederstrom, Lorelei. *Fine-Tuning the Feminine Psyche*, 63–74.

English, James F. *Comic Transactions*, 165–67.

Greene, Gayle. *Doris Lessing*, 50–56.

Schneider, Karen. *Loving Arms*, 146–48.

The Sentimental Agents, 1983

Cederstrom, Lorelei. *Fine-Tuning the Feminine Psyche*, 203–5.

Shikasta, 1979

Cederstrom, Lorelei. *Fine-Tuning the Feminine Psyche*, 192–96.

Fahim, Shadia S. *Doris Lessing*, 153–234.

Franko, Carol. "Dialogic Narration and Ambivalent Utopian Hope in Lessing's *Shikasta* and Le Guin's *Always Coming Home." J of the Fantastic in the Arts* 2:3 (1990), 23–33.

Hanley, Lynne. "Sleeping with the Enemy: Doris Lessing in the Century of Destruction," in John Richetti et al., eds., *The Columbia History*, 921–23.

Ingersoll, Earl G. "The Engendering of Narrative in Doris Lessing's *Shikasta* and Margaret Atwood's *The Handmaid's Tale,"* in Allienne R. Becker, ed., *Visions of the Fantastic*, 39–46.

The Sirian Experiments, 1981

Cederstrom, Lorelei. *Fine-Tuning the Feminine Psyche*, 198–202.

Hanley, Lynne. "Sleeping with the Enemy: Doris Lessing in the Century of Destruction," in John Richetti et al., eds., *The Columbia History*, 930–32.

Turner, Martha A. *Mechanism and the Novel,* 158–61.

The Summer Before the Dark, 1973

Cederstrom, Lorelei. *Fine-Tuning the Feminine Psyche*, 151–67.

Greene, Gayle. *Doris Lessing*, 123–39.

Rowe, Margaret Moan. *Doris Lessing*, 67–70.
Saxton, Ruth. "The Female Body Veiled: From Crocus to Clitoris," in
Ruth Saxton and Jean Tobin, eds., *Woolf and Lessing*, 118–20.

CHARLES LEVER

Harry Lorrequer, 1839
McCormack, W. J. *From Burke to Beckett*, 185–89.
Luttrell of Arran, 1865
McCormack, W. J. *From Burke to Beckett*, 189–91.

JUNE LEVINE

A Season of Weddings, 1992
Conrad, Kathryn. "Occupied Country: The Negotiation of Lesbianism
in Irish Feminist Narrative." *Eire-Ireland* 31:1–2 (1996), 130–32.

AMY LEVY

Reuben Sachs, 1888
Nord, Deborah Epstein. *Walking the Victorian Streets,* 202–4.
The Romance of a Shop, 1889
Nord, Deborah Epstein. *Walking the Victorian Streets,* 200–202.

C. S. LEWIS

The Chronicles of Narnia
Christopher, Joe R. "Alice's Adventures in Narnia; or, Through the
Wardrobe, and What Alice Found There." *Jabberwocky* 22:3 (1993),
3–13.
Hooper, Walter. *C. S. Lewis*, 397–451.
Myers, Doris T. *C. S. Lewis in Context*, 126–81.
The Dark Tower, 1977
Hooper, Walter. *C. S. Lewis*, 215–19.
The Horse and His Boy, 1954
Myers, Doris T. *C. S. Lewis in Context*, 156–65.
The Last Battle, 1956
Knowles, Murray, and Kirsten Malmkjær. *Language and Control,*
249–51.
Myers, Doris T. *C. S. Lewis in Context*, 174–81.

The Lion, the Witch, and the Wardrobe, 1950

>   Albu, Rodica. *"The Lion, the Witch and the Wardrobe:* or How a Roma-
>   nian Adult in the '90s Reads a British Book for Children Written in
>   1950." *Inklings* 11 (1993), 39–48.
>
>   Green, Roger Lancelyn, and Walter Hooper. *C. S. Lewis,* 237–44.
>
>   Knowles, Murray, and Kirsten Malmkjær. *Language and Control,*
>   248–49.
>
>   Myers, Doris T. *C. S. Lewis in Context,* 127–32.

The Magician's Nephew, 1955

>   Manlove, C. N. "The Birth of a Fantastic World: C. S. Lewis's *The Ma-
>   gician's Nephew." J of the Fantastic in the Arts* 1:1 (1988), 71–84.
>
>   Myers, Doris T. *C. S. Lewis in Context,* 167–74.

Out of the Silent Planet, 1938

>   Hannay, Margaret. "The Mythology of *Out of the Silent Planet." Myth-
>   lore* 76 (1994), 20–22.
>
>   Hooper, Walter. *C. S. Lewis,* 205–14.
>
>   Myers, Doris T. *C. S. Lewis in Context,* 39–56.
>
>   Sayer, George. *Jack,* 254–57.

Perelandra, 1943

>   Christensen, Inger. " 'Thy Great Deliverer': Christian Hero and Epic
>   Convention in John Milton's *Paradise Lost* and C. S. Lewis's *Per-
>   elandra,"* in Andrew Kennedy and Orm Øverland, eds., *Excursions in
>   Fiction,* 68–85.
>
>   Cutsinger, James S. "Angels and Inklings." *Mythlore* 19:2 (1993),
>   57–60.
>
>   Green, Roger Lancelyn, and Walter Hooper. *C. S. Lewis,* 169–71.
>
>   Hooper, Walter. *C. S. Lewis,* 220–30.
>
>   Myers, Doris T. *C. S. Lewis in Context,* 56–71.
>
>   Navarette, Susan J. "The Fine Reality of Hunger Satisfied: Food and
>   Desire in C. S. Lewis's *Perelandra,"* in Gary Westfahl et al., eds.,
>   *Foods of the Gods,* 97–112.
>
>   Sayer, George. *Jack,* 297–300.

Prince Caspian, 1951

>   Guroian, Vigen. "Faith and the Journey to Aslan's Kingdom." *Mod Age*
>   37 (1994), 54–62.
>
>   Myers, Doris T. *C. S. Lewis in Context,* 132–40.

The Silver Chair, 1953

>   Johnston, Richard J. "Orthodoxy and *The Silver Chair." Chesterton R*
>   19 (1993), 350–54.
>
>   Myers, Doris T. *C. S. Lewis in Context,* 150–56.

That Hideous Strength, 1945

>   Antor, Heinz. *Der englische Universitätsroman,* 539–43.
>
>   Branson, David A. "Arthurian Elements in *That Hideous Strength."
>   Mythlore* 19:4 (1993), 20–21.

Green, Roger Lancelyn, and Walter Hooper. *C. S. Lewis*, 174–79.

Hooper, Walter. *C. S. Lewis*, 231–42.

Jenkins, Philip. "Naming the Beast: Contemporary Apocalyptic Novels." *Chesterton R* 22 (1996), 493–94.

Myers, Doris T. *C. S. Lewis in Context*, 84–111.

Myers, Doris T. "Law and Disorder: Two Settings in *That Hideous Strength.*" *Mythlore* 19:1 (1993), 9–14.

Nicholson, Mervyn. "Bram Stoker and C. S. Lewis: *Dracula* as a Source for *That Hideous Strength.*" *Mythlore* 19:3 (1993), 16–22.

Sayer, George. *Jack*, 292–97.

Till We Have Faces, 1956

Green, Roger Lancelyn, and Walter Hooper. *C. S. Lewis*, 261–67.

Hooper, Walter. *C. S. Lewis*, 243–63.

Myers, Doris T. *C. S. Lewis in Context*, 190–213.

Sayer, George. *Jack*, 383–87.

Watson, Thomas Ramey. "Enlarging Augustinian Systems: C. S. Lewis' *The Great Divorce* and *Till We Have Faces.*" *Renascence* 46 (1994), 169–74.

The Voyage of the "Dawn Treader," 1952

Myers, Doris T. *C. S. Lewis in Context*, 140–48.

CECIL DAY LEWIS

The Beast Must Die, 1938

Freier, Mary P. "The First Six in a Series: Nicholas Blake," in Mary Jean DeMarr, ed., *In the Beginning*, 77–89.

Gindin, James. "C. Day Lewis: Moral Doubling in Nicholas Blake's Detective Fiction of the 1930s," in Patrick J. Quinn, ed., *Recharting the Thirties*, 152–55.

The Corpse in the Snowman, 1941

Freier, Mary P. "The First Six in a Series: Nicholas Blake," in Mary Jean DeMarr, ed., *In the Beginning*, 77–89.

Mahoney, MaryKay. "C. Day Lewis and Nicholas Blake: The Case of the Partially-Concealed Poet." *Clues* 15:2 (1994), 56–58.

Head of a Traveler, 1949

Mahoney, MaryKay. "C. Day Lewis and Nicholas Blake: The Case of the Partially-Concealed Poet." *Clues* 15:2 (1994), 58–61.

A Penknife in My Heart, 1958

Mahoney, MaryKay. "Patricia Highsmith, Nicholas Blake, and the Case of the Duplicate Murder." *Univ of Mississippi Stud in Engl* 11–12 (1993–95), 81–87.

A Question of Proof, 1935

Freier, Mary P. "The First Six in a Series: Nicholas Blake," in Mary Jean DeMarr, ed., *In the Beginning*, 77–89.

Gindin, James. "C. Day Lewis: Moral Doubling in Nicholas Blake's Detective Fiction of the 1930s," in Patrick J. Quinn, ed., *Recharting the Thirties*, 147–49.

The Smiler with the Knife, 1939

Freier, Mary P. "The First Six in a Series: Nicholas Blake," in Mary Jean DeMarr, ed., *In the Beginning*, 77–89.

There's Trouble Brewing, 1937

Freier, Mary P. "The First Six in a Series: Nicholas Blake," in Mary Jean DeMarr, ed., *In the Beginning*, 77–89.

Thou Shell of Death, 1936

Freier, Mary P. "The First Six in a Series: Nicholas Blake," in Mary Jean DeMarr, ed., *In the Beginning*, 77–89.

Gindin, James. "C. Day Lewis: Moral Doubling in Nicholas Blake's Detective Fiction of the 1930s," in Patrick J. Quinn, ed., *Recharting the Thirties*, 147–49.

Mahoney, MaryKay. "C. Day Lewis and Nicholas Blake: The Case of the Partially-Concealed Poet." *Clues* 15:2 (1994), 54–58.

MATTHEW GREGORY LEWIS

The Jewish Maiden, 1830

Galchinsky, Michael. *The Origin of the Modern Jewish Woman Writer*, 53–58.

The Monk, 1796

Andriano, Joseph. *Our Ladies of Darkness*, 31–45.

Botting, Fred. *Gothic*, 76–80.

Botting, Fred. "Power in the Darkness: Heterotopias, Literature and Gothic Labyrinths." *Genre* 26 (1993), 263–65.

Cavaliero, Glen. *The Supernatural and English Fiction*, 28–29.

Euridge, Gareth M. "The Company We Keep: Comic Function in M. G. Lewis's *The Monk,*" in Joe Sanders, ed., *Functions of the Fantastic*, 83–90.

Haggerty, George E. "The Gothic Novel, 1764–1824," in John Richetti et al., eds., *The Columbia History*, 235–37.

Howard, Jacqueline. *Reading Gothic Fiction*, 183–237.

Hushahn, Helga. "Nature and Psychology in Radcliffe and Lewis," in Valeria Tinkler-Villani and Peter Davidson, eds., *Exhibited by Candlelight*, 94–98.

Johnson, Anthony. "Gaps and Gothic Sensibility: Walpole, Lewis, Mary Shelley, and Maturin," in Valeria Tinkler-Villani and Peter Davidson, eds., *Exhibited by Candlelight*, 10–24.

Kauhl, Gudrun. "Myths of Enclosure and Myths of the Open in *The Monk* and *Wuthering Heights,*" in Valeria Tinkler-Villani and Peter Davidson, eds., *Exhibited by Candlelight*, 183–87.

Kilgour, Maggie. *The Rise of the Gothic Novel*, 142–76.

Letellier, Robert Ignatius. *Sir Walter Scott and the Gothic Novel*, 59–62, 76–81, 86–89, 105–8, 131–35, 152–57.

Meyer, Michael. "Let's Talk About Sex: Confessions and Vows in *The Monk.*" *Arbeiten aus Anglistik und Amerikanistik* 20 (1995), 307–16.

Richter, David H. *The Progress of Romance*, 93–95.

Voller, Jack G. *The Supernatural Sublime*, 61–74.

WYNDHAM LEWIS

The Apes of God, 1930

Anspaugh, Kelly. " 'Jean qui rit' and 'Jean qui pleure': James Joyce, Wyndham Lewis and the High Modern Grotesque," in Michael J. Meyer, ed., *Literature and the Grotesque*, 139–48.

English, James F. *Comic Transactions*, 67–97.

Klein, Scott W. *The Fictions of James Joyce and Wyndham Lewis*, 115–52.

Perrino, Mark. "Marketing Insults: Wyndham Lewis and the Arthur Press." *Twentieth Cent Lit* 41 (1995), 54–77.

Perrino, Mark. *The Poetics of Mockery*, 1–160.

Enemy of the Stars, 1932

Trotter, David. *The English Novel in History*, 280–83.

Tarr, 1918

Conroy, Mark. "Wyndham Lewis' Authoritarian Temptation." *Southern Hum R* 30 (1996), 24–27.

Levenson, Michael. *Modernism and the Fate of Individuality,* 121–44.

Peppis, Paul. "Anti-Individualism and the Fictions of National Character in Wyndham Lewis's *Tarr.*" *Twentieth Cent Lit* 40 (1994), 226–52.

Trotter, David. *The English Novel in History*, 284–86.

Wutz, Michael. "The Energetics of *Tarr:* The Vortex-Machine Kreisler." *Mod Fiction Stud* 38 (1992), 845–65.

FRANCES LIARDET

The Game, 1994

Smith, Jonathan. "Dissolving Adultery: Domesticity and Obscenity in *The Game,* " in Nicholas White and Naomi Segal, eds., *Scarlet Letters*, 214–27.

DAVID LINDSAY

Devil's Tor, 1932

D'Arcy, Julian Meldon. *Scottish Skalds and Sagamen*, 142–46.

The Haunted Woman, 1922

Cavaliero, Glen. *The Supernatural and English Fiction,* 84–85.
Punter, David. "The Passions of Gothic," in Allan Lloyd Smith and Victor Sage, eds., *Gothick Origins and Innovations,* 224–28.

A Voyage to Arcturus, 1920

D'Arcy, Julian Meldon. *Scottish Skalds and Sagamen,* 136–42.
Pick, J. B. *The Great Shadow House,* 73–88, 89–96.
Tigges, Wim. "The Split Personality and Other Gothic Elements in David Lindsay's *A Voyage to Arcturus,*" in Valeria Tinkler-Villani and Peter Davidson, eds., *Exhibited by Candlelight,* 243–54.

The Witch, 1976

D'Arcy, Julian Meldon. *Scottish Skalds and Sagamen,* 146–51.

ERIC LINKLATER

The Dark of Summer, 1956

D'Arcy, Julian Meldon. *Scottish Skalds and Sagamen,* 234–38.

Magnus Merriman, 1934

D'Arcy, Julian Meldon. *Scottish Skalds and Sagamen,* 222–27.

The Men of Ness, 1932

D'Arcy, Julian Meldon. *Scottish Skalds and Sagamen,* 205–14.

White-maa's Saga, 1929

D'Arcy, Julian Meldon. *Scottish Skalds and Sagamen,* 217–22.

ELIZA LINTON

The Autobiography of Christopher Kirkland, 1885

Sanders, Valerie. *Eve's Renegades,* 105–7, 180–82.

Realities, 1851

Anderson, Nancy Fix. "Eliza Lynn Linton: *The Rebel of the Family* (1880) and Other Novels," in Barbara Leah Harman and Susan Meyer, eds., *The New Nineteenth Century,* 120–24.

The Rebel of the Family, 1880

Anderson, Nancy Fix. "Eliza Lynn Linton: *The Rebel of the Family* (1880) and Other Novels," in Barbara Leah Harman and Susan Meyer, eds., *The New Nineteenth Century,* 117–31.
Sanders, Valerie. *Eve's Renegades,* 68–71.

The True History of Joshua Davidson, Christian and Communist, 1872

Anderson, Nancy Fix. "Eliza Lynn Linton: *The Rebel of the Family* (1880) and Other Novels," in Barbara Leah Harman and Susan Meyer, eds., *The New Nineteenth Century,* 124–27.

PENELOPE LIVELY

According to Mark, 1984

Moran, Mary Hurley. *Penelope Lively*, 96–110.

City of the Mind, 1991

Moran, Mary Hurley. *Penelope Lively*, 139–51.

Preston, Peter, and Paul Simpson-Housley. "Introduction: Writing the City," in Preston and Simpson-Housley, eds., *Writing the City,* 7–9.

Cleopatra's Sister, 1993

Jackson, Tony E. "The Consequences of Chaos: *Cleopatra's Sister* and Postmodern Historiography." *Mod Fiction Stud* 42 (1996), 397–417.

Juhasz, Suzanne. *Reading from the Heart,* 242–44.

Judgment Day, 1980

Moran, Mary Hurley. *Penelope Lively*, 53–69.

The Moon Tiger, 1987

McGuirk, Carol. "Drabble to Carter: Fiction by Women, 1962–1992," in John Richetti et al., eds., *The Columbia History,* 941–42.

Moran, Mary Hurley. *Penelope Lively*, 111–27.

Raschke, Debrah. "Penelope Lively's *Moon Tiger:* Re-envisioning a 'history of the world.' " *Ariel* 26:4 (1995), 115–31.

Next to Nature, Art, 1982

Moran, Mary Hurley. *Penelope Lively*, 70–79.

Passing On, 1989

Moran, Mary Hurley. *Penelope Lively*, 128–39.

Perfect Happiness, 1983

Moran, Mary Hurley. *Penelope Lively*, 80–95.

The Road to Lichfield, 1977

Moran, Mary Hurley. *Penelope Lively*, 29–39.

Treasures of Time, 1979

Moran, Mary Hurley. *Penelope Lively*, 39–52.

CHARLES LLOYD

Edmund Oliver, 1798

Allen, Richard C. "Charles Lloyd, Coleridge, and *Edmund Oliver.*" *Stud in Romanticism* 35 (1996), 245–94.

JOHN GIBSON LOCKHART

Reginald Dalton, 1823

Antor, Heinz. *Der englische Universitätsroman,* 112–15, 207–8.

DAVID LODGE

The British Museum Is Falling Down, 1965
> Pfandl-Buchegger, Ingrid. *David Lodge als Literaturkritiker,* 233–51.

Changing Places, 1975
> Pfandl-Buchegger, Ingrid. *David Lodge als Literaturkritiker,* 279–309.
> Spiering, M. *Englishness,* 48–50, 79–91.

Ginger, You're Barmy, 1962
> Pfandl-Buchegger, Ingrid. *David Lodge als Literaturkritiker,* 214–31.
> Taylor, D. J. *After the War,* 85–87.

How Far Can You Go?, 1980
> Chouleur, Jacques. "L'Introuvable juste milieu (ou la mutation des Catholiques anglais dans *How Far Can You Go,* roman de David Lodge)." *Mythes, Croyances et Religions dans le Monde Anglo-Saxon* 5 (1987), 49–57.
> Pfandl-Buchegger, Ingrid. *David Lodge als Literaturkritiker,* 310–56.

Nice Work, 1988
> Antor, Heinz. *Der englische Universitätsroman,* 666–69, 686–92.
> Böhm, Rudolf. "Universität und Industrie: 'Zwei Nationen' in David Lodges *Nice Work,*" in Konrad Groß et al., eds., *Das Natur/Kultur-Paradigma,* 222–36.
> Burton, Robert S. "Standoff at the Crossroads: When Town Meets Gown in David Lodge's *Nice Work.*" *Critique* (Washington, DC) 35 (1994), 237–42.
> Carbone, Paola. "Musa industriale e malattia post-moderna: l'elemento meta-letterario in *Nice Work* di David Lodge." *Confronto Letterario* 9:18 (1992), 345–76.
> Connor, Steven. *The English Novel in History,* 74–82.
> Lodge, David. "Adapting *Nice Work* for Television," in Peter Reynolds, ed., *Novel Images,* 191–203.
> Schütz, Erhard. "Aus der Arbeitswelt: Literaturprofessoren und andere Müßiggänger—David Lodge, *Nice Work,* und Thomas Mann, *Der Zauberberg,*" in Eberhard Lämmert and Barbara Naumann, eds., *Wer sind wir?,* 229–37.
> Schwend, Joachim. "Angewandte Literaturwissenschaft? *Nice Work* als Schlüsselroman für das literarische und kritische Werk von David Lodge." *Anglistik* 6:2 (1995), 76–92.

Out of the Shelter, 1970
> Pfandl-Buchegger, Ingrid. *David Lodge als Literaturkritiker,* 252–78.

The Picturegoers, 1960
> Pfandl-Buchegger, Ingrid. *David Lodge als Literaturkritiker,* 193–213.

Small World, 1984
> Maack, Annegret. "Die *romance* als postmoderne Romanform?" *Literatur in Wissenschaft und Unterricht* 26 (1993), 274–76.

Pfandl-Buchegger, Ingrid. *David Lodge als Literaturkritiker*, 357–461.

Schütz, Erhard. "Aus der Arbeitswelt: Literaturprofessoren und andere Müßiggänger—David Lodge, *Nice Work*, und Thomas Mann, *Der Zauberberg*," in Eberhard Lämmert and Barbara Naumann, eds., *Wer sind wir?*, 221–29.

THOMAS LODGE

A Margarite of America, 1596

Relihan, Constance C. *Fashioning Authority*, 18–20.

Robin the Devil, 1591

Cantar, Brenda. "Monstrous Conceptions and Lodge's *Robin the Devil*." *Stud in Engl Lit, 1500–1900* 37 (1997), 39–51.

Rosalynde, 1590

Relihan, Constance C. *Fashioning Authority*, 85–87.

Stanivukovic, Goran V. "Rhetoric as a Narrative Instrument in Thomas Lodge's *Rosalynde*," in Wolfgang Görtschacher and Holger Klein, eds., *Narrative Strategies*, 225–38.

MALCOLM LOWRY

Dark as the Grave Wherein My Friend Is Laid, 1968

McCarthy, Patrick A. *Forests of Symbols*, 141–54.

Lunar Caustic, 1968

Filipczak, Dorota. "Theology in Asylum: The Failure of Salvific Story in Malcolm Lowry's *Lunar Caustic*." *Lit and Theology* 8 (1994), 394–404.

McAlice, Edward. "A Cocteau Allusion in Lowry's *Lunar Caustic*." *Notes on Contemp Lit* 25:3 (1995), 6–7.

McCarthy, Patrick A. *Forests of Symbols*, 35–43.

October Ferry to Gabriola, 1970

McCarthy, Patrick A. *Forests of Symbols*, 166–75.

Ultramarine, 1933

Kim, Suzanne. "*A Portrait of the Artist as a Young Man* and *Ultramarine*: Two Exercises in Identification," in Patrick A. McCarthy and Paul Tiessen, eds., *Joyce/Lowry*, 109–24.

McCarthy, Patrick A. *Forests of Symbols*, 16–20, 34–36.

Under the Volcano, 1947

Ackerley, Chris. " 'Well, of course, if we knew all the things': Coincidence and Design in *Ulysses* and *Under the Volcano*," in Patrick A. McCarthy and Paul Tiessen, eds., *Joyce/Lowry*, 41–58.

Bock, Martin. "Syphilisation and Its Discontents: Somatic Indications of

Psychological Ills in Joyce and Lowry," in Patrick A. McCarthy and Paul Tiessen, eds., *Joyce/Lowry*, 132–34, 136–37.

Costa, Richard Hauer. *An Appointment with Somerset Maugham*, 143–60.

Cross, Richard K. "*Ulysses* and *Under the Volcano:* The Difficulty of Loving," in Patrick A. McCarthy and Paul Tiessen, eds., *Joyce/Lowry*, 63–79.

Duplay, Mathieu. "Les apories du personnage dans *Under the Volcano.*" *Recherches Anglaises et Nord-Américaines* 28 (1995), 65–79.

Grace, Sherrill. "Midsummer Madness and the Day of the Dead: Joyce, Lowry, and Expressionism," in Patrick A. McCarthy and Paul Tiessen, eds., *Joyce/Lowry*, 9–18.

Hughes, Rebecca, and Kieron O'Hara. "The Filmmaker as Critic: Huston's *Under the Volcano* and *The Dead,*" in Patrick A. McCarthy and Paul Tiessen, eds., *Joyce/Lowry*, 177–95.

Lawn, Jennifer. "Four Characters in Search of a Narrator: Focalization and the Representation of Consciousness in *Under the Volcano.*" *Stud in Canadian Lit* 18:2 (1993), 110–31.

McCarthy, Patrick A. *Forests of Symbols*, 2–10, 44–115.

McCarthy, Patrick A. "The World as Book, the Book as Machine: Art and Life in Joyce and Lowry," in Patrick A. McCarthy and Paul Tiessen, eds., *Joyce/Lowry*, 145–56.

Norton, Andrew. "Deconstructing the Oedipus Myth in Malcolm Lowry's *Under the Volcano.*" *Acta Litteraria Academiae Scientiarum Hungaricae* 32 (1990), 451–56.

O'Hara, Kieron. " 'You Do Not Know *Why* You Dance': Comedy in *Under the Volcano,* 'Through the Panama,' and 'Tender Is the Night.' " *Malcolm Lowry R* 31–32 (1992–93), 68–84.

Shaffer, Brian W. "Nationalism at the Bar: Anti-Semitism in *Ulysses* and *Under the Volcano,*" in Patrick A. McCarthy and Paul Tiessen, eds., *Joyce/Lowry*, 84–93.

Stevenson, Randall. *A Reader's Guide*, 88–90.

Vice, Sue. "The Construction of Femininity in *Ulysses* and *Under the Volcano:* A Bakhtinian Analysis of the Late Draft Versions," in Patrick A. McCarthy and Paul Tiessen, eds., *Joyce/Lowry*, 96–106.

Voelker, Joseph C. "Clown Meets Cops: Comedy and Paranoia in *Under the Volcano* and *Ulysses,*" in Patrick A. McCarthy and Paul Tiessen, eds., *Joyce/Lowry*, 21–39.

JOHN LYLY

Euphues, 1578

García Lorenzo, Juan Carlos. "Aspects of the Syntax of Finite Complement Clauses as Subjects in John Lyly's *Euphues: The Anatomy of Wyt.*" *Atlantis* 15:1–2 (1993), 135–52.

Pincombe, Michael. "Lyly's *Euphues:* Anatomy or Peep-Show?," in

Wolfgang Görtschacher and Holger Klein, eds., *Narrative Strategies*, 103–12.

ROSE MACAULAY

Abbots Verney, 1906
  Crawford, Alice. *Paradise Pursued*, 27–32.

And No Man's Wit, 1940
  Crawford, Alice. *Paradise Pursued*, 130–35.

Crewe Train, 1926
  Crawford, Alice. *Paradise Pursued*, 99–102.
  Thomas, Sue. "Libertarian Liberalism and the Comic Mode: Rose Macauley's Fiction of the 1920s." *Durham Univ J* 86 (1994), 99.

Dangerous Ages, 1921
  Crawford, Alice. *Paradise Pursued*, 80–85.
  Thomas, Sue. "Libertarian Liberalism and the Comic Mode: Rose Macauley's Fiction of the 1920s." *Durham Univ J* 86 (1994), 100.

The Furnace, 1907
  Crawford, Alice. *Paradise Pursued*, 32–36.

Going Abroad, 1934
  Crawford, Alice. *Paradise Pursued*, 121–27.

I Would Be Private, 1937
  Crawford, Alice. *Paradise Pursued*, 127–30.

Keeping Up Appearances, 1928
  Crawford, Alice. *Paradise Pursued*, 102–6.
  Thomas, Sue. "Libertarian Liberalism and the Comic Mode: Rose Macauley's Fiction of the 1920s." *Durham Univ J* 86 (1994), 102–3.

The Lee Shore, 1912
  Crawford, Alice. *Paradise Pursued*, 45–49.

Orphan Island, 1924
  Crawford, Alice. *Paradise Pursued*, 96–99.
  Thomas, Sue. "Libertarian Liberalism and the Comic Mode: Rose Macauley's Fiction of the 1920s." *Durham Univ J* 86 (1994), 98–99.

Potterism, 1920
  Crawford, Alice. *Paradise Pursued*, 62–65.
  Thomas, Sue. "Libertarian Liberalism and the Comic Mode: Rose Macauley's Fiction of the 1920s." *Durham Univ J* 86 (1994), 96–98.

The Secret River, 1909
  Crawford, Alice. *Paradise Pursued*, 36–39.

Staying With Relations, 1930
  Crawford, Alice. *Paradise Pursued*, 106–11.

They Were Defeated, 1932
> Crawford, Alice. *Paradise Pursued,* 116–21.

Told by an Idiot, 1923
> Crawford, Alice. *Paradise Pursued,* 85–88.

The Towers of Trebizond, 1956
> Crawford, Alice. *Paradise Pursued,* 148–56.

The Valley Captives, 1911
> Crawford, Alice. *Paradise Pursued,* 40–45.

Views and Vagabonds, 1912
> Crawford, Alice. *Paradise Pursued,* 49–53.

The World My Wilderness, 1950
> Crawford, Alice. *Paradise Pursued,* 142–46.

PATRICK MCCABE

The Butcher Boy, 1992
> Hurley, Vincent. "Recent Fictional Perspectives on Provincial Ireland." *Colby Q* 31 (1995), 27–29.

GEORGE MACDONALD

Alec Forbes of Howglen, 1865
> Boice, Daniel. "A Kind of Sacrament: Books and Libraries in the Fiction of George MacDonald." *Stud in Scottish Lit* 27 (1992), 74–75.
> Horsman, Alan. *The Victorian Novel,* 252–54.

The Golden Key, 1867
> Riso, Mary. "Awakening in Fairyland: The Journey of a Soul in George MacDonald's *The Golden Key.*" *Mythlore* 20:4 (1995), 46–51.

Lilith, 1895
> Boice, Daniel. "A Kind of Sacrament: Books and Libraries in the Fiction of George MacDonald." *Stud in Scottish Lit* 27 (1992), 77–79.
> Cavaliero, Glen. *The Supernatural and English Fiction,* 98–99.
> Pick, J. B. *The Great Shadow House,* 30–37.

Phantastes, 1858
> Gray, William N. "George MacDonald, Julia Kristeva, and the Black Sun." *Stud in Engl Lit, 1500–1900* 36 (1996), 877–91.
> Gunther, Adrian. "*Phantastes:* The First Two Chapters." *Scottish Liter J* 21:1 (1994), 32–43.

The Princess and Curdie, 1883
> Knowles, Murray, and Kirsten Malmkjær. *Language and Control,* 164–67, 170–74, 184–88.

Pennington, John. "Muscular Spirituality in George MacDonald's Curdie Books," in Donald E. Hall, ed., *Muscular Christianity*, 140–48.

The Princess and the Goblin, 1872

Cavaliero, Glen. *The Supernatural and English Fiction*, 96–97.

Knowles, Murray, and Kirsten Malmkjær. *Language and Control*, 170–72, 182–87.

Pennington, John. "Muscular Spirituality in George MacDonald's Curdie Books," in Donald E. Hall, ed., *Muscular Christianity*, 136–40.

Sillars, Stuart. *Visualisation in Popular Fiction*, 60–62.

What's Mine's Mine, 1886

Harper, Marjory. " Adventure or Exile? The Scottish Emigrant in Fiction." *Scottish Liter J* 23:1 (1996), 25–26.

Wilfrid Cumbermede, 1872

Boice, Daniel. "A Kind of Sacrament: Books and Libraries in the Fiction of George MacDonald." *Stud in Scottish Lit* 27 (1992), 75–76.

TOM MACDONALD

The Albannach, 1932

Pick, J. B. *The Great Shadow House*, 110–13.

And the Cock Crew, 1945

Pick, J. B. *The Great Shadow House*, 113–15.

The Ministers, 1979

Pick, J. B. *The Great Shadow House*, 116–18.

IAN MCEWAN

Black Dogs, 1992

Delrez, Marc. "Escape into Innocence: Ian McEwan and the Nightmare of History." *Ariel* 26:2 (1995), 7–9, 16–22.

Delville, Michel. "Marsilio Ficino and Political Syncretism in Ian McEwan's *Black Dogs*." *Notes on Contemp Lit* 26:3 (1996), 11–12.

Ryan, Kiernan. *Ian McEwan*, 61–68.

Slay, Jack, Jr. *Ian McEwan*, 140–45.

The Cement Garden, 1978

Ryan, Kiernan. *Ian McEwan*, 19–24.

Slay, Jack, Jr. *Ian McEwan*, 35–50.

Wood, Michael. "The Contemporary Novel," in John Richetti et al., eds., *The Columbia History*, 966–69.

The Child in Time, 1987

Delrez, Marc. "Escape into Innocence: Ian McEwan and the Nightmare of History." *Ariel* 26:2 (1995), 9–14.

Edwards, Paul. "Time, Romanticism, Modernism and Moderation in Ian McEwan's *The Child in Time.*" *English* 44 (1995), 41–55.

Ryan, Kiernan. *Ian McEwan*, 48–54.

Slay, Jack, Jr. *Ian McEwan*, 115–33.

Slay, Jack, Jr. "Vandalizing Time: Ian McEwan's *The Child in Time.*" *Critique* (Washington, DC) 35 (1994), 205–18.

The Comfort of Strangers, 1981

Delrez, Marc. "Escape into Innocence: Ian McEwan and the Nightmare of History." *Ariel* 26:2 (1995), 14–16.

Ryan, Kiernan. *Ian McEwan*, 33–39.

Slay, Jack, Jr. *Ian McEwan*, 72–88.

The Innocent, 1989

Ledbetter, Mark. *Victims and the Postmodern Narrative*, 88–102.

Ryan, Kiernan. *Ian McEwan*, 55–60.

Slay, Jack, Jr. *Ian McEwan*, 134–40.

Wood, Michael. "The Contemporary Novel," in John Richetti et al., eds., *The Columbia History*, 967–69.

JOHN MCGAHERN

Amongst Women, 1990

Hurley, Vincent. "Recent Fictional Perspectives on Provincial Reland." *Colby Q* 31 (1995), 24–26.

Sampson, Denis. *Outstaring Nature's Eye*, 215–41.

The Barracks, 1963

Chevalier, Jean-Louis. "Childhood in *The Barracks.*" *Etudes Irlandaises* 21:2 (1996), 171–81.

Fierobe, Claude. "Loin de Dieu, près des hommes: *The Barracks* de John McGahern." *Etudes Anglaises* 47 (1994), 445–53.

Grennan, Eamon. "John McGahern: Vision and Revisionism." *Colby Q* 31 (1995), 30–31.

O'Brien, Veronica. "*The Barracks:* What to Put Next." *Etudes Irlandaises* 21:2 (1996), 163–70.

Sampson, Denis. *Outstaring Nature's Eye*, 33–60.

The Dark, 1965

Cahalan, James M. "Female and Male Perspectives on Growing Up Irish in Edna O'Brien, John McGahern and Brian Moore." *Colby Q* 31 (1995), 62–65, 69–71.

Sampson, Denis. *Outstaring Nature's Eye*, 61–84.

The Leavetaking, 1974

Cronin, John. "John McGahern: A New Image?," in Jacqueline Genet and Wynne Hellegouarc'h, eds., *Irish Writers*, 114–16.

Grennan, Eamon. "John McGahern: Vision and Revisionism." *Colby Q* 31 (1995), 31–33.

Sampson, Denis. *Outstaring Nature's Eye*, 109–36.

The Pornographer, 1979
   Grennan, Eamon. "John McGahern: Vision and Revisionism." *Colby Q*
      31 (1995), 33–35.
   Sampson, Denis. *Outstaring Nature's Eye,* 137–61.

PATRICK MACGILL

Children of the Dead End, 1914
   Fox, Pamela. *Class Fictions,* 180–84.
The Rat-Pit, 1915
   Fox, Pamela. *Class Fictions,* 127–29.

ARTHUR MACHEN

The Great God Pan, 1894
   Hurley, Kelly. *The Gothic Body,* 46–49.
   Valentine, Mark. *Arthur Machen,* 25–34.
The Great Return, 1915
   Valentine, Mark. *Arthur Machen,* 94–96.
The Hill of Dreams, 1907
   Cavaliero, Glen. *The Supernatural and English Fiction,* 73–76.
   Valentine, Mark. *Arthur Machen,* 49–57.
   Wandrei, Donald. "Arthur Machen and *The Hill of Dreams.*" *Stud in
      Weird Fiction* 15 (1994), 27–30.
The Secret Glory, 1922
   Cavaliero, Glen. *The Supernatural and English Fiction,* 78–79.
   Valentine, Mark. *Arthur Machen,* 86–94.
The Three Imposters, 1895
   Hurley, Kelly. *The Gothic Body,* 159–67.
   Willis, Martin T. "Scientific Portraits in Magical Frames: The Construc-
      tion of Preternatural Narrative in the Work of E. T. A. Hoffmann and
      Arthur Machen." *Extrapolation* 35 (1994), 193–99.

COLIN MACINNES

Absolute Beginners, 1959
   Connor, Steven. *The English Novel in History,* 89–94.

SHENA MACKAY

Dunedin, 1992
   Smith, Penny. "Hell innit: The Millennium in Alasdair Gray's *Lanark,*
      Martin Amis's *London Fields,* and Shena Mackay's *Dunedin,*" in Lau-
      rel Brake, ed., *The Endings of Epochs,* 123–28.

COMPTON MACKENZIE

Sinister Street, 1913

Antor, Heinz. *Der englische Universitätsroman,* 499–501.

HENRY MACKENZIE

The Man of Feeling, 1771

Benedict, Barbara M. *Framing Feeling,* 117–26.

Dolan, John. "Poetry, 'Fiction' and Prose in Found Texts of the 1760s." *Genre* 28 (1995), 38–47.

Dykstal, Timothy. "The Sentimental Novel as Moral Philosophy: The Case of Henry Mackenzie." *Genre* 27 (1994), 59–78.

Gaston, Patricia S. *Prefacing the Waverley Prefaces,* 82–86.

Haggerty, George E. "Amelia's Nose; or, Sensibility and Its Symptoms." *Eighteenth Cent* 36 (1995), 143–44, 145–51.

Harkin, Maureen. "Mackenzie's *Man of Feeling:* Embalming Sensibility." *ELH* 61 (1994), 317–37.

Harries, Elizabeth Wanning. *The Unfinished Manner,* 110–13.

Hollahan, Eugene. *Crisis-Consciousness,* 44–47.

Richter, David H. *The Progress of Romance,* 74–76.

Spiegel, Maura. "Unfelt Feelings: An Evolving Grammar of Hidden Motives." *Victorian Lit and Culture* 23 (1995), 251–56.

Starr, G. A. "Sentimental Novels of the Later Eighteenth Century," in John Richetti et al., eds., *The Columbia History,* 186–90.

Van Sant, Ann Jessie. *Eighteenth-Century Sensibility,* 118–21.

Williams, Anne Patricia. "Description and Tableau in the Eighteenth-Century British Sentimental Novel." *Eighteenth-Cent Fiction* 8 (1996), 478–82.

BERNARD MACLAVERTY

Cal, 1983

Brienzo, Gary. "Belfast: Bernard Mac Laverty's Heart of Darkness," in Peter Preston and Paul Simpson-Housley, eds., *Writing the City,* 17–19, 21–27.

Simpson, Paul, and Martin Montgomery. "Language, Literature and Film: The Stylistics of Bernard MacLaverty's *Cal,*" in Peter Verdonk and Jean Jacques Weber, eds., *Twentieth-Century Fiction,* 138–61, 163–64.

Watt, Stephen. "The Politics of Bernard Mac Laverty's *Cal.*" *Eire-Ireland* 28:3 (1993), 130–46.

Lamb, 1980

Brienzo, Gary. "Belfast: Bernard Mac Laverty's Heart of Darkness," in Peter Preston and Paul Simpson-Housley, eds., *Writing the City,* 22–24.

Watt, Stephen. "The Politics of Bernard Mac Laverty's *Cal.*" *Eire-Ireland* 28:3 (1993), 138–46.

SARA MAITLAND

Three Times Table, 1991

Wisker, Gina. "Weaving Our Own Web: Demythologising/Remythologising and Magic in the Work of Contemporary Women Writers," in Wisker, ed., *It's My Party,* 122–25.

Virgin Territory, 1985

Gasiorek, Andrzej. *Post-War British Fiction,* 139–44.

THOMAS MALORY

Le Morte Darthur, 1485

Butt, Catherine. " 'Hand for Hand' and 'Body for Body': Aspects of Malory's Vocabulary of Identity and Integrity with Regard to Gareth and Lancelot." *Mod Philology* 91 (1994), 269–87.

Dauby, Hélène. "Lancelot dans *Le Morte Darthur* de Malory," in Danielle Buschinger and Michel Zink, eds., *Lancelot-Lanzelet,* 123–31.

Dimassa, Michael V. "Malory's Courteous Knights?: Gareth, Launcelot, and the Disintegration of Courtesy in the *Morte Darthur.*" *Poetica* (Tokyo) 43 (1995), 19–35.

Field, P. J. C. " 'Above Rubies': Malory and *Morte Arthure* 2559–61." *Notes and Queries* 42 (1995), 29–30.

Field, P. J. C. "The Earliest Texts of Malory's *Morte Darthur.*" *Poetica* (Tokyo) 38 (1993), 18–31.

Field, P. J. C. "Malory and the French Prose *Lancelot.*" *Bull of the John Rylands Univ Lib of Manchester* 75:1 (1993), 79–102.

Fletcher, Alan J. "King Arthur's Passing in the *Morte D'Arthur.*" *Engl Lang Notes* 31:4 (1994), 19–24.

Grimm, Kevin T. "Fellowship and Envy: Structuring the Narrative of Malory's *Tale of Sir Tristram.*" *Fifteenth-Cent Stud* 20 (1993), 77–98.

Hares-Stryker, Carolyn. "Lily Maids and Watery Rests: Elaine of Astolat." *Victorian Lit and Culture* 22 (1994), 129–50.

Harris, E. Kay. "Evidence against Lancelot and Guinevere in Malory's *Morte Darthur:* Treason by Imagination." *Exemplaria* 7:1 (1995), 179–208.

Ihle, Sandra. "Invention of Character in Malory's Grail Book," in Keith Busby and Norris J. Lacy, eds., *Conjunctures,* 181–92.

McCarthy, Terence. "*Beowulf*'s Bairns: Malory's Sterner Knights," in Leo Carruthers, ed., *Heroes and Heroines,* 149–59.

Milin, Gaël. "Le Bon Chevalier loup-garou et la mauvaise femme: L'Histoire de Sir Marrok dans *La Mort d'Arthur* de Thomas Malory." *Le Moyen Âge* 100 (1994), 65–80.

Ono, Shigeru. "Ambiguity in Malory's Language with Reference to Lancelot." *Poetica* (Tokyo) 37 (1993), 58–64.

Ross, Charles. *The Custom of the Castle*, 18–36.

Saunders, Corinne J. "Malory's *Book of Huntynge:* The Tristram Section of the *Morte Darthur.*" *Medium Ævum* 62 (1993), 270–84.

Sklar, Elizabeth S. "The Undoing of Romance in Malory's *Morte Darthur.*" *Fifteenth-Cent Stud* 20 (1993), 309–27.

Swanson, Keith. " 'God Woll Have a Stroke': Judicial Combat in the *Morte Darthur.*" *Bull of the John Rylands Univ Lib of Manchester* 74:1 (1992), 155–73.

Wimsatt, James I. "Type Conceptions of the Good Knight in the French Arthurian Cycles, Malory and Chaucer," in Leo Carruthers, ed., *Heroes and Heroines*, 137–48.

BERNARD MANDEVILLE

The Virgin Unmasked, 1709

Nelson, T. G. A. *Children, Parents, and the Rise of the Novel*, 101–4, 134–37.

MARY DELARIVIERE MANLEY

The Adventures of Rivella, 1714

Ballaster, Ros. *Seductive Forms,* 147–52.

Ballaster, Ros. "Seizing the Means of Seduction: Fiction and Feminine Identity in Aphra Behn and Delarivier Manley," in Isobel Grundy and Susan Wiseman, eds., *Women, Witing, History*, 104–8.

Ballaster, Rosalind. "Manl(e)y Forms: Sex and the Female Satirist," in Clare Brant and Diane Purkiss, eds., *Women, Texts and Histories*, 217–18, 236–37

Fabricant, Carole. "The Shared Worlds of Manley and Swift," in Donald C. Mell, ed., *Pope, Swift, and Women Writers*, 161–63, 165–67.

MacCarthy, B. G. *The Female Pen,* 207–11.

Todd, Janet. *The Sign of Angellica*, 95–98.

Memoirs of Europe, 1710

Ballaster, Rosalind. "Manl(e)y Forms: Sex and the Female Satirist," in Clare Brant and Diane Purkiss, eds., *Women, Texts and Histories*, 234–36.

The New Atalantis, 1709

Ballaster, Ros. *Seductive Forms,* 114–16, 132–36, 138–42.

Ballaster, Ros. "Seizing the Means of Seduction: Fiction and Feminine Identity in Aphra Behn and Delarivier Manley," in Isobel Grundy and Susan Wiseman, eds., *Women, Witing, History*, 103–4.

Ballaster, Rosalind. "Manl(e)y Forms: Sex and the Female Satirist," in

Clare Brant and Diane Purkiss, eds., *Women, Texts and Histories*, 226–28, 230–34.

Bowers, Toni O'Shaughnessy. "Sex, Lies, and Invisibility: Amatory Fiction from the Restoration to Mid-Century," in John Richetti et al., eds., *The Columbia History*, 61–63.

Ducrocq, Jean. "Du bon usage de la fiction: *The New Atalantis* de Delarivière Manley." *Recherches Anglaises et Nord-Américaines* 26 (1993), 63–74.

Gonda, Caroline. *Reading Daughters' Fictions*, 46–51.

MacCarthy, B. G. *The Female Pen*, 196–205.

Rabb, Melinda Alliker. "The Manl(e)y Style: Delariviere Manley and Jonathan Swift," in Donald C. Mell, ed., *Pope, Swift, and Women Writers*, 131–33, 135–42.

Todd, Janet. *The Sign of Angellica*, 87–96.

FREDERIC MANNING

Her Privates We, 1930

Raleigh, John Henry. " 'The finest and noblest book of men in war': Frederic Manning's *Her Privates We,*" in Robert M. Polhemus and Roger B. Henkle, eds., *Critical Reconstructions*, 231–50.

OLIVIA MANNING

The Doves of Venus, 1955

Taylor, D. J. *After the War*, 247–50.

THOMAS MANTE

Lucinda; or, The Self-Devoted Daughter, 1781

Cole, Richard Cargill. *Thomas Mante*, 139–47.

The Siege of Aubigny: An Historical Tale, 1782

Cole, Richard Cargill. *Thomas Mante*, 147–54.

FLORENCE MARRYAT

The Blood of the Vampire, 1897

Malchow, H. L. *Gothic Images of Race*, 168–72.

The Strange Transformation of Hannah Stubbs, 1896

Dickerson, Vanessa D. *Victorian Ghosts in the Noontide*, 143–46.

FREDERICK MARRYAT

Frank Mildmay, 1829

Horsman, Alan. *The Victorian Novel*, 13–14.

RICHARD MARSH

The Beetle, 1897
>Cavaliero, Glen. *The Supernatural and English Fiction,* 49–51.
>Hurley, Kelly. *The Gothic Body,* 124–41.

ARCHIBALD MARSHALL

Peter Binney, Undergraduate, 1899
>Antor, Heinz. *Der englische Universitätsroman,* 373–76.

FRANCES MARSHALL

A Fellow of Trinity, 1890
>Antor, Heinz. *Der englische Universitätsroman,* 335–37.

HARRIET MARTINEAU

Deerbrook, 1842
>Hobart, Ann. "Harriet Martineau's Political Economy of Everyday Life." *Victorian Stud* 37 (1994), 240–49.
>Horsman, Alan. *The Victorian Novel,* 40–42.
>Hunter, Shelagh. *Harriet Martineau,* 184–86.
>Kahn, Jacque. "Disruption and Disclosure: Women's Associations in Harriet Martineau's *Deerbrook.*" *Victorian Lit and Culture* 23 (1995), 215–29.
>Rees, Joan. *Writings on the Nile,* 22–25.

The Hour and the Man, 1841
>Rees, Joan. *Writings on the Nile,* 25–27.

JOHN CECIL MASTERMAN

An Oxford Tragedy, 1933
>Antor, Heinz. *Der englische Universitätsroman,* 531–32, 558–60.

JOHN MASTERS

Nightrunners of Bengal, 1951
>Hand, Felicity. "In the Shadow of the Mutiny: Reflections on Two Post Independence Novels on the 1857 Uprising," in Susana Onega, ed., *Telling Histories,* 65–70.

CHARLES ROBERT MATURIN

Melmoth the Wanderer, 1820

Cavaliero, Glen. *The Supernatural and English Fiction,* 29–33.

Haggerty, George E. "The Gothic Novel, 1764–1824," in John Richetti et al., eds., *The Columbia History,* 237–40.

Haslam, Richard. "Maturin and the 'Calvinist Sublime,' " in Allan Lloyd Smith and Victor Sage, eds., *Gothick Origins and Innovations,* 44–56.

Johnson, Anthony. "Gaps and Gothic Sensibility: Walpole, Lewis, Mary Shelley, and Maturin," in Valeria Tinkler-Villani and Peter Davidson, eds., *Exhibited by Candlelight,* 10–24.

Kullmann, Thomas. "Nature and Psychology in *Melmoth the Wanderer* and *Wuthering Heights,*" in Valeria Tinkler-Villani and Peter Davidson, eds., *Exhibited by Candlelight,* 100–102.

Lew, Joseph W. " 'Unprepared for Sudden Transformations': Identity and Politics in *Melmoth the Wanderer.*" *Stud in the Novel* 26 (1994), 173–93.

Oost, Regina B. " 'Servility and Command': Authorship in *Melmoth the Wanderer.*" *Papers on Lang and Lit* 31 (1995), 291–312.

Richter, David H. *The Progress of Romance,* 79–81.

Robertson, Fiona. *Legitimate Histories,* 82–85, 98–100.

Zeender, Marie-Noëlle. "John Melmoth and Dorian Gray: The Two-Faced Mirror," in C. George Sandulescu, ed., *Rediscovering Oscar Wilde,* 432–39.

The Milesian Chief, 1812

Ferris, Ina. "Narrating Cultural Encounter: Lady Morgan and the Irish National Tale." *Nineteenth-Cent Lit* 51 (1996), 301–3.

Leerssen, Joep. *Remembrance and Imagination,* 45–46.

Robertson, Fiona. *Legitimate Histories,* 216–25.

Small, Helen. *Love's Madness,* 112–17.

The Wild Irish Boy, 1808

Leerssen, Joep. *Remembrance and Imagination,* 42–45.

CONSTANCE MAUD

No Surrender, 1911

Miller, Jane Eldridge. *Rebel Women,* 144–47.

WILLIAM SOMERSET MAUGHAM

Cakes and Ale, 1930

Costa, Richard Hauer. *An Appointment with Somerset Maugham,* 16–19.

Kohl, Stephan. "Rural England in Moderne und Zwischenkriegszeit: Zur Nachgeschichte eines literarischen Konstrukts." *Poetica* (Munich) 27 (1995), 386–87.

The Moon and Sixpence, 1919

> Holden, Philip. *Orienting Masculinity*, 33–44.
> Liebman, Sheldon W. "Fiction as Fantasy: The Unreliable Narrator in *The Moon and Sixpence.*" *Engl Lit in Transition, 1880–1920* 38 (1995), 329–41.

The Narrow Corner, 1932

> Holden, Philip. *Orienting Masculinity*, 115–30.

Of Human Bondage, 1915

> Loss, Archie K. *"Of Human Bondage,"* 15–88.

The Painted Veil, 1925

> Holden, Philip. "An Area of Whiteness: The Empty Sign of *The Painted Veil.*" *Engl Stud in Canada* 20 (1994), 61–76.
> Holden, Philip. *Orienting Masculinity*, 79–93.

The Razor's Edge, 1944

> Cadogan, Mary. *And Then Their Hearts Stood Still*, 148–50.
> Holden, Philip. *Orienting Masculinity*, 131–44.

WILLIAM HAMILTON MAXWELL

O'Hara; or, 1798, 1825

> Spence, Joseph. "Allegories for a Protestant Nation: Irish Tory Historical Fiction, 1820–1850." *Rel and Lit* 28:2–3 (1996), 60–63.

FLORA MACDONALD MAYOR

The Rector's Daughter, 1929

> Joannou, Maroula. *'Ladies, Please Don't Smash These Windows,'* 89–99.
> Miller, Jane Eldridge. *Rebel Women*, 96–98.

The Third Miss Symons, 1913

> Miller, Jane Eldridge. *Rebel Women*, 96–99.

ANNA MEADES

The History of Sir William Harrington, 1771

> Dussinger, John A. "Anna Meades, Samuel Richardson and Thomas Hull: The Making of *The History of Sir Charles Grandison,*" in Albert J. Rivero, ed., *New Essays*, 177–87.

GEORGE MEREDITH

The Amazing Marriage, 1895

> Argyle, Gisela. "Meredith's 'Readable Marriage': A Polyphony of Texts." *Essays in Lit* (Macomb, IL) 22 (1995), 244–52.
> Horsman, Alan. *The Victorian Novel*, 415–17.

Beauchamp's Career, 1875

    Horsman, Alan. *The Victorian Novel,* 391–97.

    Wilding, Michael. *Social Visions,* 29–55.

Diana of the Crossways, 1885

    Horsman, Alan. *The Victorian Novel,* 407–10.

    Kranidis, Rita S. *Subversive Discourse,* 121–23.

    Lang, Claire. "Le marriage-prison dans l'œuvre de George Meredith." *Cahiers Victoriens et Edouardiens* 43 (1996), 62–63.

The Egoist, 1879

    Hollahan, Eugene. *Crisis-Consciousness,* 101–7.

    Horsman, Alan. *The Victorian Novel,* 397–404.

    Lang, Claire. "Le marriage-prison dans l'œuvre de George Meredith." *Cahiers Victoriens et Edouardiens* 43 (1996), 55–61.

    O'Hara, Patricia. "Primitive Marriage, Civilized Marriage: Anthropology, Mythology, and *The Egoist.*" *Victorian Lit and Culture* 20 (1992), 1–24.

    Smith, Jonathan. " 'The Cock of Lordly Plume': Sexual Selection and *The Egoist.*" *Nineteenth-Cent Lit* 50 (1995), 51–77.

    Turner, Martha A. *Mechanism and the Novel,* 112–18.

    Vrettos, Athena. *Somatic Fictions,* 136–42.

    Wheeler, Michael. *English Fiction of the Victorian Period,* 165–67.

Evan Harrington, 1861

    Horsman, Alan. *The Victorian Novel,* 379–80.

    Wheeler, Michael. *English Fiction of the Victorian Period,* 158–69.

One of Our Conquerors, 1891

    Brosch, Renate. "Der Anfang von *One of Our Conquerors:* Funktionalisierte Obskurität im Roman." *Literatur in Wissenschaft und Unterricht* 29 (1996), 161–70.

    Horsman, Alan. *The Victorian Novel,* 410–14.

The Ordeal of Richard Feverel, 1859

    Horsman, Alan. *The Victorian Novel,* 376–80.

    Millard, Kenneth. "My Father's Will: Self-determination and Mental Breakdown in *Basil, The Professor,* and *The Ordeal of Richard Feverel.*" *English* 44 (1995), 62–78.

    Stewart, Garrett. *Dear Reader,* 283–91.

    Turner, Martha A. *Mechanism and the Novel,* 100–112.

    Vrettos, Athena. *Somatic Fictions,* 134–36.

    Wheeler, Michael. *English Fiction of the Victorian Period,* 160–65.

Rhoda Fleming, 1865

    Cohen, Michael. *Sisters,* 146–52.

    Horsman, Alan. *The Victorian Novel,* 383–85.

    Lerner, Laurence. "Stereotypes of Woman in Victorian England," in John Morris, ed., *Exploring Stereotyped Images,* 46–48.

Swann, Charles. "A George Eliot Debt to George Meredith: From *Rhoda Fleming* to *Daniel Deronda.*" *Notes and Queries* 43 (1996), 46–47.
Sandra Belloni, 1886
Horsman, Alan. *The Victorian Novel*, 380–83.
Vittoria, 1867
Horsman, Alan. *The Victorian Novel*, 385–88.

HERMAN CHARLES MERIVALE

Faucit of Balliol, 1882
Antor, Heinz. *Der englische Universitätsroman*, 358–60.

A. A. MILNE

Winnie–the–Pooh, 1926
Connolly, Paula T. *"Winnie-the-Pooh,"* 41–116.
Hunt, Peter. *An Introduction to Children's Literature*, 112–15.
Wullschläger, Jackie. *Inventing Wonderland*, 188–91.

JAMES LESLIE MITCHELL

Grey Granite, 1934
McKenna, Brian. "The British Communist Novel of the 1930s and 1940s: A 'Party of Equals'? (And Does That Matter?)." *R of Engl Stud* 47 (1996), 375–77.
A Scots Quair, 1932–1934
Clough, R. F. *"A Scots Quair:* Ewan's Rejection of Ellen." *Scottish Liter J* 20:2 (1993), 41–48.
D'Arcy, Julian Meldon. " Chris Guthrie, Ellen Johns and the Two Ewan Tavendales: Significant Parallels in *A Scots Quair.*" *Scottish Liter J* 23:1 (1996), 42–49.
D'Arcy, Julian Meldon. *Scottish Skalds and Sagamen*, 53–63.
Fox, Pamela. *Class Fictions,* 89–93, 193–200.
Murray, Isobel. "Selves, Names and Roles: Willa Muir's *Imagined Corners* Offers Some Inspiration for *A Scots Quair.*" *Scottish Liter J* 21:1 (1994), 56–63.

NAOMI MITCHISON

The Bull Calves, 1947
Plain, Gill. *Women's Fiction of the Second World War*, 139–65.
The Land the Ravens Found, 1955
D'Arcy, Julian Meldon. *Scottish Skalds and Sagamen*, 170–74.

Memoirs of a Spacewoman, 1962

Elphinstone, Margaret. "Contemporary Feminist Fantasy in the Scottish Literary Tradition," in Robert A. Latham and Robert A. Collins, eds., *Modes of the Fantastic,* 88–90.

Lefanu, Sarah. "Difference and Sexual Politics in Naomi Mitchison's *Solution Three,*" in Jane L. Donawerth and Carol A. Kolmerten, eds., *Utopian and Science Fiction,* 153–55.

Solution Three, 1975

Lefanu, Sarah. "Difference and Sexual Politics in Naomi Mitchison's *Solution Three,*" in Jane L. Donawerth and Carol A. Kolmerten, eds., *Utopian and Science Fiction,* 158–65.

Travel Light, 1952

D'Arcy, Julian Meldon. *Scottish Skalds and Sagamen,* 165–70.

We Have Been Warned, 1935

Maslen, Elizabeth. "Sizing Up: Women, Politics and Parties," in Sarah Sceats and Gail Cunningham, eds., *Image and Power,* 200–202.

TIMOTHY MO

An Insular Possession, 1986

Yee Lin Ho, Elaine. "How Not to Write History: Timothy Mo's *An Insular Possession.*" *Ariel* 25:3 (1994), 51–63.

Todd, Richard. *Consuming Fictions,* 221–24.

Sour Sweet, 1981

Connor, Steven. *The English Novel in History,* 98–104.

Mergenthal, Silvia. "Acculturation and Family Structure: Mo's *Sour Sweet,* Kureishi's *The Buddha of Suburbia,* Ishiguro's *A Pale View of Hills,*" in Eckhard Breitinger, ed., *Defining New Idioms,* 119–22.

FRANCES MOLLOY

No Mate for the Magpie, 1985

Weekes, Anne Owens. "Ordinary Women: Themes in Contemporary Fiction by Irish Women." *Colby Q* 31 (1995), 93–94.

FLORENCE MONTGOMERY

Misunderstood, 1869

Brown, Penny. *The Captured World,* 107–10.

ROBERT BRUCE MONTGOMERY

The Case of the Gilded Fly, 1944

Antor, Heinz. *Der englische Universitätsroman,* 488–90, 597–99.

GEORGE MOORE

Aphrodite in Aulis, 1930

Christensen, Peter G. "The Aestheticized Image of Aphrodite in George Moore's *Aphrodite in Aulis." Classical and Mod Lit* 14 (1994), 127–40.

The Brook Kerith, 1916

Gray, Tony. *A Peculiar Man,* 291–97.
Grubgeld, Elizabeth. *George Moore and the Autogenous Self,* 240–42.
Welch, Robert. *Changing States,* 50–53.

Confessions of a Young Man, 1888

Gray, Tony. *A Peculiar Man,* 149–55.
Grubgeld, Elizabeth. *George Moore and the Autogenous Self,* 1–4, 36–63.

A Drama in Muslin, 1886

Bensyl, Stacia L. "Cecilia: Irish Catholicism in George Moore's *A Drama in Muslin." Eire-Ireland* 29:2 (1994), 65–76.
Gray, Tony. *A Peculiar Man,* 136–39.
Grubgeld, Elizabeth. *George Moore and the Autogenous Self,* 2–21, 65–67.
Murphy, James H. *Catholic Fiction and Social Reality in Ireland,* 29–31.

Esther Waters, 1894

Alvarez, David. "The Case of the Split Self: George Moore's Debt to Schopenhauer in *Esther Waters." Engl Lit in Transition, 1880–1920* 38 (1995), 169–82.
Gray, Tony. *A Peculiar Man,* 186–88.
Grubgeld, Elizabeth. *George Moore and the Autogenous Self,* 64–87, 200–203.
Hollahan, Eugene. *Crisis-Consciousness,* 108–10.
Kranidis, Rita S. *Subversive Discourse,* 116–18.
Lamarque, Peter, and Stein Haugom Olsen. *Truth, Fiction, and Literature,* 78–79, 83–84, 87–88.
Mothersole, Brenda. "The 'Fallen Woman' in the Victorian Novel," in John Morris, ed., *Exploring Stereotyped Images,* 208–12.
Trotter, David. "The Avoidance of Naturalism: Gissing, Moore, Grand, Bennett, and Others," in John Richetti et al., eds., *The Columbia History,* 616–18.
Trotter, David. *The English Novel in History,* 119–20.
Welch, Robert. *Changing States,* 37–39.

Evelyn Innes, 1898

Gray, Tony. *A Peculiar Man,* 264–66.
Grubgeld, Elizabeth. *George Moore and the Autogenous Self,* 204–11.

"Hail and Farewell," 1911–1914

    Gray, Tony. *A Peculiar Man*, 3–6, 35–37, 204–6, 278–80.

    Grubgeld, Elizabeth. *George Moore and the Autogenous Self*, 27–29, 103–73.

    Welch, Robert. *Changing States*, 47–50.

The Lake, 1905

    Gray, Tony. *A Peculiar Man*, 236–38.

    Grubgeld, Elizabeth. *George Moore and the Autogenous Self*, 210–31.

    Welch, Robert. *Changing States*, 45–47.

A Mummer's Wife, 1885

    Gray, Tony. *A Peculiar Man*, 126–30.

    Grubgeld, Elizabeth. *George Moore and the Autogenous Self*, 232–34.

    Mitchell, Judith. "Naturalism in George Moore's *A Mummer's Wife* (1885)," in Barbara Leah Harman and Susan Meyer, eds., *The New Nineteenth Century*, 159–76.

Sister Teresa, 1901

    Gray, Tony. *A Peculiar Man*, 264–66.

    Grubgeld, Elizabeth. *George Moore and the Autogenous Self*, 204–11.

JOHN MOORE

Zeluco, 1789

    Spacks, Patricia Meyer. *Desire and Truth*, 190–95.

HANNAH MORE

Coelebs in Search of a Wife, 1809

    Demers, Patricia. *The World of Hannah More*, 88–98.

    Gonda, Caroline. *Reading Daughters' Fictions*, 179–81.

    Tobin, Beth Fowkes. "*Mansfield Park,* Hannah More, and the Evangelical Redefinition of Virtue." *Stud on Voltaire and the Eighteenth Cent* 304 (1992), 787.

SYDNEY MORGAN

The Missionary, 1811

    Rajan, Balachandra. "Feminizing the Feminine: Early Women Writers on India," in Alan Richardson and Sonia Hofkosch, eds., *Romanticism, Race, and Imperial Culture*, 159–67.

The Wild Irish Girl, 1806

    Ferris, Ina. *The Achievement of Literary Authority*, 122–33.

    Ferris, Ina. "Narrating Cultural Encounter: Lady Morgan and the Irish National Tale." *Nineteenth-Cent Lit* 51 (1996), 295–300.

Leerssen, Joep. *Remembrance and Imagination*, 53–64.

Mellor, Anne K. "A Novel of Their Own: Romantic Women's Fiction, 1790–1830," in John Richetti et al., eds., *The Columbia History*, 344–46.

Rajan, Balachandra. "Feminizing the Feminine: Early Women Writers on India," in Alan Richardson and Sonia Hofkosch, eds., *Romanticism, Race, and Imperial Culture*, 159–61.

JAMES MORIER

The Adventures of Hajji Baba of Ispahan, 1824

Brantlinger, Patrick. "The Nineteenth-Century Novel and Empire," in John Richetti et al., eds., *The Columbia History*, 567–68.

WILLIAM MORRIS

A Dream of John Ball, 1888

Wesseling, Elisabeth. *Writing History as a Prophet*, 97–99.

News from Nowhere, 1890

Dentith, Simon. "Imagination and Inversion in Nineteenth-Century Utopian Writing," in David Seed, ed., *Anticipations,* 144–51.

Derry, Stephen. "The Time Traveller's Utopian Books and his Reading of the Future." *Foundation* 65 (1995), 16–18.

Dowling, Linda. *The Vulgarization of Art,* 69–73.

Kelsall, Malcolm. *The Great Good Place,* 138–47.

Kumar, Krishan. "A Pilgrimage of Hope: William Morris's Journey to Utopia." *Utopian Stud* 5:1 (1994), 89–107.

Mineo, Ady. "The Reverse of Salem House: The Holistic Process of Education in *News from Nowhere." J of the William Morris Soc* 11:1 (1994), 6–14.

Nellist, Brian. "Imagining the Future: Predictive Fiction in the Nineteenth Century," in David Seed, ed., *Anticipations,* 129–35.

Nichols, Ashton. "Liberationist Sexuality and Nonviolent Resistance: The Legacy of Blake and Shelley in Morris's *News from Nowhere." J of the William Morris Soc* 10:4 (1994), 20–26.

The Roots of the Mountains, 1889

Hansen, Regina. "Forms of Friendship in *The Roots of the Mountains." J of the William Morris Soc* 11:3 (1995), 19–21.

The Water of the Wondrous Isles, 1897

Boos, Florence. "The Socialist 'New Woman' and William Morris's *The Water of the Wondrous Isles." Victorian Lit and Culture* 23 (1995), 159–73.

The Well at the World's End, 1896

> Baker, Lesley A. "Romantic Realities." *J of the William Morris Soc* 10:1 (1992), 10–12.
>
> Kooistra, Lorraine Janzen. *The Artist as Critic*, 172–84.

The Wood Beyond the World, 1894

> Walter, Kay. "William Morris, *The Wood Beyond the World,* and Changing Genres in Victorian England." *Publs of the Arkansas Philol Assoc* 21:1 (1995), 99–107.

ARTHUR MORRISON

A Child of the Jago, 1896

> Fox, Pamela. *Class Fictions,* 109–18.
>
> Greenfield, John. "Ideology of Naturalism and Representation of Class in Arthur Morrison's *A Child of the Jago." Stud in the Liter Imagination* 29:1 (1996), 89–101.
>
> Kijinski, John L. "Ethnography in the East End: Native Customs and Colinial Solutions in *A Child of the Jago." Engl Lit in Transition, 1880–1920* 37 (1994), 490–500.

PENELOPE MORTIMER

The Pumpkin Eater, 1962

> Würzbach, Natascha. "The Mother Image as Cultural Concept and Literary Theme in the Nineteenth- and Twentieth-Century English Novel: A Feminist Reading within the Context of New Historicism and the History of Mentalities," in Rüdiger Ahrens and Laurenz Volkmann, eds., *Why Literature Matters*, 385.

RALPH HALE MOTTRAM

Europe's Beast, 1930

> Trout, Steven. "R. H. Mottram: The Great War and *Europe's Beast,"* in Patrick J. Quinn, ed., *Recharting the Thirties*, 54–61.

The Spanish Farm Trilogy, 1927

> Cecil, Hugh. *The Flower of Battle*, 109–16.
>
> Trout, Steven. "R. H. Mottram: The Great War and *Europe's Beast,"* in Patrick J. Quinn, ed., *Recharting the Thirties*, 52–53.

EDWIN MUIR

The Marionette, 1927

> McCulloch, Margery. *Edwin Muir*, 21–24.
>
> Pick, J. B. *The Great Shadow House*, 106–8.

Poor Tom, 1942

McCulloch, Margery. *Edwin Muir,* 28–32.

The Three Brothers, 1931

McCulloch, Margery. *Edwin Muir,* 24–28.

WILLA MUIR

Imagined Corners, 1931

Murray, Isobel. "Selves, Names and Roles: Willa Muir's *Imagined Corners* Offers Some Inspiration for *A Scots Quair.*" *Scottish Liter J* 21:1 (1994), 56–63.

ROSA MULHOLLAND

Marcella Grace, 1886

Murphy, James H. *Catholic Fiction and Social Reality in Ireland,* 20–21, 44–47.

Murphy, James H. "Rosa Mulholland, W. P. Ryan and Irish Catholic Fiction at the Time of the Anglo-Irish Revival," in Joep Leerssen et al., eds., *Forging in the Smithy,* 220–24.

The Return of Mary O'Murrough, 1908

Murphy, James H. *Catholic Fiction and Social Reality in Ireland,* 69–71.

DINAH MARIA MULOCK

Hannah, 1871

Chambers, Diane M. "Triangular Desire and the Sororal Bond: The 'Deceased Wife's Sister Bill.' " *Mosaic* 29:1 (1996), 32–35.

John Halifax, Gentleman, 1856

Lerner, Laurence. *Angels and Absences,* 126–28.

The Ogilvies, 1849

Perkin, J. Russell. "Locking George Sand in the Attic: Female Passion and Domestic Realism in the Victorian Novel." *Univ of Toronto Q* 63 (1993–94), 421–25.

IRIS MURDOCH

An Accidental Man, 1971

Gordon, David J. *Iris Murdoch's Fables of Unselfing,* 94–98.

Heusel, Barbara Stevens. *Patterned Aimlessness,* 100–117.

The Bell, 1958

Gordon, David J. *Iris Murdoch's Fables of Unselfing,* 28–32.

O'Connor, Patricia J. *To Love the Good,* 244–72.

Spear, Hilda D. *Iris Murdoch,* 27–32.

The Black Prince, 1973

> Alexander, Flora. "Iris Murdoch's Moral Comedy," in Theresa O'Connor, ed., *The Comic Tradition,* 105–6.
> Gordon, David J. *Iris Murdoch's Fables of Unselfing,* 52–60, 84–86.
> Heusel, Barbara Stevens. *Patterned Aimlessness,* 127–39, 176–88.
> Spear, Hilda D. *Iris Murdoch,* 75–81.

The Book and the Brotherhood, 1987

> Gordon, David J. *Iris Murdoch's Fables of Unselfing,* 172–76.

Bruno's Dream, 1969

> Gordon, David J. *Iris Murdoch's Fables of Unselfing,* 139–42.
> Spear, Hilda D. *Iris Murdoch,* 64–67.

A Fairly Honourable Defeat, 1970

> Gordon, David J. *Iris Murdoch's Fables of Unselfing,* 34–37, 64–68, 142–46.
> Spear, Hilda D. *Iris Murdoch,* 67–71.

The Flight from the Enchanter, 1956

> Gordon, David J. *Iris Murdoch's Fables of Unselfing,* 120–23.
> Spear, Hilda D. *Iris Murdoch,* 24–26.

The Good Apprentice, 1985

> Gordon, David J. *Iris Murdoch's Fables of Unselfing,* 164–71.
> Spear, Hilda D. *Iris Murdoch,* 100–105.
> Turner, Jack. "Iris Murdoch and the Good Psychoanalyst." *Twentieth Cent Lit* 40 (1994), 300–316.

The Green Knight, 1993

> Gordon, David J. *Iris Murdoch's Fables of Unselfing,* 178–82.
> Spear, Hilda D. *Iris Murdoch,* 109–20.

Henry and Cato, 1976

> Gordon, David J. *Iris Murdoch's Fables of Unselfing,* 151–55.
> Heusel, Barbara Stevens. *Patterned Aimlessness,* 227–29.
> Spear, Hilda D. *Iris Murdoch,* 82–87.

The Message to the Planet, 1989

> Heusel, Barbara Stevens. *Patterned Aimlessness,* 49–81, 143–55.
> Rice, Thomas J. "Iris Murdoch and Chaos: *The Message to the Planet.*" *REAL: Yrbk of Res in Engl and Am Lit* 9 (1993), 188–238.
> Sturrock, June. "Murdoch's Leech Gatherer: Interpretation in *The Message to the Planet.*" *Engl Stud in Canada* 19 (1993), 457–67.

The Nice and the Good, 1968

> Gordon, David J. *Iris Murdoch's Fables of Unselfing,* 109–15.

Nuns and Soldiers, 1980

> Gordon, David J. *Iris Murdoch's Fables of Unselfing,* 159–63.
> Heusel, Barbara Stevens. *Patterned Aimlessness,* 54–69, 140–43, 200–206.

The Philosopher's Pupil, 1983

> Gordon, David J. *Iris Murdoch's Fables of Unselfing,* 100–104.
> Heusel, Barbara Stevens. *Patterned Aimlessness,* 118–25.

The Red and the Green, 1965

> Alexander, Flora. "Iris Murdoch's Moral Comedy," in Theresa O'Connor, ed., *The Comic Tradition,* 103–5.
> Gordon, David J. *Iris Murdoch's Fables of Unselfing,* 132–34.
> Sharrock, Roger. *New Insights on English Authors,* 147–48.
> Spear, Hilda D. *Iris Murdoch,* 51–54.
> Taylor, D. J. *After the War,* 53–56.

The Sacred and Profane Love Machine, 1974

> Gordon, David J. *Iris Murdoch's Fables of Unselfing,* 89–91, 147–49.
> Siegel, Carol. *Male Masochism,* 100–102.

The Sandcastle, 1957

> Gordon, David J. *Iris Murdoch's Fables of Unselfing,* 26–28.
> Spear, Hilda D. *Iris Murdoch,* 26–27.

The Sea, the Sea, 1978

> Cavaliero, Glen. *The Supernatural and English Fiction,* 200–201.
> Gordon, David J. *Iris Murdoch's Fables of Unselfing,* 43–46, 156–59.
> Heusel, Barbara Stevens. *Patterned Aimlessness,* 69–81, 188–200.
> Nicol, Bran J. "Anticipating Retrospection: The First-Person Retrospective Novel and Iris Murdoch's *The Sea, the Sea." J of Narrative Technique* 26 (1996), 196–205.
> Sage, Lorna. *Women in the House of Fiction,* 81–82.
> Spear, Hilda D. *Iris Murdoch,* 92–100.

A Severed Head, 1961

> Siegel, Carol. *Male Masochism,* 95–100.
> Spear, Hilda D. *Iris Murdoch,* 39–46.

A Time of the Angels, 1966

> Gordon, David J. *Iris Murdoch's Fables of Unselfing,* 134–37.
> Spear, Hilda D. *Iris Murdoch,* 56–63.

Under the Net, 1954

> Alexander, Flora. "Iris Murdoch's Moral Comedy," in Theresa O'Connor, ed., *The Comic Tradition,* 100–103.
> Nicol, Bran J. "Anticipating Retrospection: The First-Person Retrospective Novel and Iris Murdoch's *The Sea, the Sea." J of Narrative Technique* 26 (1996), 192–96.
> O'Connor, Patricia J. *To Love the Good,* 231–44.
> Spear, Hilda D. *Iris Murdoch,* 20–24, 33–35.

The Unicorn, 1963

> Cavaliero, Glen. *The Supernatural and English Fiction,* 197–99.
> Gordon, David J. *Iris Murdoch's Fables of Unselfing,* 129–32.
> Spear, Hilda D. *Iris Murdoch,* 46–50.

An Unofficial Rose, 1962

> Byatt, A. S., and Ignês Sodré. *Imagining Characters*, 152–91.
> Gordon, David J. *Iris Murdoch's Fables of Unselfing,* 126–29.

A Word Child, 1975

> Gordon, David J. *Iris Murdoch's Fables of Unselfing,* 98–100.
> Heusel, Barbara Stevens. *Patterned Aimlessness*, 43–53, 158–76.

V. S. NAIPAUL

A Bend in the River, 1979

> Berger, Roger A. "Writing Without a Future: Colonial Nostalgia in V. S. Naipaul's *A Bend in the River." Essays in Lit* (Macomb, IL) 22 (1995), 144–53.
> Fersch, Annabelle F. "V. S. Naipaul's *A Bend in the River* and the Art of Re-Reading." *Commonwealth Novel in Engl* 5:2 (1992), 1–8.
> Gasiorek, Andrzej. *Post-War British Fiction,* 54–56.
> Gorra, Michael. *After Empire*, 97–99, 103–10.
> Gorra, Michael. "Rudyard Kipling to Salman Rushdie: Imperialism to Postcolonialism," in John Richetti et al., eds., *The Columbia History*, 651–54.
> Mustafa, Fawzia. *V. S. Naipaul*, 141–52.
> Narasimhaiah, C. D. *Essays in Commonwealth Literature*, 216–17.
> Sarvan, Charles. "Naipaul's *A Bend in the River:* A First-Person Narrator and the Subversion of the Text by Form," in Gordon Collier, ed., *Us/ Them*, 351–57.

The Enigma of Arrival, 1987

> Birbalsingh, Frank. "The West Indies," in Bruce King, ed., *The Commonwealth Novel*, 67–71.
> Gasiorek, Andrzej. *Post-War British Fiction,* 56–58.
> Griffiths, M. "Great English Houses/New Homes in England?: Memory and Identity in Kazuo Ishiguro's *The Remains of the Day* and V. S. Naipaul's *The Enigma of Arrival." SPAN* 36 (1993), 488–503.
> Hooker, Jeremy. *Writers in a Landscape*, 147–61.
> Levy, Judith. *V. S. Naipaul,* 97–116.
> Mustafa, Fawzia. *V. S. Naipaul*, 168–77.
> Nixon, Rob. *London Calling*, 159–63, 167–69.
> Rigik, Elnora. "Autobiography in the Fiction of V. S. Naipaul." *CEA Critic* 58:1 (1995), 55–56.
> Weiss, Timothy. "V. S. Naipaul's 'Fin de Siecle': *The Enigma of Arrival* and *A Way in the World." Ariel* 27:3 (1996), 112–16.
> Zaman, Niaz. "*The Enigma of Arrival:* Or, A Place for Mr. Naipaul," in Niaz Zaman et al., eds., *Other Englishes*, 125–35.

Guerillas, 1975

> Brice-Finch, Jacqueline. "V. S. Naipaul's Dystopic Vision in *Guerillas." Stud in the Liter Imagination* 26:2 (1993), 33–42.

Mustafa, Fawzia. *V. S. Naipaul*, 125–32.

Newman, Judie. *The Ballistic Bard*, 117–41.

Zahlan, Anne R. "Literary Murder: V. S. Naipaul's *Guerrillas*." *South Atlantic R* 59:4 (1994), 89–104.

A House for Mr. Biswas, 1961

Bahari, Razif Bin. "The Colonized Subject's Multiple and Transversal Struggle for Selfhood: The Case of *A House for Mr. Biswas*." *SPAN* 34–35 (1992–93), 16–36.

Fraser, Robert. "Fathers and Sons: Mr Biswas and Mr Soyinka." *J of Commonwealth Lit* 28:2 (1993), 93–107.

Gorra, Michael. *After Empire*, 64–69, 89–91.

Habib, Imtiaz. "Interrogating Cultures: Hybrid Subjectivity as Third Space in R. K. Narayan's *The Guide*, V. S. Naipaul's *A House for Mr. Biswas*, and Salman Rushdie's *Midnight's Children*." *Stud in the Hum* 23:1 (1996), 31–47.

Haque, Rebecca. "A Tribute to the Other Parent: The Mother in V. S. Naipaul's *A House for Mr Biswas*," in Niaz Zaman et al., eds., *Other Englishes*, 113–23.

Kapadia, Novy. "In Search of Order: A Study of V. S. Naipaul and Attia Hosain," in R. K. Dhawan and L. S. R. Krishna Sastry, eds., *Commonwealth Writing*, 113–19.

Levy, Judith. *V. S. Naipaul*, 1–37.

Mustafa, Fawzia. *V. S. Naipaul*, 58–77.

Watson, William L. "The Return of the Subaltern: The Politics of the Autonomous Self in *A House for Mr. Biswas*." *Works and Days* 22 (1993), 61–75.

Miguel Street, 1959

Gorra, Michael. *After Empire*, 81–83.

Mustafa, Fawzia. *V. S. Naipaul*, 33–44.

Narasimhaiah, C. D. *Essays in Commonwealth Literature*, 231–33.

Rao, C. Vimala. "Parallel Symmetries: Seepersad Naipaul's *The Adventures of Gurudeva* and V. S. Naipaul's *Miguel Street*," in P. K. Rajan et al., eds., *Commonwealth Literature*, 160–66.

The Mimic Men, 1967

Dhareshwar, Vivek. "Self-fashioning, Colonial Habitus, and Double Exclusion: V. S. Naipaul's *The Mimic Men*," in Arthur F. Marotti et al., eds., *Reading with a Difference*, 329–53.

Gasiorek, Andrzej. *Post-War British Fiction*, 50–54.

Mustafa, Fawzia. *V. S. Naipaul*, 100–106.

Mr. Stone and the Knights Companion, 1963

Mustafa, Fawzia. *V. S. Naipaul*, 90–92

The Mystic Masseur, 1957

Mustafa, Fawzia. *V. S. Naipaul*, 44–48, 51–54

The Suffrage of Elvira, 1958

Mustafa, Fawzia. *V. S. Naipaul*, 54–56.

A Way in the World, 1994

Rigik, Elnora. "Autobiography in the Fiction of V. S. Naipaul." *CEA Critic* 58:1 (1995), 56–59.

Weiss, Timothy. "V. S. Naipaul's 'Fin de Siecle': *The Enigma of Arrival* and *A Way in the World.*" *Ariel* 27:3 (1996), 116–22.

THOMAS NASHE

The Unfortunate Traveller, 1594

Barbour, Reid. *Deciphering Elizabethan Fiction,* 82–90.

Bauer, Matthias. *Der Schelmenroman,* 166–68.

Dorangeon, Simone. "Nashe's Unfortunate Traveller, or Absence of Narrative Consistency Disguised as Wit," in Wolfgang Görtschacher and Holger Klein, eds., *Narrative Strategies,* 259–71.

Fludernik, Monika. "Narrative Strategies in Early English Fiction: From Renaissance Prose to Aphra Behn," in Wolfgang Görtschacher and Holger Klein, eds., *Narrative Strategies,* 15–18.

Keller, James R. "Thomas Nashe's *The Unfortunate Traveler:* Taming the Spirit of Discontent." *Elizabethan R* 1:2 (1993), 7–17.

Rehder, Robert. "Realism Again: Flaubert's Barometer and *The Unfortunate Traveller,*" in Wolfgang Görtschacher and Holger Klein, eds., *Narrative Strategies,* 241–57.

Relihan, Constance C. *Fashioning Authority,* 129–30.

JOHN HENRY NEWMAN

Callista, 1856

Litvack, Leon B. "Callista, Martyrdom, and the Early Christian Novel in the Victorian Age." *Nineteenth-Cent Contexts* 17 (1993), 159–62, 167–70.

Loss and Gain: The Story of a Convert, 1848

Antor, Heinz. *Der englische Universitätsroman,* 160–63.

Heidt, Edward R. *The Image of the Church Minister,* 38–40.

BEVERLEY NICHOLS

Patchwork, 1921

Antor, Heinz. *Der englische Universitätsroman,* 481–85, 495–96, 499–501.

CAROLINE NORTON

Stuart of Dunleath, 1851

Stuart, Barbara. "Lawless Mothers," in Barbara Thaden, ed., *New Essays on the Maternal Voice,* 64–74.

MARY NORTON

Are All the Giants Dead?, 1975
  Stott, Jon C. *Mary Norton*, 109–25.
Bonfires and Broomsticks, 1957
  Stott, Jon C. *Mary Norton*, 26–34.
The Borrowers, 1952
  Stott, Jon C. *Mary Norton*, 35–66.
The Borrowers Afield, 1955
  Stott, Jon C. *Mary Norton*, 74–84.
The Borrowers Afloat, 1959
  Stott, Jon C. *Mary Norton*, 84–89.
The Borrowers Aloft, 1961
  Stott, Jon C. *Mary Norton*, 89–95.
The Borrowers Avenged, 1982
  Stott, Jon C. *Mary Norton*, 95–108.
The Magic Bed-Knob, 1943
  Stott, Jon C. *Mary Norton*, 14–26.

EDNA O'BRIEN

The Country Girls, 1960
  Cahalan, James M. "Female and Male Perspectives on Growing Up Irish
    in Edna O'Brien, John McGahern and Brian Moore." *Colby Q* 31
    (1995), 59–62.
  Otten, Kurt. "Das gespaltene Ich in Edna O'Briens Romantrilogie *The
    Country Girls.*" *Literatur in Wissenschaft und Unterricht* 27 (1994),
    79–90.
Girls in Their Married Bliss, 1964
  Cahalan, James M. "Female and Male Perspectives on Growing Up Irish
    in Edna O'Brien, John McGahern and Brian Moore." *Colby Q* 31
    (1995), 69–71.
  Otten, Kurt. "Das gespaltene Ich in Edna O'Briens Romantrilogie *The
    Country Girls.*" *Literatur in Wissenschaft und Unterricht* 27 (1994),
    79–90.
The High Road, 1988
  Conrad, Kathryn. "Occupied Country: The Negotiation of Lesbianism
    in Irish Feminist Narrative." *Eire-Ireland* 31:1–2 (1996), 128–32.
The Lonely Girl, 1962
  Cahalan, James M. "Female and Male Perspectives on Growing Up Irish
    in Edna O'Brien, John McGahern and Brian Moore." *Colby Q* 31
    (1995), 59–62.

Otten, Kurt. "Das gespaltene Ich in Edna O'Briens Romantrilogie *The Country Girls.*" *Literatur in Wissenschaft und Unterricht* 27 (1994), 79–90.

A Pagan Place, 1970

Herman, David. "Textual *You* and Double Deixis in Edna O'Brien's *A Pagan Place.*" *Style* 28 (1994), 378–404.

FLANN O'BRIEN

At Swim-Two-Birds, 1939

Booker, M. Keith. *Flann O'Brien*, 28–45, 122–25, 136–38.

Cohen, David. "An Anatomy of the Novel: Flann O'Brien's *At Swim-Two-Birds.*" *Twentieth Cent Lit* 39 (1993), 208–28.

Deane, Seamus. *Strange Country*, 157–64.

Esty, Joshua D. "Flann O'Brien's *At Swim-Two-Birds* and the Post-Post Debate." *Ariel* 26:4 (1995), 23–42.

Ferrari, Roberta. "Il labirinto diegetico: le strategie narrative in *At Swim-Two-Birds* di Flann O'Brien." *Lettore di Provincia* 24 (1992), 75–87.

McMullen, Kim. "Culture as Colloquy: Flann O'Brien's Postmodern Dialogue with Irish Tradition." *Novel* 27 (1993), 62–81.

Río Alvaro, Constanza del. "Narrative Embeddings in Flann O'Brien's *At Swim-Two-Birds.*" *Miscelanea* 15 (1994), 502–31.

Shea, Thomas F. "Patrick McGinley's Impressions of Flann O'Brien: *The Devil's Diary* and *At Swim-Two-Birds.*" *Twentieth Cent Lit* 40 (1994), 272–80.

Sturgess, Philip J. M. *Narrativity,* 235–52.

The Dalkey Archive, 1964

Booker, M. Keith. *Flann O'Brien*, 13–15, 105–20.

The Hard Life, 1961

Booker, M. Keith. *Flann O'Brien*, 85–104.

The Poor Mouth, 1941

Booker, M. Keith. *Flann O'Brien*, 66–84.

The Third Policeman, 1967

Booker, M. Keith. *Flann O'Brien*, 9–11, 17–20, 23–25, 46–65, 125–38.

Spencer, Andrew. "Many Worlds: The New Physics in Flann O'Brien's *The Third Policeman.*" *Eire-Ireland* 30:1 (1995), 145–58.

KATE O'BRIEN

The Ante-Room, 1934

Fogarty, Anne. " 'The Business of Attachment': Romance and Desire in the Novels of Kate O'Brien," in Eibhear Walshe, ed., *Ordinary Poeople Dancing*, 109–11.

Roche, Anthony. "*The Ante-Room* as Drama," in Eibhear Walshe, ed., *Ordinary Poeople Dancing*, 85–100.

As Music and Splendour, 1958

Donoghue, Emma. " 'Out of Order': Kate O'Brien's Lesbian Fictions," in Eibhear Walshe, ed., *Ordinary Poeople Dancing*, 50–56.

Feehan, Fanny. "Kate O'Brien and the Splendour of Music," in Eibhear Walshe, ed., *Ordinary Poeople Dancing*, 120–27.

The Flower of May, 1953

Walshe, Eibhear. "Lock Up Your Daughters: From Ante-Room to Interior Castle," in Walshe, ed., *Ordinary Poeople Dancing*, 158–59.

The Land of Spices, 1941

Breen, Mary. "Something Understood? Kate O'Brien and *The Land of Spices,*" in Eibhear Walshe, ed., *Ordinary Poeople Dancing*, 167–89.

Coughlan, Patricia. "Kate O'Brien: Feminine Beauty, Feminist Writing and Sexual Role," in Eibhear Walshe, ed., *Ordinary Poeople Dancing*, 79–82.

The Last of Summer, 1943

Fogarty, Anne. " 'The Business of Attachment': Romance and Desire in the Novels of Kate O'Brien," in Eibhear Walshe, ed., *Ordinary Poeople Dancing*, 113–15.

Mary Lavelle, 1936

Coughlan, Patricia. "Kate O'Brien: Feminine Beauty, Feminist Writing and Sexual Role," in Eibhear Walshe, ed., *Ordinary Poeople Dancing*, 67–76.

Donoghue, Emma. " 'Out of Order': Kate O'Brien's Lesbian Fictions," in Eibhear Walshe, ed., *Ordinary Poeople Dancing*, 41–48.

Fogarty, Anne. " 'The Business of Attachment': Romance and Desire in the Novels of Kate O'Brien," in Eibhear Walshe, ed., *Ordinary Poeople Dancing*, 112–13.

Pray for the Wanderer, 1938

Walshe, Eibhear. "Lock Up Your Daughters: From Ante-Room to Interior Castle," in Walshe, ed., *Ordinary Poeople Dancing*, 152–55.

That Lady, 1946

Walshe, Eibhear. "Lock Up Your Daughters: From Ante-Room to Interior Castle," in Walshe, ed., *Ordinary Poeople Dancing*, 159–65.

Without My Cloak, 1931

Coughlan, Patricia. "Kate O'Brien: Feminine Beauty, Feminist Writing and Sexual Role," in Eibhear Walshe, ed., *Ordinary Poeople Dancing*, 65–67.

Fogarty, Anne. " 'The Business of Attachment': Romance and Desire in the Novels of Kate O'Brien," in Eibhear Walshe, ed., *Ordinary Poeople Dancing*, 107–9.

R. B. O'BRIEN

Jack Hazlitt, 1874
   Murphy, James H. *Catholic Fiction and Social Reality in Ireland,* 55–57.

JULIA O'FAOLAIN

No Country for Young Men, 1980
   O'Connor, Theresa. "History, Gender, and the Postcolonial Condition: Julia O'Faolain's Comic Rewriting of *Finnegans Wake,"* in O'Connor, ed., *The Comic Tradition,* 124–47.

LIAM O'FLAHERTY

The Assassin, 1928
   Friberg, Hedda. *An Old Order and a New,* 109–15.
The Black Soul, 1924
   Friberg, Hedda. *An Old Order and a New,* 70–84.
The Ecstasy of Angus, 1931
   Friberg, Hedda. *An Old Order and a New,* 189–92.
Famine, 1937
   Friberg, Hedda. *An Old Order and a New,* 200–220.
Hollywood Cemetery, 1935
   Friberg, Hedda. *An Old Order and a New,* 192–98.
The House of Gold, 1929
   Friberg, Hedda. *An Old Order and a New,* 144–62.
The Informer, 1925
   Friberg, Hedda. *An Old Order and a New,* 89–99.
Insurrection, 1950
   Friberg, Hedda. *An Old Order and a New,* 241–49.
Land, 1946
   Friberg, Hedda. *An Old Order and a New,* 221–41.
The Martyr, 1933
   Deane, Paul. "The Ambiguous Rebel: Liam O'Flaherty's *The Martyr."* *Notes on Mod Irish Lit* 7:2 (1995), 22–28.
   Friberg, Hedda. *An Old Order and a New,* 177–87.
Mr. Gilhooley, 1926
   Friberg, Hedda. *An Old Order and a New,* 99–109.
The Puritan, 1931
   Friberg, Hedda. *An Old Order and a New,* 116–23.

Return of the Brute, 1929
  Friberg, Hedda. *An Old Order and a New,* 123–28.
Skerrett, 1932
  Friberg, Hedda. *An Old Order and a New,* 162–76.
Thy Neighbour's Wife, 1923
  Friberg, Hedda. *An Old Order and a New,* 60–69.
The Wilderness, 1927
  Friberg, Hedda. *An Old Order and a New,* 130–43.

MARGARET OLIPHANT

The Athelings, 1856–1857
  Martin, Carol A. *George Eliot's Serial Fiction,* 59–62.
A Beleaguered City, 1880
  Fielding, Penny. *Writing and Orality,* 207–21.
  Schor, Esther H. "The Haunted Interpreter in Oliphant's Supernatural Fiction," in D. J. Trela, ed., *Margaret Oliphant,* 97–106.
A Country Gentleman and His Family, 1886
  Williams, Merryn. "Feminist or Antifeminist? Oliphant and the Woman Question," in D. J. Trela, ed., *Margaret Oliphant,* 174–75.
The Curate in Charge, 1876
  Sanders, Valerie. *Eve's Renegades,* 71–73, 113–14, 176–77.
Hester, 1883
  Dickerson, Vanessa D. "Feminine Transactions: Money and Nineteenth-Century British Women Writers," in John Louis DiGaetani, ed., *Money,* 236–40.
  Kranidis, Rita S. *Subversive Discourse,* 92–93.
  Peterson, Linda. "The Female *Bildungsroman:* Tradition and Revision in Oliphant's Fiction," in D. J. Trela, ed., *Margaret Oliphant,* 78–81.
  Smalley, Ruth Anne. "Mothering and Mentoring: Margaret Oliphant and Surrogate Motherhood," in Barbara Thaden, ed., *New Essays on the Maternal Voice,* 100–105.
Kirsteen, 1890
  Peterson, Linda. "The Female *Bildungsroman:* Tradition and Revision in Oliphant's Fiction," in D. J. Trela, ed., *Margaret Oliphant,* 81–87.
  Smalley, Ruth Anne. "Mothering and Mentoring: Margaret Oliphant and Surrogate Motherhood," in Barbara Thaden, ed., *New Essays on the Maternal Voice,* 105–11.
  Williams, Merryn. "Feminist or Antifeminist? Oliphant and the Woman Question," in D. J. Trela, ed., *Margaret Oliphant,* 175–76.
  Williams, Merryn. "The Scottish Stories of Margaret Oliphant," in Norman Page and Peter Preston, eds., *The Literature of Place,* 83–85.

The Marriage of Elinor, 1892

Williams, Merryn. "Feminist or Antifeminist? Oliphant and the Woman Question," in D. J. Trela, ed., *Margaret Oliphant,* 176–77.

Miss Marjoribanks, 1866

O'Mealy, Joseph H. "Mrs. Oliphant, *Miss Marjoribanks* (1866), and the Victorian Canon," in Barbara Leah Harman and Susan Meyer, eds., *The New Nineteenth Century,* 63–75.

Peterson, Linda. "The Female *Bildungsroman:* Tradition and Revision in Oliphant's Fiction," in D. J. Trela, ed., *Margaret Oliphant,* 67–73.

Sanders, Valerie. *Eve's Renegades,* 73–77.

Williams, Merryn. "Feminist or Antifeminist? Oliphant and the Woman Question," in D. J. Trela, ed., *Margaret Oliphant,* 170–71.

Winston, Elizabeth. "Revising *Miss Marjoribanks." Nineteenth Cent Stud* 9 (1995), 85–94.

The Perpetual Curate, 1864

Sanders, Valerie. *Eve's Renegades,* 110–12.

Shattock, Joanne. "The Making of a Novelist: Oliphant and John Black-wood at Work on *The Perpetual Curate,"* in D. J. Trela, ed., *Margaret Oliphant,* 113–22.

Phoebe, Junior, 1876

Peterson, Linda. "The Female *Bildungsroman:* Tradition and Revision in Oliphant's Fiction," in D. J. Trela, ed., *Margaret Oliphant,* 73–78.

Sanders, Valerie. *Eve's Renegades,* 77–79.

Salem Chapel, 1863

Sanders, Valerie. *Eve's Renegades,* 110–13, 174–76.

A Son of the Soil, 1866

Williams, Merryn. "The Scottish Stories of Margaret Oliphant," in Norman Page and Peter Preston, eds., *The Literature of Place,* 81–83.

AMELIA OPIE

Adeline Mowbray; or, Mother and Daughter, 1801

Eberle, Roxanne. "Amelia Opie's *Adeline Mowbray:* Diverting the Libertine Gaze; or, The Vindication of a Fallen Woman." *Stud in the Novel* 26 (1994), 121–46.

MacCarthy, B. G. *The Female Pen,* 443–45.

Mellor Anne K. " 'Am I Not a Woman, and a Sister?': Slavery, Romanticism, and Gender," in Alan Richardson and Sonia Hofkosch, eds., *Romanticism, Race, and Imperial Culture,* 322–23.

The Father and Daughter, 1812

Staves, Susan. "British Seduced Maidens," in Carla H. Hay and Syndy M. Conger, eds., *The Past as Prologue,* 92–94.

JOE ORTON

Head to Toe, 1971

Nieragden, Goran. "Neglected Yet Respectable: Joe Orton's *Head to Toe* as Political Satire." *Engl Stud* (Amsterdam) 75 (1994), 350–55.

GEORGE ORWELL

Burmese Days, 1934

Davison, Peter. *George Orwell,* 45–54.
Fowler, Roger. *The Language of George Orwell,* 68–70, 119–35.

A Clergyman's Daughter, 1935

Davison, Peter. *George Orwell,* 62–65.
Fowler, Roger. *The Language of George Orwell,* 101–6, 109–18.

Coming Up for Air, 1939

Fowler, Roger. *The Language of George Orwell,* 65–68, 148–58.
McCartney, George. "Satire between the Wars: Evelyn Waugh and Others," in John Richetti et al., eds., *The Columbia History,* 872–73.

Down and Out in Paris and London, 1933

Coombes, John E. "Construction of Poverty: Around Orwell's *Down and Out in Paris and London." Cycnos* 11:2 (1994), 75–83.
Davison, Peter. *George Orwell,* 30–37, 43–45.
Fowler, Roger. *The Language of George Orwell,* 70–79, 93–95, 99–101.

Homage to Catalonia, 1938

Baxter, Gisèle Marie. "The Generous Spirit: The Moral and Physical Experience of a Man at War in *Homage to Catalonia* and *For Whom the Bell Tolls." Dalhousie R* 73 (1993), 368–78.
Davison, Peter. *George Orwell,* 79–87.
Foster, Kevin. "Silent Homage: Orwell in Catalonia." *Southern R* (Adelaide) 29 (1996), 19–31.
Fowler, Roger. *The Language of George Orwell,* 79–80.
Sayre, Robert. "Guerre d'Espagne et politique chez les intellectuels de gauche européens: Le Témoignage exemplaire d'Orwell." *Cycnos* 11:2 (1994), 101–12.

Keep the Aspidistra Flying, 1936

Davison, Peter. *George Orwell,* 58–62.
Fowler, Roger. *The Language of George Orwell,* 140–48.

Nineteen Eighty-Four, 1948

Aldiss, Brian W. *The Detached Retina,* 92–100.
Aragay I Sastre, Mireia. "Satire Betrayed: A Look at Orwell's *Nineteen Eighty-Four." Atlantis* 12:1 (1990), 65–76.
Booker, M. Keith. *The Dystopian Impulse in Modern Literature,* 69–89.
Connor, Steven. *The English Novel in History,* 206–13.

Davison, Peter. *George Orwell*, 129–39.

Fowler, Roger. *The Language of George Orwell*, 181–227.

Johae, Anthony. "The Russian Sources of George Orwell's *Nineteen Eighty-Four.*" *New Comparison* 17 (1994), 138–49.

Kearney, Anthony. "Orwell's *Animal Farm* and *1984.*" *Explicator* 54 (1996), 238–39.

Lamarque, Peter, and Stein Haugom Olsen. *Truth, Fiction, and Literature*, 301–4.

Loewenstein, Andrea Freud. "The Protection of Masculinity: Jews as Projective Pawns in the Texts of William Gerhardi and George Orwell," in Bryan Cheyette, ed., *Between 'Race' and Culture*, 161–64.

McCartney, George. "Satire between the Wars: Evelyn Waugh and Others," in John Richetti et al., eds., *The Columbia History*, 873–74, 888–90.

McKay, George. "Metapropaganda: Self-Reading Dystopian Fiction—Burdekin's *Swastika Night* and Orwell's *Nineteen Eighty-Four.*" *Science-Fiction Stud* 21 (1994), 302–12.

Maule, Victoria. "On the Subversion of Character in the Literature of Identity Anxiety," in Derek Littlewood and Peter Stockwell, eds., *Impossibility Fiction*, 109–12.

Milner, Andrew. *Literature, Culture, and Society*, 116–18.

Plank, Robert. *George Orwell's Guide Through Hell*, 11–125.

Regard, Frédéric. "Time for Feeling: The Structure of George Orwell's Archaic Postmodernism." *Cycnos* 11:2 (1994), 3–15.

Roger, Hélène. "De *Big Brother* au temps des *Small Brothers.*" *Cycnos* 11:2 (1994), 147–63.

Scherer, Thomas. "Die Geschichte des O: Die pornographische Dimension von George Orwells *Nineteen Eighty-Four.*" *Zeitschrift für Anglistik und Amerikanistik* 43 (1995), 145–58.

Schmidt, Mark Ray. "Rebellion, Freedom, and Other Philosophical Issues in Orwell's *1984.*" *Publs of the Arkansas Philol Assoc* 22:1 (1996), 79–85.

Simon-Vandenbergen, Anne-Marie. "Speech, Music and Dehumanisation in George Orwell's *Nineteen Eighty-Four.*" *Lang and Lit* 2 (1993), 157–82.

West, W. J. *The Larger Evils*, 1–194.

Zelter, Joachim. *Sinnhafte Fiktion und Wahrheit*, 197–204.

The Road to Wigan Pier, 1937

Bonifas, Gilbert. "Portrait of the Fascist in *The Road to Wigan Pier:* George Orwell and *G. K.'s Weekly.*" *Cycnos* 11:2 (1994), 93–99.

Curcuru, Monique. "La Classe ouvrière dans *The Road to Wigan Pier.*" *Cycnos* 11:2 (1994), 85–91.

Davison, Peter. *George Orwell*, 67–78.

Fowler, Roger. *The Language of George Orwell*, 55–59, 81–86.

MORTIMER O'SULLIVAN

The Nevilles of Garretstown, 1860

> Spence, Joseph. "Allegories for a Protestant Nation: Irish Tory Historical Fiction, 1820–1850." *Rel and Lit* 28:2–3 (1996), 67–70.

'OUIDA'

Moths, 1880

> Cadogan, Mary. *And Then Their Hearts Stood Still,* 69–72.

Under Two Flags, 1867

> Cadogan, Mary. *And Then Their Hearts Stood Still,* 65–68.

ROBERT PALTOCK

Peter Wilkins, 1750

> Baines, Paul. " 'Able Mechanick': *The Life and Adventures of Peter Wilkins* and the Eighteenth-Century Fantastic Voyage," in David Seed, ed., *Anticipations,* 13–21.
>
> Merchant, Peter. "Robert Paltock and the Refashioning of 'Inkle and Yarico.' " *Eighteenth-Cent Fiction* 9 (1996), 37–50.

MOLLIE PANTER-DOWNES

One Fine Day, 1946

> Taylor, D. J. *After the War,* 29–31.

ELIZA PARSONS

The Valley of Saint-Gothard, 1799

> Séjourné, Philippe. "Feminine Sentimental Fiction Renovated: Mrs. Eliza Parsons' *The Valley of Saint-Gothard." Caliban* 33 (1996), 43–50.

WALTER HORATIO PATER

Gaston de Latour, 1896

> Weir, David. *Decadence and the Making of Modernism,* 79–81.

Marius the Epicurean, 1885

> Adams, James Eli. *Dandies and Desert Saints,* 187–95.
>
> Adams, James Eli. "Pater's Muscular Aestheticism," in Donald E. Hall, ed., *Muscular Christianity,* 227–30.

Bizup, Joseph. "Walter Pater and the Ruskinian Gentleman." *Engl Lit in Transition, 1880–1920* 38 (1995), 56–67.

Brake, Laurel. *Walter Pater*, 42–44.

Kabel, Ans. "The Influence of Walter Pater in *Dr Jekyll and Mr Hyde* and *The Picture of Dorian Gray,*" in Peter Liebregts and Wim Tigges, eds., *Beauty and the Beast*, 139–47.

Lubbock, Jules. "Walter Pater's *Marius the Epicurean:* The Imaginary Portrait as Cultural History." *J of the Warburg and Courtauld Institutes* 46 (1983), 166–90.

Weir, David. *Decadence and the Making of Modernism*, 71–79.

PHYLLIS PAUL

Camilla, 1949

Cavaliero, Glen. *The Supernatural and English Fiction*, 174–75.

The Lion of Cooling Bay, 1953

Cavaliero, Glen. *The Supernatural and English Fiction*, 176–78.

Twice Lost, 1960

Cavaliero, Glen. *The Supernatural and English Fiction*, 178–80.

THOMAS LOVE PEACOCK

Gryll Grange, 1860

Antor, Heinz. *Der englische Universitätsroman*, 364–67.

The Misfortunes of Elphin, 1829

Gallon, David. "The Presence of Myth in T. L. Peacock's *The Misfortunes of Elphin,*" in Neil Thomas and Françoise Le Saux, eds., *Myth and Its Legacy*, 9–25.

Nightmare Abbey, 1818

Dyer, Gary R. "Peacock and the 'Philosophical Gas' of the Illuminati," in Marie Mulvey Roberts and Hugh Ormsby-Lennon, eds., *Secret Texts*, 188–204.

Mulvihill, James. "Peacock's *Nightmare Abbey* and the 'shapes' of Imposture." *Stud in Romanticism* 34 (1995), 553–68.

MERVYN PEAKE

Gormenghast, 1950

Ciambezi, Luisella. "The Description of Rituals in *Gormenghast.*" *Peake Stud* 3:4 (1994), 17–20.

Yeoman, Ann. " 'Arabesque in Motion': The Dreamscape of *Gormenghast.*" *Peake Stud* 4:1 (1994), 7–29.

Titus Alone, 1959

> Goodacre, Selwyn. "A Christian View of the Titus Books." *Peake Stud* 3:2 (1993), 5–8.
> Le Cam, Pierre-Yves. "Peake's Fantastic Realism in the Titus Books." *Peake Stud* 3:4 (1994), 5–15.
> Mason, Desmond. "The Green Peake of *Titus Alone.*" *Peake Stud* 3:1 (1992), 17–20.

Titus Groan, 1946

> Goodacre, Selwyn. "A Christian View of the Titus Books." *Peake Stud* 3:2 (1993), 5–8.
> Le Cam, Pierre-Yves. "Peake's Fantastic Realism in the Titus Books." *Peake Stud* 3:4 (1994), 5–15.

HAROLD PINTER

The Dwarfs, 1990

> Knowles, Ronald. *Understanding Harold Pinter,* 72–75.
> Regal, Martin S. *Harold Pinter,* 42–48.

JANE PORTER

The Scottish Chiefs, 1808

> Batchelor, Rhonda. "The Rise and Fall of the Eighteenth Century's Authentic Feminine Voice." *Eighteenth-Cent Fiction* 6 (1994), 355–57, 361–62, 366–67.

ANTHONY POWELL

The Acceptance World, 1955

> Brennan, Neil. *Anthony Powell,* 84–91.

Afternoon Men, 1931

> Bowen, John. "The Melancholia of Modernity: Anthony Powell's Early Fiction," in Patrick J. Quinn, ed., *Recharting the Thirties,* 105–9.
> Brennan, Neil. *Anthony Powell,* 29–44.

Agents and Patients, 1936

> Bowen, John. "The Melancholia of Modernity: Anthony Powell's Early Fiction," in Patrick J. Quinn, ed., *Recharting the Thirties,* 116–18.
> Brennan, Neil. *Anthony Powell,* 57–64.

At Lady Molly's, 1957

> Brennan, Neil. *Anthony Powell,* 91–97.

Books Do Furnish a Room, 1971

> Brennan, Neil. *Anthony Powell,* 116–21.

A Buyer's Market, 1952
   Brennan, Neil. *Anthony Powell,* 79–84.

Casanova's Chinese Restaurant, 1960
   Brennan, Neil. *Anthony Powell,* 97–99.

A Dance to the Music of Time, 1951–1975
   Brennan, Neil. *Anthony Powell,* 67–135.
   Felber, Lynette. *Gender and Genre,* 119–61.
   Joyau, Isabelle. *Investigating Powell's "A Dance to the Music of Time,"*
      1–163.

The Fisher King, 1986
   Brennan, Neil. *Anthony Powell,* 161–67.

From a View to a Death, 1933
   Bowen, John. "The Melancholia of Modernity: Anthony Powell's Early
      Fiction," in Patrick J. Quinn, ed., *Recharting the Thirties,* 113–16.
   Brennan, Neil. *Anthony Powell,* 48–57.

Hearing Secret Harmonies, 1975
   Brennan, Neil. *Anthony Powell,* 127–35.

The Kindly Ones, 1962
   Brennan, Neil. *Anthony Powell,* 100–104.

The Military Philosophers, 1968
   Brennan, Neil. *Anthony Powell,* 112–16.

O, How the Wheel Becomes It!, 1983
   Brennan, Neil. *Anthony Powell,* 155–61.

A Question of Upbringing, 1951
   Brennan, Neil. *Anthony Powell,* 67–79.

The Soldier's Art, 1966
   Brennan, Neil. *Anthony Powell,* 107–12.
   Taylor, D. J. *After the War,* 15–20.

Temporary Kings, 1973
   Brennan, Neil. *Anthony Powell,* 121–27.

The Valley of Bones, 1964
   Brennan, Neil. *Anthony Powell,* 104–7.

Venusberg, 1932
   Bowen, John. "The Melancholia of Modernity: Anthony Powell's Early
      Fiction," in Patrick J. Quinn, ed., *Recharting the Thirties,* 109–12.
   Brennan, Neil. *Anthony Powell,* 45–48.

What's Become of Waring, 1939
   Bowen, John. "The Melancholia of Modernity: Anthony Powell's Early
      Fiction," in Patrick J. Quinn, ed., *Recharting the Thirties,* 118–21.
   Brennan, Neil. *Anthony Powell,* 64–66.

JOHN COWPER POWYS

Ducdame, 1925

Cavaliero, Glen. *The Supernatural and English Fiction,* 146–48.

A Glastonbury Romance, 1932

Birns, Nicholas. " 'A Peculiar Blending': Powys's Anglo-American Synthesis in *A Glastonbury Romance* and the *Autobiography.*" *Powys Notes* 8:1–2 (1992), 37–52.

Cavaliero, Glen. *The Supernatural and English Fiction,* 148–51.

Rands, Susan. "The Topicality of *A Glastonbury Romance.*" *Powys R* 7:3–4 (1992–93), 42–53.

Robinson, Jeremy. *Sensualism and Mythology,* 26–28.

Maiden Castle, 1936

Hooker, Jeremy. *Writers in a Landscape,* 119–38.

Robinson, Jeremy. *Sensualism and Mythology,* 30–32.

Owen Glendower, 1940

Duncan, Ian. "The Mythology of Escape: *Owen Glendower* and the Failure of Historical Romance." *Powys Notes* 8:1–2 (1992), 53–81.

Porius, 1951

Cavaliero, Glen. *The Supernatural and English Fiction,* 152–53.

Weymouth Sands, 1935

Nordius, Janina. "Hav och sten: Ensamheter I *Weymouth Sands.*" *Studiekamraten* 74:2–3 (1992), 10–12.

Robinson, Jeremy. *Sensualism and Mythology,* 28–30.

Wolf Solent, 1929

Börge, Göran. "*Wolf Solent:* en modern Hamlet." *Studiekamraten* 74:2–3 (1992), 14–15.

Geijerstam, Carl-Erik af. "En satyriskt uppsluppem ensamvandrare." *Studiekamraten* 74:2–3 (1992), 7.

Nydahl, Mikael. "Emerson och *Wolf Solent.*" *Studiekamraten* 74:2–3 (1992), 26–27.

Robinson, Jeremy. *Sensualism and Mythology,* 24–26.

THEODORE FRANCIS POWYS

Mr. Weston's Good Wine, 1927

Gervais, David. "T. F. Powys: Invention and Myth." *English* 45 (1996), 62–78.

SAMUEL JACKSON PRATT

Shenstone-Green; or, The New Paradise Lost, 1779

Perry, Ruth. "Bluestockings in Utopia," in Beth Fowkes Tobin, ed., *History, Gender, and Eighteenth-Century Literature,* 166–69.

J. B. PRIESTLEY

The Good Companions, 1929
  Holdsworth, Peter. *The Rebel Tyke*, 78–82.

BARBARA PYM

An Academic Question, 1986
  Antor, Heinz. *Der englische Universitätsroman*, 695–97.

Excellent Women, 1952
  Allen, Orphia Jane. *Barbara Pym*, 70–76.

A Few Green Leaves, 1980
  Allen, Orphia Jane. *Barbara Pym*, 114–23.
  Bellringer, Alan W. "A Fistful of Pyms: Barbara Pym's Use of Cross-over Characters." *Yrbk of Engl Stud* 26 (1996), 206–7.
  McGuirk, Carol. "Drabble to Carter: Fiction by Women, 1962–1992," in John Richetti et al., eds., *The Columbia History*, 945–46, 948–49, 957–58.

A Glass of Blessings, 1958
  Allen, Orphia Jane. *Barbara Pym*, 86–90.
  Bellringer, Alan W. "A Fistful of Pyms: Barbara Pym's Use of Cross-over Characters." *Yrbk of Engl Stud* 26 (1996), 202–4.
  McGuirk, Carol. "Drabble to Carter: Fiction by Women, 1962–1992," in John Richetti et al., eds., *The Columbia History*, 960–61.

Jane and Prudence, 1953
  Allen, Orphia Jane. *Barbara Pym*, 76–81.

Less Than Angels, 1955
  Allen, Orphia Jane. *Barbara Pym*, 81–86.
  Bellringer, Alan W. "A Fistful of Pyms: Barbara Pym's Use of Cross-over Characters." *Yrbk of Engl Stud* 26 (1996), 201–2.

No Fond Return of Love, 1961
  Allen, Orphia Jane. *Barbara Pym*, 90–96.
  Bellringer, Alan W. "A Fistful of Pyms: Barbara Pym's Use of Cross-over Characters." *Yrbk of Engl Stud* 26 (1996), 204–5.

Quartet in Autumn, 1977
  Allen, Orphia Jane. *Barbara Pym*, 109–14.
  McGuirk, Carol. "Drabble to Carter: Fiction by Women, 1962–1992," in John Richetti et al., eds., *The Columbia History*, 958–59.

Some Tame Gazelle, 1950
  Allen, Orphia Jane. *Barbara Pym*, 66–69.

The Sweet Dove Died, 1978
  Allen, Orphia Jane. *Barbara Pym*, 104–9.
  Bellringer, Alan W. "A Fistful of Pyms: Barbara Pym's Use of Cross-over Characters." *Yrbk of Engl Stud* 26 (1996), 205–6.

McGuirk, Carol. "Drabble to Carter: Fiction by Women, 1962–1992," in John Richetti et al., eds., *The Columbia History*, 946–47, 958–59.

An Unsuitable Attachment, 1982

Allen, Orphia Jane. *Barbara Pym*, 96–104.

ARTHUR QUILLER-COUCH

The Splendid Spur, 1889

Orel, Harold. *The Historical Novel*, 70–86.

ANN RADCLIFFE

The Castles of Athlin and Dunbayne, 1789

Miles, Robert. *Ann Radcliffe*, 73–86.

Gaston de Blondeville, 1826

Michasiw, Kim Ian. "Ann Radcliffe and the Terrors of Power." *Eighteenth-Cent Fiction* 6 (1994), 343–46.

The Italian, 1797

Batchelor, Rhonda. "The Rise and Fall of the Eighteenth Century's Authentic Feminine Voice." *Eighteenth-Cent Fiction* 6 (1994), 351–52, 360–61, 365–66.

Berglund, Birgitta. *Woman's Whole Existence*, 47–44, 56–60.

Canuel, Mark. " 'Holy Hypocrisy' and the Government of Belief: Religion and Nationalism in the Gothic." *Stud in Romanticism* 34 (1995), 522–30.

Gonda, Caroline. *Reading Daughters' Fictions*, 144–49.

Henderson, Andrea. " 'An Embarrassing Subject': Use Value and Exchange Value in Early Gothic Characterization," in Mary A. Favret and Nicola J. Watson, eds., *At the Limits of Romanticism*, 232–40.

Hushahn, Helga. "Nature and Psychology in Radcliffe and Lewis," in Valeria Tinkler-Villani and Peter Davidson, eds., *Exhibited by Candlelight*, 92–93.

Kaufmann, David. *The Business of Common Life*, 77–87.

Keane, Angela. "Resisting Arrest: The National Constitution of Picturesque and Gothic in Radcliffe's Romances." *News from Nowhere* 1995: 96–116.

Kilgour, Maggie. *The Rise of the Gothic Novel*, 169–86.

MacCarthy, B. G. *The Female Pen*, 409–14.

Magnier, Mireille. "L'*Italian* ou le confessional des Pénitents Noirs: Reussite majeure de Mrs. Radcliffe." *Mythes, Croyances et Religions dans le Monde Anglo-Saxon* 5 (1987), 111–17.

Michasiw, Kim Ian. "Ann Radcliffe and the Terrors of Power." *Eighteenth-Cent Fiction* 6 (1994), 337–42.

Miles, Robert. *Ann Radcliffe*, 149–73.

Sage, Victor. "Gothic Laughter: Farce and Horror in Five Texts," in

Allan Lloyd Smith and Victor Sage, eds., *Gothick Origins and Innovations*, 190–93.

Saglia, Diego. "Looking at the Other: Cultural Difference and the Traveller's Gaze in *The Italian.*" *Stud in the Novel* 28 (1996), 12–34.

Schmitt, Cannon. "Techniques of Terror, Technologies of Nationality: Ann Radcliffe's *The Italian.*" *ELH* 61 (1994), 853–72.

Spacks, Patricia Meyer. *Desire and Truth,* 150–56, 162–67.

The Mysteries of Udolpho, 1794

Benedict, Barbara M. *Framing Feeling,* 172–95.

Berglund, Birgitta. *Woman's Whole Existence,* 32–37, 45–56, 64–77.

Botting, Fred. *Gothic,* 65–71.

Haggerty, George E. "The Gothic Novel, 1764–1824," in John Richetti et al., eds., *The Columbia History,* 227–28.

Howard, Jacqueline. *Reading Gothic Fiction,* 106–44.

Hushahn, Helga. "Nature and Psychology in Radcliffe and Lewis," in Valeria Tinkler-Villani and Peter Davidson, eds., *Exhibited by Candlelight,* 90–92.

Keane, Angela. "Resisting Arrest: The National Constitution of Picturesque and Gothic in Radcliffe's Romances." *News from Nowhere* 1995: 96–116.

Kilgour, Maggie. *The Rise of the Gothic Novel,* 113–43, 171–74.

Letellier, Robert Ignatius. *Sir Walter Scott and the Gothic Novel,* 63–66, 76–79, 88–90, 96–98, 152–55, 193–200, 207–11.

MacCarthy, B. G. *The Female Pen,* 406–9.

Mellor, Anne K. "A Novel of Their Own: Romantic Women's Fiction, 1790–1830," in John Richetti et al., eds., *The Columbia History,* 340–44.

Michasiw, Kim Ian. "Ann Radcliffe and the Terrors of Power." *Eighteenth-Cent Fiction* 6 (1994), 331–36.

Miles, Robert. *Ann Radcliffe,* 129–48.

Nollen, Elizabeth Mahn. "Female Detective Figures in British Fiction: Coping with Madness and Imprisonment." *Clues* 15:2 (1994), 39–42.

Pinch, Adela. *Strange Fits of Passion,* 112–19, 121–36.

Richter, David H. *The Progress of Romance,* 116–18.

Robertson, Fiona. *Legitimate Histories,* 77–80.

Scott, Linda Kane. "The Wages of Sin in *Udolpho,*" in Deborah D. Rogers, ed., *The Critical Response,* 29–30.

Spacks, Patricia Meyer. *Desire and Truth,* 156–60, 166–74.

Todd, Janet. *The Sign of Angellica,* 261–68.

Voller, Jack G. *The Supernatural Sublime,* 47–59.

Whiting, Patricia. "Literal and Literary Representations of the Family in *The Mysteries of Udolpho.*" *Eighteenth-Cent Fiction* 8 (1996), 485–501.

Williams, Anne. "Ann Radcliffe's Female Plot." *Stud on Voltaire and the Eighteenth Cent* 304 (1992), 823–25.

Wolf, Werner. "Angst und Schrecken als Attraktion: Zu einer genderorientierten Funktionsgeschichte des englischen Schauerromans im 18. und frühen 19. Jahrhundert." *Zeitschrift für Anglistik und Amerikanistik* 43 (1995), 44–49, 53–57.

The Romance of the Forest, 1791

Benedict, Barbara M. *Framing Feeling,* 172–95.

Berglund, Birgitta. *Woman's Whole Existence,* 34–35, 46–56.

Bronfen, Elisabeth. "The Perforated Text of Origins: Radcliffe Camera." *Swiss Papers in Engl Lang and Lit* 8 (1995), 40–58.

Haggerty, George E. "The Gothic Novel, 1764–1824," in John Richetti et al., eds., *The Columbia History,* 228–30.

Haggerty, George E. "Sensibility and Sexuality in *The Romance of the Forest,*" in Deborah D. Rogers, ed., *The Critical Response,* 8–15.

Keane, Angela. "Resisting Arrest: The National Constitution of Picturesque and Gothic in Radcliffe's Romances." *News from Nowhere* 1995: 96–116.

Letellier, Robert Ignatius. *Sir Walter Scott and the Gothic Novel,* 63–65.

MacCarthy, B. G. *The Female Pen,* 400–406.

Miles, Robert. *Ann Radcliffe,* 110–27.

Ogée, Frédéric. "Les songes d'Adeline: quelques remarques sur les lieux du gothique dans *The Romance of the Forest* d'Ann Radcliffe." *Caliban* 33 (1996), 29–41.

Todd, Janet. *The Sign of Angellica,* 255–59, 262–68.

Yurchuk, Maryanne. "Emotion and Reason in *The Romance of the Forest,*" in Deborah D. Rogers, ed., *The Critical Response,* 7–8.

A Sicilian Romance, 1790

Canuel, Mark. " 'Holy Hypocrisy' and the Government of Belief: Religion and Nationalism in the Gothic." *Stud in Romanticism* 34 (1995), 519–22.

Gonda, Caroline. *Reading Daughters' Fictions,* 153–55.

MacCarthy, B. G. *The Female Pen,* 399–400, 404–5.

Miles, Robert. *Ann Radcliffe,* 86–99.

MARY-ANNE RADCLIFFE

Manfroné, or The One-Handed Monk, 1809

Haggerty, George E. "The Gothic Novel, 1764–1824," in John Richetti et al., eds., *The Columbia History,* 230–32.

IRENE RATHBONE

October, 1934

Zilboorg, Caroline. "Irene Rathbone: The Great War and Its Aftermath," in Patrick J. Quinn, ed., *Recharting the Thirties,* 73–76.

They Call It Peace, 1936

Zilboorg, Caroline. "Irene Rathbone: The Great War and Its Aftermath," in Patrick J. Quinn, ed., *Recharting the Thirties*, 68–73.

We That Were Young, 1932

Zilboorg, Caroline. "Irene Rathbone: The Great War and Its Aftermath," in Patrick J. Quinn, ed., *Recharting the Thirties*, 66–68.

CHARLES READE

The Cloister and the Hearth, 1861

Cohen, Monica F. "Professing Renunciation: Domesticity in *The Cloister and the Hearth* and *Felix Holt.*" *Victorian Lit and Culture* 23 (1995), 275–79.

Griffith Gaunt, 1866

horsman, Alan. *The Victorian Novel*, 239–41.

Korobkin, Laura Hanft. "Silent Woman, Speaking Fiction: Charles Reade's Griffith Gaunt (1866) at the Adultery Trial of Henry Ward Beecher," in Barbara Leah Harman and Susan Meyer, eds., *The New Nineteenth Century*, 45–59.

Hard Cash, 1863

Horsman, Alan. *The Victorian Novel*, 238–39.

It Is Never Too Late to Mend, 1856

Horsman, Alan. *The Victorian Novel*, 235–36.

Thompson, Nicola. " 'Virile' Creators Versus 'Twaddlers Tame and Soft': Gender and the Reception of Charles Reade's *It Is Never Too Late to Mend.*" *Victorians Inst J* 23 (1995), 193–212.

A Woman Hater, 1876

Finkelstein, David. "A Woman Hater and Women Healers: John Blackwood, Charles Reade, and the Victorian Women's Medical Movement." *Victorian Periodicals R* 28 (1995), 335–48.

CLARA REEVE

The Old English Baron, 1778

Botting, Fred. *Gothic*, 54–56.

Canuel, Mark. " 'Holy Hypocrisy' and the Government of Belief: Religion and Nationalism in the Gothic." *Stud in Romanticism* 34 (1995), 516–17.

Howard, Jacqueline. *Reading Gothic Fiction*, 33–36.

MacCarthy, B. G. *The Female Pen,* 378–80.

Voller, Jack G. *The Supernatural Sublime*, 43–50.

MARY RENAULT

The Bull from the Sea, 1962
  Sweetman, David. *Mary Renault,* 208–10.
Fire from Heaven, 1970
  Sweetman, David. *Mary Renault,* 256–58.
The Friendly Young Ladies, 1944
  Sweetman, David. *Mary Renault,* 99–101.
Kind Are Her Answers, 1940
  Sweetman, David. *Mary Renault,* 79–82.
The King Must Die, 1958
  Sweetman, David. *Mary Renault,* 178–81.
The Last of the Wine, 1956
  Sweetman, David. *Mary Renault,* 156–62.
The Mask of Apollo, 1966
  Sweetman, David. *Mary Renault,* 240–44.
North Face, 1948
  Sweetman, David. *Mary Renault,* 111–13.
The Persian Boy, 1972
  Sweetman, David. *Mary Renault,* 268–70.
Purposes of Love, 1939
  Sweetman, David. *Mary Renault,* 61–68, 70–77.
Return to Night, 1947
  Sweetman, David. *Mary Renault,* 106–9.

JEAN RHYS

After Leaving Mr. Mackenzie, 1931
    Althoff, Gabriele. " 'Ich bin wirklicher als du': Zu Weiblichkeit und
      Kunst bei Jean Rhys und Georg Simmel," in Corina Caduff and Sigrid
      Weigel, eds., *Das Geschlecht der Künste,* 137–44.
    Berry, Betsy. " 'Between Dog and Wolf': Jean Rhys's Version of Natu-
      ralism in *After Leaving Mr Mackenzie." Stud in the Novel* 27 (1995),
      544–59.
    Druxes, Helga. *Resisting Bodies,* 50–59, 76–78, 80–84.
    Friedman, Ellen G. " 'Utterly Other Discourse': The Anticanon of Ex-
      perimental Women Writers from Dorothy Richardson to Christine
      Brooke-Rose," in Ellen G. Friedman and Richard Martin, eds., *Utterly
      Other Discourse,* 222–23.
    García Rayego, Rosa. "*After Leaving Mr. Mackenzie* de Jean Rhys: Una
      lectura existencialista del tiempo." *Atlantis* 12:1 (1990), 103–8.

Gregg, Veronica Marie. *Jean Rhys's Historical Imagination*, 146–53.
Sternlicht, Sanford. *Jean Rhys*, 52–69.

Good Morning, Midnight, 1939

Carr, Helen. *Jean Rhys*, 46–76.
Gregg, Veronica Marie. *Jean Rhys's Historical Imagination*, 153–61.
Rodrigues Flora, Luisa Maria. "Jean Rhys: Composition in Shadows and Surfaces," in Patrick J. Quinn, ed., *Recharting the Thirties*, 268–75.
Sternlicht, Sanford. *Jean Rhys*, 88–103.

Quartet, 1928

Sternlicht, Sanford. *Jean Rhys*, 32–51.

Voyage in the Dark, 1934

Carr, Helen. *Jean Rhys*, 78–80, 84–88.
Druxes, Helga. *Resisting Bodies*, 55–57, 72–73, 81–85.
Gregg, Veronica Marie. *Jean Rhys's Historical Imagination*, 115–35.
Sternlicht, Sanford. *Jean Rhys*, 70–87.
Thomas, Glen. " 'The One with the Beastly Lives': Gender and Textuality in Jean Rhys's *Voyage in the Dark.*" *Kunapipi* 17:3 (1995), 27–36.
Wheeler, Kathleen. *'Modernist' Women Writers*, 103–16.

Wide Saragasso Sea, 1966

Barreca, Regina. "Writing as Voodoo: Sorcery, Hysteria, and Art," in Sarah Webster Goodwin and Elisabeth Bronfen, eds., *Death and Representation*, 179–84.
Carr, Helen. *Jean Rhys*, 84–88.
Choudhoury, Romita. " 'Is there a ghost, a zombie there?': Postcolonial Intertextuality and Jean Rhys's *Wide Saragasso Sea.*" *Textual Practice* 10 (1996), 315–26.
Díaz Fernández, José Ramón. "Jean Rhys y *Wide Saragasso Sea.*" *Atlantis* 12:1 (1990), 77–102.
Ferguson, Moira. *Colonialism and Gender Relations,* 90–115.
Forrester, Faizal. "Who Stole the Soul in *Wide Saragasso Sea*?" *J of West Indian Lit* 6:2 (1994), 32–42.
Friedman, Ellen G. " 'Utterly Other Discourse': The Anticanon of Experimental Women Writers from Dorothy Richardson to Christine Brooke-Rose," in Ellen G. Friedman and Richard Martin, eds., *Utterly Other Discourse*, 223–24.
Gregg, Veronica Marie. *Jean Rhys's Historical Imagination*, 82–115.
Huggan, Graham. "A Tale of Two Parrots: Walcott, Rhys, and the Uses of Colonial Mimicry." *Contemp Lit* 35 (1994), 650–58.
Hulme, Peter. "The Locked Heart: The Creole Family Romance of *Wide Saragasso Sea*," in Francis Barker et al., eds., *Colonial Discourse/ Postcolonial Theory,* 72–85.
Humm, Maggie. "Jean Rhys: Race, Gender and History," in Gina Wisker, ed., *It's My Party*, 46–58, 60–62, 65–67, 70–72.
James, Louis. "How Many Islands Are There in Jean Rhys's *Wide Saragasso Sea*?" *Kunapipi* 16:2 (1994), 77–81.

Kamel, Rose. " 'Before I Was Set Free': The Creole Wife in *Jane Eyre* and *Wide Saragasso Sea.*" *J of Narrative Technique* 25 (1995), 1–18.

Kendrick, Robert. "Edward Rochester and the Margins of Masculinity in *Jane Eyre* and *Wide Saragasso Sea.*" *Papers on Lang and Lit* 30 (1994), 235–55.

Lalla, Barbara. "Discourse of Dispossession: Ex-centric Journeys of the Un-living in *Wide Saragasso Sea* and the Old English 'The Wife's Lament.' " *Ariel* 24:3 (1993), 55–72.

Louvel, Liliane. "Jean Rhys, *Wide Saragasso Sea:* The Locket and the Shamrock." *Etudes Anglaises* 48 (1995), 160–71.

Newman, Judie. *The Ballistic Bard*, 13–25.

Nixon, Nicola. "*Wide Saragasso Sea* and Jean Rhys's Interrogation of the 'nature wholly alien' in *Jane Eyre.*" *Essays in Lit* (Macomb, IL) 21 (1994), 267–82.

Piela, Catherine Horbury. "Finding Order: A Note on Rhys' *Wide Saragasso Sea.*" *Notes on Contemp Lit* 24:2 (1994), 9–11.

Renk, Kathleen J. "Genesis of the Gods: The Cosmic Visions of Jean Rhys and Wilson Harris." *Southern R* (Adelaide) 27 (1994), 479–84.

Rody, Caroline. "Burning Down the House: The Revisionary Paradigm of Jean Rhys's *Wide Saragasso Sea,*" in Alison Booth, ed., *Famous Last Words*, 300–318.

Sage, Lorna. *Women in the House of Fiction*, 50–52.

Smith, R. McClure. " 'I don't dream about it any more': The Textual Unconscious in Jean Rhys's *Wide Saragasso Sea.*" *J of Narrative Technique* 26 (1996), 113–30.

Sternlicht, Sanford. *Jean Rhys*, 104–21.

Tong, Q. S., and Jane Roberts. "Diachronyed Synchrony: A Comparative Study of the Opening Paragraphs of *Jane Eyre* and *Wide Saragasso Sea.*" *Anglistik* 6:2 (1995), 64–74.

Winterhalter, Teresa. "Narrative Technique and the Rage for Order in *Wide Saragasso Sea.*" *Narrative* 2 (1994), 214–27.

DOROTHY RICHARDSON

Pilgrimage, 1915–1967

Bluemel, Kristin. "Missing Sex in Dorothy Richardson's *Pilgrimage.*" *Engl Lit in Transition, 1880–1920* 39 (1996), 20–33.

Felber, Lynette. *Gender and Genre*, 75–117.

Friedman, Ellen G. " 'Utterly Other Discourse': The Anticanon of Experimental Women Writers from Dorothy Richardson to Christine Brooke-Rose," in Ellen G. Friedman and Richard Martin, eds., *Utterly Other Discourse*, 215–18.

Hidalgo, Pilar. "Female *Flânerie* in Dorothy Richardson's *Pilgrimage.*" *Revista Alicantina de Estudios Ingleses* 6 (1993), 93–98.

Loeffelholz, Mary. *Experimental Lives*, 58–61.

Michael, Magali Cornier. *Feminism and the Postmodern Impulse*, 50–52.

Podnieks, Elizabeth. "The Ultimate Astonisher: Dorothy Richardson's *Pilgrimage."* *Frontiers* 14:3 (1994), 67–94.

Radford, Jean. *Dorothy Richardson*, 6–138.

Rose, Jacqueline. "Dorothy Richardson and the Jew," in Bryan Cheyette, ed., *Between 'Race' and Culture*, 114–28.

Stevenson, Randall. *A Reader's Guide*, 37–39.

Thomson, George H. "Dorothy Richardson's Foreword to *Pilgrimage."* *Twentieth Cent Lit* 42 (1996), 344–55.

Thomson, George H. *A Reader's Guide*, 1–10, 18–56.

SAMUEL RICHARDSON

Clarissa, 1748

Aikins, Janet E. "*Clarissa* and the New Woman: Contexts for Richardson Scholarship." *Stud in the Liter Imagination* 28:1 (1995), 67–83.

Alliston, April. *Virtue's Faults*, 92–94.

Anderson, Antje Schaum. "Gendered Pleasure, Gendered Plot: Defloration as Climax in *Clarissa* and *Memoirs of a Woman of Pleasure."* *J of Narrative Technique* 25 (1995), 121–31.

Backscheider, Paula R. " 'The Woman's Past': Richardson, Defoe, and the Horrors of Marriage," in Carla H. Hay and Syndy M. Conger, eds., *The Past as Prologue*, 205–31.

Barchas, Janine. "The Engraved Score in *Clarissa:* An Intersection of Music, Narrative, and Graphic Design." *Eighteenth-Cent Life* 20:2 (1996), 1–16.

Bartolomeo, Joseph F. "Female Quixotism v. 'Feminine' Tragedy: Lennox's Comic Revision of *Clarissa,"* in Albert J. Rivero, ed., *New Essays*, 163–73.

Beasley, Jerry C. "Richardson's Girls: The Daughters of Patriarchy in *Pamela, Clarissa* and *Sir Charles Grandison,"* in Albert J. Rivero, ed., *New Essays*, 41–45.

Bellamy, Liz. "Private Virtues, Public Vices: Commercial Morality in the Novels of Samuel Richardson." *Lit and Hist* 5:2 (1996), 30–34.

Bond, Clinton. "Representing Reality: Strategies of Realism in the Early English Novel." *Eighteenth-Cent Fiction* 6 (1994), 125–40.

Bowers, Toni. *The Politics of Motherhood*, 196–224.

Brown, Murray L. "*Emblemata Rhetorica:* Glossing Emblematic Discourse in Richardson's *Clarissa."* *Stud in the Novel* 27 (1995), 455–69.

Bueler, Lois E. *"Clarissa' "s Plots,* 11–157.

Cook, Elizabeth Heckendorn. *Epistolary Bodies*, 71–113.

Cornett, Judy M. "The Treachery of Perception: Evidence and Experience in *Clarissa."* *Univ of Cincinnati Law R* 63:1 (1994), 165–93.

Courington, Chella. "From *Clarissa* to *Mrs. Dalloway*: Woolf's (Re)Vision of Richardson," in Eileen Barrett and Patricia Cramer, eds., *Re: Reading*, 95–101.

Doody, Margaret Anne. "Heliodorus Rewritten: Samuel Richardson's *Clarissa* and Frances Burney's *Wanderer*," in James Tatum, ed., *The Search for the Ancient Novel*, 117–30.

Dussinger, John A. "*Clarissa*, Jacobitism, and the 'Spirit of the University.' " *Stud in the Liter Imagination* 28:1 (1995), 55–62.

Fasick, Laura. *Vessels of Meaning*, 24–28, 36–48.

Frega, Donnalee. "Speaking in Hunger: Conditional Consumption as Discourse in *Clarissa*." *Stud in the Liter Imagination* 28:1 (1995), 87–101.

Fulton, Gordon D. "Why Look at Clarissa?" *Eighteenth-Cent Life* 20:2 (1996), 21–31.

Ghabris, Maryam. "Les Passions dans *Clarissa*." *Bull de la Société d'Etudes Anglo-Américaines des XVIIe et XVIIIe Siècles* 39 (1994), 143–57.

Ghabris, Maryam. "Richardson pédagogue." *Bull de la Société d'Etudes Anglo-Américaines des XVIIe et XVIIIe Siècles* 34 (1992), 57–65.

Glaser, Brigitte. *The Body in Samuel Richardson's "Clarissa,"* 108–201.

Gonda, Caroline. *Reading Daughters' Fictions*, 71–82.

Hansen, Klaus P. "Bürgerliche und unbürgerliche Empfindsamkeit in England," in Hansen, ed., *Empfindsamkeiten*, 58–59.

Harries, Elizabeth Wanning. *The Unfinished Manner*, 129–38.

Harris, Jocelyn. "Grotesque, Classical and Pornographic Bodies in *Clarissa*," in Albert J. Rivero, ed., *New Essays*, 101–14.

Hensley, David C. "*Clarissa*, Coleridge, Kant, and Klopstock: Emotionalism as Pietistic Intertext in Anglo-German Romanticism." *Stud in the Liter Imagination* 28:1 (1995), 125–42.

Hollahan, Eugene. *Crisis-Consciousness*, 36–44.

Hopkins, Lisa. "The Transference of *Clarissa*: Psychoanalysis and the Realm of the Feminine." *Crit Survey* 6 (1994), 218–25.

Keymer, Tom. "Jane Collier, Reader of Richardson, and the Fire Scene in *Clarissa*," in Albert J. Rivero, ed., *New Essays*, 141–56.

Keymer, Tom. *Richardson's "Clarissa,"* 45–244.

Kittredge, Katharine. "Men-Women and Womanish Men: Androgyny in Richardson's *Clarissa*." *Mod Lang Stud* 24:2 (1994), 20–26.

Koehler, Martha J. "Epistolary Closure and Triangular Return in Richardson's *Clarissa*." *J of Narrative Technique* 24 (1994), 153–69.

Lambert, Ellen Zetzel. *The Face of Love*, 51–54.

Lawson, Jacqueline Elaine. *Domestic Misconduct*, 73–109.

Lee, Joy Kyunghae. "The Commodification of Virtue: Chastity and the Virginal Body in Richardson's *Clarissa*." *Eighteenth Cent* 36 (1995), 38–52.

McCrea, Brian. "Clarissa's Pregnancy and the Fate of Patriarchal Power." *Eighteenth-Cent Fiction* 9 (1997), 125–48.

Myer, Valerie Grosvenor. *Ten Great English Novelists*, 17–22.

Nelson, T. G. A. *Children, Parents, and the Rise of the Novel*, 121–27.

Petter, Henri. "Clarissa's Family: False Friends, Fair Friends." *Swiss Papers in Engl Lang and Lit* 9 (1996), 65–74.

Pettit, Alexander. "Wit, Satire, and Comedy: *Clarissa* and the Problem of Literary Precedent." *Stud in the Liter Imagination* 28:1 (1995), 35–50.

Rain, D. C. "Deconstructing Richardson: Terry Castle and *Clarissa's Ciphers.*" *Engl Stud* (Amsterdam) 76 (1995), 520–31.

Rain, D. C. "Richardson's *Clarissa.*" *Explicator* 52 (1993), 20–22.

Rees, Christine. *Utopian Imagination and Eighteenth-Century Fiction*, 191–96.

Richetti, John. "Lovelace Goes Shopping at Smith's: Power, Play, and Class Privilege in *Clarissa.*" *Stud in the Liter Imagination* 28:1 (1995), 23–32.

Spacks, Patricia Meyer. *Desire and Truth,* 57–79.

Spacks, Patricia Meyer. "The Grand Misleader: Self-Love and Self-Division in *Clarissa.*" *Stud in the Liter Imagination* 28:1 (1995), 7–19.

Stephanson, Raymond. "Richardson's 'Nerves': The Physiology of Sensibility in *Clarissa.*" *J of the Hist of Ideas* 49 (1988), 267–85.

Stevenson, John Allen. " 'Alien Spirits': The Unity of Lovelace and Clarissa," in Albert J. Rivero, ed., *New Essays*, 85–96.

Stovel, Bruce. "Clarissa's Ignorance." *Man and Nature* 11 (1992), 99–110.

Strauch, Gérard. "Richardson et le style indirect libre." *Recherches Anglaises et Nord-Américaines* 26 (1993), 87–100.

Stuber, Florian. "*Clarissa:* A Religious Novel?" *Stud in the Liter Imagination* 28:1 (1995), 105–22.

Suarez, Michael F., S.J. "Asserting the Negative: 'Child' Clarissa and the Problem of the 'Determined Girl,' " in Albert J. Rivero, ed., *New Essays*, 69–83.

Turner, James Grantham. "Richardson and His Circle," in John Richetti et al., eds., *The Columbia History*, 77–80, 87–100.

Van Sant, Ann Jessie. *Eighteenth-Century Sensibility,* 62–82.

Weinbrot, Howard D. "*Clarissa,* Elias Brand and Death by Parentheses," in Albert J. Rivero, ed., *New Essays*, 117–36.

Weisser, Susan Ostrov. *A "Craving Fancy,"* 40–52, 105–8.

Woodward, Carolyn. " 'My Heart So Wrapt': Lesbian Disruptions in Eighteenth-Century British Fiction." *Signs* 18 (1993), 857–60.

Zomchick, John P. *Family and the Law,* 58–103.

Pamela, 1740

Aikins, Janet E. "Pamela's Use of Locke's Words." *Stud in Eighteenth-Cent Culture* 25 (1996), 75–93.

Beasley, Jerry C. "Richardson's Girls: The Daughters of Patriarchy in *Pamela, Clarissa* and *Sir Charles Grandison,*" in Albert J. Rivero, ed., *New Essays*, 38–41.

Bellamy, Liz. "Private Virtues, Public Vices: Commercial Morality in the Novels of Samuel Richardson." *Lit and Hist* 5:2 (1996), 31–34.

Bond, Clinton. "Representing Reality: Strategies of Realism in the Early English Novel." *Eighteenth-Cent Fiction* 6 (1994), 121–25.

Bony, Alain. " 'Go, Happy Paper'?: *Pamela* et les stratégies richardsoniennes de dépossession et de réappropriation autoriales." *Bull de la Société d'Etudes Anglo-Américaines des XVIIe et XVIIIe Siècles* 39 (1994), 87–106.

Bowers, Toni. " 'A Point of Conscience': Breastfeeding and Maternal Authority in *Pamela* 2." *Eighteenth-Cent Fiction* 7 (1995), 259–78.

Bowers, Toni. *The Politics of Motherhood*, 153–56, 167–96.

Burnham, Michelle. "Between England and America: Captivity, Sympathy, and the Sentimental Novel," in Deidre Lynch and William B. Warner, eds., *Cultural Institutions of the Novel*, 47–49, 63–68.

Campbell, Jill. "Fielding and the Novel at Mid-Century," in John Richetti et al., eds., *The Columbia History*, 110–13, 118–20.

Chaber, Lois A. " 'This Affecting Subject': An 'Interested' Reading of Childbearing in Two Novels by Samuel Richardson." *Eighteenth-Cent Fiction* 8 (1996), 198–208, 225–50.

Détis, Elisabeth. "Pour une étude sémiologique des personnages de *Pamela.*" *Bull de la Société d'Etudes Anglo-Américaines des XVIIe et XVIIIe Siècles* 39 (1994), 117–32.

Fasick, Laura. *Vessels of Meaning*, 20–24, 34–36, 42–43, 146–55.

Forbes, Joan. "Anti-Romantic Discourse as Resistance: Women's Fiction 1775–1820," in Lynne Pearce and Jackie Stacey, eds., *Romance Revisited*, 295–96.

Ghabris, Maryam. "Richardson pédagogue." *Bull de la Société d'Etudes Anglo-Américaines des XVIIe et XVIIIe Siècles* 34 (1992), 57–65.

Gooding, Richard. *"Pamela, Shamela,* and the Politics of the *Pamela* Vogue." *Eighteenth-Cent Fiction* 7 (1995), 109–25.

Hansen, Klaus P. "Bürgerliche und unbürgerliche Empfindsamkeit in England," in Hansen, ed., *Empfindsamkeiten*, 54–58.

Keymer, Tom. "*Pamela*'s Fables: Aesopian Writing and Political Implication in Samuel Richardson and Sir Roger L'Estrange." *Bull de la Société d'Etudes Anglo-Américaines des XVIIe et XVIIIe Siècles* 41 (1995), 81–101.

Keymer, Tom. *Richardson's "Clarissa,"* 19–32.

Maaouni, Jamila. "La Technique épistolaire dans *Pamela* (1740)." *Bull de la Société d'Etudes Anglo-Américaines des XVIIe et XVIIIe Siècles* 39 (1994), 133–41.

MacCarthy, B. G. *The Female Pen*, 241–44.

Martin, Catherine. "On the Persistence of Quest-Romance in the Romantic Genre: The Strange Case of *Pamela.*" *Poetics Today* 12:1 (1991), 87–109.

Müller, Wolfgang G. "The Homology of Syntax and Narrative Form in English and American Fiction," in Herbert Foltinek et al., eds., *Tales and "their telling difference,"* 87–88.

Myer, Valerie Grosvenor. *Ten Great English Novelists*, 14–16.

Nelson, T. G. A. *Children, Parents, and the Rise of the Novel*, 110–19.

Pickering, Samuel F., Jr. *Moral Instruction and Fiction for Children*, 98–124.

Pierce, John B. "Pamela's Textual Authority." *Eighteenth-Cent Fiction* 7 (1995), 131–46.

Rader, Ralph W. "The Emergence of the Novel in England: Genre in History vs. History of Genre." *Narrative* 1 (1993), 72–79.

Richter, David H. *The Progress of Romance*, 34–36, 84–86.

Rivero, Albert J. "The Place of Sally Godfrey in Richardson's *Pamela.*" *Eighteenth-Cent Fiction* 6 (1993), 29–46.

Schellenberg, Betty A. *The Conversational Circle*, 36–50.

Sharrock, Roger. *New Insights on English Authors*, 45–54.

Soupel, Serge. "*Pamela:* Paradoxes et ironies." *Bull de la Société d'Etudes Anglo-Américaines des XVIIe et XVIIIe Siècles* 39 (1994), 107–15.

Spacks, Patricia Meyer. *Desire and Truth,* 87–95.

Stadler, Eva Maria. "Addressing Social Boundaries: Dressing the Female Body in Early Realist Fiction," in Margaret R. Higonnet and Joan Templeton, eds., *Reconfigured Spheres*, 28–34.

Strauch, Gérard. "Richardson et le style indirect libre." *Recherches Anglaises et Nord-Américaines* 26 (1993), 87–100.

Stuber, Florian. "*Pamela II:* 'Written in Imitation of the Manner of Cervantes,' " in Albert J. Rivero, ed., *New Essays*, 53–66.

Todd, Janet. *Gender, Art and Death,* 63–80.

Toise, David W. " 'A More Culpable Passion': *Pamela, Joseph Andrews,* and the History of Desire." *Clio* 25 (1996), 397–409.

Turner, James Grantham. "Novel Panic: Picture and Performance in the Reception of Richardson's *Pamela.*" *Representations* 48 (1994), 70–92.

Turner, James Grantham. "Richardson and His Circle," in John Richetti et al., eds., *The Columbia History*, 81–87.

de Voogd, Peter. "Sentimental Horrors: Feeling in the Gothic Novel," in Valeria Tinkler-Villani and Peter Davidson, eds., *Exhibited by Candlelight*, 78–80.

Weisser, Susan Ostrov. *A "Craving Fancy,"* 39–43, 45–47.

Sir Charles Grandison, 1754

Beasley, Jerry C. "Richardson's Girls: The Daughters of Patriarchy in *Pamela, Clarissa* and *Sir Charles Grandison,*" in Albert J. Rivero, ed., *New Essays*, 35–37, 45–48.

Bellamy, Liz. "Private Virtues, Public Vices: Commercial Morality in the Novels of Samuel Richardson." *Lit and Hist* 5:2 (1996), 26–34.

Brown, Murray L. "Sir Hargrave Pollexfen, William Hogarth and 'that Obelisk behind us': Sexual Violence in *Sir Charles Grandison.*" *Philol Q* 75 (1996), 455–66.

Chaber, Lois A. "*Sir Charles Grandison* and the Human Prospect," in Albert J. Rivero, ed., *New Essays*, 193–205.

Chaber, Lois A. " 'This Affecting Subject': An 'Interested' Reading of

Childbearing in Two Novels by Samuel Richardson." *Eighteenth-Cent Fiction* 8 (1996), 208–50.

Fasick, Laura. *Vessels of Meaning*, 28–30, 40–41, 47–48.

Ghabris, Maryam. "Richardson pédagogue." *Bull de la Société d'Etudes Anglo-Américaines des XVIIe et XVIIIe Siècles* 34 (1992), 57–65.

Gonda, Caroline. *Reading Daughters' Fictions*, 93–104.

Jones, Wendy. "The Dialectic of Love in *Sir Charles Grandison.*" *Eighteenth-Cent Fiction* 8 (1995), 15–34.

Keymer, Tom. *Richardson's "Clarissa,"* 72–76.

Myer, Valerie Grosvenor. *Ten Great English Novelists*, 20–22.

Nelson, T. G. A. *Children, Parents, and the Rise of the Novel*, 181–85.

Price, Leah. "*Sir Charles Grandison* and the Executor's Hand." *Eighteenth-Cent Fiction* 8 (1996), 329–42.

Rees, Christine. *Utopian Imagination and Eighteenth-Century Fiction*, 196–200.

Rivero, Albert J. "Representing Clementina: 'Unnatural' Romance and the Ending of *Sir Charles Grandison,*" in Rivero, ed., *New Essays*, 193–205.

Schellenberg, Betty A. *The Conversational Circle*, 51–68.

Schellenberg, Betty A. "Using 'Femalities' to 'Make Fine Men': Richardson's *Sir Charles Grandison* and the Feminization of Narrative." *Stud in Engl Lit, 1500–1900* 34 (1994), 599–613.

Strauch, Gérard. "Richardson et le style indirect libre." *Recherches Anglaises et Nord-Américaines* 26 (1993), 87–100.

Turner, James Grantham. "Richardson and His Circle," in John Richetti et al., eds., *The Columbia History*, 79–81.

GRAEME RIGBY

The Black Cook's Historian, 1993

Sarvan, Charles. "Paradigms of the Slave Trade in Two British Novels." *Intl Fiction R* 23 (1996), 1–6.

JOAN RILEY

Romance, 1988

Duncker, Patricia. *Sisters and Strangers*, 247–49.

Waiting in the Twilight, 1987

Duncker, Patricia. *Sisters and Strangers*, 245–47.

MRS. DAVID G. RITCHIE

The New Warden, 1918

Antor, Heinz. *Der englische Universitätsroman*, 475–77, 511–13.

MICHELE ROBERTS

Daughters of the House, 1993

Luckhurst, Roger. " 'Impossible Mourning' in Toni Morrison's *Beloved* and Michèle Roberts's *Daughters of the House." Critique* (Washington, DC) 37 (1996), 251–58.

The Wild Girl, 1984

Rowland, Susan. "The Body's Sacred: Romance and Sacrifice in Religious and Jungian Narratives." *Lit and Theology* 10 (1996), 163–70.

ELIZABETH ROBINS

The Convert, 1907

Miller, Jane Eldridge. *Rebel Women,* 132–36.

PATRICIA ROBINS

Lady Chatterley's Daughter, 1961

Laing, Stuart. "Authenticating Romantic Fiction: *Lady Chatterley's Daughter,"* in Gina Wisker, ed., *It's My Party,* 14–26.

MARILYNNE ROBINSON

Housekeeping, 1981

Lomax, Marion. "Gendered Writing and the Writer's Stylistic Identity," in Katie Wales, ed., *Feminist Linguistics in Literary Criticism,* 13–15.

MARY ROBINSON

The False Friend, 1799

Ford, Susan Allen. " 'A name more dear': Daughters, Fathers, and Desire in *A Simple Story, The False Friend,* and *Mathilda,"* in Carol Shiner Wilson and Joel Haefner, eds., *Re-Visioning Romanticism,* 56–67.

Vancenza, or the Dangers of Credulity, 1792

MacCarthy, B. G. *The Female Pen,* 325–27.

REGINA MARIA ROCHE

The Children of the Abbey, 1796

Derry, Stephen. "Harriet Smith's Reading." *Persuasions* 14 (1992), 70–72.

Mellor, Anne K. "A Novel of Their Own: Romantic Women's Fiction,

1790–1830," in John Richetti et al., eds., *The Columbia History*, 339–40.

Clermont, 1798

Botting, Fred. *Gothic*, 71–75.

BERTA RUCK

The Bridge of Kisses, 1917

Cadogan, Mary. *And Then Their Hearts Stood Still*, 60–61.

SALMAN RUSHDIE

Grimus, 1975

Harrison, James. *Salman Rushdie*, 30–40.

Hume, Kathryn. "Taking a Stand While Lacking a Center: Rushdie's Postmodern Politics." *Philol Q* 74 (1995), 210–15.

Rao, M. Madhusudhana. *Salman Rushdie's Fiction*, 1–12, 42–56, 95–106.

Syed, Mujeebuddin. "Warped Mythologies: Salman Rushdie's *Grimus.*" *Ariel* 25:4 (1994), 135–49.

Haroun and the Sea of Stories, 1990

Aji, Aron R. " 'All Names Mean Something': Salman Rushdie's *Haroun* and the Legacy of Islam." *Contemp Lit* 36 (1995), 103–27.

Durix, Jean-Pierre. " 'The Gardener of Stories': Salman Rushdie's *Haroun and the Sea of Stories.*" *J of Commonwealth Lit* 28:1 (1993), 114–22.

Hume, Kathryn. "Taking a Stand While Lacking a Center: Rushdie's Postmodern Politics." *Philol Q* 74 (1995), 215–24.

Krishnan, R. S. "Telling of the Tale: Text, Context, and Narrative Act in Rushdie's *Haroun and the Sea of Stories.*" *Intl Fiction R* 22 (1995), 67–73.

Rangachari, Latha, and Evangelini Manickam. "The Story Teller Silenced: A Study of Rushdie's *Haroun and The Sea of Stories.*" *Liter Criterion* 30:4 (1995), 15–24.

Sen, Suchismita. "Memory, Language, and Society in Salman Rushdie's *Haroun and the Sea of Stories.*" *Contemp Lit* 36 (1995), 654–74.

Todd, Richard. *Consuming Fictions*, 299–301.

Midnight's Children, 1981

Booker, M. Keith. "Decolonizing Literature: *Ulysses* and the Postcolonial Novel in English," in Robert Newman, ed., *Pedagogy, Praxis, "Ulysses,"* 139–44.

Connor, Steven. *The English Novel in History*, 30–33.

Forsyth, Neil, and Martine Hennard. " 'Mr Mustapha Aziz and Fly': Defamiliarization of 'family' in Salman Rushdie's *Midnight's Children.*" *Swiss Papers in Engl Lang and Lit* 9 (1996), 197–205.

Gasiorek, Andrzej. *Post-War British Fiction,* 165–69.

Gorra, Michael. *After Empire,* 111–48.

Gorra, Michael. "Rudyard Kipling to Salman Rushdie: Imperialism to Postcolonialism," in John Richetti et al., eds., *The Columbia History,* 654–55.

Habib, Imtiaz. "Interrogating Cultures: Hybrid Subjectivity as Third Space in R. K. Narayan's *The Guide,* V. S. Naipaul's *A House for Mr. Biswas,* and Salman Rushdie's *Midnight's Children." Stud in the Hum* 23:1 (1996), 33–47.

Harris, Michael. *Outsiders and Insiders,* 31–45.

Harrison, James. *Salman Rushdie,* 41–68.

Hawes, Clement. "Leading History by the Nose: The Turn to the Eighteenth Century in *Midnight's Children." Mod Fiction Stud* 39 (1993), 147–65.

Hume, Kathryn. "Taking a Stand While Lacking a Center: Rushdie's Postmodern Politics." *Philol Q* 74 (1995), 210–15.

Juan-Navarro, Santiago. "The Dialogic Imagination of Salman Rushdie and Carlos Fuentes: National Allegories and the Scene of Writing in *Midnight's Children* and *Cristóbal Nonato." Neohelicon* 20:2 (1993), 264–70, 281–87, 294–301, 306–8.

Juarez Hervas, Luisa. "An Irreverent Chronicle: History and Fiction in Salman Rushdie's *Midnight's Children,"* in Susana Onega, ed., *Telling Histories,* 73–84.

Kane, Jean M. "The Migrant Intellectual and the Body of History: Salman Rushdie's *Midnight's Children." Contemp Lit* 37 (1996), 94–116.

Kortenaar, Neil ten. "*Midnight's Children* and the Allegory of History." *Ariel* 26:2 (1995), 41–60.

McGee, Patrick. *Telling the Other,* 139–45.

Millward, Celia. "Games with Names in *Midnight's Children." Names* 42 (1994), 91–98.

Narasimhaiah, C. D. *Essays in Commonwealth Literature,* 123–25.

Noor, Ronny. "Misrepresentation of History in Salman Rushdie's *Midnight's Children." Notes on Contemp Lit* 26:2 (1996), 7–8.

Price, David W. "Salman Rushdie's 'Use and Abuse of History' in *Midnight's Children." Ariel* 25:2 (1994), 91–106.

Rao, M. Madhusudhana. *Salman Rushdie's Fiction,* 12–21, 38–42, 56–71, 106–9, 123–30.

Syed, Mujeebuddin. "*Midnight's Children* and Its Indian Con-Texts." *J of Commonwealth Lit* 29:2 (1994), 95–107.

Todd, Richard. *Consuming Fictions,* 286–90.

White, Jonathan. "Politics and the Individual in the Modernist Historical Novel: Gordimer and Rushdie," in White, ed., *Recasting the World,* 226–39.

Williams, Mark. "The Novel as National Epic: Wilson Harris, Salman Rushdie, Keri Hulme," in Bruce King, ed., *The Commonwealth Novel,* 192–97.

Wood, Michael. "The Contemporary Novel," in John Richetti et al., eds., *The Columbia History*, 977–78.

The Moor's Last Sigh, 1995

Todd, Richard. *Consuming Fictions*, 301–3.

The Satanic Verses, 1988

Al-Raheb, Hani. "Salman Rushdie's *The Satanic Verses:* Fantasy for Religious Satire." *New Comparison* 19 (1995), 183–91.

Balasubramanian, Radha. "The Similarities Between Mikahil Bulgakov's *The Master and Margarita* and Salman Rushdie's *The Satanic Verses."* *Intl Fiction R* 22 (1995), 37–46.

Börner, Klaus H. "Salman Rushdie, *Satanic Verses:* Observations on Cultural Hybridity," in Eckhard Breitinger, ed., *Defining New Idioms*, 107–17.

Connor, Steven. *The English Novel in History*, 112–27.

Davies, J. M. Q. "Aspects of the Grotesque in Rushdie's *The Satanic Verses*." *AUMLA* 85 (1996), 29–35.

English, James F. *Comic Transactions*, 206–37.

Gasiorek, Andrzej. *Post-War British Fiction*, 170–74.

Gorra, Michael. *After Empire*, 149–56.

Gorra, Michael. "Rudyard Kipling to Salman Rushdie: Imperialism to Postcolonialism," in John Richetti et al., eds., *The Columbia History*, 653–56.

Hanne, Michael. *The Power of the Story*, 191–237.

Harrison, James. *Salman Rushdie*, 89–124.

Henry, Richard. *Pretending and Meaning*, 1–6, 8–10, 18–21.

Hume, Kathryn. "Taking a Stand While Lacking a Center: Rushdie's Postmodern Politics." *Philol Q* 74 (1995), 215–24.

Mann, Harveen Sachdeva. " 'Being Borne across': Translation and Salman Rushdie's *The Satanic Verses."* *Criticism* 37 (1995), 281–303.

Mishra, Vijay. "Postcolonial Differend: Diasporic Narratives of Salman Rushdie." *Ariel* 26:3 (1995), 12–43.

Parameswaran, Uma. "The We/They Paradigm in Rushie's *The Satanic Verses,"* in Gordon Collier, ed., *Us/Them*, 189–99.

Phillips, Kathy J. "Salman Rushdie's *The Satanic Verses* as a Feminist Novel," in Cristina Bacchilega and Cornelia N. Moore, eds., *Constructions and Confrontations*, 103–7.

Samuel, Julian. "Salman Rushie in the Age of Reason," in Gordon Collier, ed., *Us/Them*, 201–7.

Todd, Richard. *Consuming Fictions*, 295–99.

Wood, Michael. "The Contemporary Novel," in John Richetti et al., eds., *The Columbia History*, 977–79.

Shame, 1983

Harrison, James. *Salman Rushdie*, 69–88.

Hume, Kathryn. "Taking a Stand While Lacking a Center: Rushdie's Postmodern Politics." *Philol Q* 74 (1995), 210–15.

Rao, M. Madhusudhana. *Salman Rushdie's Fiction*, 21–28, 71–82, 109–18, 130–34.

Steinig, Swenta. "Houses: To Build is to Demolish—A Study of Salman Rushdie's *Shame* and Shashi Deshpende's *Roots and Shadows*," in Eckhard Breitinger, ed., *Defining New Idioms*, 97–105.

Todd, Richard. *Consuming Fictions*, 290–94.

W. P. RYAN

The Plough and the Cross, 1910

Murphy, James H. "Rosa Mulholland, W. P. Ryan and Irish Catholic Fiction at the Time of the Anglo-Irish Revival," in Joep Leerssen et al., eds., *Forging in the Smithy*, 225–28.

Starlight Through the Roof, 1895

Murphy, James H. *Catholic Fiction and Social Reality in Ireland*, 107–10.

RAFAEL SABATINI

The Hounds of God, 1928

Hughes, Helen. *The Historical Romance*, 76–80.

The Sea-Hawk, 1915

Orel, Harold. *The Historical Novel*, 151–58.

The Trampling of the Lilies, 1906

Hughes, Helen. *The Historical Romance*, 58–63.

MICHAEL SADLEIR

Hyssop, 1915

Antor, Heinz. *Der englische Universitätsroman*, 514–16.

SIEGFRIED SASSOON

The Complete Memoirs of George Sherston, 1928–1936

Sternlicht, Sanford. *Siegfried Sassoon*, 82–91.

DOROTHY L. SAYERS

Busman's Honeymoon, 1937

Lewis, Terrance L. *Dorothy L. Sayers' Wimsey*, 7–11.

Plain, Gill. *Women's Fiction of the Second World War*, 51–54, 62–64.

Gaudy Night, 1936

Antor, Heinz. *Der englische Universitätsroman,* 513–14, 571–82.

Campbell, SueEllen. "The Detective Heroine and the Death of Her Hero: Dorothy Sayers to P. D. James," in Glenwood Irons, ed., *Feminism in Women's Detective Fiction,* 12–17.

Clark, S. L. "*Gaudy Night'*s Legacy: P. D. James' *An Unsuitable Job for a Woman.*" *Sayers R* 4 (Sept. 1980), 1–12.

Klein, Kathleen Gregory. "Dorothy L. Sayers: From First to Last," in Mary Jean DeMarr, ed., *In the Beginning,* 13–16.

Lewis, Terrance L. *Dorothy L. Sayers' Wimsey,* 121–24.

Loeffelholz, Mary. *Experimental Lives,* 149–50.

Plain, Gill. *Women's Fiction of the Second World War,* 56–61.

Thormählen, Marianne. "The Idea of Academe in Dorothy L. Sayers' *Gaudy Night*—and How It Strikes a Contemporary," in Christopher Dean, ed., *Studies in Sayers,* 21–26.

Have His Carcase, 1932

Lewis, Terrance L. *Dorothy L. Sayers' Wimsey,* 93–96.

Murder Must Advertise, 1933

Lewis, Terrance L. *Dorothy L. Sayers' Wimsey,* 39–43.

The Nine Tailors, 1934

Beach, Sarah. "Harriet in Rehearsal: Hilary Thorpe in *The Nine Tailors.*" *Mythlore* 19:3 (1993), 37–39.

Strong Poison, 1930

Loeffelholz, Mary. *Experimental Lives,* 148–49.

Plain, Gill. *Women's Fiction of the Second World War,* 52–54.

Unnatural Death, 1927

Lewis, Terrance L. *Dorothy L. Sayers' Wimsey,* 34–36.

The Unpleasantness at the Bellona Club, 1928

Lewis, Andrew. " 'The Gladsome Light of Jurisprudence': Lord Peter's Library of Roman Law," in Christopher Dean, ed., *Studies in Sayers,* 13–18.

Lewis, Terrance L. *Dorothy L. Sayers' Wimsey,* 1–3, 36–39.

Whose Body?, 1923

Dean, Christopher. "The Character of Lord Peter Wimsey in *Whose Body?*" *Inklings* 12 (1994), 11–26.

Klein, Kathleen Gregory. "Dorothy L. Sayers: From First to Last," in Mary Jean DeMarr, ed., *In the Beginning,* 7–9.

OLIVE SCHREINER

From Man to Man, 1926

Casey, Janet Galligani. "Power, Agency, Desire: Olive Schreiner and the Pre-Modern Narrative Moment." *Narrative* 4 (1996), 124–39.

Horton, Susan R. *Difficult Women, Artful Lives*, 69–70, 98–99, 131–33, 203–4.

LeFew, Penelope A. "Schopenhauerian Pessimism in Olive Schreiner's *A Story of an African Farm* and *From Man to Man.*" *Engl Lit in Transition, 1880–1920* 37 (1994), 303–15.

Steele, Murray. "A Humanist Bible: Gender Roles, Sexuality and Race in Olive Schreiner's *From Man to Man,*" in Christopher Parker, ed., *Gender Roles and Sexuality,* 95–98.

The Story of an African Farm, 1883

Brantlinger, Patrick. "The Nineteenth-Century Novel and Empire," in John Richetti et al., eds., *The Columbia History*, 575–76.

Dutta, Shanta. "Sue's 'Obscure' Sisters." *Thomas Hardy J* 12:2 (1996), 60–70.

Horton, Susan R. *Difficult Women, Artful Lives*, 179–81.

Kahane, Claire. *Passions of the Voice*, 80–98.

Lawson, Elizabeth. "Of Lies and Memory: *The Story of an African Farm,* Book of the White Feather." *Cahiers Victoriens et Edouardiens* 44 (1996), 111–24.

LeFew, Penelope A. "Schopenhauerian Pessimism in Olive Schreiner's *A Story of an African Farm* and *From Man to Man.*" *Engl Lit in Transition, 1880–1920* 37 (1994), 303–15.

McMurry, Andrew. "Figures in a Ground: An Ecofeminist Study of Olive Schreiner's *The Story of an African Farm.*" *Engl Stud in Canada* 20 (1994), 431–46.

Miller, Jane Eldridge. *Rebel Women,* 117–19.

Mohr, Hans-Ulrich. "Drei Konstrukte weiblicher Verhaltensräume: Charlotte Smith, Olive Schreiner, Angela Carter." *Arbeiten aus Anglistik und Amerikanistik* 20 (1995), 317–33.

Monsman, Gerald. "Olive Schreiner's Allegorical Vision." *Victorian R* 18:2 (1992), 49–61.

Rowe, Margaret Moan. *Doris Lessing*, 16–20.

Sheckels, Theodore F., Jr. *The Lion on the Freeway*, 21–27.

Trooper Peter Halket, 1897

Chrisman, Laura. "Colonialism and Feminism in Olive Schreiner's 1890s Fiction." *Engl in Africa* 20:1 (1993), 33–37.

Undine, 1929

Horton, Susan R. *Difficult Women, Artful Lives*, 143–49, 154–62.

CAROLINE LUCY SCOTT

The Old Grey Church, 1856

Tush, Susan Rowland. *George Eliot and . . . Popular Women's Fiction*, 15–36.

PAUL SCOTT

The Bender, 1963

Kumar, Manjushree S. "Self-Transcendence through Work in Paul Scott's Novels." *Liter Criterion* 30:4 (1995), 27–30.

The Day of the Scorpion, 1968

Gorra, Michael. *After Empire,* 52–55.

Gorra, Michael. "Rudyard Kipling to Salman Rushdie: Imperialism to Postcolonialism," in John Richetti et al., eds., *The Columbia History,* 646–47.

A Division of the Spoils, 1975

Gorra, Michael. "Rudyard Kipling to Salman Rushdie: Imperialism to Postcolonialism," in John Richetti et al., eds., *The Columbia History,* 643–44.

The Jewel in the Crown, 1966

Gorra, Michael. *After Empire,* 15–18, 37–42, 44–50, 59–61.

A Male Child, 1956

Kumar, Manjushree S. "Self-Transcendence through Work in Paul Scott's Novels." *Liter Criterion* 30:4 (1995), 32–33.

The Mark of the Warrior, 1958

Kumar, Manjushree S. "Self-Transcendence through Work in Paul Scott's Novels." *Liter Criterion* 30:4 (1995), 31–32.

The Raj Quartet, 1976

Gorra, Michael. *After Empire,* 15–61.

Gorra, Michael. "Rudyard Kipling to Salman Rushdie: Imperialism to Postcolonialism," in John Richetti et al., eds., *The Columbia History,* 643–47.

Kumar, Manjushree S. "Self-Transcendence through Work in Paul Scott's Novels." *Liter Criterion* 30:4 (1995), 33–40.

Moore, Robin. "Paul Scott and the Raj as Metaphor," in Annie Greet et al., eds., *Raj Nostalgia,* 135–50.

Sharrad, Paul. "The Books Behind the Film: Paul Scott's *The Raj Quartet,*" in Annie Greet et al., eds., *Raj Nostalgia,* 123–33.

The Raj Quintet, 1977

Brann, Eva T. H. "Paul Scott's Raj Quintet: Real Politics in Imagined Gardens," in Joseph M. Knippenberg and Peter Augustine Lawler, eds., *Poets, Princes, and Private Citizens,* 191–208.

SARAH SCOTT

A Description of Millenium Hall, 1762

Cruise, James. "A House Divided: Sarah Scott's *Millenium Hall.*" *Stud in Engl Lit, 1500–1900* 35 (1995), 555–70.

Dunne, Linda. "Mothers and Monsters in Sarah Robinson Scott's *Millenium Hall*," in Jane L. Donawerth and Carol A. Kolmerten, eds., *Utopian and Science Fiction,* 54–72.

Elliott, Dorice Williams. "Sarah Scott's *Millenium Hall* and Female Philanthropy." *Stud in Engl Lit, 1500–1900* 35 (1995), 535–51.

Lewes, Darby. *Dream Revisionaries,* 38–39, 81–83.

Macey, J. David, Jr. "Eden Revisited: Re-visions of the Garden in Astell's *Serious Proposal,* Scott's *Millenium Hall,* and Graffigny's *Lettres d'une péruvienne.*" *Eighteenth-Cent Fiction* 9 (1997), 168–74.

Perry, Ruth. "Bluestockings in Utopia," in Beth Fowkes Tobin, ed., *History, Gender, and Eighteenth-Century Literature,* 159–63.

Rees, Christine. *Utopian Imagination and Eighteenth-Century Fiction,* 216–27, 229–34.

Schellenberg, Betty A. *The Conversational Circle,* 88–101.

Smith, Johanna M. "Philanthropic Community in *Millenium Hall* and the York Ladies Committee." *Eighteenth Cent* 36 (1995), 266–80.

Stoddard, Eve Walsh. "The Politics of Sentiment: Sarah Scott's *Millenium Hall.*" *Stud on Voltaire and the Eighteenth Cent* 304 (1992), 795–98.

Woodward, Carolyn. " 'My Heart So Wrapt': Lesbian Disruptions in Eighteenth-Century British Fiction." *Signs* 18 (1993), 855–57.

The History of Sir George Ellison, 1766

Stoddard, Eve W. "A Serious Proposal for Slavery Reform: Sarah Scott's *Sir George Ellison.*" *Eighteenth-Cent Stud* 28 (1995), 379–93.

The Test of Filial Duty, 1772

Gonda, Caroline. *Reading Daughters' Fictions,* 107–9.

WALTER SCOTT

The Abbot, 1820

Johnson, Christopher. "The Relationship Between *The Monastery* and *The Abbot.*" *Scottish Liter J* 20:2 (1993), 31–39.

Anne of Geierstein, 1829

Robertson, Fiona. *Legitimate Histories,* 239–45.

Tait, Margaret. "*Anne of Geierstein.*" *Scott Newsl* 28 (1996), 17–18.

The Antiquary, 1816

Caracciolo, Peter L. "Wilkie Collins and 'The God Almighty of Novelists': The Example of Scott in *No Name* and *Armadale,*" in Nelson Smith and R. C. Terry, eds., *Wilkie Collins to the Forefront,* 168–70.

Gordon, Jan B. *Gossip and Subversion,* 22–24.

Gordon, Jan B. " 'Liquidating the Sublime': Gossip in Scott's Novels," in Mary A. Favret and Nicola J. Watson, eds., *At the Limits of Romanticism,* 259–61.

Hartveit, Lars. " 'Silent Intercourse': The Impact of the 18th-Century Conceptual Heritage in *The Antiquary* and *St. Ronan's Well.*" *Engl Stud* (Amsterdam) 77 (1996), 32–44.

Kaufmann, David. *The Business of Common Life,* 114–22.

Robertson, Fiona. *Legitimate Histories*, 197–205.

Wilt, Judith. "Walter Scott: Narrative, History, Synthesis," in John Richetti et al., eds., *The Columbia History*, 305–6.

The Bride of Lammermoor, 1819

Chandler, James. "Scott and the Scene of Explanation: Framing Contextuality in *The Bride of Lammermoor." Stud in the Novel* 26 (1994), 69–94.

Ferris, Ina. *The Achievement of Literary Authority*, 220–22.

Robertson, Fiona. *Legitimate Histories*, 214–25.

Small, Helen. *Love's Madness*, 123–38.

Turner, Martha A. *Mechanism and the Novel,* 63–78.

The Fair Maid of Perth, 1828

Robertson, Fiona. *Legitimate Histories*, 138–41.

The Fortunes of Nigel, 1822

Gordon, Jan B. *Gossip and Subversion*, 31–33.

Robertson, Fiona. *Legitimate Histories*, 225–33.

Guy Mannering, 1815

Gordon, Jan B. *Gossip and Subversion*, 16–20.

Gordon, Jan B. " 'Liquidating the Sublime': Gossip in Scott's Novels," in Mary A. Favret and Nicola J. Watson, eds., *At the Limits of Romanticism,* 255–57.

The Heart of Midlothian, 1818

Cohen, Michael. *Sisters*, 118–24.

Edgecombe, R. S. "Two Female Saviours in Nineteenth-Century Fiction: Jeanie Deans and Mary Barton." *Engl Stud* (Amsterdam) 77 (1996), 48–58.

Gordon, Jan B. *Gossip and Subversion*, 25–27.

Gordon, Jan B. " 'Liquidating the Sublime': Gossip in Scott's Novels," in Mary A. Favret and Nicola J. Watson, eds., *At the Limits of Romanticism,* 261–62.

Henderson, Andrea K. *Romantic Identities*, 130–62.

Hollahan, Eugene. *Crisis-Consciousness*, 49–54.

Monk, Leland. "The Novel as Prison: Scott's *The Heart of Midlothian." Novel* 27 (1994), 287–302.

Murphy, Peter. "Scott's Disappointments: Reading *The Heart of Midlothian." Mod Philology* 92 (1994), 179–98.

Newman, Beth. "*The Heart of Midlothian* and the Masculinization of Fiction." *Criticism* 36 (1994), 521–37.

Robertson, Fiona. *Legitimate Histories*, 205–14.

Secor, Marie. "Jeanie Deans and the Nature of True Eloquence," in Don H. Bialostosky and Lawrence D. Needham, eds., *Rhetorical Traditions,* 250–63.

Spacks, Patricia Meyer. *Desire and Truth,* 224–31.

Sutherland, John. *Is Heathcliff a Murderer?,* 20–23.

Tysdahl, Bjørn. "Scott's Imagery: The Beast and the Body," in Andrew Kennedy and Orm Øverland, eds., *Excursions in Fiction*, 232–39, 250–51.

Wallace, Miriam L. "Nationalism and the Scottish Subject: The Uneasy Marriage of London and Edinburgh in Sir Walter Scott's *The Heart of Midlothian." Hist of European Ideas* 16:1–3 (1993), 41–47.

Ivanhoe, 1819

Ferris, Ina. *The Achievement of Literary Authority*, 224–28, 237–56.

Galchinsky, Michael. *The Origin of the Modern Jewish Woman Writer*, 45–49.

Kaufmann, David. *The Business of Common Life,* 122–37.

Lackey, Lionel. "Vainly Expected Messiahs: Christianity, Chivalry and Charity in *Ivanhoe." Stud in Scottish Lit* 27 (1992), 150–66.

Lambert, Ellen Zetzel. *The Face of Love,* 32–40.

Millgate, Jane. "Making It New: Scott, Constable, Ballantyne, and the Publication of *Ivanhoe." Stud in Engl Lit, 1500–1900* 34 (1994), 795–808.

Ragussis, Michael. *Figures of Conversion*, 58–61, 89–129, 185–92.

Rignall, John. *Realist Fiction*, 29–31.

Wilt, Judith. "Walter Scott: Narrative, History, Synthesis," in John Richetti et al., eds., *The Columbia History*, 315–17.

The Legend of Montrose, 1819

Ferris, Ina. *The Achievement of Literary Authority*, 207–17.

The Monastery, 1820

Fielding, Penny. *Writing and Orality*, 58–73.

Johnson, Christopher. "The Relationship Between *The Monastery* and *The Abbot." Scottish Liter J* 20:2 (1993), 31–39.

Old Mortality, 1816

Ferris, Ina. *The Achievement of Literary Authority*, 140–60, 161–94.

Peveril of the Peake, 1822

Robertson, Fiona. *Legitimate Histories*, 188–95.

Singer, Daniella E. "Scott's Analysis of Justice, Law, and Equity in *Peveril of the Peak:* The Significance of Martindale." *Studia Neophilologica* 68 (1996), 61–70.

Slagle, Judith Bailey. "Shadwell's *Volunteers* through the Centuries: Power Structures Adapted in Scott's *Peveril of the Peak* and Churchill's *Serious Money." Restoration* 20 (1996), 236–45.

Tait, Margaret. "*Peveril of the Peake." Scott Newsl* 27 (1995), 13–14.

The Pirate, 1821

Robertson, Fiona. *Legitimate Histories*, 169–77.

Redgauntlet, 1824

Brown, Homer Obed. *Institutions of the English Novel*, 145–70.

Ferns, Chris. "That Obscure Object of Desire: Sir Walter Scott and the Borders of Gender." *Engl Stud in Canada* 22:1–3 (1996), 149–64.

Kaufmann, David. *The Business of Common Life,* 110–12.

Rignall, John. *Realist Fiction*, 31–36.

Robertson, Fiona. *Legitimate Histories*, 246–64.

Rob Roy, 1817

Brown, Homer Obed. *Institutions of the English Novel*, 145–70.

Ferns, Chris. "That Obscure Object of Desire: Sir Walter Scott and the Borders of Gender." *Engl Stud in Canada* 22:1–3 (1996), 150–64.

Fielding, Penny. *Writing and Orality*, 153–55.

Robertson, Fiona. *Legitimate Histories*, 177–87.

St. Ronan's Well, 1824

Ferris, Ina. *The Achievement of Literary Authority*, 253–55.

Hartveit, Lars. " 'Silent Intercourse': The Impact of the 18th-Century Conceptual Heritage in *The Antiquary* and *St. Ronan's Well.*" *Engl Stud* (Amsterdam) 77 (1996), 32–44.

The Surgeon's Daughter, 1827

Harper, Marjory. " Adventure or Exile? The Scottish Emigrant in Fiction." *Scottish Liter J* 23:1 (1996), 22–23.

The Talisman, 1825

Hopkins, Lisa. "Clothes and the Body of the Knight: The Making of Men in Sir Walter Scott's *The Talisman.*" *Wordsworth Circle* 27 (1996), 21–24.

Wilt, Judith. "Walter Scott: Narrative, History, Synthesis," in John Richetti et al., eds., *The Columbia History*, 318–20.

Waverley, 1814

Brown, Homer Obed. *Institutions of the English Novel*, 138–70.

Buzard, James. "Translation and Tourism: Scott's *Waverley* and the Rendering of Culture." *Yale J of Criticism* 8:2 (1995), 31–54.

Davis, Paul A. "Scott's Histories and Fiction in *Waverley* and the 'Fictional Essays.' " *REAL: Yrbk of Res in Engl and Am Lit* 9 (1993), 21–32.

Dixon, Robert. *Writing the Colonial Adventure*, 15–20.

Ferns, Chris. "That Obscure Object of Desire: Sir Walter Scott and the Borders of Gender." *Engl Stud in Canada* 22:1–3 (1996), 150–64.

Ferris, Ina. *The Achievement of Literary Authority*, 79–104, 108–33.

Ferris, Ina. "Translation from the Borders: Encounter and Recalcitrance in *Waverley* and *Clan-Albin.*" *Eighteenth-Cent Fiction* 9 (1997), 207–22.

Gordon, Jan B. *Gossip and Subversion*, 1–6.

Gordon, Jan B. " 'Liquidating the Sublime': Gossip in Scott's Novels," in Mary A. Favret and Nicola J. Watson, eds., *At the Limits of Romanticism,* 247–52.

Hamilton, Paul. "*Waverley:* Scott's Romantic Narrative and Revolutionary Historiography." *Stud in Romanticism* 33 (1994), 611–34.

Kaufmann, David. *The Business of Common Life,* 103–14.

Kropf, David Glenn. *Authorship as Alchemy*, 105–50.

Makdisi, Saree. "Colonial Space and the Colonization of Time in Scott's *Waverley.*" *Stud in Romanticism* 34 (1995), 155–87.

Malzahn, Manfred. "Exorcising the Past: Scottish Gentlemen and Gentleman Savages." *Scott Newsl* 29/30 (1996/97), 1–11.

Mergenthal, Silvia. "Un-twisting the Three Serpents: A Comment on a Passage in Scott's *Waverley.*" *Scott Newsl* 19 (1991), 4–6.

Ragussis, Michael. *Figures of Conversion*, 97–99.

Rignall, John. *Realist Fiction*, 22–28.

Spacks, Patricia Meyer. *Desire and Truth,* 206–13.

Sutherland, John. *Is Heathcliff a Murderer?,* 10–13.

Wilt, Judith. "Walter Scott: Narrative, History, Synthesis," in John Richetti et al., eds., *The Columbia History*, 309–12.

Wolf, Werner. "Die Domestizierung der Geschichte: Eine These zur Funktion des englischen historischen Romans im 19. Jahrhundert am Beispiel von Scott, Thackeray und Dickens." *Archiv für das Studium der neueren Sprachen und Literaturen* 231 (1994), 275–81.

Waverley Novels

Ferris, Ina. *The Achievement of Literary Authority*, 89–94, 100–102, 199–222, 242–52.

Gaston, Patricia S. *Prefacing the Waverley Prefaces*, 1–159.

Letellier, Robert Ignatius. *Sir Walter Scott and the Gothic Novel*, 125–204.

Stevenson, A. G. "Law Officers and Deforcement in the Waverley Novels." *Scott Newsl* 25/26 (1994/95), 6–9.

Trumpener, Katie. "The Abbotsford Guide to India: Romantic Fictions of Empire and the Narratives of Canadian Literature," in Deidre Lynch and William B. Warner, eds., *Cultural Institutions of the Novel*, 195–98.

Wesseling, Elisabeth. *Writing History as a Prophet*, 35–49.

Wilt, Judith. "Walter Scott: Narrative, History, Synthesis," in John Richetti et al., eds., *The Columbia History*, 303–5, 308–15, 321–25.

Woodstock, 1826

Robertson, Fiona. *Legitimate Histories*, 265–73.

Tysdahl, Bjørn. "Scott's Imagery: The Beast and the Body," in Andrew Kennedy and Orm Øverland, eds., *Excursions in Fiction*, 240–51.

ADELINE SERGEANT

The Story of a Penitent Soul, 1892

Nelson, Carolyn Christensen. *British Women Fiction Writers*, 61–65.

ANNA SEWARD

Louisa: A Poetical Novel in Four Epistles, 1784

Robinson, Daniel. "Forging the Poetical Novel: The Elision of Form in Anna Seward's *Louisa.*" *Wordsworth Circle* 27 (1996), 25–29.

ELIZABETH SEWELL

The Experience of Life, or Aunt Sarah, 1853
  Brown, Penny. *The Captured World,* 103–5.
Katharine Ashton, 1854
  Horsman, Alan. *The Victorian Novel,* 244–46.

PETER SHAFFER

Withered Murder, 1956
  Bach, Susanne. "*Withered Murder:* Peter Shaffer as Novelist." *Arbeiten aus Anglistik und Amerikanistik* 19:1 (1994), 27–40.

WILLIAM SHARP

The Mountain Lovers, 1895
  Pick, J. B. *The Great Shadow House,* 43–44.

GEORGE BERNARD SHAW

Cashel Byron's Profession, 1886
  Dietrich, Richard Farr. *Bernard Shaw's Novels,* 4–7, 129–44.
  Gordon, David J. *Bernard Shaw and the Comic Sublime,* 73–74.
  Weintraub, Stanley. *Shaw's People,* 5–6.
Immaturity, 1930
  Dietrich, Richard Farr. *Bernard Shaw's Novels,* 78–94, 174–78.
  Gordon, David J. *Bernard Shaw and the Comic Sublime,* 70–71.
  Griffith, Gareth. *Socialism and Superior Brains,* 193–95.
  Koritz, Amy. *Gendering Bodies/Performing Art,* 111–13.
  Mercier, Vivian. *Modern Irish Literature,* 120–23.
  Weintraub, Stanley. *Shaw's People,* 129–30.
The Irrational Knot, 1905
  Dietrich, Richard Farr. *Bernard Shaw's Novels,* 95–114.
  Gordon, David J. *Bernard Shaw and the Comic Sublime,* 71–72.
  Mercier, Vivian. *Modern Irish Literature,* 121–27.
Love Among the Artists, 1900
  Dietrich, Richard Farr. *Bernard Shaw's Novels,* 114–28.
  Gordon, David J. *Bernard Shaw and the Comic Sublime,* 72–73.
An Unsocial Socialist, 1887
  Dietrich, Richard Farr. *Bernard Shaw's Novels,* 145–65.
  Gordon, David J. *Bernard Shaw and the Comic Sublime,* 74–76.
  Griffith, Gareth. *Socialism and Superior Brains,* 26–28.
  Mercier, Vivian. *Modern Irish Literature,* 125–27.

MARY SHELLEY

Falkner, 1837

> Hill-Miller, Katherine C. *"My Hideous Progeny,"* 165–201.
> Smith, Johanna M. *Mary Shelley,* 111–18.

Frankenstein, 1818

> Aldiss, Brian W. *The Detached Retina,* 56–63, 75–80.
> Auerbach, Nina. *Our Vampires, Ourselves,* 19–21.
> Bahar, Saba. *"Frankenstein,* Family Politics and Population Politics." *Swiss Papers in Engl Lang and Lit* 9 (1996), 129–39.
> Batchelor, Rhonda. "The Rise and Fall of the Eighteenth Century's Authentic Feminine Voice." *Eighteenth-Cent Fiction* 6 (1994), 352–55, 357–59, 362–63, 367–68.
> Berthin, Christine. "Insémination et dissémination: *Frankenstein* ou l'imagination au féminin." *Bull de la Société d'Etudes Anglo-Américaines des XVIIe et XVIIIe Siècles* 37 (1993), 103–18.
> Bohls, Elizabeth A. "Standards of Taste, Discourses of 'Race,' and the Aesthetic Education of a Monster: Critique of Empire in *Frankenstein." Eighteenth Cent Life* 18:3 (1994), 23–34.
> Botting, Fred. "Frankenstein, Werther and the Monster of Love." *News from Nowhere* 1995: 157–85.
> Botting, Fred. *Gothic,* 101–6.
> Brewer, William D. "Mary Shelley on Dreams." *Southern Hum R* 29 (1995), 109–10.
> Burwick, Roswitha. "Goethe's *Werther* and Mary Shelley's *Frankenstein." Wordsworth Circle* 24 (1993), 47–52.
> Campbell, Ian. "Jekyll, Hyde, Frankenstein and the Uncertain Self." *Cahiers Victoriens et Edouardiens* 40 (1994), 51–62.
> Cavaliero, Glen. *The Supernatural and English Fiction,* 60–63.
> Clayton, Jay. "Concealed Circuits: Frankenstein's Monster, the Medusa, and the Cyborg." *Raritan* 15:4 (1996), 53–69.
> Connor, Steven. *The English Novel in History,* 169–77.
> Craig, Siobhan. "Monstrous Dialogues: Erotic Discourse and the Dialogic Constitution of the Subject in *Frankenstein,"* in Karen Hohne and Helen Wussow, eds., *A Dialogue of Voices,* 83–95.
> Crawford, Barry. "The Science Fiction of the House of Saul: From Frankenstein's Monster to Lazarus Long," in George Slusser et al., eds., *Immortal Engines,* 147–50, 153–54.
> Dickerson, Vanessa D. "The Ghost of a Self: Female Identity in Mary Shelley's *Frankenstein." J of Popular Culture* 27:3 (1993), 79–90.
> Duyfhuizen, Bernard. "Periphrastic Naming in Mary Shelley's *Frankenstein." Stud in the Novel* 27 (1995), 477–90.
> Fredricks, Nancy. "On the Sublime and Beautiful in Shelley's *Frankenstein." Essays in Lit* (Macomb, IL) 23 (1996), 178–87.
> Frost, R. J. " 'It's Alive!': *Frankenstein*—The Film, the Feminist Novel and Science Fiction." *Foundation* 67 (1996), 75–92.

Goldner, Ellen J. "Monstrous Body, Tortured Soul: *Frankenstein* at the Juncture between Discourses," in Lee Quinby, ed., *Genealogy and Literature,* 28-46.

Gomel, Elana. "The Body of Parts: Dickens and the Poetics of Synecdoche." *J of Narrative Technique* 26 (1996), 53–54, 58–59.

Goodson, A. C. "Frankenstein in the Age of Prozac." *Lit and Medicine* 14–15 (1995–96), 17–30.

Halberstam, Judith. *Skin Shows,* 28–52.

Harris, Steven B. "The Immortality Myth and Technology," in George Slusser et al., eds., *Immortal Engines,* 52–54.

Hill-Miller, Katherine C. *"My Hideous Progeny,"* 59–100.

Hollinger, Veronica. "Putting On the Feminine: Gender and Negativity in *Frankenstein* and *The Handmaid's Tale,"* in Daniel Fischlin, ed., *Negation, Critical Theory, and Postmodern Textuality,* 209–15.

Howard, Jacqueline. *Reading Gothic Fiction,* 238–84.

Huet, Marie-Hélène. *Monstrous Imagination,* 129–62.

Jacobs, Naomi. "The Frozen Landscape in Women's Utopian and Science Fiction," in Jane L. Donawerth and Carol A. Kolmerten, eds., *Utopian and Science Fiction,* 192–94.

Johnson, Anthony. "Gaps and Gothic Sensibility: Walpole, Lewis, Mary Shelley, and Maturin," in Valeria Tinkler-Villani and Peter Davidson, eds., *Exhibited by Candlelight,* 10–24.

Kaufmann, David. *The Business of Common Life,* 30–36, 57–64.

Kearns, Katherine. *Nineteenth-Century Literary Realism,* 119–43.

Kercsmar, Rhonda Ray. "Displaced Apocalypse and Eschatological Anxiety in *Frankenstein." South Atlantic Q* 95 (1996), 729–47.

Ketterer, David. "Frankenstein's 'Conversion' from Natural Magic to Modern Science—and a *Shifted* (and Converted) Last Draft Insert." *Science-Fiction Stud* 24:1 (1997), 57–71.

Kilgour, Maggie. *The Rise of the Gothic Novel,* 39–41, 190–217.

Knoepflmacher, U. C. "Afterword: Endings as Beginnings," in Alison Booth, ed., *Famous Last Words,* 350–51, 353–55.

Lansdown, Richard. "Beginning Life: Mary Shelley's Introduction to *Frankenstein." Crit R* 35 (1995), 81–94.

Leader, Zachary. *Revision and Romantic Authorship,* 167–205.

McLane, Maureen Noelle. "Literate Species: Populations, 'Humanities,' and *Frankenstein." ELH* 63 (1996), 959–83.

Macovski, Michael. *Dialogue and Literature,* 105–33.

Maertz, Gregory. "Family Resemblances: Intertextual Dialogue Between Father and Daughter Novelists in Godwin's *St. Leon* and Shelley's *Frankenstein." Univ of Mississippi Stud in Engl* 11–12 (1993–95), 303–17.

Malchow, H. L. *Gothic Images of Race,* 9–40.

Marshall, Tim. *"Frankenstein* and the 1832 Anatomy Act," in Allan Lloyd Smith and Victor Sage, eds., *Gothick Origins and Innovations,* 57–64.

Marshall, Tim. *Murdering to Dissect,* 11–16, 50–60, 141–50, 177–328.

Maule, Victoria. "On the Subversion of Character in the Literature of Identity Anxiety," in Derek Littlewood and Peter Stockwell, eds., *Impossibility Fiction*, 116–17.

May, Leila Silvana. "Sibling Revelry in Mary Shelley's *Frankenstein*." *Stud in Engl Lit, 1500–1900* 35 (1995), 669–81.

Mellor, Anne K. "A Novel of Their Own: Romantic Women's Fiction, 1790–1830," in John Richetti et al., eds., *The Columbia History*, 346–49.

Michie, Elsie B. *Outside the Pale*, 14–16, 20–45.

Miller, Elizabeth. "*Frankenstein* and *Dracula*: The Question of Influence," in Allienne R. Becker, ed., *Visions of the Fantastic*, 123–29.

Milner, Andrew. *Literature, Culture, and Society*, 149–60, 162–67.

Moretti, Franco. *Signs Taken For Wonders*, 88–91, 105–7.

Neff, D. S. "The 'Paradise of the Mothersons': *Frankenstein* and *The Empire of the Nairs*." *JEGP* 95 (1996), 210–22.

Neilson, Heather. " 'The face at the window': Gothic Thematics in *Frankenstein, Wuthering Heights,* and *The Turn of the Screw*." *Sydney Stud in Engl* 19 (1993–94), 76–80.

Purinton, Marjean D. "Ideological Revision: Cross-Gender Characterization in Mary Shelley's *Frankenstein*." *CEA Critic* 56:1 (1993), 53–62.

Rauch, Alan. "The Monstrous Body of Knowledge in Mary Shelley's *Frankenstein*." *Stud in Romanticism* 34 (1995), 227–53.

Richardson, Alan. *Literature, Education, and Romanticism*, 204–12.

Richter, David H. *The Progress of Romance*, 101–3.

Rose, Ellen Cronan. "Custody Battles: Reproducing Knowledge about *Frankenstein*." *New Liter Hist* 26 (1995), 809–29.

Salotto, Eleanor. "*Frankenstein* and Dis(re)membered Identity." *J of Narrative Technique* 24 (1994), 190–207.

Sanderson, Richard K. "Glutting the Maw of Death: Suicide and Procreation in *Frankenstein*." *South Central R* 9:2 (1992), 49–64.

Sayres, William G. "Compounding the Crime: Ingratitude and the Murder Conviction of Justine Moritz in *Frankenstein*." *Engl Lang Notes* 31:4 (1994), 48–53.

Shattuck, Roger. *Forbidden Knowledge*, 84–86, 93–95, 97–100.

Smith, Johanna M. *Mary Shelley*, 40–48.

Smith, Mark Trevor. *"All Nature Is But Art,"* 91–114.

Stableford, Brian. "Frankenstein and the Origins of Science Fiction," in David Seed, ed., *Anticipations*, 46–57.

Stewart, Garrett. *Dear Reader*, 113–32.

Sutherland, John. *Is Heathcliff a Murderer?*, 24–34.

Thompson, Terry W. "Wrapped in Darkness: Hecate in Chapter Sixteen of *Frankenstein*." *Engl Lang Notes* 33:3 (1996), 28–32.

Voller, Jack G. *The Supernatural Sublime*, 159–69, 175–78.

Willis, Martin. "*Frankenstein* and the Soul." *Essays in Criticism* 45 (1995), 24–34.

Wilson, Jean. "Romanticism's Real Women," in David L. Clark and Donald C. Goellnicht, eds., *New Romanticisms*, 259–60.

Zwickel, Carol. "The Functions of the Narratees in Mary Shelley's *Frankenstein.*" *Bull of the West Virginia Assoc of Coll Engl Teachers* 13:1 (1991), 69–75.

The Last Man, 1826

Aldiss, Brian W. *The Detached Retina,* 63–68.

Bradshaw, Michael. "Mary Shelley's *The Last Man:* The End of the World as We Know It," in Derek Littlewood and Peter Stockwell, eds., *Impossibility Fiction,* 163–75.

Jacobus, Mary. *First Things,* 106–23.

Nellist, Brian. "Imagining the Future: Predictive Fiction in the Nineteenth Century," in David Seed, ed., *Anticipations,* 114–17.

Parrinder, Patrick. "From Mary Shelley to *The War of the Worlds:* The Thames Valley Catastrophe," in David Seed, ed., *Anticipations,* 65–67.

Schor, Esther. *Bearing the Dead,* 235–40.

Smith, Johanna M. *Mary Shelley,* 48–54.

Stewart, Garrett. *Dear Reader,* 114–16, 126–30, 166–68.

Lodore, 1835

Hill-Miller, Katherine C. *"My Hideous Progeny,"* 128–64.

Smith, Johanna M. *Mary Shelley,* 105–11.

Mathilda, 1959

Brewer, William D. "Mary Shelley on Dreams." *Southern Hum R* 29 (1995), 110–13.

Brewer, William D. "Mary Shelley on the Therapeutic Value of Language." *Papers on Lang and Lit* 30 (1994), 390–406.

Ford, Susan Allen. " 'A name more dear': Daughters, Fathers, and Desire in *A Simple Story, The False Friend,* and *Mathilda,*" in Carol Shiner Wilson and Joel Haefner, eds., *Re-Visioning Romanticism,* 57–67.

Gonda, Caroline. *Reading Daughters' Fictions,* 164–69.

Henderson, Andrea K. *Romantic Identities,* 120–29.

Hill-Miller, Katherine C. *"My Hideous Progeny,"* 101–27.

McKeever, Kerry. "Naming the Daughter's Suffering: Melancholia in Mary Shelley's *Mathilda.*" *Essays in Lit* (Macomb, IL) 23 (1996), 190–205.

Rajan, Tilottama. "Mary Shelley's *Mathilda:* Melancholy and the Political Economy of Romanticism." *Stud in the Novel* 26 (1994), 43–61.

Smith, Johanna M. *Mary Shelley,* 94–96.

Perkin Warbeck, 1830

Santagostino, Federica. "Storia e *fiction* in *Perkin Warbeck* di Mary Shelley." *Confronto Letterario* 11:21 (1994), 111–18.

Smith, Johanna M. *Mary Shelley,* 81–92.

Valperga, 1823

Brewer, William D. "Mary Shelley on Dreams." *Southern Hum R* 29 (1995), 113–18.

Brewer, William D. "Mary Shelley's *Valperga:* The Triumph of Eutha-
nasia's Mind." *European Romantic R* 5 (1995), 133–48.

Rajan, Tilottama. "Mary Shelley's *Mathilda:* Melancholy and the Political Economy of Romanticism." *Stud in the Novel* 26 (1994), 62–65.

Smith, Johanna M. *Mary Shelley,* 68–76.

PERCY BYSSHE SHELLEY

St. Irvyne, 1811

Voller, Jack G. *The Supernatural Sublime,* 169–72.

FRANCES SHERIDAN

The Memoirs of Miss Sidney Bidulph, 1761–1767

Harries, Elizabeth Wanning. *The Unfinished Manner,* 144–48.

MacCarthy, B. G. *The Female Pen,* 310–15.

Spacks, Patricia Meyer. *Desire and Truth,* 134–40.

Spacks, Patricia Meyer. "Oscillations of Sensibility." *New Liter Hist* 25
(1994), 508–11.

Todd, Janet. *The Sign of Angellica,* 166–75.

MARY MARTHA SHERWOOD

Fairchild Family, 1818

Brown, Penny. *The Captured World,* 44–47.

Richardson, Alan. *Literature, Education, and Romanticism,* 137–40.

The History of Henry Milner, 1823–1837

Brown, Penny. *The Captured World,* 48–49.

M. P. SHIEL

The Purple Cloud, 1901

Keep, C. J. "Cross-Dressing at the End of Time: Orientalism and Apocalypse in M. P. Shiel's *The Purple Cloud." Frontenac R* 10–11 (1993–
94), 129–49.

PHILIP SIDNEY

Arcadia, 1598

Biester, James. " 'A Pleasant and Terrible Reverence': Maintenance of
Majesty in Sidney's *New Arcadia." Philol Q* 72 (1993), 419–38.

Cantar, Brenda. "Charmed Circles of Enchantment: Pre-Oedipal Fantasies in Sir Philip Sidney's *Arcadia." Sidney Newsl* 12:1 (1992), 3–20.

Carver, Robert H. F. " 'Valiant Aristomenes': A Messenian Hero in Sidney's *Old Arcadia* ." *Notes and Queries* 41 (1994), 26–28.

Casaregola, Vincent. "Unstable Elements: The Explosion of the '*Arcadia* Project,' " in Wolfgang Görtschacher and Holger Klein, eds., *Narrative Strategies*, 147–63.

Dickson, Lynne. "Sidney's Grotesque Muse: Fictional Excess and the Feminine in the *Arcadias.*" *Renaissance Papers* 1992, 41–55.

Hopkins, Lisa. "The Disguised Royalty Motif in the *Arcadia,*" in Wolfgang Görtschacher and Holger Klein, eds., *Narrative Strategies*, 187–93.

Hunt, Maurice. "*The Countess of Pembroke's Arcadia,* Shakespeare's *A Midsummer Night's Dream,* and the School of Night: An Intertextual Nexus." *Essays in Lit* (Macomb, IL) 23 (1996), 3–16.

Iser, Wolfgang. "Liebe und Verwandlung im Schäferroman: Zur Poetologie des Fiktiven," in Herbert Foltinek et al., eds., *Tales and "their telling difference,"* 154–56, 160–63.

Kegl, Rosemary. *The Rhetoric of Concealment*, 45–75.

Kinney, Clare R. "Chivalry Unmasked: Courtly Spectacle and the Abuses of Romance in Sidney's *New Arcadia.*" *Stud in Engl Lit, 1500–1900* 35 (1995), 35–50.

Lamb, Mary Ellen. "Exhibiting Class and Displaying the Body in Sidney's *Countess of Pembroke's Arcadia.*" *Stud in Engl Lit, 1500–1900* 37 (1997), 55–69.

Partee, Morriss Henry. "Sir Philip Sidney and the Lure of Beauty." *Publs of the Arkansas Philol Assoc* 19:2 (1993), 53–69.

Relihan, Constance C. "The Geography of the Arcadian Landscape: Constructing Otherness, Preserving Europe," in Wolfgang Görtschacher and Holger Klein, eds., *Narrative Strategies*, 167–83.

Roberts, Katherine J. *Fair Ladies: Sir Philip Sidney's Female Characters*.

Saupe, Karen. "Trial, Error, and Revision in Sidney's *Arcadias.*" *Sidney Newsl* 12:2 (1993), 22–29.

Skretkowicz, Victor. "Categorising Redirection in Sidney's *New Arcadia,*" in Wolfgang Görtschacher and Holger Klein, eds., *Narrative Strategies*, 290–96.

Sussman, Anne. " 'Sweetly Ravished': Sidney's *Old Arcadia* and the Poetics of Sexual Violence." *Renaissance Papers* 1994, 55–66.

White, R. S. *Natural Law*, 137–48.

Worden, Blair. *The Sound of Virtue*, 3–354.

ALAN SILLITOE

The Death of William Posters, 1965

García Tortosa, Francisco. "*Ellos* y *nosotros* en Alan Sillitoe," in Juan Bargalló, ed., *Identidad y Alteridad*, 77–79.

Wilding, Michael. *Social Visions*, 120–25.

The Flame of Life, 1974
  Wilding, Michael. *Social Visions,* 130–39.
Key to the Door, 1961
  Wilding, Michael. *Social Visions,* 107–20.
Saturday Night and Sunday Morning, 1958
  Taylor, D. J. *After the War,* 105–9, 111–23, 125–28.
  Wilding, Michael. *Social Visions,* 95–107.
A Tree on Fire, 1967
  Wilding, Michael. *Social Visions,* 125–30.

CATHERINE SINCLAIR

Holiday House: A Book for the Young, 1839
  Brown, Penny. *The Captured World,* 95–98.

MAY SINCLAIR

The Creators, 1910
  Harris, Janice H. "Challenging the Script of the Heterosexual Couple: Three Marriage Novels by May Sinclair." *Papers on Lang and Lit* 29 (1993), 452–56.
  Miller, Jane Eldridge. *Rebel Women,* 189–94.
The Helpmate, 1907
  Harris, Janice H. "Challenging the Script of the Heterosexual Couple: Three Marriage Novels by May Sinclair." *Papers on Lang and Lit* 29 (1993), 439–48.
Kitty Tailleur, 1908
  Harris, Janice H. "Challenging the Script of the Heterosexual Couple: Three Marriage Novels by May Sinclair." *Papers on Lang and Lit* 29 (1993), 448–52.
Life and Death of Harriet Frean, 1922
  Phillips, Terry. "Battling with the Angel: May Sinclair's Powerful Mothers," in Sarah Sceats and Gail Cunningham, eds., *Image and Power,* 134–37.
  Würzbach, Natascha. "The Mother Image as Cultural Concept and Literary Theme in the Nineteenth- and Twentieth-Century English Novel: A Feminist Reading within the Context of New Historicism and the History of Mentalities," in Rüdiger Ahrens and Laurenz Volkmann, eds., *Why Literature Matters,* 382.
Mary Olivier, 1919
  Phillips, Terry. "Battling with the Angel: May Sinclair's Powerful Mothers," in Sarah Sceats and Gail Cunningham, eds., *Image and Power,* 129–34.

Würzbach, Natascha. "The Mother Image as Cultural Concept and Literary Theme in the Nineteenth- and Twentieth-Century English Novel: A Feminist Reading within the Context f New Historicism and the History of Mentalities," in Rüdiger Ahrens and Laurenz Volkmann, eds., *Why Literature Matters*, 381–82.

The Romantic, 1920

Goldman, Dorothy. *Women Writers and the Great War*, 60–62.

The Three Sisters, 1914

Miller, Jane Eldridge. *Rebel Women,* 194–200.

CHARLOTTE SMITH

The Banished Man, 1794

Fry, Carrol L. *Charlotte Smith*, 84–88.

Celestina, 1791

Fry, Carrol L. *Charlotte Smith*, 45–47.

Desmond, 1792

Conway, Alison. "Nationalism, Revolution, and the Female Body: Charlotte Smith's *Desmond." Women's Stud* 24 (1995), 395–406.

Fry, Carrol L. *Charlotte Smith*, 65–80.

MacCarthy, B. G. *The Female Pen,* 392–94.

Rogers, Katharine M. "Romantic Aspirations, Restricted Possibilities: The Novels of Charlotte Smith," in Carol Shiner Wilson and Joel Haefner, eds., *Re-Visioning Romanticism*, 74–80.

Ty, Eleanor. *Unsex'd Revolutionaries,* 130–42.

Emmeline, 1788

Forbes, Joan. "Anti-Romantic Discourse as Resistance: Women's Fiction 1775–1820," in Lynne Pearce and Jackie Stacey, eds., *Romance Revisited*, 294–304.

Fry, Carrol L. *Charlotte Smith*, 42–44, 60–63.

Mohr, Hans-Ulrich. "Drei Konstrukte weiblicher Verhaltensräume: Charlotte Smith, Olive Schreiner, Angela Carter." *Arbeiten aus Anglistik und Amerikanistik* 20 (1995), 317–33.

Rogers, Katharine M. "Romantic Aspirations, Restricted Possibilities: The Novels of Charlotte Smith," in Carol Shiner Wilson and Joel Haefner, eds., *Re-Visioning Romanticism*, 72–78.

Ty, Eleanor. *Unsex'd Revolutionaries,* 115–29.

Ethelinde, 1789

Fry, Carrol L. *Charlotte Smith*, 44–45.

Marchmont, 1796

Fry, Carrol L. *Charlotte Smith*, 100–104.

Montalbert, 1795

Fry, Carrol L. *Charlotte Smith*, 124–29.

Rogers, Katharine M. "Romantic Aspirations, Restricted Possibilities:

The Novels of Charlotte Smith," in Carol Shiner Wilson and Joel Haefner, eds., *Re-Visioning Romanticism*, 75–79.

The Old Manor House, 1793

Fletcher, Loraine. "Charlotte Smith's Emblematic Castles." *Crit Survey* 4 (1992), 3–8.

Fry, Carrol L. *Charlotte Smith*, 90–96.

MacCarthy, B. G. *The Female Pen*, 394–98.

Mellor, Anne K. "A Novel of Their Own: Romantic Women's Fiction, 1790–1830," in John Richetti et al., eds., *The Columbia History*, 330–31.

Spacks, Patricia Meyer. "Novels of the 1790s: Action and Impasse," in John Richetti et al., eds., *The Columbia History*, 265–67.

The Wanderings of Warwick, 1794

Fry, Carrol L. *Charlotte Smith*, 96–97.

The Young Philosopher, 1798

Fry, Carrol L. *Charlotte Smith*, 104–8, 130–32.

Rogers, Katharine M. "Romantic Aspirations, Restricted Possibilities: The Novels of Charlotte Smith," in Carol Shiner Wilson and Joel Haefner, eds., *Re-Visioning Romanticism*, 79–83, 85–87.

Ty, Eleanor. *Unsex'd Revolutionaries*, 143–54.

JOAN SMITH

A Masculine Ending, 1987

Antor, Heinz. *Der englische Universitätsroman*, 706–8.

PAUL SMITH

The Countrywoman, 1962

Emprin, Jacques. "*The Countrywoman* de Paul Smith: Représentation du paupérisme dublinois dans les années 1920." *Etudes Irlandaises* 21:2 (1996), 56–65.

STEVIE SMITH

The Holiday, 1949

Civello, Catherine A. "Stevie Smith's *Ecriture Féminine:* Pre-Oedipal Desires and Wartime Realities." *Mosaic* 28:2 (1995), 118–21.

Schneider, Karen. *Loving Arms*, 70–72.

Severin, Laura. "Recovering the Serious Antics of Stevie Smith's Novels." *Twentieth Cent Lit* 40 (1994), 463–74.

Novel on Yellow Paper, 1936

Civello, Catherine A. "Stevie Smith's *Ecriture Féminine:* Pre-Oedipal Desires and Wartime Realities." *Mosaic* 28:2 (1995), 110–14.

Lassner, Phyllis. " 'The Milk of Our Mother's Kindness Has Ceased to Flow': Virginia Woolf, Stevie Smith, and the Representation of the Jew," in Bryan Cheyette, ed., *Between 'Race' and Culture*, 139–44.

Over the Frontier, 1938

Civello, Catherine A. "Stevie Smith's *Ecriture Féminine:* Pre-Oedipal Desires and Wartime Realities." *Mosaic* 28:2 (1995), 114–18.

Lassner, Phyllis. " 'The Milk of Our Mother's Kindness Has Ceased to Flow': Virginia Woolf, Stevie Smith, and the Representation of the Jew," in Bryan Cheyette, ed., *Between 'Race' and Culture*, 139–44.

Plain, Gill. *Women's Fiction of the Second World War*, 68–84.

Schneider, Karen. *Loving Arms*, 61–70.

Wheeler, Kathleen. *'Modernist' Women Writers*, 148–61.

TOBIAS SMOLLETT

Ferdinand Count Fathom, 1753

Donoghue, Frank. *The Fame Machine*, 125–32, 140–43.

Douglas, Aileen. *Uneasy Sensations*, 96–116.

Rousseau, G. S. "From Swift to Smollett: The Satirical Tradition in Prose Narrative," in John Richetti et al., eds., *The Columbia History*, 141–44.

Skinner, John. *Constructions of Smollett*, 119–40.

Spector, Robert D. *Smollett's Women*, 39–46, 85–92, 117–19.

The History and Adventures of an Atom, 1769

Douglas, Aileen. *Uneasy Sensations*, 130–61.

Rousseau, G. S. "From Swift to Smollett: The Satirical Tradition in Prose Narrative," in John Richetti et al., eds., *The Columbia History*, 146–47.

Skinner, John. *Constructions of Smollett*, 161–76.

Humphry Clinker, 1771

Bony, Alain. "*The Expedition of Humphry Clinker,* ou le corps du roman: Théorie et pratique de l'écriture romanesque selon Smollett." *Recherches Anglaises et Nord-Américaines* 26 (1993), 113–36.

Bulckaen, Denise. "De l'autre au soi: Le Vrai Voyage dans *Humphry Clinker.*" *Bull de la Société d'Etudes Anglo-Américaines des XVIIe et XVIIIe Siècles* 35 (1992), 91–104.

Bulckaen, Denise. "Savoir ou être: Réévaluation de l'itinéraire éducatif du héros smollettien (l'exemple de *Humphry Clinker*)." *Bull de la Société d'Etudes Anglo-Américaines des XVIIe et XVIIIe Siècles* 34 (1992), 67–84.

Cantrell, Pamela. "Writing the Picture: Fielding, Smollett, and Hogarthian Pictorialism." *Stud in Eighteenth-Cent Culture* 24 (1995), 72–80.

Donoghue, Frank. *The Fame Machine*, 150–58.

Douglas, Aileen. *Uneasy Sensations*, 162–84.

Haggerty, George E. "Amelia's Nose; or, Sensibility and Its Symptoms." *Eighteenth Cent* 36 (1995), 144–45.

Jacobsen, Susan L. " 'The Tinsel of the Times': Smollett's Argument against Conspicuous Consumption in *Humphry Clinker.*" *Eighteenth-Cent Fiction* 9 (1996), 71–88.

McCrea, Brian. "*Roderick Random*'s 'Agreeable Lassitude' and Smollett's Anamnestic Fiction." *J of Narrative Technique* 25 (1995), 167–71.

Miles, Peter. "The Bookhood of *Humphry Clinker:* The Editor, the Publisher, and the Law." *Eighteenth Cent Life* 18:1 (1994), 48–62.

Miles, Peter. "Smollett, Rowlandson, and a Problem of Identity: Decoding Names, Bodies, and Gender in *Humphry Clinker.*" *Eighteenth-Cent Life* 20:1 (1996), 1–20.

Rousseau, G. S. "From Swift to Smollett: The Satirical Tradition in Prose Narrative," in John Richetti et al., eds., *The Columbia History*, 147–52.

Schellenberg, Betty A. *The Conversational Circle*, 102–16.

Schwarzschild, Edward L. " 'I Will Take the Whole Upon My Own Shoulders': Collections and Corporeality in *Humphry Clinker.*" *Criticism* 36 (1994), 541–64.

Sharp, Andrew. "Scots, Savages, and Barbarians: *Humphry Clinker* and the Scots' Philosophy." *Eighteenth Cent Life* 18:3 (1994), 65–76.

Skinner, John. *Constructions of Smollett*, 188–215.

Spector, Robert D. *Smollett's Women,* 60–80, 144–60.

Sussman, Charlotte. "Lismahago's Captivity: Transculturation in *Humphry Clinker.*" *ELH* 61 (1994), 597–616.

Vivies, Jean. "Savoir-faire ancien ou savoir-faire nouveau? Le Dénouement de *Humphry Clinker.*" *Bull de la Société d'Etudes Anglo-Américaines des XVIIe et XVIIIe Siècles* 41 (1995), 123–33.

Warner, John M. *Joyce's Grandfathers*, 73–88.

Peregrine Pickle, 1751

Bauer, Matthias. *Im Fuchsbau der Geschichten*, 116–20.

Bauer, Matthias. *Der Schelmenroman*, 178–79.

Brack, O. M., Jr. "Smollett's *Peregrine Pickle* Revisited." *Stud in the Novel* 27 (1995), 260–70.

Cantrell, Pamela. "Writing the Picture: Fielding, Smollett, and Hogarthian Pictorialism." *Stud in Eighteenth-Cent Culture* 24 (1995), 84–86.

Donoghue, Frank. *The Fame Machine*, 125–32, 136–40.

Douglas, Aileen. *Uneasy Sensations,* 70–94.

Nelson, T. G. A. *Children, Parents, and the Rise of the Novel*, 152–59, 205–8.

Rousseau, G. S. "From Swift to Smollett: The Satirical Tradition in Prose Narrative," in John Richetti et al., eds., *The Columbia History*, 137–43.

Skinner, John. *Constructions of Smollett*, 67–106.

Spector, Robert D. *Smollett's Women,* 20–22, 46–60, 132–38.

Warner, John M. *Joyce's Grandfathers,* 66–72.

Roderick Random, 1748

Bauer, Matthias. *Im Fuchsbau der Geschichten,* 116–20.

Bauer, Matthias. *Der Schelmenroman,* 177–78.

Beasley, Jerry C. "Translation and Cultural *Translatio,*" in Carmen Benito-Vessels and Michael Zappala, eds., *The Picaresque,* 98–105.

Bruhm, Steven. "Roderick Random's Closet." *Engl Stud in Canada* 19 (1993), 401–13.

Donoghue, Frank. *The Fame Machine,* 125–29, 133–36.

Douglas, Aileen. *Uneasy Sensations,* 43–69.

McCrea, Brian. "*Roderick Random*'s 'Agreeable Lassitude' and Smollett's Anamnestic Fiction." *J of Narrative Technique* 25 (1995), 154–67.

Nelson, T. G. A. *Children, Parents, and the Rise of the Novel,* 202–5.

Phillips, Jerry. "Narrative, Adventure, and Schizophrenia: From Smollett's *Roderick Random* to Melville's *Omoo.*" *J of Narrative Technique* 25 (1995), 177–84.

Rousseau, G. S. "From Swift to Smollett: The Satirical Tradition in Prose Narrative," in John Richetti et al., eds., *The Columbia History,* 133–37.

Skinner, John. *Constructions of Smollett,* 31–66.

Skinner, John. "*Roderick Random* and the Fiction of Autobiography." *Auto/Biography Stud* 9:1 (1994), 98–114.

Spector, Robert D. *Smollett's Women,* 20–22, 26–34, 92–99.

Warner, John M. *Joyce's Grandfathers,* 58–66.

Zomchick, John P. *Family and the Law,* 105–29.

Sir Launcelot Greaves, 1762

Cantrell, Pamela. "Writing the Picture: Fielding, Smollett, and Hogarthian Pictorialism." *Stud in Eighteenth-Cent Culture* 24 (1995), 81–84.

Donoghue, Frank. *The Fame Machine,* 146–51.

Douglas, Aileen. *Uneasy Sensations,* 116–29.

Punday, Daniel. "Satiric Method and the Reader in *Sir Launcelot Greaves.*" *Eighteenth-Cent Fiction* 6 (1994), 169–88.

Rousseau, G. S. "From Swift to Smollett: The Satirical Tradition in Prose Narrative," in John Richetti et al., eds., *The Columbia History,* 144–45.

Skinner, John. *Constructions of Smollett,* 140–61.

Spector, Robert D. *Smollett's Women,* 34–39, 126–28.

C. P. SNOW

The Affair, 1960

Eriksson, Bo H. T. *The "Structuring Forces" of Detection,* 60–71.

A Coat of Varnish, 1978

    Eriksson, Bo H. T. *The "Structuring Forces" of Detection,* 99–120.

Death under Sail, 1932

    Eriksson, Bo H. T. *The "Structuring Forces" of Detection,* 33–49.

The Masters, 1951

    Antor, Heinz. *Der englische Universitätsroman,* 654–56.

New Lives for Old, 1933

    Rabinovitz, Rubin. "The Reaction against Modernism: Amis, Snow, Wilson," in John Richetti et al., eds., *The Columbia History,* 908–9.

The Sleep of Reason, 1968

    Eriksson, Bo H. T. *The "Structuring Forces" of Detection,* 71–98.

Strangers and Brothers, 1940–1970

    Eriksson, Bo H. T. *The "Structuring Forces" of Detection,* 50–60.

ROBERT SOUTHEY

The Doctor, etc., 1834

    Shortland, Michael. "Robert Southey's *The Doctor, etc.:* Anonymity and Authorship." *Engl Lang Notes* 31:4 (1994), 54–61.

MURIEL SPARK

The Comforters, 1957

    Cavaliero, Glen. *The Supernatural and English Fiction,* 203–4.

The Driver's Seat, 1970

    Cavaliero, Glen. *The Supernatural and English Fiction,* 206–7.

The Hothouse by the East River, 1973

    Cavaliero, Glen. *The Supernatural and English Fiction,* 205–6.

    Meaney, Gerardine. *(Un)Like Subjects,* 161–63, 180–85, 187–91, 196–216.

Memento Mori, 1959

    Edgecombe, Rodney Stenning. "Muriel Spark, Cardinal Newman and an Aphorism in *Memento Mori.*" *Notes on Contemp Lit* 24:1 (1994), 12.

The Prime of Miss Jean Brodie, 1961

    Ashworth, Ann. "The Betrayal of the Mentor in *The Prime of Miss Jean Brodie.*" *J of Evolutionary Psych* 16:1–2 (1995), 37–46.

    Whiteley, Patrick J. "The Social Framework of Knowledge: Muriel Spark's *The Prime of Miss Jean Brodie.*" *Mosaic* 29:4 (1996), 79–99.

Symposium, 1990

    Monterrey, Tomás. "Old and New Elements in Muriel Spark's *Symposium.*" *Stud in Scottish Lit* 27 (1992), 175–88.

HENRY DEVERE STACPOOLE

The Blue Lagoon, 1908

Hardin, Richard F. "The Man Who Wrote *The Blue Lagoon:* Stacpoole's Pastoral Center." *Engl Lit in Transition, 1880–1920* 39 (1996), 205–19.

DOROTHY STANLEY

Miss Pim's Camouflage, 1918

Goldman, Dorothy. *Women Writers and the Great War*, 55–57.

OLAF STAPLEDON

Darkness and the Light, 1942

Crossley, Robert. *Olaf Stapledon*, 275–78.

Last and First Men, 1930

Crossley, Robert. *Olaf Stapledon*, 182–200.

Last Men in London, 1932

Crossley, Robert. *Olaf Stapledon*, 198–204.

A Man Divided, 1950

Crossley, Robert. *Olaf Stapledon*, 389–91.

Odd John, 1935

Crossley, Robert. *Olaf Stapledon*, 220–31.

Sirius, 1944

Crossley, Robert. *Olaf Stapledon*, 292–96, 302–4, 308–12.

The Star Maker, 1937

Aldiss, Brian W. *The Detached Retina*, 41–43.
Crossley, Robert. *Olaf Stapledon*, 228–33, 239–50, 275–78.

CHRISTINA STEAD

Cotters' England, 1967

Blake, Ann. "Christina Stead's Tyneside Novel: *Cotters' England.*" *Durham Univ J* 86 (1994), 271–79.

FLORA ANNIE STEEL

On the Face of the Waters, 1896

Paxton, Nancy L. "Mobilizing Chivalry: Rape in Flora Annie Steel's *On the Face of the Waters* (1896) and Other British Novels about the Indian Uprising of 1857," in Barbara Leah Harman and Susan Meyer, eds., *The New Nineteenth Century*, 266–71.

JAMES STEPHENS

The Charwoman's Daughter, 1912
  Martin, Augustine. *Bearing Witness,* 73–75.
The Crock of Gold, 1912
  Martin, Augustine. *Bearing Witness,* 115–28.

LAURENCE STERNE

A Sentimental Journey, 1768
  Battestin, Martin C. "*A Sentimental Journey:* Sterne's 'Work of Redemption.' " *Bull de la Société d'Etudes Anglo-Américaines des XVIIe et XVIIIe Siècles* 38 (1994), 189–204.
  Battestin, Martin C. "Sterne among the *Philosophes:* Body and Soul in *A Sentimental Journey.*" *Eighteenth-Cent Fiction* 7 (1994), 17–36.
  Benedict, Barbara M. *Framing Feeling,* 88–92.
  Chézaud, Patrick. "Langage naturel et art du roman chez Laurence Sterne." *Bull de la Société d'Etudes Anglo-Américaines des XVIIe et XVIIIe Siècles* 41 (1995), 113–22.
  Davidson, Elizabeth. "*A Sentimental Journey,* Volume I: Yorick's Apprenticeship of Manners." *Coll Lang Assoc J* 37 (1994), 453–66.
  Denizot, Paul. "Ecriture et peinture dans *Le Voyage sentimental.*" *Bull de la Société d'Etudes Anglo-Américaines des XVIIe et XVIIIe Siècles* 40 (1995), 35–46.
  Denizot, Paul. "Singulier et pluriel dans *A Sentimental Journey.*" *Bull de la Société d'Etudes Anglo-Américaines des XVIIe et XVIIIe Siècles* 37 (1993), 73–83.
  Descargues, Madeleine. "*A Sentimental Journey,* ou le cas d'indélicatesse." *Etudes Anglaises* 46 (1993), 407–19.
  Donoghue, Frank. *The Fame Machine,* 82–85.
  Dupas, Jean-Claude. "L''Innomable': Le *Sentiment* dans *A Sentimental Journey.*" *Bull de la Société d'Etudes Anglo-Américaines des XVIIe et XVIIIe Siècles* 37 (1993), 85–102.
  Dupas, Jean-Claude. "*A Sentimental Journey:* 'Hint(ing) at the Circumstances Which Make It So.' " *Bull de la Société d'Etudes Anglo-Américaines des XVIIe et XVIIIe Siècles* 38 (1994), 205–16.
  Fuchs, Anne. "Sterne's *Sentimental Journey* and Goethe's *Italian Journey:* Two Models of the Non-Perception of Otherness." *New Comparison* 16 (1993), 26–42.
  Gould, Rebecca. "Sterne's Sentimental Yorick as Male Hysteric." *Stud in Engl Lit, 1500–1900* 36 (1996), 641–51.
  Haggerty, George E. "Amelia's Nose; or, Sensibility and Its Symptoms." *Eighteenth Cent* 36 (1995), 139–43.
  Hansen, Klaus P. "Bürgerliche und unbürgerliche Empfindsamkeit in England," in Hansen, ed., *Empfindsamkeiten,* 60–62.
  Harries, Elizabeth Wanning. *The Unfinished Manner,* 41–47, 53–55.

Keymer, Tom. "Marvell, Thomas Hollis, and Sterne's Maria: Parody in *A Sentimental Journey*." *Shandean* 5 (1993), 9–26.

Kraft, Elizabeth. *Laurence Sterne Revisited*, 105–28.

Miller, Eric. "The Insufficiency, Success, and Significance of Natural History." *Stud in Engl Lit, 1500–1900* 35 (1995), 519–31.

Mullan, John. "Sterne's Comedy of Sentiments." *Bull de la Société d'Etudes Anglo-Américaines des XVIIe et XVIIIe Siècles* 38 (1994), 233–41.

Myer, Valerie Grosvenor. *Ten Great English Novelists*, 51–53.

Potkay, Adam. *The Fate of Eloquence*, 142–53.

Starr, G. A. "Sentimental Novels of the Later Eighteenth Century," in John Richetti et al., eds., *The Columbia History*, 191–94.

Van Sant, Ann Jessie. *Eighteenth-Century Sensibility*, 96–102, 106–10.

Vivies, Jean. "*A Sentimental Journey*, or Reading Rewarded." *Bull de la Société d'Etudes Anglo-Américaines des XVIIe et XVIIIe Siècles* 38 (1994), 243–53.

de Voogd, Peter. "Sentimental Horrors: Feeling in the Gothic Novel," in Valeria Tinkler-Villani and Peter Davidson, eds., *Exhibited by Candlelight*, 75–78.

Warner, John M. *Joyce's Grandfathers*, 110–20.

Tristram Shandy, 1760–1767

Bandry, Anne. "Les Faux Volumes de *Tristram Shandy*." *Bull de la Société d'Etudes Anglo-Américaines des XVIIe et XVIIIe Siècles* 36 (1993), 25–42.

Bandry, Anne. "*Tristram Shandy:* un protocole caracolant." *Recherches Anglaises et Nord-Américaines* 26 (1993), 103–11.

Bauer, Matthias. *Im Fuchsbau der Geschichten*, 120–41.

Bauer, Matthias. *Der Schelmenroman*, 180–83.

Benedict, Barbara M. *Framing Feeling*, 69–88.

Bowden, Martha F. "The Interdependence of Women in *Tristram Shandy:* A Chapter of Eyes, Sausages and Sciatica." *Engl Lang Notes* 31:4 (1994), 40–46.

Bowden, Martha F. "The Liturgical Shape of Life at Shandy Hall." *Shandean* 7 (1995), 43–59.

Brown, Homer Obed. *Institutions of the English Novel*, 116–37.

Chalker, John. "The Death of Sterne's Yorick." *Notes and Queries* 42 (1995), 461–62.

Chézaud, Patrick. "Langage naturel et art du roman chez Laurence Sterne." *Bull de la Société d'Etudes Anglo-Américaines des XVIIe et XVIIIe Siècles* 41 (1995), 113–22.

Descargues, Madeleine. "In Pursuit of Sterne's Epistolary Persona." *Shandean* 4 (1992), 167–79.

Donoghue, Frank. *The Fame Machine*, 56–63, 73–85.

Gervais, Bertrand. "Reading Tensions: Of Sterne, Klee, and the Secret Police." *New Liter Hist* 26 (1995), 858–61.

Harries, Elizabeth Wanning. *The Unfinished Manner*, 40–53, 166–72.

King, Ross. *"Tristram Shandy* and the Wound of Language." *Stud in Philology* 92 (1995), 291–310.

Kraft, Elizabeth. *Laurence Sterne Revisited*, 47–104, 129–42.

Loverso, Marco. "Integrated Consciousness and Dialectical Structure in *Tristram Shandy."* *Engl Stud in Canada* 20 (1994), 377–92.

Marques de Azevedo, Mail. "Aspectos de comicidade em *A vida e as opiniões do Cavalheiro Tristram Shandy* e *Memórias Postumas de Brás Cubas."* *Revista Letras* (Paraná) 45 (1996), 11–19.

Maybach, Heike. *Der erzählte Leser,* 50–57.

Moglen, Helene. "(W)holes and Noses: The Indeterminacies of *Tristram Shandy."* *Lit and Psych* 41:3 (1995), 44–70.

Myer, Valerie Grosvenor. *Ten Great English Novelists*, 41–49.

New, Melvyn. "The Odd Couple: Laurence Sterne and John Norris of Bemerton." *Philol Q* 75 (1996), 363–80.

New, Melvyn. *"Tristram Shandy,"* 25–134.

Parnell, J. T. "Swift, Sterne, and the Skeptical Tradition." *Stud in Eighteenth-Cent Culture* 23 (1994), 221–39.

Pinnegar, Fred C. "The Groin Wounds of Tristram and Uncle Toby." *Shandean* 7 (1995), 87–99.

Potkay, Adam. *The Fate of Eloquence*, 151–58.

Rosenblum, Michael. "Why What Happens in Shandy Hall Is Not 'A Matter for the Police.' " *Eighteenth-Cent Fiction* 7 (1995), 147–64.

Sherbert, Garry. *Menippean Satire,* 119–43, 149–87.

Simms, Norman. "The Missing Jews and Jewishness in *Tristram Shandy."* *Shandean* 4 (1992), 135–48.

Somerlate Barbosa, Maria José. "Sterne and Machado: Parodic and Intertextual Play in *Tristram Shandy* and *Memórias."* *Comparatist* 16 (1992), 24–48.

Soud, Stephen. " 'Weavers, Gardeners, and Gladiators': Labyrinths in *Tristram Shandy."* *Eighteenth-Cent Stud* 28 (1995), 397–408.

Spacks, Patricia Meyer. *Desire and Truth,* 38–43.

Spies, Bernhard. "Feuer im Palast zu Lilliput: Überlegungen zu Satire und Groteske im Jahrhundert der Aufklärung." *Arcadia* 30 (1995), 310–15.

Stevenson, John Allen. "Sterne: Comedian and Experimental Novelist," in John Richetti et al., eds., *The Columbia History*, 154–57, 162–78.

Warner, John M. *Joyce's Grandfathers*, 89–106.

Watts, Carol. "The Modernity of *Tristram Shandy."* *Shandean* 6 (1994), 99–116.

Williams, Anne Patricia. "Description and Tableau in the Eighteenth-Century British Sentimental Novel." *Eighteenth-Cent Fiction* 8 (1996), 473–75.

Wolff, Erwin. "Falling and the Fall in Sterne's *Tristram Shandy,"* in Elmar Lehmann and Bernd Lenz, eds., *Telling Stories*, 97–108.

Zander, Horst. " 'Non enim adiectivo haec ejus, sed opus ipsum est': Überlegungen zum Paratext in *Tristram Shandy."* *Poetica* (Munich) 28 (1996), 132–53.

Zwanefeld, Agnes. "The Rhetoric of Tristram Shandy's First Chapter." *Shandean* 4 (1992), 66–80.

ROBERT LOUIS STEVENSON

The Black Arrow, 1888

Nollen, Scott Allen. *Robert Louis Stevenson*, 150–53.

Catriona, 1891

Federico, Annette. "Books for Boys: Violence and Representation in *Kidnapped* and *Catriona.*" *Victorians Inst J* 22 (1994), 118–28.

Houppermans, Sjef. "Robert, Alexandre, Marcel, Henri, Jean et les autres: R. L. Stevenson and his 'French Connections,' " in Peter Liebregts and Wim Tigges, eds., *Beauty and the Beast*, 198–99.

Nollen, Scott Allen. *Robert Louis Stevenson*, 249–56.

Sandison, Alan. *Robert Louis Stevenson*, 204–13.

Dr. Jekyll and Mr. Hyde, 1886

Arata, Stephen D. "The Sedulous Ape: Atavism, Professionalism, and Stevenson's *Jekyll and Hyde.*" *Criticism* 37 (1995), 233–54.

Armitt, Lucie. *Theorising the Fantastic*, 119–33.

Bailin, Miriam. *The Sickroom in Victorian Fiction*, 14–15.

Botting, Fred. *Gothic*, 138–42.

Campbell, Ian. "Jekyll, Hyde, Frankenstein and the Uncertain Self." *Cahiers Victoriens et Edouardiens* 40 (1994), 51–62.

Clarke, Bruce. *Allegories of Writing*, 6–9, 76–81, 140–44.

Clunas, Alex. "Comely External Utterance: Reading Space in *The Strange Case of Dr Jekyll and Mr Hyde.*" *J of Narrative Technique* 24 (1994), 173–86.

Connor, Steven. *The English Novel in History*, 178–82.

Elphinstone, Margaret. "Contemporary Feminist Fantasy in the Scottish Literary Tradition," in Robert A. Latham and Robert A. Collins, eds., *Modes of the Fantastic*, 85–87.

Foss, Chris. "Xenophobia, Duality, and the 'Other' Side of Nationalism: A Reading of Stevenson's *Jekyll and Hyde.*" *Cahiers Victoriens et Edouardiens* 40 (1994), 63–76.

Greenslade, William. *Degeneration, Culture, and the Novel*, 83–85.

Halberstam, Judith. *Skin Shows*, 53–85.

Hendershot, Cyndy. "Overdetermined Allegory in *Jekyll and Hyde.*" *Victorian Newsl* 84 (1993), 35–38.

Hubbard, Tom. *Seeking Mr Hyde*, 21–31, 33–72 .

Jagoda, Susan Heseltine. "A Psychiatric Interpretation of Dr. Jekyll's 'Case.' " *Victorian Newsl* 89 (1996), 31–33.

Kabel, Ans. "The Influence of Walter Pater in *Dr Jekyll and Mr Hyde* and *The Picture of Dorian Gray*," in Peter Liebregts and Wim Tigges, eds., *Beauty and the Beast*, 142–47.

Mack, Douglas S. "Dr Jekyll, Mr Hyde, and Count Dracula," in Peter Liebregts and Wim Tigges, eds., *Beauty and the Beast*, 152–56.

Naugrette, Jean-Pierre. *"The Strange Case of Dr Jekyll and Mr Hyde:* essai d'onomastique." *Cahiers Victoriens et Edouardiens* 40 (1994), 77–90.

Nollen, Scott Allen. *Robert Louis Stevenson*, 155–226.

Persak, Christine. "Spencer's Doctrines and Mr. Hyde: Moral Evolution in Stevenson's 'Strange Case.' " *Victorian Newsl* 86 (1994), 13–17.

Pick, J. B. *The Great Shadow House*, 25–29.

Robertson, Patricia R. "An Issue of Will: *Dr. Jekyll and Mr. Hyde."* *Publs of the Arkansas Philol Assoc* 18:1 (1992), 65–74.

Sandison, Alan. *Robert Louis Stevenson*, 215–65.

Seed, David. "Behind Closed Doors: The Management of Mystery in *The Strange Case of Dr. Jekyll and Mr. Hyde,"* in Allan Lloyd Smith and Victor Sage, eds., *Gothick Origins and Innovations*, 180–89.

Stewart, Garrett. *Dear Reader*, 359–76.

Sutherland, John. *Is Heathcliff a Murderer?*, 184–88.

Williams, M. Kellen. " 'Down With the Door, Poole': Designating Deviance in Stevenson's *Strange Case of Dr. Jekyll and Mr Hyde."* *Engl Lit in Transition, 1880–1920* 39 (1996), 412–26.

Wright, Daniel L. " 'The Prisonhouse of My Disposition': A Study of the Psychology of Addiction in *Dr. Jekyll and Mr. Hyde."* *Stud in the Novel* 26 (1994), 254–63.

Youngs, Tim. "Stevenson's Monkey-Business: The Strange Case of Dr Jekyll and Mr Hyde," in Peter Liebregts and Wim Tigges, eds., *Beauty and the Beast*, 157–70.

The Ebb-Tide, 1894

Derry, Stephen. *"The Island of Doctor Moreau* and Stevenson's *The Ebb-Tide."* *Notes and Queries* 43 (1996), 437.

Hubbard, Tom. *Seeking Mr Hyde*, 101–4.

Nollen, Scott Allen. *Robert Louis Stevenson*, 309–24.

Sandison, Alan. *Robert Louis Stevenson*, 317–66.

Watts, Cedric. *"The Ebb-Tide* and *Victory."* *Conradiana* 28 (1996), 133–36.

Kidnapped, 1886

Federico, Annette. "Books for Boys: Violence and Representation in *Kidnapped* and *Catriona."* *Victorians Inst J* 22 (1994), 118–28.

Nollen, Scott Allen. *Robert Louis Stevenson*, 227–80.

Sandison, Alan. *Robert Louis Stevenson*, 179–204.

The Master of Ballantrae, 1889

Amalric, Jean-Claude. *"The Master of Ballantrae:* un conte d'hiver? Note sur un sous-titre." *Cahiers Victoriens et Edouardiens* 40 (1994), 119–24.

Clunas, Alexander B. " 'A Double Word': Writing and Justice in *The Master of Ballantrae."* *Stud in Scottish Lit* 28 (1993), 55–74.

Eigner, Edwin M. *"The Master of Ballantrae* as Elegiac Romance." *Cahiers Victoriens et Edouardiens* 40 (1994), 99–105.

Fielding, Penny. *Writing and Orality*, 153–78.

Houppermans, Sjef. "Robert, Alexandre, Marcel, Henri, Jean et les autres: R. L. Stevenson and his 'French Connections,' " in Peter Liebregts and Wim Tigges, eds., *Beauty and the Beast*, 201–3.

Jumeau, Alain. *"The Master of Ballantrae:* roman d'aventures ou tragédie?" *Cahiers Victoriens et Edouardiens* 40 (1994), 107–18.

Nollen, Scott Allen. *Robert Louis Stevenson*, 281–97.

Orel, Harold. *The Historical Novel*, 42–49.

Sandison, Alan. *Robert Louis Stevenson*, 270–315.

Sutherland, John. *Is Heathcliff a Murderer?*, 189–95.

Prince Otto, 1885

Nollen, Scott Allen. *Robert Louis Stevenson*, 341–42.

Sandison, Alan. *Robert Louis Stevenson*, 145–77.

Treasure Island, 1883

Cole, David L. "Maps and the Discovery Motif in *Treasure Island, King Solomon's Mines,* and *The Treasure of the Sierra Madre." Illinois Engl Bull* 83:2 (1996), 2–4.

Davies, Hunter. *The Teller of Tales*, 134–38.

Dekker, George. "James and Stevenson: The Mixed Current of Realism and Romance," in Robert M. Polhemus and Roger B. Henkle, eds., *Critical Reconstructions*, 130–39.

Dixon, Robert. *Writing the Colonial Adventure*, 30–32.

Nollen, Scott Allen. *Robert Louis Stevenson*, 83–119.

Rose, Jacqueline. *The Case of Peter Pan*, 78–80.

Sandison, Alan. *Robert Louis Stevenson*, 48–80.

Sutton, Max. "Jim Hawkins and the Faintly Inscribed Reader in *Treasure Island." Cahiers Victoriens et Edouardiens* 40 (1994), 37–45.

Wright, Terence. "Doing and Being: The Place of Romance in the Novel Tradition." *Durham Univ J* 86 (1994), 84–85.

Weir of Hermiston, 1896

Fielding, Penny. *Writing and Orality*, 179–98.

Nollen, Scott Allen. *Robert Louis Stevenson*, 344–47.

Sandison, Alan. *Robert Louis Stevenson*, 369–413.

Sutherland, John. *Is Heathcliff a Murderer?*, 224–27.

J. I. M. STEWART

Death at the President's Lodging, 1936

Antor, Heinz. *Der englische Universitätsroman*, 584–90.

Operation Pax, 1952

Antor, Heinz. *Der englische Universitätsroman*, 645–47.

MARY STEWART

Madam, Will You Talk?, 1955

Cadogan, Mary. *And Then Their Hearts Stood Still*, 24–27.
Watson, Daphne. *Their Own Worst Enemies*, 31–33.

BRAM STOKER

Dracula, 1897

Andriano, Joseph. *Our Ladies of Darkness*, 105–16.
Auerbach, Nina. *Our Vampires, Ourselves*, 6–8, 13–15, 29–32, 34–36, 63–98, 101–6, 111–13, 119–28, 130–37, 139–141.
Belford, Barbara. *Bram Stoker*, 211–47, 251–88, 323–31.
Botting, Fred. *Gothic*, 145–54.
Brederoo, N. J. "Dracula in Film," in Valeria Tinkler-Villani and Peter Davidson, eds., *Exhibited by Candlelight*, 271–81.
Case, Alison. "Tasting the Original Apple: Gender and the Struggle for Narrative Authority in *Dracula.*" *Narrative* 1 (1993), 223–40.
Cavaliero, Glen. *The Supernatural and English Fiction*, 45–49.
Cusick, Edmund. "Stoker's Languages of the Supernatural: A Jungian Approach to the Novels," in Allan Lloyd Smith and Victor Sage, eds., *Gothick Origins and Innovations*, 140–44.
Deane, Seamus. *Strange Country*, 89–94.
DeNaples, Frederick L. "Unearthing Holmes: 1890s Interpretations of the Great Detective," in Nikki Lee Manos and Meri-Jane Rochelson, eds., *Transforming Genres*, 228–30.
Dickens, David B. "Bürger's Ballad 'Lenore': En Route to *Dracula,*" in Allienne R. Becker, ed., *Visions of the Fantastic*, 131–37.
Dixon, Robert. *Writing the Colonial Adventure*, 100–111.
Geary, Robert F. "The Powers of Dracula." *J of the Fantastic in the Arts* 4:1 (1991), 81–91.
Glover, David. " 'Our enemy is not merely spiritual': Degeneration and Modernity in Bram Stoker's *Dracula.*" *Victorian Lit and Culture* 22 (1994), 249–63.
Glover, David. *Vampires, Mummies, and Liberals*, 32–47, 58–81, 92–99, 138–40.
Gutjahr, Paul. "Stoker's *Dracula.*" *Explicator* 52 (1993), 36–38.
Halberstam, Judith. *Skin Shows*, 86–106.
Halberstam, Judith. "Technologies of Monstrosity: Bram Stoker's *Dracula.*" *Victorian Stud* 36 (1993), 333–50.
Hall, Jasmine Yong. "Solicitors Soliciting: The Dangerous Circulations of Professionalism in *Dracula* (1897)," in Barbara Leah Harman and Susan Meyer, eds., *The New Nineteenth Century*, 97–113.
Hennelly, Mark M., Jr. "The Victorian Book of the Dead: *Dracula*, Part III." *J of Evolutionary Psych* 14:1–2 (1993), 143–57.
Hughes, William. " 'So Unlike the Normal Lunatic': Abnormal Psychol-

ogy in Bram Stoker's *Dracula.*" *Univ of Mississippi Stud in Engl* 11–12 (1993–95), 1–9.

Hurley, Kelly. *The Gothic Body*, 18–20.

Jurkiewicz, Kenneth. "Francis Coppola's Secret Gardens: *Bram Stoker's Dracula* and the Auteur as Decadent Visionary," in Allienne R. Becker, ed., *Visions of the Fantastic*, 167–71.

Kane, Michael. "Insiders/Outsiders: Conrad's *The Nigger of the 'Narcissus'* and Bram Stoker's *Dracula.*" *Mod Lang R* 92 (1997), 7–21.

Krumm, Pascale. "Metamorphosis as Metaphor in Bram Stoker's *Dracula.*" *Victorian Newsl* 88 (1995), 5–10.

Krumm, Pascale. "La peur de l'autre dans 'le Horla' de Maupassant et *Dracula* de Stoker." *Neophilologus* 79 (1995), 541–50.

McDonald, Jan. " 'The Devil Is Beautiful': *Dracula*—Freudian Novel and Feminist Drama," in Peter Reynolds, ed., *Novel Images*, 80–103.

Mack, Douglas S. "Dr Jekyll, Mr Hyde, and Count Dracula," in Peter Liebregts and Wim Tigges, eds., *Beauty and the Beast*, 149–51.

Malchow, H. L. *Gothic Images of Race*, 125–68.

Miller, Elizabeth. "*Frankenstein* and *Dracula:* The Question of Influence," in Allienne R. Becker, ed., *Visions of the Fantastic*, 123–29.

Moretti, Franco. *Signs Taken For Wonders,* 95–99, 104–7.

Morrison, Ronald D. "Reading Barthes and Reading *Dracula:* Between Work and Text." *Kentucky Philol R* 9 (1994), 23–28.

Nicholson, Mervyn. "Bram Stoker and C. S. Lewis: *Dracula* as a Source for *That Hideous Strength.*" *Mythlore* 19:3 (1993), 16–22.

Palumbo, Donald. "Sexuality and the Allure of the Fantastic in Literature," in Palumbo, ed., *Erotic Universe*, 17–18.

Richards, Jeffrey. "Gender, Race and Sexuality in Bram Stoker's Other Novels," in Christopher Parker, ed., *Gender Roles and Sexuality,* 143–45, 148–50.

Richter, David H. *The Progress of Romance*, 141–43.

Sage, Victor. "Gothic Laughter: Farce and Horror in Five Texts," in Allan Lloyd Smith and Victor Sage, eds., *Gothick Origins and Innovations*, 197–201.

Schaffer, Talia. " 'A Wilde Desire Took Me': The Homoerotic History of *Dracula.*" *ELH* 61 (1994), 381–420.

Schmitt, Cannon. "Mother Dracula: Orientalism, Degeneration, and Anglo-Irish National Subjectivity at the Fin de Siècle," in John S. Rickard, ed., *Irishness and (Post)Modernism*, 25–39.

Signorotti, Elizabeth. "Repossessing the Body: Transgressive Desire in 'Carmilla' and *Dracula.*" *Criticism* 38 (1996), 619–28.

Smart, Robert A. "Blood and Money in Bram Stoker's *Dracula:* The Struggle Against Monopoly," in John Louis DiGaetani, ed., *Money*, 253–60.

Stavick, J. e. d.. "Love at First Beet: Vegetarian Critical Theory Meats *Dracula.*" *Victorian Newsl* 89 (1996), 23–29.

Stewart, Garrett. " 'Count Me In': *Dracula,* Hypnotic Participation, and the Late-Victorian Gothic of Reading." *LIT: Literature, Interpretation, Theory* 5 (1994), 1–17.

Stewart, Garrett. *Dear Reader*, 377–83.

Stewart, Garrett. "Film's Victorian Retrofit." *Victorian Stud* 38 (1995), 184–95.

Stott, Rebecca. *The Fabrication*, 52–87.

Sutherland, John. *Is Heathcliff a Murderer?*, 233–38.

Thompson, David. "Supinely Anticipating Red-Eyed Shadows: A Jungian Analysis of Bram Stoker's *Dracula*." *J of Evolutionary Psych* 15 (1994), 289–301.

Vrettos, Athena. *Somatic Fictions*, 165–75.

The Jewel of Seven Stars, 1903

Cusick, Edmund. "Stoker's Languages of the Supernatural: A Jungian Approach to the Novels," in Allan Lloyd Smith and Victor Sage, eds., *Gothick Origins and Innovations*, 144–47.

Glover, David. *Vampires, Mummies, and Liberals*, 81–93.

Hughes, William. "Profane Resurrections: Bram Stoker's Self-Censorship in *The Jewel of Seven Stars*," in Allan Lloyd Smith and Victor Sage, eds., *Gothick Origins and Innovations*, 132–39.

Lady Athlyne, 1908

Glover, David. *Vampires, Mummies, and Liberals*, 127–35.

Richards, Jeffrey. "Gender, Race and Sexuality in Bram Stoker's Other Novels," in Christopher Parker, ed., *Gender Roles and Sexuality*, 157–60.

The Lady of the Shroud, 1909

Glover, David. *Vampires, Mummies, and Liberals*, 51–57.

The Lair of the White Worm, 1911

Richards, Jeffrey. "Gender, Race and Sexuality in Bram Stoker's Other Novels," in Christopher Parker, ed., *Gender Roles and Sexuality*, 150–52.

Stott, Rebecca. *The Fabrication*, 62–64, 76–78.

The Man, 1905

Glover, David. *Vampires, Mummies, and Liberals*, 106–27.

Richards, Jeffrey. "Gender, Race and Sexuality in Bram Stoker's Other Novels," in Christopher Parker, ed., *Gender Roles and Sexuality*, 160–61.

Miss Betty, 1898

Richards, Jeffrey. "Gender, Race and Sexuality in Bram Stoker's Other Novels," in Christopher Parker, ed., *Gender Roles and Sexuality*, 155–56.

The Mystery of the Sea, 1902

Richards, Jeffrey. "Gender, Race and Sexuality in Bram Stoker's Other Novels," in Christopher Parker, ed., *Gender Roles and Sexuality*, 168–69.

The Shoulder of Shasta, 1895

Richards, Jeffrey. "Gender, Race and Sexuality in Bram Stoker's Other Novels," in Christopher Parker, ed., *Gender Roles and Sexuality,* 155–57.

The Snake's Pass, 1890

Daly, Nicholas. "Irish Roots: The Romance of History in Bram Stoker's *The Snake's Pass." Lit and Hist* 4:2 (1995), 42–67.

Glover, David. *Vampires, Mummies, and Liberals,* 29–53.

Richards, Jeffrey. "Gender, Race and Sexuality in Bram Stoker's Other Novels," in Christopher Parker, ed., *Gender Roles and Sexuality,* 152–53.

DAVID STOREY

This Sporting Life, 1960

Schiffer, Jürgen. "Körperlichkeit und Sport in David Storeys Roman *This Sporting Life." Arete* 4:1 (1986), 87–104.

NOEL STREATFEILD

Aunt Clara, 1952

Huse, Nancy. *Noel Streatfeild,* 101–2.

I Ordered a Table for Six, 1942

Huse, Nancy. *Noel Streatfeild,* 62–63.

Judith, 1956

Huse, Nancy. *Noel Streatfeild,* 103–4.

Luke, 1939

Huse, Nancy. *Noel Streatfeild,* 55–59.

Mothering Sunday, 1950

Huse, Nancy. *Noel Streatfeild,* 99–101.

Myra Carroll, 1944

Huse, Nancy. *Noel Streatfeild,* 63–64.

Parson's Nine, 1932

Huse, Nancy. *Noel Streatfeild,* 32–33.

Saplings, 1945

Huse, Nancy. *Noel Streatfeild,* 64–67.

A Shepherdess of Sheep, 1934

Huse, Nancy. *Noel Streatfeild,* 35–36.

The Silent Speaker, 1961

Huse, Nancy. *Noel Streatfeild,* 104–5.

Tops and Bottoms, 1933
   Huse, Nancy. *Noel Streatfeild,* 34–35.
The Whicharts, 1931
   Huse, Nancy. *Noel Streatfeild,* 27–32.
The Winter Is Past, 1940
   Huse, Nancy. *Noel Streatfeild,* 60–61.

[MISS STREET]

The Recluse of the Appenines, 1793
   Shaffer, Julie. "Non-Canonical Women's Novels of the Romantic Era:
   Romantic Ideologies and the Problematics of Gender and Genre." *Stud
   in the Novel* 28 (1996), 480–84.

JANE MARGARET STRICKLAND

Adonijah: A Tale of the Jewish Dispersion, 1856
   Tush, Susan Rowland. *George Eliot and . . . Popular Women's Fiction,*
   51–58.

FRANCIS STUART

Black List, Section H, 1971
   McCartney, Anne. "Francis Stuart and Religion: Sharing the Leper's
   Lair," in Robert Welch, ed., *Irish Writers and Religion,* 138–39, 143.
   Welch, Robert. *Changing States,* 149–53.
A Hole in the Head, 1977
   Welch, Robert. *Changing States,* 156–61.
Pigeon Irish, 1932
   Welch, Robert. *Changing States,* 153–56.
The Pillar of Cloud, 1948
   McCartney, Anne. "Francis Stuart and Religion: Sharing the Leper's
   Lair," in Robert Welch, ed., *Irish Writers and Religion,* 139–40,
   142–43.
   Welch, Robert. *Changing States,* 138–44.

GRAHAM SWIFT

Ever After, 1992
   Hartung-Brückner, Heike. " 'Histrionics': Varianten und Implikationen
   der Auseinandersetzung mit Geschichte im erzählerischen Werk von
   Graham Swift—Gestützt auf ein Interview mit dem Autor." *Germanisch-Romanische Monatsschrift* 46 (1996), 467–69.

Holmes, Frederick M. "The Representation of History as Plastic: The Search for the Real Thing in Graham Swift's *Ever After*." *Ariel* 27:3 (1996), 25–42.

Janik, Del Ivan. "No End of History: Evidence from the Contemporary English Novel." *Twentieth Cent Lit* 41 (1995), 183–86.

Maack, Annegret. "Die *romance* als postmoderne Romanform?" *Literatur in Wissenschaft und Unterricht* 26 (1993), 279–82.

Out of This World, 1988

Bernard, Catherine. "Dismembering/Remembering Mimesis: Martin Amis, Graham Swift," in Theo D'haen and Hans Bertens, eds., *British Postmodern Fiction*, 124–44.

Hartung-Brückner, Heike. " 'Histrionics': Varianten und Implikationen der Auseinandersetzung mit Geschichte im erzählerischen Werk von Graham Swift—Gestützt auf ein Interview mit dem Autor." *Germanisch-Romanische Monatsschrift* 46 (1996), 466–67.

Shuttlecock, 1981

Hartung-Brückner, Heike. " 'Histrionics': Varianten und Implikationen der Auseinandersetzung mit Geschichte im erzählerischen Werk von Graham Swift—Gestützt auf ein Interview mit dem Autor." *Germanisch-Romanische Monatsschrift* 46 (1996), 464–65.

The Sweet-Shop Owner, 1980

Hartung-Brückner, Heike. " 'Histrionics': Varianten und Implikationen der Auseinandersetzung mit Geschichte im erzählerischen Werk von Graham Swift—Gestützt auf ein Interview mit dem Autor." *Germanisch-Romanische Monatsschrift* 46 (1996), 464.

Waterland, 1983

Bernard, Catherine. "Dismembering/Remembering Mimesis: Martin Amis, Graham Swift," in Theo D'haen and Hans Bertens, eds., *British Postmodern Fiction*, 123–44.

Cooper, Pamela. "Imperial Topographies: The Spaces of History in *Waterland*." *Mod Fiction Stud* 42 (1996), 371–95.

Elias, Amy J. "Meta-*mimesis*? The Problem of British Postmodern Realism," in Theo D'haen and Hans Bertens, eds., *British Postmodern Fiction*, 14–16.

Gasiorek, Andrzej. *Post-War British Fiction*, 149–58.

Haefner, Gerhard. "Geschichte und Natur in Graham Swifts *Waterland*," in Konrad Groß et al., eds., *Das Natur/Kultur-Paradigma*, 208–21.

Hartung-Brückner, Heike. " 'Histrionics': Varianten und Implikationen der Auseinandersetzung mit Geschichte im erzählerischen Werk von Graham Swift—Gestützt auf ein Interview mit dem Autor." *Germanisch-Romanische Monatsschrift* 46 (1996), 465–66.

Janik, Del Ivan. "No End of History: Evidence from the Contemporary English Novel." *Twentieth Cent Lit* 41 (1995), 177–82.

Kubíková, Magdaléna. "The Space of Time and Timelessness: Reflections on Graham Swift's *Waterland.*" *Litteraria Pragensia* 6 (1993), 78–87.

Lord, Geoffrey. "Mystery and History, Discovery and Recovery in Thomas Pynchon's *The Crying of Lot 49* and Graham Swift's *Waterland.*" *Neophilologus* 81 (1997), 145–59.

Marsh, Kelly A. "The Neo-Sensation Novel: A Contemporary Genre in the Victorian Tradition." *Philol Q* 74 (1995), 99–121.

Murphy, Sean P. "In the Middle of Nowhere: The Interpellative Force of Experimental Narrative Structure in Graham Swift's *Waterland.*" *Stud in the Hum* 23:1 (1996), 70–81.

Schad, John. "The End of the End of History: Graham Swift's *Waterland.*" *Mod Fiction Stud* 38 (1992), 911–23.

Todd, Richard. *Consuming Fictions*, 235–41.

Wilt, Judith. *Abortion, Choice, and Contemporary Fiction,* 111–18.

Wood, Michael. "The Contemporary Novel," in John Richetti et al., eds., *The Columbia History*, 973–74.

JONATHAN SWIFT

Gulliver's Travels, 1726

Argent, Joseph E. "The Etymology of a Dystopia: Laputa Reconsidered." *Engl Lang Notes* 34:1 (1996), 36–39.

Baines, Paul. " 'Able Mechanick': *The Life and Adventures of Peter Wilkins* and the Eighteenth-Century Fantastic Voyage," in David Seed, ed., *Anticipations,* 9–13.

Boucé, Paul-Gabriel. "The Rape of Gulliver Reconsidered." *Swift Stud* 11 (1996), 98–114.

Brantlinger, Patrick. *Fictions of State*, 65–73.

Chalmers, Alan D. *Jonathan Swift and the Burden of the Future,* 86–129.

Chase, Jefferson S. "Lying in Swift's *Gulliver's Travels* and Heine's *Atta Troll.*" *Compar Lit* 45 (1993), 330–44.

Cleary, Thomas R. "Big People and Little People: Size, Distance and Value in Gulliver's Travels and Baroque *trompe-l'œil.*" *Stud on Voltaire and the Eighteenth Cent* 305 (1992), 1493–96.

Crider, Richard. "Yahoo (Yahu): Notes on the Name of Swift's Yahoos." *Names* 41 (1993), 103–7.

Donoghue, Denis. "The Brainwashing of Lemuel Gulliver." *Southern R* (Baton Rouge, LA) 32 (1996), 128–46.

Doody, Margaret Anne. "Swift and Romance," in Christopher Fox and Brenda Tooley, eds., *Walking Naboth's Vineyard*, 98–122.

Ehrenpreis, Irvin. "Show and Tell in *Gulliver's Travels.*" *Swift Stud* 8 (1993), 18–33.

Fabricant, Carole. "Swift as Irish Historian," in Christopher Fox and Brenda Tooley, eds., *Walking Naboth's Vineyard*, 54–55.

Francus, Marilyn. *The Converting Imagination*, 26–28, 50, 58–59, 63, 66, 68, 101-4, 138–39, 146–47, 153–54, 157–60.

Freedman, William. "Swift's Struldbruggs, Progress, and the Analogy of History." *Stud in Engl Lit, 1500–1900* 35 (1995), 457–69.

Gardiner, Anne Barbeau. "Licking the Dust in Luggnagg: Swift's Reflections on the Legacy of King William's Conquest of Ireland." *Swift Stud* 8 (1993), 35–44.

Guthke, Karl S. *The Last Frontier*, 298–301.

Higgins, Ian. *Swift's Politics,* 144–96.

Lamarque, Peter, and Stein Haugom Olsen. *Truth, Fiction, and Literature*, 128–29, 423–25.

McMinn, Joseph. *Jonathan's Travels*, 86–88.

Mandell, Laura. "Demystifying (with) the Repugnant Female Body: Mary Leapor and Feminist Literary History." *Criticism* 38 (1996), 558–61.

Marshall, Tim. *Murdering to Dissect*, 72–74.

Montag, Warren. *The Unthinkable Swift,* 124–56.

Morvan, Alain. "Swift's *Gulliver's Travels."* *Explicator* 51 (1993), 219–20.

Nelson, T. G. A. *Children, Parents, and the Rise of the Novel*, 105–8.

Nicholson, Colin. *Writing and the Rise of Finance*, 91–122.

Palmer, Frank. *Literature and Moral Understanding,* 159–61.

Palmeri, Frank. "The Metamorphoses of Satire in Eighteenth-Century Narrative." *Compar Lit* 48 (1996), 240–51.

Phiddian, Robert. "The English Swift/the Irish Swift," in Paul Hyland and Neil Sammells, eds., *Irish Writing*, 40–43.

Phiddian, Robert. *Swift's Parody*, 175–77.

Rees, Christine. *Utopian Imagination and Eighteenth-Century Fiction*, 123–63.

Rennie, Neil. *Far-Fetched Facts*, 61–64, 76–82.

Ritchie, Daniel E. *Reconstructing Literature in an Ideological Age*, 39–58.

Roberts, Marie Mulvey. "Science, Magic and Masonry: Swift's Secret Texts," in Marie Mulvey Roberts and Hugh Ormsby-Lennon, eds., *Secret Texts*, 102–4.

Rousseau, G. S. "From Swift to Smollett: The Satirical Tradition in Prose Narrative," in John Richetti et al., eds., *The Columbia History*, 130–31.

Sicker, Philip. "Leopold's Travels: Swiftian Optics in Joyce's 'Cyclops.' " *Joyce Stud Annual 1995*, 59–78.

Spies, Bernhard. "Feuer im Palast zu Lilliput: Überlegungen zu Satire und Groteske im Jahrhundert der Aufklärung." *Arcadia* 30 (1995), 306–7, 314–15.

Stannard, Michael. "The '*South-East* Point of *New-Holland*' as Noplace: A Possible Solution to a Textual Problem in the Fourth Voyage of *Gulliver's Travels." Notes and Queries* 43 (1996), 297–99.

Stroud, Theodore A. "The Symmetry of *Gulliver's Travels." Hypotheses* 1 (1992), 6–7.

Terry, Richard. "*Gulliver's Travels* and the Savage-Critic Topos." *Swift Stud* 11 (1996), 115–31.

Todd, Dennis. *Imagining Monsters*, 140–78.

Treadwell, Michael. "The Text of *Gulliver's Travels,* Again." *Swift Stud* 10 (1995), 62–78.

Wagner, Peter. *Reading Iconotexts*, 37–73.

Ward, Ian. *Law and Literature*, 112–17.

Washington, Gene. "Swift's *Gulliver's Travels,* bk. 4, ch. 1." *Explicator* 52 (1994), 75–76.

Washington, Gene. "Swift's *Gulliver's Travels,* Bk. 2, Ch. 1." *Explicator* 52 (1994), 214–15.

Wilding, Michael. *Social Visions*, 3–28.

Wintle, Sarah. "If Houyhnhnms were Horses: Thinking with Animals in Book IV of *Gulliver's Travels.*" *Crit R* 34 (1994), 3–19.

ALGERNON CHARLES SWINBURNE

Lesbia Brandon, 1952

Rooksby, Rikky. "A. C. Swinburne's *Lesbia Brandon* and the Death of Edith Swinburne." *Notes and Queries* 40 (1993), 487–90.

NETTA SYRETT

Anne Page, 1908

Ardis, Ann. "Toward a Redefinition of 'Experimental Writing': Netta Syrett's Realism," in Alison Booth, ed., *Famous Last Words*, 265–68.

Three Women, 1912

Ardis, Ann. "Toward a Redefinition of 'Experimental Writing': Netta Syrett's Realism," in Alison Booth, ed., *Famous Last Words*, 268–72.

MEADOWS TAYLOR

Confessions of a Thug, 1839

Brantlinger, Patrick. "The Nineteenth-Century Novel and Empire," in John Richetti et al., eds., *The Columbia History*, 570–72.

Williams, Robert Grant. "Shadows of Imperialism: Canonical Typology in Taylor's *Confessions of a Thug.*" *Dalhousie R* 72 (1992–93), 482–92.

Seeta, 1872

Paxton, Nancy L. "Mobilizing Chivalry: Rape in Flora Annie Steel's *On the Face of the Waters* (1896) and Other British Novels about the Indian Uprising of 1857," in Barbara Leah Harman and Susan Meyer, eds., *The New Nineteenth Century*, 259–63.

SIMON TAYLOR

Mortimer's Deep, 1992

> Whyte, Christopher. "Postmodernism, Gender and Belief in Recent
> Scottish Fiction." *Scottish Liter J* 23:1 (1996), 55–63.

ROWENA TENET

Bewitching Imposter, 1983

> Hughes, Helen. *The Historical Romance,* 124–30.

EMMA TENNANT

Two Women of London, 1978

> Connor, Steven. *The English Novel in History,* 178–82.
> Elphinstone, Margaret. "Contemporary Feminist Fantasy in the Scottish
> Literary Tradition," in Robert A. Latham and Robert A. Collins, eds.,
> *Modes of the Fantastic,* 86–88.

WILLIAM MAKEPEACE THACKERAY

Catherine, 1840

> Clarke, Micael M. *Thackeray and Women,* 47–55.
> Horsman, Alan. *The Victorian Novel,* 77–78.
> McKendy, Thomas. "Sources of Parody in Thackeray's *Catherine.*"
> *Dickens Stud Annual* 23 (1994), 287–300.

Denis Duval, 1864

> Reed, John R. *Dickens and Thackeray,* 464–69.

Henry Esmond, 1852

> Chrétien, Maurice. "De Finibus." *Cahiers Victoriens et Edouardiens* 38
> (1993), 18–21.
> Clarke, Micael M. *Thackeray and Women,* 114–36.
> Ferris, Ina. "Thackeray and the Ideology of the Gentleman," in John
> Richetti et al., eds., *The Columbia History,* 421–22.
> Horsman, Alan. *The Victorian Novel,* 87–90.
> Lerner, Laurence. "The Unsaid in *Henry Esmond.*" *Essays in Criticism*
> 45 (1995), 141–57.
> McKnight, Natalie J. *Suffering Mothers,* 104–9.
> Myer, Valerie Grosvenor. *Ten Great English Novelists,* 91–93.
> Reed, John R. *Dickens and Thackeray,* 377–99.
> Sutherland, John. *Is Heathcliff a Murderer?,* 84–89.
> Sutherland, John. *Victorian Fiction,* 16–27.
> Wheeler, Michael. *English Fiction of the Victorian Period,* 58–61.
> Winnifrith, Tom. *Fallen Women,* 78–81.

Wolf, Werner. "Die Domestizierung der Geschichte: Eine These zur Funktion des englischen historischen Romans im 19. Jahrhundert am Beispiel von Scott, Thackeray und Dickens." *Archiv für das Studium der neueren Sprachen und Literaturen* 231 (1994), 282–87.

The Luck of Barry Lyndon, 1844

    Bauer, Matthias. *Im Fuchsbau der Geschichten,* 141–43.

    Clarke, Micael M. *Thackeray and Women,* 59–68.

    Fletcher, Robert P. " 'Proving a thing even while you contradict it': Fictions, Beliefs, and Legitimation in *The Memoirs of Barry Lyndon, Esq.*" *Stud in the Novel* 27 (1995), 493–509.

The Newcomes, 1854–1855

    Chrétien, Maurice. "De Finibus." *Cahiers Victoriens et Edouardiens* 38 (1993), 21–25.

    Clarke, Micael M. *Thackeray and Women,* 137–68.

    Ferris, Ina. "Thackeray and the Ideology of the Gentleman," in John Richetti et al., eds., *The Columbia History,* 420–22.

    Hall, Donald E. *Fixing Patriarchy,* 87–106.

    Horsman, Alan. *The Victorian Novel,* 90–92.

    McMaster, R. D. "London as a System of Signs in Thackeray's *The Newcomes.*" *Victorian R* 16:1 (1990), 1–19.

    Perera, Suvendrini. *Reaches of Empire,* 62–64.

    Reed, John R. *Dickens and Thackeray,* 400–422.

    Skilton, David. *Anthony Trollope and His Contemporaries,* 85–88.

    Winnifrith, Tom. *Fallen Women,* 81–86.

Pendennis, 1849–1850

    Antor, Heinz. *Der englische Universitätsroman,* 200–202.

    Birken, William J. "Thackeray's Medical Fathers." *Victorians Inst J* 21 (1993), 71–87.

    Clarke, Micael M. *Thackeray and Women,* 137–68.

    Cronin, Mark. "The Rake, The Writer, and *The Stranger:* Textual Relations between *Pendennis* and *David Copperfield.*" *Dickens Stud Annual* 24 (1996), 215–37.

    Ermarth, Elizabeth Deeds. *The English Novel in History,* 17–19.

    Fasick, Laura. *Vessels of Meaning,* 84–89.

    Ferris, Ina. "Thackeray and the Ideology of the Gentleman," in John Richetti et al., eds., *The Columbia History,* 423–24.

    Fisher, Judith L. "Image versus Text in the Illustrated Novels of William Makepeace Thackeray," in Carol T. Christ and John O. Jordan, eds., *Victorian Literature,* 69–72.

    Horsman, Alan. *The Victorian Novel,* 85–87.

    McKnight, Natalie J. *Suffering Mothers,* 99–104.

    Reed, John R. *Dickens and Thackeray,* 353–76.

    Sutherland, John. *Is Heathcliff a Murderer?,* 123–28.

    Sutherland, John. *Victorian Fiction,* 6–11, 13–15.

    Winnifrith, Tom. *Fallen Women,* 78–80.

Philip, 1862

> Birken, William J. "Thackeray's Medical Fathers." *Victorians Inst J* 21 (1993), 71–87.
>
> Chrétien, Maurice. "De Finibus." *Cahiers Victoriens et Edouardiens* 38 (1993), 27–29.
>
> Reed, John R. *Dickens and Thackeray,* 442–60.

Rebecca and Rowena, 1850

> McMaster, R. D. *"Rebecca and Rowena* and Bakhtin." *Cahiers Victoriens et Edouardiens* 38 (1993), 49–68.

The Rose and the Ring, 1854

> Wilson, Anita C. "The Shining Garb of Wonder: The Paradox of Literary Fairy Tales in Mid-Victorian England." *Cahiers Victoriens et Edouardiens* 37 (1993), 87–89.

Vanity Fair, 1848

> Brantlinger, Patrick. *Fictions of State,* 154–57.
>
> Bruce, Cicero. "Thackeray's *Vanity Fair." Explicator* 53 (1995), 85–87.
>
> Byerly, Alison. " 'The Masquerade of Existence': Thackeray's Theatricality." *Dickens Stud Annual* 23 (1994), 259–82.
>
> Clarke, Micael M. *Thackeray and Women,* 69–113.
>
> Ermarth, Elizabeth Deeds. *The English Novel in History,* 17–24.
>
> Ferris, Ina. "Thackeray and the Ideology of the Gentleman," in John Richetti et al., eds., *The Columbia History,* 410–20.
>
> Fisher, Judith L. "Image versus Text in the Illustrated Novels of William Makepeace Thackeray," in Carol T. Christ and John O. Jordan, eds., *Victorian Literature,* 62–69.
>
> Hanley, Matthew M. "The Vain Narrative of *Vanity Fair." Lang and Culture* 25 (1993), 15–26.
>
> Harden, Edgar F. *"Vanity Fair": A Novel without a Hero,* 21–119.
>
> Heglar, Charles J. "Rhoda Swartz in *Vanity Fair:* A Doll Without Admirers." *Coll Lang Assoc J* 37 (1994), 336–47.
>
> Horsman, Alan. *The Victorian Novel,* 82–85.
>
> Jadwin, Lisa. "Clytemnestra Rewarded: The Double Conclusion of *Vanity Fair,"* in Alison Booth, ed., *Famous Last Words,* 35–57.
>
> Jumeau, Alain. "Le dialogue entre le texte et l'image au chapitre 67 de *Vanity Fair." Cahiers Victoriens et Edouardiens* 38 (1993), 31–47.
>
> Kaye, Richard A. "A Good Woman on Five Thousand Pounds: *Jane Eyre, Vanity Fair,* and Literary Rivalry." *Stud in Engl Lit, 1500–1900* 35 (1995), 723–35.
>
> Litvak, Joseph. "Miss Me, Stupid: Sophistication, Sexuality, and *Vanity Fair." Novel* 29 (1996), 223–41.
>
> McKnight, Natalie J. *Suffering Mothers,* 92–99.
>
> Marks, Patricia. *"'Mon Pauvre Prisonnier':* Becky Sharp and the Triumph of Napoleon." *Stud in the Novel* 28 (1996), 76–88.
>
> Myer, Valerie Grosvenor. *Ten Great English Novelists,* 84–90.
>
> Norton, Sandy Morey. "The Ex-Collector of Boggley-Wollah: Colonialism in the Empire of *Vanity Fair." Narrative* 1 (1993), 124–35.

Peck, John. "Middle-Class Life in *Vanity Fair*." *English* 43 (1994), 1–15.

Perera, Suvendrini. *Reaches of Empire,* 94–102.

Perkin, J. Russell. "Thackeray and Imperialism: A Response to Sandy Morey Norton." *Narrative* 2 (1994), 161–65.

Schad, John. "Reading the Long Way Round: Thackeray's *Vanity Fair.*" *Yrbk of Engl Stud* 26 (1996), 25–33.

Stewart, Garrett. *Dear Reader,* 49–54, 68–70, 277–83.

Sutherland, John. *Is Heathcliff a Murderer?,* 66–72.

Thornton, Sara. "*Vanity Fair* ou 'l'illusion comique.' " *Cahiers Victoriens et Edouardiens* 38 (1993), 71–82.

Véga-Ritter, Max. "Manhood in *Vanity Fair.*" *Cahiers Victoriens et Edouardiens* 38 (1993), 87–102.

Wheat, Patricia H. *The Adytum of the Heart,* 57–73.

Wheeler, Michael. *English Fiction of the Victorian Period,* 52–58.

The Virginians, 1958–1959

Chrétien, Maurice. "De Finibus." *Cahiers Victoriens et Edouardiens* 38 (1993), 25–27.

Reed, John R. *Dickens and Thackeray,* 423–41.

Winnifrith, Tom. *Fallen Women,* 86–90.

D. M. THOMAS

Summit, 1987

Fletcher, M. D. "Thomas' Satire in *Summit.*" *Stud in Contemp Satire* 18 (1991–92), 9–17.

The White Hotel, 1981

Bartkowski, Frances, and Catherine Stearns. "The Lost Icon in *The White Hotel.*" *J of the Hist of Sexuality* 1 (1990), 283–95.

Granofsky, Ronald. *The Trauma Novel,* 131–49.

Ledbetter, Mark. *Victims and the Postmodern Narrative,* 72–86.

MacInnes, John. "The Case of Anna G.: *The White Hotel* and Acts of Understanding." *Soundings* 77 (1994), 253–69.

Wesseling, Elisabeth. *Writing History as a Prophet,* 123–25.

Wren, James A. "Thomas's *The White Hotel.*" *Explicator* 54 (1996), 123–26.

DYLAN THOMAS

Adventures in the Skin Trade, 1955

Sangalli, Romilde. "Dylan Thomas: *Adventures in the Skin Trade.*" *Confronto Letterario* 9 (1992), 437–53.

EDWARD THOMAS

The Happy-Go-Lucky Morgans, 1913
    Hooker, Jeremy. *Writers in a Landscape,* 72–75, 79–80.

EDWARD THOMPSON

An End of the Hours, 1938
    Nagarajan, S. "The Englishman as a Teacher of English Literature
    Abroad," in Annie Greet et al., eds., *Raj Nostalgia,* 61–72.

GUY THORNE

Not in Israel, 1913
    Holmes, Colin, and Gina Mitchell. "*When It Was Dark:* Jews in the Lit-
    erature of Guy Thorne," in John Morris, ed., *Exploring Stereotyped
    Images,* 236–40.
When It Was Dark, 1903
    Holmes, Colin, and Gina Mitchell. "*When It Was Dark:* Jews in the Lit-
    erature of Guy Thorne," in John Morris, ed., *Exploring Stereotyped
    Images,* 232–36.

WILLIAM EDWARDS TIREBUCK

Miss Grace of All Souls, 1895
    Fox, Pamela. *Class Fictions,* 118–23.

J. R. R. TOLKIEN

The Fellowship of the Ring, 1954
    Obertino, James. "Tolkien's *The Fellowship of the Ring.*" *Explicator* 54
    (1996), 230–32.
    Stevens, David, and Carol D. Stevens. *J. R. R. Tolkien,* 70–89.
The Hobbit, 1937
    Collins, David R. *J. R. R. Tolkien,* 74–83.
    Glenn, Jonathan A. "To Translate a Hero: *The Hobbit* as *Beowulf* Re-
    told." *Publs of the Arkansas Philol Assoc* 17:2 (1991), 13–30.
    Green, William H. *"The Hobbit,"* 37–123.
    Hopkins, Lisa. "Bilbo Baggins as a Burglar." *Inklings* 10 (1992), 93–
    101.
    Ratcliff, John, and Christina Scull. "*The Hobbit* and Tolkien's Other Pre-
    War Writings." *Mallorn* 30 (1993), 14–20.

Sarjeant, Williams A. S. "Where Did the Dwarves Come From?" *Mythlore* 19:1 (1993), 43, 64.

Stevens, David, and Carol D. Stevens. *J. R. R. Tolkien*, 59–66.

The Lord of the Rings, 1966

Collins, David R. *J. R. R. Tolkien*, 82–88.

Ellison, John. " 'Before Defended Walls': Hill-Forts and Fortified Sites in Northern Eriador in the Second and Third Ages." *Mallorn* 31 (1994), 20–28.

Hardgrave, Martin. "Bells and Bell-Ringing in Middle-Earth." *Mallorn* 31 (1994), 15–19.

Helms, Philip W. *Tolkien's Peaceful War*, 18–35.

Hood, Gwyneth. "Nature and Technology: Angelic and Sacrificial Strategies in Tolkien's *The Lord of the Rings.*" *Mythlore* 19:4 (1993), 6–12.

Keene, Louise E. "The Restoration of Language in Middle-Earth." *Mythlore* 20:4 (1995), 6–13.

Lacon, Ruth. "Notes toward a History of the Easterlings." *Mallorn* 32 (1995), 28–35.

Langford, Jonathan. "Sitting Down to the Sacramental Feast: Food and Cultural Diversity in *The Lord of the Rings,*" in Gary Westfahl et al., eds., *Foods of the Gods*, 117–38.

Lewis, Alex. "Boromir's Journey." *Inklings* 10 (1992), 135–43.

McComas, Alan. "Negating and Affirming Spirit through Language: The Integration of Character, Magic, and Story in *The Lord of the Rings.*" *Mythlore* 19:2 (1993), 4–14.

Nagel, Rainer. "Normenvorgabe in der literarischen Übersetzung: Illustriert an den Eigennamen in J. R. R. Tolkiens *The Lord of the Rings.*" *Zeitschrift für Anglistik und Amerikanistik* 43 (1995), 1–8.

Nelson, Charles W. "But Who Is Rose Cotton?: Love and Romance in *The Lord of the Rings.*" *J of the Fantastic in the Arts* 3:3 (1994), 6–20.

Sanford, Len. "The Fall from Grace—Decline and Fall in Middle-Earth: Metaphors for Nordic and Christian Theology in *The Lord of the Rings* and *The Silmarillion.*" *Mallorn* 32 (1995), 15–20.

Stevens, David, and Carol D. Stevens. *J. R. R. Tolkien*, 68–135.

Zgorzelski, Andrzej. "A Fairy Tale Modified: Time and Space as Syncretic Factors in J. R. R. Tolkien's Trilogy." *LiLi* 92 (1993), 126–40.

The Return of the King, 1955

Stevens, David, and Carol D. Stevens. *J. R. R. Tolkien*, 107–35.

Silmarillion, 1977

Collins, David R. *J. R. R. Tolkien*, 85–86.

Cutsinger, James S. "Angels and Inklings." *Mythlore* 19:2 (1993), 57–60.

Houghton, John. "Augustine and the Ainulindale." *Mythlore* 21:1 (1995), 4–8.

Sanford, Len. "The Fall from Grace—Decline and Fall in Middle-Earth:

Metaphors for Nordic and Christian Theology in *The Lord of the Rings* and *The Silmarillion." Mallorn* 32 (1995), 15–20.

Stevens, David, and Carol D. Stevens. *J. R. R. Tolkien*, 39–58.

The Two Towers, 1955

Stevens, David, and Carol D. Stevens. *J. R. R. Tolkien*, 90–106.

CHARLOTTE ELIZABETH TONNA

Helen Fleetwood, 1841

Brown, Penny. *The Captured World,* 72–74.
Harsh, Constance D. *Subversive Heroines,* 30–32, 55–57, 87–91.
Horsman, Alan. *The Victorian Novel,* 42–44.

Judah's Lion, 1843

Ragussis, Michael. *Figures of Conversion,* 44–51.

ROSE TREMAIN

Restoration, 1989

Rozett, Martha Tuck. "Constructing a World: How Postmodern Historical Fiction Reimagines the Past." *Clio* 25 (1996), 160–62.

ROBERT TRESSELL

The Ragged Trousered Philanthropists, 1914

Fox, Pamela. *Class Fictions,* 63–79.
Trotter, David. *The English Novel in History,* 30–32.

WILLIAM TREVOR

Reading Turgenev, 1991

Fitzgerald-Hoyt, Mary. "William Trevor's Protestant Parables." *Colby Q* 31 (1995), 40–45.
Hurley, Vincent. "Recent Fictional Perspectives on Provincial Ireland." *Colby Q* 31 (1995), 26–27.

ANTHONY TROLLOPE

The American Senator, 1877

Blaicher, Günther. "Die Problematik internationaler Kritik in Trollopes *The American Senator." Literaturwissenschaftliches Jahrbuch im Auftrage der Görres-Gesellschaft* 36 (1995), 177–93.
Nardin, Jane. *Trollope and Victorian Moral Philosophy,* 121–25.

Ayala's Angel, 1881

> Miller, J. Hillis. "Literary Study in the Age of Electronic Reproduction," in Rüdiger Ahrens and Laurenz Volkmann, eds., *Why Literature Matters,* 298–310.

Barchester Towers, 1857

> Antor, Heinz. *Der englische Universitätsroman,* 329–30, 349–51, 379–81.
>
> Hall, Donald E. *Fixing Patriarchy,* 199–202.
>
> Heidt, Edward R. *The Image of the Church Minister,* 33–37.
>
> Horsman, Alan. *The Victorian Novel,* 335–37.
>
> Kucich, John. *The Power of Lies,* 63–68.
>
> Lawson, Kate. "Abject and Defiled: Signora Neroni's Body and the Question of Domestic Violence in *Barchester Towers.*" *Victorian R* 21 (1995), 53–67.
>
> Ragussis, Michael. *Figures of Conversion,* 238–41.
>
> Skilton, David. *Anthony Trollope and His Contemporaries,* 5–7, 79–82.
>
> York, R. A. *Strangers and Secrets,* 89–103.

Can You Forgive Her?, 1864

> Craig, Randall. "Rhetoric and Courtship in *Can You Forgive Her?*" *ELH* 62 (1995), 217–32.
>
> Felber, Lynette. *Gender and Genre,* 31–66.
>
> Hall, Donald E. *Fixing Patriarchy,* 202–3.
>
> Horsman, Alan. *The Victorian Novel,* 346–48.
>
> Skilton, David. *Anthony Trollope and His Contemporaries,* 40–42.
>
> Walton, Priscilla L. *Patriarchal Desire and Victorian Discourse,* 21–41.

The Claverings, 1867

> Horsman, Alan. *The Victorian Novel,* 349–50.
>
> Skilton, David. *Anthony Trollope and His Contemporaries,* 24–28.

Cousin Henry, 1879

> Nardin, Jane. *Trollope and Victorian Moral Philosophy,* 87–98.

Doctor Thorne, 1858

> Horsman, Alan. *The Victorian Novel,* 337–39.
>
> Skilton, David. *Anthony Trollope and His Contemporaries,* 10–12, 95–98.

Dr. Wortle's School, 1881

> Nardin, Jane. *Trollope and Victorian Moral Philosophy,* 99–101, 105–9.

The Duke's Children, 1880

> Ermarth, Elizabeth Deeds. *The English Novel in History,* 218–20.
>
> Felber, Lynette. *Gender and Genre,* 31–74.
>
> Franklin, J. Jeffrey. "The Victorian Discourse of Gambling: Speculations on *Middlemarch* and *The Duke's Children.*" *ELH* 61 (1994), 899–918.
>
> Horsman, Alan. *The Victorian Novel,* 370–71.

Walton, Priscilla L. *Patriarchal Desire and Victorian Discourse*, 139–61.

The Eustace Diamonds, 1872

Brantlinger, Patrick. "Cashing in on the Real: Money and the Failure of Mimesis in Defoe and Trollope." *Stud in the Liter Imagination* 29:1 (1996), 13–19.

Cohen, William A. *Sex Scandal*, 161–90.

Cohen, William A. "Trollope's Trollop." *Novel* 28 (1995), 237–55.

Felber, Lynette. *Gender and Genre*, 31–47.

Horsman, Alan. *The Victorian Novel*, 359–61.

Nardin, Jane. *Trollope and Victorian Moral Philosophy*, 41–50.

Ragussis, Michael. *Figures of Conversion*, 242–45.

Skilton, David. *Anthony Trollope and His Contemporaries*, 70–74.

Walton, Priscilla L. *Patriarchal Desire and Victorian Discourse*, 64–87.

The Fixed Period, 1882

Birns, Nicholas. "The Empire Turned Upside Down: The Colonial Fictions of Anthony Trollope." *Ariel* 27:3 (1996), 15–22.

Nardin, Jane. *Trollope and Victorian Moral Philosophy*, 110–21.

Framley Parsonage, 1861

Hall, N. John. "Trollope," in John Richetti et al., eds., *The Columbia History*, 469–71.

Horsman, Alan. *The Victorian Novel*, 339–41.

Horwitz, Barbara. "*Pride and Prejudice* and *Framley Parsonage:* A Structural Resemblance." *Persuasions* 15 (1993), 32–35.

Kucich, John. *The Power of Lies*, 54–62, 67–69.

Harry Heathcote, 1874

Birns, Nicholas. "The Empire Turned Upside Down: The Colonial Fictions of Anthony Trollope." *Ariel* 27:3 (1996), 9–15.

He Knew He Was Right, 1869

Hamer, Mary. "No Fairy-Tale: The Story of Marriage in Trollope's *He Knew He Was Right,"* in Nicholas White and Naomi Segal, eds., *Scarlet Letters*, 149–58.

Horsman, Alan. *The Victorian Novel*, 356–57.

Jones, Wendy. "Feminism, Fiction and Contract Theory: Trollope's *He Knew He Was Right." Criticism* 36 (1994), 401–11.

Oberhelman, David D. "Trollope's Insanity Defense: Narrative Alienation in *He Knew He Was Right." Stud in Engl Lit, 1500–1900* 35 (1995), 789–802.

Skilton, David. *Anthony Trollope and His Contemporaries*, 42–45.

Wiesenthal, C. S. "The Body Melancholy: Trollope's *He Knew He Was Right." Dickens Stud Annual* 23 (1994), 227–54.

Is He Popenjoy?, 1878

Cooksey, Thomas L. "Mrs Bond's Ducks and Trollope's *Popenjoy." Notes and Queries* 43 (1996), 48.

Sutherland, John. *Is Heathcliff a Murderer?*, 168–75.

John Caldigate, 1879

Nardin, Jane. *Trollope and Victorian Moral Philosophy,* 75–86.

The Kellys and the O'Kellys, 1848

Horsman, Alan. *The Victorian Novel,* 332–34.
Skilton, David. *Anthony Trollope and His Contemporaries,* 2–4.

Lady Anna, 1874

Nardin, Jane. *Trollope and Victorian Moral Philosophy,* 65–74.
Skilton, David. *Anthony Trollope and His Contemporaries,* 95–98.

The Last Chronicle of Barset, 1867

Hall, N. John. "Trollope," in John Richetti et al., eds., *The Columbia History,* 466–67.
Horsman, Alan. *The Victorian Novel,* 351–54.

The Macdermotts of Ballycloran, 1847

Skilton, David. *Anthony Trollope and His Contemporaries,* 1–3.

Marion Fay, 1882

Skilton, David. *Anthony Trollope and His Contemporaries,* 95–98.

Miss Mackenzie, 1865

Hall, N. John. "Trollope," in John Richetti et al., eds., *The Columbia History,* 462–63.
Skilton, David. *Anthony Trollope and His Contemporaries,* 79–87.
Swann, Charles. "Miss Harleth, Miss Mackenzie: Mirror Images?" *Notes and Queries* 43 (1996), 47–48.

Mr. Scarborough's Family, 1883

Horsman, Alan. *The Victorian Novel,* 373–74.
Nardin, Jane. *Trollope and Victorian Moral Philosophy,* 126–37.

Nina Balatka, 1867

Baumgarten, Murray. "Seeing Double: Jews in the Fiction of F. Scott Fitzgerald, Charles Dickens, Anthony Trollope, and George Eliot," in Bryan Cheyette, ed., *Between 'Race' and Culture,* 54–61.

Orley Farm, 1862

Fisichelli, Glynn-Ellen. "The Language of Law and Love: Anthony Trollope's *Orley Farm.*" *ELH* 61 (1994), 635–52.
Horsman, Alan. *The Victorian Novel,* 341–44.
Skilton, David. *Anthony Trollope and His Contemporaries,* 24–28, 91–93.

Phineas Finn, 1869

Felber, Lynette. *Gender and Genre,* 5157.
Horsman, Alan. *The Victorian Novel,* 354–56.
Skilton, David. *Anthony Trollope and His Contemporaries,* 24–29.
Sutherland, John. *Is Heathcliff a Murderer?,* 139–45.
Walton, Priscilla L. *Patriarchal Desire and Victorian Discourse,* 42–63.
Wolfreys, Julian. *Being English,* 154–69.

Wolfreys, Julian. "Reading Trollope: Whose Englishness Is It Anyway?" *Dickens Stud Annual* 22 (1993), 306–20.

Phineas Redux, 1874

Felber, Lynette. *Gender and Genre,* 31–35, 56–57.
Horsman, Alan. *The Victorian Novel,* 361–63.
Nardin, Jane. *Trollope and Victorian Moral Philosophy,* 51–62.
Walton, Priscilla L. *Patriarchal Desire and Victorian Discourse,* 88–112.

The Prime Minister, 1876

Felber, Lynette. *Gender and Genre,* 37–58.
Hall, Donald E. *Fixing Patriarchy,* 204–6.
Horsman, Alan. *The Victorian Novel,* 367–69.
Ragussis, Michael. *Figures of Conversion,* 249–59.
Sutherland, John. *Is Heathcliff a Murderer?,* 163–67.
Walton, Priscilla L. *Patriarchal Desire and Victorian Discourse,* 113–38.
Wolfreys, Julian. *Being English,* 169–76.
Wolfreys, Julian. "Reading Trollope: Whose Englishness Is It Anyway?" *Dickens Stud Annual* 22 (1993), 321–28.

Rachel Ray, 1863

Horsman, Alan. *The Victorian Novel,* 345–46.
Sutherland, John. *Is Heathcliff a Murderer?,* 133–37.

Sir Harry Hotspur, 1870

Skilton, David. *Anthony Trollope and His Contemporaries,* 119–21.

The Small House at Allington, 1864

Horsman, Alan. *The Victorian Novel,* 343–45.
Skilton, David. *Anthony Trollope and His Contemporaries,* 140–43.
Turner, Mark W. "Gendered Issues: Intertextuality and *The Small House at Allington* in *Cornhill Magazine.*" *Victorian Periodicals R* 26 (1993), 228–34.

The Warden, 1855

Floyd, Kevin. "Discerning Motive: Another Look at Trollope's *Warden.*" *Univ of Mississippi Stud in Engl* 11–12 (1993–95), 88–95.
Hall, N. John. "Trollope," in John Richetti et al., eds., *The Columbia History,* 460–61.
Horsman, Alan. *The Victorian Novel,* 334–36.
Lambert, Ellen Zetzel. *The Face of Love,* 76–77.
Wheeler, Michael. *English Fiction of the Victorian Period,* 124–27.

The Way We Live Now, 1875

Brantlinger, Patrick. *Fictions of State,* 165–68.
Horsman, Alan. *The Victorian Novel,* 363–67.
Ragussis, Michael. *Figures of Conversion,* 246–49.
Skilton, David. *Anthony Trollope and His Contemporaries,* 64–67, 73–78.

Smith, Monika Rydygier. "Trollope's Dark Vision: Domestic Violence in *The Way We Live Now*." *Victorian R* 22 (1996), 13–26.

Sutherland, John. *Is Heathcliff a Murderer?*, 156–62.

Sutherland, John. *Victorian Fiction*, 114–32.

Wheeler, Michael. *English Fiction of the Victorian Period*, 129–31.

FRANCES TROLLOPE

The Attractive Man, 1846

Ransom, Teresa. *Fanny Trollope*, 160–61.

The Barnabys in America, 1843

Ellis, Linda Abess. *Frances Trollope's America*, 81–90, 100–112, 123–26, 132–34.

Kissel, Susan S. *In Common Cause*, 48–50.

Charles Chesterfield, 1841

Ransom, Teresa. *Fanny Trollope*, 137–39.

Fashionable Life, or Paris and London, 1856

Ransom, Teresa. *Fanny Trollope*, 213–15.

Jessie Phillips, 1843

Ransom, Teresa. *Fanny Trollope*, 150–52.

Jonathan Jefferson Whitlaw, 1836

Button, Marilyn D. "Reclaiming Mrs. Frances Trollope: British Abolitionist and Feminist." *Coll Lang Assoc J* 38 (1994), 73–86.

Ellis, Linda Abess. *Frances Trollope's America*, 63–67, 82–84, 107–12, 120–24.

Kissel, Susan S. *In Common Cause*, 75–79.

Michael Armstrong, 1840

Brown, Penny. *The Captured World*, 69–72.

Harsh, Constance D. *Subversive Heroines*, 38–41, 79–81.

Kissel, Susan S. *In Common Cause*, 74–77, 82–86.

Ransom, Teresa. *Fanny Trollope*, 127–30.

The Old World and the New, 1849

Ellis, Linda Abess. *Frances Trollope's America*, 86–93, 100–102, 121–24, 131–34.

The Refugee in America, 1832

Ellis, Linda Abess. *Frances Trollope's America*, 46–48, 51–54; 62–63, 69–71, 86–89, 93–95, 101–3, 113–15, 121–24, 130–34.

Kissel, Susan S. *In Common Cause*, 118–20.

Uncle Walter, 1852

Kissel, Susan S. *In Common Cause*, 47–48, 75–78, 80–81.

Ransom, Teresa. *Fanny Trollope*, 200–204.

JOANNA TROLLOPE

A Village Affair, 1989
Cadogan, Mary. *And Then Their Hearts Stood Still,* 245–46.

RICHARD ST. JOHN TYRWHITT

Hugh Heron, 1880
Antor, Heinz. *Der englische Universitätsroman,* 367–69.

BARRY UNSWORTH

Sacred Hunger, 1992
Sarvan, Charles. "Paradigms of the Slave Trade in Two British Novels." *Intl Fiction R* 23 (1996), 1–6.

EDWARD UPWARD

Journey to the Border, 1938
Quinn, Patrick. "At the Frontier: Edward Upward's *Journey to the Border,*" in Patrick J. Quinn, ed., *Recharting the Thirties,* 234–45.

COLWYN EDWARD VULLIAMY

Don Among the Dead Men, 1952
Antor, Heinz. *Der englische Universitätsroman,* 648–50.

JOHN WAIN

Hurry on Down, 1953
Taylor, D. J. *After the War,* 70–73, 77–79.

HORACE WALPOLE

The Castle of Otranto, 1765
Boone, Troy. "Narrating the Apparition: Glanvill, Defoe, and the Rise of Gothic Fiction." *Eighteenth Cent* 35 (1994), 183–88.
Botting, Fred. *Gothic,* 48–54.
Canuel, Mark. " 'Holy Hypocrisy' and the Government of Belief: Religion and Nationalism in the Gothic." *Stud in Romanticism* 34 (1995), 516–17.
Cavaliero, Glen. *The Supernatural and English Fiction,* 24–26.
Clery, Emma. "Against Gothic," in Allan Lloyd Smith and Victor Sage, eds., *Gothick Origins and Innovations,* 34–43.

Dolan, John. "Poetry, 'Fiction' and Prose in Found Texts of the 1760s." *Genre* 28 (1995), 47–50.

Gonda, Caroline. *Reading Daughters' Fictions*, 142–44.

Haggerty, George E. "The Gothic Novel, 1764–1824," in John Richetti et al., eds., *The Columbia History*, 220–23.

Hogle, Jerrold E. "The Ghost of the Counterfeit in the Genesis of the Gothic," in Allan Lloyd Smith and Victor Sage, eds., *Gothick Origins and Innovations*, 23–33.

Howard, Jacqueline. *Reading Gothic Fiction*, 30–36, 90–92.

Johnson, Anthony. "Gaps and Gothic Sensibility: Walpole, Lewis, Mary Shelley, and Maturin," in Valeria Tinkler-Villani and Peter Davidson, eds., *Exhibited by Candlelight*, 10–24.

Kilgour, Maggie. *The Rise of the Gothic Novel*, 17–22.

Magnier, Mireille. "Sir Horace Walpole: *Le Château d'Otrante,* ébauche d'un retour au moyen âge des merveilles." *Mythes, Croyances et Religions dans le Monde Anglo-Saxon* 4 (1986), 98–108.

Richter, David H. *The Progress of Romance*, 66–71, 78–82, 86–88.

de Voogd, Peter. "Sentimental Horrors: Feeling in the Gothic Novel," in Valeria Tinkler-Villani and Peter Davidson, eds., *Exhibited by Candlelight*, 80–86.

MAURICE WALSH

The Small Dark Man, 1929

Judge, E. J. "The Location of *The Small Dark Man.*" *Scottish Liter J* 20:2 (1993), 49–60.

MRS. HUMPHRY WARD

The Case of Richard Meynell, 1911

Wilt, Judith. "The Romance of Faith: Mary Ward's Robert Elsmere and Richard Meynell." *Lit and Theology* 10 (1996), 33–42.

The Coryston Family, 1913

Sanders, Valerie. *Eve's Renegades*, 192–93.
Sutherland, John. *Mrs Humphry Ward*, 328–30.

Daphne; or, Marriage a La Mode, 1909

Harris, Janice Hubbard. *Edwardian Stories of Divorce,* 127–32.

David Grieve, 1892

Sutherland, John. *Mrs Humphry Ward*, 133–40.

Delia Blanchflower, 1914

Miller, Jane Eldridge. *Rebel Women,* 156–59.

Eleanor, 1900

Sutherland, John. *Mrs Humphry Ward*, 232–37.

Helbeck of Bannisdale, 1898

Sanders, Valerie. *Eve's Renegades*, 84–86, 188–92.
Sutherland, John. *Mrs Humphry Ward*, 153–59.

Lady Connie, 1916

Antor, Heinz. *Der englische Universitätsroman*, 492–94, 563–66.

Lady Rose's Daughter, 1903

Sutherland, John. *Mrs Humphry Ward*, 238–41.

Marcella, 1894

Herrero, M. Dolores. "Defiance in Disguise: Mary Ward's Ambivalent Concept of Woman as Reflected in *Marcella.*" *Engl Lit in Transition, 1880–1920* 38 (1995), 445–63.
Sanders, Valerie. *Eve's Renegades*, 80–83.
Sutherland, John. *Mrs Humphry Ward*, 140–48.
Trotter, David. *The English Novel in History*, 83–86.
Wilt, Judith. " 'Transition Time': The Political Romances of Mrs. Humphry Ward's *Marcella* (1894) and *Sir George Tressady* (1896)," in Barbara Leah Harman and Susan Meyer, eds., *The New Nineteenth Century*, 225–36.

Miss Bretherton, 1884

Sutherland, John. *Mrs Humphry Ward*, 100–105.
Sutherland, John. *Victorian Fiction,* 133–45.

Robert Elsmere, 1888

Hapgood, Lynne. " 'The Reconceiving of Christianity': Secularisation, Realism and the Religious Novel: 1888–1900." *Lit and Theology* 10 (1996), 331–40.
Herrero Granado, María Dolores. "Fiction through History and/or History through Fiction: Mary A. Ward's Theism as Reflected in Robert Elsmere—An Illustration of the Ultimate Hegelian Paradox," in Susana Onega, ed., *Telling Histories*, 31–47.
Jenkins, Ruth Y. *Reclaiming Myths of Power,* 147–49.
Sanders, Valerie. *Eve's Renegades*, 116–17, 186–88.
Spacks, Patricia Meyer. " 'A Dull Book is Easily Renounced.'" *Victorian Lit and Culture* 22 (1994), 287–301.
Sutherland, John. *Mrs Humphry Ward*, 106–31.
Wilt, Judith. "The Romance of Faith: Mary Ward's Robert Elsmere and Richard Meynell." *Lit and Theology* 10 (1996), 33–42.

Sir George Tressady, 1896

Sutherland, John. *Mrs Humphry Ward*, 149–52.
Wilt, Judith. " 'Transition Time': The Political Romances of Mrs. Humphry Ward's *Marcella* (1894) and *Sir George Tressady* (1896)," in Barbara Leah Harman and Susan Meyer, eds., *The New Nineteenth Century*, 225–29, 236–45.

MARINA WARNER

Indigo, 1992

Connor, Steven. *The English Novel in History*, 186–97.

Korte, Barbara. "Kulturwissenschaft *in* der Literaturwissenschaft: Am Beispiel von Marina Warners Roman *Indigo.*" *Anglia* 114 (1996), 431–45.

López Rodríguez, Marta Sofía. "*Indigo*, de Marina Warner: re-escribiendo la historia colonial," in José Romera Castillo et al., eds., *La novela histórica*, 285–91.

Todd, Richard. *Consuming Fictions*, 203–11.

Zabus, Chantal. "What Next Miranda? Marina Warner's *Indigo.*" *Kunapipi* 16:3 (1994), 81–92.

REX WARNER

The Aerodrome, 1941

Coombes, John. "The Novels of Rex Warner," in Patrick J. Quinn, ed., *Recharting the Thirties*, 229–31.

The Wild Goose Chase, 1937

Coombes, John. "The Novels of Rex Warner," in Patrick J. Quinn, ed., *Recharting the Thirties*, 222–29.

SYLVIA TOWNSEND WARNER

After the Death of Don Juan, 1938

Hopkins, Chris. "Sylvia Townsend Warner and the Marxist Historical Novel." *Lit and Hist* 4:1 (1995), 61–63.

McKenna, Brian. "The British Communist Novel of the 1930s and 1940s: A 'Party of Equals'? (And Does That Matter?)." *R of Engl Stud* 47 (1996), 381–82.

Maslen, Elizabeth. "Sizing Up: Women, Politics and Parties," in Sarah Sceats and Gail Cunningham, eds., *Image and Power*, 199–200.

The Corner That Held Them, 1948

McKenna, Brian. "The British Communist Novel of the 1930s and 1940s: A 'Party of Equals'? (And Does That Matter?)." *R of Engl Stud* 47 (1996), 382–85.

Lolly Willowes, 1926

Hopkins, Chris. "Sylvia Townsend Warner and the Marxist Historical Novel." *Lit and Hist* 4:1 (1995), 54–55.

Knoll, Bruce. " 'An Existence Doled Out': Passive Resistance as a Dead End in Sylvia Townsend Warner's *Lolly Willowes.*" *Twentieth Cent Lit* 39 (1993), 344–62.

Summer Will Show, 1936

Foster, Thomas. " 'Dream Made Flesh': Sexual Difference and Narratives of Revolution in Sylvia Townsend Warner's *Summer Will Show."* *Mod Fiction Stud* 41 (1995), 531–54.

Hopkins, Chris. "Sylvia Townsend Warner and the Marxist Historical Novel." *Lit and Hist* 4:1 (1995), 55–61.

McKenna, Brian. "The British Communist Novel of the 1930s and 1940s: A 'Party of Equals'? (And Does That Matter?)." *R of Engl Stud* 47 (1996), 377–80.

Maslen, Elizabeth. "Sizing Up: Women, Politics and Parties," in Sarah Sceats and Gail Cunningham, eds., *Image and Power*, 197–98.

KEITH WATERHOUSE

Billy Liar, 1959

Taylor, D. J. *After the War*, 69–72.

ALEC WAUGH

Island in the Sun, 1956

Harris, Michael. *Outsiders and Insiders*, 143–58.

EVELYN WAUGH

Black Mischief, 1932

Gorra, Michael. "Rudyard Kipling to Salman Rushdie: Imperialism to Postcolonialism," in John Richetti et al., eds., *The Columbia History*, 648–49.

Hastings, Selina. *Evelyn Waugh*, 259–63.

Brideshead Revisited, 1945

Bittner, David. "Advantage, Lady Marchmain." *Evelyn Waugh Newsl* 27:3 (1993), 6–7.

Bittner, David. "Mr. Ryder—Daddy Dearest." *Evelyn Waugh Newsl* 30:3 (1996), 4–5.

Bittner, David. "On the Road to Morocco: The Hospital in *Brideshead."* *Evelyn Waugh Newsl* 29:1 (1995), 1–2.

Core, Deborah. *"Brideshead Revisited:* Waugh's 'War Novel'?" *Evelyn Waugh Newsl* 28:2 (1994), 5–7.

Golub, Spencer. "Spies in the House of Quality: The American Reception of *Brideshead Revisited,"* in Peter Reynolds, ed., *Novel Images*, 139–55.

Hastings, Selina. *Evelyn Waugh*, 482–91.

Hennessy, Edmund A. "The Farthing Dinner Party in *Brideshead."* *Evelyn Waugh Newsl* 29:2 (1995), 1–2.

Higdon, David Leon. "Gay Sebastian and Cheerful Charles: Homoeroticism in Waugh's *Brideshead Revisited.*" *Ariel* 25:4 (1994), 77–87.

Holmes, Daryl. "The Uses of Games in *Brideshead Revisited.*" *Evelyn Waugh Newsl* 30:2 (1996), 1–6, and 30:3 (1996), 1–4.

Lynch, Richard P. "Evelyn Waugh's Early Novels: The Limits of Fiction." *Papers on Lang and Lit* 30 (1994), 384–86.

McCartney, George. "Satire between the Wars: Evelyn Waugh and Others," in John Richetti et al., eds., *The Columbia History*, 890–92.

Mooneyham, Laura. "The Triple Conversions of *Brideshead Revisited.*" *Renascence* 45 (1993), 225–35.

Osborne, John. "The Character of Lord Marchmain." *Evelyn Waugh Newsl* 27:3 (1993), 5–6.

Osborne, John W. "The Character of Cordelia in *Brideshead Revisited.*" *Evelyn Waugh Newsl* 29:3 (1995), 1–2.

Rothstein, David. "*Brideshead Revisited* and the Modern Historicization of Memory." *Stud in the Novel* 25 (1993), 318–30.

Wilson, John Howard. "Brothers, War, and Succession in *Brideshead Revisited* and *Sword of Honour.*" *Evelyn Waugh Newsl* 28:1 (1994), 1–4.

Decline and Fall, 1928

Bogaards, Winnifred M. "Evelyn Waugh's England: Class in *Decline and Fall.*" *Swansea R* 1994, 129–38.

Hastings, Selina. *Evelyn Waugh*, 169–75.

Loe, Thomas. "Design and Satire in *Decline and Fall.*" *Stud in Contemp Satire* 17 (1990), 31–41.

Lynch, Richard P. "Evelyn Waugh's Early Novels: The Limits of Fiction." *Papers on Lang and Lit* 30 (1994), 380–83.

McCartney, George. "Satire between the Wars: Evelyn Waugh and Others," in John Richetti et al., eds., *The Columbia History*, 869–70, 878–79, 881–82.

Patey, Douglas Lane. "Penology, Pride, and a Historical Original for Sir Wilfred Lucas-Dockery in *Decline and Fall.*" *Evelyn Waugh Newsl* 28:3 (1994), 4–7.

Robinson, Daniel. "Evelyn Waugh in 'The Best of All Possible Worlds': *Decline and Fall*, a Comedy of Theodicy." *Engl Lang Notes* 34:1 (1996), 77–85.

A Handful of Dust, 1934

Bittner, David. "Tony as Hero of *A Handful of Dust;* or 'Last' But Not Least." *Evelyn Waugh Newsl* 28:1 (1994), 4–6.

Davis, Robert Murray. "Brenda Last's Reading." *Evelyn Waugh Newsl* 30:2 (1996), 7–8.

Hastings, Selina. *Evelyn Waugh*, 307–12.

Lynch, Richard P. "Evelyn Waugh's Early Novels: The Limits of Fiction." *Papers on Lang and Lit* 30 (1994), 377–79, 383–84.

McCartney, George. "Satire between the Wars: Evelyn Waugh and Others," in John Richetti et al., eds., *The Columbia History*, 882–85.

Marx, Sam. "Evelyn Waugh and *A Handful of Dust.*" *Evelyn Waugh Newsl* 28:1 (1994), 6–7.

Helena, 1950

McCartney, George. "Satire between the Wars: Evelyn Waugh and Others," in John Richetti et al., eds., *The Columbia History,* 890–91.

The Loved One, 1948

Allen, Brooke. "Waugh's *The Loved One:* A Classic/Romantic Paradigm." *Univ of Mississippi Stud in Engl* 11–12 (1993–95), 344–50.

Hastings, Selina. *Evelyn Waugh,* 519–21.

Ross, T. J. "Reconsidering Evelyn Waugh's *The Loved One.*" *Mod Age* 37 (1995), 156–62.

Spiering, M. *Englishness,* 41–43, 45–50, 66–79.

Men at Arms, 1952

Hastings, Selina. *Evelyn Waugh,* 546–49.

The Ordeal of Gilbert Pinfold, 1957

Cavaliero, Glen. *The Supernatural and English Fiction,* 208–9.

Johnson, R. Neill. "Shadowed by the Gaze: Evelyn Waugh's *Vile Bodies* and *The Ordeal of Gilbert Pinfold.*" *Mod Lang R* 91 (1996), 15–19.

McCartney, George. "Satire between the Wars: Evelyn Waugh and Others," in John Richetti et al., eds., *The Columbia History,* 877–79.

Scoop, 1938

Hastings, Selina. *Evelyn Waugh,* 367–73.

Sword of Honour, 1965

McCartney, George. "Satire between the Wars: Evelyn Waugh and Others," in John Richetti et al., eds., *The Columbia History,* 884–86.

Taylor, D. J. *After the War,* 13–15.

Wilson, John Howard. "Brothers, War, and Succession in *Brideshead Revisited* and *Sword of Honour.*" *Evelyn Waugh Newsl* 28:1 (1994), 1–4.

Unconditional Surrender, 1961

Hastings, Selina. *Evelyn Waugh,* 594–98.

McCartney, George. "Satire between the Wars: Evelyn Waugh and Others," in John Richetti et al., eds., *The Columbia History,* 886–87.

Vile Bodies, 1930

Allen, Brooke. "*Vile Bodies:* A Futurist Fantasy." *Twentieth Cent Lit* 40 (1994), 318–27.

Hastings, Selina. *Evelyn Waugh,* 206–11.

Hopkins, Chris. "Evelyn Waugh, Henri Bergson and *Vile Bodies.*" *Evelyn Waugh Newsl* 29:1 (1995), 6–8.

Johnson, R. Neill. "Shadowed by the Gaze: Evelyn Waugh's *Vile Bodies* and *The Ordeal of Gilbert Pinfold.*" *Mod Lang R* 91 (1996), 9–15.

McCartney, George. "Satire between the Wars: Evelyn Waugh and Others," in John Richetti et al., eds., *The Columbia History,* 867–69.

MARY WEBB

The Golden Arrow, 1915

Cavaliero, Glen. *The Supernatural and English Fiction,* 144–45.

Gone to Earth, 1917

Siegel, Carol. *Male Masochism,* 34–47.

Sillars, Stuart. *Visualisation in Popular Fiction,* 93–112.

Precious Bane, 1924

Barreca, Regina. "Writing as Voodoo: Sorcery, Hysteria, and Art," in Sarah Webster Goodwin and Elisabeth Bronfen, eds., *Death and Representation,* 185–87.

Cadogan, Mary. *And Then Their Hearts Stood Still,* 109–12.

FAY WELDON

The Cloning of Joanna May, 1989

Brooks, Marilyn. "From Vases to Tea-Sets: Screening Women's Writing," in Gina Wisker, ed., *It's My Party,* 135–39.

Doody, Margaret Anne. "Classic Weldon," in Regina Barreca, ed., *Fay Weldon's Wicked Fictions,* 42–44.

Ford, Betsy. "Belladonna Speaks: Fay Weldon's *Waste Land* Revision in *The Cloning of Joanna May.*" *West Virginia Univ Philol Papers* 38 (1992), 322–33.

Quiello, Rose. "Going to Extremes: The Foreign Legion of Women in Fay Weldon's *The Cloning of Joanna May,*" in Regina Barreca, ed., *Fay Weldon's Wicked Fictions,* 83–91.

Darcy's Utopia, 1990

Barreca, Regina. *Untamed and Unabashed,* 150–52.

Female Friends, 1975

Sage, Lorna. *Women in the House of Fiction,* 153–58.

Growing Rich, 1992

Wisker, Gina. "Weaving Our Own Web: Demythologising/Remythologising and Magic in the Work of Contemporary Women Writers," in Wisker, ed., *It's My Party,* 119–21.

The Heart of the Country, 1987

Barreca, Regina. "Writing as Voodoo: Sorcery, Hysteria, and Art," in Sarah Webster Goodwin and Elisabeth Bronfen, eds., *Death and Representation,* 178–79.

Smith, Patricia Juliana. " 'And I Wondered If She Might Kiss Me': Lesbian Panic as Narrative Strategy in British Women's Fiction." *Mod Fiction Stud* 41 (1995), 592–602.

Leader of the Band, 1988

Glavin, John. "Fay Weldon, Leader of the Frivolous Band," in Regina Barreca, ed., *Fay Weldon's Wicked Fictions,* 139–47.

The Life and Loves of a She-Devil, 1983

> Bronfen, Elisabeth. " 'Say Your Goodbyes and Go': Death and Women's Power in Fay Weldon's Fiction," in Regina Barreca, ed., *Fay Weldon's Wicked Fictions,* 78–82.
>
> Brooks, Marilyn. "From Vases to Tea-Sets: Screening Women's Writing," in Gina Wisker, ed., *It's My Party,* 139–43.
>
> Cadogan, Mary. *And Then Their Hearts Stood Still,* 258–59.
>
> Glavin, John. "Fay Weldon, Leader of the Frivolous Band," in Regina Barreca, ed., *Fay Weldon's Wicked Fictions,* 136–40.
>
> Katz, Pamela. "They Should Have Called It 'She-Angel,' " in Regina Barreca, ed., *Fay Weldon's Wicked Fictions,* 114–29.
>
> McGuirk, Carol. "Drabble to Carter: Fiction by Women, 1962–1992," in John Richetti et al., eds., *The Columbia History,* 950–52.
>
> McKinstrey, Susan Jaret. "Fay Weldon's *Life and Loves of a She-Devil:* The Speaking Body," in Regina Barreca, ed., *Fay Weldon's Wicked Fictions,* 104–13.
>
> Mergenthal, Silvia. " 'Seeing Is Believing': The Rhetoric of Looking in Angela Carter's *Nights at the Circus* and Fay Weldon's *Life and Loves of a She-Devil." GRAAT* 11 (1993), 105–17.
>
> Nash, Julie. " 'Energy and Brashness' and Fay Weldon's Tricksters," in Regina Barreca, ed., *Fay Weldon's Wicked Fictions,* 93–98.
>
> Sage, Lorna. *Women in the House of Fiction,* 158–60.
>
> Smith, Patricia Juliana. "Weldon's *The Life and Loves of a She-Devil." Explicator* 51 (1993), 255–57.
>
> Walker, Nancy A. "Witch Weldon: Fay Weldon's Use of the Fairy Tale Tradition," in Regina Barreca, ed., *Fay Weldon's Wicked Fictions,* 13–15.

Life Force, 1992

> Nash, Julie. " 'Energy and Brashness' and Fay Weldon's Tricksters," in Regina Barreca, ed., *Fay Weldon's Wicked Fictions,* 98–102.

Praxis, 1978

> Barreca, Regina. "It's the End of the World as We Know It: Bringing Down the House in Fay Weldon's Fiction," in Barreca, ed., *Fay Weldon's Wicked Fictions,* 181–84.
>
> Sage, Lorna. *Women in the House of Fiction,* 153–58.

Puffball, 1980

> Cosslett, Tess. *Women Writing Childbirth,* 34–37, 69–75.
>
> Doody, Margaret Anne. "Classic Weldon," in Regina Barreca, ed., *Fay Weldon's Wicked Fictions,* 44–46.

Remember Me, 1976

> Bronfen, Elisabeth. " 'Say Your Goodbyes and Go': Death and Women's Power in Fay Weldon's Fiction," in Regina Barreca, ed., *Fay Weldon's Wicked Fictions,* 75–78.

Words of Advice, 1977

> Walker, Nancy A. "Witch Weldon: Fay Weldon's Use of the Fairy Tale Tradition," in Regina Barreca, ed., *Fay Weldon's Wicked Fictions,* 17–19.

H. G. WELLS

All Aboard for Ararat, 1941

> Foot, Michael. *The History of Mr Wells,* 264–69.

Ann Veronica, 1909

> Brink, Andrew. *Obsession and Culture,* 65–67.
>
> Foot, Michael. *The History of Mr Wells,* 99–103.
>
> Miller, Jane Eldridge. *Rebel Women,* 165–72.
>
> Montgomery, Fiona. " 'Women who Dids, and all that kind of thing. . . .' Male Perceptions of 'Wholesome' Literature," in Christopher Parker, ed., *Gender Roles and Sexuality,* 172–74.
>
> Simpson, Anne B. "Architects of the Erotic: H. G. Wells's 'New Women,' " in Carola M. Kaplan and Anne B. Simpson, eds., *Seeing Double,* 41–46.
>
> Trotter, David. *The English Novel in History,* 130–32.

Babes in the Darkling Wood, 1940

> Foot, Michael. *The History of Mr Wells,* 269–72.

Boon, 1915

> Foot, Michael. *The History of Mr Wells,* 154–58.

The Bulpington of Blup, 1932

> Worthen, John. "Orts and Slarts: Two Biographical Pieces on D. H. Lawrence." *R of Engl Stud* 46 (1995), 26–32.

The Croquet Player, 1936

> Parrinder, Patrick. *Shadows of the Future,* 31–33.

The First Men in the Moon, 1901

> Myers, Doris T. *C. S. Lewis in Context,* 39–47.
>
> Parrinder, Patrick. *Shadows of the Future,* 76–77.

The History of Mr. Polly, 1910

> Foot, Michael. *The History of Mr Wells,* 104–6.

In the Days of the Comet, 1906

> Brink, Andrew. *Obsession and Culture,* 63–65.
>
> Foot, Michael. *The History of Mr Wells,* 73–76.
>
> Parrinder, Patrick. *Shadows of the Future,* 105–6.

The Invisible Man, 1897

> Sutherland, John. *Is Heathcliff a Murderer?,* 228–32.

The Island of Dr. Moreau, 1896

> Derry, Stephen. *"The Island of Doctor Moreau* and Stevenson's *The Ebb-Tide." Notes and Queries* 43 (1996), 437.

Gomel, Elana. "The Body of Parts: Dickens and the Poetics of Synecdoche." *J of Narrative Technique* 26 (1996), 54–56, 58–59.

Hammond, J. R. "*The Island of Doctor Moreau:* A Swiftian Parable." *Wellsian* 16 (1993), 30–40.

Hendershot, Cyndy. "The Animal Without: Masculinity and Imperialism in *The Island of Doctor Moreau* and 'The Adventure of the Speckled Band.' " *Nineteenth Cent Stud* 10 (1996), 1–23.

Hurley, Kelly. *The Gothic Body*, 102–13, 122–24, 155–57.

Parrinder, Patrick. *Shadows of the Future*, 56–64.

Schenkel, Elmar. "Die verkehrte Insel: *The Tempest* und H. G. Wells' *The Island of Dr Moreau.*" *Anglia* 111 (1993), 39–58.

Joan and Peter, 1918

Foot, Michael. *The History of Mr Wells,* 164–68, 169–76.

Kipps, 1905

Foot, Michael. *The History of Mr Wells,* 62–64.

Marriage, 1912

Foot, Michael. *The History of Mr Wells,* 113–23.

Harris, Janice H. "Wifely Silence and Speech in Three Marriage Novels by H. G. Wells." *Stud in the Novel* 26 (1994), 406–10.

Miller, Jane Eldridge. *Rebel Women,* 173–80.

Mr. Blettsworthy on Rampole Island, 1928

Foot, Michael. *The History of Mr Wells,* 206–8.

Mr. Britling Sees It Through, 1916

Foot, Michael. *The History of Mr Wells,* 157–61, 163–65.

A Modern Utopia, 1905

Parrinder, Patrick. *Shadows of the Future,* 96–112.

The New Machiavelli, 1910

Brink, Andrew. *Obsession and Culture,* 70–73.

Foot, Michael. *The History of Mr Wells,* 106–12.

The Passionate Friends, 1913

Foot, Michael. *The History of Mr Wells,* 128–39.

Harris, Janice H. "Wifely Silence and Speech in Three Marriage Novels by H. G. Wells." *Stud in the Novel* 26 (1994), 410–12.

The Research Magnificent, 1915

Foot, Michael. *The History of Mr Wells,* 144–48.

The Shape of Things to Come, 1933

Turner, Arthur Campbell. "Armed Conflict in the Science Fiction of H. G. Wells," in George Slusser and Eric S. Rabkin, eds., *Fights of Fancy,* 73–77.

Star Begotten, 1937

Foot, Michael. *The History of Mr Wells,* 244–46.

The Time Machine, 1895

Alkon, Paul. "Cannibalism in Science Fiction," in Gary Westfahl et al., eds., *Foods of the Gods*, 142–44, 146–57.

Baxter, Stephen. "Further Visions: Sequels to *The Time Machine.*" *Foundation* 65 (1995), 41–49.

Crossley, Robert. "In the Palace of Green Porcelain: Artifacts from the Museums of Science Fiction," in George Slusser and Eric S. Rabkin, eds., *Styles of Creation*, 210–12.

Foot, Michael. *The History of Mr Wells*, 29–35.

Hammond, J. R. "The Significance of Weena." *Wellsian* 18 (1995), 19–22.

Huntington, John. "*The Time Machine* and Wells's Social Trajectory." *Foundation* 65 (1995), 6–13.

Hurley, Kelly. *The Gothic Body*, 79–88.

James, Edward. *Science Fiction in the Twentieth Century*, 28–30.

Myers, Doris T. *C. S. Lewis in Context*, 56–63.

Palumbo, Donald E. "The Politics of Entropy: Revolution vs. Evolution in George Pal's 1960 Film Version of H. G. Wells's *The Time Machine,*" in Robert A. Latham and Robert A. Collins, eds., *Modes of the Fantastic*, 204–11.

Parrinder, Patrick. *Shadows of the Future*, 34–64, 73–75.

Russell, W. M. S. "Time Before and After *The Time Machine.*" *Foundation* 65 (1995), 24–37.

Sommerville, Bruce David. "*The Time Machine:* A Chronological and Scientific Revision." *Wellsian* 17 (1994), 11–27.

Trotter, David. "The Avoidance of Naturalism: Gissing, Moore, Grand, Bennett, and Others," in John Richetti et al., eds., *The Columbia History*, 619–20.

Tono-Bungay, 1909

Born, Daniel. *The Birth of Liberal Guilt,* 140–64.

Brantlinger, Patrick. *Fictions of State*, 207–11.

Cash, Eric. "Confessions of a Skirt-Chasing Feminist: Wells's *Tono Bungay* and the Idea of a New Woman ." *Wellsian* 17 (1994), 32–43.

Foot, Michael. *The History of Mr Wells*, 92–99.

Kohl, Stephan. "Rural England in Moderne und Zwischenkriegzeit: Zur Nachgeschichte eines literarischen Konstrukts." *Poetica* (Munich) 27 (1995), 382–83.

Lucas, John. "The Sunlight on the Garden," in Carola M. Kaplan and Anne B. Simpson, eds., *Seeing Double*, 70–71.

Parrinder, Patrick. *Shadows of the Future*, 23–24, 88–89.

Simpson, Anne B. "H. G. Wells's *Tono-Bungay:* Individualism and Difference." *Essays in Lit* (Macomb, IL) 22 (1995), 75–84.

Squillace, Robert. "Bennett, Wells, and the Persistence of Realism," in John Richetti et al., eds., *The Columbia History*, 664–74.

The War of the Worlds, 1898

Guthke, Karl S. *The Last Frontier*, 386–91.

Maule, Victoria. "On the Subversion of Character in the Literature of

Identity Anxiety," in Derek Littlewood and Peter Stockwell, eds., *Impossibility Fiction*, 113–16.

Parrinder, Patrick. "From Mary Shelley to *The War of the Worlds:* The Thames Valley Catastrophe," in David Seed, ed., *Anticipations,* 67–72.

The Wife of Sir Isaac Harman, 1914

Harris, Janice H. "Wifely Silence and Speech in Three Marriage Novels by H. G. Wells." *Stud in the Novel* 26 (1994), 412–17.

Miller, Jane Eldridge. *Rebel Women,* 181–88.

Simpson, Anne B. "Architects of the Erotic: H. G. Wells's 'New Women,' " in Carola M. Kaplan and Anne B. Simpson, eds., *Seeing Double*, 46–53.

The World Set Free, 1914

Foot, Michael. *The History of Mr Wells,* 140–42.

REBECCA WEST

The Fountain Overflows, 1956

Adamson, Jane. "States of Soul, Styles of Mind: Rebecca West's *The Fountain Overflows." Crit R* 32 (1992), 114–41.

Harriet Hume, 1929

Scott, Bonnie Kime. *Refiguring Modernism,* 139–45.

The Judge, 1922

Scott, Bonnie Kime. *Refiguring Modernism,* 130–39.

The Return of the Soldier, 1918

Cadogan, Mary. *And Then Their Hearts Stood Still,* 103–4.

The Thinking Reed, 1936

Joannou, Maroula. *'Ladies, Please Don't Smash These Windows,'* 127–58.

Loeffelholz, Mary. *Experimental Lives,* 83–85.

STANLEY J. WEYMAN

The Abbess of Vlaye, 1904

Hughes, Helen. *The Historical Romance*, 52–57.

The Castle Inn, 1898

Tarr, C. Anita. "A Twisted Romance: Abduction and Rape in Stanley John Weyman's *The Castle Inn." Engl Lit in Transition, 1880–1920* 39 (1996), 63–71.

A Gentleman of France, 1893

Orel, Harold. *The Historical Novel,* 102–14.

Starvecrow Farm, 1905

> Hughes, Helen. *The Historical Romance,* 109–15.

T. H. WHITE

The Once and Future King, 1958

> Bewer, Elisabeth. *T. H. White's "The Once and Future King,"* 17–225.
> Blake, Andrew. "T. H. White, Arnold Bax, and the Alternative History of Britain," in Derek Littlewood and Peter Stockwell, eds., *Impossibility Fiction,* 29–32.

WILLIAM HALE WHITE

The Autobiography of Mark Rutherford, 1881

> Swann, Charles. *"Miriam's Schooling and Other Papers:* Historical Fictions Ancient and Modern, Sacred and Secular." *Mod Lang R* 90 (1995), 847–60.
> Swann, Charles. "William Cowper's *Adelphi* and William Hale White's *The Autobiography of Mark Rutherford:* Parallels or Influence?" *Notes and Queries* 42 (1995), 198–99.

RICHARD WHITEING

The Island, 1888

> Hapgood, Lynne. "Regaining a Focus: New Perspectives on the Novels of Richard Whiteing, 1888–1899," in Nikki Lee Manos and Meri-Jane Rochelson, eds., *Transforming Genres,* 174–81.

No. 5 John Street, 1899

> Hapgood, Lynne. "Regaining a Focus: New Perspectives on the Novels of Richard Whiteing, 1888–1899," in Nikki Lee Manos and Meri-Jane Rochelson, eds., *Transforming Genres,* 181–89.

OSCAR WILDE

The Picture of Dorian Gray, 1891

> Adams, James Eli. *Dandies and Desert Saints,* 217–21.
> Allen, Dennis W. *Sexuality in Victorian Fiction,* 110–36.
> Brînzeu, Pia. "Dorian Gray's Rooms and Cyberspace," in C. George Sandulescu, ed., *Rediscovering Oscar Wilde,* 21–28.
> Bruhm, Steven. "Taking One to Know One: Oscar Wilde and Narcissism." *Engl Stud in Canada* 21 (1995), 170–83.
> Cavaliero, Glen. *The Supernatural and English Fiction,* 69–70.
> Cohen, William A. *Sex Scandal,* 215–18.

Dale, Peter Allan. "Oscar Wilde: Crime and the 'Glorious Shapes of Art.' " *Victorian Newsl* 88 (1995), 2–4.

D'Alessandro, Jean M. Ellis. "Intellectual Wordplay in Wilde's Characterization of Henry Wotton," in C. George Sandulescu, ed., *Rediscovering Oscar Wilde*, 61–73.

Danson, Lawrence. " 'Each Man Kills the Thing He Loves': The Impermanence of Personality in Oscar Wilde," in C. George Sandulescu, ed., *Rediscovering Oscar Wilde*, 85–92.

Danson, Lawrence. *Wilde's Intentions*, 13–16, 51–53, 130–36.

Foster, John Wilson. "Against Nature? Science and Oscar Wilde." *Univ of Toronto Q* 63 (1993–94), 328–41.

Fraile Murlanch, Isabel. "Taking Risks: A Reading of Oscar Wilde's *The Picture of Dorian Gray.*" *Miscelanea* 15 (1994), 219–34.

Gillespie, Michael Patrick. "Ethics and Aesthetics in *The Picture of Dorian Gray,*" in C. George Sandulescu, ed., *Rediscovering Oscar Wilde*, 137–54.

Gillespie, Michael Patrick. *Oscar Wilde and the Poetics of Ambiguity*, 46–74.

Gillespie, Michael Patrick. *"The Picture of Dorian Gray,"* 33–106.

Gillespie, Michael Patrick. " 'What's in a Name?': Representing *The Picture of Dorian Gray,*" in John S. Rickard, ed., *Irishness and (Post)-Modernism*, 44–59.

Goedegebuure, Jaap. "The New Man: Moral Aspects of Decadent Literature." *New Comparison* 14 (1992), 161–62.

González, Antonio Ballesteros. "The Mirror of Narcissus in *The Picture of Dorian Gray,*" in C. George Sandulescu, ed., *Rediscovering Oscar Wilde*, 1–10.

Gordon, Jan B. *Gossip and Subversion*, 295–99, 312–18, 326–46.

Halberstam, Judith. *Skin Shows,* 53–85.

Hammond, Paul. *Love between Men*, 175–81.

Hasseler, Terri A. "The Physiological Determinism Debate in Oscar Wilde's *The Picture of Dorian Gray.*" *Victorian Newsl* 84 (1993), 31–35.

Kabel, Ans. "The Influence of Walter Pater in *Dr Jekyll and Mr Hyde* and *The Picture of Dorian Gray,*" in Peter Liebregts and Wim Tigges, eds., *Beauty and the Beast*, 143–47.

Knox, Melissa. *Oscar Wilde*, 48–49, 56–57, 60–63, 82–83.

Lane, Christopher. "Framing Fears, Reading Designs: The Homosexual Art of Painting in James, Wilde, and Beerbohm." *ELH* 61 (1994), 936–43.

Lawler, Donald. "The Gothic Wilde," in C. George Sandulescu, ed., *Rediscovering Oscar Wilde*, 249–53.

McCollister, Deborah. "Wilde's *The Picture of Dorian Gray.*" *Explicator* 54 (1996), 17–20.

Mahaffey, Vicki. "Père-version and Im-mère-sion: Idealized Corruption in *A Portrait of the Artist as a Young Man* and *The Picture of Dorian Gray.*" *James Joyce Q* 31:3 (1994), 197–202.

Milligan, Barry. *Pleasures and Pains,* 111–13.

Murray, Isobel. "Oscar Wilde in His Literary Element: Yet Another Source for *Dorian Gray?,*" in C. George Sandulescu, ed., *Rediscovering Oscar Wilde,* 283–95.

Nassaar, Christopher S. "Wilde's *The Picture of Dorian Gray* and *Lady Windermere's Fan." Explicator* 54 (1996), 20–24.

Nassaar, Christopher S. "Wilde's *The Picture of Dorian Gray* and *Salome." Explicator* 53 (1995), 217–20.

Nunokawa, Jeff. "The Importance of Being Bored: The Dividends of Ennui in *The Picture of Dorian Gray." Stud in the Novel* 28 (1996), 357–70.

Nunokawa, Jeff. *Oscar Wilde,* 69–75.

Ostermann, Sylvia. "Eros and Thanatos in *The Picture of Dorian Gray,*" in C. George Sandulescu, ed., *Rediscovering Oscar Wilde,* 297–303.

Pine, Richard. *The Thief of Reason,* 161–63, 226–27, 334–36.

Rabaté, Jean-Michel. "On Joycean and Wildean Sodomy." *James Joyce Q* 31:3 (1994), 162–65.

Richter, David H. *The Progress of Romance,* 139–42.

Satzinger, Christa. *The French Influences,* 99–187.

Schmidgall, Gary. *The Stranger Wilde,* 22–26, 297–300.

Sinfield, Alan. *The Wilde Century,* 99–105.

Smith, Elaine. "Oscar Wilde's *The Picture of Dorian Gray:* A Decadent Portrait of Life in Art—or Art in Life." *Publs of the Arkansas Philol Assoc* 19:1 (1993), 23–31.

Stewart, Garrett. *Dear Reader,* 346–52.

Stewart, Garrett. "Reading Figures: The Legible Image of Victorian Textuality," in Carol T. Christ and John O. Jordan, eds., *Victorian Literature,* 347–49.

Sutherland, John. *Is Heathcliff a Murderer?,* 196–201.

Theoharis, Theoharis Constantine. "Will to Power, Poetic Justice, and Mimesis in *The Picture of Dorian Gray,*" in C. George Sandulescu, ed., *Rediscovering Oscar Wilde,* 397–404.

Thomas, Martine. *"The Picture of Dorian Gray:* la création du 'héros' eponyme." *Recherches Anglaises et Nord-Américaines* 28 (1995), 17–35.

Trotter, David. "The Avoidance of Naturalism: Gissing, Moore, Grand, Bennett, and Others," in John Richetti et al., eds., *The Columbia History,* 618–19.

Upchurch, David A. *Wilde's Use of Irish Celtic Elements in "The Picture of Dorian Gray."*

Waldrep, Shelton. "The Aesthetic Realism of Oscar Wilde's *Dorian Gray." Stud in the Liter Imagination* 29:1 (1996), 103–10.

Weir, David. *Decadence and the Making of Modernism,* 109–13.

Willoughby, Guy. *Art and Christhood,* 62–75.

Witt, Amanda. "Blushings and Palings: The Body as Text in Wilde's *The Picture of Dorian Gray." Publs of the Arkansas Philol Assoc* 19:2 (1993), 85–95.

Zeender, Marie-Noëlle. "John Melmoth and Dorian Gray: The Two-Faced Mirror," in C. George Sandulescu, ed., *Rediscovering Oscar Wilde*, 432–39.

ELLEN WILKINSON

Clash, 1929

Fox, Pamela. *Class Fictions,* 85–89, 169–76.

Fox, Pamela. "The 'Revolt of the Gentle': Romance and the Politics of Resistance in Working-Class Women's Writing." *Novel* 27 (1994), 156–59.

CHARLES WILLIAMS

All Hallows' Eve, 1945

Cavaliero, Glen. *The Supernatural and English Fiction,* 112–13.

Davidson, Alice E. "Language and Meaning in the Novels of Charles Williams," in Charles A. Huttar and Peter J. Schakel, eds., *The Rhetoric of Vision,* 44–48.

Medcalf, Stephen. "The Athanasian Principle in Williams' Use of Images," in Charles A. Huttar and Peter J. Schakel, eds., *The Rhetoric of Vision,* 40–43.

Peckham, Robert W. "Rhetoric and the Supernatural in the Novels of Charles Williams." *Renascence* 45 (1993), 245–46.

Scheper, George L. "*All Hallows' Eve:* The Cessation of Rhetoric and the Redemption of Language," in Charles A. Huttar and Peter J. Schakel, eds., *The Rhetoric of Vision,* 132–61.

Willard, Thomas. "Acts of the Companions: A. E. Waite's Fellowship of the Rosy Cross and the Novels of Charles Williams," in Marie Mulvey Roberts and Hugh Ormsby-Lennon, eds., *Secret Texts,* 291–94.

Descent into Hell, 1937

Cavaliero, Glen. *The Supernatural and English Fiction,* 110–12.

Davidson, Alice E. "Language and Meaning in the Novels of Charles Williams," in Charles A. Huttar and Peter J. Schakel, eds., *The Rhetoric of Vision,* 48–50, 54–58.

Kollmann, Judith J. "Complex Rhetoric for a Simple Universe: *Descent into Hell,*" in Charles A. Huttar and Peter J. Schakel, eds., *The Rhetoric of Vision,* 113–31.

Peckham, Robert W. "Rhetoric and the Supernatural in the Novels of Charles Williams." *Renascence* 45 (1993), 243–45.

Smith, Evans Lansing. "The Mythical Method of *Descent into Hell.*" *Mythlore* 76 (1994), 10–15.

Tilley, Elizabeth. "Religion and Popular Culture: Charles Williams's *Descent into Hell,*" in Patrick J. Quinn, ed., *Recharting the Thirties,* 248–61.

The Greater Trumps, 1932

> Beach, Charles. " 'Courtesy' in Charles Williams' *The Greater Trumps.*" *Mythlore* 19:1 (1993), 16–20.
>
> Henry, Richard. "Charles Williams and the Aesthetic Ideal of Friedrich von Schiller." *Extrapolation* 35 (1994), 271–80.
>
> Medcalf, Stephen. "The Athanasian Principle in Williams' Use of Images," in Charles A. Huttar and Peter J. Schakel, eds., *The Rhetoric of Vision,* 30–33.
>
> Peckham, Robert W. "Rhetoric and the Supernatural in the Novels of Charles Williams." *Renascence* 45 (1993), 240–43.

Many Dimensions, 1931

> Bosky, Bernadette. "Charles Williams: Occult Fantasies/Occult Fact," in Robert A. Latham and Robert A. Collins, eds., *Modes of the Fantastic,* 181–83.
>
> Flieger, Verlyn. "Time in the Stone of Sulliman," in Charles A. Huttar and Peter J. Schakel, eds., *The Rhetoric of Vision,* 78–89.
>
> Peckham, Robert W. "Rhetoric and the Supernatural in the Novels of Charles Williams." *Renascence* 45 (1993), 238–39.

The Place of the Lion, 1931

> Cutsinger, James S. "Angels and Inklings." *Mythlore* 19:2 (1993), 57–60.
>
> Filmer-Davies, Cath. "Charles Williams, a Prophet for Postmodernism: Skepticism and Belief in *The Place of the Lion,*" in Charles A. Huttar and Peter J. Schakel, eds., *The Rhetoric of Vision,* 103–12.
>
> Medcalf, Stephen. "The Athanasian Principle in Williams' Use of Images," in Charles A. Huttar and Peter J. Schakel, eds., *The Rhetoric of Vision,* 33–36.

Shadows of Ecstasy, 1933

> Bosky, Bernadette. "Charles Williams: Occult Fantasies/Occult Fact," in Robert A. Latham and Robert A. Collins, eds., *Modes of the Fantastic,* 180–82.
>
> Peckham, Robert W. "Rhetoric and the Supernatural in the Novels of Charles Williams." *Renascence* 45 (1993), 237–38.

War in Heaven, 1930

> Bosky, Bernadette. "Charles Williams: Occult Fantasies/Occult Fact," in Robert A. Latham and Robert A. Collins, eds., *Modes of the Fantastic,* 181–83.
>
> Cavaliero, Glen. *The Supernatural and English Fiction,* 108–9.
>
> Willard, Thomas. "Acts of the Companions: A. E. Waite's Fellowship of the Rosy Cross and the Novels of Charles Williams," in Marie Mulvey Roberts and Hugh Ormsby-Lennon, eds., *Secret Texts,* 286–88.

HELEN MARIA WILLIAMS

Julia, 1790

> MacCarthy, B. G. *The Female Pen,* 322–25.
>
> Ty, Eleanor. *Unsex'd Revolutionaries,* 75–84.

NIGEL WILLIAMS

Jack Be Nimble, 1980
> Taylor, D. J. *After the War,* 261–64.

ANGUS WILSON

Hemlock and After, 1952
> Whitebrook, Maureen. *Real Toads in Imaginary Gardens,* 39–57.

No Laughing Matter, 1967
> Erzgräber, Willi. "Zwischen Viktorianismus und Moderne: Zu Angus Wilsons Roman *No Laughing Matter.*" *Germanisch-Romanische Monatsschrift* 45 (1995), 88–102.
> Gasiorek, Andrzej. *Post-War British Fiction,* 101–10.

Old Men at the Zoo, 1961
> Rabinovitz, Rubin. "The Reaction against Modernism: Amis, Snow, Wilson," in John Richetti et al., eds., *The Columbia History,* 913–14.
> Spiering, M. *Englishness,* 129–32, 143–46.
> Whitebrook, Maureen. *Real Toads in Imaginary Gardens,* 61–76.

COLIN WILSON

The Space Vampires, 1976
> Hollinger, Veronica. "The Vampire and/as the Alien." *J of the Fantastic in the Arts* 5:3 (1993), 5–17.

JEANETTE WINTERSON

Art and Lies, 1994
> Burns, Christy L. "Fantastic Language: Jeanette Winterson's Recovery of the Postmodern Word." *Contemp Lit* 37 (1996), 278–84, 293–304.

Oranges Are Not the Only Fruit, 1985
> Bollinger, Laurel. "Models for Female Loyalty: The Biblical Ruth in Jeanette Winterson's *Oranges Are Not the Only Fruit.*" *Tulsa Stud in Women's Lit* 13 (1994), 363–77.
> Brinks, Ellen, and Lee Talley. "Unfamiliar Ties: Lesbian Constructions of Home and Family in Jeanette Winterson's *Oranges Are Not the Only Fruit* and Jewelle Gomez's *The Gilda Stories,*" in Catherine Wiley and Fiona R. Barnes, eds., *Homemaking,* 147–57.
> Brooks, Marilyn. "From Vases to Tea-Sets: Screening Women's Writing," in Gina Wisker, ed., *It's My Party,* 131–35.
> Burns, Christy L. "Fantastic Language: Jeanette Winterson's Recovery of the Postmodern Word." *Contemp Lit* 37 (1996), 284–85.
> Duncker, Patricia. *Sisters and Strangers,* 178–80.

Griffin, Gabriele. "Acts of Defiance: Celebrating Lesbians," in Gina Wisker, ed., *It's My Party,* 81–98.

Griffin, Gabriele. *Heavenly Love?,* 63–69.

Onega, Susana. " 'I'm Telling Youy Stories, Trust Me': History/Story-telling in Jeanette Winterson's *Oranges Are Not the Only Fruit,"* in Onega, ed., *Telling Histories*, 135–47.

The Passion, 1987

Burns, Christy L. "Fantastic Language: Jeanette Winterson's Recovery of the Postmodern Word." *Contemp Lit* 37 (1996), 288–92.

Sexing the Cherry, 1989

Burns, Christy L. "Fantastic Language: Jeanette Winterson's Recovery of the Postmodern Word." *Contemp Lit* 37 (1996), 285–88.

Langland, Elizabeth. "Sexing the Text: Narrative Drag as Feminist Poetics and Politics in Jeanette Winterson's *Sexing the Cherry." Narrative* 5:1 (1997), 99–106.

Lozano, María. " 'How You Cuddle in the Dark Governs How You See the History of the World': A Note on Some Obsessions in Recent British Fiction," in Susana Onega, ed., *Telling Histories*, 129–34.

Rozett, Martha Tuck. "Constructing a World: How Postmodern Historical Fiction Reimagines the Past." *Clio* 25 (1996), 159–60.

Written on the Body, 1992

Haines-Wright, Lisa, and Traci Lynn Kyle. "From He and She to You and Me: Grounding Fluidity, Woolf's *Orlando* to Winterson's *Written on the Body,"* in Beth Rigel Daugherty and Eileen Barrett, eds., *Virginia Woolf,* 177–82.

Lanser, Susan S. "Queering Narratology," in Kathy Mezei, ed., *Ambiguous Discourse,* 250–60.

NICHOLAS WISEMAN

Fabiola; or, The Church of the Catacombs, 1854

Litvack, Leon B. "Callista, Martyrdom, and the Early Christian Novel in the Victorian Age." *Nineteenth-Cent Contexts* 17 (1993), 165–67.

MARY WOLLSTONECRAFT

Maria, or The Wrongs of Woman, 1798

Batchelor, Rhonda. "The Rise and Fall of the Eighteenth Century's Authentic Feminine Voice." *Eighteenth-Cent Fiction* 6 (1994), 348–51, 359–60, 364–65.

Berglund, Birgitta. *Woman's Whole Existence,* 78–80, 106–20.

Fry, Carrol L. *Charlotte Smith,* 130–32.

Gonda, Caroline. *Reading Daughters' Fictions*, 157–58.

Goodwin, Sarah Webster. "Romanticism and the Ghost of Prostitution:

Freud, *Maria*, and 'Alice Fell,' " in Sarah Webster Goodwin and Elisabeth Bronfen, eds., *Death and Representation*, 159–63.

Homans, Margaret. "Feminist Fictions and Feminist Theories of Narrative." *Narrative* 2 (1994), 3–6.

Johnson, Nancy E. "Rights, Property and the Law in the English Jacobin Novel." *Mosaic* 27:4 (1994), 106–11.

Kawatsu, Masae. "Self and Society: Wollstonecraft's Dilemma in *The Wrongs of Woman*," in Kenkishi Kamijima, ed., *Centre and Circumference*, 638–53.

Kilgour, Maggie. *The Rise of the Gothic Novel*, 75–96.

Lenz, Bernd. "Popularisierung und Wandlung der Empfindsamkeit im englischen Roman des 18. Jahrhunderts," in Klaus P. Hansen, ed., *Empfindsamkeiten*, 72–74.

MacCarthy, B. G. *The Female Pen*, 427–29.

Mellor, Anne K. "Righting the Wrongs of Woman: Mary Wollstonecraft's *Maria*." *Nineteenth-Cent Contexts* 19 (1996), 413–23.

Robinson, Daniel. "Theodicy versus Feminist Strategy in Mary Wollstonecraft's Fiction." *Eighteenth-Cent Fiction* 9 (1997), 183–202.

Small, Helen. *Love's Madness*, 28–31.

Spacks, Patricia Meyer. "Novels of the 1790s: Action and Impasse," in John Richetti et al., eds., *The Columbia History*, 258–60.

Sudan, Rajani. "Mothering and National Identity in the Works of Mary Wollstonecraft," in Alan Richardson and Sonia Hofkosch, eds., *Romanticism, Race, and Imperial Culture*, 82–87.

Todd, Janet. *Gender, Art and Death*, 120–23.

Ty, Eleanor. *Unsex'd Revolutionaries*, 31–45.

Wilson, Jean. "Romanticism's Real Women," in David L. Clark and Donald C. Goellnicht, eds., *New Romanticisms*, 260–62.

Mary, A Fiction, 1787

Berglund, Birgitta. *Woman's Whole Existence*, 78–106.

Lenz, Bernd. "Popularisierung und Wandlung der Empfindsamkeit im englischen Roman des 18. Jahrhunderts," in Klaus P. Hansen, ed., *Empfindsamkeiten*, 72–74.

Robinson, Daniel. "Theodicy versus Feminist Strategy in Mary Wollstonecraft's Fiction." *Eighteenth-Cent Fiction* 9 (1997), 183–202.

Sudan, Rajani. "Mothering and National Identity in the Works of Mary Wollstonecraft," in Alan Richardson and Sonia Hofkosch, eds., *Romanticism, Race, and Imperial Culture*, 80–82.

EMMA CAROLINE WOOD

East Lynne, 1861

Horsman, Alan. *The Victorian Novel*, 222–23.

Kucich, John. *The Power of Lies*, 161–95.

Vrettos, Athena. *Somatic Fictions*, 44–47.

Sorrow on the Sea, 1868

   Matus, Jill. " 'The Unnaturalness of her Crime': Mid-Victorian Representations of Maternal Deviance," in Barbara Thaden, ed., *New Essays
   on the Maternal Voice,* 89–95.

   Matus, Jill L. *Unstable Bodies,* 179–86.

LEONARD SIDNEY WOOLF

The Village in the Jungle, 1913

   Thompson, Theresa M. "Confronting Modernist Racism in the Post-Colonial Classroom: Teaching Virginia Woolf's *The Voyage Out* and Leonard Woolf's *The Village in the Jungle,*" in Eileen Barrett and
   Patricia Cramer, eds., *Re: Reading,* 241–50.

The Wise Virgins, 1914

   Reid, Panthea. *Art and Affection,* 144–50.

VIRGINIA WOOLF

Between the Acts, 1941

   Apstein, Barbara. "Chaucer, Virginia Woolf and *Between the Acts.*"
   Woolf Stud Annual 2 (1996), 117–32.

   Beer, John. *Romantic Influences,* 188–91.

   Bezrucka, Yvonne. "Assenza, violenza, proliferazione dei sensi in *Between the Acts* di Virginia Woolf." *Quaderni di Lingue e Letterature*
   19 (1994), 97–107.

   Clarke, Stuart N. "The Horse with a Green Tail." *Virginia Woolf Misc*
   34 (1990), 3–4.

   Cramer, Patricia. "Virginia Woolf's Matriarchal Family of Origins in
   Between the Acts." *Twentieth Cent Lit* 39 (1993), 166–82.

   English, James F. *Comic Transactions,* 108–27.

   Erzgräber, Willi. "Zwischen Viktorianismus und Moderne: Zu Angus
   Wilsons Roman *No Laughing Matter.*" *Germanisch-Romanische Monatsschrift* 45 (1995), 96–98.

   Goodenough, Elizabeth. " 'We Haven't the Words': The Silence of Children in the Novels of Virginia Woolf," in Goodenough et al., eds.,
   Infant Tongues, 187–88.

   Hanson, Clare. *Virginia Woolf,* 182–200.

   Harris, Ann. "Scraps and Fragments of Empire: The Pageant as Metaphor in Woolf and Walcott," in Beth Rigel Daugherty and Eileen Barrett, eds., *Virginia Woolf,* 210–15.

   Herman, David. *Universal Grammar and Narrative Form,* 139–81.

   Kautz, Elizabeth Dolan. "The Anti-Tyranny Aesthetic of *Between the
   Acts.*" *Virginia Woolf Misc* 44 (1994), 3.

   Lambert, Elizabeth. "Unsocial Impulses and Writhing Dinosaurs: Evolution as Fiction in Virginia Woolf's Novels." *CEA Critic* 58:1 (1995), 91–94.

Lassner, Phyllis. " 'The Milk of Our Mother's Kindness Has Ceased to Flow': Virginia Woolf, Stevie Smith, and the Representation of the Jew," in Bryan Cheyette, ed., *Between 'Race' and Culture*, 136–38.

Mahaffey, Vicki. "Virginia Woolf," in John Richetti et al., eds., *The Columbia History*, 814–17.

Michael, Magali Cornier. *Feminism and the Postmodern Impulse*, 70–76.

Michael, Magali Cornier. "Woolf's *Between the Acts* and Lessing's *The Golden Notebook:* From Modern to Postmodern Subjectivity," in Ruth Saxton and Jean Tobin, eds., *Woolf and Lessing*, 39–46.

Miller, Marlowe A. "Between the Acts of Modernism and Postmodernism." *Virginia Woolf Misc* 44 (1994), 4.

Newman, Herta. *Virginia Woolf and Mrs. Brown*, 123–33.

Painter, Penny. "The Summer of 1897: The Origin of Some Character and Place Names in Virginia Woolf's *Between the Acts." Virginia Woolf Misc* 35 (1990), 6–7.

Parkes, Adam. *Modernism and the Theater of Censorship,* 178–79.

Phillips, Kathy J. *Virginia Woolf against Empire,* 200–220.

Pike, David L. *Passage through Hell,* 186–88.

Plain, Gill. *Women's Fiction of the Second World War,* 124–37.

Pridmore-Brown, Michele. "The Politics of Theatre: Virginia Woolf's *Between the Acts." Virginia Woolf Misc* 47 (1996), 1–2.

Reese, Judy S. *Recasting Social Values,* 135–47.

Rosenberg, Beth Carole. *Virginia Woolf and Samuel Johnson,* 106–14.

Schneider, Karen. *Loving Arms,* 110–32.

Schroeder, Steven. *Virginia Woolf's Subject,* 221–26.

Scott, Bonnie Kime. *Refiguring Modernism,* 51–70, 172–75.

Seeley, Tracy. "(Un)Weaving the Shroud of the Fathers: 'A Woman's Sentence' in *Between the Acts." Crit Matrix* 7:1 (1993), 81–97.

Stonebridge, Lyndsey. "Rhythm: Breaking the Illusion," in Helen Wussow, ed., *New Essays on Virginia Woolf*, 107–12.

Usui, Masami. "Making a Mask of Her Own in Virginia Woolf's *Between the Acts* and in Fumiko Enchi's *The Waiting Years." Virginia Woolf R* 12 (1995), 61–71.

Vandivere, Julie. "Waves and Fragments: Linguistic Construction as Subject Formation in Virginia Woolf." *Twentieth Cent Lit* 42 (1996), 226–31.

Wiley, Catherine. "Making History Unrepeatable in Virginia Woolf's *Between the Acts." Clio* 25 (1995), 3–20.

Wilt, Judith. *Abortion, Choice, and Contemporary Fiction,* 29–31.

Wirth-Nesher, Hana. "Final Curtain on the War: Figure and Ground in Virginia Woolf's *Between the Acts." Style* 28 (1994), 183–98.

Jacob's Room, 1922

Booth, Allyson. "The Architecture of Loss: Teaching *Jacob's Room* as a War Novel," in Eileen Barrett and Patricia Cramer, eds., *Re: Reading*, 65–71.

Brunkhorst, Martin. "Virginia Woolf und die Restaurationskomödie." *Sprachkunst* 24:1 (1993), 73–86.

Carpentier, Martha C. "Why An Old Shoe? Teaching *Jacob's Room* as *l'écriture féminine*," in Eileen Barrett and Patricia Cramer, eds., *Re: Reading*, 142–48.

Delorey, Denise. "Parsing the Female Sentence: The Paradox of Containment in Virginia Woolf's Narratives," in Kathy Mezei, ed., *Ambiguous Discourse*, 95–100.

Fisher, Jane. "*Jacob's Room* and the Canon: Teaching Woolf During the Culture Wars," in Eileen Barrett and Patricia Cramer, eds., *Re: Reading*, 290–92.

Froula, Christine. "War, Civilization, and the Conscience of Modernity: Views from *Jacob's Room*," in Beth Rigel Daugherty and Eileen Barrett, eds., *Virginia Woolf*, 280–94.

Galef, David. *The Supporting Cast*, 113–61.

Goodenough, Elizabeth. " 'We Haven't the Words': The Silence of Children in the Novels of Virginia Woolf," in Goodenough et al., eds., *Infant Tongues*, 199–200.

Hanson, Clare. *Virginia Woolf*, 42–57.

Loeffelholz, Mary. *Experimental Lives*, 63–65.

Mahaffey, Vicki. "Virginia Woolf," in John Richetti et al., eds., *The Columbia History*, 797–801.

Moore, Madeline. "Virginia Woolf and the Good Brother," in Beth Rigel Daugherty and Eileen Barrett, eds., *Virginia Woolf*, 168–70.

Newman, Herta. *Virginia Woolf and Mrs. Brown*, 31–40.

Olin-Hitt, Michael R. "Power, Discipline, and Individuality: Subversive Characterization in *Jacob's Room*," in Beth Rigel Daugherty and Eileen Barrett, eds., *Virginia Woolf*, 128–33.

Phillips, Kathy J. *Virginia Woolf against Empire*, 121–53.

Pike, David L. *Passage through Hell*, 167–70, 173–75.

Reese, Judy S. *Recasting Social Values*, 119–24.

Reid, Panthea. *Art and Affection*, 258–60.

Schroeder, Steven. *Virginia Woolf's Subject*, 143–48.

Smith, Susan Bennett. "What the Duke of Wellington Is Doing in *Jacob's Room*." *Virginia Woolf Misc* 36 (1991), 2.

Usui, Masami. "The German Raid on Scarborough in *Jacob's Room*." *Virginia Woolf Misc* 35 (1990), 7.

Zappa, Stephanie. "Woolf, Women, and War: From Statement in *Three Guineas* to Impression in *Jacob's Room*," in Beth Rigel Daugherty and Eileen Barrett, eds., *Virginia Woolf*, 274–79.

Mrs. Dalloway, 1925

Allan, Tuzyline Jita. *Womanist and Feminist Aesthetics*, 19–44.

Backus, Margot Gayle. "Exploring the Ethical Implications of Narrative in a Sophomore-level Course on Same-sex Love: *Mrs. Dalloway* and *The Last September*," in Eileen Barrett and Patricia Cramer, eds., *Re: Reading*, 102–5.

Brantlinger, Patrick. *Fictions of State*, 223–34.

Courington, Chella. "From *Clarissa* to *Mrs. Dalloway*: Woolf's (Re)Vision of Richardson," in Eileen Barrett and Patricia Cramer, eds., *Re: Reading*, 95–101.

Curd, Patricia Kenig. "Aristotelian Visions of Moral Character in Virginia Woolf's *Mrs. Dalloway*." *Engl Lang Notes* 33:1 (1995), 40–54.

Darrohn, Christine. " 'In a third class railway carriage': Class, the Great War, and *Mrs. Dalloway*," in Beth Rigel Daugherty and Eileen Barrett, eds., *Virginia Woolf*, 99–103.

Delorey, Denise. "Parsing the Female Sentence: The Paradox of Containment in Virginia Woolf's Narratives," in Kathy Mezei, ed., *Ambiguous Discourse*, 100–104.

Fulker, Teresa. "Virginia Woolf's Daily Drama of the Body." *Woolf Stud Annual* 1 (1995), 9–24.

Goodenough, Elizabeth. " 'We Haven't the Words': The Silence of Children in the Novels of Virginia Woolf," in Goodenough et al., eds., *Infant Tongues*, 194–97.

Greenslade, William. *Degeneration, Culture, and the Novel*, 230–33.

Hanson, Clare. *Virginia Woolf*, 55–72.

Hauck, Christina. " 'To Escape the Horror of Family Life': Virginia Woolf and the British Birth Control Debate," in Helen Wussow, ed., *New Essays on Virginia Woolf*, 21–26.

Hoff, Molly. "A Feast of Words in *Mrs. Dalloway*." *Woolf Stud Annual* 1 (1995), 89–103.

Hoff, Molly. "The Music Hall in *Mrs. Dalloway*." *Virginia Woolf Misc* 41 (1993), 6–7.

Hoff, Molly. "People like Ott." *Virginia Woolf Misc* 37 (1991), 2–3.

Hoff, Molly. "Who Is Sylvia?" *Virginia Woolf Misc* 40 (1993), 4–5.

Hoff, Molly. "Woolf's *Mrs. Dalloway*." *Explicator* 53 (1995), 108–11.

Hotchkiss, Lia M. "Writing the Jump Cut: *Mrs. Dalloway* in the Context of Cinema," in Beth Rigel Daugherty and Eileen Barrett, eds., *Virginia Woolf*, 134–39.

Jackson, Tony E. *The Subject of Modernism*, 113–38.

Jacobsen, Sally A. "Using Bloomsbury Art to Teach *Mrs. Dalloway*, *To the Lighthouse*, and *The Waves*: A New Historical Approach," in Eileen Barrett and Patricia Cramer, eds., *Re: Reading*, 48–50.

Kennard, Jean E. "Power and Sexual Ambiguity: The *Dreadnought* Hoax, *The Voyage Out*, *Mrs. Dalloway* and *Orlando*." *J of Mod Lit* 20 (1996), 156–61.

Lambert, Elizabeth. "Unsocial Impulses and Writhing Dinosaurs: Evolution as Fiction in Virginia Woolf's Novels." *CEA Critic* 58:1 (1995), 91–94.

Levenback, Karen L. "Clarissa Dalloway, Doris Kilman and the Great War." *Virginia Woolf Misc* 37 (1991), 3–4.

Levenback, Karen L. "Virginia Woolf and Returning Soldiers: The Great War and the Reality of Survival in *Mrs. Dalloway* and *The Years*." *Woolf Stud Annual* 2 (1996), 75–80.

Littleton, Jacob. "*Mrs. Dalloway:* Portrait of the Artist as a Middle-Aged Woman." *Twentieth Cent Lit* 41 (1995), 36–53.

Luftig, Victor. *Seeing Together,* 192–96.

McPherson, Karen S. *Incriminations,* 130–57.

Mahaffey, Vicki. "Virginia Woolf," in John Richetti et al., eds., *The Columbia History,* 800–806.

Matson, Patricia. "The Terror and Ecstasy: The Textual Politics of Virginia Woolf's *Mrs. Dalloway,*" in Kathy Mezei, ed., *Ambiguous Discourse,* 162–81.

Meyerowitz, Selma. "Portraying Mrs Dalloway." *Virginia Woolf Misc* 37 (1991), 4–5.

Mezei, Kathy. "Who Is Speaking Here? Free Indirect Discourse, Gender, and Authority in *Emma, Howards End,* and *Mrs. Dalloway,*" in Mezei, ed., *Ambiguous Discourse,* 81–86.

Morgan, Geneviève Sanchis. "Performance Art and Tableau Vivant—The Case of Clarissa Dalloway and Mrs. Ramsay," in Beth Rigel Daugherty and Eileen Barrett, eds., *Virginia Woolf,* 268–72.

Nalbantian, Suzanne. *Aesthetic Autobiography,* 158–65.

Naumann, Barbara. "Illusionen der Identität: Virginia Woolf, *Mrs. Dalloway,* und Nathalie Sarraute, *Portrait d'un inconnu,*" in Eberhard Lämmert and Barbara Naumann, eds., *Wer sind wir?,* 163–77.

Neverow-Turk, Vara. " 'Mrs. Rayley is out, Sir': Re-reading that Hole in Minta's Stocking." *Virginia Woolf Misc* 39 (1992), 9.

Newman, Herta. *Virginia Woolf and Mrs. Brown,* 43–50.

Peitrequin, Raymond. "The Beggar's Song in *Mrs Dalloway:* An Analysis with Some Views on the Poetics of Empathy." *Etudes de Lettres* 3 (1993), 121–37.

Phillips, Kathy J. *Virginia Woolf against Empire,* 1–26.

Rao, Eleonora. "Un triangolo narrativo in *Mrs Dalloway* di Virginia Woolf." *Anglistica* 27:2 (1984), 65–91.

Reed, Donna K. "Merging Voices: *Mrs. Dalloway* and *No Place on Earth.*" *Compar Lit* 47 (1995), 118–33.

Reese, Judy S. *Recasting Social Values,* 91–99, 107–10.

Rignall, John. *Realist Fiction,* 152–56.

Rosenberg, Beth Carole. *Virginia Woolf and Samuel Johnson,* 77–84.

Schröder, Leena Kore. "*Mrs Dalloway* and the Female Vagrant." *Essays in Criticism* 45 (1995), 324–43.

Schroeder, Steven. *Virginia Woolf's Subject,* 152–54.

Scott, Bonnie Kime. *Refiguring Modernism,* 8–18.

Sizemore, Christine W. "The 'Outsider-Within': Virginia Woolf and Doris Lessing as Urban Novelists in *Mrs. Dalloway* and *The Four-Gated City,*" in Ruth Saxton and Jean Tobin, eds., *Woolf and Lessing,* 59–66.

Smith, Laura A. "Who Do We Think Clarissa Dalloway is Anyway? Re-Search Into Seventy Years of Woolf Criticism," in Eileen Barrett and Patricia Cramer, eds., *Re: Reading,* 215–20.

Smith, Susan Bennett. "Reinventing Grief Work: Virginia Woolf's Feminist Representations of Mourning in *Mrs. Dalloway* and *To the Light-house." Twentieth Cent Lit* 41 (1995), 313–18.

Sprague, Claire. "Multipersonal and Dialogic Modes in *Mrs. Dalloway* and *The Golden Notebook,"* in Ruth Saxton and Jean Tobin, eds., *Woolf and Lessing*, 3–8.

Tate, Trudi. *"Mrs Dalloway* and the Armenian Question." *Textual Practice* 8 (1994), 467–81.

Tyler, Lisa. "Mother-Daughter Passion and Rapture: The Demeter Myth in the Fiction of Virginia Woolf and Doris Lessing," in Ruth Saxton and Jean Tobin, eds., *Woolf and Lessing*, 81–83.

Viola, André. " 'Buds on the Tree of Life': A Recurrent Mythological Image in Virginia Woolf's *Mrs. Dalloway." J of Mod Lit* 20 (1996), 239–47.

Webb, Caroline. "Life After Death: The Allegorical Progress of *Mrs. Dalloway." Mod Fiction Stud* 40 (1994), 279–96.

Wicke, Jennifer. *"Mrs. Dalloway* Goes to Market: Woolf, Keynes, and Modern Markets." *Novel* 28 (1994), 5–22.

Williams-Gualandi, Debra. "A Dialogical Introduction to Mrs. Clarissa Dalloway." *Etudes Anglaises* 48 (1995), 277–86.

Night and Day, 1919

Cooley, Elizabeth. " 'The Medicine She Trusted To': Communication in *The Voyage Out* and *Night and Day,"* in Janet Doubler Ward and Jo-Anna Stephens Mink, eds., *Communication and Women's Friendships*, 70–75.

Luftig, Victor. *Seeing Together*, 177–89.

Phillips, Kathy J. *Virginia Woolf against Empire,* 79–94.

Reid, Panthea. *Art and Affection,* 211–13.

Orlando, 1928

Barrett, Eileen. "Response: Decamping Sally Potter's *Orlando,"* in Eileen Barrett and Patricia Cramer, eds., *Re: Reading*, 197–99.

Benzel, Kathryn N. "Reading Readers in Virginia Woolf's *Orlando: A Biography." Style* 28 (1994), 169–80.

Berman, Jessica. "Reading Beyond the Subject: Virginia Woolf's Constructions of Community," in Helen Wussow, ed., *New Essays on Virginia Woolf*, 50–53.

Burns, Christy L. "Re-Dressing Feminist Identities: Tensions Between Essential and Constructed Selves in Virginia Woolf's *Orlando." Twentieth Cent Lit* 40 (1994), 342–59.

Caramagno, Thomas C. "Laterality and Sexuality: The Transgressive Aesthetics of *Orlando,"* in Beth Rigel Daugherty and Eileen Barrett, eds., *Virginia Woolf,* 183–88.

Cervetti, Nancy. "In the Breeches, Petticoats, and Pleasures of *Orlando." J of Mod Lit* 20 (1996), 165–75.

Cuddy-Keane, Melba, Natasha Aleksiuk, Kay Li, Morgan Love, Chris Rose, and Andrea Williams. "The Heteroglossia of History, Part One:

The Car," in Beth Rigel Daugherty and Eileen Barrett, eds., *Virginia Woolf*, 77–79.

Dresner, Lisa M. "The Body and the Letter: The Fragmentation of the Male Subject in Woolf's *Orlando*," in Eileen Barrett and Patricia Cramer, eds., *Re: Reading*, 53–57.

Garvey, Johanna X. K. " 'If We Were All Suddenly Somebody Else': *Orlando* as the New *Ulysses*." *Women's Stud* 23 (1994), 1–13.

Haines-Wright, Lisa, and Traci Lynn Kyle. "From He and She to You and Me: Grounding Fluidity, Woolf's *Orlando* to Winterson's *Written on the Body*," in Beth Rigel Daugherty and Eileen Barrett, eds., *Virginia Woolf*, 177–82.

Hankins, Leslie K. "Redirections: Challenging the Class Axe and Lesbian Erasure in Potter's *Orlando*," in Eileen Barrett and Patricia Cramer, eds., *Re: Reading*, 168–80.

Hanson, Clare. *Virginia Woolf*, 94–111.

Hecht, Roger. " 'I am Nature's Bride': *Orlando* and the Female Pastoral," in Eileen Barrett and Patricia Cramer, eds., *Re: Reading*, 22–27.

Hill, Marylu. "Mothering Her Text: Woolf and the Maternal Paradigm of Biography." *Virginia Woolf Misc* 46 (1995), 3.

Joannou, Maroula. *'Ladies, Please Don't Smash These Windows,'* 102–26.

Jones, Ellen Carol. "The Flight of a Word: Narcissism and the Masquerade of Writing in Virginia Woolf's *Orlando*." *Women's Stud* 23 (1994), 155–72.

Kelsall, Malcolm. *The Great Good Place,* 177–80.

Kennard, Jean E. "Power and Sexual Ambiguity: The *Dreadnought* Hoax, *The Voyage Out, Mrs. Dalloway* and *Orlando*." *J of Mod Lit* 20 (1996), 161–64.

Lawrence, Karen R. *Penelope Voyages*, 179–206.

Levine, Michael L. "*Orlando* on Screen: Three Hundred Years of Nothing Happening." *Virginia Woolf Misc* 42 (1994), 3–4.

Mahaffey, Vicki. "Virginia Woolf," in John Richetti et al., eds., *The Columbia History*, 789–90.

Mason, D. G. "Woolf, Carlyle, and the Writing of *Orlando*." *Engl Stud in Canada* 19 (1993), 329–37.

Michael, Magali Cornier. *Feminism and the Postmodern Impulse*, 67–70.

Moore, Madeline. "Virginia Woolf and Sally Potter: The Play of Opposites and the Modern Mind in *Orlando*," in Eileen Barrett and Patricia Cramer, eds., *Re: Reading*, 184–95.

Nalbantian, Suzanne. *Aesthetic Autobiography*, 165–68.

Olin-Hitt, Michael R. "Desire, Death, and Plot: The Subversive Play of *Orlando*." *Women's Stud* 24 (1995), 483–94.

Parkes, Adam. "Lesbianism, History, and Censorship: *The Well of Loneliness* and the Suppressed Randiness of Virginia Woolf's *Orlando*." *Twentieth Cent Lit* 40 (1994), 446–57.

Parkes, Adam. *Modernism and the Theater of Censorship,* 162–78.

Phillips, Kathy J. *Virginia Woolf against Empire*, 184–200.

Pike, David L. *Passage through Hell*, 171–73, 183–85, 188–90, 194–201.

Rado, Lisa. "Would the Real Virginia Woolf Please Stand Up? Feminist Criticism, the Androgyny Debates, and Orlando." *Women's Stud* 26 (1997), 147–66.

Schroeder, Steven. *Virginia Woolf's Subject*, 109–16, 159–62.

Scott, Bonnie Kime. *Refiguring Modernism*, 26–28.

Sproles, Karyn. "Orlando's Self-Conscious Biographer and Challenges to the Patriarchy." *Virginia Woolf Misc* 46 (1995), 2.

Squier, Susan M. "Virginia Woolf's London and the Feminist Revision of Modernism," in Mary Ann Caws, ed. *City Images*, 111–14.

Stockton, Sharon. "Virginia Woolf and The Renaissance: The Promise of Capital and the Violence of Materialism." *Clio* 24 (1995), 245–50.

Sun Yom, Sue. "Bio-graphy and the Quantum Leap: Waves, Particles, and Light as a Theory of Writing the Human Life," in Beth Rigel Daugherty and Eileen Barrett, eds., *Virginia Woolf*, 145–47.

Thompson, Nicola. "Some Theories of One's Own: *Orlando* and the Novel." *Stud in the Novel* 25 (1993), 306–15.

Webb, Caroline. "Listing to the Right: Authority and Inheritance in *Orlando* and *Ulysses*." *Twentieth Cent Lit* 40 (1994), 190–202.

Wussow, Helen. "Virginia Woolf and the Problematic Nature of the Photographic Image." *Twentieth Cent Lit* 40 (1994), 3–5.

To the Lighthouse, 1927

Anspaugh, Kelly. "Traveling to the Lighthouse with Woolf and Johnson." *Virginia Woolf Misc* 45 (1995), 4–5.

Banerjee, Jacqueline. "Grief and the Modern Writer." *English* 43 (1994), 23–26.

Barzilai, Shuli. "The Politics of Quotation in *To the Lighthouse:* Mrs. Woolf Resites Mr. Tennyson and Mr. Cowper." *Lit and Psych* 41:3 (1995), 22–39.

Bernstein, Stephen. "Modernist Spatial Nostalgia: Forster, Conrad, Woolf," in Beth Rigel Daugherty and Eileen Barrett, eds., *Virginia Woolf*, 40–44.

Brantlinger, Patrick. *Fictions of State*, 223–34.

Brivic, Sheldon. "Love as Destruction in Woolf's *To the Lighthouse*." *Mosaic* 27:3 (1994), 65–83.

Delorey, Denise. "Parsing the Female Sentence: The Paradox of Containment in Virginia Woolf's Narratives," in Kathy Mezei, ed., *Ambiguous Discourse*, 104–6.

Diment, Galya. *The Autobiographical Novel,* 3–10, 61–108, 145–47.

Doyle, Laura. " 'These Emotions of the Body': Intercorporeal Narrative in *To the Lighthouse*." *Twentieth Cent Lit* 40 (1994), 42–68.

Ender, Evelyne. "A Writer's Birthpains: Virginia Woolf and the Mother's Share." *Swiss Papers in Engl Lang and Lit* 9 (1996), 258–70.

Gliserman, Martin. *Psychoanalysis, Language, and the Body of the Text,* 112–38.

Glorie, Josephine Carubia. "Mapping the Epistemic Terrain in Virginia Woolf's *To the Lighthouse*," in Eileen Barrett and Patricia Cramer, eds., *Re: Reading*, 155–61.

Goodenough, Elizabeth. " 'We Haven't the Words': The Silence of Children in the Novels of Virginia Woolf," in Goodenough et al., eds., *Infant Tongues*, 184–86, 197–98.

Handley, William R. "The Housemaid and the Kitchen Table: Incorporating the Frame in *To the Lighthouse." Twentieth Cent Lit* 40 (1994), 15–39.

Hanson, Clare. *Virginia Woolf*, 72–94.

Hauck, Christina. " 'To Escape the Horror of Family Life': Virginia Woolf and the British Birth Control Debate," in Helen Wussow, ed., *New Essays on Virginia Woolf*, 26–32.

Holmesland, Oddvar. "Paradoxes of Artistic Unification: A Study of *To the Lighthouse,"* in Andrew Kennedy and Orm Øverland, eds., *Excursions in Fiction*, 108–22.

Hussey, Mark. "*To the Lighthouse* and Physics: The Cosmology of David Bohm and Virginia Woolf," in Helen Wussow, ed., *New Essays on Virginia Woolf*, 79–94.

Jacobsen, Sally A. "Using Bloomsbury Art to Teach *Mrs. Dalloway, To the Lighthouse*, and *The Waves:* A New Historical Approach," in Eileen Barrett and Patricia Cramer, eds., *Re: Reading*, 48–50.

Kanwar, Anju. "Briscoe's *alt[a]r*native: *Durga* or *Sati*? Woolf and Hinduism in *To the Lighthouse,"* in Beth Rigel Daugherty and Eileen Barrett, eds., *Virginia Woolf*, 104–9.

Klein, Jürgen. "Gesellschaftskritik und Sinnsuche in Virginia Woolfs Roman *To the Lighthouse." Anglistik* 6:2 (1995), 52–64.

Knoepflmacher, U. C. "Afterword: Endings as Beginnings," in Alison Booth, ed., *Famous Last Words*, 347–51.

Kochersperger, Reba. "Woolf's *To the Lighthouse." Explicator* 52 (1994), 229–30.

Levenson, Michael. *Modernism and the Fate of Individuality,* 166–216.

Levy, Eric P. "Woolf's Metaphysics of Tragic Vision in *To the Lighthouse." Philol Q* 75 (1996), 109–28.

Loeffelholz, Mary. *Experimental Lives*, 66–70.

Low, Lisa. " 'Two Figures in Dense Violet Night': Virginia Woolf, John Milton, and the Epic Vision of Marriage." *Woolf Stud Annual* 1 (1995), 72–86.

Luftig, Victor. *Seeing Together*, 203–9.

McKenna, Kathleen. "The Language of Orgasm," in Eileen Barrett and Patricia Cramer, eds., *Re: Reading*, 29–37.

MacMaster, Anne. "Anguished Love for the Angel of the House: *To the Lighthouse* and the Women's Studies Generations Paper," in Eileen Barrett and Patricia Cramer, eds., *Re: Reading*, 269–72.

Mahaffey, Vicki. "Virginia Woolf," in John Richetti et al., eds., *The Columbia History*, 805–9.

Marret, Sophie. "Deuil et vision dans *To the Lighthouse.*" *Q/W/E/R/T/Y* 5 (1995), 215–26.

Morgan, Geneviève Sanchis. "Performance Art and Tableau Vivant—The Case of Clarissa Dalloway and Mrs. Ramsay," in Beth Rigel Daugherty and Eileen Barrett, eds., *Virginia Woolf,* 268–72.

Morgan, Margaret M. "A Rhetorical Context for Virginia Woolf," in Beth Rigel Daugherty and Eileen Barrett, eds., *Virginia Woolf,* 16–20.

Nalbantian, Suzanne. *Aesthetic Autobiography,* 140–58.

Newman, Herta. *Virginia Woolf and Mrs. Brown,* 83–93.

Nussbaum, Martha C. "The Window: Knowledge of Other Minds in Virginia Woolf's *To the Lighthouse.*" *New Liter Hist* 26 (1995), 731–52.

Phillips, Kathy J. *Virginia Woolf against Empire,* 94–120.

Rapaport, Herman. *Between the Sign and the Gaze,* 214–16.

Reese, Judy S. *Recasting Social Values,* 124–26, 129–35.

Reid, Panthea. *Art and Affection,* 301–5.

Rosenberg, Beth Carole. *Virginia Woolf and Samuel Johnson,* 84–92.

Rubenstein, Roberta. "Fixing the Past: Yearning and Nostalgia in Woolf and Lessing," in Ruth Saxton and Jean Tobin, eds., *Woolf and Lessing,* 27–29.

Saxton, Ruth. "The Female Body Veiled: From Crocus to Clitoris," in Ruth Saxton and Jean Tobin, eds., *Woolf and Lessing,* 105–10.

Schroeder, Steven. *Virginia Woolf's Subject,* 154–57.

Scott, Bonnie Kime. *Refiguring Modernism,* 18–26.

Smith, Grady. "Virginia Woolf: The Narrow Bridge of Art." *Mod Age* 36 (1993), 39–46.

Smith, Susan Bennett. "Reinventing Grief Work: Virginia Woolf's Feminist Representations of Mourning in *Mrs. Dalloway* and *To the Lighthouse.*" *Twentieth Cent Lit* 41 (1995), 318–23.

Stevenson, Randall. *A Reader's Guide,* 29–33.

Stevenson, Randall, and Jane Goldman. " 'But what? Elegy?': Modernist Reading and the Death of Mrs Ramsay." *Yrbk of Engl Stud* 26 (1996), 173–86.

Swanson, Diana L. "The Lesbian Feminism of Woolf's *To the Lighthouse,*" in Eileen Barrett and Patricia Cramer, eds., *Re: Reading,* 38–43.

Tratner, Michael. "Figures in the Dark: Working Class Women in *To the Lighthouse.*" *Virginia Woolf Misc* 40 (1993), 3–4.

Tratner, Michael. *Modernism and Mass Politics,* 48–75.

Tyler, Lisa. "Mother-Daughter Passion and Rapture: The Demeter Myth in the Fiction of Virginia Woolf and Doris Lessing," in Ruth Saxton and Jean Tobin, eds., *Woolf and Lessing,* 79–81.

Wareham, John. "Woolf's *To the Lighthouse.*" *Explicator* 52 (1994), 167–69.

Wilson, Deborah. "Fishing for Woolf's Submerged Lesbian Text," in Eileen Barrett and Patricia Cramer, eds., *Re: Reading,* 121–26.

Winston, Janet. " 'Something Out of Harmony': *To the Lighthouse* and the Subject(s) of Empire." *Woolf Stud Annual* 2 (1996), 39–67.

Würzbach, Natascha. "The Mother Image as Cultural Concept and Literary Theme in the Nineteenth- and Twentieth-Century English Novel: A Feminist Reading within the Context of New Historicism and the History of Mentalities," in Rüdiger Ahrens and Laurenz Volkmann, eds., *Why Literature Matters*, 383–84.

The Voyage Out, 1915

Cooley, Elizabeth. " 'The Medicine She Trusted To': Communication in *The Voyage Out* and *Night and Day,*" in Janet Doubler Ward and Jo-Anna Stephens Mink, eds., *Communication and Women's Friendships*, 65–70.

Cummins, June. "Death and the Maiden Voyage: Mapping the Junction of Feminism and Postcolonial Theory in *The Voyage Out,*" in Beth Rigel Daugherty and Eileen Barrett, eds., *Virginia Woolf*, 204–10.

Friedman, Susan Stanford. "Spatialization, Narrative Theory, and Virginia Woolf's *The Voyage Out,*" in Kathy Mezei, ed., *Ambiguous Discourse*, 109–32.

Goodenough, Elizabeth. " 'We Haven't the Words': The Silence of Children in the Novels of Virginia Woolf," in Goodenough et al., eds., *Infant Tongues*, 188–94.

Hanle, James M. "Virginia Woolf's Revisions of *The Voyage Out*: Some New Evidence." *Twentieth Cent Lit* 42 (1996), 309–19.

Hanson, Clare. *Virginia Woolf*, 28–39.

Kahane, Claire. *Passions of the Voice*, 99–126.

Kennard, Jean E. "Power and Sexual Ambiguity: The *Dreadnought* Hoax, *The Voyage Out, Mrs. Dalloway* and *Orlando.*" *J of Mod Lit* 20 (1996), 153–56.

Lawrence, Karen R. *Penelope Voyages*, 154–79.

Levy, Heather. "*The Voyage Out* of Women's Silence," in Eileen Barrett and Patricia Cramer, eds., *Re: Reading*, 273–78.

Lewis, Andrea. "The Visual Politics of Empire and Gender in Virginia Woolf's *The Voyage Out*." *Woolf Stud Annual* 1 (1995), 106–19.

MacMaster, Anne. "Beginning with the Same Ending: Virginia Woolf and Edith Wharton," in Beth Rigel Daugherty and Eileen Barrett, eds., *Virginia Woolf*, 216–22.

Mahaffey, Vicki. "Virginia Woolf," in John Richetti et al., eds., *The Columbia History*, 789–90.

Phillips, Kathy J. *Virginia Woolf against Empire,* 52–79.

Reese, Judy S. *Recasting Social Values,* 83–90.

Reid, Panthea. *Art and Affection,* 93–95.

Rosenberg, Beth Carole. " '. . . in the wake of the matrons': Virginia Woolf's Rewriting of Fanny Burney," in Beth Rigel Daugherty and Eileen Barrett, eds., *Virginia Woolf*, 118–22.

Saxton, Ruth. "The Female Body Veiled: From Crocus to Clitoris," in Ruth Saxton and Jean Tobin, eds., *Woolf and Lessing*, 97–105.

Stockton, Sharon. "Virginia Woolf and The Renaissance: The Promise of Capital and the Violence of Materialism." *Clio* 24 (1995), 236–45.

Swanson, Diana L. " 'My boldness terrifies me': Sexual Abuse and Female Subjectivity in *The Voyage Out.*" *Twentieth Cent Lit* 41 (1995), 284–306.

Thompson, Theresa M. "Confronting Modernist Racism in the Post-Colonial Classroom: Teaching Virginia Woolf's *The Voyage Out* and Leonard Woolf's *The Village in the Jungle*," in Eileen Barrett and Patricia Cramer, eds., *Re: Reading*, 241–50.

Tratner, Michael. *Modernism and Mass Politics*, 84–97.

Tucker, Louise. "Voyages and Vagabonds: Sex and Text in Virginia Woolf and Colette." *New Comparison* 15 (1993), 110–19.

Tyler, Lisa. " 'I Am Not What You Supposed': Walt Whitman's Influence on Virginia Woolf," in Beth Rigel Daugherty and Eileen Barrett, eds., *Virginia Woolf*, 110–16.

Tyler, Lisa. "Mother-Daughter Passion and Rapture: The Demeter Myth in the Fiction of Virginia Woolf and Doris Lessing," in Ruth Saxton and Jean Tobin, eds., *Woolf and Lessing*, 77–79, 81–83.

Tyler, Lisa. " 'Nameless Atrocities' and the Name of the Father: Literary Allusion and Incest in Virginia Woolf's *The Voyage Out.*" *Woolf Stud Annual* 1 (1995), 26–42.

Vlasopolos, Anca. "Staking Claims for No Territory: The Sea as Woman's Space," in Margaret R. Higonnet and Joan Templeton, eds., *Reconfigured Spheres*, 76–77, 80–84.

The Waves, 1931

Berman, Jessica. "Reading Beyond the Subject: Virginia Woolf's Constructions of Community," in Helen Wussow, ed., *New Essays on Virginia Woolf*, 53–55.

Booker, M. Keith. *Literature and Domination*, 42–69.

Burns, Betty-Ann. "Against Diagnosis: Multiple Personality Response in the Life and Work of Virginia Woolf," in Helen Wussow, ed., *New Essays on Virginia Woolf*, 123–25.

Doyle, Laura. "Sublime Barbarians in the Narrative of Empire; or, Longinus at Sea in *The Waves.*" *Mod Fiction Stud* 42 (1996), 323–45.

Erzgräber, Willi. "Zwischen Viktorianismus und Moderne: Zu Angus Wilsons Roman *No Laughing Matter.*" *Germanisch-Romanische Monatsschrift* 45 (1995), 93–96.

Goldman, Jane. " 'Purple Buttons on her Bodice': Feminist History and Iconography in *The Waves.*" *Woolf Stud Annual* 2 (1996), 3–23.

Goodenough, Elizabeth. " 'We Haven't the Words': The Silence of Children in the Novels of Virginia Woolf," in Goodenough et al., eds., *Infant Tongues*, 198–99.

Hackett, Robin. "Shakespeare's Sonnet 7 in Woolf's *The Waves.*" *Virginia Woolf Misc* 36 (1991), 6.

Hanson, Clare. *Virginia Woolf*, 125–48.

Hild, Allison. "Community/Communication in Woolf's *The Waves:* The Language of Motion." *J of Narrative Technique* 24 (1994), 69–78.

Jackson, Tony E. *The Subject of Modernism*, 139–62.

Jacobsen, Sally A. "Using Bloomsbury Art to Teach *Mrs. Dalloway*, *To the Lighthouse*, and *The Waves*: A New Historical Approach," in Eileen Barrett and Patricia Cramer, eds., *Re: Reading*, 48–50.

Kane, Julie. "Varieties of Mystical Experience in the Writings of Virginia Woolf." *Twentieth Cent Lit* 41 (1995), 336–47.

Katz, Tamar. "Modernism, Subjectivity, and Narrative Form: Abstraction in *The Waves*." *Narrative* 3 (1995), 232–48.

McGee, Patrick. *Telling the Other*, 110–14, 116–20.

Mahaffey, Vicki. "Virginia Woolf," in John Richetti et al., eds., *The Columbia History*, 810–14.

Miltner, Robert. "Re:Writing and Re:Teaching Virginia Woolf's *The Waves*," in Eileen Barrett and Patricia Cramer, eds., *Re: Reading*, 45–48.

Moore, Madeline. "Virginia Woolf and the Good Brother," in Beth Rigel Daugherty and Eileen Barrett, eds., *Virginia Woolf*, 170–74.

Newman, Herta. *Virginia Woolf and Mrs. Brown*, 55–63.

Paccaud-Huguet, Josiane. "The Crowded Dance of Words: Language and Jouissance in *The Waves*." *Q/W/E/R/T/Y* 5 (1995), 227–40.

Phillips, Gyllian. "Re(de)composing the Novel: *The Waves*, Wagnerian Opera and Percival/Parsifal." *Genre* 28 (1995), 119–43.

Phillips, Kathy J. *Virginia Woolf against Empire*, 121–26, 153–84.

Pike, David L. *Passage through Hell*, 186–92.

Reese, Judy S. *Recasting Social Values*, 101–5, 126–28.

Reid, Panthea. *Art and Affection*, 333–45.

Roe, Sue. "The Mind in Visual Form: Sketching *The Waves*." *Q/W/E/R/T/Y* 5 (1995), 241–51.

Rosenberg, Beth Carole. *Virginia Woolf and Samuel Johnson*, 93–102.

Roughley, Neil. " 'A Sort of Death? A New Assembly of Elements?': Zum 'Tod des Subjekts' in Virginia Woolfs *The Waves*." *Anglia* 112 (1994), 364–89.

Schapiro, Barbara Ann. "Attunement and Interpretation: Reading Virginia Woolf," in Daniel Rancour-Laferriere, ed., *Self-Analysis in Literary Study*, 182–88.

Schiff, Karen. "Finding the Reader in *The Waves*: Bernard's Dinner Party," in Eileen Barrett and Patricia Cramer, eds., *Re: Reading*, 137–40.

Schroeder, Steven. *Virginia Woolf's Subject*, 175–79.

Scott, Bonnie Kime. *Refiguring Modernism*, 26–51.

Smith, Marilyn Schwinn. "Virginia Woolf and Marina Tsvetaeva: Female Bards in Modernity," in Eileen Barrett and Patricia Cramer, eds., *Re: Reading*, 265–68.

Sun Yom, Sue. "Bio-graphy and the Quantum Leap: Waves, Particles, and Light as a Theory of Writing the Human Life," in Beth Rigel Daugherty and Eileen Barrett, eds., *Virginia Woolf*, 147–50.

Tobin, Jean. "On Creativity: Woolf's *The Waves* and Lessing's *The Golden Notebook*," in Ruth Saxton and Jean Tobin, eds., *Woolf and Lessing*, 151–60.

Topia, André. "*The Waves:* l'œil et le monde." *Etudes Anglaises* 48 (1995), 430–41.

Tratner, Michael. *Modernism and Mass Politics*, 217–40.

Vandivere, Julie. "Waves and Fragments: Linguistic Construction as Subject Formation in Virginia Woolf." *Twentieth Cent Lit* 42 (1996), 221–26.

Vandivere, Julie. "Woolf's *The Waves.*" *Explicator* 53 (1994), 47–50.

Vanita, Ruth. " 'Throwing Caution to the Winds': Homoerotic Patterns in *The Waves*," in Eileen Barrett and Patricia Cramer, eds., *Re: Reading*, 299–304.

The Years, 1937

Backus, Margot Gayle. " 'Looking for that Dead Girl': Incest, Pornography and the Capitalist Family Romance in *Nightwood, The Years* and *Tar Baby.*" *Am Imago* 51 (1994), 425–32.

Erzgräber, Willi. "Zwischen Viktorianismus und Moderne: Zu Angus Wilsons Roman *No Laughing Matter.*" *Germanisch-Romanische Monatsschrift* 45 (1995), 91–93.

Friedman, Ellen G. " 'Utterly Other Discourse': The Anticanon of Experimental Women Writers from Dorothy Richardson to Christine Brooke-Rose," in Ellen G. Friedman and Richard Martin, eds., *Utterly Other Discourse*, 220–21.

Hanson, Clare. *Virginia Woolf*, 148–67.

Lassner, Phyllis. " 'The Milk of Our Mother's Kindness Has Ceased to Flow': Virginia Woolf, Stevie Smith, and the Representation of the Jew," in Bryan Cheyette, ed., *Between 'Race' and Culture*, 134–36.

Levenback, Karen L. "Placing the First 'Enormous Chunk' deleted from *The Years.*" *Virginia Woolf Misc* 42 (1994), 8–9.

Levenback, Karen L. "Virginia Woolf and Returning Soldiers: The Great War and the Reality of Survival in *Mrs. Dalloway* and *The Years.*" *Woolf Stud Annual* 2 (1996), 80–85.

Mahaffey, Vicki. "Virginia Woolf," in John Richetti et al., eds., *The Columbia History*, 789–96.

Phillips, Kathy J. *Virginia Woolf against Empire*, 26–51.

Pike, David L. *Passage through Hell*, 192–96.

Plain, Gill. *Women's Fiction of the Second World War*, 85–115.

Schroeder, Steven. *Virginia Woolf's Subject*, 189–97, 199–209.

Swanson, Diana L. "An Antigone Complex? Psychology and Politics in *The Years* and *Three Guineas*," in Beth Rigel Daugherty and Eileen Barrett, eds., *Virginia Woolf*, 35–39.

LADY MARY WROTH

Urania, 1621

Carrell, Jennifer Lee. "A Pack of Lies in a Looking Glass: Lady Mary Wroth's *Urania* and the Magic Mirror of Romance." *Stud in Engl Lit, 1500–1900* 34 (1994), 79–102.

Fendler, Susanne. "Questioning the Knight's Quest: The Narrator as Judge in Two Imitations of Sidney's *Arcadia*," in Wolfgang Görtschacher and Holger Klein, eds., *Narrative Strategies*, 290–96.

Hackett, Helen. "The Torture of Limena: Sex and Violence in Lady Mary Wroth's *Urania*," in Kate Chedgzoy et al., eds., *Voicing Women*, 93–108.

Hackett, Helen. " 'Yet Tell Me Some Such Fiction': Lady Mary Wroth's *Urania* and the 'Femininity' of Romance," in Clare Brant and Diane Purkiss, eds., *Women, Texts and Histories*, 39–64.

Hall, Kim F. *Things of Darkness*, 187–210.

Hanson, Ellis. "Sodomy and Kingcraft in *Urania* and *Antony and Cleopatra*," in Claude J. Summers, ed., *Homosexuality*, 138–44.

MacCarthy, B. G. *The Female Pen*, 42–50.

Miller, Naomi J. *Changing the Subject*, 54–63, 133–42, 170–81, 216–33.

Roberts, Josephine A. "Lady Mary Wroth's *Urania*: A Response to Jacobean Censorship," in W. Speed Hill, ed., *New Ways of Looking at Old Texts*, 125–29.

Todd, Janet. *The Sign of Angellica*, 46–48.

Walker, Kim. *Women Writers of the English Renaissance*, 175–90.

Waller, Gary. *The Sidney Family Romance*, 247–81.

JOHN WYNDHAM

The Day of the Triffids, 1951

Manlove, C. N. "Everything Slipping Away: John Wyndham's *The Day of the Triffids.*" *J of the Fantastic in the Arts* 4:1 (1991), 29–53.

V. M. YEATES

Winged Victory, 1934

Cecil, Hugh. *The Flower of Battle*, 64–73.

CHARLOTTE YONGE

The Clever Woman of the Family, 1865

Demoor, Marysa. "Women Authors and their Selves: Autobiography in the Work of Charlotte Yonge, Rhoda Broughton, Mary Cholmondeley and Lucy Clifford." *Cahiers Victoriens et Edouardiens* 39 (1994), 54–55.

Sanders, Valerie. *Eve's Renegades*, 61–67.

Sturrock, June. *"Heaven and Home,"* 48–73.

Sturrock, June. "Something to Do: Charlotte Yonge, Tractarianism and the Question of Women's Work." *Victorian R* 18:2 (1992), 28–45.

Wheatley, Kim. "Death and Domestication in Charlotte M. Yonge's *The*

Clever Woman of the Family." Stud in Engl Lit, 1500–1900 36 (1996), 895–913.

The Daisy Chain, 1856

Brown, Penny. *The Captured World,* 100–102.
Sanders, Valerie. *Eve's Renegades,* 61–64, 100–102, 169–70.
Sturrock, June. *"Heaven and Home,"* 29–47.

The Heir of Redclyffe, 1853

Cadogan, Mary. *And Then Their Hearts Stood Still,* 38–40.
Horsman, Alan. *The Victorian Novel,* 247–48.

The Pillars of the House, 1873

Sturrock, June. "Something to Do: Charlotte Yonge, Tractarianism and the Question of Women's Work." *Victorian R* 18:2 (1992), 35–45.

The Three Brides, 1876

Sturrock, June. *"Heaven and Home,"* 74–97.

ISRAEL ZANGWILL

The Big Bow Mystery, 1891

DeNaples, Frederick L. "Unearthing Holmes: 1890s Interpretations of the Great Detective," in Nikki Lee Manos and Meri-Jane Rochelson, eds., *Transforming Genres,* 217–22.
Rochelson, Meri-Jane. *"The Big Bow Mystery:* Jewish Identity and the English Detective Novel." *Victorian R* 17:2 (1991), 11–19.

ANONYMOUS NOVELS

The Adventures of Oxymel Classic, Esq., 1768

> Antor, Heinz. *Der englische Universitätsroman,* 39–42, 48–50, 53–55, 64–68, 80–82.

College Debts, 1870

> Antor, Heinz. *Der englische Universitätsroman,* 332–35.

The Enigma: A Leaf from the Archives of the Wolcherley House, 1856

> Tush, Susan Rowland. *George Eliot and . . . Popular Women's Fiction,* 63–106.

Laura Gay, 1856

> Tush, Susan Rowland. *George Eliot and . . . Popular Women's Fiction,* 147–66.

Rank and Beauty; or, The Young Baroness, 1856

> Tush, Susan Rowland. *George Eliot and . . . Popular Women's Fiction,* 111–26.

Romance of the Pyrenees, 1803

> Besson, Françoise. "Une mathématique de l'eau étrange dans *Romance of the Pyrenees." Caliban* 33 (1996), 63–71.

The Travels and Adventures of Mademoiselle de Richelieu, 1744

> Woodward, Carolyn. " 'My Heart So Wrapt': Lesbian Disruptions in Eighteenth-Century British Fiction." *Signs* 18 (1993), 838–55.

LIST OF BOOKS INDEXED

Abbott, H. Porter. *Beckett Writing Beckett: The Author in the Autograph.* Ithaca (NY) and London: Cornell University Press, 1996.

Acheson, James. *Samuel Beckett's Artistic Theory and Practice: Criticism, Drama and Early Fiction.* London: Macmillan; New York: St. Martin's, 1997.

Adams, Alice E. *Reproducing the Womb: Images of Childbirth in Science, Feminist Theory, and Literature.* Ithaca (NY) and London: Cornell University Press, 1994.

Adams, James Eli. *Dandies and Desert Saints: Styles of Victorian Masculinity.* Ithaca (NY) and London: Cornell University Press, 1995.

Ahrens, Rüdiger, and Laurenz Volkmann, eds. *Why Literature Matters: Theories and Functions of Literature.* Heidelberg: Universitätsverlag C. Winter, 1996.

Aldiss, Brian W. *The Detached Retina: Aspects of SF and Fantasy.* Syracuse, NY: Syracuse University Press, 1995.

Allan, Tuzyline Jita. *Womanist and Feminist Aesthetics: A Comparative View.* Athens: Ohio University Press, 1995.

Allen, Dennis W. *Sexuality in Victorian Fiction.* Norman and London: University of Oklahoma Press, 1993.

Allen, Orphia Jane. *Barbara Pym: Writing a Life.* Metuchen (NJ) and London: Scarecrow Press, 1994.

Alliston, April. *Virtue's Faults: Correspondences in Eighteenth-Century British and French Women's Fiction.* Stanford, CA: Stanford University Press, 1996.

Almond, Barbara, and Richard Almond. *The Therapeutic Narrative: Fictional Relationships and the Process of Psychological Change.* Westport (CT) and London: Praeger, 1996.

Ambrosetti, Ronald J. *Eric Ambler.* New York: Twayne, 1994.

Anderson, David R., and Gwin J. Kolb, eds. *Approaches to Teaching the Works of Samuel Johnson.* New York: Modern Language Association of America, 1993.

Andrews, Malcolm. *Dickens and the Grown-up Child.* London: Macmillan, 1994.

Andriano, Joseph. *Our Ladies of Darkness: Feminine Daemonology in Male Gothic Fiction*. University Park: Pennsylvania State University Press, 1993.

Antor, Heinz. *Der englische Universitätsroman: Bildungskonzepte und Erziehungsziele*. Heidelberg: Universitätsverlag C. Winter, 1996.

Arlett, Robert. *Epic Voices: Inner and Global Impulse in the Contemporary American and British Novel*. Selinsgrove, PA: Susquehanna University Press; London: Associated University Presses, 1996.

Armitt, Lucie. *Theorising the Fantastic*. London: Arnold, 1996.

Atkinson, Michael. *The Secret Marriage of Sherlock Holmes and Other Eccentric Readings*. Ann Arbor: University of Michigan Press, 1996.

Auerbach, Nina. *Our Vampires, Ourselves*. Chicago and London: University of Chicago Press, 1995.

Azim, Firdous. *The Colonial Rise of the Novel*. London and New York: Routledge, 1993.

Bacchilega, Cristina, and Cornelia N. Moore, eds. *Constructions and Confrontations: Changing Representations of Women and Feminisms, East and West*. Honolulu: College of Languages, Linguistics and Literature (University of Hawai'i), 1996.

Bailin, Miriam. *The Sickroom in Victorian Fiction: The Art of Being Ill*. Cambridge: Cambridge University Press, 1994.

Bakewell, Michael. *Lewis Carroll: A Biography*. London: Heinemann, 1996.

Baldridge, Cates. *The Dialogics of Dissent in the English Novel*. Hanover (NH) and London: Middlebury College Press, 1994.

Ballaster, Ros. *Seductive Forms: Women's Amatory Fiction from 1684 to 1740*. Oxford: Clarendon, 1992.

Barbour, Reid. *Deciphering Elizabethan Fiction*. Newark: University of Delaware Press; London and Toronto: Associated University Presses, 1993.

Bargalló, Juan, ed. *Identidad y Alteridad: Aproximación al tema del doble*. Sevilla: Ediciones Alfar, 1994.

Barker, Francis, Peter Hulme, and Margaret Iversen, eds. *Colonial Discourse/ Postcolonial Theory*. Manchester and New York: Manchester University Press, 1994.

Barreca, Regina. *Untamed and Unabashed: Essays on Women and Humor in British Literature*. Detroit, MI: Wayne State University Press, 1994.

Barreca, Regina, ed. *Fay Weldon's Wicked Fictions*. Hanover (NH) and London: University Press of New England, 1994.

Barrett, Eileen, and Patricia Cramer, eds. *Re: Reading, Re: Writing, Re: Teaching Virginia Woolf—Selected Papers from the Fourth Annual Conference on Virginia Woolf*. (Bard College, Annandale-on-Hudson, New York, June 9–12, 1994.) New York: Pace University Press, 1995.

Barta, Peter I. *Bely, Joyce, and Döblin: Peripatetics in the City Novel*. Gainesville: University Press of Florida, 1996.

Batchelor, John. *The Life of Joseph Conrad: A Critical Biography*. Oxford (UK) and Cambridge (MA): Blackwell, 1994.

Bauer, Matthias. *Im Fuchsbau der Geschichten: Anatomie des Schelmenromans*. Stuttgart and Weimar: J. B. Metzler, 1993.

Birch, Sarah. *Christine Brooke-Rose and Contemporary Fiction.* Oxford: Clarendon, 1994.

Bivona, Daniel. *Desire and Contradiction: Imperial Visions and Domestic Debates in Victorian Literature.* Manchester and New York: Manchester University Press, 1990.

Björkén, Cecilia. *Into the Isle of Self: Nietzschean Patterns and Contrasts in D. H. Lawrence's "The Trespasser."* Lund: Lund University Press, 1996.

Black, Martha Fodaski. *Shaw and Joyce: 'The Last Word in Stolentelling.'* Gainesville: University Press of Florida, 1995.

Blamires, Harry. *The New Bloomsday Book: A Guide through "Ulysses."* 3rd ed. London and New York: Routledge, 1996.

Blewett, David. *The Illustration of "Robinson Crusoe," 1719–1920.* Gerrards Cross (UK): Colin Smythe, 1995.

Blum, Virginia L. *Hide and Seek: The Child between Psychoanalysis and Fiction.* Urbana and Chicago: University of Illinois Press, 1995.

Bodenheimer, Rosemarie. *The Real Life of Mary Ann Evans: George Eliot, Her Letters and Fiction.* Ithaca (NY) and London: Cornell University Press, 1994.

Boesky, Amy. *Founding Fictions: Utopias in Early Modern England.* Athens (GA) and London: University of Georgia Press, 1996.

Bolt, Sydney. *A Preface to James Joyce.* 2nd ed. London and New York: Longman, 1992.

Bonaparte, Felicia. *The Gypsy-Bachelor of Manchester: The Life of Mrs. Gaskell's Demon.* Charlottesville and London: University Press of Virginia, 1992.

Booker, M. Keith. *The Dystopian Impulse in Modern Literature: Fiction as Social Criticism.* Westport (CT) and London: Greenwood Press, 1994.

Booker, M. Keith. *Flann O'Brien, Bakhtin, and Menippean Satire.* Syracuse, NY: Syracuse University Press, 1995.

Booker, M. Keith. *Joyce, Bakhtin, and the Literary Tradition: Toward a Comparative Cultural Poetics.* Ann Arbor: University of Michigan Press, 1995.

Booker, M. Keith. *Literature and Domination: Sex, Knowledge, and Power in Modern Fiction.* Gainesville: University Press of Florida, 1993.

Booth, Alison, ed. *Famous Last Words: Changes in Gender and Narrative Closure.* Charlottesville and London: University Press of Virginia, 1993.

Born, Daniel. *The Birth of Liberal Guilt in the English Novel: Charles Dickens to H. G. Wells.* Chapel Hill and London: University of North Carolina Press, 1995.

Bornstein, George, ed. *Representing Modernist Texts: Editing as Interpretation.* Ann Arbor: University of Michigan Press, 1991.

Botting, Fred. *Gothic.* London and New York: Routledge, 1996.

Bowen, Zack. *Bloom's Old Sweet Song: Essays on Joyce and Music.* Gainesville: University Press of Florida, 1995.

Bowers, Toni. *The Politics of Motherhood: British Writing and Culture, 1680–1760.* Cambridge: Cambridge University Press, 1996.

Brake, Laurel. *Walter Pater.* Plymouth (UK): Northcote House, 1994.

Caduff, Corina, and Sigrid Weigel, eds. *Das Geschlecht der Künste*. Cologne: Böhlau Verlag, 1996.

Calderaro, Michela A. *A Silent New World: Ford Madox Ford's "Parade's End."* Bologna: CLUEB, 1993.

Campbell, Jill. *Natural Masques: Gender and Identity in Fielding's Plays and Novels*. Stanford, CA: Stanford University Press, 1995.

Campbell, Joseph. *Mythic Worlds, Modern Words: On the Art of James Joyce*. Ed. Edmund L. Epstein. New York: HarperCollins, 1993.

Carabine, Keith, Owen Knowles, and Wieslaw Krajka, eds. *Conrad's Literary Career*. Lublin: Maria Curie-Sklodowska University; Boulder, CO: East European Monographs (New York: Columbia University Press), 1992.

Carabine, Keith, Owen Knowles, and Wieslaw Krajka, eds. *Contexts for Conrad*. Lublin: Maria Curie-Sklodowska University; Boulder, CO: East European Monographs (New York: Columbia University Press), 1993.

Carr, Helen. *Jean Rhys*. Plymouth (UK): Northcote House, 1996.

Carré, Jacques, ed. *The Crisis of Courtesy: Studies in the Conduct-Book in Britain, 1600–1900*. Leiden: E. J. Brill, 1994.

Carroll, David. *George Eliot and the Conflict of Interpretations: A Reading of the Novels*. Cambridge: Cambridge Unversity Press, 1992.

Carruthers, Leo, ed. *Heroes and Heroines in Medieval English Literature*. Cambridge: D. S. Brewer, 1994.

Cavaliero, Glen. *The Supernatural and English Fiction*. Oxford and New York: Oxford University Press, 1995.

Caws, Mary Ann, ed. *City Images: Perspectives from Literature, Philosophy, and Film*. Langhorne, PA: Gordon and Breach, 1991.

Cecil, Hugh. *The Flower of Battle: British Fiction Writers of the First World War*. London: Secker & Warburg, 1995.

Cederstrom, Lorelei. *Fine-Tuning the Feminine Psyche: Jungian Patterns in the Novels of Doris Lessing*. New York: Peter Lang, 1990.

Chalmers, Alan D. *Jonathan Swift and the Burden of the Future*. Newark: University of Delaware Press; London: Associated University Presses, 1995.

Chambers, Douglas. *The Reinvention of the World: English Writing, 1650–1750*. London: Edward Arnold, 1996.

Chedgzoy, Kate, Melanie Hansen, and Suzanne Trill, eds. *Voicing Women: Gender and Sexuality in Early Modern Writing*. Keele (UK): Keele University Press, 1996.

Cheng, Vincent J. *Joyce, Race, and Empire*. Cambridge: Cambridge University Press, 1995.

Cheyette, Bryan, ed. *Between 'Race' and Culture: Representations of 'the Jew' in English and American Literature*. Stanford, CA: Stanford University Press, 1996.

Childers, Joseph W. *Novel Possibilities: Fiction and the Formation of Early Victorian Culture*. Philadelphia: University of Pennsylvania Press, 1995.

Ching-Liang Low, Gail. *White Skins/Black Masks: Representation and Colonialism*. London and New York: Routledge, 1996.

Cronin, Anthony. *Samuel Beckett: The Last Modernist*. London: HarperCollins, 1996.

Crossley, Robert. *Olaf Stapledon: Speaking for the Future*. Syracuse, NY: Syracuse University Press, 1994.

Culleton, Claire A. *Names and Naming in Joyce*. Madison: University of Wisconsin Press, 1994.

Danson, Lawrence. *Wilde's Intentions: The Artist in his Criticism*. Oxford: Clarendon, 1997.

D'Arcy, Julian Meldon. *Scottish Skalds and Sagamen: Old Norse Influence on Modern Scottish Literature*. East Lothian (Scotland): Tuckwell Press, 1996.

Daugherty, Beth Rigel, and Eileen Barrett, eds. *Virginia Woolf: Texts and Contexts—Selected Papers from the Fifth Annual Conference on Virginia Woolf*. (Otterbein College, Westerville, Ohio, June 15–18, 1995.) New York: Pace University Press, 1996.

David, Deirdre. *Rule Britannia: Women, Empire, and Victorian Writing*. Ithaca (NY) and London: Cornell University Press, 1995.

Davies, Hunter. *The Teller of Tales: In Search of Robert Louis Stevenson*. London: Sinclair-Stevenson, 1994.

Davies, Paul. *The Ideal Real: Beckett's Fiction and Imagination*. Rutherford, NJ: Fairleigh Dickinson University Press; London and Toronto: Associated University Presses, 1994.

Davison, Neil R. *James Joyce, "Ulysses," and the Construction of Jewish Identity: Culture, Biography, and "The Jew" in Modernist Europe*. Cambridge: Cambridge University Press, 1996.

Davison, Peter. *George Orwell: A Literary Life*. New York: St. Martin's, 1996.

Dean, Christopher, ed. *Studies in Sayers: Essays Presented to Dr Barbara Reynolds on Her 80th Birthday*. Hurstpierpoint (UK): Dorothy L. Sayers Society, 1994.

Deane, Seamus. *Strange Country: Modernity and Nationhood in Irish Writing since 1790*. Oxford: Clarendon, 1997.

Deery, June. *Aldous Huxley and the Mysticism of Science*. London: Macmillan; New York: St. Martin's, 1996.

DeMaria, Robert, Jr. *The Life of Samuel Johnson: A Critical Biography*. Oxford (UK) and Cambridge (MA): Blackwell, 1993.

DeMarr, Mary Jean. *In the Beginning: First Novels in Mystery Series*. Bowling Green, OH: Bowling Green State University Popular Press, 1995.

Demers, Patricia. *The World of Hannah More*. Lexington: University Press of Kentucky, 1996.

Dettmar, Kevin J. H. *The Illicit Joyce of Postmodernism: Reading against the Grain*. Madison and London: University of Wisconsin Press, 1996.

D'haen, Theo, and Hans Bertens, eds. *British Postmodern Fiction*. Amsterdam and Atlanta: Rodopi, 1993.

Dhawan, R. K., and L. S. R. Krishna Sastry, eds. *Commonwealth Writing: A Study in Expatriate Experience*. Delhi: Prestige, 1994.

DiBattista, Maria, and Lucy McDiarmid, eds. *High and Low Moderns: Liter-*

Ellis, Linda Abess. *Frances Trollope's America: Four Novels*. New York: Peter Lang, 1993.

English, James F. *Comic Transactions: Literature, Humor, and the Politics of Community in Twentieth-Century Britain*. Ithaca (NY) and London: Cornell University Press, 1994.

Eriksen, Roy, ed. *Contexts of Pre-Novel Narrative: The European Tradition*. Berlin: Mouton de Gruyter, 1994.

Eriksson, Bo H. T. *The "Structuring Forces" of Detection: The Cases of C. P. Snow and John Fowles*. Uppsala: Reklam & Katalogtryck ab, 1995.

Ermarth, Elizabeth Deeds. *The English Novel in History, 1840–1895*. London and New York: Routledge, 1997.

Fahim, Shadia S. *Doris Lessing: Sufi Equilibrium and the Form of the Novel*. London: Macmillan; New York: St. Martin's, 1994.

Fairhall, James. *James Joyce and the Question of History*. Cambridge: Cambridge University Press, 1993.

Fasick, Laura. *Vessels of Meaning: Women's Bodies, Gender Norms, and Class Bias from Richardson to Lawrence*. DeKalb: Northern Illinois University Press, 1997.

Favret, Mary A., and Nicola J. Watson, eds. *At the Limits of Romanticism: Essays in Cultural, Feminist, and Materialist Criticism*. Bloomington and Indianapolis: Indiana University Press, 1994.

Feinstein, Elaine. *Lawrence and the Women: The Intimate Life of D. H. Lawrence*. New York: HarperCollins, 1993.

Felber, Lynette. *Gender and Genre in Novels Without End: The British 'Roman-Fleuve.'* Gainesville: University Press of Florida, 1995.

Ferguson, Moira. *Colonialism and Gender Relations from Mary Wollstonecraft to Jamaica Kincaid: East Caribbean Connections*. New York: Columbia University Press, 1993.

Ferres, Kay. *Christopher Isherwood: A World in Evening*. San Bernardino, CA: Borgo Press, 1994.

Ferris, David. *Theory and the Evasion of History*. Baltimore and London: Johns Hopkins University Press, 1993.

Ferris, Ina. *The Achievement of Literary Authority: Gender, History, and the Waverley Novels*. Ithaca (NY) and London: Cornell University Press, 1991.

Ferris, Kathleen. *James Joyce and the Burden of Disease*. Lexington: University Press of Kentucky, 1995.

Fielding, Penny. *Writing and Orality: Nationality, Culture, and Nineteenth-Century Scottish Fiction*. Oxford: Clarendon, 1996.

Filmer-Davies, Kath. *Fantasy Fiction and Welsh Myth: Tales of Belonging*. London: Macmillan; New York: St. Martin's, 1996.

Fischer, Andreas, ed. *Repetition*. Tübingen: Gunter Narr Verlag, 1994.

Fischlin, Daniel, ed. *Negation, Critical Theory, and Postmodern Textuality*. Dordrecht (Netherlands): Kluwer Academic Publishers, 1994.

Fisher, Joe. *The Hidden Hardy*. New York: St. Martin's, 1992.

Fjågesund, Peter. *The Apocalyptic World of D. H. Lawrence*. Oslo: Norwegian University Press, 1991.

Tongues: The Voice of the Child in Literature. Detroit, MI: Wayne State University Press, 1994.

Goodwin, Sarah Webster, and Elisabeth Bronfen, eds. *Death and Representation*. Baltimore and London: Johns Hopkins University Press, 1993.

Gordon, David J. *Bernard Shaw and the Comic Sublime*. New York: St. Martin's, 1990.

Gordon, David J. *Iris Murdoch's Fables of Unselfing*. Columbia and London: University of Missouri Press, 1995.

Gordon, Haim. *Fighting Evil: Unsung Heroes in the Novels of Graham Greene*. Westport (CT) and London: Greenwood Press, 1997.

Gordon, Jan B. *Gossip and Subversion in Nineteenth-Century British Fiction: Echo's Economies*. London: Macmillan; New York: St. Martin's, 1996.

Gordon, Lyndall. *Charlotte Brontë: A Passionate Life*. London: Chatto & Windus, 1994.

Gorman, Anita G. *The Body in Illness and Health: Themes and Images in Jane Austen*. New York: Peter Lang, 1993.

Gorra, Michael. *After Empire: Scott, Naipaul, Rushdie*. Chicago and London: University of Chicago Press, 1997.

Görtschacher, Wolfgang, and Holger Klein, eds. *Narrative Strategies in Early English Fiction*. Lewiston (NY) and Salzburg: Edwin Mellen Press, 1995.

Gottfried, Roy. *Joyce's Iritis and the Irritable Text: The Dis-lexic "Ulysses."* Gainesville: University Press of Florida, 1995.

Granlund, Helena. *The Paradox of Self-Love: Christian Elements in George Eliot's Treatment of Egoism*. Stockholm: Almqvist & Wiksell International, 1994.

Granofsky, Ronald. *The Trauma Novel: Contemporary Symbolic Depictions of Collective Disaster*. New York: Peter Lang, 1995.

Gray, Tony. *A Peculiar Man: A Life of George Moore*. London: Sinclair-Stevenson, 1996.

Green, Roger Lancelyn, and Walter Hooper. *C. S. Lewis: A Biography*. Rev. ed. San Diego, CA: Harcourt Brace & Company, 1994.

Green, William H. *"The Hobbit": A Journey into Maturity*. New York: Twayne, 1995.

Greene, Gayle. *Doris Lessing: The Poetics of Change*. Ann Arbor: University of Michigan Press, 1994.

Greenslade, William. *Degeneration, Culture, and the Novel, 1880–1940*. Cambridge: Cambridge University Press, 1994.

Greet, Annie, Syd Harrex, and Susan Hosking, eds. *Raj Nostalgia: Some Literary and Critical Implications*. Adelaide: Flinders Press, 1992.

Gregg, Veronica Marie. *Jean Rhys's Historical Imagination: Reading and Writing the Creole*. Chapel Hill and London: University of North Carolina Press, 1995.

Griffin, Gabriele. *Heavenly Love? Lesbian Images in Twentieth-Century Women's Writing*. Manchester and New York: Manchester University Press, 1993.

Griffith, Gareth. *Socialism and Superior Brains: The Political Thought of Bernard Shaw*. London and New York: Routledge, 1993.

Griffith, John W. *Joseph Conrad and the Anthropological Dilemma: 'Bewildered Traveller.'* Oxford: Clarendon, 1995.

Groß, Konrad, Kurt Müller, and Meinhard Winkgens, eds. *Das Natur/Kultur-Paradigma in der englischsprachigen Erzählliteratur des 19. und 20. Jahrhunderts: Festschrift zum 60. Geburtstag von Paul Goetsch*. Tübingen: Gunter Narr, 1994.

Grubgeld, Elizabeth. *George Moore and the Autogenous Self: The Autobiography and Fiction*. Syracuse, NY: Syracuse University Press, 1994.

Grundy, Isobel, and Susan Wiseman, eds. *Women, Writing, History: 1640–1740*. Athens: University of Georgia Press, 1992.

Guthke, Karl S. *The Last Frontier: Imagining Other Worlds, from the Copernican Revolution to Modern Science Fiction*. Trans. Helen Atkins. Ithaca (NY) and London: Cornell University Press, 1990.

Guy, Josephine M. *The Victorian Social-Problem Novel: The Market, the Individual and Communal Life*. New York: St. Martin's, 1996.

Halberstam, Judith. *Skin Shows: Gothic Horror and the Technology of Monsters*. Durham (NC) and London: Duke University Press, 1995.

Hall, Donald E. *Fixing Patriarchy: Feminism and Mid-Victorian Male Novelists*. New York: New York University Press, 1996.

Hall, Donald E., ed. *Muscular Christianity: Embodying the Victorian Age*. Cambridge: Cambridge University Press, 1994.

Hall, Kim F. *Things of Darkness: Economies of Race and Gender in Early Modern England*. Ithaca (NY) and London: Cornell University Press, 1995.

Hammond, Paul. *Love betwen Men in English Literature*. New York: St. Martin's, 1996.

Hands, Timothy. *Thomas Hardy*. New York: St. Martin's, 1995.

Hanne, Michael. *The Power of the Story: Fiction and Political Change*. Providence (RI) and Oxford: Berghahn Books, 1994.

Hansen, Klaus P., ed. *Empfindsamkeiten*. Passau: Wissenschaftsverlag Richard Rothe, 1990.

Hanson, Clare. *Virginia Woolf*. New York: St. Martin's, 1994.

Harden, Edgar F. *"Vanity Fair": A Novel without a Hero*. New York: Twayne, 1995.

Harman, Barbara Leah, and Susan Meyer, eds. *The New Nineteenth Century: Feminist Readings of Underread Victorian Fiction*. New York and London: Garland, 1996.

Haroian-Guerin, Gil. *The Fatal Hero: Diana, Deity of the Moon, as an Archetype of the Modern Hero in English Literature*. New York: Peter Lang, 1996.

Harpham, Geoffrey Galt. *One of Us: The Mastery of Joseph Conrad*. Chicago and London: University of Chicago Press, 1996.

Harries, Elizabeth Wanning. *The Unfinished Manner: Essays on the Fragment in the Later Eighteenth Century*. Charlottesville and London: University Press of Virginia, 1994.

Harris, Janice Hubbard. *Edwardian Stories of Divorce*. New Brunswick, NJ: Rutgers University Press, 1996.

Harris, Michael. *Outsiders and Insiders: Perspectives of Third World Culture in British and Post-Colonial Fiction*. New York: Peter Lang, 1992.

Harrison, James. *Salman Rushdie*. New York: Twayne, 1992.

Harrison, Robert Pogue. *Forests: The Shadow of Civilization*. Chicago and London: University of Chicago Press, 1992.

Harsh, Constance D. *Subversive Heroines: Feminist Resolutions of Social Crisis in the Condition-of-England Novel*. Ann Arbor: University of Michigan Press, 1994.

Harter, Deborah A. *Bodies in Pieces: Fantastic Narrative and the Poetics of the Fragment*. Stanford, CA: Stanford University Press, 1996.

Harty, John, III, ed. *James Joyce's "Finnegans Wake": A Casebook*. New York and London: Garland, 1991.

Hastings, Selina. *Evelyn Waugh: A Biography*. London: Sinclair-Stevenson, 1994.

Hay, Carla H., and Syndy M. Conger, eds. *The Past as Prologue: Essays to Celebrate the Twenty-Fifth Anniversary of ASECS*. New York: AMS Press, 1995.

Heidt, Edward R. *The Image of the Church Minister in Literature*. Lewiston, NY: Edwin Mellen Press, 1994.

Heller, Vivian. *Joyce, Decadence, and Emancipation*. Urbana and Chicago: University of Illinois Press, 1995.

Helms, Philip W. (with Kerry Elizabeth Thompson). *Tolkien's Peaceful War: A History and Explanatiopn of Tolkien Fandom and War*. Ed. Paul S. Ritz. Highland, MI: American Tolkien Society, 1994.

Helsinger, Elizabeth K. *Rural Scenes and National Representation: Britain, 1815–1850*. Princeton, NJ: Princeton University Press, 1997.

Henderson, Andrea K. *Romantic Identities: Varieties of Subjectivity, 1774–1830*. Cambridge: Cambridge University Press, 1996.

Henry, Richard. *Pretending and Meaning: Toward a Pragmatic Theory of Fictional Discourse*. Westport (CT) and London: Greenwood Press, 1996.

Herman, David. *Universal Grammar and Narrative Form*. Durham (NC) and London: Duke University Press, 1995.

Herz, Judith Scherer. *"A Passage to India": Nation and Narration*. New York: Twayne, 1993.

Heusel, Barbara Stevens. *Patterned Aimlessness: Iris Murdoch's Novels of the 1970s and 1980s*. Athens (GA) and London: University of Georgia Press, 1995.

Heyns, Michiel. *Expulsion and the Nineteenth-Century Novel: The Scapegoat in English Realist Fiction*. Oxford: Clarendon, 1994.

Higgins, Ian. *Swift's Politics: A Study in Disaffection*. Cambridge: Cambridge University Press, 1994.

Higonnet, Margaret R., and Joan Templeton, eds. *Reconfigured Spheres: Feminist Explorations of Literary Space*. Amherst: University of Massachusetts Press, 1994.

Hill, W. Speed, ed. *New Ways of Looking at Old Texts*. Binghamton, NY: Medieval and Renaissance Texts and Studies, 1993.

Hill-Miller, Katherine C. *"My Hideous Progeny": Mary Shelley, William Godwin, and the Father-Daughter Relationship*. Newark: University of Delaware Press; London: Associated University Presses, 1995.

Hinnant, Charles H. *'Steel for the Mind': Samuel Johnson and Critical Discourse*. Newark: University of Delaware Press; London and Toronto: Associated University Presses, 1994.

Hoeveler, Diane Long, and Beth Lau, eds. *Approaches to Teaching Brontë's "Jane Eyre."* New York: Modern Language Association of America, 1993.

Hofheinz, Thomas C. *Joyce and the Invention of Irish History: "Finnegans Wake" in Context*. Cambridge: Cambridge University Press, 1995.

Hogan, Patrick Colm. *Joyce, Milton, and the Theory of Influence*. Gainesville: University Press of Florida, 1995.

Hohne, Karen, and Helen Wussow, eds. *A Dialogue of Voices: Feminist Literary Theory and Bakhtin*. Minneapolis and London: University of Minnesota Press, 1994.

Holden, Philip. *Orienting Masculinity, Orienting Nation: W. Somerset Maugham's Exotic Fiction*. Westport (CT) and London: Greenwood Press, 1996.

Holdsworth, Peter. *The Rebel Tyke: Bradford and J. B. Priestley*. Bradford (UK): Bradford Libraries, 1994.

Hollahan, Eugene. *Crisis-Consciousness and the Novel*. Newark: University of Delaware Press; London and Toronto: Associated University Presses, 1992.

Hoogland, Renée C. *Elizabeth Bowen: A Reputation in Writing*. New York and London: New York University Press, 1994.

Hoogland, Renée C. *Lesbian Configurations*. New York: Columbia University Press, 1997.

Hooker, Jeremy. *Writers in a Landscape*. Cardiff: University of Wales Press, 1996.

Hooper, Walter. *C. S. Lewis: A Companion and Guide*. New York: HarperCollins, 1996.

Horsman, Alan. *The Victorian Novel*. Oxford: Clarendon, 1990.

Horton, Susan R. *Difficult Women, Artful Lives: Olive Schreiner and Isak Dinesen, In and Out of Africa*. Baltimore and London: Johns Hopkins University Press, 1995.

Houston, Gail Turley. *Consuming Fictions: Gender, Class, and Hunger in Dickens's Novels*. Carbondale and Edwardsville: Southern Illinois University Press, 1994.

Howard, Jacqueline. *Reading Gothic Fiction: A Bakhtinian Approach*. Oxford: Clarendon, 1994.

Hubbard, Tom. *Seeking Mr Hyde: Studies in Robert Louis Stevenson, Symbolism, Myth and the Pre-Modern*. Frankfurt: Peter Lang, 1995.

Huet, Marie-Hélène. *Monstrous Imagination*. Cambridge (MA) and London: Harvard University Press, 1993.

ativity in George Eliot's Fiction. New York and London: New York University Press, 1994.

Jones, W. Gareth, ed. *Tolstoi and Britain.* Oxford: Berg, 1995.

Jordan, Elaine, ed. *Joseph Conrad.* London: Macmillan, 1996.

Jordan, Heather Bryant. *How Will the Heart Endure: Elizabeth Bowen and the Landscape of War.* Ann Arbor: University of Michigan Press, 1992.

Josipovici, Gabriel. *The World and the Book: A Study of Modern Fiction.* 3rd ed. London: Macmillan, 1994.

Joyau, Isabelle. *Investigating Powell's "A Dance to the Music of Time."* London: Macmillan; New York: St. Martin's, 1994.

Juhasz, Suzanne. *Reading from the Heart: Women, Literature, and the Search for True Love.* New York: Viking, 1994.

Kaczvinsky, Donald P. *Lawrence Durrell's Major Novels, or The Kingdom of the Imagination.* Selinsgrove, PA: Susquehanna University Press; London: Associated University Presses, 1997.

Kahane, Claire. *Passions of the Voice: Hysteria, Narrative, and the Figure of the Speaking Woman, 1850–1915.* Baltimore and London: Johns Hopkins University Press, 1995.

Kamijima, Kenkishi, ed. *Centre and Circumference: Essays in English Romanticism.* Tokyo: Kirihara, 1995.

Kaplan, Carola M., and Anne B. Simpson, eds. *Seeing Double: Revisioning Edwardian and Modernist Literature.* New York: St. Martin's, 1996.

Kaufmann, David. *The Business of Common Life: Novels and Classical Economics between Revolution and Reform.* Baltimore and London: Johns Hopkins University Press, 1995.

Kearns, Katherine. *Nineteenth-Century Literary Realism: Through the Looking-Glass.* Cambridge: Cambridge University Press, 1996.

Keck, Annette, and Dietmar Schmidt, eds. *Auto(r)erotik: Gegenstandslose Liebe als literarisches Projekt.* Berlin: Erich Schmidt Verlag, 1994.

Kegl, Rosemary. *The Rhetoric of Concealment: Figuring Gender and Class in Renaissance Literature.* Ithaca (NY) and London: Cornell University Press, 1994.

Kelly, Kathleen Coyne. *A. S. Byatt.* New York: Twayne; London: Prentice Hall International, 1996.

Kelsall, Malcolm. *The Great Good Place: The Country House and English Literature.* New York: Harvester Wheatsheaf, 1993.

Kennedy, Andrew, and Orm Øverland, eds. *Excursions in Fiction: Essays in Honour of Professor Lars Hartveit on His 70th Birthday.* Oslo: Novus Press, 1994.

Kennedy, Judith, ed. *Victorian Authors and their Works: Revision, Motivations, and Modes.* Athens: Ohio University Press, 1991.

Kershner, R. B., ed. *Joyce and Popular Culture.* Gainesville: University Press of Florida, 1996.

Keymer, Tom. *Richardson's "Clarissa" and the Eighteenth-Century Reader.* Cambridge: Cambridge University Press, 1992.

Kilgour, Maggie. *The Rise of the Gothic Novel.* London and New York: Routledge, 1995.

King, Bruce, ed. *The Commonwealth Novel since 1960*. London: Macmillan, 1991.

Kissel, Susan S. *In Common Cause: The 'Conservative' Frances Trollope and the 'Radical' Frances Wright*. Bowling Green, OH: Bowling Green State University Popular Press, 1993.

Klein, Scott W. *The Fictions of James Joyce and Wyndham Lewis: Monsters of Nature and Design*. Cambridge: Cambridge University Press, 1994.

Knippenberg, Joseph M., and Peter Augustine Lawler, eds. *Poets, Princes, and Private Citizens: Literary Alternatives to Postmodern Politics*. Lanham, MD: Rowman & Littlefield, 1996.

Knowles, Murray, and Kirsten Malmkjær. *Language and Control in Children's Literature*. London and New York: Routledge, 1996.

Knowles, Ronald. *Understanding Harold Pinter*. Columbia: University of South Carolina Press, 1995.

Knowlson, James. *Damned to Fame: The Life of Samuel Beckett*. New York: Simon & Schuster, 1996.

Knox, Melissa. *Oscar Wilde: A Long and Lovely Suicide*. New Haven (CT) and London: Yale University Press, 1994.

Kooistra, Lorraine Janzen. *The Artist as Critic: Bitextuality in "Fin-de-Siècle" Illustrated Books*. Aldershot (UK) and Brookfield (VT): Scolar Press, 1995.

Koritz, Amy. *Gendering Bodies/Performing Arts: Dance and Literature in Early Twentieth-Century British Culture*. Ann Arbor: University of Michigan Press, 1995.

Kostelanetz, Richard. *An ABC of Contemporary Reading*. San Diego, CA: San Diego State University Press, 1995.

Kraft, Elizabeth. *Laurence Sterne Revisited*. New York: Twayne; London: Prentice Hall International, 1996.

Kranidis, Rita S. *Subversive Discourse: The Cultural Production of Late Victorian Feminist Novels*. London: Macmillan, 1995.

Kropf, David Glenn. *Authorship as Alchemy: Subversive Writing in Pushkin, Scott, Hoffmann*. Stanford, CA: Stanford University Press, 1994.

Kucich, John. *The Power of Lies: Transgression in Victorian Fiction*. Ithaca (NY) and London: Cornell University Press, 1994.

LaChapelle, Dolores. *D. H. Lawrence: Future Primitive*. Denton: University of North Texas Press, 1996.

Lago, Mary. *E. M. Forster: A Literary Life*. New York: St. Martin's, 1995.

Lamarque, Peter, and Stein Haugom Olsen. *Truth, Fiction, and Literature: A Philosophical Perspective*. Oxford: Clarendon, 1994.

Lambert, Ellen Zetzel. *The Face of Love: Feminism and the Beauty Question*. Boston: Beacon Press, 1995.

Lämmert, Eberhard, and Barbara Naumann, eds. *Wer sind wir? Europäische Phänotypen im Roman des zwanzigsten Jahrhunderts*. Munich: Wilhelm Fink, 1996.

Lane, Maggie. *Jane Austen and Food*. London and Rio Grande (OH): Hambledon Press, 1995.

Langbaum, Robert. *Thomas Hardy in Our Time*. London: Macmillan; New York: St. Martin's, 1995.

Latham, Robert A., and Robert A. Collins, eds. *Modes of the Fantastic: Selected Essays from the Twelfth International Conference on the Fantastic in the Arts*. Westport (CT) and London: Greenwood Press, 1995.

Lawrence, Karen R. *Penelope Voyages: Women and Travel in the British Literary Tradition*. Ithaca (NY) and London: Cornell University Press, 1994.

Lawson, Jacqueline Elaine. *Domestic Misconduct in the Novels of Defoe, Richardson, and Fielding*. Lewiston, NY: Mellen University Press, 1994.

Leader, Zachary. *Revision and Romantic Authorship*. Oxford: Clarendon, 1996.

Lecercle, Jean-Jacques. *Philosophy of Nonsense: The Intuitions of Victorian Nonsense Literature*. London and New York: Routledge, 1994.

Ledbetter, Mark. *Victims and the Postmodern Narrative, or, Doing Violence to the Body: An Ethic of Reading and Writing*. London: Macmillan; New York: St. Martin's, 1996.

Lee, A. Robert, ed. *Other Britain, Other British: Contemporary Multicultural Fiction*. London and East Haven (CT): Pluto Press, 1995.

Lee, Hsiao-Hung. *"Possibilities of Hidden Things": Narrative Transgression in Victorian Fictional Autobiographies*. New York: Peter Lang, 1996.

Leerssen, Joep. *Remembrance and Imagination: Patterns in the Historical and Literary Representation of Ireland in the Nineteenth Century*. Cork: Cork University Press, 1996.

Leerssen, Joep, A. H. van der Weel, and Bart Westerweel, eds. *Forging in the Smithy: National Identity and Representation in Anglo-Irish Literary History*. Amsterdam and Atlanta: Rodopi, 1995.

Lefkovitz, Lori Hope, ed. *Textual Bodies: Changing Boundaries of Literary Representation*. Albany: State University of New York Press, 1997.

Lehmann, Elmar, and Bernd Lenz, eds. *Telling Stories: Studies in Honour of Ulrich Broich on the Occasion of His 60th Birthday*. Amsterdam: B. R. Grüner, 1992.

Lerner, Laurence. *Angels and Absences: Child Deaths in the Nineteenth Century*. Nashville (TN) and London: Vanderbilt University Press, 1997.

Letellier, Robert Ignatius. *Sir Walter Scott and the Gothic Novel*. Lewiston, NY: Edwin Mellen Press, 1995 (c. 1994).

Levenson, Michael. *Modernism and the Fate of Individuality: Character and Novelistic Form from Conrad to Woolf*. Cambridge: Cambridge University Press, 1991.

Levitt, Annette Shandler. *The Intertextuality of Joyce Cary's "The Horse's Mouth."* Lewiston, NY: Edwin Mellen Press, 1993.

Levy, Judith. *V. S. Naipaul: Displacement and Autobiography*. New York and London: Garland, 1995.

Lewes, Darby. *Dream Revisionaries: Gender and Genre in Women's Utopian Fiction, 1870–1920*. Tuscaloosa and London: University of Alabama Press, 1995.

Lewiecki-Wilson, Cynthia. *Writing Against the Family: Gender in Lawrence*

Nixon, Rob. *London Calling: V. S. Naipaul, Postcolonial Mandarin.* New York and Oxford: Oxford University Press, 1992.

Nolan, Emer. *James Joyce and Nationalism.* London and New York: Routledge, 1995.

Nollen, Scott Allen. *Robert Louis Stevenson: Life, Literature and the Silver Screen.* Jefferson (NC) and London: McFarland & Co., 1994.

Nord, Deborah Epstein. *Walking the Victorian Streets: Women, Representation, and the City.* Ithaca (NY) and London: Cornell University Press, 1995.

Novy, Marianne. *Engaging with Shakespeare: Responses of George Eliot and Other Women Novelists.* Athens (GA) and London: University of Georgia Press, 1994.

Nugel, Bernfried, ed. *Now More Than Ever: Proceedings of the Aldous Huxley Centenary Symposium, Münster 1994.* Frankfurt: Peter Lang, 1995.

Nunokawa, Jeff. *Oscar Wilde.* New York and Philadelphia: Chelsea House, 1995.

O'Connor, Patricia J. *To Love the Good: The Moral Philosophy of Iris Murdoch.* New York: Peter Lang, 1996.

O'Connor, Theresa, ed. *The Comic Tradition in Irish Women Writers.* Gainesville: University Press of Florida, 1996.

Onega, Susana, ed. *Telling Histories: Narrativizing History, Historicizing Literature.* Amsterdam and Atlanta: Rodopi, 1995.

Oppenheim, Lois, and Marius Buning, eds. *Beckett On and On . . . .* Madison and Teaneck, NJ: Fairleigh Dickinson University Press; London: Associated University Presses, 1996.

Orel, Harold. *The Historical Novel from Scott to Sabatini: Changing Attitudes toward a Literary Genre, 1814–1920.* London: Macmillan; New York: St. Martin's, 1995.

Osteen, Mark. *The Economy of "Ulysses": Making Both Ends Meet.* Syracuse, NY: Syracuse University Press, 1995.

Otis, Laura. *Organic Memory: History and the Body in the Late Nineteenth and Early Twentieth Centuries.* Lincoln and London: University of Nebraska Press, 1994.

Page, Norman, and Peter Preston, eds. *The Literature of Place.* London: Macmillan, 1993.

Palmer, Frank. *Literature and Moral Understanding: A Philosophical Essay on Ethics, Aesthetics, Education, and Culture.* Oxford: Clarendon, 1992.

Palumbo, Donald, ed. *Erotic Universe: Sexuality and Fantastic Literature.* New York: Greenwood Press, 1986.

Parker, Christopher, ed. *Gender Roles and Sexuality in Victorian Literature.* Aldershot (UK): Scolar Press, 1995.

Parkes, Adam. *Modernism and the Theater of Censorship.* New York and Oxford: Oxford University Press, 1996.

Parrinder, Patrick. *Shadows of the Future: H. G. Wells, Science Fiction, and Prophecy.* Syracuse, NY: Syracuse University Press, 1995.

Pearce, Joseph. *Wisdom and Innocence: A Life of G. K. Chesterton.* London: Hodder & Stoughton, 1996.

Polhemus, Robert M., and Roger B. Henkle, eds. *Critical Reconstructions: The Relationship of Fiction and Life*. Stanford, CA: Stanford University Press, 1994.

Potkay, Adam. *The Fate of Eloquence in the Age of Hume*. Ithaca (NY) and London: Cornell University Press, 1994.

Preston, Peter, and Paul Simpson-Housley, eds. *Writing the City: Eden, Babylon and the New Jerusalem*. London and New York: Routledge, 1994.

Prince, Michael. *Philosophical Dialogue in the British Enlightenment: Theology, Aesthetics, and the Novel*. Cambridge: Cambridge University Press, 1996.

Purdy, Anthony, ed. *Literature and Money*. Amsterdam and Atlanta: Rodopi, 1993.

Pyle, Forest. *The Ideology of Imagination: Subject and Society in the Discourse of Romanticism*. Stanford, CA: Stanford University Press, 1995.

Quinby, Lee, ed. *Genealogy and Literature*. Minneapolis and London: University of Minnesota Press, 1995.

Quinn, Patrick J., ed. *Recharting the Thirties*. Selinsgrove, PA: Susquehanna University Press; London: Associated University Presses, 1996.

Rackin, Donald. *"Alice's Adventures in Wonderland" and "Through the Looking-Glass": Nonsense, Sense, and Meaning*. New York: Twayne, 1991.

Radford, Jean. *Dorothy Richardson*. Bloomington and Indianapolis: Indiana University Press, 1991.

Ragussis, Michael. *Figures of Conversion: 'The Jewish Question' and English National Identity*. Durham (NC) and London: Duke University Press, 1995.

Rajan, P. K., A. Jameela Begum, K. M. George, and K. Radha, eds. *Commonwealth Literature: Themes and Techniques—Essays in Honour of Prof. K. Ayyappa Paniker*. Delhi: Ajanta, 1993.

Rancour-Laferriere, Daniel, ed. *Self-Analysis in Literary Study: Exploring Hidden Agendas*. New York and London: New York University Press, 1994.

Ransom, Teresa. *Fanny Trollope: A Remarkable Life*. New York: St. Martin's, 1995.

Rao, M. Madhusudhana. *Salman Rushdie's Fiction: A Study ("Satanic Verses" Excluded)*. New Delhi: Sterling Publishers, 1992.

Rapaport, Herman. *Between the Sign and the Gaze*. Ithaca (NY) and London: Cornell University Press, 1994.

Raper, Julius Rowan, Melody L. Enscore, and Paige Matthey Bynum, eds. *Lawrence Durrell: Comprehending the Whole*. Columbia and London: University of Missouri Press, 1995.

Ray, Martin. *Joseph Conrad*. London: Edward Arnold, 1993.

Readings, Bill, and Bennet Schaber, eds. *Postmodernism Across the Ages: Essays for a Postmodernity That Wasn't Born Yesterday*. Syracuse, NY: Syracuse University Press, 1993.

Reed, John R. *Dickens and Thackeray: Punishment and Forgiveness*. Athens: Ohio University Press, 1995.

Rees, Christine. *Utopian Imagination and Eighteenth-Century Fiction*. London and New York: Longman, 1996.

Rees, Joan. *Writings on the Nile: Harriet Martineau, Florence Nightingale, Amelia Edwards*. London: Rubicon Press, 1995.

Reese, Judy S. *Recasting Social Values in the Work of Virginia Woolf*. Selinsgrove, PA: Susquehanna University Press; London: Associated University Presses, 1996.

Regal, Martin S. *Harold Pinter: A Question of Timing*. London: Macmillan; New York: St. Martin's, 1995.

Reid, Panthea. *Art and Affection: A Life of Virginia Woolf*. New York and Oxford: Oxford University Press, 1996.

Relihan, Constance C. *Fashioning Authority: The Development of Elizabethan Novelistic Discourse*. Kent (OH) and London: Kent State University Press, 1994.

Rennie, Neil. *Far-Fetched Facts: The Literature of Travel and the Idea of the South Seas*. Oxford: Clarendon, 1995.

Reynolds, Kimberley, and Nicola Humble. *Victorian Heroines: Representations of Femininity in Nineteenth-Century Literature and Art*. New York: New York University Press, 1993.

Reynolds, Peter, ed. *Novel Images: Literature in Performance*. London and New York: Routledge, 1993.

Rice, Thomas Jackson. *Joyce, Chaos, and Complexity*. Urbana and Chicago: University of Illinois Press, 1997.

Richardson, Alan. *Literature, Education, and Romanticism: Reading as Social Practice, 1780–1832*. Cambridge: Cambridge University Press, 1994.

Richardson, Alan, and Sonia Hofkosh, eds. *Romanticism, Race, and Imperial Culture, 1780–1834*. Bloomington and Indianapolis: Indiana University Press, 1996.

Richetti, John, John Bender, Deirdre David, and Michael Seidel, eds. *The Columbia History of the British Novel*. New York: Columbia University Press, 1994.

Richter, David H. *The Progress of Romance: Literary Historiography and the Gothic Novel*. Columbus: Ohio State University Press, 1996.

Rickard, John S., ed. *Irishness and (Post)Modernism*. Lewisburg, PA: Bucknell University Press; London and Toronto: Associated University Presses, 1994.

Ricks, Christopher. *Beckett's Dying Words: The Clarendon Lectures, 1990*. Oxford: Clarendon, 1993.

Ricks, Christopher. *Essays in Appreciation*. Oxford: Clarendon, 1996.

Rignall, John. *Realist Fiction and the Strolling Spectator*. London and New York: Routledge, 1992.

Rignall, John, ed. *George Eliot and Europe*. Brookfield, VT: Scolar Press, 1997.

Ritchie, Daniel E. *Reconstructing Literature in an Ideological Age: A Biblical Poetics and Literary Studies from Milton to Burke*. Grand Rapids (MI) and Cambridge (UK): William B. Eerdmans, 1996.

Rivero, Albert J., ed. *New Essays on Samuel Richardson*. New York: St. Martin's, 1996.

Roberts, Katherine J. *Fair Ladies: Sir Philip Sidney's Female Characters*. New York: Peter Lang, 1993.

Roberts, Marie Mulvey, and Hugh Ormsby-Lennon, eds. *Secret Texts: The Literature of Secret Societies*. New York: AMS Press, 1995.

Robertson, Fiona. *Legitimate Histories: Scott, Gothic, and the Authorities of Fiction*. Oxford: Clarendon, 1994.

Robinson, Jeremy. *Sensualism and Mythology: The Wessex Novels of John Cowper Powys*. Kidderminster (UK): Crescent Moon Publishing, 1990.

Robson, W. W. *Critical Enquiries: Essays on Literature*. New York: St. Martin's, 1993.

Rogers, Deborah D., ed. *The Critical Response to Ann Radcliffe*. Westport (CT) and London: Greenwood Press, 1994.

Romera Castillo, José, Mario García-Page, and Francisco Gutiérrez Carbajo, eds. *Bajtín y la literatura*. Madrid: Visor, 1995.

Romera Castillo, José, Francisco Gutiérrez Carbajo, and Mario García-Page, eds. *La novela histórica a finales del siglo XX: Actas del V Seminario Internacional del Instituto de Semiótica Literaria y Tetral de la UNED*. Madrid: Visor, 1996.

Rose, Danis. *The Textual Diaries of James Joyce*. Dublin: Lilliput Press, 1995.

Rose, Jacqueline. *The Case of Peter Pan, or The Impossibility of Children's Fiction*. Rev. ed. London: Macmillan, 1992.

Rosenberg, Beth Carole. *Virginia Woolf and Samuel Johnson: Common Readers*. New York: St. Martin's, 1995.

Rosenberg, Brian. *Little Dorrit's Shadows: Character and Contradiction in Dickens*. Columbia and London: University of Missouri Press, 1996.

Rosenthal, Lynne M. *Rumer Godden Revisited*. New York: Twayne; London: Prentice Hall International, 1996.

Ross, Charles. *The Custom of the Castle: From Malory to Macbeth*. Berkeley: University of California Press, 1997.

Ross, Charles L., and Dennis Jackson, eds. *Editing D. H. Lawrence: New Versions of a Modern Author*. Ann Arbor: University of Michigan Press, 1995.

Rothfield, Lawrence. *Vital Signs: Medical Realism in Nineteenth-Century Fiction*. Princeton, NJ: Princeton University Press, 1992.

Rowe, Margaret Moan. *Doris Lessing*. New York: St. Martin's, 1994.

Ryan, Kiernan. *Ian McEwan*. Plymouth (UK): Northcote House, 1994.

Sacco, Teran Lee. *A Transcription and Analysis of Jane Austen's Last Work, "Sanditon."* Lewiston, NY: Edwin Mellen Press, 1995.

Sadrin, Anny. *Parentage and Inheritance in the Novels of Charles Dickens*. Cambridge: Cambridge University Press, 1994.

Sage, Lorna. *Angela Carter*. Plymouth (UK): Northcote House, 1994.

Sage, Lorna. *Women in the House of Fiction: Post-War Women Novelists*. New York: Routledge, 1992.

Enlightenment to Victoria. Princeton, NJ: Princeton University Press, 1994.

Schroeder, Steven. *Virginia Woolf's Subject and the Subject of Ethics: Notes Toward a Poetics of Persons.* Lewiston, NY: Edwin Mellen Press, 1996.

Scott, Bonnie Kime. *Refiguring Modernism—Volume 2: Postmodern Feminist Readings of Woolf, West, and Barnes.* Bloomington and Indianapolis: Indiana University Press, 1995.

Seed, David. *James Joyce's "A Portrait of the Artist as a Young Man."* New York: St. Martin's, 1992.

Seed, David, ed. *Anticipations: Essays on Early Science Fiction and its Precursors.* Syracuse, NY: Syracuse University Press, 1995.

Selig, Robert L. *George Gissing.* Rev. ed. New York: Twayne, 1995.

Senn, Fritz. *Inductive Scrutinies: Focus on Joyce.* Ed. Christine O'Neill. Dublin: Lilliput Press, 1995.

Seymour-Smith, Martin. *Hardy.* London: Bloomsbury Publishing, 1994.

Shankman, Steven. *In Search of the Classic: Reconsidering the Greco-Roman Tradition, Homer to Valéry and Beyond.* University Park: Pennsylvania State University Press, 1994.

Sharrock, Roger. *New Insights on English Authors from Marvell to Larkin: An English Variety.* Lewiston, NY: Edwin Mellen Press, 1995.

Shattuck, Roger. *Forbidden Knowledge: From Prometheus to Pornography.* New York: St. Martin's, 1996.

Sheckels, Theodore F., Jr. *The Lion on the Freeway: A Thematic Introduction to Contemporary South African Literature in English.* New York: Peter Lang, 1996.

Shelden, Michael. *Graham Greene: The Enemy Within.* New York: Random House, 1994.

Sherbert, Garry. *Menippean Satire and the Poetics of Wit: Ideologies of Self-Consciousness in Dunton, D'Urfey, and Sterne.* New York: Peter Lang, 1996.

Sherry, Vincent. *James Joyce: "Ulysses."* Cambridge: Cambridge University Press, 1994.

Shuttleworth, Sally. *Charlotte Brontë and Victorian Psychology.* Cambridge: Cambridge University Press, 1996.

Siegel, Carol. *Male Masochism: Modern Revisions of the Story of Love.* Bloomington and Indianapolis: Indiana University Press, 1995.

Sillars, Stuart. *Visualisation in Popular Fiction, 1860–1960: Graphic Narratives, Fictional Images.* London and New York: Routledge, 1995.

Sinfield, Alan. *The Wilde Century: Effeminacy, Oscar Wilde and the Queer Moment.* New York: Columbia University Press, 1994.

Singley, Carol J., and Susan Elizabeth Sweeney, eds. *Anxious Power: Reading, Writing, and Ambivalence in Narrative by Women.* Albany: State University of New York Press, 1993.

Sjöholm, Christina. *"The Vice of Wedlock": The Theme of Marriage in George Gissing's Novels.* Stockholm: Almqvist & Wiksell, 1994.

Skilton, David. *Anthony Trollope and His Contemporaries: A Study in the*

Spoo, Robert. *James Joyce and the Language of History: Daedalus's Nightmare.* New York and Oxford: Oxford University Press, 1994.

Sprechman, Ellen Lew. *Seeing Women as Men: Role Reversal in the Novels of Thomas Hardy.* Lanham, MD: University Press of America, 1995.

Stape, J. H., ed. *The Cambridge Companion to Joseph Conrad.* Cambridge: Cambridge University Press, 1996.

Stave, Shirley A. *The Decline of the Goddess: Nature, Culture, and Women in Thomas Hardy's Fiction.* Westport, CT: Greenwood Press, 1995.

Steiner, Wendy. *Pictures of Romance: Form against Context in Painting and Literature.* Chicago and London: University of Chicago Press, 1988.

Stephan, Inge, Sabine Schilling, and Sigrid Weigel, eds. *Jüdische Kultur und Weiblichkeit in der Moderne.* Cologne: Böhlau Verlag, 1994.

Sternlicht, Sanford. *Jean Rhys.* New York: Twayne; London: Prentice Hall International, 1997.

Sternlicht, Sanford. *Siegfried Sassoon.* New York: Twayne, 1993.

Stevens, David, and Carol D. Stevens. *J. R. R. Tolkien: The Art of the Myth-Maker.* Ed. Roger C. Schlobin. San Bernardino, CA: Borgo Press, 1993.

Stevenson, Randall. *A Reader's Guide to the Twentieth-Century Novel in Britain.* Lexington: University Press of Kentucky, 1993.

Stewart, Garrett. *Dear Reader: The Conscripted Audience in Nineteenth-Century British Fiction.* Baltimore and London: Johns Hopkins University Press, 1996.

Stone, Harry. *The Night Side of Dickens: Cannibalism, Passion, Necessity.* Columbus: Ohio State University Press, 1994.

Stott, Jon C. *Mary Norton.* New York: Twayne, 1994.

Stott, Rebecca. *The Fabrication of the Late Victorian "Femme Fatale": The Kiss of Death.* London: Macmillan, 1992.

Sturgess, Philip J. M. *Narrativity: Theory and Practice.* Oxford: Clarendon, 1992.

Sturrock, June. *"Heaven and Home": Charlotte M. Yonge's Domestic Fiction and the Victorian Debate over Women.* Victoria, BC: English Literary Studies, University of Victoria, 1995.

Suchoff, David. *Critical Theory and the Novel: Mass Society and Cultural Criticism in Dickens, Melville, and Kafka.* Madison: University of Wisconsin Press, 1994.

Summers, Claude J., ed. *Homosexuality in Renaissance and Enlightenment England: Literary Representations in Historical Context.* New York: Haworth Press, 1992.

Sutherland, John. *Is Heathcliff a Murderer? Great Puzzles in Nineteenth-Century Literature.* Oxford and New York: Oxford University Press, 1996.

Sutherland, John. *Mrs Humphry Ward: Eminent Victorian, Pre-eminent Edwardian.* Oxford: Clarendon, 1990.

Sutherland, John. *Victorian Fiction: Writers, Publishers, Readers.* New York: St. Martin's, 1995.

Sweetman, David. *Mary Renault: A Biography.* New York: Harcourt Brace & Co., 1993.

Swinden, Patrick. *"Silas Marner": Memory and Salvation.* New York: Twayne, 1992.

Tambling, Jeremy. *Dickens, Violence and the Modern State: Dreams of the Scaffold.* London: Macmillan; New York: St. Martin's, 1995.

Tatum, James, ed. *The Search for the Ancient Novel.* Baltimore and London: Johns Hopkins University Press, 1994.

Taylor, D. J. *After the War: The Novel and English Society since 1945.* London: Chatto & Windus, 1993.

Thaden, Barbara, ed. *New Essays on the Maternal Voice in the Nineteenth Century.* Dallas: Contemporary Research Press, 1995.

Thomas, Brian. *"The Return of the Native": Saint George Defeated.* New York: Twayne; London: Prentice Hall International, 1995.

Thomas, Donald. *Lewis Carroll: A Portrait with Background.* London: John Murray, 1996.

Thomas, Neil, and Françoise Le Saux, eds. *Myth and Its Legacy in European Literature.* Durham (UK): University of Durham Modern Languages Series, 1996.

Thompson, Jon. *Fiction, Crime, and Empire: Clues to Modernity and Postmodernism.* Urbana and Chicago: University of Illinois Press, 1993.

Thomson, George H. *A Reader's Guide to Dorothy Richardson's "Pilgrimage."* Greensboro, NC: ELT Press, 1996.

Thornton, Weldon. *The Antimodernism of Joyce's "Portrait of the Artist as a Young Man."* Syracuse, NY: Syracuse University Press, 1994.

Tinkler-Villani, Valeria, and Peter Davidson, eds. *Exhibited by Candlelight: Sources and Developments in the Gothic Tradition.* Amsterdam and Atlanta: Rodopi, 1995.

Tobin, Beth Fowkes, ed. *History, Gender, and Eighteenth-Century Literature.* Athens (GA) and London: University of Georgia Press, 1994.

Todd, Dennis. *Imagining Monsters: Miscreations of the Self in Eighteenth-Century England.* Chicago and London: University of Chicago Press, 1995.

Todd, Janet. *Gender, Art and Death.* New York: Continuum, 1993.

Todd, Janet. *The Sign of Angellica: Women, Writing and Fiction, 1660–1800.* New York: Columbia University Press, 1989.

Todd, Richard. *Consuming Fictions: The Booker Prize and Fiction in Britain Today.* London: Bloomsbury Publishing, 1996.

Tomarken, Edward. *A History of the Commentary on Selected Writings of Samuel Johnson.* Columbia, SC: Camden House, 1994.

Tratner, Michael. *Modernism and Mass Politics: Joyce, Woolf, Eliot, Yeats.* Stanford, CA: Stanford University Press, 1995.

Tredell, Nicolas. *Caute's Confrontations: A Study of the Novels of David Caute.* Nottingham (UK): Paupers' Press, 1994.

Treip, Andrew, ed. *Finnegans Wake: "teems of times."* Amsterdam and Atlanta: Rodopi, 1994.

Trela, D. J., ed. *Margaret Oliphant: Critical Essays on a Gentle Subversive.* Selinsgrove, PA: Susquehanna University Press; London: Associated University Presses, 1995.

Tristram, Hildegard L. C., ed. *(Re)Oralisierung*. Tübingen: Gunter Narr Verlag, 1996.

Trotter, David. *The English Novel in History, 1895–1920*. London and New York: Routledge, 1993.

Tucker, George Holbert. *Jane Austen the Woman: Some Biographical Insights*. New York: St. Martin's, 1994.

Turner, Martha A. *Mechanism and the Novel: Science in the Narrative Process*. Cambridge: Cambridge University Press, 1993.

Tush, Susan Rowland. *George Eliot and the Conventions of Popular Women's Fiction: A Serious Literary Response to the "Silly Novels by Lady Novelists."* New York: Peter Lang, 1993.

Ty, Eleanor. *Unsex'd Revolutionaries: Five Women Novelists of the 1790s*. Toronto: University of Toronto Press, 1993.

Tymoczko, Maria. *The Irish "Ulysses."* Berkeley: University of California Press, 1994.

Uglow, Jenny. *Henry Fielding*. Plymouth (UK): Northcote House, 1995.

Upchurch, David A. *Wilde's Use of Irish Celtic Elements in "The Picture of Dorian Gray."* New York: Peter Lang, 1992.

Valente, Joseph. *James Joyce and the Problem of Justice: Negotiating Sexual and Colonial Difference*. Cambridge: Cambridge University Press, 1995.

Valentine, Mark. *Arthur Machen*. Mid Glamorgan: Seren (Poetry Wales Press), 1995.

Van Dover, J. K. *You Know My Method: The Science of the Detective*. Bowling Green, OH: Bowling Green State University Popular Press, 1994.

Van Sant, Ann Jessie. *Eighteenth-Century Sensibility and the Novel: The Senses in Social Context*. Cambridge: Cambridge University Press, 1993.

Verdonk, Peter, and Jean Jacques Weber, eds. *Twentieth-Century Fiction: From Text to Context*. London and New York: Routledge, 1995.

Vickers, Ilse. *Defoe and the New Sciences*. Cambridge: Cambridge University Press, 1996.

Vitaglione, Daniel. *George Eliot and George Sand*. New York: Peter Lang, 1993.

Voller, Jack G. *The Supernatural Sublime: The Metaphysics of Terror in Anglo-American Romanticism*. DeKalb: Northern Illinois University Press, 1994.

Vos, Alvin, ed. *Place and Displacement in the Renaissance*. Binghamton, NY: Medieval and Renaissance Texts and Studies, 1995.

Vrettos, Athena. *Somatic Fictions: Imagining Illness in Victorian Culture*. Stanford, CA: Stanford University Press, 1995.

Wagner, Peter. *Reading Iconotexts: From Swift to the French Revolution*. London: Reaktion Books, 1995.

Wales, Katie, ed. *Feminist Linguistics in Literary Criticism*. Cambridge: D. S. Brewer, 1994.

Walker, Kim. *Women Writers of the English Renaissance*. New York: Twayne; London: Prentice Hall International, 1996.

Wallace, Tara Ghoshal. *Jane Austen and Narrative Authority*. London: Macmillan; New York: St. Martin's, 1995.

Waller, Gary. *The Sidney Family Romance: Mary Wroth, William Herbert, and the Early Modern Construction of Gender*. Detroit, MI: Wayne State University Press, 1993.

Walshe, Eibhear, ed. *Ordinary People Dancing: Essays on Kate O'Brien*. Cork: Cork University Press, 1993.

Walton, Priscilla L. *Patriarchal Desire and Victorian Discourse: A Lacanian Reading of Anthony Trollope's Palliser Novels*. Toronto: University of Toronto Press, 1995.

Ward, Ian. *Law and Literature: Possibilities and Perspectives*. Cambridge: Cambridge University Press, 1995.

Ward, Janet Doubler, and JoAnna Stephens Mink, eds. *Communication and Women's Friendships: Parallels and Intersections in Literature and Life*. Bowling Green, OH: Bowling Green State University Popular Press, 1993.

Warner, John M. *Joyce's Grandfathers: Myth and History in Defoe, Smollett, Sterne, and Joyce*. Athens (GA) and London: University of Georgia Press, 1993.

Watson, Daphne. *Their Own Worst Enemies: Women Writers of Women's Fiction*. London and Boulder (CO): Pluto Press, 1995.

Watson, G. J. *Irish Identity and the Literary Revival: Synge, Yeats, Joyce and O'Casey*. 2nd ed. Washington, DC: Catholic University of America Press, 1994.

Weintraub, Stanley. *Shaw's People: Victoria to Churchill*. University Park: Pennsylvania State University Press, 1996.

Weir, David. *Decadence and the Making of Modernism*. Amherst: University of Massachusetts Press, 1995.

Weir, David. *James Joyce and the Art of Mediation*. Ann Arbor: University of Michigan Press, 1996.

Weisser, Susan Ostrov. *A "Craving Vacancy": Women and Sexual Love in the British Novel, 1740–1880*. Washington Square: New York University Press, 1997.

Weisser, Susan Ostrov, and Jennifer Fleischner, eds. *Feminist Nightmares: Feminism and the Problem of Sisterhood*. New York and London: New York University Press, 1994.

Welch, Robert. *Changing States: Transformations in Modern Irish Writing*. London and New York: Routledge, 1993.

Welch, Robert, ed. *Irish Writers and Religion*. Savage, MD: Barnes & Noble, 1992.

Wennö, Elisabeth. *Ironic Formula in the Novels of Beryl Bainbridge*. Göteborg: Acta Universitatis Gothoburgensis, 1993.

Wesseling, Elisabeth. *Writing History as a Prophet: Postmodernist Innovations of the Historical Novel*. Amsterdam and Philadelphia: John Benjamins, 1991.

West, W. J. *The Larger Evils: "Nineteen Eighty-Four"—The Truth Behind the Satire*. Edinburgh: Canongate Press, 1992.

Westfahl, Gary, George Slusser, and Eric S. Rabkin, eds. *Foods of the Gods:*

Eating and the Eaten in Fantasy and Science Fiction. Athens (GA) and London: University of Georgia Press, 1996.

Wexler, Joyce Piell. *Who Paid for Modernism? Art, Money, and the Fiction of Conrad, Joyce, and Lawrence.* Fayetteville: University of Arkansas Press, 1997.

Wheat, Patricia H. *The Adytum of the Heart: The Literary Criticism of Charlotte Brontë.* Rutherford, NJ: Fairleigh Dickinson University Press; London and Toronto: Associated University Presses, 1992.

Wheeler, Kathleen. *'Modernist' Women Writers and Narrative Art.* Washington Square: New York University Press, 1994.

Wheeler, Michael. *English Fiction of the Victorian Period: 1830–1890.* 2nd ed. London and New York: Longman, 1994.

Whistler, Theresa. *Imagination of the Heart: The Life of Walter de la Mare.* London: Duckworth, 1993.

White, Jonathan, ed. *Recasting the World: Writing after Colonialism.* Baltimore and London: Johns Hopkins University Press, 1993.

White, Nicholas, and Naomi Segal, eds. *Scarlet Letters: Fictions of Adultery from Antiquity to the 1990s.* London: Macmillan; New York: St. Martin's, 1997.

White, R. S. *Natural Law in English Renaissance Literature.* Cambridge: Cambridge University Press, 1996.

Whitebrook, Maureen. *Real Toads in Imaginary Gardens: Narrative Accounts of Liberalism.* Lanham, MD: Rowman & Littlefield, 1995.

Whitlock, Gillian, and Helen Tiffin, eds. *Re-Siting Queen's English: Text and Tradition in Post-Colonial Literatures—Essays Presented to John Pengwerne Matthews.* Amsterdam and Atlanta: Rodopi, 1992.

Whittier-Ferguson, John. *Framing Pieces: Designs of the Gloss in Joyce, Woolf, and Pound.* New York and Oxford: Oxford University Press, 1996.

Widdowson, Peter, ed. *D. H. Lawrence.* London and New York: Longman, 1992.

Widdowson, Peter, ed. *"Tess of the d'Urbervilles": Thomas Hardy.* London: Macmillan, 1993.

Wilding, Michael. *Social Visions.* Sydney: Sydney Studies, 1993.

Wiley, Catherine, and Fiona R. Barnes, eds. *Homemaking: Women Writers and the Politics and Poetics of Home.* New York and London: Garland, 1996.

Willoughby, Guy. *Art and Christhood: The Aesthetics of Oscar Wilde.* Rutherford, NJ: Fairleigh Dickinson University Press; London and Toronto: Associated University Presses, 1993.

Wilson, Carol Shiner, and Joel Haefner, eds. *Re-Visioning Romanticism: British Women Writers, 1776–1837.* Philadelphia: University of Pennsylvania Press, 1994.

Wilson, Robert. *Joseph Conrad, Sources and Traditions.* Rogers, AR: Weir Press, 1995.

Wilt, Judith. *Abortion, Choice, and Contemporary Fiction: The Armageddon of the Maternal Instinct.* Chicago and London: University of Chicago Press, 1990.

Wiltshire, John. *Samuel Johnson in the Medical World: The Doctor and the Patient.* Cambridge: Cambridge University Press, 1991.

Winnifrith, Thomas John, ed. *Critical Responses on Emily Brontë.* New York: G. K. Hall; London: Prentice Hall International, 1997.

Winnifrith, Tom. *Fallen Women in the Nineteenth-Century Novel.* London: Macmillan; New York: St. Martin's, 1994.

Wisker, Gina, ed. *It's My Party: Reading Twentieth-Century Women's Writing.* London and Boulder (CO): Pluto Press, 1994.

Wolfe, Peter. *Alarms and Epitaphs: The Art of Eric Ambler.* Bowling Green, OH: Bowling Green State University Popular Press, 1993.

Wolfreys, Julian. *Being English: Narratives, Idioms, and Performances of National Identity from Coleridge to Trollope.* Albany: State University of New York Press, 1994.

Wood, Nigel, ed. *"Mansfield Park."* Buckingham (UK) and Philadelphia: Open University Press, 1993.

Woodmansee, Martha, and Peter Jaszi, eds. *The Construction of Authorship: Textual Appropriation in Law and Literature.* Durham (NC) and London: Duke University Press, 1994.

Worden, Blair. *The Sound of Virtue: Philip Sidney's "Arcadia" and Elizabethan Politics.* New Haven (CT) and London: Yale University Press, 1996.

Worthen, John. *D. H. Lawrence.* London: Edward Arnold, 1991.

Wright, Adrian. *Foreign Country: The Life of L. P. Hartley.* London: André Deutsch, 1996.

Wright, Terence. *Elizabeth Gaskell: 'We are not angels'—Realism, Gender, Values.* London: Macmillan; New York: St. Martin's, 1995.

Wullschläger, Jackie. *Inventing Wonderland: The Lives and Fantasies of Lewis Carroll, Edward Lear, J. M. Barrie, Kenneth Grahame and A. A. Milne.* New York: Free Press, 1995.

Wussow, Helen, ed. *New Essays on Virginia Woolf.* Dallas, TX: Contemporary Research Press, 1995.

Wyatt, Jean. *Reconstructing Desire: The Role of the Unconscious in Women's Reading and Writing.* Chapel Hill and London: University of North Carolina Press, 1990.

Yee, Cordell D. K. *The Word according to James Joyce: Reconstructing Representation.* Lewisburg, PA: Bucknell University Press; London: Associated University Presses, 1997.

York, R. A. *Strangers and Secrets: Communication in the Nineteenth-Century Novel.* Rutherford, NJ: Fairleigh Dickinson University Press; London and Toronto: Associated University Presses, 1994.

Zaman, Niaz, Shawkat Hussain, Firdous Azim, Kaiser Haq, and Syed Manzoorul Islam, eds. *Other Englishes: Essays in Commonwealth Writing.* Dhaka (Bangladesh): University Press Limited, 1991.

Zelter, Joachim. *Sinnhafte Fiktion und Wahrheit: Untersuchungen zur ästhetischen und epistemologischen Problematik des Fiktionsbegriffs im Kon-*

text europäischer Ideen- und englischer Literaturgeschichte. Tübingen: Max Niemeyer, 1994.

Zhang, Zaixin. *Voices of the Self in Daniel Defoe's Fiction: An Alternative Marxist Approach.* Frankfurt: Peter Lang, 1993.

Zomchick, John P. *Family and the Law in Eighteenth-Century Fiction.* Cambridge: Cambridge University Press, 1993.

INDEX

441

REFERENCE